From Self to Sources

Instructor's Annotated Edition

Instructor's Annotated Edition

From Self

to Sources

Essays and Beyond

Lee Brandon
Mt. San Antonio College

Houghton Mifflin Company   Boston   New York

To Sharon

Editor in Chief: Patricia A. Coryell
Senior Sponsoring Editor: Mary Jo Southern
Development Editor: Kellie Cardone
Editorial Assistant: Peter Mooney
Senior Project Editor: Kathryn Dinovo
Cover Design Manager: Diana Coe
Senior Manufacturing Coordinator: Marie Barnes
Marketing Manager: Annamarie Rice

Cover image: © 2002 Miles Hyman

Printed in the U.S.A.

Library of Congress Control Number: 2002101698

Student Text ISBN: 0-618-15064-1
Instructor's Annotated Edition ISBN: 0-618-15065-X

123456789-VHG-06 05 04 03 02

Contents

Chapter 6   Description: Moving Through Space   132

Chapter 7   Exemplification: Writing with Examples   165

Chapter 9   Classification: Establishing Groups   221

you fantasize about while pummeling the punching bag at the gym."

"In fact, all of the women you're going to learn to avoid have some very attractive qualities, qualities that many men instinctively fall for. That's what makes it so critical for you to avoid them."

"It is vital that everyone understand the different emotional states cessation of smoking can cause. . . . [They are] those of the zealot, the evangelist, the elect, and the serene."

"Extending an empty hand to show that you have no weapon, grasping another's hand to signify your human bond—you have to admit the handshake has impeccable symbolic credentials."

"As a cornerback, I finally discovered an effective process, one that begins with preparation before the game and ends with strategic action on the field during a pass play."

"Strategically, I will make sure that our tour ends in the
kitchen, because most important decisions in families are
made at the kitchen table."

"You should already have extensive drawings for your
fresco—these will be much sought by scholars and collectors in centuries to come."

"The first thing I did when I returned to work the next morning was search the Web for information on Bell's palsy—
beginning a series of self-misdiagnoses that did more lasting
damage than the palsy itself."

"Each player is responsible for his or her own attitude. . . .
Spit frequently. Spit at all crucial moments. Spit correctly. Spit
should be *blown,* not ptuied weakly with the lips, which often
results in dribble."

"A star starts out life from what seems like nothing at all.
Stars are born in huge clouds of gas that are actually far less
dense than the space immediately surrounding Earth."

Chapter 11   *Comparison and Contrast: Showing Similarities and Differences*   281

Chapter 12 Cause and Effect: Determining Reasons and Outcomes *316*

Chapter 14   Argument: Writing to Persuade   387

Appendixes

Thematic Contents

The questions accompanying these five thematic groupings will help you understand some of the relationships among the sources and will also help you relate your own insights and experiences to the sources. Moreover, the questions will help you formulate topics for your reading-related writing based on a combination of your views and the ideas in the selections. Your writing may mix patterns of writing or primarily use a single pattern such as narration, cause and effect, or comparison and contrast. Keep in mind that even the most specific uses of single patterns are almost never pure.

Childhood and Growing Up

What in your childhood shaped you, limited you, or strengthened you? What still lives with you as childhood pivotal experiences? What lingers as memories, sweet or sour? How were the following authors affected in childhood? How does time change one's perception of events so that something that was once painful is now humorous or something that seemed slight then is profoundly important now?

Struggle with Dignity

Some people deal with adversity better than others. How do individuals in the following sources deal with difficult predicaments, the problems of their everyday lives, and the threat of death? What instances do you find of dignity, heroism, panic, resignation, and struggle? Do you have absolute definitions of *hero* and *dignity,* or do the definitions depend on the circumstances? Which of these sources is the most realistic reaction to a perceived hardship? Which is the most praiseworthy?

Work

In what ways do work and the workplace define, limit, and change individuals? What can make life at work generally pleasant or unpleasant? Do the following sources remind you of any of your work experiences?

The Confrontational Society

What behavior or attitudes are obnoxious in society, and how are they related to freedom, respect for others, and responsibility? What is the most constructive way to complain? Or in some cases are the troubling situations mostly hopeless? How have you on specific occasions dealt with irritating situations?

Gender

Judging from the following reading selections, could one argue that a woman's life—social, work, and love—can be, in some ways, more complicated and difficult than a man's? How are men represented in the following sources?

Preface

Designed for use in either developmental or freshman composition courses, *From Self to Sources: Essays and Beyond* contains comprehensive writing instruction, a systematic research paper guide, a basic handbook, and abundant, engaging readings.

Writing Instruction

Writing instruction includes explanations, examples, and exercises at the sentence, paragraph, and essay levels, with concentration on the essay and the documented essay.

Chapters 1 through 3 define the essay and the documented essay, and explain the writing process.

Chapter 4 covers critical reading, summarizing, paraphrasing, and synthesizing. It shows how students can incorporate ideas from single and multiple sources into their essays and how they can critique or merely explain reading selections.

Chapters 5 through 14 present the patterns of writing exemplified by both the undocumented and the documented essay. This arrangement allows instructors, at any point, to choose an assignment with or without documentation, perhaps beginning with the simple personal essay and advancing toward a more complicated essay of documentation. It even permits the instructor teaching students with disparate writing abilities to mix complexities of assignments within a class.

Here is one available option for instructors using *From Self to Sources:*

- Begin with simple undocumented essays that are related to reading selections in this book; the content in those essays should be parallel or clearly tangential.

- Progress to assignments of documented essays with closer textual ties to single sources, including a few references and a quotation or two. Use MLA style or informal acknowledgment of textbook sources.

- Continue with the assignment of documented essays, using thematically grouped reading assignments and perhaps asking students to find other related material in the library or on the Internet. Students would print out or photocopy the outside material and submit it with their assignments.

- As students become more confident in their abilities and more comfortable with documentation (how to incorporate information and credit sources), begin the research paper unit, which now is only a simple, logical, and highly accessible extension of the classwork rather than a set of intimidating new skills.

Topic suggestions at the ends of chapters include reading-related, career-related, and general topics so that instructors can specify one type or can mix types for class assignments.

Chapter 15, The Research Paper, demonstrates in ten illustrated steps how to write a research paper. This chapter includes MLA documentation style as well as a discussion of libraries, online searching, plagiarism, and other research-related topics.

Chapter 16 is a handbook that includes explanation, examples, and exercises. Answers to half of the exercises appear in the Answer Key, allowing for both classroom work and independent study.

Reading Selections

Selected as exemplary models of writing on stimulating topics, forty-two professional and twenty-three student essays are integrated with writing instruction. Numerous thematically grouped sources with guidelines allow students to consider different perspectives and to develop their own. Each of Chapters 5 through 14 contains both an undocumented and a documented essay by a student writer. The sources are culturally diverse and varied in subject material, so they will appeal to students of different backgrounds—generational, ethnic, gender, and regional—while stressing the commonality of experience. Cartoons by Buddy Hickerson support chapter themes and instruction.

Guide questions following the selections direct students to analyze the readings for form and to react critically to the content. Reading-related writing suggestions direct students to parallel experiences, evaluations, and analyses.

Special Features

- The best integration of reading selections and writing instruction on the market

- Reading-related writing instruction that helps students build confidence and skills with documented writing before working on a research paper

- Practical exercises in organization and revision

- Demonstrations of student essays showing the prewriting and writing stages

- Computer-related writing tips incorporated into the text

- A Writing Process Worksheet suitable for photocopying and intended to provide guidance for students and to save time and effort for instructors

- Extended instruction in writing the summary, paraphrase, and synthesis

- A chapter on the research paper organized around a student demonstration presented in Ten Steps to Writing a Research Paper

- Sentence-writing exercises with material for individual and group work
- A Self-Evaluation Chart to help students track their needs and goals and to promote self-reliance

Support Material for Instructors

The Instructor's Annotated Edition (IAE) contains immediate answers for exercises and activities, along with the following support:

- The Instructor's Guide (all parts included in the IAE)
- Reproducible quizzes for Chapter 16, Handbook, and many professional essays
- Suggestions for effective and time-saving approaches to instruction
- A sample syllabus

Software Resources

- Houghton Mifflin Grammar CD-Rom for PC and Macintosh. Teaches and reinforces the basics of grammar, punctuation, and mechanics.
- Expressways, Version 4.0, for PC, Macintosh, and Windows. Guides students as they write and revise paragraphs and essays.

Acknowledgments

I am profoundly indebted to the following instructors who have reviewed this textbook: Dr. Catherine Packard of Southeastern Illinois College; Joanna Tardoni of Western Wyoming Community College; Kathleen Rice of Community College of Indiana; Carol Miter of Riverside Community College; Thomas Beery of Lima Technical College; Janet Cutshall of Sussex County Community College; Jill A. Lahnstein of Cape Fear Community College; Athene W. Sallee of Forsyth Technical Community College; and Julie Nichols of Okaloosa-Walton Community College. Thanks also to the faculty members at Mt. San Antonio College, with special recognition to the Basic Courses Review Committee.

I deeply appreciate the work of freelance editors Ann Marie Radaskewicz and Mary Dalton Hoffman, Nancy Benjamin of Books By Design, as well as my colleagues at Houghton Mifflin: Mary Jo Southern, Kellie Cardone, Anna Rice, Danielle Richardson, Peter Mooney, and Kathryn Dinovo.

I am especially grateful to my family of wife, children and their spouses, and grandchildren for their cheerful, inspiring support: Sharon, Kelly, Erin, Jeanne, Michael, Shane, Lauren, Jarrett, and Matthew.

Lee Brandon

Student Overview

THE QUIGMANS   by Buddy Hickerson

"I know you love me, Francine ... I
just need it in writing."

Practice with Principles

S ome will tell you that to become a better writer you should practice. Others will say that to become a better writer you should learn the principles of writing.

Each view is a half-truth. If you practice without knowing what to do, you'll get better only within your own limitations; any bad habits are likely to become more ingrained. If you learn the principles of writing and do not practice them, they will never become a functioning part of your skills. Making that connection of practice and principles is now within your grasp as you gaze at a book with a well-rounded approach to writing. Combining sound techniques and ample writing practice, *From Self to Sources: Essays and Beyond* is designed for use both in class and on your own.

The subtitle might suggest two subjects to you. The word *beyond* refers to documented essays. Actually, essays and documented essays are quite similar. An *essay* is a group of paragraphs, each of which supports a single idea. A *documented essay* is the same, except that it includes some acknowledged content from another source or sources. The borrowed material may be as little as a single idea taken from one source in this textbook, or it may be many ideas pulled together into a research paper.

It is not difficult to incorporate the views of others into your essay. Moreover, the procedure for giving credit to your source or sources is easy. One premise of this book is that as you write some short documented essays during the first part of the course, you will become comfortable with the process. Later in the course, writing a longer documented essay, the research paper, will be merely the next step. The progression will be logical. The step will be easily accessible.

Each chapter in this book begins with a list of chapter topics.

Chapters 1 through 3 discuss the essay, the documented essay, and the writing process, including a detailed student example.

Chapter 4 explains reading-related writing: reading critically, underlining, annotating, outlining, note taking, summarizing, paraphrasing, synthesizing, evaluating, and documenting.

Chapters 5 through 14 focus on forms of discourse, commonly called patterns of development: narration, description, exposition (explaining), and argumentation. Each chapter includes a student essay and a student documented essay.

Chapter 15 presents a discussion of the research paper.

Chapter 16, the handbook, offers instruction in fundamentals, sentence writing, spelling, and ESL problems.

The Appendixes cover the Writing Process Worksheet, taking tests, and writing job applications and résumés.

Strategies for Self-Improvement

Here are some strategies you can follow to make the best use of this book and to jump-start the improvement in your writing skills.

1. *Be active and systematic in learning.* Take advantage of your instructor's expertise by being an active class member—one who takes notes, asks questions, and contributes to discussion. Become dedicated to systematic learning: Determine your needs, decide what to do, and do it. Make learning a part of your everyday thinking and behavior.

2. *Read widely.* Samuel Johnson, a great English scholar, once said he didn't want to read anything by people who had written more than they had read. William Faulkner, a Nobel Prize winner in literature, said, "Read, read, read. Read everything—trash, classics, good and bad, and see how writers do it." Read to learn technique, to acquire ideas, and to be stimulated to write. Especially read to satisfy your curiosity and to receive pleasure. If reading is a main component of your course, approach it as systematically as you do writing.

3. *Keep a journal.* Keep a journal even though it may not be required in your particular class. It is a good practice to jot down your observations in a notebook. Here are some topics for daily, or almost daily, journal writing:

   • Summarize, evaluate, or react to reading assignments.

   • Summarize, evaluate, or react to what you see on television and in movies, and to what you read in newspapers and in magazines.

   • Describe and narrate situations or events you experience.

   • Write about career-related matters you encounter in other courses or on the job.

   Your journal entries may read like an intellectual diary, a record of what you are thinking about at certain times. Keeping a journal will help you to understand reading material better, to develop more language skills, and to think more clearly—as well as to become more confident and to write more easily so that writing becomes a comfortable, everyday activity. Your entries may also provide subject material for longer, more carefully crafted pieces. The most important thing is to get into the habit of writing something each day.

4. *Evaluate your writing skills.* Use the Self-Evaluation Chart inside the front cover of this book to assess your writing skills by listing problem areas you need to work on. You may be adding to these lists throughout the entire term. Drawing on your instructor's comments, make notes on matters such as organization, development, content, spelling, vocabulary, diction, grammar, sentence structure, punctuation, and capitalization. Use this chart for self-motivated

study assignments and as a checklist in all stages of writing. As you master each problem area, you can erase it or cross it out.

Most of the elements you record in your Self-Evaluation Chart probably are covered in *From Self to Sources*. The table of contents, the index, and the Correction Chart on the inside back cover of the book will direct you to the additional instruction you decide you need.

- *Organization/Development/Content:* List aspects of your writing, including the techniques of all stages of the writing process, such as freewriting, brainstorming, and clustering; the phrasing of a good topic sentence or thesis; and the design, growth, and refinement of your ideas.

- *Spelling/Vocabulary/Diction:* List common spelling words marked as incorrect on your college assignments. Here, *common* means words that you use often. If you are misspelling these words now, you may have been doing so for years. Look at your list. Is there a pattern to your misspellings? Consult the Improving Spelling section in Chapter 16 for a set of useful rules. Whatever it takes, master the words on your list. Continue to add troublesome words as you accumulate assignments. If your vocabulary is imprecise or your diction is inappropriate (if you use slang, trite expressions, or words that are too informal), note those problems as well.

- *Grammar/Sentence Structure:* List recurring problems in your grammar or sentence structure. Use the symbols and page references listed on the Correction Chart (inside back cover of this book) or look up the problem in the index.

- *Punctuation/Capitalization:* Treat these problems the same way you treat grammar problems. Note that the Mastering Punctuation and Conquering Capitalization sections in Chapter 16 number some rules; therefore, you can often give exact locations of the remedies for your problems.

Here is an example of how your chart might be used.

Self-Evaluation Chart

Organization/ Development/ Content	Spelling/ Vocabulary/ Diction	Grammar/ Sentence Structure	Punctuation/ Capitalization
needs more specific support such as examples, 166	avoid slang, 53	fragments, 480	difference between semicolons and commas, 507
refine outline, 39	avoid clichés such as "be there for me," 53	subject-verb agreement, 489	
		comma splice, 481	comma after long introductory modifier, 506
use clear topic sentence, 14	it's, its, 521		
	rec*ei*ve, rule on, 517	vary sentence patterns, 58	

5. *Use the Writing Process Worksheet.* Record details about each of your assignments, such as the due date, topic, length, and form. The worksheet will also remind you of the stages of the writing process: explore, organize, and write. A blank Writing Process Worksheet for you to photocopy for assignments appears on page 31 and in Appendix A, page 531. Discussed in Chapters 2 and 3, it illustrates student work in almost every chapter. Your instructor may ask you to complete the form and submit it with your assignments.

6. *Take full advantage of technology.* Although using a word processor will not by itself make you a better writer, it will enable you to write and revise more swiftly as you move, alter, and delete material with a few keystrokes. Devices such as the thesaurus, spell checker, grammar checker, and style checker will help you revise and edit. Many colleges have writing labs with good instruction and facilities for networking and researching complicated topics. The Internet, used wisely, can provide resource materials for compositions.

7. *Be positive.* To improve your English skills, write with freedom, but revise and edit with rigor. Work with your instructor to set attainable goals, and proceed at a reasonable pace. Soon, seeing what you have mastered and checked off your list will give you a sense of accomplishment.

While you progress in your English course, notice how you are getting better at content, organization, and mechanics as you read, think, and write.

Consequently, you can expect writing to become a highly satisfying pleasure. After all, once you learn to write well, writing can be just as enjoyable as talking.

Finally, don't compare yourself with others. Compare yourself with yourself and, as you improve, consider yourself what you are—a student on the path toward more effective writing, a student on the path toward success.

1

The Essay and Its Parts

THE QUIGMANS   by Buddy Hickerson

© Tribune Media Services, Inc. All Rights Reserved. Reprinted with permission.

his book begins with the assumption that you have these questions about writing an essay:

- What do you mean by *essay?*
- How do I write an essay?
- How do I use sources in writing essays?

These questions are answered directly in the first four chapters. Chapter 1 defines the word *essay,* examines its parts, and provides an example. Chapters 2 and 3 discuss a system called the writing process. Chapter 4 addresses the use of sources in writing, with an emphasis on connecting reading and writing. All of this instruction is accompanied by exercises that will engage you in the most important part of learning to write well: writing itself.

The Essay Defined

Writing an essay is remarkably similar to other writing you have done. Whether you are composing a friendly e-mail, a job application, a customer complaint, an accident report, or a college essay, you are likely to follow a similar pattern. In some way, you will probably introduce your subject, discuss it, and end on a note of finality.

An essay is a group of paragraphs, each of which supports a controlling idea called a thesis. The length of an essay varies, but in college writing the number of paragraphs in a short essay is likely to be between three and nine. Many short essays are about five paragraphs long, often because of the nature of the assignment and time limitations, but there is no special significance in the number five.

Figure 1.1 shows the essay in its simplest form.

Essays and Documented Essays

You are probably most familiar with the simple personal essay, a relatively independent piece of writing derived from reflection or experience—for example, how you have been influenced by one individual or what you learned from a part-time job. Because it is based on your perceptions and contains no references to sources, it is called an undocumented essay or, simply, an essay.

However, as you move deeper into your college program, you increasingly will be expected to support your ideas by referring to sources, especially reading material. The result will be a documented essay or a research paper. That work will be either informally or formally

Figure 1.1
Essay Pattern

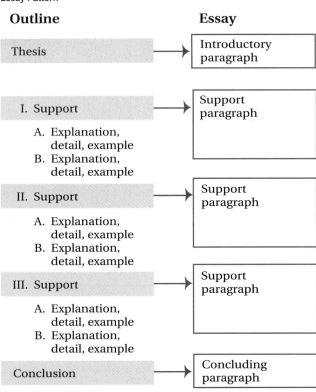

documented, meaning that you will indicate, in some way, where you found the ideas you borrowed.

The basic form of documented or undocumented essays is about the same, and is similar to that in the following example, although the number of support paragraphs may vary.

Student Essay

Student Lvette Lohayza wrote her simple personal essay in response to this assignment:

> Write an essay about how to do something or about how something was done. For example, you might write about how your family cooks and serves a special holiday meal. Placed within a cultural framework, it could interestingly provide information about both the process and the culture, blending the two.

The parts of the essay are marked to show the structure of both the essay and the supporting paragraphs.

Tamales, a Family Production

Lvette Lohayza

Christmas Eve at Grandma's house is a joyous time, especially for the females of my family. <u>That is the time when we assist</u> **Thesis** <u>Grandma in making her wonderfully palatable tamales.</u> Beginning at daybreak and ending after darkness, it is an occasion of bonding **Introductory** and reunion. Grandma always greets us with a freshly brewed pot **paragraph** of coffee and some *dulce.* The next eight hours will be a whirlwind of lively talk and cooperative work.

Topic sentence 　　<u>Soon after our coffee, we drive off to a special market called the</u> <u>*mercado,* where Grandma leads us in shopping for the items we</u> <u>need.</u> First, we visit the butcher, whose name is Pepé. He is await- ing Grandma's arrival, as he does every year. He has put aside his freshest beefsteaks just for her. She carefully chooses the red- **Support paragraph** dest and the most visibly fat-free meat available. According to Grandma, the meat must be bright red because that is a clear indi- cation of its freshness, and freshness is especially what her tamales depend on. Next, we follow Grandma to an aisle where she exam- ines piles of *ojas,* or corn husks, which are used for wrapping and cooking the tamales. We help her select and count out an equal number of large and medium husks. Then we stop at the canned- food section for what is known as *chili de las palmas,* a hot and spicy red sauce. Finally, we reach the section of the market that prepares and sells *masa,* a cornmeal substance for encasing the meat in the tamales. Shopping as a group has brought us closer together and reminded us of the complete annual event, which will now include the cooking and later will end at the dinner table.

Topic sentence 　　<u>As soon as we return, at nearly eight in the morning, Grandma,</u> <u>like a colonel, delegates duties for the first stage of our work.</u> A vet- eran crew boils the meat in black cast-iron pots, each large piece **Support paragraph** with a clove of garlic embedded in it for flavor. Several older women sort out the corn husks, large from medium, as the younger girls wash them and put them in separate stacks to dry on a six-foot table. By the time the husks have dried, the boiled meat is ready for shredding. With Grandma watching over our shoulders, the room is full of laughter and talk and enjoyable industry. Grandma herself sets two twenty-five-gallon shining steel pots onto burners and pours in about four inches of water. Then she drops in racks that will be used for steaming the tamales. Meanwhile, as the spicy aroma fills the kitchen, and the ambiance becomes ever more cheerful, we all gather around the table and shred the meat with our bare hands.

Topic sentence	<u>After the meat has been shredded, we mix it with chili sauce and olives and begin forming the tamales on the large table, where the dry corn husks lie in stacks of medium and large.</u> The first step is to use a butter knife to spread *masa* on a large corn husk. Next,
Support paragraph	we fork a couple of heaps of meat onto the *masa.* Then we add another generous layer of *masa* and cap it with a medium corn husk. Carefully, we roll the edges of the larger leaf over the edges of the medium leaf to seal the tamale, so that no meat or *masa* leaks out while cooking. This continual spreading, stuffing, and rolling of the tamales will go on for the next two to three hours.
Topic sentence	<u>Once all of the tamales have been rolled, they are carefully stacked in the large cooking pots and a wet hand towel is placed on</u>
Support paragraph	<u>top of the tamales to trap the steam while they are cooking.</u> Four to six hours of steam-cooking pass before the tamales are ready for consumption.
Concluding paragraph	By this time, we all have insatiable appetites and are ready for this well-deserved meal. Smiling broadly and listening to compliments as she takes orders, meaning requests, Grandma is the main server. The children, who have been peeking into the kitchen and begging for bites, are served at their own table. Standing in line with plates, the men are calling out the numbers of tamales they need to satisfy their prodigious appetites. The young men, who are, in their own way, part of the group effort because they provided valet parking as families arrived, follow their fathers and uncles in line. We females, independent as some of us may be most of the year, are fortunate in that we get to enjoy the whole process as team members with Grandma and family, and for that experience, the eating of the Christmas tamales is all the better.

The Parts of an Essay

The main components in an essay are the introduction, support paragraphs, transitions, and the conclusion.

- The *introduction* is usually only one paragraph that includes the thesis, which states the controlling idea.

- *Support paragraphs,* sometimes called the body, offer evidence and reasoning.

- *Transition paragraphs* are single, brief paragraphs that point out divisions of the essay. (They are seldom used in the short essay.)

- The *conclusion* provides an appropriate ending—often a restatement of or a reflection on the thesis.

The Thesis Defined

The six most important words this book can offer you are *State your thesis and support it.* It is not surprising, therefore, that the thesis is an essential part of your introduction and probably the most important sentence in your essay.

Origin of the Thesis

The thesis of an essay can come from different sources. You may generate it early on through prewriting, you may develop it from something you have read, or you may be assigned a topic. In any case, you need to work on your thesis statement—just that one sentence—until you have developed an interesting subject and a well-focused treatment. Your working thesis may differ from the one you finally use in your essay, but it can easily be reworded once you begin writing and revising.

Writing the Thesis

An effective thesis is one that can be developed with supporting information. *It has both a subject **and** a treatment. The **subject** is what you intend to write about. The **treatment** is what you intend to do with your subject.*

> **Example:** Glendora High School   offers a well-balanced
> subject   treatment
> academic program.

In some instances the subject will follow the treatment:

> The time has come for a national law legalizing
> treatment
> physician-assisted suicide for the terminally ill.
> subject

In other instances the subject will divide the treatment:

> Four factors establish Elvis Presley as the greatest
> treatment   subject   treatment
> entertainer of the twentieth century: appearance,
> singing ability, style, and influence.

An ineffective thesis usually presents a treatment that is vague, too broad, or too narrow. It may also have a subject that is too general or too broad.

Vague: The Santa Anita Mall is great. (The word *great* is
<u>subject</u>   <u>treatment</u>
imprecise.)

Better: The Santa Anita Mall allows me to purchase all of my
<u>subject</u>   <u>treatment</u>
clothing needs in one location. (The treatment specifies
something that can be developed.)

Too broad: Shopping malls have caused trouble. (The phrase
<u>subject</u>   <u>treatment</u>
shopping malls is general, meaning all malls, and the
treatment is imprecise.)

Better: The development of the Santa Anita Mall contributed
<u>subject</u>   <u>treatment</u>
to the decline of several nearby downtown retail centers.
(The subject has been restricted from all malls to one mall,
and the concern is now specified as *development;* the
treatment, *have caused trouble,* is made more specific.)

Too narrow: The Santa Anita Mall is located in Arcadia,
<u>subject</u>   <u>treatment</u>
California. (This is only a fact, something that can be
verified but not developed.)

Better: The Santa Anita Mall was built at a location
<u>subject</u>   <u>treatment</u>
highly accessible to urban shoppers. (This adjustment
indicates that the location is highly important to urban
shoppers, an idea that can be developed.)

Exercise 1   **EVALUATING THESES**

In the following theses, underline and label the subjects (S) and treatments (T). Also judge each one as effective (E) or ineffective (I).

Example:

___I___   *Moby Dick* is an interesting book.
S   T

___E___   1. Pop music is a reflection of contemporary values.
S   T

___I___   2. William Faulkner was born in Mississippi.
S   T

_____E_____ 3. <u>Education</u> has value beyond <u>money</u>.
  S T

_____E_____ 4. <u>Hope</u> is not the same as <u>expectation</u>.
  S T

_____E_____ 5. <u>Individuals</u> do not have the right to <u>select the laws they</u>
  S T
will obey.

_____I_____ 6. <u>I</u> was born in <u>Brooklyn</u>.
  S T

_____I_____ 7. <u>Greece</u> has <u>a long history</u>.
  S T

_____I_____ 8. <u>Sacramento</u> is the <u>capital of California</u>.
  S T

_____E_____ 9. <u>Knowledge</u> is not the same as <u>wisdom</u>.
  S T

_____I_____ 10. <u>The history of organically grown foods</u> is <u>fascinating</u>.
  S T

| **Exercise 2** | **EVALUATING THESES** |

Complete the following entries to make each one an effective thesis.
Answers will vary.
1. Puppy love is based on <u>physical attraction.</u>

   _____

2. Sports at the professional level are becoming <u>far too commercial.</u>

   _____

3. Tattoos are more expensive to remove <u>than to acquire.</u>

   _____

4. Heredity and environment are both important in <u>the formation of character</u>
   <u>and personality.</u>

5. Exercise can become <u>a preoccupation.</u>

   _____

6. Toxic waste occurs in <u>the air, in water, and on the land.</u>

   _____

7. Television commercials are often <u>misleading.</u>

   _____

8. People who grow up economically deprived <u>are likely to be thrifty.</u>

   _____

9. My unreasonable boss gave me <u>more work than I could do.</u>

_____

10. My part-time job has taught me <u>self-sufficiency.</u>

_____

Exercise 3	**WRITING THESES**

For each subject, add a treatment to create an effective thesis. You may also restrict or alter the subject by making it more specific. The subject need not be the first word in your thesis.
Answers will vary.

1. Cell phones <u>should be banned in restaurants.</u>

_____

2. Skateboards <u>offer youth an opportunity to pursue a sport without adult interference.</u>

_____

3. SUVs <u>are a subject of controversy.</u>

_____

4. Madonna <u>thrives on controversy.</u>

_____

5. Elvis <u>came from country, blues, and gospel music roots.</u>

_____

6. Human clones <u>can be used someday as a solution to infertility.</u>

_____

7. Textbooks <u>are the highest form of artistic expression.</u>

_____

8. Truthfulness <u>at the expense of hurt feelings is not a good policy.</u>

_____

9. Humor <u>can diffuse tense situations.</u>

_____

10. Divorce <u>is sometimes the best solution to a bad marriage.</u>

_____

Forms of Support for the Thesis

Some essay assignments benefit from a rich combination of supporting forms for the organization of content. Others require an emphasis on a particular form, as instructors ask students to discuss causes, to show effects, to argue a position, to examine parts of a whole unit, to define concepts, to explain a process, to compare ideas, and so on. Those particular forms will be our main concern in this book. The following basic outlines show some of the most common ways for dividing and organizing ideas. Keep in mind that these are only frameworks for essays and that, in writing, forms will overlap in varying degrees. For instance, you might be comparing and contrasting ideas, but you could still use examples, description, and definitions for further support. In the outlines, each Roman numeral heading represents one or more paragraphs of support. Although the outlines are, by their nature, mechanical, the well-written finished essay submerges the form in flowing content.

- *Narration:* division of time or incident to tell a story
    - I. Situation
    - II. Conflict
    - III. Struggle
    - IV. Outcome
    - V. Meaning

- *Exemplification:* division into several examples or sets of examples
    - I. First example (or a set of examples)
    - II. Second example (or a set of examples)
    - III. Third example (or a set of examples)

- *Process analysis:* division into steps, telling how something is done (the form used in the student essay on pp. 9–10)
    - I. Preparation
    - II. Steps
        - A. Step 1
        - B. Step 2
        - C. Step 3

- *Analysis by division:* division of a unit into parts (for example, an essay has an introduction, development of a thesis, and a conclusion).
    - I. First part
    - II. Second part
    - III. Third part

- *Causes and effects:* division into causes or effects
  - I. Cause (or effect) one
  - II. Cause (or effect) two
  - III. Cause (or effect) three

These forms, as well as description, classification, comparison and contrast, definition, and argument are the subjects of individual chapters in this book.

Special Paragraphs Within the Essay

Understanding the function and structure of the three main components of an essay—paragraphs of introduction, support, and conclusion—will help you in both planning and writing your assignments.

Introductory Paragraphs

A good introductory paragraph does many things. It attracts the reader's interest, states or points toward the thesis, and moves the reader smoothly into the support, or developmental, paragraphs. Introductory methods include

- a direct statement of the thesis
- background
- definition of term(s)
- quotation(s)
- a shocking statement
- question(s)
- a combination of two or more methods in this list

You should not decide that some of the methods are good and some are bad. Indeed, all are valid, and the most common one is the last, the combination. Use the approach that best fits each essay. Resist the temptation to use the same kind of introduction in every essay you write.

Each of the following statements is an introductory paragraph. The thesis is the same in all of them, yet each uses a different introductory method. Notice the great variety here.

Direct Statement of the Thesis:

Anyone on the road in any city near midnight on Friday and Saturday is among dangerous people. They're not the product of the witching hour; they're the product of the "happy hour."

Subject
Treatment

They're called drunk drivers. <u>These threats to our lives and limbs need to be controlled by federal laws with strong provisions.</u>

Background:

In one four-year period in California (1995–1998), 15,363 people were injured and 5,954 were killed by drunk drivers. Each year, the same kinds of figures come in from all our states. The state laws vary. The federal government does virtually nothing. Drunk driving has reached the point of being a national problem of huge proportions. <u>This slaughter of innocent citizens should be stopped by following the lead of many other nations and passing federal legislation with strong provisions.</u>

Subject
Treatment

Definition of Terms:

Here's a recipe. Take two thousand pounds of plastic, rubber, and steel, pour in ten gallons of gas, and start the engine. Then take one human being of two hundred pounds of flesh, blood, and bones, pour in two glasses of beer in one hour, and put him or her behind the wheel. Mix the two together, and the result may be a drunken driver ready to cause death and destruction. <u>This problem of drunk driving</u> can and should be controlled by federal legislation with strong provisions.

Subject
Treatment

Quotation:

The National Highway Traffic Safety Administration has stated that 50 percent of all fatal accidents involve intoxicated drivers and that "75 percent of those drivers have a blood alcohol content of .10 percent or greater." That kind of information is widely known, yet the carnage on the highways continues. <u>This problem of drunk driving</u> should be addressed by a federal law with strict provisions.

Subject
Treatment

Shocking Statement and Questions:

Almost 60,000 Americans were killed in the Vietnam War. What other war kills more than that number every four years? Give up? It's the war with drunk drivers. The war in Vietnam ended about three decades ago, but our DUI war goes on, and the drunks are winning. <u>This deadly conflict</u> should be controlled by a federal law with strong provisions.

Subject
Treatment

Questions and a Definition:

What is a drunk driver? In California it's a person with a blood alcohol content of .08 percent or more who is operating a motor vehicle. What do those drivers do? Some of them kill. Every year more than 16,000 people nationwide die. Those are easy ques-

**Subject
Treatment**

tions. The difficult one is, What can be done? One answer is clear: <u>Drunk drivers</u> <u>should be controlled by federal laws with strong provisions.</u>

All these introductory methods are effective. Some others, however, are ineffective because they are too vague to carry the thesis or because they carry the thesis in a mechanical way. The mechanical approach may be direct and explicit, but it usually numbs the reader's imagination and interest.

Avoid: The purpose of this essay is to write about the need for strong national laws against drunk driving.

Avoid: I will now write a paper about the need for strong national laws against drunk driving.

The length of an introduction can vary, but the typical length for the introductory paragraph of a student essay is three to five sentences. If your introduction is shorter than three sentences, be certain that it conveys all that you want to say. If it is longer than five, be certain that it only introduces and does not try to expand on ideas. That function is reserved for the developmental paragraphs; a long and complicated introduction may make your essay top-heavy.

Exercise 4   **WRITING AN INTRODUCTION**

Pick one of the following theses (altering it a bit to suit your own ideas, if you like) and write at least two introductions for it, using a different method for each one. Underline the thesis in each paragraph, and label the subject and treatment parts.
Answers will vary.

1. Owning a home makes more sense than renting an apartment.

2. The extent of student cheating is unknown by most instructors.

3. Much sexual harassment goes unreported for understandable reasons.

4. Hunting is not regarded as a sport by animals in the wild.

5. Balancing parts of one's life is a major problem for most students I know.

6. Fanatics are troubled people, even if they are engaged in worthwhile concerns.

7. Heroes exist in everyday life.

8. The ethnic makeup of my neighborhood has changed in the last ten years.

9. Getting a job at _____ is a matter of following certain guidelines.

10. A career choice should be based on factors other than money.

Support Paragraphs

Support paragraphs, also called developmental paragraphs, form the body of an essay and provide information and reasoning that justify the thesis contained in the paragraph of introduction.

The following paragraph is both a definition and an example of the developmental paragraph:

Topic sentence

Support
Support

Support

<u>The developmental paragraph contains three parts: the subject, the topic sentence, and the support.</u> The *subject* is what you will write about. It is likely to be broad and must be focused or qualified for specific treatment. The *topic sentence* contains both the subject and the treatment—what you will do with the subject. It carries the central idea to which everything else in the paragraph is subordinated. For example, the first sentence of this paragraph is a topic sentence. Even when not stated, the topic sentence as an underlying idea unifies the paragraph. The *support* is the evidence or reasoning by which a topic sentence is developed. It comes in several basic patterns and serves any of

the four forms of expression: narration, description, exposition, and argumentation. These forms, which are usually combined in writing, will be presented with both student and professional examples in the following chapters. <u>The developmental paragraph, therefore, is a group of sentences, each with the function of supporting a controlling idea called the topic sentence.</u>

Concluding sentence *(margin note)*

Concluding Paragraphs

Your concluding paragraph should give the reader the feeling that you have said all you want to say about your subject. Like introductory paragraphs, concluding paragraphs are of various types. Here are some effective ways of concluding an essay:

- Conclude with a final paragraph or sentence that is a logical part of the body of the essay; that is, it functions as part of the support. In the following example, there is no formal conclusion. This form is more common in the published essay than in the student essay.

    One day he hit me. He said he was sorry and even cried, but I could not forgive him. We got a divorce. It took me a while before I could look back and see what the causes really were, but by then it was too late to make any changes.

    Maria Campos, "A Divorce with Reasons" *(margin note)*

- Conclude with a restatement of the thesis in slightly different words, perhaps pointing out its significance and/or making applications.

    Don't blame it on the referee. Don't even blame it on the fight managers. Put the blame where it belongs—on the prevailing mores that regard prize fighting as a perfectly proper enterprise and vehicle of entertainment. No one doubts that many people enjoy prize fighting and will miss it if it should be thrown out. And that is precisely the point.

    Norman Cousins, "Who Killed Benny Paret?" *(margin note)*

- Conclude with a review of the main points of the discussion—a kind of summary. This is appropriate only if the complexity of the essay makes a summary necessary.

    As we have been made all too aware lately in this country, the more energy we conserve now, the more we'll have for the future. The same holds true for skiing. So take the Soft Path of energy conservation as you ski. You'll not only be able to make longer nonstop runs, but you'll have more energy to burn on the dance floor.

    Carl Wingus, "Conserving Energy as You Ski" *(margin note)*

- Conclude with an anecdote related to the thesis.

    Over the harsh traffic sounds of motors and horns and blaring radios came the faint whang-whang of a would-be musician with a beat-up guitar and a money-drop hat turned up at his feet. It all reminded me of when I had first experienced the conglomeration of things that now assailed my senses. This jumbled mixture of things both human and nonhuman was, in fact, the reason I had come to live here. Then it was different and exciting. Later it was the reason I was leaving.

Brian Maxwell, "Leaving Los Angeles"

• Conclude with a quotation related to the thesis.

    More than half the fatal traffic accidents involve intoxicated drivers, according to the National Highway Traffic Safety Administration. Cavenaugh and Associates, research specialists, say that drunk drivers killed 47,000 people in California in the five-year period from 1993 through 1997. They go on to say that intoxicated drivers cost us somewhere between eleven billion and twenty-four billion dollars each year. It is time to give drunk drivers a message: "Stay off the road. You are costing us pain, injury, and death, and no one has the right to do that."

Daniel Humphries, "Get Them Off the Road"

There are also many ineffective ways of concluding an essay. Do not conclude with the following:

• a summary when a summary is unnecessary.

• a complaint about the assignment or an apology about the quality of the work.

• an afterthought—that is, something you forgot to discuss in the body of the paper.

• a tagged conclusion—that is, a sentence beginning with such phrases as *In conclusion, To conclude,* or *I would like to conclude this discussion,* or *Last but not least.*

• a conclusion that raises additional problems that should have been settled during the discussion.

The conclusion is an integral part of the essay and is often a reflection of the introduction. If you have trouble with the conclusion, reread your introduction. Then work for a roundness or completeness in the whole paper.

Exercise 5   WRITING A CONCLUDING PARAGRAPH

For Exercise 4, you wrote two introductions. Select the better one, consider the basic information you would probably use for support (jotting down a few ideas if you like), and then write a simple conclusion of three to five sentences. This is an exercise to demonstrate that the conclusion connects with the introduction, is a consequence of the development of the essay, and ends on a note of finality. Of course, in your regular assignments, you will not write your conclusion until after you have written the other paragraphs.

Answers will vary.

| Exercise 6 | **EVALUATING AN ESSAY** |

Mark the following essay in this way:

- *Circle the introductory paragraph.*
- *Enclose the concluding paragraph in a rectangle.*
- *Double underline the thesis.*
- *Underline the topic sentence for each support paragraph.*

She Came a Long Way

Shontel Jasper

Introductory paragraph

Eyelids closed, she lay in the white hospital bed in the intensive care ward, her lungs filling with water and collapsing. In three days she would be dead, but she wouldn't go easily. <u>She would go out as</u>

Thesis

<u>she had lived, for she had no choice.</u>

Topic sentence

<u>She could have been an aged poster child for emphysema and lung cancer.</u> Her face was drawn around her skull, her head was hairless from chemotherapy, the lines around her eyes revealed years of squinting through tobacco smoke, and her lips were dry and flaky like scales of a dead fish lying in the sun. A thin plastic belt hung loosely under her slack jowls like a necklace and the pendant was a clear plastic plug with a hole in it. The plug had been inserted into an incision in the woman's throat to aid her in breathing, and the air now whistled in and out irregularly. At the head of her bed stood an oxygen bottle like a cold and impersonal sentinel.

Topic sentence

The nurse had just checked off items on the chart and left the room. <u>Slowly, warily, the patient opened her eyes, and seeing no one in the room, immediately began her caper.</u> Because of her shallow, rapid breathing, she was a study in slow movement. First there was a faint stirring under the sheet and then the sound of crackling cellophane. Then her hands emerged, holding a crumpled pack of Camels, from which she took a crooked cigarette before putting the remainder back under the covers. Next she removed the thin book of matches from her pillowcase. With the cigarette and matches clutched in her right hand, she fingered the control button to raise the head of her bed to almost ninety degrees. Laboriously, she swung her legs over the edge of the mattress, and choked back a fit of wheezy coughing that made the plug sound like a toddler playing a penny whistle.

Topic sentence

Heading for the rest room, she knew exactly what she would do, because she had done it before. After closing the door behind herself, she turned on the exhaust fan. She then popped the insert from the plug and licked the paper at the end of her cigarette. When she raised her chin, the raw flesh showed through the transparent plastic, looking like a gill slit, into which she placed her cigarette and pinched the plastic around the part she had just licked. With trembling hands she scratched a match to flame and raised it awkwardly toward the cigarette. Instinctively, she looked above the commode for a mirror, but there was none. The hospital doesn't want patients in this ward to see their own images.

Concluding paragraph

> At last the moment of enjoyment had arrived. After taking a deep drag and removing the cigarette, she coughed, and the smoke streamed out of the hole and billowed. It looked white and vaporous as if she were an internal-combustion engine with a blown head gasket. She held her chin high, and lined up the hole carefully to receive the treat once more.

Basic Paragraph Patterns

Two effective patterns of conventional paragraph structure are shown in Figure 1.2. Pattern A merely states the controlling idea, the topic sentence, and develops it; Pattern B adds a concluding sentence following the topic development. Two other forms of paragraph structure—the paragraph with an unstated but implied topic sentence and the paragraph with the topic sentence at the end of the paragraph—are used less frequently in college writing.

Figure 1.2
Paragraph Patterns

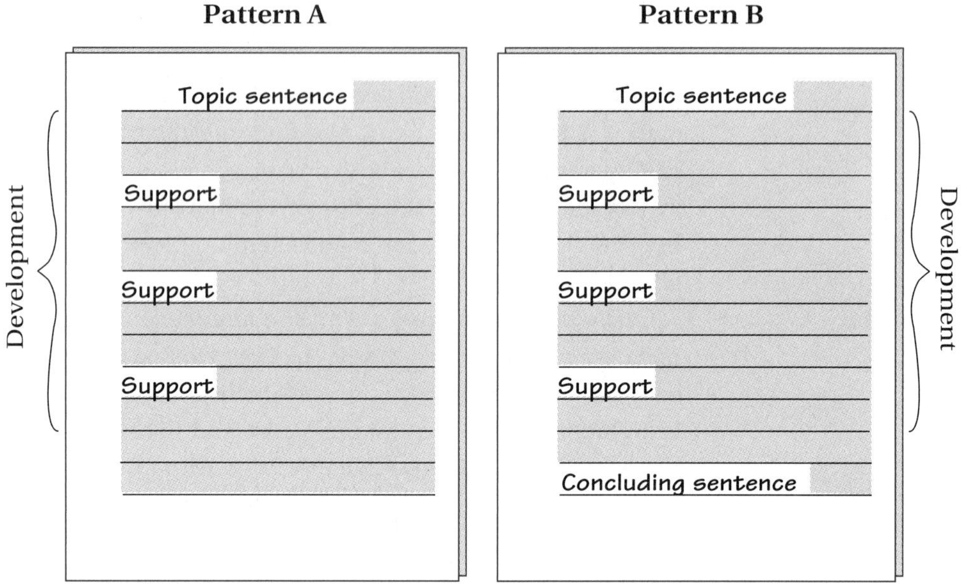

Pattern A

Development

Topic sentence

Support

Support

Support

Pattern B

Development

Topic sentence

Support

Support

Support

Concluding sentence

Example of Pattern A:

Pity, Anger, and Achievement Performance

Topic sentence
Support

It is generally thought that pity and sympathy are "good" emotions and that anger is a "bad" emotion. <u>However, attribution theorists have pointed out that the consequences of these emotional expressions are complex. In one investigation,</u> Graham (1984) gave subjects (twelve-year-old children) false failure feedback during an achievement task. For some children, this was accompanied by the remark: "I feel sorry for you" as well as body postures and facial gestures that accompany sympathy (head down, hands folded, etc.). To other students, the experimenter said: "I am angry with you." Students receiving the pity feedback tended to blame the failure on themselves (low ability) and their performance declined. On the other hand, students receiving anger feedback attributed their failure to lack of effort

Support

and their performance subsequently increased. <u>This is not to advocate that sympathy is always detrimental and anger always facilitative.</u> Rather, the consequences of feedback depend on how that feedback is construed and what it means to the recipient of the communication. Other kinds of feedback, such as praise for success at an easy task and excessive and unsolicited helping, also tend to convey that the student is "unable" and therefore have some negative consequences.

Seymour Feshbach and
Bernard Weiner, *Personality*

Example of Pattern B:

Primitive Methods of Lie Detection

Topic sentence

<u>Throughout history there have been efforts to distinguish the guilty from the innocent and to tell the liars from the truthful.</u>

Support

For example, <u>a method of lie detection practiced in Asia</u> involved giving those suspected of a crime a handful of raw rice to chew. After chewing for some time, the persons were instructed to spit out the rice. The innocent person was anticipated to do this easily, whereas the guilty party was expected to have grains of rice sticking to the roof of the mouth and tongue. This technique relied on the increased sympathetic nervous system activity in the presumably fearful and guilty person. This activity would result in the drying up of saliva that, in turn, would cause grains of rice to stick in the mouth.

Support

<u>A similar but more frightening technique</u> involved placing a heated knife blade briefly against the tongue, another method used for criminal detection. An innocent person would not be burned while the guilty party would immediately feel pain, again because of the relative dryness of the mouth.

Concluding sentence

<u>Many of these methods relied (unknowingly) on the basic physiological principles that also guided the creation of the polygraph.</u>

Seymour Feshbach and
Bernard Weiner, *Personality*

Exercise 7   **ANALYZING A PARAGRAPH**

1. Is the following paragraph developed in Pattern A (topic sentence/ development) or Pattern B (topic sentence/development/concluding sentence)?
   Pattern A

2. Identify the parts of the paragraph pattern by underlining the topic sentence and the concluding sentence, if any, and annotating the support in the left margin. Use the two example paragraphs as models.

Topic sentence

Support (example)

Support (example)

Support (example)

Support (example)

<u>But now I can say that I am a Japanese-American.</u> It means I have a place here in this country, too. I have a place here on the East Coast, where our neighbor is so much a part of our family that my mother never passes her house at night without glancing at the lights to see if she is home and safe; where my parents have hauled hundreds of pounds of rocks from fields and arduously planted Christmas trees and blueberries, lilacs, asparagus, and crab apples, where my father still dreams of angling a stream to a new bed so that he can dig a pond in the field and fill it with water and fish. "The neighbors already came for their Christmas tree?" he asks in December. "Did they like it? Did they like it?"

Kesaya E. Noda,
"Growing Up Asian in America"

Exercise 8   **ANALYZING A PARAGRAPH**

1. Is the following paragraph developed in Pattern A (topic sentence/ development) or Pattern B (topic sentence/development/concluding sentence)?
Pattern B

2. Identify the parts of the paragraph pattern by underlining the topic sentence and the concluding sentence, if any, and annotating the support in the left margin. Use the two example paragraphs as models.

Topic sentence

  <u>I can see myself today as a person historically defined by law and custom as being forever alien.</u> Being neither "free white," nor "African," our people in California were deemed "aliens, ineligible for citizenship," no matter how long they intended to stay here. Aliens ineligible for citizenship were prohibited from

Support

owning, buying, or leasing land. They did not and could not belong here. The voice in me remembers that I am always a *Japanese*-American in the eyes of many. A third-generation German-American is an American. A third-generation Japanese-American is a Japanese-American. Being Japanese means being a danger to the country during the war and knowing how to use

Concluding sentence

chopsticks. <u>I wear this history on my face.</u>

Kesaya E. Noda,
"Growing Up Asian in America"

Writer's Guidelines: The Essay and Its Parts

1. An essay is a group of paragraphs, each of which supports a controlling statement called a thesis.

2. Each paragraph in an essay is almost always one of three types: introductory, support, or concluding.

3. An effective thesis has both a subject and a treatment. The subject is what you intend to write about. The treatment is what you intend to do with your subject.

   Example: <u>Bidwell Elementary School</u> <u>is too crowded.</u>
                           subject   **treatment**

4. An effective thesis presents a treatment that can be developed with supporting information.

5. An ineffective thesis is vague, too broad, or too narrow.

6. Supporting information is often presented in patterns, such as narration, exemplification, process analysis, analysis by division, and cause and effect.

7. A good introductory paragraph attracts the reader's interest, states or points toward the thesis, and moves the reader smoothly into the support, or developmental, paragraphs.

8. Introductory methods include a direct statement of the thesis, background, definition of term(s), quotation(s), a shocking statement, question(s), and a combination of two or more methods in this list.

9. Your concluding paragraph should give the reader the feeling that you have said all you want to say about your subject.

10. Some effective methods of concluding are a restatement of the thesis in slightly different words, perhaps pointing out its significance or making applications of it; a review of the main points; an anecdote related to the thesis; and a quotation.

2

The Writing Process: Prewriting

THE QUIGMANS   by Buddy Hickerson

Camping with a hack writer.

Chapter 1 focused on the parts of an essay. However, it stopped short of presenting an overall plan for completing a specific writing assignment. The reason for that omission is simple. Each assignment has its own guidelines that vary according to the topic, the source of ideas, the time permitted, the conditions for writing, and the purpose. Any writing system must be flexible, because a technique that is an asset for one assignment may be a burden for another. Therefore, a good writer should know numerous techniques, treating each as a tool to be used when needed. All of these tools are in the same box, one labeled "The Writing Process."

The Writing Process Defined

The writing process consists of strategies that can help you proceed from your purpose or initial idea to a final developed essay. Those strategies can be divided into prewriting techniques and writing stages. Using prewriting techniques, you explore, experiment, gather information, formulate your thesis, and develop and organize your support. In the writing stages, you write a first draft, revise your draft as many times as necessary, and edit your writing. For the typical college writing assignment, the writing process looks like this:

1. Prewriting
   - Exploring, experimenting, and gathering information
   - Writing the thesis and organizing and developing support (especially by outline)
2. Writing
   - Drafting, revising, and editing

The process of writing is *recursive,* which means "going back and forth." If, for example, you have begun your essay only to discover that your subject is too broadly considered, you may decide to back up and narrow your thesis and adjust your outline.

Prewriting is discussed in this chapter; writing is discussed in Chapter 3. The writing process is demonstrated in "Prison as a Community" by Tanya. She wrote the essay while she was enrolled in a small, low-cost college program at the California Institution for Women, where she was incarcerated. Her name has been changed to protect her privacy, but the prison she wrote about so colorfully is very real.

The Writing Process Worksheet

An uninterrupted copy of Tanya's complete demonstration of the writing process can be found in Appendix B, page 532. It is presented according to the Writing Process Worksheet, a form providing space to record important information and guidance for you in prewriting and writing. For your instructor, it is a record of the progress of your work. A blank worksheet is provided in Appendix A, page 531, for enlargement and duplication for those who wish to use it. Figure 2.1 also shows a reduced image.

These are the main features highlighted in the form:

1. *Assignment:* Record the particulars of the assignment, all too frequently the most neglected aspect of a writing project. If you do not know, or later cannot recall, specifically what you are supposed to write and when you are to submit it, you cannot do satisfactory work. An otherwise excellent composition on a misunderstood assignment may get you a failing grade, a regrettable situation for both you and your instructor.

2. *Prewriting:* On this form, prewriting is divided into two stages.

   - Stage One: Record the appropriate strategies as you explore, experiment, and gather information. This part may take the form of freewriting, brainstorming, clustering, note taking, or a combination of these strategies, depending on your assignment.

   - Stage Two: Write your thesis and an outline or an outline alternative such as a cluster or a list.

3. *Writing:* This portion of the worksheet encompasses writing from the first to the final draft, including all revision and editing.

   - Stage Three: By providing two easily remembered acronyms, the Writing Process Worksheet reminds you of necessary skills of revision—<u>c</u>oherence, <u>l</u>anguage, <u>u</u>nity, <u>e</u>mphasis, <u>s</u>upport, and <u>s</u>entences (CLUESS)—and of editing—<u>c</u>apitalization, <u>o</u>missions, <u>p</u>unctuation, and <u>s</u>pelling (COPS).

Prewriting

Certain strategies commonly grouped under the heading *prewriting* can help you get started, define your topic, and develop your ideas. These strategies—freewriting, brainstorming, clustering, gathering information, writing the thesis, and outlining—are very much a part of writing. The understandable desire to skip to the finished statement is what causes the most common student-writer grief: that of not filling the blank sheet or of filling it but not significantly improving on the blankness. The prewriting strategies described in this section will help you attack the blank sheet constructively with imaginative thought, analysis, and experimentation. They can lead to clear, effective communication. Gathering information is taken up separately in detail in Chapters 4 and 15.

Freewriting

Freewriting is a prewriting strategy that its originator, Peter Elbow, has called "babbling in print." In freewriting, you write without stopping,

Writing Process Worksheet

TITLE _____

NAME _____   DUE DATE _____

ASSIGNMENT   In the space below, write whatever you need to know about your assignment, including information about the topic, audience, pattern of writing, length, whether to include a rough draft or revised drafts, and whether your paper must be typed.

PREWRITING STAGE ONE   **Explore**   Freewrite, brainstorm (list), cluster, or gather information as directed by your instructor. Use the back of this page or separate paper if you need more space.

PREWRITING STAGE TWO   **Organize**   Write a topic sentence or thesis; label the subject and the treatment parts.

Write an outline or an outline alternative.

WRITING STAGE THREE   **Write**   On separate paper, write and then revise your paper as many times as necessary for coherence, language (usage, tone, and diction), unity, emphasis, support, and sentences (CLUESS). Read your paper aloud to hear and correct any grammatical errors or awkward-sounding sentences.

Edit any problems in fundamentals, such as capitalization, omissions, punctuation, and spelling (COPS).

Figure 2.1
Writing Process Worksheet

letting your ideas tumble forth. You do not concern yourself with the fundamentals of writing, such as punctuation and spelling. Freewriting is an adventure into your memory and imagination. It is discovery, invention, and exploration. If you are at a loss for words on your subject, write down a comment such as "I don't know what is coming next" or "blah, blah, blah," and continue when relevant words come. It is important to keep writing. Freewriting immediately eliminates the blank page and thereby helps you break through an emotional barrier, but that is not the only benefit. The words that you sort through in that idea kit will include some you can use. You can then underline or circle those words and even add notes on the side so that the freewriting continues to grow even after its initial, spontaneous expression.

The way you proceed depends on the type of assignment. You might

- work with a topic of your choice.
- work from a restricted list of topics.
- work with a prescribed topic.

Working with the *topic of your choice* gives you the greatest freedom of exploration. You would probably select a subject that interests you and freewrite about it, allowing your mind to wander among its many parts, perhaps mixing fact and fantasy, direct experience, and hearsay. Freewriting about music might uncover areas of special interest and knowledge, such as jazz or folk rock, that you would want to pursue further in freewriting or other prewriting strategies.

Working from a *restricted list of topics* requires a more focused kind of freewriting. With the list, you can, of course, experiment with several topics to discover which is most suitable for you. If, for example, "career choice," "career preparation," "career guidance," and "career prospects" are on the restricted list, you would probably select one and freewrite about that. If it works well for you, you would probably proceed with the next step of your prewriting. If you are not satisfied with what you uncover in freewriting, you would explore another item from the restricted list.

Working with a *prescribed topic,* you focus on a particular topic and try to restrict your freewriting to its boundaries. If your topic specifies a division of a subject area such as "political involvement of your generation," then you would tie those key words to your own information, critical thinking, and imaginative responses. If the topic is restricted to a particular reading selection such as your reactions to a poem, then that poem would give you a framework for freewriting about your own experiences, creations, and opinions. An analysis of the piece would probably include underlining pertinent ideas, annotating it (writing in the margins), and even taking notes on it.

Freewriting can help you get words on paper to generate topics, develop new insights, and explore ideas. Freewriting can lead to other stages of prewriting and writing, and it can also provide content for details and insights as you develop your topic.

Tanya had received this assignment from her freshman composition instructor:

Write an essay of 500 to 800 words on a specific group of people who function as a unit, such as a family, a work team, a sports team, a committee, an organization, or some kind of community. Consider social units you have studied or are studying in history, sociology, and psychology courses. Submit the Writing Process Worksheet and at least one preliminary draft with your final typed draft. List any sources you have used.

Tanya's freewriting (a partial example) explains how she settled on her topic and, in this case, provides the reader with perspective for her work.

Writing about a group of people gives me a lot of things to think about from where I am in my situation here in prison. I could write about gangs and there are plenty of them around and I could write about prison families and lots of different work stations all over the grounds and I could even write about the guards or correctional officers as they like to be called. And I could find a lot in my other classes that would give me information or at least some definitions and frameworks to work from. One thing I read about in my history book last week made me think even before this assignment. And that was <u>the walled cities</u> that sprung up in Europe more than a thousand years ago. They were little <u>communities. All inside walls.</u> Just <u>like the place where I live now.</u> When I came to prison I'd never been locked up before and I didn't know about prison and I guess I just thought of prison as a place where a bunch of people are locked up and sort of herded around. Then I came here and discovered that <u>prison is like</u> a <u>little town</u> in some ways and it has walls or fences just like the walled city I read about in my history book. Its just that <u>some one of them walled people out</u> and <u>one of them walls people in.</u> Reading the book made me think about my place here and how youve got most <u>everything here that you'll find in a regular city.</u> You've got <u>government,</u> <u>schools,</u> <u>churches,</u> a <u>post office,</u> a <u>hospital,</u> <u>rec space,</u> and <u>citizens</u> and a lot more. The place is called <u>the California Institution</u> for Women, but until about a year ago it had its own name, Frontera, with a separate zip code.

Unit

Walls
and
fences

Town

Walling in

Parts

After her freewriting session, Tanya examined what she had written for possible ideas to develop for a writing assignment. As she recognized those ideas, she underlined key words and phrases and made a few notes in the margins. By reading only the underlined words in her freewrite, you can understand what is important to Tanya; it was not necessary for her to underline whole sentences.

In addition to putting words on that dreaded blank sheet of paper, Tanya discovered that she had quite a lot to say about the prison and that she had selected a favorable topic to develop. The entire freewriting process took no more than five minutes. Had she found only a few ideas or no promising ideas at all, she might have freewritten on another topic. In going back over her work, she saw some errors, especially in wording and sentence structure, but she did not correct them because the purpose of freewriting is discovery, not revising or correcting grammar, punctuation, and spelling. Tanya was confident that she could continue with the process of writing a paper.

Exercise 1	FREEWRITING

Try freewriting on a broad topic such as one of the following:

an event that was important to you in your youth
a concert, a movie, or a television program
the ways you use your computer
drugs—causes, effects, a friend with a problem
gangs—causes, effects, an experience
the benefits of using a word processor
ways of disciplining children
why a person is a hero or role model to you
a great or terrible party
a bad or good day at school
why a college education is important

Following the example in Tanya's freewriting, underline and annotate the phrases that may lead to ideas you could explore further.

Brainstorming and Listing

Brainstorming is a strategy for coming up with fresh, new ideas in a hurry. What key words and phrases pop into your mind when you think about your topic? One effective way to get started brainstorming is to ask the big-six questions about your subject area: Who? What? Where? When? Why? and How? Then let your mind run free as you jot down answers in single entries or lists. Using the big-six questions also helps you begin to organize ideas for your writing. Some of the questions may not fit, and some may be more important than others, depending on the purpose of your writing. For example, if you were writing about the causes of an accident, the Why? question could be more important than the others. If you were concerned with how to succeed in college, the How? question would predominate. If you were writing in response to a reading selection, you would confine your thinking to questions related to the content of the reading selection.

Whatever the focus of the six questions, the result is likely to be numerous ideas that will provide information for continued exploration and development of your topic. Thus your pool of information for writing widens and deepens.

An alternative to the big-six-questions approach is simply to make a list of words and phrases related to your subject area or specific topic.

Tanya continued with the subject of the prison, and her topic tightened to focus on particular areas. Although she could have listed the annotations and the words she underlined in her freewriting, she instead used the big-six questions for her framework.

Who?	People at the California Institution for Women
What?	A community with parts: government, education, religion, services, business, citizens, housing
Where?	Inside the fence
When?	All the time
Why?	Because the people make up a unit, a community
How?	As each part of the prison relates to other parts

Notice that each question is answered in this example, but with some topics some questions may not fit. As Tanya addressed the What? question, her brainstorming produced a long list, suggesting an area with strong possibilities for the focus of her paper.

Listing is another effective way to brainstorm, especially if you have a defined topic and a storehouse of information. Skip the big-six-questions approach and simply make a list of words and phrases related to your topic. This strategy is favored by many writers.

Thinking from the outset that she was concerned mainly with prison as a community, Tanya might have gone directly to making a list indicating the components and their relationships.

(churches)

(schools)

(government)

cops

post office

hospital

cafeteria

laundry

(service providers)

(citizens)

recreation

housing

(industry)

stores

maintenance

Exercise 2   **BRAINSTORMING**

Further explore the topic you worked with in Exercise 1 by first answering the big-six questions and then by making a list.

Big-Six Questions

Who? _____

What? _____

Where? _____

When? _____

Why? _____

How? _____

List

_____

_____

_____

_____

_____

_____

_____

_____

_____

_____

Clustering

Clustering is another prewriting technique. Start by double-bubbling your topic; that is, write it down in the middle of the page and draw a double circle around it, like the hub of a wheel. Then respond to the question What comes to mind? Draw a single bubble around other ideas on spokes radiating from the hub. Any bubble can lead to another bubble or to numerous bubbles in the same way. This strategy is sometimes used instead of an outline or it is used before making an outline to organize and develop ideas.

The more specific the topic inside the double bubble, the fewer the number of spokes that will radiate from it. For example, a topic such as "high school dropouts" would have more spokes than "reasons for dropping out of high school."

Here is Tanya's cluster on the subject of prison as a community. She has drawn dotted lines around subclusters that seem to relate to a workable, unified topic.

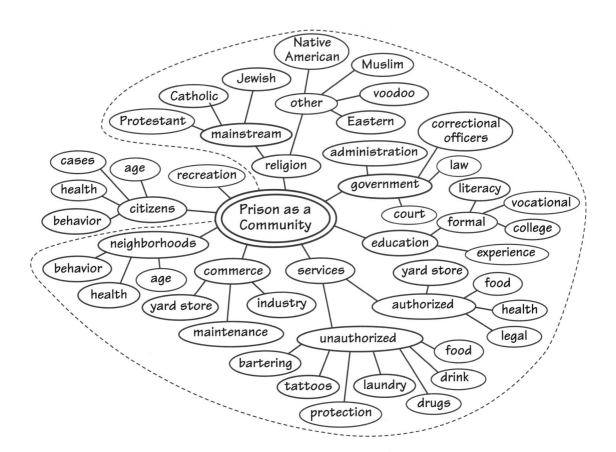

Exercise 3	**CLUSTERING**

Continuing with your topic, develop a cluster of related ideas. Draw dotted lines around subclusters that have potential for focus and more development.

Composing the Thesis

Your thesis can come from any of several places. You may be able to generate it in your initial freewriting, brainstorming, clustering, or information gathering, or you may be given an assigned topic. In any case, your procedure is the same at this point. You need to work on your thesis—just that one sentence—until you have developed an interesting subject and a well-focused treatment. That statement may be a bit more mechanical than the one you actually use in your essay, but it can easily be reworded once you are engaged in writing, revising, and editing.

The controlling idea will probably not pop into your head full-blown. It is more likely to be the result of repeated revisions. Even when you are revising a paper you have written, you may go back and rephrase your topic sentence or thesis. That is part of the back-and-forth (recursive) nature of the writing process.

Note how Tanya reworks her thesis several times before she settles on a well-focused statement capable of being developed.

This prison is a complete community.

Except for freedom, this prison is a microcosm of American society.

subject   treatment

Except for freedom, <u>this prison</u> <u>has all the components of a typical</u> <u>community outside the fence.</u>

Exercise 4	**COMPOSING A THESIS**

After consulting your freewriting, brainstorming or listing, and clustering, write a thesis. Label the subject and treatment parts. Refer to Chapter 1, page 11, if you need more guidance.

Outlining

Outlining is the tool that most people think of in connection with organizing an essay. *Outlining* divides the controlling idea into sections of support material, divides those sections further, and establishes sequence.

An outline is a kind of framework that can be used in two ways: It can indicate the plan for an essay you intend to write, and it can show the organization of a passage you are reading. The outline of a reading passage and the outline as a plan for writing are identical in form. If you intend to write a summary of a reading selection, then a single outline might be used for both purposes.

The two main outline forms are the *sentence outline* (each entry is a complete sentence) and the *topic outline* (each entry is a key word or phrase). The topic outline is more common in writing essays.

In the following topic outline, notice first how the parts are arranged on the page: the indentations, the number and letter sequences, the punctuation, and the placement of words. Then read the outline and see how the ideas relate to one another.

Main idea (usually the thesis for an essay)

    I. Major support
        A. Minor support
            1. Explanation, detail, example
            2. Explanation, detail, example

B. Minor support

    1. Explanation, detail, example

    2. Explanation, detail, example

II. Major support

  A. Minor support

    1. Explanation, detail, example

    2. Explanation, detail, example

  B. Minor support

    1. Explanation, detail, example

    2. Explanation, detail, example

Tanya's next task was to organize her material. For this strategy, she went back to her bubble cluster, which she had divided into eight major parts. She had already decided she wanted to work with the idea of prison as a community and explain it from her perspective. Therefore, she focused on only one part of the cluster—the part indicated by the broken boundary line to enclose "neighborhoods," "commerce," "services," "education," "government," and "religion."

With her divisions selected, Tanya might have started to write a first draft at this point, but instead she decided she wanted to recall and organize more detail, so she began an outline. She used her own memory and private reference sources for information. In her second draft of her outline, she combined "commerce" and "services." If she had been working on a source-based topic, she would have gone back to the reading. If she had been working on a topic requiring research, she would have consulted library and Internet sources.

                     subject   **treatment**

Thesis: Except for freedom, <u>this prison</u> <u>has all the components of a typical community outside the fence.</u>

  I. Government as laws

    A. Administration

    B. Correctional officers

    C. Convicts

 II. Housing

    A. Assignments

      1. Based on behavior

      2. Based on age

      3. Based on health

    B. Special units

III. Commerce and services

    A. Regular jobs

        1. Industry

           a. Free enterprise

           b. Prison products

        2. Prison operation

    B. Underground services

        1. Hustles

        2. Extent

IV. Religion

    A. Larger groups

        1. Protestant

        2. Catholic

        3. Jewish

    B. Others in smaller numbers

        1. Sweat lodge folks

        2. Muslims

        3. Inmate preacher

        4. Voodoo practitioner

V. Education

    A. Formal

        1. Literacy

        2. Vocational

        3. College

    B. Informal

        1. Survival

        2. Life improvement

Exercise 5   **COMPLETING OUTLINES**

Fill in the missing parts of the following outline. Consider whether you are dealing with time, examples, causes, effects, parts, or steps.

Answers will vary.

1. Too many of us are preoccupied with material things.

    I. Clothing

    II. Cars

    III. <u>Housing</u> _____

2. Television sitcoms may vary, but every successful show has certain components.

    I. Good acting

    II. Good characters _____

    III. Good situations

    IV. Good writing _____

3. A person who is trying to discourage unwanted sexual advances should take several measures.

    I. Choose dates carefully _____

    II. Set clear boundaries

    III. Avoid compromising situations

4. Concentrating during reading involves various techniques.

    I. Preview material

    II. Pose questions

    III. Underline material _____

5. Crime has some bad effects on a nearby neighborhood.

    I. People fearful

        A. Don't go out at night

        B. Put bars on windows _____

    II. People without love for neighborhood

        A. Have rundown, ill-kept property _____

        B. Put houses up for sale

    III. People as victims

        A. Loss of possessions

        B. Harm to individuals _____

6. Exercising can improve a person's life.

    I. Looks better

        A. Skin

        B. Physique _____

    II. Feels better

        A. Mind _____

        B. Body

    III. Performs better

        A. Work

        B. Play and social _____

7. Shoppers in department stores can be grouped according to needs.

    I. <u>Lookers</u>

    II. Specific needs

    III. Bargain hunters

8. There are different kinds of intelligence based on situations.

    I. Street-smart

    II. Common sense

    III. <u>Academic</u>

9. Smoking should be discouraged.

    I. Harm to smokers

        A. <u>Respiratory problems</u>

        B. Cancer risk

    II. Harm to those around smokers

        A. <u>Family and loved ones</u>

        B. Fellow workers

    III. Cost

        A. Industry—production and absenteeism

        B. <u>Health care</u>

10. An excellent police officer must have six qualities.

    I. <u>Fairness</u>

    II. Knowledge of law

    III. <u>Physical soundness</u>

    IV. Emotional soundness

    V. Skill in using weapons

    VI. <u>Good judgment</u>

Exercise 6   **WRITING AN OUTLINE**

Working with the thesis you developed in Exercise 4, write an outline. The thesis may suggest a particular pattern of development. Following the lead of that thesis, the Roman numeral headings will often indicate divisions of time or place, steps, causes, effects, or parts of a unit. For example, if you have selected your favorite retail store for your subject and your reasons for choosing it as the treatment, then those reasons would be indicated with Roman numeral headings.

Writer's Guidelines: The Writing Process—Prewriting

1. The writing process consists of strategies that can help you produce a polished essay. *Prewriting* includes exploring, experimenting, gathering information, writing the thesis, and organizing and developing support. *Writing* includes drafting, revising, and editing.

2. Prewriting includes one or more of the following strategies:

   Freewriting: writing without stopping so that you can explore, experiment, and invent

   Brainstorming and listing: responding to *Who? What? Where? When? Why? How?* questions or making lists on likely divisions of your subject

Clustering: showing related ideas by double-bubbling a subject and then connecting single bubbles of related ideas on spokes radiating out and branching from the hub

Gathering information: underlining, annotating, and note taking. (These techniques are explored in Chapters 4 and 15.)

Composing the thesis: writing a sentence that has two parts—the subject (what you are writing about) and the treatment (what you will do with the subject)

Outlining: dividing the controlling idea into sections of support material, dividing those sections further, and establishing a workable sequence

3

The Writing Process: Writing, Revising, and Editing

THE QUIGMANS   by Buddy Hickerson

© Tribune Media Services, Inc. All Rights Reserved. Reprinted with permission.

Writing the First Draft

O nce you have developed your thesis and your outline (or list), you are ready to begin writing your essay. The initial writing is called the first, or rough, draft. Your thesis statement is likely to be at or near the beginning of your essay and will be followed by your support as ordered by your outline. As you write, refer to your thesis often and write a clear topic sentence for each paragraph.

Following your outline for basic organization, you should proceed without worrying about the refinements of writing. This is not the time to concern yourself with perfect spelling, grammar, or punctuation. After you have finished that first draft, read it carefully. If your thesis is sound and your outline has served you well, you now have a basic discussion. You have made a statement and supported it.

Don't be embarrassed by the roughness of your work. You should be embarrassed only if you leave it that way. You are seeing the reason why a first draft is called "rough." Famous authors have said publicly that they wouldn't show their rough drafts even to their closest, most forgiving friends.

Whether you write in longhand or on a computer depends on what works best for you. Some writers prefer to do a first draft by hand, mark it up, and then go to the computer. Computers save you time in all aspects of your writing, especially revision.

The following paragraphs from Tanya's essay show how she wrote her first draft. Notice how the paragraphs follow the order of topics in her outline; they also include some new ideas. The excerpt includes paragraph 2 and part of paragraph 3.

It all begins with rules.   n

CIW has a goverment, one that is totalitarian not democratic.

prison
The constitution is a set of laws passed by the state of California.

I. Government as laws
A. Administration
associates
The warden and her ~~deputies~~ administer the law with wisdom. The

B. Correctional officers
with grace
correctional officers enforce the laws fairly. The convicts obey ~~without~~

C. Convicts
acquaintances with bunco experience
~~complaining.~~ If you believe all of that, I have some ~~friends~~ around here

II. Housing
A. Assignments
1. Based on behavior
2. Based on age
3. Based on health
a bundle of
who just found ~~some~~ cash and would like to share it with you.

where we live
These laws also govern ~~housing~~ in the prison. It is said that the

two most important things in prison are where one lives and where

one works. An inmate's address at prison can be determined by

B. Special units —— several factors/~~such as~~ behavior, reputation, age, and health/ there-

fore, one can be assigned to a cell block with designations such as

ordinary (general dorm, room, or cell), honors, geriatrics, convales-

cent, protective custody, or psychiatric. At times special living units

are formed/ ~~o~~nce there was a living unit at CIW called the AIDS

ward, for convicts who were HIV positive. ~~A strange procedure~~

~~developed.~~ If somebody approached these women as they were . . .

The Recursive Factor

The process of writing can be called *recursive,* which means "going back and forth." In this respect, writing is like reading. If you do not understand what you have read, you back up and read it again. After you have read an entire passage, you may need to read it again selectively. The same can be said of writing. If, for example, after having developed an outline and started writing your first draft, you discover that your subject is too broad, you will have to back up, narrow your thesis, and then adjust your outline. You may even want to return to an early cluster of ideas to see how you can use a smaller grouping of them. Revision is usually the most recursive of all parts of the writing process. You will go over your material again and again until you are satisfied that you have expressed yourself as well as you possibly can.

Your Audience

When you speak to a person, you routinely adjust what you say and how you say it. You should do the same for your audience when you write. To the extent that you can, consider the needs, interests, knowledge, and abilities of your intended readers and appropriately adjust your subject, explanations, style, and word choice.

Exercise 1   **WRITING YOUR ROUGH DRAFT**

Using the thesis you developed in Chapter 2, write a rough draft of an essay as directed by your instructor.

Revising

The term *first draft* suggests quite accurately that there will be other drafts, or versions, of your writing. Only in the most dire situations, such as an in-class examination when you have time for only one draft, should you be satisfied with a single effort.

What you do beyond the first draft is revision and editing. Revision includes organization, content, and language effectiveness. Editing (discussed later in this chapter) involves a final correction of simple mistakes and fundamentals such as spelling, punctuation, and capitalization. In practice, editing and revising are not always separate activities, although writers usually wait until the next-to-the-last draft to edit minor details and attend to other small points that can be easily overlooked.

Successful revision almost always involves intense, systematic rewriting. You should learn to look for certain aspects of skillful writing as you enrich and repair your first draft. To help you recall these aspects so that you can keep them in mind and examine your material in a comprehensive fashion, this textbook offers a memory device—an acronym in which each letter suggests an important feature of good writing and revision. This device enables you to memorize the features of good writing quickly. Soon you will be able to recall and refer to them automatically. These features need not be attended to individually when you revise your writing, although they may be, and they need not be attended to in the order presented here. The acronym is CLUESS (pronounced "clues"), which provides this guide:

Coherence

Language

Unity

Emphasis

Support

Sentences

Each of these features of good writing can be approached with a set of techniques you can apply easily to your first draft. They are presented here with some details, examples, and supporting exercises. The Writer's Guidelines at the end of this chapter provide a concise list of these features and a set of questions you can apply to your own writing and to peer editing.

Coherence

Coherence is the orderly relationship of ideas, each leading smoothly and logically to the next. You must weave your ideas together so skillfully that the reader can easily see how one idea connects to another and to the central thought. This central thought, of course, is expressed in the topic sentence for a paragraph and in the thesis for an essay. You can achieve coherence efficiently by using the following:

overall pattern

transitional terms

repetition of key words and ideas

pronouns

consistent point of view

Overall Pattern

Several chapters in this book discuss strategies for an overall pattern of organization or order. Three basic patterns prevail: *time* (chronology), *space* (spatial arrangement), and *emphasis* (stress on ideas). Sometimes you will combine patterns. The coherence of each can be strengthened by using transitional words such as the following:

Time: *first, then, soon, later, following, after, at that point*

Space: *up, down, right, left, beyond, behind, above, below*

Emphasis: *first, second, third, most, more*

Transitional Terms

By using transitional terms, you can help your readers move easily from one idea to another. Each of the following sentences has one of these terms.

First, I realized I had to get a job to stay in school.

At the same time, my track coach wanted the team to spend more hours working out.

We were, *after all,* the defending champions.

Finally, I dropped one of my courses.

Repetition of Key Words and Ideas

Repeat key words and phrases to keep the main subject in the reader's mind and to maintain the continuity necessary for a smooth flow of logical thought. (See the section on Emphasis on page 55.)

Pronouns

Pronouns, such as *he, her, them,* and *it,* provide natural connecting links in your writing. Why? Every pronoun refers to an earlier noun (called the *antecedent* of the pronoun) and thus carries the reader back to that earlier thought. Here are some examples.

> I tried to buy *tickets* for the concert, but *they* were all sold.

> Assertive *people* tend to make decisions quickly. However, *they* may not make the wisest decisions.

> *Roger* painted a picture of *his* father's pickup truck. *It* was so good that *his* professor asked *him* to enter *it* in an art show.

Consistent Point of View

Point of view shows the writer's relationship to the material, the subject, and it usually does not change within a passage.

If you are conveying personal experience, the point of view will be *first person,* or *I,* which can be either involved (a participant) or detached (an observer).

The second person, *you* and *your,* is usually reserved for how-to writing in college assignments.

If you are presenting something from a distance, geographical or historical (for example, telling a story about George Washington), the point of view will be *third person,* and the participants will be referred to as *he, she,* and *they.*

Along with the consistency of perspective, you should avoid shifts in number (*she* to *they*) and verb tense (*is* to *was*).

Being consistent in these matters will promote coherence.

Language

In the revision process, the word *language* takes on a special meaning, referring to usage, tone, and diction. If you are writing with a computer, consider using the thesaurus feature, but keep in mind that no two words share precisely the same meaning.

Usage

Usage is the kind or general style of language we use. All or almost all of us operate on the principle of appropriateness. If I used *ain't* as part of my explanations in this textbook, you would be surprised and probably disappointed; you would think about my word choice rather than what I have to say. Why would you be surprised? Because *ain't* is not appropriate for my audience in this situation. If you write an essay containing slang, you will probably be understood, but if the slang is not appropriate, you will draw unfavorable attention to your message. That does not mean that slang does not have its place—it does. It can be imaginative and colorful. Often, though, it is only a weak substitute for a more precise vocabulary.

Usage is an important part of writing and revising. Judge what is appropriate for your audience and your purpose. What kind of language is expected? What kind of language is best suited for accomplishing your purpose?

Most of the material in Chapter 16, Handbook: Writing Effective Sentences, is grammatical explanation of standard, mainly formal, English. Using standard verb tenses and pronoun cases will help you to write effectively. Chapter 16 offers clear explanations and examples. It also provides exercises supported by answers in the Answer Key. As you practice the principles of standard English in your writing and revising, you will master them.

Tone

Have you ever heard someone say, "Don't talk to me in that tone of voice" or "I accepted what she was saying, but I didn't like the tone she used when she told me"? *Tone* in these contexts means that the sound of the speaker's voice and maybe the language choices conveyed disrespect to the listener. The tone could have represented any number of feelings about the subject matter and the audience. Tone can have as many variations as you can have feelings: It can, for example, be sarcastic, humorous, serious, cautionary, objective, groveling, angry, bitter, sentimental, enthusiastic, somber, outraged, or loving.

Let's say you are getting a haircut. Looking in those panoramic mirrors bordered with pictures of people with different styles of haircuts, you see that the hair stylist is cutting off too much hair. You could use different tones in giving him or her some timely how-to instructions.

> *Objective:* "If you don't mind, what I meant to say was that I would like a haircut proportioned similar to that one there in the picture of Tom Cruise from *Jerry Maguire.*"

> *Humorous:* "I hesitate to make suggestions to someone who is standing at my back and holding a sharp instrument near my throat, but I'm letting my hair grow out a bit. I don't want you to take off a lot in the back and on the sides."

> *Angry and sarcastic:* "Look man, when I sat down, I said I wanted my hair cut in the design of Tom Cruise in *Jerry Maguire.* The way you're hacking at it, you must've thought I said *Top Gun.*"

> *Servile:* "I really like the way you cut my hair, and I can see that you are proportioning it with great care, but I would like my hair to be a bit longer than the style that I think you're working on. Do you remember how I used to get my hair cut about a year ago, a little longer on the sides and more bushy on top? You came up with a great style that everyone liked. Could you give me one similar to that?"

Overbearing: "Damn it, buddy. Will you watch what you're doing! I asked for a haircut, not a shave. If God had wanted me to have bare skin above my shoulders, he would've put the hair on my feet."

In speech, feelings and attitudes are represented by inflection, loudness, word choice, and language patterns. In writing, tone is conveyed mainly by word choice and order; it is closely related to style—the variations in the way you write, depending on your purpose. Your purpose is simply to present a particular idea in a particular context. The context implies the audience; it is important to use the tone appropriate to your audience.

Usually your tone will be consistent throughout your presentation, although for the informal essay often assigned in college, you may choose to begin in a lighthearted, amusing tone before switching to a more serious, objective mode.

Diction

Diction is word choice. If you use good diction, you are finding the best words for a particular purpose in addressing a certain audience. There is some overlap, therefore, between usage and diction. I may look at an area in the subway and present my reaction in the following way:

Poor Diction:

This part of the subway is really a mess. Everywhere I look I can see things people have thrown away, which have fallen through the grates above. Along with the solid items are liquids. On the walls are a hodgepodge of posters and writing. The whole area is very dirty and very unpleasant.

Note how the scene comes to life with better word choice:

Good Diction:

[Before me I saw] an unspeakable mass of congealed oil, puddles of dubious liquid, and a mishmash of old cigarette packets, mutilated and filthy newspapers, and the debris that filtered down from the street above. [The walls were a display of posters]— here a text from the Bible, there a half-naked girl, here a pair of girl's legs walking up the keys of a cash register—all scribbled over with unknown names and well-known obscenities. . . .

Gilbert Highet, "Subway Station"

The difference between these two passages is obvious. The first is general. Terms such as "very dirty" and "very unpleasant" carry little meaning. The author has not made us see. The word *very* is an empty modifier. The second passage is specific. You can visualize what the writer is saying through the specific diction, the detail. The first is general and, for content, hardly goes beyond a single phrase—mess in the subway.

The following chart shows the difference between general and specific words.

General	Specific	More Specific
food	fruit	juicy, ripe peach
mess	litter	candy wrappers; empty cans
drink	soda	Diet Pepsi
odor	kitchen smell	aroma of coffee brewing

Another aspect of diction is freshness and originality of expression. To achieve those distinctions, avoid clichés, which are trite, familiar phrases. Consider this sentence:

> When the Prince married Cinderella, her sisters went <u>green with envy</u> because she was now <u>on easy street,</u> leaving them <u>out in the cold.</u>

Those words were written by a person who doesn't care about communicating in a clear and interesting manner. It would be far better to say:

> When the Prince married Cinderella, her sisters were envious because they had no suitors.

This list shows some clichés to avoid:

young at heart	quick as a flash
rotten to the core	slow but sure
uphill battle	other side of the coin
more than meets the eye	breathless silence
bitter end	acid test
as luck would have it	better late than never
last but not least	six of one, half dozen of the other

These are ready-made expressions. A cliché master manipulates language as if it were a prefabricated building going up, not bothering to use any imagination and leaving little opportunity for his or her audience to use theirs. Good diction, however, reflects the writer as an individual and is fresh, original, and clear.

Unity

A controlling idea, stated or implied, unifies every piece of good writing. It is the central point around which the supporting material revolves. For a paragraph, the elements are the topic sentence and the supporting sentences. For an essay, the elements are the thesis and the supporting developmental paragraphs. All the supporting material should be related to the topic sentence or thesis, and it should all be subordinate to the topic sentence or thesis. Unity can be strengthened and made more apparent if you restate the topic sentence or thesis at the end of the unit and if you repeat key words and phrases from time to time. A good check on unity is to ask yourself if everything in your paragraph or essay is subordinate to and derived from the controlling idea.

Don't confuse unity and coherence. Whereas coherence involves the clear movement of thought from sentence to sentence or paragraph to paragraph, unity means staying on the topic. A unified and coherent outline would become incoherent if the parts were scrambled, but the outline technically would still be unified. These qualities of writing go together. You should stay on the topic and make clear connections.

Emphasis

Emphasis, a feature of most good writing, helps the reader focus on the main ideas. It can be achieved in several ways but mainly through placement of key ideas and through repetition.

Placement of Ideas

The most emphatic part of any passage, whether a sentence or a book, is the last part, because we usually remember most easily what we read last. The second most emphatic part of a passage is the beginning, because our mind is relatively uncluttered when we read it. For these reasons, among others, the topic sentence or thesis is usually at the beginning of a piece, and it is often restated at the end in an echoing statement.

Repetition of Key Words and Ideas

Repetition is one of the simplest devices in your writer's toolbox. The words repeated may be single words, phrases, slightly altered sentences, or synonyms. Repetition keeps the dominant subject in the reader's mind and maintains the continuity necessary for a smooth flow of logical thought.

You can use this valuable technique easily. If, as is done in the following example, you are discussing the effects of the school dropout problem, then the words *effect(s),* along with synonyms such as *result(s)* or *consequence(s),* and *school dropout(s)* are likely to be repeated several times. Moreover, phrases giving insight into the issue may be repeated, perhaps with slight variation.

The causes of the school <u>dropout</u> problem have received much attention recently, but the <u>effects</u> are just as important. One obvious <u>result</u> is that of unemployment or low-paying employment. The student who <u>drops out</u> of school is likely to be <u>dropping</u> into poverty, perhaps even into a lifelong condition. Another <u>effect</u> is juvenile crime. The young person who has no prospects for a good job and no hope all too frequently turns to illegal activities. A third <u>result</u> concerns the psychological well-being of the <u>dropout</u>. Although <u>withdrawing</u> from school seems to offer a quick, viable solution to perceived problems, it almost immediately has <u>consequences</u> for the <u>dropout</u>'s self-esteem. Of course, these <u>effects</u> may also be tied to causes, such as drugs, poverty, crime, or psychological problems, but devastating <u>repercussions</u> are there at the far end of the causes-and-effects continuum, and youngsters who are contemplating <u>dropping out</u> should consider them with care.

The effective use of word and phrase repetition should not be confused with an irritating misuse of word repetition. We all at times get hung up on certain words, and the result is a negative response from our audience. Consider this awkward use of repetition:

> She looked at him and frowned. He returned the look and then looked away at a stranger looking for his lost keys.

That's too many *look*'s. Consider this version:

> She looked at him [*or, even better,* She frowned at him]. He glared back and then glanced away at a stranger searching for his lost keys.

The second version preserves the idea of people "looking" by using synonyms. It is more precise, and does not grate on the reader's mind as the first does.

Support

How much support does a piece of writing need? A good developmental paragraph fulfills its function by developing the topic sentence. An essay is complete when it fulfills its function of developing a thesis. Obviously, you will have to judge what is complete. With some subjects, you will need little supporting and explanatory material. With others, you will need much more. Incompleteness, not overdevelopment, is more common among beginning writers. Besides having enough support, be sure that the points of support are presented in the best possible sequence.

Consider the following paragraph. Is it complete? Does the writer make the main idea clear and provide adequate support for it? Are the ideas in the right order?

> A cat's tail is a good barometer of its intentions. By various movements of its tail a cat will signal many of its wants. Other

movements indicate its attitudes. An excited or aggressively aroused cat will whip its entire tail back and forth.

At first glance, this paragraph seems complete. It begins with a concise topic sentence telling us that a cat's tail is a good barometer of its intentions. It adds information of a general nature in the following two sentences. Then it presents a supporting example about the aggressively aroused cat. But the paragraph is not explicit; there is insufficient supporting material for the opening generalization. The paragraph leaves the reader with too much information to fill in. What are some other ways that cats communicate their intentions with their tails? How do they communicate specific wishes or desires? Is their communication effective? If the passage is to answer these questions that may come into the reader's mind, it must present more material to support the beginning generalization. The original paragraph that follows begins with a concise topic sentence that is then supported with details.

A cat's tail is a good barometer of its intentions. An excited or aggressively aroused cat will whip its entire tail back and forth. When I talk to Sam, he holds up his end of the conversation by occasionally flicking the tip of his tail. Mother cats move their tails back and forth to invite their kittens to play. A kitten raises its tail perpendicularly to beg for attention; older cats may do so to beg for food. When your cat holds its tail aloft while criss-crossing in front of you, it is trying to say, "Follow me"—usually to the kitchen, or more precisely, to the refrigerator. Unfortunately, many cats have lost their tails in refrigerator doors as a consequence.

Michael W. Fox, "What Is Your Pet Trying to Tell You?"

We can strengthen our understanding of good support by analyzing the structure of the model paragraph, putting to use the information we have assimilated to this point in the discussion. The paragraph begins with the highest generalization (the main idea in the topic sentence): "A cat's tail is a good barometer of its intentions." It follows immediately with six supporting statements and ends with a final sentence to add humor to the writing. If we place this material in outline form, we can easily see the recurrent pattern in the flow of thought from general to particular.

Topic sentence (highest generalization)

A cat's tail is a good barometer of its intentions.

Major support

A. An excited or aggressively aroused cat will whip its entire tail back and forth.

Major support

B. When I talk to Sam, he holds up his end of the conversation by occasionally flicking the tip of his tail.

Major support

C. Mother cats move their tails back and forth to invite their kittens to play.

Major support

D. A kitten raises its tail perpendicularly to beg for attention;

Major support	E. older cats may do so to beg for food.
Major support	F. When your cat holds its tail aloft while crisscrossing in front of you, it is trying to say, "Follow me"—usually to the kitchen, or more precisely, to the refrigerator.
Added for humor	Unfortunately, many cats have lost their tails in refrigerator doors as a consequence.

Sentences

In the revision process, the term *sentences* pertains to the variety of sentence patterns and the correctness of sentence structure.

Variety of Sentences

A passage that offers a variety of simple and complicated sentences satisfies the reader, just as a combination of simple and complicated foods go together in a good meal. The writer can introduce variety by including both short and long sentences, by using different sentence patterns, and by beginning sentences in different ways.

Length

In revising, examine your writing to make sure that sentences vary in length. A series of short sentences is likely to make the flow seem choppy and the thoughts disconnected. However, single short sentences often work very well. Because they are uncluttered with supporting points and qualifications, they are often direct and forceful. Consider using short sentences to emphasize points and to introduce ideas. Use longer sentences to provide details or show how ideas are related.

Variety of Sentence Patterns

Good writing includes a variety of sentence patterns. Although there is no limit to the number of sentences you can write, you may be pleased to discover that the conventional English sentence appears in only four basic patterns.

Simple:	She did the work well.
Compound:	She did the work well, and she was well paid.
Complex:	Because she did the work well, she was well paid.
Compound-complex:	Because she did the work well, she was well paid, and she was satisfied

An analysis of these patterns with suggestions and exercises for combining sentences is given in Chapter 16.

Each of the four sentence patterns listed has its own purposes and strengths. The simple sentence conveys a single idea. The compound sentence shows, by its structure, that two somewhat equal ideas are connected. The complex sentence shows that one idea is less important than another; that is, it is dependent on, or subordinate to, the idea in the main clause. The compound-complex sentence has the scope of both the compound sentence and the complex sentence.

Variety of Sentence Beginnings

Another way to provide sentence variety is to use different kinds of beginnings. A new beginning may or may not be accompanied by a changed sentence pattern. Among the most common beginnings, other than starting with the subject of the main clause, are those using a prepositional phrase, a dependent clause, or a conjunctive adverb such as *therefore, however,* or *in fact.*

- Prepositional phrase

    In your fantasy, you are the star.

    Like casino owners, game show hosts want you to be cheery.

- Dependent clause

    When the nighttime "Wheel of Fortune" debuted, the slot was occupied by magazine shows.

    As Pat Sajak noted, viewers often solve the puzzle before the contestants do.

- Conjunctive adverb

    Now you know.

    Therefore, you feel happy, excited, and a bit superior.

Problems with Sentences

A complete sentence must generally include an independent clause, which is a group of words that contains a subject and a verb and can stand alone. Some groups of words may sound interesting, but they are not really sentences. Three common problem groupings are the fragment, the comma splice, and the run-on.

- *Fragment:* A word grouping that is structurally incomplete is only a fragment of a sentence.

    Because he left. (This is a dependent clause, not a complete sentence.)

Went to the library. (This has no subject.)

She being the only person there. (This has no verb.)

Waiting there for help. (This phrase has neither subject nor verb.)

In the back seat under a book. (This contains two phrases but no subject or verb.)

- *Comma splice:* The comma splice consists of two independent clauses with only a comma between them.

The weather was bad, we canceled the picnic. (A comma by itself cannot join two independent clauses.)

- *Run-on:* The run-on differs from the comma splice in only one way: It has no comma between the independent clauses.

The weather was bad we canceled the picnic.

Fragments, comma splices, and run-ons can easily be fixed (see Chapter 16) during the revising and editing stages of your writing. A computerized grammar checker may help you find these problems.

If you frequently have problems with sentence structure and awkwardness of phrasing, be especially suspicious of long sentences. Test each sentence of fifteen or more words for flaws. Try writing shorter, more direct sentences until you gain confidence and competency. Then work with sophisticated patterns.

See the Writer's Guidelines at the end of this chapter for a concise summary of the strategies for effective revision.

Editing

Editing, the final stage of the writing process, involves a careful examination of your work. Look for problems with capitalization, omissions, punctuation, and spelling (COPS).

Because you can find spelling errors in writing by others more easily than you can in your own, try to have someone you know read your draft and help you locate misspellings. Also, a computerized spell checker is quite useful. However, it will not detect wrong words that are correctly spelled, so you should always proofread. It is often helpful to leave the piece for a few hours or a day, then reread it as if it were someone else's work.

Before you submit your writing to your instructor, do what almost all professional writers do before sending their material along: Read it aloud, to yourself or to a willing audience. Reading material aloud will help you catch any awkwardness of expression, omission and misplacement of words, and other problems that are easily overlooked by an author.

As you can see, writing is a process and is not a matter of just sitting down and banging out a statement. The parts of the process from prewriting to revising to editing are connected, and your movement is ultimately forward, but this process allows you to go back and forth in the recursive manner discussed earlier in this chapter. If your outline is not working, perhaps the flaw is in your thesis. You may need to go back and fix it. If one section of your essay is skimpy, perhaps you will have to go back and reconsider the pertinent material in your outline or clustering. There you might find more details or alter a statement so that you can move into more fertile areas of thought.

The following is her first *draft* that shows Tanya's revision process. The draft also includes some editing (COPS).

Prison as a Community

Few free world citizens ~~look at~~ regard the California Institution for

Women as a walled city but that's what it is. Before I was sent here,

I ~~thought of~~ imagined prison as a bunch of scared and scary people in a fenced pen. Then I

became a resident and discovered that, except for freedom, this

place has all the parts of a community outside the fence. ~~It was an~~

~~important discovery.~~

It all begins with rules.

CIW has a goverment, one that is totalitarian not democratic.

The prison constitution is a set of laws passed by the state of California.

The warden and her ~~deputies~~ associates administer the laws ~~with wisdom~~. The

correctional officers enforce the laws ~~fairly~~. The convicts obey

~~without complaining~~ with grace. If you believe all of that, I have some ~~friends~~ acquaintances with bunco experience

around here who just found ~~some~~ a bundle of cash and would like to share it

with you.

These laws also govern ~~housing~~ where we live in the prison. It is said that the

two most important things in prison are where one lives and where

one works. An inmate's address at prison can be determined by several factors/ ~~such as~~ behavior, reputation, age, and health/ there-fore, one can be assigned to a cell block with designations such as ordinary (general dorm, room, or cell), honors, geriatrics, *solitary,* convales-cent, protective custody, or psychiatric. At times special living units are formed/ *O*nce there was a living unit at CIW called the AIDS ward, for convicts who were HIV positive. ~~A strange procedure developed.~~ If somebody approached these women as they were being escorted across the yard *;* a correctional officer would blow a whistle and shout, "Stay away! These inmates have AIDS! These inmates have AIDS!" The HIV positive women now live in housing for the general population, and staff is more enlightened.

The other part of the ~~mentioned~~ saying "where you work" is tied in with both *free world* ~~street~~ industry and the operation of the prison. For years CIW has produced clothing for the California Transportation *We have also manufactured jeans and underwear for California prisons for men.* Agency (CalTrans), made mostly of heavy orange fabric. Most jobs relate to food, laundry, maintenance, and clerical *services, such as* ~~services~~. All able-bodied women, even those in educational programs, must work. Some jobs provide *compensation* ~~money~~, the so-called *"* pay slots *"*, but prison work is almost never connected with vocational training or with *post-parole* ~~street~~ jobs. The money *, usually about fifteen to thirty dollars a month,* is placed in a trust fund and can be used in the prison store for treats, smokes, *health aids,* hygiene items, or the like. Another part of "work" at the prison ~~is tied~~ *relates* to the underground activities and economy. ~~No one keeps written records of these trans-~~

~~actions.~~ The hustles include tattooing, gambling, drugs, food running, strong-arming laundry service, body guarding, and hootch making *(a homemade alcohol product)*. That list tells

you more about prison than does the official line offered to the

public.

In *addition to the commonplace housing and the above and below ground work,* CIW also offers religion a la carte. ~~Religion is really important.~~

Convicts have three full-time chaplains. Anyone can attend a Jew-

ish Sed*e*r, a Catholic mass, or a protestant spectacular. Last Sunday,

I attended a foot-stomping, *woman-wailing* Gospel Bonanza put on by outside evan-

gelists, the men in spandex and the women with big hair. The pro-

gram rivaled any free world revival in a three-post tent. *A*lso avail-

able are sweat lodge rituals for the Native Americans and services

for Muslims.

Like the commercial and service areas, religion also has its

underground activities. ~~There are several examples.~~ Currently an

inmate *, who was an ordained minister on the streets,* has been baptizing women in the shower (total immersion,

she argues) marrying lesbians, and performing exorcisms (including

one on a schizoid yard cat named Blue Eyes). *Equally well known* A voodooist has *recently* con-

structed personalized images for putting a hex on those she believes

have offended her, leading a number of terrified women to dispose

of hair and other byproducts of personal hyg*ie*ne only by the toilet

flushing technique.

Another component of the community ~~Then there~~ is school. It may be on an academically low level,

such as literacy, or somewhat advanced, such as the GED program.

Small college programs, such as the one I am now enrolled in, depend on state funding, which in our case will be withdrawn next year.

At the practical level, in recent years, several vocational programs have been offered and then discontinued: plumbing, graphic arts, and hair styling.

Naturally, the other side of formal education at CIW is informal education. No one leaves the same as she was upon entering. Each inmate will learn from the prison and become *either* better or worse. I wish I could say that life improvement usually wins out over other forces. It does sometimes happen in this best of all criminal schools. *For myself, against odds, I intend to make it so.*

Yes, CIW is more than a holding pen for criminal types. It really is a community/ *B* but being a social unit does not make it a nice place to live. The average person stays here for three to five years and moves on, ~~which is~~ about the average for movement on the street.

And not all is bad. Some of us convicts do save ourselves. We occasionally get some help. *For most, the help is not enough.*

After two more revisions with editing, Tanya typed this *final draft,* proofread it once again, read it aloud, and, satisfied, submitted it to her instructor.

Prison as a Community

Tanya

Few free world citizens regard the California Institution for Women as a walled city, but that's what it is. Before I was sent here, I imagined prison as a bunch of scared and scary people in a fenced pen. Then I became a resident and discovered that, except for freedom, this place has all the parts of a community outside the fence.

It all begins with rules. CIW has a government, one that is totalitarian, not democratic. The constitution is a set of laws passed by the state of California. The warden and her associates administer the laws. The correctional officers enforce the laws. The convicts obey—or else.

These laws also govern where we live in the prison. It is said that the two most important things in prison are where one lives and where one works. An inmate's address at prison can be determined by several factors: behavior, reputation, age, and health. Therefore, one can be assigned to a cell block with designations such as ordinary (general dorm, room, or cell), honors, geriatrics, solitary, convalescent, protective custody, or psychiatric. At times special living units are formed. Once there was a living unit at CIW called the AIDS ward, for convicts who were HIV positive. If somebody approached these women as they were being escorted across the yard, a correctional officer would blow a whistle and shout, "Stay away! These inmates have AIDS! These inmates have AIDS!" The HIV positive women now live in housing for the general population, and staff is more enlightened.

The other part of the saying, "where you work," is tied in with both free world industry and the operation of the prison. For years CIW has produced clothing for the California Transportation Agency (CalTrans), made mostly of heavy orange fabric. We have also manufactured Levis and underwear for California prisons for men. Most jobs relate to services, such as food, laundry, maintenance, and clerical. All able-bodied women, even those in educational programs, must work. Some jobs provide compensation, the so-called "pay slots," but prison work is almost never connected with vocational training or with post-parole jobs. The money, usually about fifteen to thirty dollars a month, is placed in a trust fund and can be used in the prison store for treats, smokes, health aids, hygiene items, or the like.

Another part of "work" at the prison relates to the underground activities and economy. The hustles include tattooing, gambling, drugs, food running, laundry service, strong-arming, body guarding, and hootch (a homemade alcohol product) making. That list tells you more about prison than does the official line offered to the public.

In addition to the commonplace housing and the above and below ground work, CIW offers religion a la carte. Convicts have three full-time chaplains. Anyone can attend a Jewish Seder, a Catholic mass, or a protestant spectacular. Last Sunday, I attended a foot-stomping, woman-wailing Gospel Bonanza put on by outside evangelists, the men in spandex and the women with big hair. The program rivaled any free world revival in a three-post tent. Also available are sweat lodge rituals for the Native Americans and services for Muslims.

Like the commercial and service areas, religion has its underground activities. Currently an inmate, who was an ordained minister on the streets, has been baptizing women in the shower (total immersion, she argues), marrying lesbians, and performing exorcisms (including one on a schizoid yard cat* named Blue Eyes). Equally well known, a voodooist has recently constructed personalized images for putting a hex on those she believes have offended her, leading a number of terrified women to dispose of hair and other byproducts of personal hygiene only by the toilet-flushing technique.

Another component of the community is school. It may be on an academically low level, such as literacy, or somewhat advanced, such as the GED program. At the practical level, in recent years, several vocational programs have been offered and then discontinued: plumbing, graphic arts, and hair styling. Small college programs, such as the one I am now enrolled in, depend on state funding, which in our case will be withdrawn next year.

Naturally, the other side of formal education at CIW is informal education. No one leaves the same as she was upon entering. Each inmate will learn from the prison and become either better or worse. I wish I could say that life improvement usually wins out over other forces. It does sometimes happen in this best of all criminal schools. For myself, against odds, I intend to make it so.

Yes, CIW is more than a holding pen for criminal types. It really is a community. But being a social unit does not make it a nice place to live. The average person stays here for three to five years and moves on, about the average for movement on the street. And not all is bad. Some of us convicts do save ourselves. We occasionally get some help. For most, the help is not enough.

Exercise 2   **REVISING AND EDITING A FIRST DRAFT**

Revise the following student first draft according to CLUESS (coherence, language, unity, emphasis, support, and sentences). Then edit for COPS (capitalization, omissions, punctuation, and spelling). Space is provided for you to add, delete, move, and correct material. Divide the paragraph into a brief three-paragraph essay by placing an "X" after the introductory paragraph and another after the support, or body, paragraph.

Answers will vary.

*A yard cat is an unowned cat that runs free on the prison grounds.

Feng Shui

James Chow

When my real estate client, Mrs. Wong, asked me, "Do you

~~Of course~~
know about Feng Shui?" I smiled and said, "~~Sure enough~~." Without

       d   function in my profession Feng Shui
that knowlege I could not ~~do my deals~~. ~~It~~ is the name for Chinese

      e
superstitions/Especially those regarding the interrelationships of a

          he or she   s Thus,
person's birth chart and the home where ~~they~~ live. Describing an

ideal house to a client may be ~~a~~ more a matter of describing what it

            X
should not have rather than what it should have. These are a few of

  negative characteristics
the ~~downers~~ other than those associated with personal charts.

At the entrance heading into the front door there should be no

  because   bring death or divorce
tree, ~~but for~~ it may ~~mean you'll croak or split the blanket~~. The front

door itself should not face the stairwell because all good fortune

may roll right out of the house. The back door should also not face

                   money
the front door such an arrangement may allow the ~~dough~~ that

comes in the front door to go out the back. The house itself should

                les
sit on a lot that is square or rectangular/ sharp ang~~els~~ will bring

  bad luck
~~you down~~. The land itself should be higher along the fence behind

  Moreover, Feng Shui holds that t
the house to hold in prosperity. The house must face the right direc-

    the individual's time of birth
tion according to ~~your birthday~~. This placement can affect a person's

destiny
~~future~~. The number of the house may be more easily understood in

      has the same character as death
Chinese, the number 4 ~~means you're a goner~~. These and many,

  of feng shui
many more rules, along with common-sense requirements such as a

           functional floor plan,
bright and cheerful feeling and a ~~fine layout~~ are points Mrs. Wong

X
will consider. Because trying to follow all the rules may hold up

of feng shui
^

an excellent house
people from finding ~~a happy pad~~, I often advise clients not to take
^

miserable
them too seriously lest they make life ~~a downer~~.
^

Exercise 3   **REVISING AND EDITING YOUR PAPER**

Revise and edit the rough draft you wrote for Exercise 1.

Writer's Guidelines: Writing, Revising, and Editing

1. Writing

   Write your first draft, paying close attention to your outline, list, or cluster. Do not concern yourself with perfect spelling, grammar, or punctuation.

2. Revising

   Revise your draft, using CLUESS.

   Coherence

   - Are the ideas clearly related, each one to the others and to the central idea?
   - Is there a clear pattern of organization (time, space, or emphasis)?
   - Is the pattern supported by words that suggest the basis of that organization (time: *now, then, later;* space: *above, below, up, down;* emphasis: *first, second, last*)?
   - Is coherence enhanced by the use of transitional terms, pronouns, repetition, and a consistent point of view?

   Language

   - Is the general style of language *usage* appropriate (properly standard and formal or informal) for the purpose of the piece and the intended audience?
   - Is the *tone* (language use showing attitude toward material and audience) appropriate?
   - Is the *diction* (word choice) effective? Are the words precise in conveying meaning? Are they fresh and original?

Unity

- Are the thesis and every topic sentence clear and well stated? Do they indicate both subject and treatment?
- Are all points of support clearly related to and subordinate to the topic sentence of each paragraph and to the thesis of the essay?

Emphasis

- Are ideas properly placed (especially near the beginning and end) for emphasis?
- Are important words and phrases repeated for emphasis?

Support

- Is there adequate material—such as examples, details, quotations, and explanations—to support each topic sentence and thesis?
- Are the points of support placed in the best possible order?

Sentences

- Are the sentences varied in length and beginnings?
- Are the sentences varied in pattern (simple, compound, complex, and compound-complex)?
- Are all problems with sentence structure (fragments, comma splices, run-ons) corrected?

3. Editing

- Edit your draft for COPS. Are all problems in such areas as capitalization, omissions, punctuation, and spelling corrected?

4

Reading-Related Writing

THE QUIGMANS   by Buddy Hickerson

© Tribune Media Services, Inc. All Rights Reserved. Reprinted with permission.

Reading for Writing

ecause most college writing assignments are connected with reading, it is worthwhile to consider how to focus thoughtful attention on the written word. Of course, if you know about writing assignments or tests beforehand, your reading can be more concentrated. You should always begin a reading assignment by asking yourself why you are reading that particular material and how it relates to your course work and interests. For example, most selections in this book are presented as ideas to stimulate thought and invite reflective comparisons, to provide material for analysis and evaluation, and to show how a pattern or process of writing can be done effectively. The discussion and critical-thinking questions and activities that follow the selections arise from these purposes. Other questions raised by your instructor or on your own can also direct you in purposeful reading. Consider such questions and activities at the outset. Then, as you read, use strategies that are appropriate for the kind of assignment you are working on. Among the most common strategies are underlining, annotating, and outlining. Used correctly, they will help you attain a critical, receptive, and focused state of mind as you prepare for writing assignments.

Underlining

Imagine you are reading a chapter of several pages, and you decide to underline and write in the margins. Immediately, the underlining takes you out of the passive, television-watching frame of mind. You are involved. You are participating. It is now necessary for you to discriminate, to distinguish more important from less important ideas. Perhaps you have thought of underlining as a method designed only to help you with reviewing. That is, when you study the material the next time, you won't have to reread all of it; instead, you can focus on the most important underlined parts. While you are underlining, you are benefiting from an imposed concentration, because this procedure forces you to think, to focus. Consider the following suggestions for underlining:

1. Underline the main ideas in paragraphs. The most important statement, the topic sentence, is likely to be at the beginning of the paragraph.

2. Underline the support for those main ideas.

3. Underline answers to questions that you bring to the reading assignment. These questions may have come from the end of the chapter, from subheadings that you turn into questions, or from your independent concerns about the topic.

4. Underline only the key words. You would seldom underline all the words in a sentence and almost never a whole paragraph.

Does that fit your approach to underlining? Possibly not. Most students, in their enthusiasm to do a good job, overdo underlining.

The trick is to figure out what to underline. You would seldom underline more than about 30 percent of a passage, although the amount would depend on your purpose and the nature of the material. Following the preceding four suggestions will be useful. Learning more about the principles of sentence, paragraph, and essay organization will also be helpful.

Annotating

Annotating, writing notes in the margins, is a practice related to underlining. You can do it independently, although it usually appears in conjunction with underlining to signal your understanding and to extend your involvement in your reading.

Writing in the margins represents intense involvement because it turns a reader into a writer. If you read material and write something in the margin as a reaction to it, then in a way you have had a conversation with the author. The author has made a statement and you have responded. In fact, you may have added something to the text; therefore, for your purposes you have become a co-author or collaborator. The comments you make in the margin are of your own choosing, according to your interests and the purpose you bring to the reading assignment. Your response in the margin may merely echo the author's ideas, it may question them critically, it may relate them to something else, or it may add to them.

The comments and marks in Section 1 of the following essay will help you understand the connection between writing and reading. Both techniques—underlining to indicate main and supporting ideas and annotating to indicate their importance and relevance to the task at hand—will enhance thinking, reading, and writing.

Like, Whatever . . .
An epidemic of inarticulacy could, uh, well, suck

David Orr

Section 1: Problem and Causes [Editor's subtitle]

1

Bright student

<u>He</u> entered my office as a freshman advisee sporting <u>nearly perfect SAT scores</u> and an <u>impeccable academic record</u>—a young man of considerable promise. During a 20-minute conversation,

Self-restricted vocabulary

How typical?

however, he displayed a vocabulary that consisted mostly of two words: *cool* and *really.* Almost 800 SAT points hitched to each word. He is no aberration, but an example of diminished literacy in a culture that often fails to use words carefully.

2

Source indicating vocabulary decline?

In the past 50 years, by one reckoning, the working vocabulary of the average 14-year-old has declined from 25,000 words to 10,000. This is a decline not merely in words, but also in the capacity to think. We are losing the capacity to say what we mean, and ultimately to think about what we mean, about the things that matter most.

3

Evidence?

The problem is not confined to teenagers and young adults. A national epidemic of incoherence is evident in public discourse, street talk, movies, television, and music. Nor is the problem new. As H.L. Mencken, William Safire, and other commentators have noted, language is always coming undone. Why? First, those who intend to control others seize the words and metaphors by which people describe their world; in our time, the attackers are trying to sell one kind of quackery or another: economic, political, religious, or technological. The clarity and felicity of language—as distinct from its quantity—is devalued in an industrial-technological society. In fact, clear, artful language threatens that society.

Causes

First Cause—the controllers

4

Second cause— specialized vocabulary

Good and bad

Second, language is in decline because it is being balkanized by specialized vocabularies. The highly technical language of the expert is, of course, both bane and blessing. It is useful for describing fragments of the world, but not for describing how they fit into a coherent whole. The language of molecular biology can describe genetic engineering, but interpreting the act of re-arranging life's genetic fabric requires an altogether different language, and a mind-set that seeks to discover larger patterns.

5

Third cause—lack of direct experience

Has virtual experience no value?

Third, language reflects the range and depth of our experience. But our experience is being impoverished to the extent that it is rendered artificial and prepackaged. Most of us no longer experience skilled physical work on farms or in forests. Consequently, words and metaphors based on intimate knowledge of soils, plants, trees, animals, landscapes, and rivers have all but vanished. Recreation and software industries are engineering and shrink-wrapping our experience of an increasingly uniform and ugly world, and peddling it back to us as "fun" or "information."

6

Fourth cause—no common literature

Fourth, we are no longer held together by reading a common literature or listening to the same stories. Allusions to the Bible and great literature no longer resonate because those works are unfamiliar to a growing number of people.

7

Of the roughly 6,000 languages now spoken, linguists predict that less than half are expected to survive to the year 2050. Lan-

Language goes global and gets trimmed

guage is being <u>whittled down to</u> the <u>dimensions</u> of the <u>global economy</u> and <u>homogenized</u> to accord with the <u>"information age."</u> This represents a <u>loss of cultural information,</u> a blurring of our capacity to understand the world and our place in it, and a losing bet that <u>people armed with</u> the <u>words, metaphors,</u> and <u>mind-set</u> of <u>industry</u> and <u>technology can,</u> in fact, <u>manage</u> the <u>earth.</u>

8

Language, George Orwell once wrote, "becomes ugly and inaccurate because our thoughts are foolish, but the slovenliness of our language makes it easier for us to have foolish thoughts."

In management age, language gets managed

The <u>new class of corporate chiefs, global managers, genetic engineers,</u> and <u>money speculators</u> <u>will reduce language</u> to the <u>level of utility, function,</u> and <u>management.</u> Evil begins not only with words used with malice, but also with words that diminish people, land, and life. The prospects for evil grow as those for language decline.

9

Language and humanity

Lincoln

Churchill

Our affinity for <u>language makes us human.</u> <u>We are never better than when we use words clearly eloquently, and civilly.</u> Language can elevate thought and ennoble behavior. <u>Abraham Lincoln's words</u> at Gettysburg in 1863 gave meaning to the terrible sacrifices of the Civil War. <u>Winston Churchill's words</u> inspired a nation in the dark hours of 1940. If we intend to protect and enhance our humanity, we must first protect and enhance language and fight anything that undermines and cheapens it.

Section 2: Solutions [Editor's subtitle]

10

First solution— direct communication

But how to deal with mass population?

What does this mean? <u>First,</u> we must <u>restore</u> the <u>habit</u> of <u>talking directly to each other</u>—whatever the loss in economic efficiency. I propose that we <u>smash every communication device used in place</u> of <u>a real person,</u> <u>beginning with answering machines.</u>

11

Second solution—public reading

<u>Second,</u> we can <u>restore</u> the <u>habit of public reading.</u> One of my distinctive childhood memories is <u>attend</u>ing a <u>public reading</u> of Shakespeare by the British actor Charles Laughton. With no prop other than a book, he read with energy and passion for two hours, keeping a large audience—including at least one 8-year-old boy— enthralled. No movie was ever as memorable. Further, I propose that adults <u>turn off the television,</u> <u>unplug</u> the <u>computer,</u> and <u>read good books to</u> their <u>children.</u> I know of no better or more pleasurable way to stimulate thinking, encourage love of language, and facilitate a child's ability to form images.

Plus family reading

12

Third solution— language accountability

<u>Third,</u> we ought to <u>hold those who corrupt language accountable,</u> <u>beginning with</u> the <u>advertising industry,</u> which spends hundreds of billions of dollars each year to sell us an unconscionable amount of often useless, environmentally destructive, and un-

Methods?
Laws?

healthy stuff. We should insist that they abide by community standards of truthfulness, including full disclosure of what products do to the environment and to those who buy them.

13

Fourth solution—
protect local culture

Fourth, we need to protect local culture from domination by national media, markets, and power. Language grows from the outside in, from periphery to center. It is renewed in the vernacular, where human intentions intersect places and circumstances, and by everyday acts of authentic living and speaking. It is corrupted by contrivance, pretense, and fakery. We need to protect the independence of local newspapers and local radio stations, as well as those parts of our culture where memory, tradition, and devotion to place still exist.

Protect by law? by
education?

14

Fifth solution—education

Finally, since language is the currency of truth, we should defend the integrity and clarity of language as the highest priority for schools, colleges, and universities. As teachers, we should insist on good writing, assign readings that are well written, and restore rhetoric—the ability to speak clearly and well—to the liberal arts curriculum. And we, too, should be held accountable for what we say.

Role of teachers

15

In terms of volume, this is surely an information age. But in terms of understanding, wisdom, spiritual clarity, and civility, we have entered a darker age. We are committing what C.S. Lewis once called "verbicide." The volume of words is inversely related to our capacity to use them well, and to think clearly about what they mean. It is no wonder that in a dreary century of gulags, genocide, global wars, and nuclear weapons, our use of language has been dominated by propaganda and advertising. And what will be said in the 21st century, as the stark realities of biotic impoverishment become apparent? Can we summon the clarity of mind to speak the necessary words?

Threat of propaganda
and advertising

Outlining Source Material

After reading, underlining, and annotating the piece, the next step could be to outline it. If the piece is well organized, you should be able to reduce it to a simple outline so that you can, at a glance, see the relationship of ideas (sequence, relative importance, and interdependence). Outlining is explained on pages 39–43.

Here is an outline of Section 1 of "Like, Whatever . . ."

I. National problem with language decline

   A. Among the young

   B. Among society generally

II. Causes

    A. Word controllers

        1. Methods

        2. Agendas

    B. Specialized vocabularies

        1. Good effects

        2. Bad effects

    C. Lack of direct experience

        1. Cultural changes

        2. Engineered activities

    D. No common literature

III. Global language

    A. Homogenized process

    B. Earth managed

    C. Dehumanization

Exercise 1	**UNDERLINING, ANNOTATING, AND OUTLINING**

Complete the underlining and annotation in Section 2 of "Like, What-ever . . .". Then complete the following outline that covers the same passage.
Answers will vary.

IV. Solutions

    A. Restore direct communication

        1. Talk directly _____

        2. Smash answering machines

    B. Restore public reading

        1. Turn off electronic devices _____

        2. Read aloud _____

    C. Make violators accountable _____

        1. Impose community standards _____

        2. Require disclosure

    D. Protect local culture _____

        1. Oppose national domination _____

        2. Cherish local expression

    E. Educate

        1. Defend integrity and clarity of language _____._____

        2. Require high standards in school reading and writing _____

        3. Hold teachers accountable _____

V. The challenge
   A. Language dominated by <u>propaganda</u> and <u>advertising</u>
   B. Uncertain response

Supporting Ideas with Quotations and References

In your reading-related writing assignments, you are likely to use three methods in developing your ideas: explanation, direct reference to the reading selection, and quotation from the reading. The explanations can take different forms, such as causes or effects, comparison, definition, or exemplification. These forms are explored later in this book. The references point the reader directly toward the reading selection. The more specific the reference—including even the page number—the more helpful it is to your readers. As for quotations, remember that the words are borrowed. They can be very effective as support, but you must give credit to the original writer.

The use of quoted material is justified if it cannot be easily restated or if it carries weight because of its eloquence or origin. Usually, you should paraphrase or summarize rather than quote material to maintain the smooth flow of your thoughts. When quotation is called for, most writers use short quotations (just a few words) and blend them with paraphrase or summary; this compromise preserves the flavor and force of the original without creating an unevenness of presentation.

Basic Documentation

Borrowing words or ideas without giving credit to the source is called *plagiarism.* At best, plagiarism is sloppy scholarship; at worst, it is intellectual thievery. Therefore, your instructor will ask you to document or, in some way, to acknowledge original material in your source-based writing. Your method may be either informal or formal.

Informal Documentation

If you are writing in response to a single source—for example, from your textbook—your instructor may not ask you to indicate by page number where you found each borrowed idea. However, you will be expected to make clear, by use of quotation marks and names of authors, that you *have* borrowed ideas. If you are writing from an assigned reading selection, your references would not list your textbook as a source or use page number references unless your instructor directs you to do so. Simply writing something such as "I agree with Suzanne Britt when she says that thin people are unpleasant" would suffice.

Formal Documentation

If you are using material from sources other than your textbook, your instructor will probably ask you to use formal documentation, which includes citations and the listing of works that are cited.

Citations are acknowledgments of borrowed material. One documentation method is Modern Language Association (MLA) style. Here are some of the most common principles that can be used for textbook or other restricted sources, with some examples.

- If you use material from a source you have read, identify that source so the reader will recognize it or be able to find it.
- Document any original idea borrowed, whether it is quoted, paraphrased (written in your words but not shorter), or summarized (written in your words and shorter). Basic situations include the following:

> Normally, you need give only the author's name and a page number enclosed in parentheses: (Rivera 45).

> If you state the author's name in introducing the quotation or idea, then usually give only the page number in parentheses: (45).

> If the author has written more than one piece in the book, then a title or shortened form of the title is also required: (Rivera, *The Land* 45).

Here is an example of documenting a quotation by an author represented only once in a textbook, using the author's name to introduce:

> Suzanne Britt says that thin people have "speedy little metabolisms that cause them to bustle briskly" (297).

Following is an example of documenting an idea borrowed from an author but not quoted, using the author's name to introduce:

> Suzanne Britt believes that thin people are weak in character (299).

Here is an example of documenting an idea borrowed from another source but not using the author's name to introduce:

> Music often helps Alzheimer's patients think more clearly (Weiss 112).

MLA style also provides guidance for the listing of sources, called *Works Cited*. Here are three examples of commonly used materials.

Article in a Monthly or Bimonthly Magazine
Fallows, James. "Why Americans Hate the Media." *Atlantic Monthly* Feb. 1996: 45–64.

Newspaper Article
Gregory, Tina. "When All Else Fails." *Philadelphia Inquirer* 2 Apr. 1990: C12.

A Work in an Anthology (or in a textbook, other than by the author of that textbook)
Brock, Elizabeth. "A Bee in My Bonnet." *Paragraphs and Essays*. Ed. Lee Brandon. Boston: Houghton Mifflin Company, 2001. 106-107.

See Chapter 15, The Research Paper, for more explanation on formal documentation, including information about Internet sources.

Documentation in Action

Your essay may include ideas from newspapers, magazines, or books. To make life simpler for you, most of the reading-related assignments in this book are based on selections included in this book. When you are writing about some thing you have read, just write as you usually would, but bring in ideas and quotations from that source. You may also want to refer to more than one source. You may even use ideas from other sources to contrast with your own. For example, you may say, "Unlike Fred M. Hechlinger in 'The First Step in Improving Sex Education: Remove the Hellfire' (351), I believe that public schools should not offer sex education." Do not feel that each point you make must be directly related to sources.

Here is a paragraph by student Jackie Malone illustrating how to incorporate ideas and document them:

Sexist men are victims of their own bias against females. Because they cannot accept women as full human beings, they themselves are smaller in dimension. In Irwin Shaw's "The Girls in Their Summer Dresses," Michael looks at his wife, but he doesn't see a full human being; he just sees a sexual object: "what a pretty girl, what nice legs" (314). Because he sees her and other women that way, he cannot ever have the relationship with her that she deserves and that he would find fulfilling. Of course, thinking of women as just soft and cuddly has its effects on men in other ways. The man as father who thinks that way may very well regard his own daughter as one limited in her ranges of activities and limited in her potential. He may be one of those fathers who immediately stereotype their daughters as headed for a "life of the affections," not like a son's, "earning a living" (Lurie 249). Unfortunately, these men cannot accept females as their equals in any important respect, and, in doing so, they deprive themselves, as well as others.

Types of Reading-Related Writing

Many college assignments will require you to use source material, rather than write only about personal experience. The extent to which you write from sources will depend on your purpose in fulfilling assignments. Some assignments will be very precise, asking you to paraphrase, summarize, explain, or evaluate specific reading material. Others will ask you to relate a source or part of a source to your experiences.

These reading-related assignments will be based on single or multiple sources. All of them will require a careful reading of a source or sources. As you concentrate on your purpose, your skills in underlining, annotating, and outlining will help you to interpret material and locate useful ideas that can be borrowed for your writing.

Single-Source Writing

Writing from a single source will take one or more of the following forms:

- a *summary* (material in your own words; only main ideas)
- a *paraphrase* (material in your own words; more than main ideas)
- a *reaction* (usually ideas on how the reading relates specifically to you, your experiences, and your attitudes; it also is often a critique of the worth and logic of the reading)
- a *two-part response* (includes both a summary and a reaction, but they are separate)

Summary

A *summary* is a rewritten, shortened version of a piece of writing in which you use your own wording to express the main ideas. Learning to summarize effectively will help you in many ways. Summary writing reinforces comprehension skills in reading. It requires you to discriminate among the ideas in the reading passage. Summaries are usually written in the form of a well-designed paragraph or a cluster of brief paragraphs and are frequently used in essays and research papers.

The following rules will guide you in writing effective summaries.

1. Cite the author and title of the text.

2. Keep the length shorter than the original by about two-thirds (although the exact reduction will vary depending on the content of the original).

3. Include the main ideas. (Include details only infrequently.)

4. Change the original wording without changing the idea.

5. Do not evaluate the content or give an opinion (even if you see an error in logic or fact).

6. Do not add ideas (even if you have an abundance of related information).

7. Do not include any personal comments (do not use *I*, referring to self).

8. Use quotations sparingly. (If you do quote directly from the source, enclose the quoted material in quotation marks.)

9. Use author tags ("says York," "according to York," or "the author explains") to remind the reader(s) that you are summarizing the material of another author.

Paraphrase

A *paraphrase* is similar to a summary in that both are a recasting of a reading passage into your own words. It is different, however, in that the summary includes only main ideas, whereas the paraphrase can include the rewording of any statement. The summary is shorter than the original; the paraphrase can be longer, shorter, or about the same length. However, both forms are reworded products. Except for the rules about a summary being shorter and concentrating on main ideas, the same rules apply to writing a paraphrase.

| Exercise 2 | **EVALUATING A SUMMARY** |

Apply the rules of summary writing to the following summary of Section 1 of "Like, Whatever . . ." (p. 72). Use rule numbers (pp. 80–81) to annotate the faulty parts of the summary.

[1]"Like, Whatever . . ."

[1]The author says "a national epidemic of incoherence is evident in public discourse, street talk, movies, television, and music."[3]His main example is a 14-year-old with high SAT scores and mainly a two-word vocabulary.[5,7]It seems to me that he had to have a big vocabulary to achieve high SAT scores.[1]The author goes on to explain that four causes are evident. One, the controllers—[8]economic, political, religious, or technological—have imposed their own words to characterize their main concerns, thereby controlling the way people think

about certain things, such as abortion, industrial safety, and unemployment. Two, language has developed in certain areas to pertain only to those areas and not to relate to other concerns, thus setting up communication barriers.[1] The author could have and should have focused more here. Three, our direct experience with our physical world in nature has diminished, and with that loss goes the use of language pertaining to our direct experience.[7] I think he means we do not go camping or practice farming very much anymore. Four,[8] we are no longer held together by reading a common literature or listening to the same stories. Moreover, the problem of language decline is global. Languages are disappearing, and international business leaders are imposing their words and thought patterns on the world population. Humanity depends on us to make language strong and to [8]fight anything that undermines and cheapens it.

Following is an example of an effective summary of the Section 1 of "Like, Whatever . . .".

A Summary of "Like, Whatever . . ." by David Orr

In "Like, Whatever . . ." David Orr says the decline of language usage is a national problem that threatens our ability to think effectively. He explains that four causes are evident. One, the controllers—"economic, political, religious, or technological"—have imposed their own words to characterize their main concerns, thereby controlling the way people think about certain things. Two, language has developed in certain areas to pertain to those areas and not to relate to other concerns, thus setting up communication barriers. Three, our direct experience with our physical world in nature has diminished, and with that loss goes the use of language relating to our direct experience. Virtual experience and commercially packaged encounters do not lead to language invention. Four, we do not share a literature derived from common reading and listening experiences. Moreover, the problem of language decline is global. Languages are disappearing, and international business leaders are imposing their words and thought patterns on the world population. Humanity depends on our maintaining and improving our language skills.

Reaction

As with all reading-related assignments, after clarifying exactly what you are setting out to do in writing your reaction, you read, underline, and annotate your subject passage. You may even outline or summarize the material before you proceed to writing your response. At this time, you know the author's purpose, the main points, and the reasoning and supporting information. The focus of your reaction will depend on the author's purpose in writing the passage. All reactions will include some summary and paraphrase. Following are some of the approaches you may take:

- *Agreement or disagreement:* You may agree or disagree with the author's ideas and present your views on a point-by-point basis, typically discussing each point in a paragraph composed of a summary, probably some quotation, and your response. Or you may select only a few points for your treatment. Whatever your range, your position will be supported by your own reasoning and by your own evidence, such as examples.

- *Critique, or evaluation:* This approach usually has a broader scope than the reaction of agreement or disagreement. It emphasizes critical thinking and reveals the worth, logic, and overall effectiveness of the piece.

- *Parallel experience (sometimes called a* spin-off*):* You may concentrate on your own experience or experiences as related to one or more ideas in the passage. For example, if your subject reading selection is about a struggle over a career choice and you have had a similar struggle, you may decide to use the framework of the reading passage to guide you in discussing your struggle. You would refer specifically to the subject passage, perhaps use some quotation, and point out similarities and dissimilarities between the reading selection and your experience. Your reader would recognize your grasp of the original piece and appreciate the skill with which you relate it to your experience. This approach may use only a part of the subject work, a substantial portion, or all the major points.

The following paragraph is a reaction in which the student writer agrees with one aspect of Section 1 of "Like, Whatever . . .".

Response to "Like, Whatever . . ." by David Orr

In "Like, Whatever . . ." David Orr makes a strong case for his thesis that language usage is declining worldwide. Language is part of society and reflects all its changes and values. As the economy becomes global, so does language. As international companies advertise and use public relations techniques, everyone is exposed over and over to phrases that are carefully crafted by individuals with agendas, such as CEOs, politicians, preachers, and ad-persons. He says they want to control how we think. Orr's examples of language decline easily bring to mind other examples that bombard us daily. We are more likely to buy a car that is "preowned" than one that is "used." We would rather live in the "inner city" than a "slum" or "ghetto." It is easier for a company to "downsize" than to "fire people." It is better for a gas stove to "puff-back" than to "explode." We can hardly avoid using certain words that bother us, such as "pro-life" or "pro-choice." And we vaguely realize that as we accept words adopted and adapted by others to characterize their positions, our thoughts are being controlled. Yet we do not look around for words to fit our situations. Instead, we are provided with virtual experiences, complete with words. As with a song video, we are given the words, and we are given the pictures so we do not have to use our imagination. Almost every phase of life is becoming a video. David Orr is saying we should sing more of our own songs and write them with care.

Student author's reactions, agreeing with the subject piece and providing new examples

Two-Part Response

As you have seen, the reaction includes a partial summary or is written with the assumption that readers have read the original piece. However, your instructor may prefer that you separate each form— for example, by presenting a clear, concise summary followed by a reaction to the passage. This format is especially useful for critical examination of a text or for problem-solving assignments, because it requires you to understand and repeat another's views or experiences before responding. The two-part approach also helps you avoid the common problem of writing only a summary of the text when your instructor wants you to both summarize and evaluate or otherwise react. Before writing a summary and a reaction, ask your instructor if you should separate your summary from your response.

Following is a two-part response to Section 2 of "Like, Whatever . . .". The first paragraph is a summary of the passage, and the second is the reader's reaction to it.

Two-Part Response to Section 2 of "Like Whatever . . ."
by David Orr

Summary

In "Like, Whatever . . ." David Orr does not just describe the problem of language decline; he also offers five clear solutions. The first solution is to restore direct communication by "talking directly to each other" and forsaking electronic substitutes. The second is to bring back public reading after disconnecting such instruments as television sets and computers. The third is to make those who debase the language accountable by requiring full explanations of the harmful effects of advertised products. The fourth is to protect local customs and cultures by promoting local rather than national media. The fifth is to make effective language the primary concern in all educational institutions. Teachers themselves should require high standards in reading and writing. Orr says that our "language has been dominated by propaganda and advertising." He says we have the answers to the problem of language decline, and now he wonders if we have the strength to respond.

Reaction

In his essay "Like, Whatever . . ." David Orr details the problem of language decline and offers five solutions. One solution struck a familiar chord in my experience, that of our need to communicate directly with others and to turn off electronic devices such as the television set. When I was in the fifth grade, my school promoted an experiment. We students were asked to persuade our families to unplug our television sets for one month. It was not an easy argument to make in my household, but my family finally did agree. The result was pretty remarkable. Instead of watching reruns of "Star Trek" during dinner, we talked. At first we did not have much to say, and once my mother made out a list of topics. But soon we were talking straight through the meals, and not just during television commercials. I learned family folklore that I never would have heard about, and I still remember some of it. At times I contributed by talking more about school and what I was doing than I ever had. After dinner we played games and engaged in a lot of banter. Before bedtime, my parents and I read stories to my two younger siblings. The experiment lasted for just that one month. At the end of that one experimental month, my family talked about never plugging in the television set. Then came the professional football playoff games. My youngest sister confessed that she had been sort of cheating all along by visiting with friends to watch television. She said she had needed to watch so she would not feel like a nerd with her friends. Then I was sick for a couple of weeks. Television helped me pass the time. Soon we were a television family again. We kids were being told to hush up during the mealtime news programs. During "Wheel of Fortune," we could speak up with answers. As

Student's experience that illustrates one of Orr's basic ideas

David Orr says, we were listening to speech "dominated by propaganda and advertising." For the most part, we had made the choice. Unfortunately and regrettably, we liked it.

Multiple-Source Writing

Synthesis

A *synthesis* is the blending of two or more sources with your own commentary. The extent to which the sources are used varies. You may be writing about a controversial issue and need some expert insights or observations. You would naturally read several sources. You may even summarize some of them as you identify main ideas. In your search you may discover that one reading selection yields a single answer while another yields a different answer. A third has perhaps two solutions. From your perspective all four of the ideas are sound and you decide to show how they can work together to solve the problem.

The procedure is simple.

- Make notes from the sources. If the sources are not in your textbook, you may want to use a standard note-card form, which includes the relationship of the idea to your topic, identification of your source, location of the material within the work, and the idea as quoted or paraphrased, as shown in the following student example. (See Chapter 15, page 438, for further discussion of taking notes.)

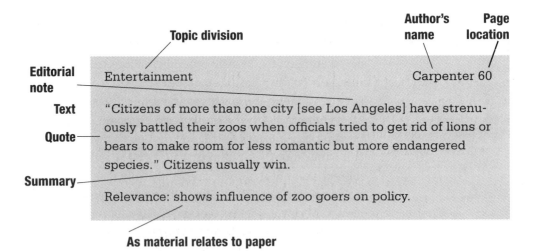

- If the sources are in your textbook, underline and mark material for use—or, even better, copy the passage you intend to quote or paraphrase—and key it to your outline by using symbols or by copying it onto your outline.

• As you present the ideas, identify them by source information in citations and discuss their relationship.

The result of this procedure may be a paragraph, with the ideas blended, or it may be an essay. The essay form might include an introduction defining the issue, a separate paragraph for each author's view, a paragraph or so for explaining precisely how the borrowed ideas relate, and then the conclusion.

Whether the blending of two or more sources occurs within a sentence, a paragraph, or an essay, it is still synthesis. The ideas are always presented in a relationship that builds an idea, discusses an idea from a different perspective, or even opposes an idea.

A synthesis can relate to the summary and the paraphrase. The summary identifies main ideas in sources. The synthesis will use one or more of those ideas to compare and contrast with other ideas from sources. The ideas themselves may be used as quotations, but they are more likely to be restated, or paraphrased.

Demonstration of Synthesis

Following is a demonstration of synthesis as it occurs in a short essay. To save space, only excerpts from three key sources are included here. The borrowed quotations are underlined and annotated. Note that each source is concerned with how to deal with youth gangs, but each has a different solution. Student Lewan Huang sees merit in all views and creates a simple synthesis. The citations, as they occur in parentheses in her essay on page 88, might not be required by some instructors if the sources are all from the same book.

Gangs and gang violence have become subjects of great interest and concern for all of Southern California. Law-enforcement agencies are expending enormous resources in their fight against gang-related crime. But, for the mothers of the targets of this law-enforcement effort, the problem is far more immediate than newspaper headlines and stories on TV news. The problem is family. . . .

Community involvement as one solution

Capt. Jack <u>Blair</u> of the <u>Pomona Police Department</u> <u>leads weekly gang-truce meetings</u> attended by <u>parents, gang members</u> and <u>local clergy.</u> In the course of his year-long involvement with the Pomona program, he has become convinced that "parents are the key to [solving] the whole problem." At his meetings, and at other meetings of parents around the county, Blair believes that parents have begun to make a difference. <u>"Once the parents unite and form groups, talking to each other and sharing information, that is threatening to the gang members.</u> They want anonymity. They don't want their tactics or activities talked about with parents of rival gangs. When the moms are saying 'Hey, don't go over to this neighborhood,' or 'I know that you went over to that neighborhood,' there is a certain amount of sport removed."   230

But in those days, most *vatos* became *veteranos* by their 20s and outgrew the crazy life. Some led a dual life, going to school or work during the week and hanging out in the neighborhood on weekends. Guns were a rare commodity and drive-bys were just beginning to be used as a gang tactic. Most *veteranos* made the transition to the work force as semiskilled and skilled laborers and as professionals. . . . Guys working for a living as did their fathers and grandfathers before them.

Economic cause

The loss of blue-collar jobs, combined with the curtailment of social spending, has eroded employment and educational opportunities for our children to the point that they are extremely marginalized. In the process, the adolescent lifestyle for many of them appears to have become a life sentence.   C3

Hundreds of young women and girls have hooked up with the Bloods and Crips in Portland, giving their boyfriends safe haven and sometimes joining them in the violence of gang culture.

Police say the future of gangs may hinge on these young women, who dress their children—especially little boys—in gang colors, teach them hand signs and nurture an allegiance to vendettas.

Enablers

"If we could get the girls to stop associating with the male gang members, we wouldn't have any gangs," policewoman Dorothy Elmore says bluntly.

"Girls are the backbone of gangs," say Elmore, who works with the Portland Police Bureau's Gang Enforcement Team.

"Girls give the males a place to lay their heads. Girls shelter them. Girls feed them. They protect them. They nurture them. Girls carry their guns and their dope. They are the key.   A3

Student Essay

Using More Than Laws Against Gangs
Lewan Huang

One of the most difficult crimes to combat is youth crime, specifically that perpetrated by gangs. If gangs could be eradicated or even if their criminal activities could be curtailed, the crime rate would drop dramatically. Incarceration is always available as a solution, but it does not get at the causes or treat the gang problems within their own communities. Broader-based solutions pertain to drug culture, families, education, and the economy.

Gang members are primarily males, but females often play the roles of enablers. Holly Gilbert says in "Girls Form Backbone of Gangs" that females are the key to gang survival. These females support their male companions, help them in crime, conceal their drugs and weapons, and bear their children. Then they dress the children in gang clothing and pass along gang behavior, traditions, and hand signs. Gilbert quotes Portland, Oregon, policewoman Dorothy Elmore as saying, "'If we could get the girls to stop associating with the male gang members, we wouldn't have any gangs'" (A3). Getting these girls to recognize how they are being used and abused would be an important step in combatting gang activity.

Another solution lies with the actual families of gang members. Gang members themselves often come from troubled families but not always. And well-meaning family members can help if they are given the opportunity through some kind of organized structure. Sue Horton, in "Mothers, Sons, and the Gangs," writes about one such program in Pomona, California. There the local police department brings together the gang members, their parents, and the clergy to discuss neighborhood problems. Captain Jack Blair says, "'Once the parents unite and form groups, talking to each other and sharing information, that is threatening to gang members'" (230). There the parents have become part of the solution.

One of the most significant causes of gang formation is economic. Carlos A. Chavez and Antonio H. Rodriguez say that gangs have long existed in Los Angeles, but now the underlying conditions have changed. In previous times, the gang members would go through a brief period of rebellion; then they would mature and join the job market for skilled and unskilled workers in factories. But those jobs are no longer available. According to Chavez and Rodriguez, "The loss of blue-collar jobs, combined with the curtailment of social spending," has reduced work and school opportunities, and gang life now extends well into maturity (C3).

These three solutions came from three different articles, but taken together they offer the multidirectional approach that is necessary. We need to educate the girlfriend enablers and to work with the family members. Beyond that, we as a society should provide educational and job opportunities. As for the gang members and their personal responsibility, they need to be receptive and adaptive. Of course, if they are not law abiding, the police should lock them up.

Works Cited

Chavez, Carlos A., and Antonio H. Rodriguez. *"La Vida Loca:* Crazy Life, Crazy Death." *Los Angeles Times* 17 Aug. 1995: C3.
Gilbert, Holly, "Girls Form Backbone of Gangs." *The Oregonian* 30 Sept. 1990: A3.
Horton, Sue. "Mothers, Sons, and the Gangs." *Celebrating Diversity.* Ed. Lee Brandon. Lexington, Mass.: D.C. Heath, 1995, 229–239.

Essays and Applications

The following paired essays demonstrate many of the elements of good writing that we have been exploring. To help you evaluate and write in response to those selections, each essay is accompanied first by a set of discussion and critical thinking questions and then by several reading-related writing suggestions. As you read, underline and annotate the material.

Cell Phones and Pagers—to Ban or Bless?

Both students and instructors are likely to react to allowing cell phones and pagers in the classroom with rapture or rage. Good representations of the opposing views on this issue, these paired informal essays by teachers Gail Washburn and Don Mack appeared on the same page of *NEA Today,* March 2001.

Allow Cell Phones and Pagers in the Classroom

Gail Washburn

Gail Washburn teaches art at Rangeland Elementary School in Louisville, Kentucky. A 21-year teaching veteran, she recently served on a National Board for Professional Teaching Standards committee, writing elementary art standards.

1   "Mom's working late tonight, son. Please wait for me by the front door of your school immediately after basketball practice.

2   "Don't play around in the gym, because I have another Association meeting this evening and your dad is working second shift."

3   If only I could give this message to my son!

4   I was always taught to be the most I could be. Get involved in your job and community, volunteer, give back. I have taught my students and children to have that same work ethic and attitude. How disconnected I feel when I can't reach my son at school to tell him of a change of plans.

5   If only I could talk to him now.

6   How many times have I left messages with an already overworked office secretary? And how often have I left notes in my school mailbox, unread for days?

7   I am a teacher, and I believe disruptive beeps and rings should be turned off and the phone set to vibrate mode during class. But in this great age of E-technology, I should be able to reach my son.

8   There are more single parents, divorced custodial parents, and workaholic parents than ever. More moms are choosing careers over staying at home. More dads are choosing to commute out-of-town for better jobs.

9   All this is juggled with after-school classes, sports, clubs, detention—what are parents to do?

10   We now have daycares at the workplace. Personal Internet camera surveillance at child-care facilities seems to improve employee morale and attendance.

11   Let's face it—parents work better when they know their kids are okay. We, as educators, want them to be more involved with their kids. And cell phones are one way to accomplish that.

12   But there's more than the parents' dilemma. Let's look at the bigger picture. Times are changing. E-commerce is on the rise. In the future, there will be telephones on wristwatches, backpacks, notebooks. Will we ban them?

13   I remember grounding my son once and telling him he couldn't use the telephone. Hearing laughter and talking coming from his room, I tiptoed up the steps and quickly opened the door. To my surprise, he was on his computer, talking to his friends face to face, voice to voice.

14   The future is now. Computers are cell phones and pagers. Students will find a way to use them, just as our generation used the once-prohibited calculators and tape recorders.

15   Finally, we say we should teach by example. Can we as teachers live without our cell phones and pagers?

16   How many times has our school telephone system blacked out because of heavy rains and strong winds (better known as long-winded teachers on the only available phone line)?

17   In case of emergencies, cell phones can be the only lifeline out of the school facility. Remember Columbine?

18   Not all cellular technology interferes with learning. With the newest technology, students can use their cell phones to connect to the Internet.

19   Let's find ways like these to incorporate cellular technology into our classroom curriculum.

Exercise 3   DISCUSSION AND CRITICAL THINKING

Purpose
1. What is Washburn's position?
    Cell phones and pagers should be allowed in classrooms.

2. Does she allow for any exceptions to her position?
    No, but she does acknowledge the need for students to avoid beeps and rings.

Support
3. What are Washburn's main points of support?
    (1) Parents and children have busy schedules and need to communicate easily with one another. (2) Other forms of communication (telephone calls through the school, notes) do not work well. (3) Cell phones and pagers are commonplace. (4) Cell phones can connect with the Internet as part of classroom learning.

Organization and Special Techniques
4. How convincing are Washburn's examples, both real and hypothetical?
    Answers will vary.

5. What comparison does she use? How apt is it?
    She compares the teachers' need for cell phones and pagers with that of students. Some might argue that the analogy is false in that teachers' circumstances (role, maturity, needs) are far different from those of students.

6. How effective is Washburn's placement of her main idea toward the middle of the essay?
    Answers will vary.

Personal Reaction
7. Are you persuaded by her argument? Why or why not? Has she overlooked any good points on her side?
    Answers will vary.

Ban Cell Phones and Pagers in Classrooms

Don Mack

Don Mack is a computer lab facilitator and chair of the learning media services department at Laramie High School in Wyoming. He has taught for 23 years. He edits the Albany County Education Association newsletter and is Wyoming's representative to the NEA Resolutions Committee.

1   Increasingly, authorities have outlawed the use of cell phones by motorists because of the risk of accidents. In a school classroom, we don't typically have students driving automobiles, but we conduct a wide variety of activities that require every bit as much attention from the student as traffic would from a motorist.

2   Schools are islands of learning where a teacher and a group of students are provided the opportunity to interact, interrupted only by the passing bell.

3   Educational professionals have campaigned long and hard to eliminate the incessant intercom and paper barrage that accosts the classroom. In many places, we have been successful, and interruptions from secretaries, counselors, and administrators have been cut to a bare minimum.

4   The incursion of cell phones and beepers could deal a severe setback to any progress that's been made to bar interruptions.

5   Early this year, a colleague's presentation was disrupted when a student's cell phone, carried into the classroom in a backpack, began ringing. Initially, both the teacher and students attempted to ignore the distraction and continued working. But after several rings, the owner of the cell phone apologized and answered the call.

6   The call was of a social nature and the student hung up as quickly as possible. But the flow of instruction was disrupted, and valuable learning time was lost. This isn't an isolated occurrence.

7   Setting the phone to vibrate instead of ring is not enough. Whether the phone beeps, squawks, belts out an N'Sync tune, or simply vibrates, the pesky little device will continue to demand attention. Very few adults will let a call go unanswered. And my observations of my own children and students indicate than an unanswered phone call drives them up a wall.

8   If the phone is answered, all learning comes to a screeching halt while a classroom full of ears listens to one side of a conversa-

tion and imagines the dialogue that must be coming from the invisible intruder.

9   By their very nature, these gadgets insist on being the controlling attraction in the classroom. For some students, the distraction comes because they don't have a cell phone or pager and wish they did. These items are also attractive to the thieves who may inhabit our hallways and prey on the unsuspecting.

10   School curriculums are created to provide the best possible education for the students. When a phone call interrupts the classroom regimen, it destroys the planning and instruction that have been carefully crafted by the educator, be it lecture, group work, test taking, or silent seat work.

11   Policies and procedures have been adopted and office personnel have been well trained in the answering of school phones and the delivery of messages. There's little in the way of emergency or critical information that can't get from a school secretary to a student in a matter of seconds, should the need arise. In our school, there is a pay phone for students who must place a call.

12   Cell phones and pagers have no place among the possessions that a student brings to school.

Exercise 4   **DISCUSSION AND CRITICAL THINKING**

Purpose

1. Which sentence most clearly states Mack's thesis?
    The last one: "Cell phones and pagers have no place among the possessions that a student brings to school."

2. Does he allow any exceptions or make any concessions?
    No.

Support

3. What are Mack's main points of support?
    (1) Cell phones and pagers interrupt learning. (2) Allowing cell phones and pagers would set back policies to bar other interruptions. (3) Cell phones and pagers are unnecessary because there are other ways to deliver messages effectively.

Organization and Special Techniques

4. Mack begins with a comparison to stress the importance of his position. Is the comparison of driving an automobile and sitting in a classroom valid?
    Certainly the consequences of a distraction in each of these settings are very different. Perhaps a comparison set in a classroom and a concert hall would have worked better.

5. Does the example in paragraph 5 work well? Explain.
    It illustrates Mack's main point and leads into further discussion of the point.

6. In paragraph 11, Mack offers a refutation to those who say that students and parents need to be able to communicate effectively. In his refutation, Mack argues that such communication occurs now without use of cell phones or pagers. Is his reasoning persuasive?
Answers will vary.

Personal Reaction

7. Relying on your experience and reasoning, evaluate Mack's argument.
Answers will vary.

| **Exercise 5** | **SUGGESTIONS FOR READING-RELATED WRITING** |

Complete one of the following reading-related responses.

1. Write a summary of one of the essays.
2. Write a reaction response to one of the essays. Be sure to incorporate your own views and discuss your experiences with cell phones and pagers.
3. Write a two-part response composed of labeled summary and reaction parts.
4. Write a synthesis on one of the following points. Refer to both sources to some extent and include citations.
   a. the use of cell phones in restaurants and movie theaters or the use of cell phones by automobile drivers (not based mainly on the two essays but sharing some points of concern)
   b. your own view on whether to allow cell phones and pagers in classrooms, perhaps including some examples from your experience

Journal Writing

Your journal entries are likely to be concerned primarily with the relationship between the reading material and you—your life experiences, your views, your imagination. The reading material will give you something of substance to write about, but you will be writing especially for yourself, developing confidence and ease in writing, so that writing becomes a comfortable part of your everyday activities, as speaking already is.

These journal entries will be part of your intellectual diary, recording what you are thinking about a certain issue. They will be of use in helping you understand the reading material, in helping you develop your writing skills, in uncovering ideas that can be used on other assignments, and in helping you think more clearly and imaginatively. Because

these entries are of a more spontaneous nature than the more structured writing assignments, organization and editing are likely to be of
less concern.

Each journal entry should be clearly dated and, if reading related,
should specify the title and author of the original piece.

Even if your instructor wants you to concentrate on what you read
for your journal writing, he or she might not want you to be restricted to
the material in this text. Fortunately, you are surrounded by reading
material in newspapers, magazines, and, of course, textbooks from
other courses. These topics can serve you well, especially if you want to
begin your journal writing now.

Career-Related Writing

This textbook includes career-related writing topics at the end of Chapters 5 through 14. They are a special feature designed to offer options to
students who would like to write about jobs they currently hold, major
areas of study, and intended careers. Because students are often studying materials in other classes and have access to other published
sources, career-related writing may include ideas from reading material.
Those ideas can be documented with a listing of the source, which usually includes the name of the author, title of the work, place of publication, publisher, date, and page numbers. The citations for quotations or
specific references can be made in the same fashion as the ones for textbook sources.

Writer's Guidelines: Reading-Related Writing

1. Underlining helps you to read with discrimination.
   - Underline the main ideas in paragraphs.
   - Underline the support for those ideas.
   - Underline answers to questions you bring to the reading assign-
     ment.
   - Underline only the key words.
2. Annotating enables you to actively engage the reading material.
   - Number parts if appropriate.
   - Make comments according to your interests and needs.
3. Outlining the passages you read sheds light on the relationship of
   ideas, including the major divisions of the passage and their relative
   importance.

4. Summarizing helps you concentrate on main ideas.
   - Cite the author and title of the text.
   - Keep the length shorter than the original by about two-thirds (although the exact reduction will vary depending on the content of the original).
   - Include the main ideas. (Include details only infrequently.)
   - Change the original wording without changing the idea.
   - Do not evaluate the content or give an opinion in any way (even if you see an error in logic or fact).
   - Do not add ideas (even if you have an abundance of related information).
   - Do not include any personal comments (Do not use *I*, referring to self.).
   - Use quotations sparingly. (If you do quote directly from the source, enclose the quoted material in quotation marks.)
   - Use author tags ("says York," "according to York," or "the author explains") to remind the reader(s) that you are summarizing the material of another author.

5. Three other types of reading-related writing are
   - the *reaction*—a discussion of how the reading relates to you, your experiences, and your attitudes; also, often your critique of the worth and logic of the piece.
   - the *two-part response*—a summary and a reaction, usually presented in separate paragraphs.
   - the *synthesis*—a blending of ideas from two or more sources.

6. Most ideas in reading-related papers are developed using one or more of these ways: explanation, direct references, and quotations.

7. Documenting is giving credit to borrowed ideas and words.

Narration: Moving Through Time

THE QUIGMANS   by Buddy Hickerson

At home with the police.

© Tribune Media Services, Inc. All Rights Reserved. Reprinted with permission.

Writing Narratives

*I*n our everyday lives, we tell stories and invite other people to do so by asking questions such as "What happened at work today?" and "What did you do last weekend?" We are disappointed when the answer is "Nothing much." We may be equally disappointed when a person doesn't give us enough details or gives us too many and spoils the effect. After all, we are interested in people's stories and in the people who tell them. We like narratives.

A *narrative* is an account of an incident or a series of incidents that make up a complete and significant action. A narrative can be as short as a joke, as long as a novel, or anything between, including a single paragraph. Each narrative has a pattern that consists of five properties: situation, conflict, struggle, outcome, and meaning.

Pattern

Situation

Situation is the background for the action. The situation may be described only briefly, or it may even be implied. ("To celebrate my seventeenth birthday, I went to the Department of Motor Vehicles to take my practical test for my driver's license.")

Conflict

Conflict is friction, such as a problem in the surroundings, with another person, or within the individual. The conflict, which is at the heart of each narrative, produces struggle. ("It was raining and my appointment was the last one of the day. The examiner was a serious, weary-looking man who reminded me of a bad boss I once had, and I was nervous.")

Struggle

Struggle, which need not be physical, is the manner of dealing with conflict. The struggle adds action or engagement and generates the plot. ("After grinding on the ignition because the engine was already on, I had trouble finding the windshield wiper control. Next I forgot to signal until after I had pulled away from the curb. As we crept slowly down the rain-glazed street, the examiner told me to take the emergency brake off. All the while I listened to his pen scratching on his clipboard. 'Pull over and park,' he said solemnly.")

Outcome

Outcome Is the result of the struggle. ("After I parked the car, the examiner told me to relax, and then he talked to me about school. When we continued, somehow I didn't make any errors, and I got my license.")

Meaning

Meaning is the significance of the story, which may be deeply philosophical or simple, stated or implied. ("Calmness promotes calmness.")

Purpose and Form

Narratives primarily inform or persuade, although they may also entertain. They make up many of the examples we use in explaining ideas, and they engage a reader's feelings and intellect as we persuade readers to accept our views. Narratives can be used in brief paragraph statements and throughout the essay: the introduction, the support paragraphs, and the conclusion.

Narratives come in different lengths and forms. Parts of short stories, novels, essays, ballads, and plays are narrative. Anecdotes and jokes are often purely narrative.

When Mark Twain was reminded of his reputation for always bothering people with his questions and observations—in short, for being a gadfly or a pest—he had this to say:

> I was always told that I was a sickly and precarious and tiresome and uncertain child, and lived mainly on allopathic medicines during the first seven years of my life. I asked my mother about this, in her old age—she was in her eighty-eighth year—and said:
> "I suppose that during all that time you were uneasy about me?"
> "Yes, the whole time."
> "Afraid I wouldn't live?"
> After a reflective pause—ostensibly to think out the facts—
> "No—afraid you would."

Thus instead of saying, "People have always regarded me as a pain in the posterior," Mark Twain told a story. His brief story is one kind of narrative, called an *anecdote*. Usually based on truth, and often experience, anecdotes frequently illustrate points and set a tone in speeches and writings.

Our conversations are filled with narratives, too. Speakers use story-based jokes to relax and engage the audience. Comedians make up stories purely for the sake of entertainment, making no significant point:

> Ugly! I was such an ugly kid my parents once took me on a vacation because they didn't want to kiss me goodbye.

> Ugly! When people called me that, I went to the dictionary to see what it meant, and I saw my picture.

But even these jokes—in, let's say, an essay about the idea "self-consciousness during youth"—could be used effectively to inform by entertaining.

Everywhere people inform, persuade, and entertain with the narrative.

Narrative Technique

Order

Narratives almost always move in chronological order. The progressive action, of course, carries that idea, but transitional words that suggest time change—such as *then, later, soon, finally, last,* and *now*—are also useful. Furthermore, you can specify time change directly by using such phrases as "the next day," "after ten minutes had passed," and "when the smoke had cleared."

Because description is so frequently an ally of narration, you may combine references to space as a technique for giving order to your writing. Space references include the specific noting of movement from place to place by using words such as *here, there,* and *beyond.*

Verb Tense

Because most narratives relate experience in time order, the verb tense is likely to be the past ("She *walked* into the room") rather than the present ("She *walks* into the room"), although you may use either. An unnecessary change in tense tends to distract or confuse readers.

Two generalizations may be useful as you work with verb tense.

- Most narratives (often summaries) based on literature are written in the *present tense.*

  Tom Sawyer *pretends* that painting the fence *is* a special pleasure. His friends *watch* him eagerly. He *talks* and *displays* his joy. They *pay* him to do his work.

- Most historical events and personal experiences are written in the *past tense.*

  The Battle of Gettysburg *was* the decisive encounter in the Civil War. Although General Lee, the Confederate general in charge of the overall strategy, *was* a wise and experienced man, he *made* some tactical blunders that *led* to a devastating victory by the Union forces.

  We *walked* down the path to the well-house, attracted by the fragrance of the honeysuckle with which it *was covered.* Someone *was drawing* water and my teacher *placed* my hand under the spout. As the cool stream *gushed* over one hand she *spelled* into the other the word *water,* first slowly, then rapidly.

Helen Keller, *The Story of My Life*

Although Helen Keller chose the conventional past tense for verbs in this passage, she might have chosen the present tense for a sense of immediacy.

The two main points about tense are the following:

- The generalizations about verb tense selection are useful: Use past for the historical and the personal, and use present for fiction.

- The verb tense in a passage should change only when the shift is needed for clarity or emphasis.

Point of View

Point of view shows the writer's relationship to the material, the subject, and it usually does not change within a passage.

If you are conveying personal experience, the point of view will be *first person,* which can be either involved (as a participant) or detached (as an observer). The involved perspective uses *I* more prominently than the detached does.

If you are presenting something from a distance—geographical or historical (for example, telling a story about George Washington)—the point of view will usually be *third person,* and the participants will be referred to as "he," "she," and "they."

Description

A good descriptive writer presents material so that the perceptive reader can read and re-experience the writer's ideas. One device important to that writer is imagery. Images can be perceived through the senses (sight, hearing, taste, smell, and touch). A good descriptive writer also gives specific details and presents concrete particulars (actual things) in a convincing way. We read, we visualize, we identify, and—*zap*—we connect with a narrative account.

In the following passage, the images are italicized to emphasize how the author has made us hear, smell, touch, and see. Also note the other specific details.

> Before she had quite arisen, she *called* our names and *issued* orders, and *pushed* her large feet into homemade slippers and *across* the *bare lye-washed wooden floor* to *light* the coal-oil lamp.
>
> The *lamplight* in the Store gave a *soft* make-believe feeling to our world which made me want to *whisper* and walk about on tiptoe. The *odors* of onions and oranges and kerosene had been *mixing* all night and wouldn't be disturbed until the wooded slat was removed from the door and the early morning air *forced* its way in with the bodies of people who had walked miles to reach the pickup place.

Maya Angelou, "Soft Mornings and Harsh Afternoons"

Note the use of specific information in the next paragraph.

> On one recent Saturday afternoon a Latino fifth-grader, wearing the same type of hightop tennis shoes I wore as a ten-year-old on that same street corner, strode up to Señor Farrillas' snow-cone pushcart. The kid pulled out a pocketful of dimes and bought two *raspadas*. One for himself, and one for his school chum—a Vietnamese kid. He was wearing hightops, too. They both ordered strawberry, as I recall.

Luis Torres, "Los Chinos Discover el Barrio"

Torres presents the material so you can visualize it. Try to picture this, instead: "The other day I saw a youngster buy a refreshment for himself and his friend." Of course, that is what happened, but very little narrative/descriptive communication takes place in this abbreviated version. In Torres's account, you know when and where the action took place. You know what the kids were wearing, and you know that the author (point of view as technique) identifies with the kids. They buy strawberry *raspadas* from Señor Farrillas. The Latino kid pays for the *raspadas* with "a pocketful of dimes." Did you ever, as a kid, put your hand in the pocket of some tight jeans and try to pull out those dimes with a balled fist? We identify, and the imagery registers. We may not have visited that street corner in reality, but vicariously we take a trip with Torres.

Dialogue

Dialogue is used purposefully in narration to characterize, particularize, and support ideas. It shows us how people talk and think, as individuals or as representatives of society. Not every narrative requires dialogue.

Note in the following paragraph that the snatches of dialogue are brief. The language will ring true to Asian immigrants and those who have been around Asian immigrants. It is starkly realistic yet sympathetically engaging in context so that we are convinced of its authenticity and drawn into the story. As narrator, the author was present when the utterances in this paragraph were made.

> My brother was even more fanatical than I about speaking English. He was especially hard on my mother, criticizing her, often cruelly, for her pidgin speech—smatterings of Chinese scattered like chop suey in her conversation. "It's not 'What it is,' Mom," he'd say in exasperation. "It's 'What *is* it, what *is* it!'" Sometimes Mom might leave out an occasional "the" or "a," or perhaps a verb of being. He would stop her in midsentence: "Say it again, Mom. Say it right." When he tripped over his own tongue, he'd blame it on her: "See, Mom, it's all your fault. You set a bad example."

Elizabeth Wong, "The Struggle to Be an All-American Girl"

Before turning to your own writing of narratives, let's look at a range of them, some composed by professional writers and some by students. These examples will show you different forms and different techniques, and they will furnish you with subject material for your own writing in essays and journals.

Connecting Sources and Writing

Student Essay

This is the topic Sandra Pei selected from a list:

> Write a narrative about two people who overcame difficulties and found genuine love.

Sandra Pei was born in Singapore and, although she now lives contentedly in America, she fondly remembers her relatives "back home." There, in the traditional Chinese culture, the family had tremendous influence in all matters, even marriage. The prospects for a loveless marriage existed, but somehow, beautifully, "love happened," even following a great disappointment.

The Switched Bride

Sandra Pei

Love in our dreams may be something that takes place in a moment, at first sight. We meet the gaze of someone across a crowded room and that's it—for life. For most people falling in love for life is much less spectacular. It may even follow disappoint-
Thesis   ments. <u>My Uncle George and Aunt Hua</u> had that <u>experience,</u> <u>and they are the leading characters in my favorite love story of</u> <u>all time</u>.

Uncle George lived in Singapore when he fell deeply in love. At
Situation   least he thought so. As a member of a traditional Chinese family, <u>he</u> <u>worked hard</u> and <u>established himself</u> in business before he would <u>permit himself</u> to <u>think about marriage</u>. When he was thirty, <u>he</u> was <u>finally secure</u>, and ready; so he started looking around and <u>discov-</u><u>ered</u> that just next door was <u>a beautiful young single woman</u>. They exchanged glances, and <u>being sure</u> that <u>he was in love</u>, <u>he asked his</u> <u>parents</u> to <u>talk to her parents</u> <u>about</u> a <u>wedding</u>.

In about two months, the arrangements had been made and Uncle George was content. He would have his beautiful bride, and life would be perfect. He worked with his family and made all the plans for a new house. He never talked directly to the girl, but he continued to look at her as she worked about her house, often accompanied by her older, plain sister.

On the day of the wedding, Uncle George was very happy, and when the music played, he entered the temple to accept his bride.
Conflict   As he joined her at the altar, he shyly turned to look at her lovely face. But to his consternation, he saw instead the plain sister. <u>Someone had switched brides</u>, and he was furious in his protest.

Struggle   The <u>families quickly called</u> a <u>conference</u> to solve the problem, and tea was served amid much talking and even yelling. The other family had switched brides with the permission of Uncle George's family. <u>They all wanted the older daughter to get married first</u>. They argued and argued and argued with Uncle George. The prospective <u>bride</u> was <u>tearful and embarrassed</u>. <u>Uncle George gave in</u> and married the plain daughter, *Hua*.

Outcome

Meaning

The word *Hua* means flower in Chinese, and that's what she was, a flower that as Uncle George's wife, blossomed and, to him, became very beautiful. <u>They have had</u> a <u>loving marriage</u> for <u>more than thirty years</u> now. To Uncle George love was not something that he saw; <u>it</u> was <u>something that happened—with a little help</u>.

| Exercise 1 | **DISCUSSION AND CRITICAL THINKING** |

Underline and then annotate Sandra Pei's essay "The Switched Bride" to show these parts: thesis, situation, conflict, struggle, outcome, and meaning.

Practicing Patterns of Narration

| Exercise 2 | **COMPLETING PATTERNS OF NARRATION** |

Fill in the blanks to complete the following outline of the narrative "The Switched Bride" by Sandra Pei.

I. Situation
- A. Uncle George is not married.
- B. Uncle George <u>falls in love</u>   .

II. Conflict
- A. A marriage is arranged.
- B. The bride <u>is switched</u>   .
- C. Uncle George discovers <u>the deception</u>   .

III. Struggle
- A. Uncle George is unhappy.
- B. Hua, the prospective bride, is <u>embarrassed</u>   .
- C. Both families argue <u>with Uncle George</u>   .

IV. Outcome
- A. Uncle George agrees to marry Hua.
- B. They <u>get married</u>   .
- C. They <u>become happy together</u>   .

V. Meaning
- A. Love may not be planned.
- B. Sometimes <u>love just happens</u>   .
- C. That love is <u>just as sweet as any other love</u>   .

Student Documented Essay

Regina Ochoa read several narrative essays in anticipation of her assignment to write a single-source essay. "The Suspected Shopper" by Ellen Goodman immediately attracted her interest. Goodman had written about a shopping experience in this age of suspicion, in which all customers are treated as if they are dishonest.

Ochoa easily remembered her own experience, one that was even more poignant than Goodman's. She had been falsely charged with shoplifting. Being detained for something one has not done, in a public place and in the presence of a parent and an older sibling, was not something she would ever forget.

Busted for No Good Reason

Regina Ochoa

Reading Ellen Goodman's "The Suspected Shopper" reminded me of the time when I was a suspected shopper. Goodman documented the way she was treated: accosted by threatening signs about shoplifting, made to check her bag, monitored while trying on clothes, keyed through at the jewelry store, and carded at the sales counter. The result was familiar, as she took "home six ounces of silk and a load of resentment." My experience was far more humiliating. I was not just suspected; I was wrongly accused.

Thesis

It was another one of those days when I was dragged out shopping with my mom and oldest sister. After we had a satisfying lunch at the food park, Mom decided to make a last stop at a nearby department store.

Situation

I decided to amuse myself by browsing around alone. I kept my eye out looking for my mom and sister, hoping they would come looking for me to tell me it was time to leave. As I turned fixtures of colorful earrings around and around, I played with the spare change in my pocket, hearing the chiming, clinking sound.

After a few minutes, which seemed like hours, had passed, I decided to go find my mom and sister. "There you are, Regina," my mom said impatiently as I came upon them. "Are you ready to go?"

She didn't even wait for my answer, but I thought to myself, "Of course, I am."

Conflict

As we were leaving the store, two men came running out after us. "Excuse me, miss," one said directly to me, "but we'd like you to come back inside for a moment." Bewildered and very confused, we all walked back into the store while the men cautiously followed behind us. It was as if they expected me to run away and hide out in the mall.

"What's wrong?" my mom asked them. "What did she do?"

"You'll see," they answered simultaneously, as if one answering wasn't emphatic enough.

Inside the elevator, one man pushed the button, taking us all the way down to the basement level. Suddenly it hit me, and I knew I was being wrongfully accused of something I did not do.

I turned to my mom and desperately said, "I swear I didn't take anything."

"I hope so, Regina, because if you did, this will be pretty embarrassing," she said, offering a bit less comfort than I wanted.

The elevator seemed to be taking forever. It was as if the walls were caving in, and the men just stared right through me as if I were a mug shot.

Finally the elevator door opened, and they took me to a small room where I watched myself on television.

There I was on the screen, browsing through earring fixtures, and my hand appeared to be stuffing something in my pocket. One couldn't quite tell because of the way the camera was positioned.

"There's nothing in my pocket but loose change," I screamed out angrily. I was already in tears. Embarrassment was all over my face. My sister reached over to help me empty my pocket, and sure enough, there was nothing but about a dozen coins.

"I was just putting my hand into my pocket to play with the change," I said to the men. This time I was the accuser.

"You owe my daughter an apology," my mom said to the man who seemed to be in charge.

"Sorry," he said. He barely whispered it. I knew he felt foolish, but at that moment I couldn't feel much pity for him.

As we all left the store in silence, I vowed to myself never to accuse anyone of anything without being absolutely certain—no, without being doubly absolutely certain.

Work Cited

Goodman, Ellen, "The Suspected Shopper." *Keeping in Touch.* Ed. Ellen Goodman. New York: Simon & Schuster, 1985, 133–134.

Exercise 3   DISCUSSION AND CRITICAL THINKING

Purpose

1. What is Ochoa's main idea?

   Being wrongly accused of shoplifting is a humiliating experience.

Support and Organization

2. Underline and annotate the essay to indicate these parts: thesis, situation, conflict, struggle, outcome, and meaning.

Special Techniques

3. Explain how each of these aspects is used:

   Verb tense: past tense

   Point of view: first person

   Dialogue: extensively among Ochoa, family, and security personnel

Personal Reaction and Interpretation

4. What conditions (her frame of mind, her clothing, her possessions) made Ochoa behave in a way that would seem suspicious to the store detectives?

   She is impatient and bored. She is watching for her mother and her sister. She is fidgeting, playing with coins in her pocket as she fingers jewelry.

5. After she was detained, what factors made the following sequence of events more dramatic?

   The detectives don't give particulars at first. They walk behind her as if she is a flight risk. They take her down in an elevator to the basement.

6. Should Ochoa's mother have required more than an apology?

   Answers will vary.

7. What does Ochoa imply about the differences between fact and opinion?

   Ochoa admits that it looks as if she is pocketing something, but then one can't really be sure. Her movements are facts; the interpretation by the detectives is opinion.

If Those Cobras Don't Get You, the Alligators Will

Richard Wolkomir

Writing in the *Smithsonian*, journalist Richard Wolkomir examines the wacky world of urban legends, where these tall but told-as-true tales speak to, and sometimes spoof, our deepest fears and cherished phobias. His main source of information is Jan Harold Brunvand—"Mr. Urban Legend"—the foremost collector of these strange stories. This essay is not one narrative; it is a collection of narratives in abbreviated forms, an essay that tells how urban legends are created.

Example

1   A woman's at the mall here last week, in that big discount store. She's looking at these rolled-up carpets from Asia. She sticks her hand into one to feel the thickness, and something pricks her finger. Then her hand swells up. Whole arm turns black. She falls on the floor dead.

2   So they unroll the carpet. Inside's a cobra, and about ten baby cobras.

3   A friend of mine told me. His cousin knows one of the sales-clerks.

4   Hey, it's a jungle out there.

5   Just ask Jan Harold Brunvand—"Mr. Urban Legend." A University of Utah folklorist, Brunvand collects modern told-as-true tall tales like the cobra-in-the-carpet story. More come in every day from his informants around the world. They are weird whoppers we tell one another, believing them to be factual. Haunted airliners. A hundred-miles-per-gallon car the oil companies keep secret. How about that guy who stole a frozen chicken at the supermarket and hid it under his hat, then fainted in the check-out line because his brain froze? And did you hear about the guy who's eating fast-food fried chicken when he sees this scaly rat's tail sticking out of the batter?

Authoritative statement

Definition

6   The Pied Piper is still piping. But in our fiber-optic age he pipes an MTV tune. "These stories are like traditional legends—they reflect our concerns," says Brunvand. "But now we live in cities and drive cars."

7   In fact, many of the 500 or so modern legends that Brunvand has collected do involve cars. In previous eras, legends were often about specters, since ghosts bred like bunnies in the dark corners of candle-lit houses. Spooks still pop up, but now they ride in

V-6's. That may be because cars offer a certain liberation. But freedom is scary. Out on that open highway, anything might happen.

8   Brunvand titled the first of his five urban legends books *The Vanishing Hitchhiker* (1981), after what he calls the classic automobile legend. Here's how it goes:

Situation

> *Well, this happened to one of my girlfriend's best friends and her father. They were driving along a country road on their way home from the cottage when they saw a young girl hitchhiking. They stopped and picked her up and she got in the back seat. She told the girl and her father that she just lived in the house about five miles up the road. She didn't say anything after that but just turned to watch out the window. When the father saw the house,*

Conflict

Struggle

> *he drove up to it and turned to tell the girl they had arrived—but she wasn't there! Both he and his daughter were really mystified and decided to knock on the door and tell the people what had happened. They told them that they had once had a daughter who answered the description of the girl they supposedly had picked*

Outcome
Meaning

> *up, but she had disappeared some years ago and had last been seen hitchhiking on this very road. Today would have been her birthday.*

9   That version, says Brunvand, came from a Toronto teenager in 1973. But the story had begun going around North America at the turn of the century. The automobile motif had taken over by the 1930s. Usually the teller cites specific local streets where the driver picks up the spectral hitchhiker. Sometimes the ghost leaves a book or scarf in the car, which the bereaved parents then identify as belonging to their lost daughter. Sometimes the driver spies the hitchhiker's photograph on the family piano, wearing the same party dress in which she died, and which she wore when he picked her up.

10   Brunvand says "The Vanishing Hitchhiker" tale evolved from earlier European stories, usually about travelers on horseback. In Hawaii, the hitchhiker became associated with the ancient volcano goddess Pele. Brunvand even cites a prototype of the story in the New Testament (Acts 8:26–39) in which an Ethiopian driving a chariot picks up the Apostle Philip, who baptizes him and then disappears.

11   In his newest book, *The Baby Train* (1993), Brunvand discusses "The Slasher Under the Car": attackers hide beneath women's cars parked at shopping malls and slash their ankles when the women return to the parking lot. Brunvand says he's been hearing these stories for years but has never found any evidence that the attacks really happened. Such tales, he says, do not report actual

events. But they are "carrying the folk news." We are issuing ourselves warnings: it's a dangerous world—watch your ankles!

12   Urban legends are kissing cousins of myths, fairy tales and rumors. Legends differ from rumors because the legends are stories, with a plot. And unlike myths and fairy tales, they are supposed to be current and true, events rooted in everyday reality that at least could happen. Like that woman given a microwave oven by her children. After bathing her poodle, she got the idea of drying it in the microwave—the poor poodle exploded! Other versions feature cats, parakeets and "one unfortunate turtle," says Brunvand. Before microwave ovens appeared, the ill-fated pets met their doom in gas ovens or clothes dryers. Apparently our appliances make us uneasy, perhaps because technology mystifies us, a sort of scientific magic.

13   Actually the entire modern world—as revealed in urban legends—is hexed. Libraries sink into the ground, and elephants mistake red Volkswagen Beetles for the stools in their circus acts and sit on them. A woman poaches her insides at a tanning parlor. And evil lurks in the night, as everyone knows who ever got the willies hearing that lover's lane classic of the repressed 1950s, "The Hook": a teenage couple is parked on a back road, when over the radio comes an announcement that a crazed killer with a hook for a hand has escaped from the insane asylum. The girl begs the boy to take her home. He gets mad, stamps on the gas and they roar away. When they get to her house, he gets out of the car and goes around to open her door. Hanging from its handle is a bloody hook.

14   People like to get scared, which is why Stephen King never misses a car payment. Teenagers in particular enjoy scary urban legends, says Brunvand, especially about kids like themselves. "As adolescents move out into the larger world, the world's dangers may close in on them," he says. The legends, he adds, deliver a warning: "Watch out! This could happen to you!"

15   Adults, too, use legends to remind themselves of dangers, such as Demon Rum. Did you hear about the drunk weaving his way home along the Interstate just south of here after an office party? A trooper pulls him over, but just then there's a fender-bender in the opposite lane. The trooper tells the driver to stay put while he attends to the accident. The driver gets out, wanders around and says to heck with it. He drives home. He tells his wife, "If the police call, say I was home all night, sober as a judge." The next morning the doorbell rings and it's two troopers, including the one who pulled him over the night before. The man claims he was home all

night. "Just ask my wife," he says. His wife backs him up. The troopers ask to look in his garage. Puzzled, the man says "Sure." They open the garage door and there's the police car, lights still flashing.

16   Such are the stories bulging the files in Jan Harold Brunvand's office in his Salt Lake City home. Every day he receives letters and telephone calls reporting the "folk news" of hospital patients who receive amputations by mistake, and Dobermans choking on what proves to be the fingers of burglars—who turn out to be cowering and bleeding in the bedroom closet.

17   Brunvand, who wears a gray mustache and hornrimmed glasses, was born in Cadillac, Michigan, in 1933. Both his parents immigrated to the United States from the small Norwegian town of Kristiansand. Brunvand earned a B.A. in journalism and an M.A. in English at Michigan State. Then, with a Fulbright scholarship, he studied folklore in Norway. "Mainly, I just wanted to spend more time in Norway," he says. But when he began work on a doctorate in English at Indiana University, Richard M. Dorson, who is a leading folklore professor, persuaded him that folklore was the hot new field.

18   He began teaching at the University of Idaho in 1961. He served in the U.S. Army, taught at Southern Illinois University, then moved to the University of Utah, in Salt Lake City. By now he had studied folklore of the American West, decoration of Romanian houses, and folklore in literature—his dissertation was on Shakespeare's *The Taming of the Shrew,* which is based on an old folktale. But he was mulling the idea of urban legends.

19   As a student he had assisted a leading folklorist with a textbook that had a chapter entitled "Urban Belief Tales." One was "The Dead Cat in the Package," about a trauma common to apartment dwellers: What do you do with a dead pet? That was in 1958. In 1959 Brunvand was stunned to see that same old tale reported on page one of a Bloomington, Indiana, newspaper as news.

> *Chamber of Commerce Manager Jules Hendricks tells about a neighbor of his in Indianapolis who found a novel way of disposing of the remains of a dead cat. Knowing the city ordinance prohibited burying the body, the woman called a friend of hers who lived in the country and asked if she could bury the body for her. The friend agreed, and they planned to meet for the exchange at a downtown department store tea room. Carrying the cat in a brown paper bag, the woman stopped to do some shopping en route to her rendezvous—and carelessly laid the bag on a counter. When she returned, the bag was gone. A clerk sympathized, explaining that the store had been having trouble with shoplifters*

lately. Her problem solved (if not in the way she had planned), the woman started home. Just outside the store, she found a crowd of people had gathered. Squeezing among them to find out what the attraction was, she saw the unconscious body of a 200-pound woman, clutching to her breast a brown paper bag from which protruded the head of the dead cat.

20   "It was living folklore," says Brunvand. "When I started teaching at the University of Idaho, I discovered that students think folklore is always about somewhere else and another time—about getting to know your grandmother—and I wanted to show that it's also about getting to know yourself."

21   He began to teach about contemporary legends and collect them. He wrote *The Vanishing Hitchhiker,* which was used as a text in his course, then marketed successfully as a book for general readers. Brunvand found himself appearing on television and radio, including five appearances on "Late Night with David Letterman," where he told a story about the popular talk-show host himself. The tale was inspired by the fact that after the show's opening monologue, the camera shifts to bandleader Paul Shaffer while Letterman takes his seat. Supposedly, Letterman's contract stipulates that Dave will never show his posterior on TV. After Brunvand related the tale, Letterman stood up, turned his back to the camera and raised his coattails, proving that this story, at least, is rooted in apocrypha.

22   Sometimes, however, these tall tales have hints of real roots. For instance, we've all heard about the alligators in the New York City sewers. Vacationers returning from Florida supposedly flush away their unwanted reptile pets, and the alligators feed on rats in the darkness under the streets. They grow into huge, blind albinos. Marijuana flourishes down there, too. "New York white" grows from seeds hastily flushed away during drug raids. But nobody dares harvest these potent plants because of the alligators.

23   Folklorists studying the alligator legend have unearthed a February 10, 1935, *New York Times* story reporting that city workers found an eight-foot alligator in a sewer. Teddy May, who was New York sewer commissioner during the 1930s, told Robert Daley, author of the 1959 book *The World Beneath the City,* that he had found alligators in the sewers but had exterminated them by 1937. However, a sewer official told Brunvand that Teddy May was "almost as much of a legend as the alligators," a spinner of colorful yarns.

24   One story, at least, Brunvand has pinned down. Ever since the hit movie *Three Men and a Baby* came out in video in 1990, view-

Quotation

ers have insisted that a ghostly boy appears in one scene, standing stiffly behind some sheer curtains. The scene is said to have been filmed in a New York apartment leased from a couple who had moved out after their son committed suicide there. But the movie was filmed on a Toronto sound stage, not in a Manhattan apartment, says Brunvand. And the "ghost" is merely a cardboard cutout of actor Ted Danson, whose character in the film, also an actor, decorated his apartment with his own advertising placard.

25 So who started the "ghost-on-the-videotape" story? Probably nobody in particular, Brunvand says. Real urban legends, he believes, are a group effort. "Most of them are communal. When a community circulates a piece of folklore, everyone participates in the creation, each performer adding something in his or her own style."

26 Legends are continually recycled. The *Three Men and a Baby* story, for example, is a version of much older stories about photographs of ghosts. Typically, says Brunvand, a house is photographed, and a strange face shows up in a window—the face of somebody murdered in the house. Or an extra person appears in a picture of lumberjacks or miners, somebody killed in an on-the-job accident.

27 Legends can be destructive. Once Brunvand served as consultant to a pizza chain that was besieged by false stories about disgruntled employees who were contaminating the food. He says such false tales of contamination are rife. Maybe we fear that beneath technological society's seeming order seethes chaos.

28 Teenagers still tell the story of the girl who teased her hair into a "beehive," a now passé style. Not wanting to mess it up, she just sprayed her hair and did not wash it. Black widow spiders nested in the beehive and bit her to death. The moral: wash your hair or you'll die.

29 "We have banished nature, but it still lurks, apparently hopping mad. That is why, in our urban legends, supermarket shoppers who reach for bananas get bitten by tarantulas. Biting ants proliferate under plaster casts. Someone brings home a potted cactus and watches, horrified, as it quivers, then splits open to spew out venomous spiders. A woman brings home a cuddly Chihuahua she found abandoned at Manhattan's South Street Seaport, only to learn months later from a veterinarian that her beloved pet actually is a sewer rat. And then there are those imported comforters that wriggle off the bed—they are stuffed with living maggots! Earwigs get in sleepers' ears and eat into their brains. The secret of successful diet pills turns out to be that

they contain tapeworms. Burger emporiums use ground-up worms. And sometimes a pickle in a pickle jar actually is a finger!

30   Brunvand's books have made urban legends—or "contemporary legends"—a growing research field for folklorists. Members of the International Society for Contemporary Legend Research bore into the stories from all sorts of angles. Their writings carry such titles as "'The Disappearing Hitchhiker': "Narrative Acculturation among the Ramah Navajo"; "'The Fast Food Ghost': A Study in the Supernatural's Capacity to Survive Secularization"; "'The Superglue Revenge': A Psychological Analysis"; "'The Devil in the Discotheque': A Semiotic Analysis of a Contemporary Legend."

31   Professor Bill Ellis of Pennsylvania State University at Hazleton edits the legend society's newsletter, *FOAFtale News.* "FOAF" stands for "friend of a friend," the usually cited source for a legend. Ellis says the stories often are true in the sense that they express real stresses in a community. Last year he turned his attention to a legend that had upset several college campuses. Supposedly, the 16th-century seer Nostradamus had prophesied that in 1991 a massacre would occur at an unspecified university on Halloween. At each university where the legend flared up, it contained details—such as a peculiar building—that clearly identified the doomed school as the very one.

32   Ellis was struck that the legend sprang up only on certain campuses. He discovered that these were schools that had previously had an episode of real violence against students, such as a mugging or rape. He theorizes that such legends serve to crystallize anxieties in the air. Before Halloween, vigilance soared on some of the affected campuses. Students telephoned campus police whenever a stray cat rustled the grass or a door slammed. But after Halloween, vigilance plummeted. Ellis says it shows how an urban legend expresses a population's anxieties, and then clears the mental air like a midsummer thunderstorm.

33   Then there were the cattle-mutilation stories that surfaced out West in the 1970s. An FBI investigation revealed that all of the carcasses bore the marks of death by natural causes. Yet rumors still abound of mysterious, perhaps alien, forces eviscerating livestock.

34   Clearly, urban legends run deep. And they keep coming, crying out for analysis. "I can't stop—as long I open my mail and answer my phone, I'm going to get more stories," says Jan Brunvand. "And when a story's hot, suddenly it's all over the country, with allusions in newspapers and on talk shows." It's fascinating to watch the stories spread, he adds. "You're seeing the living tradition as it develops and changes."

35 Which reminds him: Did you hear about the wife who used bug spray on a cockroach that was running around the toilet bowl? And then her husband went into the bathroom and lit a cigar?

36 "That one," says Brunvand with a smile, "is called 'The Exploding Toilet.'"

Exercise 4   **VOCABULARY HIGHLIGHTS**

Write a short definition of each word as it is used in the essay. (Paragraph numbers are given in parentheses.) Be prepared to use the words in your own sentences.

specters (7)	placard (24)
motif (9)	passé (28)
prototype (10)	proliferate (29)
mulling (18)	crystallize (32)
rendezvous (19)	plummeted (32)

Exercise 5   **DISCUSSION AND CRITICAL THINKING**

1. What sentence in paragraph 5 defines *urban legend?*
   The fourth.

2. Why do people create, tell, and listen to urban legends?
   People are afraid. They love to be frightened. They love good tales, especially those that are strange and supposedly true.

3. Mark *The Vanishing Hitchhiker* in paragraph 8 for these parts: situation, conflict, struggle, outcome, and meaning.

4. Wolkomir uses examples, authoritative statements, definitions, and quotations for support. Annotate one of each.

5. Which of the urban legends in this essay do you recognize?
   Answers will vary.

6. Of the three main purposes of narrative writing—to persuade, to inform, and to entertain—which two are apparent in this essay?
   To inform and to entertain.

On the Road: A City of the Mind

Sue Hubbell

As both a former trucker and a keen observer of human nature, Sue Hubbell is well qualified to analyze truck-stop culture. The all-night food-and-gas establishments she writes about cater to truckers, accept tourists as second-class citizens during daylight hours, and—in the dead of the night—become a "city of the mind" for workers and drivers. These men and women are linked by common feelings, needs, and behavior. This article appeared in "The American Scene" in *Time* magazine in 1985.

1   In the early morning there is a city of the mind that stretches from coast to coast, from border to border. Its cross streets are the interstate highways, and food, comfort, companionship are served up in its buildings, the truck stops near the exits. Its citizens are all-night drivers, the truckers and the waitresses at the stops.

2   In daylight the city fades and blurs when the transients appear, tourists who merely want a meal and a tank of gas. They file into the carpeted dining rooms away from the professional drivers' side, sit at the Formica tables set off by imitation cloth flowers in bud vases. They eat and are gone, do not return. They are not a part of the city and obscure it.

3   It is 5 A.M. in a truck stop in West Virginia. Drivers in twos, threes and fours are eating breakfast and talking routes and schedules.

4   "Truckers!" growls a manager. "They say they are in a hurry. They complain if the service isn't fast. We fix it so they can have their fuel pumped while they are eating and put in telephones on every table so they can check with their dispatchers. They could be out of here in half an hour. But what do they do? They sit and talk for two hours."

5   The truckers are lining up for seconds at the breakfast buffet (all you can eat for $3.99—biscuits with chipped-beef gravy, fruit cup, French toast with syrup, bacon, pancakes, sausage, scrambled eggs, doughnuts, Danish, cereal in little boxes).

6   The travel store at the truck stop has a machine to measure heartbeat in exchange for a quarter. There are racks of jackets, belts, truck supplies, tape cassettes. On the wall are paintings for sale, simulated wood with likenesses of John Wayne or a stag. The rack by the cash register is stuffed with Twinkies and chocolate Suzy Qs.

7　　It is 5 A.M. in New Mexico. Above the horseshoe-shaped counter on panels where a menu is usually displayed, an overhead slide show is in progress. The pictures change slowly, allowing the viewer to take in all the details. A low shot of a Peterbilt, its chrome fittings sparkling in the sunshine, is followed by one of a bosomy young woman, the same who must pose for those calendars found in auto-parts stores. She almost has on clothes, and she is offering to check a trucker's oil. The next slide is a side view of a whole tractor-trailer rig, its 18 wheels gleaming and spoked. It is followed by one of a blond bulging out of a hint of cop clothes writing a naughty trucker a ticket.

8　　The waitress looks too tired and too jaded to be offended. The jaws of the truckers move mechanically as they fork up their eggs-over-easy. They stare at the slides, glassy eyed, as intent on chrome as on flesh.

9　　It is 4 A.M. in Oklahoma. A recycled Stuckey's with blue tile roof calls itself simply Truck Stop. The sign also boasts showers, scales, truck wash and a special on service for $88.50. At a table inside, four truckers have ordered a short stack and three eggs apiece, along with bacon, sausage and coffee. (Trucker's Superbreakfast—$ 3.79).

10　　They have just started drinking their coffee, and the driver with the Roadway cap calls over the waitress, telling her there is salt in the sugar he put in his coffee. She is pale, thin, young, has dark circles under her eyes. The truckers have been teasing her, and she doesn't trust them. She dabs a bit of sugar from the canister on a finger and tastes it. Salt. She samples sugar from the other canisters. They have salt too, and she gathers them up to replace them. Someone is hazing her, breaking her into her new job. Her eyes shine with tears.

11　　She brings the food and comes back when the truckers are nearly done. She carries a water jug and coffeepot on her tray. The men are ragging her again, and her hands tremble. The tray falls with a crash. The jug breaks. Glass, water and coffee spread across the floor. She sits down in the booth, tears rolling down her cheeks.

12　　"I'm so tired. My old man . . . he left me," she says, the tears coming faster now. "The judge says he's going to take my kid away if I can't take care of him, so I stay up all day and just sleep when he takes a nap and the boss yells at me and . . . and . . . the truckers all talk dirty. . . . I'm so tired."

13　　She puts her head down on her arms and sobs luxuriously. The truckers are gone, and I touch her arm and tell her to look at what

Situation

Conflict

Struggle

Outcome

Meaning (implied)

they have left, There is a $20 bill beside each plate. She looks up, nods, wipes her eyes on her apron, pockets the tips and goes to get a broom and a mop.

14   It is 3:30 A.M. in Illinois at a glossy truck stop that offers all mechanical services, motel rooms, showers, Laundromat, game room, TV lounge, truckers' bulletin board and a stack of newspapers published by the Association of Christian Truckers. Piped-in music fills the air.

15   The waitress in the professional drivers' section is a big motherly-looking woman with red hair piled in careful curls on top of her head. She correctly sizes up the proper meal for the new customer at the counter. "Don't know what you want, honey? Try the chicken-noodle soup with a hot roll. It will stick to you like you've got something, and you don't have to worry about grease."

16   She has been waitressing 40 years, 20 of them in this truck stop. As she talks she polishes the stainless steel, fills mustard jars, adds the menu inserts for today's special (hot turkey sandwich, mashed potatoes and gravy, pot of coffee—$2.50).

17   "The big boss, well, he's a love, but some of the others aren't so hot. But it's a job. Gotta work somewhere. I need a day off though. Been working six, seven days straight lately. Got shopping to do. My lawn needs mowing."

18   Two truckers are sitting at a booth. Their faces are lined and leathery. One cap says Harley-Davidson, the other Coors.

19   Harley-Davidson calls out, "If you wasn't so mean, Flossie, you'd have a good man to take care of you and you wouldn't have to mow the damn lawn."

20   She puts down the mustard jar, walks over to Harley-Davidson and Coors, stands in front of them, hands on wide hips. "Now you listen here, Charlie, I'm good enough woman for any man but all you guys want are chippies."

21   Coors turns bright red. She glares at him. "You saw my ex in here last Saturday night with a chippie on his arm. He comes in here all the time with two, three chippies just to prove to me what a high old time he's having. If that's a good time, I'd rather baby-sit my grandkids."

22   Chippies are not a topic of conversation that Charlie and Coors wish to pursue. Coors breaks a doughnut in two, and Charlie uses his fork to make a spillway for the gravy on the double order of mashed potatoes that accompanies his scrambled eggs.

23   Flossie comes back and turns to the new customer in mirror shades at this dark hour, a young trucker with cowboy boots and hat. "John-boy. Where you been? Haven't seen you in weeks. Looks

like you need a nice omelet. Cook just made some of those bis-
cuits you like too."

24   I leave a tip for Flossie and pay my bill. In the men's room,
where I am shunted because the ladies' is closed for cleaning,
someone has scrawled poignant words: NO TIME TO EAT NOW.

Exercise 6   **VOCABULARY HIGHLIGHTS**

*Write a short definition of each word as it is used in the essay. (Paragraph
numbers are given in parentheses.) Be prepared to use the words in your
own sentences.*

transients (2)	canister (10)
Formica (2)	hazing (10)
obscure (2)	luxuriantly (13)
simulated (6)	chippie (21)
jaded (8)	poignant (24)

Exercise 7   **DISCUSSION AND CRITICAL THINKING**

1. What does the subtitle "A City of the Mind" mean? How can that
   "city" be described?
   The subtitle refers to truck-stop workers and truck drivers who are linked by common feelings,
   needs, and behavior. Those are the common denominators. The ambiance, food, and service can
   be described along with those who serve and those who receive the service.

2. Using four narrative accounts, Hubbell describes four locations, in
   no particular order. Why doesn't she place them in order according
   to time or distance?
   She jumps around in geography and time because she wants to show that the "city" is a state of
   mind that occurs simultaneously in many locations.

3. Why do tourists eat in a different section of the truck stop from the
   truck drivers?
   The truckers have special prices, sometimes special food, and a clublike (state of mind) setting.

4. How is the waitress in paragraph 10 different from the model in the
   picture in paragraph 7?
   The waitress in paragraph 10 represents reality and the model in paragraph 7 represents fantasy
   in "A City of the Mind."

5. Why is Flossie (paragraphs 14 through 24) doing better than the
   waitress in Oklahoma (paragraphs 9 through 13)?
   Flossie has been waitressing for "40 years, 20 of them in this truck stop." She has a fast tongue,
   a quick mind, and motherly charm. She can be either honey or vinegar, and the truck drivers
   know it.

6. What are the two most specific food items?

   Twinkies and chocolate Suzy Qs (paragraph 6)

7. What are other examples of very specific diction used to help the reader visualize specific items?

   "recycled Stuckey's" (paragraph 9); "likenesses of John Wayne" (paragraph 6); "Roadway cap" (paragraph 10); Harley-Davidson and Coors caps (paragraph 18)

8. Mark the narrative contained in paragraphs 9 through 13 for these parts: situation, conflict, struggle, outcome, and meaning (implied).

The Talkies

James Lileks

Columnist for the *Minneapolis Star Tribune* and contributor to the *Washington Post*, James Lileks is well known for his humorous observations on human behavior. He is the author of two novels, *Falling up the Stairs* (1988) and *Mr. Obvious* (1995), and two collections of essays: *Notes of a Nervous Man* (1991) and *Fresh Lies* (1995), which contains the following selection.

1   I am a tolerant man. Especially at the movies. I do not complain when the seats are as plush as a Baptist pew, or the buttered popcorn tastes like packing material with a drizzle of melted crayon. I don't mind that I have to cash a bond to buy a box of Dots, and if I have to use solvents to free my feet from the floor at the end of the film, that's acceptable. I'm not happy when the man with the big yellow hat from the Curious George books sits directly in front of me and blocks my view, but accept it as the price you pay for a communal experience.

2   But people who talk in movies make me turn eight shades of mad. Plunk two talkers behind me and I start to pine for a decent billy club. Something well weighted with a comfortable grip. As I see it, there are two excuses for talking during movies: (a) you are on the screen; or (b) you have a rare neurological disease that causes you to blurt out statements like "I CAN'T BELIEVE SISKEL AND EBERT GAVE THIS TWO THUMBS UP!" at inappropriate times—and so you go to movie theaters where your affliction seems less bizarre.

3   Mind you, I am not discussing those who lean to their partner and whisper a few words or observations. Most of you whisper, or

keep it to yourselves. The people to whom I refer are those who speak at a volume just a few decibels shy of the level you would use to warn someone in a crowd of a falling piano. The people who seem to expect their names to be listed in the credits under "Additional Dialogue."

4   Last week I went to see *Mississippi Burning*. I use the word "see" with precision, for I heard not a line of the dialogue. The entire row behind me talked all through the trailers. That's fine. That's what trailers are for. Go on, get it out of your system. They also talked during the opening credits, but that was acceptable; they'd arrived late—I know this because one of them hit me in the head with her purse—and they were still flush with the excitement that comes with leaving the house three minutes before the film starts.

5   But as the film progressed, it became obvious that the row behind us was a group from the Institute for Pointing Out the Obvious, off on a field trip. The first image of the film, an early '60s-model car cresting a hill, prompted the gentleman behind me to note, "That's an old car." The appearance of several more cars of the same period gave the man an empirical Epiphany, and he could not help but burst out with his conclusion:

6   "This must be set in the past."

7   There was a period of silence, during which he may or may not have whispered, "Note how reflective and rectangular the screen is," to his partner. The slack was taken up by a group to his right, who were attempting to recall what this film was about, perhaps on the assumption that the plot, due to malicious filmmakers anxious for financial ruin, would remain inscrutable for the next two hours.

8   These folk soon shut up—after my buddy had turned around, locked eyes, and given his best I-taught-Manson-all-he-knows look. But the ones behind me were just beginning.

9   Nothing escaped comment. The streets in the rural Mississippi town were unpaved? Lo, hear them discuss the volume of dust raised by a passing car. The sheriff was fat? Lend an ear to "Looka that gut," and other biting witticisms (such as, "I mean it, how can he be that fat? I'll never get that fat."). Woe to any screen characters who fail to heed their judgments, and prolonged approval of those who do.

10   Often I was treated to a critical evaluation in process. At one point, Gene Hackman drives up to the house of a woman who knows something but isn't telling the Feds. This prompts the following speech:

11   "Oh, it's broad daylight, he'd better not go up to that house. People would talk and her husband would hear about it, don't you think?"

12   "I imagine so."

13   "Well, everyone knows that's his car."

14   "See, he's leaving."

15   "Yeah, he's turning around."

16   "Good. 'Cause he'd have gotten in trouble, and so would she."

17   Turning around and shouting "SHUT UP! SHUT UP AND REMAIN IN A STATE OF SHUTUPEDNESS!" would have done no good. I had spent the previous hour turning around and glaring, but they apparently took this to mean I was angry that they were speaking too softly, and hence depriving me of their views. For a while I was turning around, glaring and turning away with a heavy sigh, but given the classical decor of the theater, they probably interpreted this as a nostalgic sigh of regret for an idealized world long passed. Nothing worked. When the man issued a few racking coughs interspersed with words, I considered lighting up a cigarette and letting the smoke waft his way, but smoking, of course, is considered discourteous to others.

18   For a while I attempted to use telekinesis to loose a piece of plaster on the ceiling directly above them, but this did not work.

19   I finally turned around and said, "Quiet!" They nodded, as though I was describing an attribute of the theater. I might as well have said "Dark!" or "Chairs in rows!" They embarked anew on another discussion of whether or not that actor was in that Jack Nicholson film.

20   Actors, incidentally, were not allowed to have roles. When they discussed the motivations of Gene Hackman's character, they addressed him as Gene Hackman. "See, Gene Hackman wants to do it his way, that's the problem." This helped all of us within hearing range maintain our suspension of disbelief. Willem Dafoe, late of *Platoon,* was known only as "the guy in the glasses." They would occasionally bring out the depth in his character by asking, "Why is he always wearing a suit? It looks so warm, doesn't he sweat?"

21   If I seem to be exaggerating, I assure you I am not. These people babbled without cease, as though the fountain at the concession stand had added sodium pentothal to their beverages. I could not move, as there was not a decent seat to be had in the theater. I could barely concentrate on the film, as I was always steeled for another pronouncement. All I could do was entertain the idea of following them home, standing in the corner of their

bedroom, and saying things like, "Oh, see, he has his arm around her shoulder, he likes her. Okay, well, she's getting ready for bed now, that's a nice set of sheets, I have ones like those at home. Say, that's quite a mole, I'd get that checked out if I had a mole like that," and so forth.

22   It would only be fair.

23   So, friends, if you're in a movie house, and you have something to say, ask yourself this: Do you, in the course of your day, constantly have to shout over the sound of a jackhammer, and should you now adjust your voice accordingly? Is what you have to say really necessary? Is the gentleman in front of you waving a flag on which is printed the nautical symbol for PUT A LID ON IT?

24   If you feel you still have to speak, ask yourself this: If this was World War II, and I was behind German lines with Nazis everywhere, could the Nazis hear me if I spoke at this level, and subsequently submit me to horrible torture? If the answer is yes, tone it down. Or write it out and hand it to your partner, with the instructions to swallow it immediately.

25   Or, go on talking. Go ahead. You paid your money. Gab it up. And make sure you kick the seat in front of you when you cross your legs. You're only conforming to ancient tradition, after all. Movies are nothing more than modern versions of cavemen telling tales around the fire, and back then there were always a couple who talked all through the story.

26   We know this because of drawings on the walls of caves where they buried the talkers.

Exercise 8   **VOCABULARY HIGHLIGHTS**

Write a short definition of each word as it is used in the essay. (Paragraph numbers are given in parentheses.) Be prepared to use the words in your own sentences.

communal (1)   decor (17)

neurological (2)   nostalgic (17)

empirical (5)   interspersed (17)

Epiphany (5)   telekinesis (18)

inscrutable (7)   sodium pentothal (21)

Exercise 9	DISCUSSION AND CRITICAL THINKING

1. Is Lileks trying to inform or to persuade his readers?

   To persuade.

2. What is his main point?

   People should not talk loudly during movies.

3. How is the title ironic?

   "Talkies" usually refers to modern movies, which added sound and replaced the silent movies, but Lileks uses "Talkies" to refer to the movie houses where the most prominent audibles come not from the screen but from the audience.

4. Of the five parts of a narrative—situation, conflict, struggle, outcome, and meaning—which occupies the greater part of this essay?

   Struggle.

5. Why is dialogue important here as a narrative technique?

   The author's concern is talking; therefore, the words document his generalization, providing the specific information to support his argument.

Soft Mornings and Harsh Afternoons

Maya Angelou

In this narrative passage from her celebrated book *I Know Why the Caged Bird Sings*, Maya Angelou introduces you to people and situations from her childhood. She also introduces you to a full range of her emotions, from reverential love to bitter anger. Early mornings and late afternoons frame the passage, but they represent more than just the time of day.

1   Each year I watched the field across from the Store turn caterpillar green, then gradually frosty white. I knew exactly how long it would be before the big wagons would pull into the front yard and load on the cotton pickers at daybreak to carry them to the remains of slavery's plantations.

2   During the picking season my grandmother would get out of bed at four o'clock (she never used an alarm clock) and creak down to her knees and chant in a sleep-filled voice, "Our Father, thank you for letting me see this New Day. Thank you that you didn't allow the bed I lay on last night to be my cooling board, nor my blanket my winding sheet. Guide my feet this day along the

straight and narrow, and help me to put a bridle on my tongue. Bless this house, and everybody in it. Thank you, in the name of your Son, Jesus Christ, Amen."

3   Before she had quite arisen, she called our names and issued orders, and pushed her large feet into homemade slippers and across the bare lye-washed wooden floor to light the coal-oil lamp.

4   The lamplight in the Store gave a soft make-believe feeling to our world which made me want to whisper and walk about on tip-toe. The odors of onions and oranges and kerosene had been mixing all night and wouldn't be disturbed until the wooded slat was removed from the door and the early morning air forced its way in with the bodies of people who had walked miles to reach the pickup place.

5   "Sister, I'll have two cans of sardines."

6   "I'm gonna work so fast today I'm gonna make you look like you standing still."

7   "Lemme have a hunk uh cheese and some sody crackers."

8   "Just gimme a coupla them fat peanut paddies." That would be from a picker who was taking his lunch. The greasy brown paper sack was stuck behind the bib of his overalls. He'd use the candy as a snack before the noon sun called the workers to rest.

9   In those tender mornings the Store was full of laughing, joking, boasting and bragging. One man was going to pick two hundred pounds of cotton, and another three hundred. Even the children were promising to bring home fo' bits and six bits.

10   The champion picker of the day before was the hero of the dawn. If he prophesied that the cotton in today's field was going to be sparce and stick to the bolls like glue, every listener would grunt a hearty agreement.

11   The sound of the empty cotton sacks dragging over the floor and the murmurs of waking people were sliced by the cash register as we rang up the five-cent sales.

12   If the morning sounds and smells were touched with the supernatural, the late afternoon had all the features of the normal Arkansas life. In the dying sunlight the people dragged, rather than their empty cotton sacks.

13   Brought back to the Store, the pickers would step out of the backs of trucks and fold down, dirt-disappointed, to the ground. No matter how much they had picked, it wasn't enough. Their wages wouldn't even get them out of debt to my grandmother, not to mention the staggering bill that waited on them at the white commissary downtown.

14   The sounds of the new morning had been replaced with grumbles about cheating houses, weighted scales, snakes, skimpy

cotton and dusty rows. In later years I was to confront the stereotyped picture of gay song-singing cotton pickers with such inordinate rage that I was told even by fellow Blacks that my paranoia was embarrassing. But I had seen the fingers cut by the mean little cotton bolls, and I had witnessed the backs and shoulders and arms and legs resisting any further demands.

15   Some of the workers would leave their sacks at the Store to be picked up the following morning, but a few had to take them home for repairs. I winced to picture them sewing the coarse material under a coal-oil lamp with fingers stiffening from the day's work. In too few hours they would have to walk back to Sister Henderson's Store, get vittles and load, again, onto the trucks. Then they would face another day of trying to earn enough for the whole year with the heavy knowledge that they were going to end the season as they started it. Without the money or credit necessary to sustain a family for three months. In cotton-picking time the late afternoons revealed the harshness of Black Southern life, which in the early morning had been softened by nature's blessing of grogginess, forgetfulness and the soft lamplight.

Exercise 10	**DISCUSSION AND CRITICAL THINKING**

1. What qualities does Angelou's grandmother represent to her?

   Her grandmother represents the dignified struggle for life; she is efficient, compassionate, stable, and wise.

2. Use short phrases to indicate the time of day associated with the narrative parts.

   situation: morning
   conflict: late afternoon
   struggle: late afternoon until sunset
   outcome: sunset
   meaning: sunset, or evening

3. Is the narrative movement time, place, or both?

   Overall it is time, but the place does shift from the store to the field and back to the store.

4. What does Angelou mean by "supernatural" and "normal" in paragraph 12?

   "Supernatural" mornings represent hope, and "normal" late afternoons represent reality.

5. What opposing feelings does Angelou express?

   She has reverence for her grandmother, compassion for the workers, and scorn for the farm owners.

✎ Topics for Writing Narration

You will find a Writing Process Worksheet in Appendix A, page 531. It can be photocopied and enlarged, filled in, and submitted with each assignment if your instructor directs you to do so.

Each essay developed from these suggested source-based topics should include at least one reference to the reading selection by the author's name and the title. Quotations should be enclosed in quotation marks. Follow your instructor's directions in documenting the ideas you borrow. Whether you use informal or formal documentation, the form is not complicated, and you will soon learn to use it for these essays without checking each time. See pages 77 and 78 for a discussion of MLA style and informal documentation.

Underlining and annotating reading selections will help you in finding support material. In prewriting brief essays, consider marking your outline to indicate where you will use quotations or other borrowed ideas. If the quotations or reworded statements are short and few, you could even insert them inside parentheses or circles in your outline; if you do, also include the author's last name and the page number. A sound system, consistently used, will save you time and ensure technically strong papers.

"The Switched Bride"

1. Write a narrative about an unusual or chance encounter that led to a satisfying relationship.

2. Write about a blind date that started badly and ended well.

3. Write about a marriage based on something else than love but that turned to love.

"Busted for No Good Reason"

4. Write a narrative about a memorable time when you or someone you know well was falsely accused (work, games, relationship, school).

5. Pretend that you were the store detective who detained Ochoa and discuss what you initially thought, what went wrong, what you now learned, and how you felt.

6. Write about a time when you or someone you know well falsely accused or suspected someone.

"If Those Cobras Don't Get You, the Alligators Will"

7. Using a definition provided by Richard Wolkomir, write an urban legend as the major part of an essay of 400 to 600 words. The essay

may be original or it may be an elaborated version of a legend found in Wolkomin's essay. Explain why you think such an urban legend is or would be appealing.

8. In a group of four or five students, develop your own urban legend. After your group has collectively come up with the basic story, each student should work independently to expand it out as an essay, with an explanation of how this has the ingredients to become an enduring urban legend.

"On the Road: A City of the Mind"

9. Hubbell's essay uses four narratives to show that truck-stop restaurants are about the same, no matter where they are located. They are, of course, staffed and frequented by real individuals. Write an essay about a restaurant you have visited, one that has its own character and stands out for its uniqueness. Your narrative would cover one trip to that establishment and would emphasize its exceptional distinctions. Consider writing about the food, surroundings, clientele, workers, and, perhaps, the owner. With references, contrast your subject with the restaurants described in Hubbell's essay.

"The Talkies"

10. Using Lileks's basic idea that self-centered or ignorant persons may spoil the enjoyment of others, discuss an experience you have had in a restaurant, a lecture hall (during a special occasion or a typical class presentation), a concert, a sporting event, a sports bar, or a church. Refer to some of Lileks's points for comparison and contrast.

"Soft Mornings and Harsh Afternoons"

11. Using Angelou's account as a basic framework, write about a group of people or a person whom you have witnessed from the early morning to the evening, from the freshness of morning to the fatigue of evening; worker exploitation may or may not be an issue. Your subject may be a family member or members, or it may be a group of people you know, who work in the fields or factories. Include descriptive details to suggest the different moods of different times of day.

12. Angelou writes reverently about her grandmother, showing her in action from getting-up time to work time and characterizing her by her movements and words. Write about someone you have known and respected. Show him or her performing some task or solving some problem. Write from a first-person point of view and indicate your feelings. You may want to point out how your subject is similar to and different from Angelou's grandmother.

Career-Related Topics

13. Write a narrative account of a work-related encounter between a manager and a worker and briefly explain the significance of the event.

14. Write a narrative account of an encounter between a customer and a salesperson. Explain what went right and what went wrong.

15. Write a narrative account of how a person solved a work-related problem perhaps by using technology.

16. Write a narrative account of a salesperson handling a customer's complaint. Critique the procedure.

General Topics

Each of the following topics concerns the writing of a narrative with meaning beyond the story itself. The narrative will be used to inform or persuade in relation to a clearly stated idea.

17. Write a narrative based on a topic sentence such as this: "One experience showed me what _____ [pain, fear, anger, love, sacrifice, dedication, joy, sorrow, shame, pride] was really like."

18. Write a simple narrative about a fire, a riot, an automobile accident, a rescue, shoplifting, or some other unusual happening you witnessed.

19. Write a narrative that supports (or opposes) the idea of a familiar saying such as one of the following:

You never know who a friend is 'til you need one.

A bird in the hand is worth two in the bush.

A person who is absent is soon forgotten.

Better to be alone than to be in bad company.

A person in a passion rides a mad horse.

Borrowing is the mother of trouble.

A person who marries for money earns it.

The person who lies down with dogs gets up with fleas.

Never give advice to a friend.

If it isn't broken, don't fix it.

Nice people finish last.

It isn't what you know, it's who you know.

Fools and their money are soon parted.

Every person has a price.

You get what you pay for.

Haste makes waste.

The greatest remedy for anger is delay.

A person full of him- or herself is empty.

To forget a wrong is the best revenge.

Money is honey, my little sonny, And a rich man's joke is always funny.

Writer's Guidelines: Narration

1. Include these points so you will be sure you have a complete narrative:
   - situation
   - conflict
   - struggle
   - outcome
   - meaning

2. Use these techniques or devices as appropriate:
   - images that appeal to the senses (sight, smell, taste, hearing, touch) and other details to advance action
   - dialogue
   - transitional devices (such as *next, soon, after, later, following*) to indicate chronological order

3. Give details concerning action.

4. Be consistent with point of view and verb tense.

5. Keep in mind that most narratives written as college assignments will have an expository purpose; that is, they explain a specific idea.

6. Consider working with a short time frame for short writing assignments. For example, writing about an entire graduation ceremony might be too complicated, but concentrating on the moment when you walked forward to receive the diploma or the moment when the relatives and friends come down on the field could work very well.

7. For source-based essays, use quotation marks around phrases and sentences you borrow and document formally or informally as directed by your instructor.

6

Description: Moving Through Space

THE QUIGMANS by Buddy Hickerson

Something in his appearance told Francine that
Sigfried had been dumped many times before.

© Tribune Media Services, Inc. All Rights Reserved. Reprinted with
permission.

Writing Description

escription is the use of words to represent the appearance or nature of something. It is not merely the work of an indifferent camera. Instead, often going beyond sight, it includes details that will convey an accurate representation. Just what details the descriptive writer selects will depend on several factors, especially the type of description and the dominant impression that the writer is trying to convey.

Types of Description

Depending on how you wish to treat your subject material, your description is likely to be either objective or subjective.

Effective *objective description* presents the subject clearly and directly as it exists outside the realm of emotions. If you are explaining the function of the heart, the characteristics of a computer chip, or the renovation of a manufacturing facility, your description will probably feature specific, impersonal details. Most technical and scientific writing is objective in this sense. It is likely to be practical and utilitarian, making little use of speculation or poetic technique and featuring mainly what can be seen.

Effective *subjective description* is also concerned with clarity and it may be direct, but it conveys a feeling about the subject and sets a mood while making a point. Because most expression involves personal views, even when it explains by analysis, subjective description (often called *emotional description*) has a broader range of uses than objective description.

Descriptive passages can be a combination of objective and subjective description; only the larger context of the passage will reveal the main intent. The following description of a baseball begins with objective treatment and then moves to subjective.

Objective treatment moving to subjective treatment

Roger Angell, "On the Ball"

> It weighs just over five ounces and measures between 2.86 and 2.94 inches in diameter. It is made of a composition-cork nucleus encased in two thin layers of rubber, one black and one red, surrounded by 121 yards of tightly wrapped blue-gray wool yarn, 45 yards of white wool yarn, 53 more yards of blue-gray wool yarn, 150 yards of fine cotton yarn, a coat of rubber cement, and a cowhide (formerly horsehide) exterior, which is held together with 216 slightly raised red cotton stitches. Printed certifications, endorsements, and outdoor advertising spherically attest to its authenticity. . . . Feel the ball, turn it over in your hand; hold it across the seam or the other way, with the seam just to the side of your middle finger. Speculation stirs. You want to get outdoors and throw this spare and sensual object to somebody or, at the very least, watch somebody else throw it. The game has begun.

The following subjective description, also on the subject of baseball, is designed to move the emotions while informing.

The following details relate to the paradoxes.

Note the emotional appeals, the subjective approach.

Paul Gallico, "Babe Ruth"

The Babe was a bundle of paradoxes. Somehow one of the most appealing things about him was that he was neither built, nor did he look like, an athlete. He did not even look like a ballplayer. Although he stood six feet two inches and weighed 220 pounds, his body was pear-shaped and even when in tip-top condition he had a bit of a belly. His barrel always seemed too much for his legs, which tapered into a pair of ankles as slender almost as those of a girl. The great head, perched upon a pair of round and unathletic shoulders, presented a moon of a face, the feature of which was the flaring nostrils of a nose that was rather like a snout. His voice was deep and hoarse, his speech crude and earthy, his ever-ready laughter a great, rumbling gurgle that arose from the caverns of his middle. He had an eye that was abnormally quick, nerves and muscular reactions to match, a supple wrist, a murderous swing, and a gorgeously truculent, competitive spirit.

Techniques of Descriptive Writing

As a writer of a description, you will need to focus your work to accomplish three specific tasks:

- Emphasize a single point (dominant impression).

- Establish a perspective from which to describe your subject (point of view).

- Position the details for coherence (order).

Dominant Impression

See if you can find the dominant impression in this description:

Please help me find my dog. He is a mongrel with the head of a poodle and the body of a wolfhound, and his fur is patchy and dingy-gray. He has only three legs, but despite his arthritis, he uses them pretty well to hobble around and scratch his fleas and mange. His one seeing eye is cloudy, so he runs with his head sideways. His ragged, twisted ears enable him to hear loud sounds, which startle his troubled nervous system and cause him to howl pitifully. If you give him a scrap of food, he will gum it up rapidly and try to wag his broken tail. He answers to the name of Lucky.

Of course, the dominant impression, what is being emphasized, is "misery," or "unlucky," not "lucky." The dominant impression emerges from a pattern of details, often involving repetition of one idea with different particulars. Word choice, which is of paramount importance, depends on your purpose in writing and on your audience.

If you are eating hamburgers in a restaurant, and you say to your companion, "This food is good," your companion may understand all he or she needs to understand on the subject. After all, your companion can see you sitting there chewing the food, smacking your lips, and wiping the sauce off your chin. But if you write that sentence and send it to someone, your reader may be puzzled. Although the reader may know you fairly well, he or she may not know the meaning of "good" (to eat? to purchase for others? to sell?) or of "this food" (What kind? Where is it? How is it special? How is it prepared? What qualities does it have?).

To convey your main concern effectively to readers, you will want to give some sensory impressions. These sensory impressions, collectively called *imagery,* refer to that which can be experienced by the senses—what we can see, smell, taste, hear, and touch. You may use *figures of speech* to convey these sensory impression; figures of speech involve comparisons of unlike things that, nevertheless, have something in common.

The imagery in this passage is italicized. The dominant impression is underscored.

<table>
<tr><td>

Topic sentence
Dominant impression

Image (touch)
Image (sight)
Image (sound)

Image (taste)
Image (smell)
Figure of speech
Note movement
through time and space
Image (sight)
Image (sound)

Dale Scott, "Hefty Burger"
</td><td>

Sitting here in Harold's Hefty Burgers at midnight, I am convinced that I am eating the <u>ultimate form of food.</u> The *buns* are *feathery soft* to the touch but *heavy* in the hand and *soggy* inside. As I take a full-mouth, no-nonsense bite, the *melted cheese* and *juices cascade* over my fingers and make little *oil slicks* on the *vinyl table* below. I *chew noisily* and happily like a puppy at a food bowl, stopping occasionally to flush down the *rich, thick taste of spicy animal fat* with a *swig* from a *chilled mug of fizzing root beer* that *prickles* my *nose.* Over at the grill, *the smell of frying onions creeps away* stealthily on *invisible feet* to conquer the neighborhood, turning hundreds of ordinary *citizens* like me into drooling, stomach growling, fast-food addicts, who *trudge* in from the night like the walking dead and *call out* the same order, time after time. "Hefty Burger." "Hefty Burger." "Hefty Burger."
</td></tr>
</table>

In reading Scott's enthusiastic endorsement of the Hefty Burger, the reader will have no trouble understanding the idea that he liked the food. Through imagery, Scott has involved the reader in what he has seen, smelled, heard, tasted, and touched. He has also used figures of speech, including these examples:

Simile: a comparison using *like* or *as*	"chew noisily and happily like a puppy"
Metaphor: a comparison using word replacement.	"feathery [instead of 'delicately'] soft"
Personification: an expression giving human characteristics to something not human.	"smell of frying onions creeps away stealthily on invisible feet to conquer" [instead of "spreads to entice"]

Subjective description is likely to make more use of imagery, figurative language, and words rich in associations than is objective description. But just as a fine line cannot always be drawn between the objective and the subjective, a fine line cannot always be drawn between word choice in one and in the other. However, we can say with certainty that whatever the type of description, careful word choice will always be important. Consider the following points about word choice (diction), point of view, and order.

Word Choice: General and Specific, Abstract and Concrete

To move from the general to the specific is to move from the whole class or group of items to individual ones; for example,

General	*Specific*	*More Specific*
food	hamburger	Hefty Burger
mess	grease	oil slicks on the table
drink	soda	mug of root beer
odor	smell from the grill	smell of frying onions

Words are classified as abstract or concrete, depending on what they refer to. *Abstract words* refer to qualities or ideas: *good, ordinary, ultimate, truth, beauty, maturity, love. Concrete words* refer to things or a substance; they have reality: *onions, grease, buns, tables, food.* Specific concrete words, sometimes called *concrete particulars,* often support generalizations effectively and convince the reader of the accuracy of the description.

Never try to give all the details in a description. Instead, be selective. Pick only those details that you need to project a dominant impression, always taking into account the knowledge and attitudes of your readers. To reintroduce an idea from the beginning of this chapter, description is not photographic. If you wish to describe a person, select the traits that will project your intended dominant impression. If you wish to describe a landscape, do not give all the details that you might find in a picture; on the contrary, pick the details that support your intended dominant impression. That extremely important dominant impression is directly linked to your purpose. It is created by the judicious choice and arrangement of images, figurative language, and revealing details.

Point of View

Point of view shows the writer's relationship to the subject, thereby establishing the perspective from which the subject is described. It rarely changes within a passage. Two terms usually associated with fiction writing, *first person* and *third person*, also pertain to descriptive writing.

If you want to convey personal experience, your point of view will be *first person*, which can be either involved (point of view of a participant) or uninvolved (point of view of an observer). The involved perspective uses *I* more prominently than the uninvolved. Student Dale Scott's paragraph "Hefty Burgers" uses first person, involved.

If you want to present something from a detached position, especially from a geographical or historical distance (see "Babe Ruth" and "On the Ball"), your point of view will be *third person*, and you will refer to your subjects by name or by third-person pronouns such as *he, she, him, her, it, they,* and *them,* without imposing yourself as an *I* person.

Order

The point of view you select may indicate or even dictate the order in which you present descriptive details. If you are describing your immediate surroundings while taking a walk (first person, involved), the descriptive account would naturally develop spatially as well as chronologically—that is, in both space and time.

- To indicate space, use terms such as *next to, below, under, above, behind, in front of, beyond, in the foreground, in the background, to the left,* and *to the right.*

- To indicate time, use words such as *first, second, then, soon, finally, while, after, next, later, now,* and *before.*

Some descriptive pieces, for example, the one on Babe Ruth, may follow an idea progression for emphasis and not move primarily through space or time. Whatever appropriate techniques you use will guide your reader and thereby aid coherence.

All three elements—dominant impression, point of view, and order—work together in a well-written description.

The dominant impression of the paragraph "On the Ball" is of an object remarkably well designed for its purpose. The point of view is third person, and the order of the description moves from the core of the baseball outward.

The paragraph "Babe Ruth" emphasizes the idea of paradox (something that appears to be a contradiction). The details are presented from a detached point of view (third person) and appear in order from physique to overall appearance to behavior. The details show a person who wasn't built like an athlete and didn't look like an athlete yet was one of the most famous athletes of all time. Collectively those details convey the dominant impression of "Ruth, the paradox."

Scott's "Hefty Burger" can also be evaluated for all three elements:

- *Dominant impression:* good food (images, figurative language, other diction). The reader experiences the incident as the writer did because of the diction. The general and abstract have been made clear by use of the specific and the concrete. Of course, not all abstract words need to be tied to the concrete, nor do all general words need to be transformed to the specific. As you describe, use your judgment to decide which words fit your purposes—those needed to enable your audience to understand your ideas and to be persuaded or informed.

- *Point of view:* first person, involved

- *Order:* spatial, from restaurant table to grill, to outside, and back to restaurant

Useful Procedure for Writing Description

A checklist may help you write a more effective description.

What is your subject? (school campus during summer vacation)

What is the dominant impression? (deserted)

What is the situation? (You are walking across the campus in early August.)

What is the order of details? (time and place)

What details of imagery support the dominant impression? (smell of flowers and cut grass rather than food and smoke and perfume; dust accumulated on white porcelain drinking fountain; sound of the wind, wildlife, and silence rather than people; crunch of dead leaves underfoot; echo of footsteps)

The cluster form may be useful. (See the Writing Process Worksheet in Appendix A.)

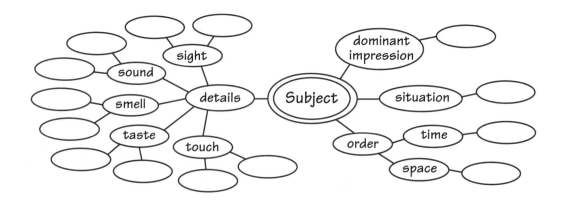

Consider giving your description a narrative framework. Include some action if it fits your purpose.

Exercise 1   **WRITING DESCRIPTIVE SENTENCES**

Improve the following sentences by supplying specific and concrete words. Use images when they serve your purposes.

Answers will vary.

Example: The animal was restless and hungry.

The gaunt lion paced about the cage and chewed hungrily on an old shoe.

1. The fans were happy. _____

2. She was in love. _____

3. Confusion surrounded him. _____

4. The traffic was congested. _____

5. The dessert impressed the diner. _____

6. The woman liked her date. _____

7. The salesman was obnoxious. _____

8. The room was cluttered. _____

9. His hair was unkempt. _____

10. The car was a mess. _____

Connecting Sources and Writing

Student Essay

One's first car usually occupies a special place in one's memory. Here, Jerry Price looks back more than twenty years, remembering nostalgically the details of a car that seems to symbolize a stage of his life.

My First—and Best—Car
Jerry Price

Personification
Metaphor
Sight

Touch
Simile

Smell

She was beautiful. The light of a full moon danced on her sleek, curved body. Her chrome wheels and bumpers shined so brightly they were almost blinding. A salesman came over and handed me the keys. I opened her door and sat in the driver's seat, which hugged my body like an expensive pair of leather gloves. Although she was a six-year-old car, the previous owner had taken excellent care of her. The interior had a slight smell of Armorall, used to preserve the seats and dashboard and make them glow.

Sound

It was love at first sight, and I knew I had to have her. After my dad arranged the deal, I drove her home for the first time. She was a beautiful car with a light-blue body and a white vinyl top. Her 350 cc engine purred like a cat when accelerated. Her three-speed automatic transmission shifted gears with ease and without hesitation.

Sight

Sight

She was a 1969 Camaro Rally Sport, the one with all the special features. The showiest feature was the special chrome detailing package. The chrome vents in front of the door and the chrome side moldings helped protect the paint and made the car shine brilliantly. Matching her vents, her three-sectioned tail brake light housing was split diagonally with chrome, a feature unique to the Rally Sport. She also had hidden headlights, which opened only when the lights were turned on. With black carpet and a black dash, the interior was immaculate. The seats were white vinyl with a black and white cloth middle. Her dash was filled only with gauges, no dummy lights.

My new car gave me many things. The most important was freedom. I was able to take out dates without begging my parents for their car. During the winter months I was able to drive up to the mountains to ski. In the summer I drove to the beach. On the weekends I could be found in my car, driving up and down Whittier Boulevard. Cruising Whittier was a great experience. All my friends would be there. We would race, talk, and meet girls. If we were unlucky, we would get a ticket from the police.

My car was not all simple enjoyment and transportation. She also gave me responsibilities. I worked as a box boy for Alpha Beta to make loan payments and buy gas. And she needed to be maintained. I had little knowledge of cars, so I went to night school and took auto shop. I learned how to repair and maintain her, and I used the school's tools to do the work. I rebuilt her engine and changed her transmission. She always ran well and never let me down. After I owned her for four years, I had to sell her to buy a truck.

Personification

Metaphor

I will never forget how she looked the first time I saw her shining in the sales lot. I'm sad to say the last time I saw her was two weeks after I'd sold her. She was sprawled in a parking lot, smashed from an accident. I wanted to buy her back and try to repair her, but she had already been sold to a junkyard for parts. I still miss her. She will be in my heart forever.

Exercise 2   **DISCUSSION AND CRITICAL THINKING**

1. Is this descriptive essay mainly subjective or objective?
   Subjective.

2. Is the third paragraph organized by space or time?
   Space.

3. Overall, is the essay organized by space or time?
   Time.

4. How are the images and figures of speech in the first paragraph different from those in the last paragraph?
   The first paragraph suggests newness: "full moon danced," "sleek, curved body," and "hugged my body." The last paragraph shows the car "sprawled in a parking lot," a casualty of a traffic accident.

5. Price refers to his car as "she" and "her" rather than "it." In your opinion, does that add to or detract from the effectiveness of the essay?
   Answers will vary.

6. Annotate the essay to show a least one example of simile, metaphor, personification, and images of sight, touch, smell, and sound.

Practicing Patterns of Description

Description, which is almost always used with other patterns, is very important and often neglected. Exercise 3 features descriptive writing that is used with a narrative account.

Exercise 3   **COMPLETING DESCRIPTIVE PATTERNS**

Fill in the blank bubbles with words from "My First—and Best—Car." In the first stage of writing a descriptive essay, this kind of structured clustering can help you recollect and organize information.

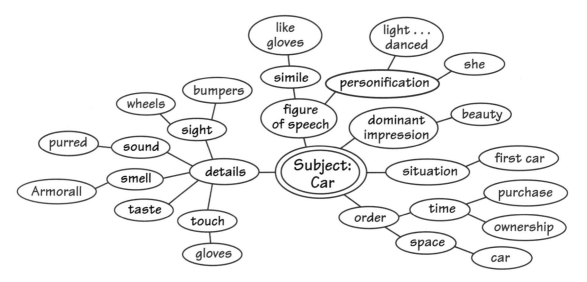

In the next stage of writing, Price used a narrative outline based on time to discuss his experience with the car. You can see how the clustering strategy provides information for development.

   I. *Sees beautiful car*
   II. *Likes it and buys it*
  III. *Enjoys the car*
  IV. *Learns responsibility from using the car*
   V. *Sells the car*
  VI. *Sad to see the car after it is wrecked.*

Student Documented Essay

This informally documented essay was written in response to the following prompt:

> In "Tuesday Morning," a chapter in *Blue Highways,* William Least Heat-Moon writes about Native Ameri-

cans who have preserved much in their culture, but have also blended their culture with that of others. Using the concept of cultural blending, write an essay of 500 to 900 words about a neighborhood, family, or home you are familiar with. Point out how your subject is similar to and different from Least Heat-Moon's subject. Consider such matters as customs, behavior, home furnishings and decorations, and appearance. ("Tuesday Morning" is also included in this chapter, pages 156–167.)

My Navajo Home in Los Angeles

Thomas Whiterock

In "Tuesday Morning," William Least Heat-Moon wrote of the Navajo and Hopi people, who lived on their reservations but selectively blended their tribal ways with outside ways. Least Heat-Moon says that "it looked as if the old categories of cowboys and Indians had merged," and that in the Hopi Cultural Center, the drawings by children contained details from their native culture and *Star Wars* (85). As a Navajo who has lived more off the reservation than on, I naturally think of how I, too, have blended the two sides of my life. The difference is that my family, especially my mother, here in Los Angeles, has surrounded me with objects to remind me of my tribal heritage. At times it is easy to take all of this family education for granted. Then a friend stops by my home to work with me on a school project, and I easily move into the role of teacher, explaining what my mother explained to me, revealing the cultural blends of my life. . . .

On a warm summer day, my friend Tung and I walk into my mother's house. It is a relief to be out of the heat and to feel the coolness of home. I immediately begin to walk across the living room to get to the stack of homework waiting for me. Out of the corner of my eye, I notice that Tung is not behind me, but is still standing in the doorway, staring toward the opposing wall. "What is that?" he asks pointing.

"That," I say, "is Navajo. Just look around, and you'll see Navajo items everywhere."

Across from where Tung stands, hangs a large painting of pottery and corn on a table top. The pottery, white and brown, is decorated with bold black lines and birds. The corn is a heap of ears, the grains colored white, yellow, maroon, brown, and black and partially wrapped in pale husks. On one side of the painting is a willow reed basket of Indian corn resting on a table. It is the same kind as that depicted in the painting. I explain that the corn is as important to our diet as rice is to his. When the white man put us on reservations to change our religion and language, he also tried to change our food. We were given corn in equal rations with wheat, which was foreign to us. We had to fight for our corn. On the other side of the painting hangs a string of long, red chili peppers. The chili was introduced to us by the Spanish and Mexicans, and today is still consumed with each meal in most Navajo families.

Next, Tung points to the ladder leaning against the wall, a crude ladder made of sections of bare wood. The rungs are held tightly in the notches with straps of leather. "Why do you have a ladder that leads nowhere?" he asks. "This, too, is Navajo," I explain. "Though there were different kinds of houses, or hogans, the most common was the square, a one-room house made of logs and adobe. These homes often had lofts for the children to sleep in, and leading up to these lofts were ladders. Even though we have no loft, the ladder is here as a relic of older times to remind us of our heritage."

Then Tung slowly walks to the corner of the room and examines a five-foot hollow cylinder of wood propped against the wall decorated by red and black Navajo rugs. This wooden object always holds the most fascination for guests, and it's something my family is accustomed to explaining. I tell him, "That is the cause of ignorant statements and stereotypes and makes Native Americans the butt of many jokes. But it also means much to my people." He moved it back and forth, listening. "Yes, there really is a rain dance," I continue. "Not like you see in cartoons or in old movies made by white men, though. That is used in a ceremony performed by the Zuni, the Hopi, and the Navajo. The dance is vital to their harvest." Tung tilts the rainstick again. As the seeds roll through the small tunnels inside, the simulated sound of rainfall makes him smile. "Better put the stick down," I joke. "That's a dangerous instrument in the hands of an amateur, unless you like flash floods."

Later I walk Tung to the door after long hours of studying. He takes another look around the room and smiles. "I like it here," he says. "It's a true home in every way, and it makes connections." I open the door. The sky has become overcast. It looks as if it just might rain after all. . . .

William Least Heat-Moon saw the other side, the Native Americans of the reservations holding onto their traditions and objects as they imported outside influences. But I am on that other side, and my mother, in her own way, helped me do some cultural blending. She set up our home like a Navajo museum—for herself but also for me. A good teacher begets a good student, and a good student will naturally become a teacher. That idea came to mind as I guided Tung through my Navajo home in Los Angeles.

Work Cited

Least Heat-Moon, William. "Tuesday Morning." *Celebrating Diversity*. Ed. Lee Brandon. Lexington, Mass.: D. C. Heath and Company, 1995. 83–88.

| **Exercise 4** | **DISCUSSION AND CRITICAL THINKING** |

1. Is the description in this essay mostly objective or subjective?
   Subjective.

2. How does the verb tense change and why does Whiterock make the change?
   The essay is framed by his references to "Tuesday Morning," which he sets off by making them mostly in the past tense as he frames the present-tense experience with his friend.

3. Is the main imagery that of sight or sound?
   Sight.

4. What is the dominant impression in this essay?
   Pride, reverence, and respect for the Navajo culture.

5. Is the order based mainly on time or space?
   Time.

6. List some words that indicate the passage of time.
   "Next," "then," "later."

7. Is the order in the fourth paragraph based mainly on time or space?
   Space.

8. List some phrases in the fourth paragraph that suggest movement through space.
   "Across from," "on one side," "on the other side."

The Grandfather

Gary Soto

Gary Soto, teacher and celebrated writer, has written poignantly about growing up near Fresno, California. Originally published in *A Summer Life* (1990), this essay is a blended objective and subjective description of Soto's grandfather in the context of relatives, trees, and rose bushes.

1   Grandfather believed a well-rooted tree was the color of money. His money he kept hidden behind portraits of sons and daughters or taped behind the calendar of an Aztec warrior. He tucked it into the sofa, his shoes and slippers, and into the tight-lipped pockets of his suits. He kept it in his soft brown wallet that was machine tooled with "MEXICO" and a *campesino* and donkey climbing a hill. He had climbed, too, out of Mexico, settled in Fresno and worked thirty years at Sun Maid Raisin, first as a packer and later, when he was old, as a watchman with a large clock on his belt.

2   After work, he sat in the backyard under the arbor, watching the water gurgle in the rose bushes that ran along the fence. A lemon tree hovered over the clothesline. Two orange trees stood near the alley. His favorite tree, the avocado, which had started in a jam jar from a seed and three toothpicks lanced in its sides, rarely bore fruit. He said it was the wind's fault, and the mayor's, who allowed office buildings so high that the haze of pollen from the countryside could never find its way into the city. He sulked about this. He said that in Mexico buildings only grew so tall. You could see the moon at night, and the stars were clear points all the way to the horizon. And wind reached all the way from the sea, which was blue and clean, unlike the oily water sloshing against a San Francisco pier.

3   During its early years, I could leap over that tree, kick my bicycling legs over the top branch and scream my fool head off because I thought for sure I was flying. I ate fruit to keep my strength up, fuzzy peaches and branch-scuffed plums cooled in the refrigerator. From the kitchen chair he brought out in the evening, Grandpa would scold, "Hijo, what's the matta with you? You gonna break it."

4   By the third year, the tree was as tall as I, its branches casting a meager shadow on the ground. I sat beneath the shade, scratching words in the hard dirt with a stick. I had learned "Nile" in summer school and a dirty word from my brother who wore granny

sunglasses. The red ants tumbled into my letters, and I buried them, knowing that they would dig themselves back into fresh air.

5   A tree was money. If a lemon cost seven cents at Hanoian's Market, then Grandfather saved fistfuls of change and more because in winter the branches of his lemon tree hung heavy yellow fruit. And winter brought oranges, juicy and large as softballs. Apricots he got by the bagfuls from a son, who himself was wise for planting young. Peaches he got from a neighbor, who worked the night shift at Sun Maid Raisin. The chile plants, which also saved him from giving up his hot, sweaty quarters, were propped up with sticks to support an abundance of red fruit.

6   But his favorite tree was the avocado because it offered hope and the promise of more years. After work, Grandpa sat in the backyard, shirtless, tired of flagging trucks loaded with crates of raisins, and sipped glasses of ice water. His yard was neat: five trees, seven rose bushes, whose fruit were the red and white flowers he floated in bowls, and a statue of St. Francis that stood in a circle of crushed rocks, arms spread out to welcome hungry sparrows.

7   After ten years, the first avocado hung on a branch, but the meat was flecked with black, an omen, Grandfather thought, a warning to keep an eye on the living. Five years later, another avocado hung on a branch, larger than the first and edible when crushed with a fork into a heated tortilla. Grandfather sprinkled it with salt and laced it with a river of chile.

8   "It's good," he said, and let me taste.

9   I took a big bite, waved a hand over my tongue, and ran for the garden hose gurgling in the rose bushes. I drank long and deep, and later ate the smile from an ice cold watermelon.

10   Birds nested in the tree, quarreling jays with liquid eyes and cool, pulsating throats. Wasps wove a horn-shaped hive one year, but we smoked them away with swords of rolled up newspapers lit with matches. By then, the tree was tall enough for me to climb to look into the neighbor's yard. But by then I was too old for that kind of thing and went about with my brother, hair slicked back and our shades dark as oil.

11   After twenty years, the tree began to bear. Although Grandfather complained about how much he lost because pollen never reached the poor part of town, because at the market he had to haggle over the price of avocados, he loved that tree. It grew, as did his family, and when he died, all his sons standing on each other's shoulders, oldest to youngest, could not reach the highest branches. The wind could move the branches, but the trunk, thicker than any waist, hugged the ground.

Exercise 5   **DISCUSSION AND CRITICAL THINKING**

1. Is Soto's purpose mainly to characterize his grandfather, the avocado tree, the family, or himself?

   Answers will vary. The title suggests the grandfather. Description focuses on the tree. Family growth parallels that of the tree. Soto is the perceptive and reverent observer and reporter.

2. How does Soto describe the avocado tree in its struggle to grow and bear fruit? Consider such matters as who plants it, what keeps it from initially being pollinated, and how it eventually produces fruit.

   It starts under difficult conditions, presumably from a seed saved by the grandfather. Then the family destroys the wasps nesting in the tree (people's problem). According to the grandfather, the high-rise buildings block the winds carrying pollen, and only in its twentieth year does it bear good fruit.

3. Why does the grandfather like the tree?

   It offers hope and the promise of more years, and it could mean money.

4. How does the grandfather change? Consider what he likes to do, what he produces, and what he could reasonably look upon with pleasure at the end of his life.

   He tends his garden, producing beauty (roses) and crops (lemons, oranges, and avocados). He relaxes in his yard and complains about the wind and the mayor. The grandfather sees his family and the tree prosper.

5. How are the family and the tree similar?

   Each grows under difficult conditions.

6. What do the trees (five) and the rose bushes (seven) represent, standing around the statue of St. Francis, arms spread "to welcome hungry sparrows"?

   As symbols, the grouping may be biblical, representing the twelve disciples. Or it may be just twelve plants and a cheap statue.

7. What gives the main order to this description—time (as the account takes place) or space (indicating directions around the yard)?

   Time.

8. What words in paragraph 2 make the description subjective?

   "Gurgle," "hovered," "lanced."

9. Why does Soto use "The Grandfather" as a title rather than "My Grandfather" or "Grandfather"? Does he suggest that this grandfather should be considered in some larger sense?

   Answers will vary. Perhaps this grandfather represented a patriarchal figure for a generation that, like the tree, struggled but then prospered.

I Was a Member of the Kung Fu Crew

Henry Han Xi Lau

Whether we like it or not, we are judged by our appearance. Some could not care less about public opinion, and they dress and groom for themselves. Most consciously make some choices in efforts to impress others. We may even dress differently for different occasions, and we dress differently for different stages of our lives. In this essay, Henry Han Xi Lau writes of the importance of clothing, grooming, and body language in his old neighborhood.

1   Chinatown is ghetto, my friends are ghetto, I am ghetto. I went away to college last year, but I still have a long strand of hair that reaches past my chin. I need it when I go back home to hang with the K.F.C.—for Kung Fu Crew, not Kentucky Fried Chicken. We all met in a Northern Shaolin kung fu class years ago. Our *si-fu** was Rocky. He told us: "In the early 1900's in China, your grand master was walking in the streets when a foreigner riding on a horse disrespected him. So then he felt the belly of the horse with his palms and left. Shortly thereafter, the horse buckled and died because our grand master had used *qi-gong*[†] to mess up the horse's internal organs." Everyone said, "Cool, I would like to do that." Rocky emphasized, "You've got to practice really hard for a long time to reach that level."

2   By the time my friends and I were in the eighth grade, we were able to do 20-plus push-ups on our knuckles and fingers. When we practiced our crescent, roundhouse and tornado kicks, we had 10-pound weights strapped to our legs. Someone once remarked, "Goddamn—that's a freaking mountain!" when he saw my thigh muscles in gym class.

3   Most Chinatown kids fall into a few general categories. There are pale-faced nerds who study all the time to get into the Ivies.[‡] There are the recent immigrants with uncombed hair and crooked teeth who sing karaoke in bars. There are the punks with highlighted hair who cut school, and the gangsters, whom everyone else avoids.

4   Then there is the K.F.C. We work hard like the nerds, but we identify with the punks. Now we are reunited, and just as in the

*Si-fu is a martial arts teacher.
[†]*Qi-gong* is the skill of attracting vital energy.
[‡]*Ivies* is slang for Ivy League universities such as Harvard.

old days we amble onto Canal Street, where we stick out above the older folks, elderly women bearing laden bags of bok choy and oranges. As an opposing crew nears us, I assess them to determine whether to grill them or not. Grilling is the fine art of staring others down and trying to emerge victorious.

5   How the hair is worn is important in determining one's order on the streets. In the 80's the dominant style was the mushroom cut, combed neatly or left wild in the front so that a person can appear menacing as he peers through his bangs. To gain an edge in grilling now, some kids have asymmetrical cuts, with long random strands sprouting in the front, sides or back. Some dye their hair blue or green, while blood red is usually reserved for gang members.

6   Only a few years ago, examination of the hair was sufficient. But now there is a second step: assessing pants. A couple of years ago, wide legs first appeared in New York City, and my friends and I switched from baggy pants. In the good old days, Merry-Go-Round in the Village sold wide legs for only $15 a pair. When Merry-Go-Round went bankrupt, Chinatown kids despaired. Wide-leg prices at other stores increased drastically as they became more popular. There are different ways of wearing wide legs. Some fold their pant legs inward and staple them at the hem. Some clip the back ends of their pants to their shoes with safety pins. Others simply cut the bottoms so that fuzzy strings hang out.

7   We grill the opposing punks. I untuck my long strand of hair so that it swings in front of my face. Nel used to have a strand, but he chewed it off one day in class by accident. Chu and Tom cut their strands off because it scared people at college. Jack has a patch of blond hair, while Tone's head is a ball of orange flame. Chi has gelled short hair, while Ken's head is a black mop. As a group, we have better hair than our rivals. But they beat us with their wide legs. In our year away at college, wide legs have gone beyond our 24-inch leg openings. Twenty-six- to 30-inch jeans are becoming the norm. If wide legs get any bigger, they will start flying up like a skirt in an updraft.

8   We have better accessories, though. Chi sports a red North Face that gives him a rugged mountain-climber look because of the jungle of straps sprouting in the back. Someone once asked Chi, "Why is the school bag so important to one's cool?" He responded, "Cuz it's the last thing others see when you walk away from them or when they turn back to look at you after you walk past them." But the other crew has female members, which augments their points. The encounter between us ends in a stalemate. But at least the K.F.C. members are in college and are not true punks.

9 In the afternoon, we decide to eat at the Chinatown McDonald's for a change instead of the Chinese bakery Maria's, our dear old hangout spot. "Mickey D's is a good sit," Nel says. I answer: "But the Whopper gots more fat and meat. It's even got more bun." Nel agrees. "True that," he says. I want the Big Mac, but I buy the two-cheeseburger meal because it has the same amount of meat but costs less.

10 We sit and talk about ghettoness again. We can never exactly articulate what being ghetto entails, but we know the spirit of it. In Chinatown toilet facilities we sometimes find footprints on the seats because F.O.B.'s (Fresh off the boats)* squat on them as they do over the holes in China. We see alternative brand names in stores like Dolo instead of Polo, and Mike instead of Nike.

11 We live by ghettoness. My friends and I walk from 80-something Street in Manhattan to the tip of the island to save a token. We gorge ourselves at Gray's Papaya because the hot dogs are 50 cents each. But one cannot be stingy all the time. We leave good tips at Chinese restaurants because our parents are waiters and waitresses, too.

12 We sit for a long time in the McDonald's, making sure that there is at least a half-inch of soda in our cups so that when the staff wants to kick us out, we can claim that we are not finished yet. Jack positions a mouse bite of cheeseburger in the center of a wrapper to support our claim.

13 After a few hours, the K.F.C. prepares to disband. I get in one of the no-license commuter vans on Canal Street that will take me to Sunset Park in Brooklyn, where my family lives now. All of my friends will leave Chinatown, for the Upper East Side and the Lower East Side, Forest Hills in Queens and Bensonhurst in Brooklyn. We live far apart, but we always come back together in Chinatown. For most of us, our homes used to be here and our world was here.

Exercise 6   **DISCUSSION AND CRITICAL THINKING**

1. What is the dominant impression of the "ghettoness" displayed by the author and his friends? In other words, how do they want others in their old neighborhood to see them?
    As menacing.

2. Underline the sight imagery in paragraphs 5, 7, and 8.

Fresh off the boats are new immigrants to America.

3. What descriptive images pertaining to grooming characterize their ghettoness?
   Unconventional hair styles.

4. What descriptive images of clothing characterize their ghettoness?
   Wide-legged pants. Chi wears a North Face school bag.

5. What descriptive images of body language characterize their ghettoness?
   They "grill," or try to stare down rival groups. The staring is accompanied by a ritualized flaunting of hair styles. Overall, the behavior is quite similar to that of feral animals in protecting territory and making sexual claims. Male red-winged blackbirds defend their nesting zones in much the same fashion.

6. How different is K.F.C. behavior from that of groups with which you are familiar?
   Answers will vary.

7. Do you see K.F.C. members as ghetto people?
   Answers will vary.

8. What do you predict as the future for the K.F.C. members?
   Answers will vary.

The Discus Thrower

Richard Selzer

We often think of pivotal experiences as stages in growing up: when we move from childhood to adulthood, when we gain strength and substance as adults, when we learn about ourselves from others. But what about the experience of death? Perhaps we think less about it because it is too painful. And, of course, our own death is something we cannot write about personally. Dr. Richard Selzer writes poignantly about the world of medicine and the ways in which people deal with suffering and death. Selzer titles this essay "The Discus Thrower." The title is also used for a famous ancient Greek sculpture in which an idealized muscular athlete is poised just before beginning his forward movement to throw the discus. Is there a connection between the two? If so, is it one of mockery or solemn admiration?

1   I spy on my patients. Ought not a doctor to observe his patients by any means and from any stance, that he might the more fully assemble evidence? So I stand in the doorways of hospital rooms and gaze. Oh, it is not all that furtive an act. Those in bed need only look up to discover me. But they never do.

2   From the doorway of Room 542 the man in the bed seems deeply tanned. Blue eyes and close-cropped white hair give him the appearance of vigor and good health. But I know that his skin is not brown from the sun. It is rusted, rather, in the last stage of containing the vile repose within. And the blue eyes are frosted, looking inward like the windows of a snowbound cottage. This man is blind. This man is also legless—the right leg missing from midthigh down, the left from just below the knee. It gives him the look of a bonsai, roots and branches pruned into the dwarfed facsimile of a great tree.

3   Propped on pillows, he cups his right thigh in both hands. Now and then he shakes his head as though acknowledging the intensity of his suffering. In all of this he makes no sound. Is he mute as well as blind?

4   The room in which he dwells is empty of all possessions—no get-well cards, small, private caches of food, day-old flowers, slippers, all the usual kick-shaws of the sickroom. There is only the bed, a chair, a nightstand, and a tray on wheels that can be swung across his lap for meals.

5   "What time is it?" he asks.

6   "Three o'clock."

7   "Morning or afternoon?"

8   "Afternoon."

9   He is silent. There is nothing else he wants to know.

10   "How are you?" I say.

11   "Who is it?" he asks.

12   "It's the doctor. How do you feel?"

13   He does not answer right away.

14   "Feel?" he says.

15   "I hope you feel better," I say.

16   I press the button at the side of the bed.

17   "Down you go," I say.

18   "Yes, down," he says.

19   He falls back upon the bed awkwardly. His stumps, unweighted by legs and feet, rise in the air, presenting themselves. I unwrap the bandages from the stumps, and begin to cut away the black scabs and dead, glazed fat with scissors and forceps. A shard of white bone comes loose. I pick it away. I wash the wounds with disinfectant and redress the stumps. All this while, he does not speak. What is he thinking behind those lids that do not blink? Is he remembering a time when he was whole? Does he dream of feet? Of when his body was not a rotting log?

20   He lies solid and inert. In spite of everything, he remains impressive, as though he were a sailor standing athwart a slanting deck.

21   "Anything more I can do for you?" I ask.

22   For a long moment he is silent.

23   "Yes," he says at last and without the least irony. "You can bring me a pair of shoes."

24   In the corridor, the head nurse is waiting for me.

25   "We have to do something about him," she says. "Every morning he orders scrambled eggs for breakfast, and, instead of eating them, he picks up the plate and throws it against the wall."

26   "Throws his plate?"

27   "Nasty. That's what he is. No wonder his family doesn't come to visit. They probably can't stand him any more than we can."

28   She is waiting for me to do something.

29   "Well?"

30   "We'll see," I say.

31   The next morning I am waiting in the corridor when the kitchen delivers his breakfast. I watch the aide place the tray on the stand and swing it across his lap. She presses the button to raise the head of the bed. Then she leaves.

32   In time the man reaches to find the rim of the tray, then on to find the dome of the covered dish. He lifts off the cover and places it on the stand. He fingers across the plate until he probes the eggs. He lifts the plate in both hands, sets it on the palm of his right hand, centers it, balances it. He hefts it up and down slightly, getting the feel of it. Abruptly, he draws back his right arm as far as he can.

33   There is the crack of the plate breaking against the wall at the foot of his bed and the small wet sound of the scrambled eggs dropping to the floor.

34   And then he laughs. It is a sound you have never heard. It is something new under the sun. It could cure cancer.

35   Out in the corridor, the eyes of the head nurse narrow.

36   "Laughed, did he?"

37   She writes something down on her clipboard.

38   A second aide arrives, brings a second breakfast tray, puts it on the nightstand, out of his reach. She looks over at me shaking her head and making her mouth go. I see that we are to be accomplices.

39   "I've got to feed you," she says to the man.

40   "Oh, no you don't," the man says.

41   "Oh, yes I do," the aide says, "after the way you just did. Nurse says so."

42   "Get me my shoes," the man says.

43   "Here's oatmeal," the aide says. "Open." And she touches the spoon to his lower lip.

44   "I ordered scrambled eggs," says the man.

45   "That's right," the aide says.

46   I step forward.

47   "Is there anything I can do?" I say.

48   "Who are you?" the man asks.

49   In the evening I go once more to that ward to make my rounds. The head nurse reports to me that Room 542 is deceased. She has discovered this quite by accident, she says. No, there had been no sound. Nothing. It's a blessing, she says.

50   I go into his room, a spy looking for secrets. He is still there in his bed. His face is relaxed, grave, dignified. After a while, I turn to leave. My gaze sweeps the wall at the foot of the bed, and I see the place where it has been repeatedly washed, where the wall looks very clean and very white.

Exercise 7   **VOCABULARY HIGHLIGHTS**

Write a short definition of each word as it is used in the essay. (Paragraph numbers are given in parentheses.) Be prepared to use the words in your own sentences.

furtive (1)   athwart (20)

facsimile (2)   hefts (32)

shard (19)

Exercise 8   **CRITICAL THINKING AND DISCUSSION**

1. Reread paragraphs 2 and 19 and underline the most striking images.

2. What is the dominant impression of the man's appearance?
   Blind amputee near death.

3. What is the dominant impression of the man's behavior?
   Incorrigibly defiant.

4. Use one word to characterize the feelings of these individuals as they observe the patient:
   nurse: irritated
   aides: detached   Answers will vary.
   doctor: empathetic

5. To what extent does Selzer's description of the patient depend on narration?

Without action the patient would be only a subject of pity.

6. To what extent does Selzer's narration depend on description?

The patient's behavior without this moving description of him would be merely childlike behavior.

7. Why is the author so fascinated with the patient?

Apparently because the patient has so little left of the senses, pleasures, and experiences that are commonly associated with being alive and human; yet, he struggles and following Dylan Thomas's admonition, will "not go gently into that good night."

8. Are the implications of the title comic or heroic?

The "Discus Thrower," a piece of sculpture from ancient Greece, represents the truly heroic. The discus thrower in art is an idealized man, everything that a person can be physically under ideal conditions. The discus thrower in the hospital is heroic in the sense that if one takes into account his limitations, one must agree that he finds his own way to express himself, to defy all, and to declare himself an individual.

Tuesday Morning

William Least Heat-Moon

William Trogdon, of English-Irish-Osage ancestry, writes under the pen name William Least Heat-Moon. Traveling around the country in the old van he named Ghost Dancing, he sought out locales on secondary highways marked in blue on road maps, and a collection of his subsequent descriptions of these adventures became the best-selling book *Blue Highways*. Here he travels across two Indian reservations as history, geography, anthropology, and whimsy merge.

1   Tuesday morning: the country east of Heber was a desert of sagebrush and globe-shaped junipers and shallow washes with signs warning of flash floods. I turned north at Snowflake, founded by Erastus Snow and Bill Flake, and headed toward the twenty-five thousand square miles of Navajo reservation (nearly equal to West Virginia) which occupies most of the northeastern corner of Arizona. The scrub growth disappeared entirely and only the distant outlines of red rock mesas interrupted the emptiness. But for the highway, the land was featureless.

2   Holbrook used to be a tough town where boys from the Hash Knife cattle outfit cut loose. Now, astride I-44 (once route 66), Holbrook was a tourist stop for women with Instamatics* and

---

*An Instamatic is a type of camera.

men with metal detectors; no longer was the big business cattle, but rather rocks and gems.

3   North of the interstate, I entered the reserve. Although the area has been part of the Navajo homeland for five hundred years, settlers of a century before, led by Kit Carson,* drove the Navajo out of Arizona in retribution for their raids against whites and other Indians alike. A few years later, survivors of the infamous "Long Walk"† returned to take up their land again. Now the Navajo possess the largest reservation in the United States and the one hundred fifty thousand descendants of the seven thousand survivors comprise far and away the largest tribe. Their reservation is the only one in the country to get bigger—five times bigger—after it was first set aside; their holdings increased largely because white men had believed Navajo land worthless. But in fact, the reservation contains coal, oil, gas, uranium, helium, and timber; these resources may explain why Navajos did not win total control over their land until 1972.

4   Liquor bottles, beercans, an occasional stripped car littered the unfenced roadside. Far off the highway, against the mesa bottoms, stood small concrete-block or frame houses, each with a television antenna, pickup, privy, and ceremonial hogan of stone, adobe, and cedar. Always the hogan doors faced east.

5   In a classic scene, a boy on a pinto pony herded a flock of sheep and goats—descendants of the Spanish breed—across the highway. A few miles later, a man wearing a straw Stetson and pegleg Levi's guided up a draw a pair of horses tied together at the neck in the Indian manner. With the white man giving up on the economics of cowpunching, it looked as if the old categories of cowboys and Indians had merged; whoever the last true cowboy in America turns out to be, he's likely to be an Indian.

6   At the center of the reservation lay Hopi territory, a large rectangle with boundaries the tribes cannot agree on because part of the increase of Navajo land has come at the expense of the Hopis. A forbidding sign in Latinate English:

> YOU ARE ENTERING THE EXCLUSIVE
> HOPI RESERVATION AREA. YOUR
> ENTRANCE CONSTITUTES CONSENT
> TO THE JURISDICTION OF THE HOPI
> TRIBE AND ITS COURTS.

*Kit Carson was a U.S. frontiersman, scout, and Indian agent.
†The Long Walk was part of the forced removal of American Indians to reservations.

7   Although the Hopi have lived here far longer than any other surviving people and consider their mile-high spread of rock and sand, wind and sun, the center of the universe, they are now, by Anglo decree, surrounded by their old enemies, the Navajo, a people they see as latecomers. In 1880, Hopis held two and one half million acres; today it has decreased to about a half million.

8   Holding on to their land has been a long struggle for the Hopi. Yet for a tribe whose name means "well behaved," for Indians without war dances, for a group whose first defense against the conquistadors was sprinkled lines of sacred cornmeal, for a people who protested priestly corruption (consorting with Hopi women and whipping men) by quietly pitching a few padres over the cliffs, Hopis have done well. But recently they have fought Navajo expansion in federal courts, and a strange case it is: those who settled first seeking judgment from those who came later through laws of those who arrived last.

9   Because the Navajo prefer widely dispersed clusters of clans to village life, I'd seen nothing resembling a hamlet for seventy-five miles. But Hopi Polacca almost looks like a Western town in spite of Indian ways here and there: next to a floral-print bedsheet on a clothesline hung a coyote skin, and beside box houses were adobe bread ovens shaped like skep* beehives. The Navajo held to his hogan, the Hopi his oven. Those things persisted.

10   Like bony fingers, three mesas reached down from larger Black Mesa into the middle of Hopi land; not long ago, the only way onto these mesas was by handholds in the steep rock heights. From the tops, the Hopi look out upon a thousand square miles. At the heart of the reservation, topographically and culturally, was Second Mesa. Traditionally, Hopis, as do the eagles they hold sacred, prefer to live on precipices; so it was not far from the edge of Second Mesa that they built the Hopi Cultural Center. In the gallery were drawings of mythic figures by Hopi children who fused centuries and cultures with grotesque Mudhead Kachinas wearing large terra-cotta masks and jack-o-lantern smiles, dancing atop spaceships with Darth Vader and Artoo Deetoo.*

11   At the Center, I ate *nokquivi,* a good hominy stew with baked chile peppers, but I had no luck in striking up a conversation. I drove on toward the western edge of the mesa. Not far from the tribal garage (TRIBAL VEHICLES ONLY) stood small sandstone houses, their slabs precisely cut and fitted as if by ancient Aztecs, a people related to the Hopi. The solid houses blended with the tawny land

*Skep refers to straw.
*Darth Vader and Artoo Deetoo are characters in the film *Star Wars.*

so well they appeared part of the living rock. All were empty. The residents had moved to prefabs and double-wides.

12   I couldn't see how anyone could survive a year in this severe land, yet Hopis, like other desert life, are patient and clever and not at all desperate; they have lasted here for ten centuries by using tiny terraced plots that catch spring rain and produce a desert-hardy species of blue corn, as well as squash, onions, beans, peppers, melons, apricots, peaches. The bristlecone pine of American Indians, Hopis live where almost nothing else will, thriving long in adverse conditions: poor soil, drought, temperature extremes, high winds. Those give life to the bristlecone and the Hopi.

13   Clinging to the southern lip of Third Mesa was ancient Oraibi, most probably the oldest continuously occupied village in the United States. Somehow the stone and adobe have been able to hang on to the precipitous edge since the twelfth century. More than eight hundred Hopis lived at Oraibi in 1901—now only a few. All across the reservation I'd seen no more than a dozen people, and on the dusty streets of the old town I saw just one bent woman struggling against the wind. But somewhere there must have been more.

14   To this strangest of American villages the Franciscan Father, Tomás Garces, came in 1776 from Tucson with gifts and "true religion." Hopis permitted him to stay at Oraibi, looking then as now if you excluded an occasional television antenna, but they refused his gifts and god, and, on the fourth day of July, sent him off disheartened. To this time, no other North American tribe has held closer to its own religion and culture. Although the isolated Hopi had no knowledge of the importance of religious freedom to the new nation surrounding them, several generations successfully ignored "the code of religious offenses"—laws designed by the Bureau of Indian Affairs to destroy the old rituals and way of life—until greater bureaucratic tolerance came when Herbert Hoover* appointed two Quakers to direct the BIA.

15   A tribal squadcar checked my speed at Hotevilla, where the highway started a long descent off the mesa. The wind was getting up, and tumbleweed bounded across the road, and sand hummed against the Ghost. West, east, north, south—to each a different weather: sandstorm, sun, rain, and bluish snow on the San Francisco Peaks, that home of the Kachinas who are the spiritual forces of Hopi life.

*Herbert Hoover was president of the United States from 1929 to 1933.

16   Tuba City, founded by Mormon missionaries as an agency and named after a Hopi chieftain although now mostly a Navajo town, caught the sandstorm full face. As I filled the gas tank, I tried to stay behind the van, but gritty gusts whipped around the corners and stung me and forced my eyes shut. School was just out, and children, shirts pulled over their heads, ran for the trading post, where old Navajo men who had been sitting outside took cover as the sand changed the air to matter. I ducked in too. The place was like an A&P, TG&Y,* and craft center.

17   In viridescent velveteen blouses and violescent nineteenth-century skirts, Navajo women of ample body, each laden with silver and turquoise bracelets, necklaces, and rings—not the trading post variety but heavy bands gleaming under the patina of long wear—reeled off yards of fabric. The children, like schoolkids anywhere, milled around the candy; they spoke only English. But the old men, now standing at the plate glass windows and looking into the brown wind, popped and puffed out the ancient words. I've read that Navajo, a language related to that of the Indians of Alaska and northwest Canada, has no curse words unless you consider "coyote" cursing. By comparison with other native tongues, it's remarkably free of English and Spanish; a Navajo mechanic, for example, has more than two hundred purely Navajo terms to describe automobile parts. And it might be Navajo that will greet the first extraterrestrial ears to hear from planet Earth: on board each *Voyager* spacecraft traveling toward the edge of the solar system and beyond is a gold-plated, long-playing record: following an aria from Mozart's *Magic Flute* and Chuck Berry's "Johnny B. Goode," is a Navajo night chant, music the conquistadors heard.

18   Intimated by my ignorance of Navajo and by fear of the contempt that full-bloods often show lesser bloods, I again failed to stir a conversation. After the storm blew on east, I followed the old men back outside, where they squatted to watch the day take up the weather of an hour earlier. To one with a great round head like an earthen pot, I said, "Is the storm finished now?" He looked at me, then slowly turned his head, while the others examined before them things in the air invisible to me.

19   I took a highway down the mesa into a valley of the Painted Desert, where wind had textured big drifts of orange sand into rills, U.S. 89 ran north along the Echo Cliffs. Goats grazed in stubble by the roadsides, and to the west a horseman moved his sheep. Hogans here stood alone; they were not ceremonial lodges but homes. For miles at the highway edges sat little cardboard

*A&P is a grocery store; TG&Y is a variety store, also called a "five and dime."

and scrapwood ramadas, each with a windblasted sign advertising jewelry and cedar beads. In another era, white men came in wagons to trade beads to Indians; now they came in stationwagons and bought beads. History may repeat, but sometimes things get turned around in the process.

Exercise 9　　**CRITICAL THINKING AND DISCUSSION**

1. Why must William Least Heat-Moon, himself a Native American, write about these reservations as an outsider?

   He is an Osage, a member of a different tribe.

2. What does he say about the role of cowboys and Indians in paragraph 5?

   He says that the Indians are the true cowboys now, a role reversal.

3. What specific items from nontraditional Native American culture are mentioned in paragraphs 4 and 5?

   "Liquor bottles," "beer cans," "stripped cars," "concrete-block or frame houses," "television antenna, pickup," "Stetson," "Levi's."

4. How do the cultures merge in paragraph 10?

   The children combine designs from contemporary media ("Darth Vader and Artoo Deetoo") with traditional Kachina art.

5. In what way are the Hopis the "bristlecone pines" of American Indians (paragraph 12)?

   They endure over long periods of time under harsh conditions.

6. What types of images (sight, sound, touch, taste, smell) are used in paragraphs 16 and 17?

   Touch—"gritty"; sight—"sand changed the air to matter," "Navajo women of ample body"; sound—"popped . . . out the ancient words."

7. What role reversal is mentioned in the last paragraph?

   The Indians now sell beads to the whites.

✎ Topics for Writing Description

Writing Process Worksheet

You will find a Writing Process Worksheet in Appendix A, page 531. It can be photocopied and enlarged, filled in, and submitted with each assignment if your instructor directs you to do so.

Source-Based Topics

Each essay developed from these suggested source-based topics should include at least one reference to the reading selection by the author's name and the title. Quotations should be enclosed in quotation marks. Follow your instructor's directions in documenting the ideas you borrow. Whether you use informal or formal documentation, the form is not complicated, and you will soon learn to use it for these essays without

checking each time. See pages 77 and 78 for a discussion of MLA style and informal documentation.

Underlining and annotating reading selections will help you in finding support material. In prewriting brief essays, consider marking your outline to indicate where you will use quotations or other borrowed ideas. If the quotations or reworded statements are short and few, you could even insert them inside parentheses or circles in your outline; if you do, also include the author's last name and the page number. A sound system, consistently used, will save you time and ensure technically strong papers.

"My First—and Best—Car"

1. Using this essay as a model, describe your first car or your first bike.

"My Navajo Home in Los Angeles"

2. Write about your own home, discussing art, pictures, furniture, and other items that show the cultural diversity of your household.

3. If you know an interracial family, write a descriptive essay to show how more than one culture is represented in the customs and home furnishings of that family.

"The Grandfather"

4. Often a person can be described and defined by the details of his or her surroundings, such as the items the person has selected for the yard, the house, the work area, or the interior of an automobile. For the grandfather, it was the yard, mainly the avocado tree; the plant matured as he grew old and one learns about him as one learns about the tree. Consider using that concept—one item (car, plant, collection, wardrobe, equipment) in relation to one person you know well.

"I Was a Member of the Kung Fu Crew"

5. Write about a group of which you have been a member or a group with which you are familiar. Describe how their clothing, grooming, and behavior have been chosen for the purpose of group identity. Explain how your group is different from the K.F.C.

"The Discus Thrower"

6. Assume the person of the nurse and describe the patient in the same narrative framework. Include details about the patient's medical condition, his appearance, and his behavior. Pretend that you, as the nurse, just happened to read the doctor's account and now want to explain from the perspective of somebody who had to clean up the patient's messes.

7. Write a descriptive narrative about someone you know or have known who suffered greatly but struggled to express himself or herself. Point out how your subject is different from and similar to the patient in Selzer's essay.

"Tuesday Morning"

8. Write a descriptive narrative about a drive through an area you are familiar with. Use cultural blending as your dominant impression and discuss values and customs that are related to the details of your description. Use Least Heat-Moon's essay as a model.

Career-Related Topics

9. Describe a well-furnished, well-functioning office or other work area. Be specific.

10. Describe a computer-related product; give special attention to the dominant trait that gives the product its reputation.

11. Describe a person groomed and attired for a particular job or interview. Provide details pertaining to the person as well as the place or situation. Describe yourself from a detached point of view if you like.

General Topics

Objective Description

Give your topic some kind of framework or purpose beyond simply writing a description. As you develop your purpose, consider the knowledge and attitudes of your readers. You might be describing a lung for a biology instructor, a geode for a geology instructor, a painting for an art instructor, or a comet for an astronomy instructor. Or maybe you could pose as the seller of an object, such as a desk, a table, or a bicycle. Describe one of the following topics:

12. A simple object, such as a pencil, cup, sock, dollar bill, coin, ring, or notebook.

13. A human organ, such as a heart, liver, lung, or kidney.

14. A visible part of your body, such as a toe, finger, ear, nose, or eye.

15. A construction, such as a room, desk, chair, commode, or table.

16. A mechanism, such as a bicycle, tricycle, wagon, car, motorcycle, can opener, or stapler.

Subjective Description

The following topics also should be developed with a purpose other than merely writing a description. Your intent can be as simple as giving a subjective reaction to your topic. However, unless you are dealing with a topic you can present reflectively or a topic as interesting in itself as the one in "On the Ball" (p. 133), you will usually need some kind of situation. The narrative framework (something happening) is especially useful in providing order and vitality to writing. Here are three possibilities for you to consider:

17. Personalize a trip to a supermarket, a stadium, an airport, an unusual house, a mall, the beach, a court, a church, a club, a business, the library, or the police station. Describe a simple conflict in one of those places while emphasizing descriptive details.

18. Pick a high point in any event and describe the most important few seconds. Think how a scene can be captured by a video camera and then give focus by applying the dominant impression principle, using relevant images of sight, sound, taste, touch, and smell. The event might be a ball game, a graduation ceremony, a wedding ceremony, a funeral, a dance, a concert, a family gathering, a class meeting, a rally, a riot, a robbery, a fight, a proposal, or a meal. Focus on subject material that you can cover effectively in the passage you write.

19. Pick a moment when you were angry, sad, happy, confused, lost, rattled, afraid, courageous, meek, depressed, or elated. Describe how the total context of the situation contributed to your feeling.

Writer's Guidelines: Description

1. In objective description, use direct, practical language appealing mainly to the sense of sight.

2. In subjective description, appeal to the reader's feelings, especially through the use of figurative language and through images of sight, sound, smell, taste, and touch.

3. Use concrete, specific words if appropriate.

4. Apply these questions to your writing:

   • What is the dominant impression I am trying to convey?

   • What details support the dominant impression?

   • What is the order of the details?

   • What is the point of view? Is it first or third person? Involved or objective?

5. Consider giving the description a narrative framework. Include some action.

Exemplification: Writing with Examples

THE QUIGMANS by Buddy Hickerson

"So what do you have that's fresh?"

Surveying Exposition

ith this chapter on exemplification, we turn to *exposition,* a form of writing whose main purpose is to explain. This and the following six chapters will explore these questions:

Exemplification	Can you give me an example or examples of what you mean?
Analysis by Division	How do the parts work together?
Classification	What types of things are these?
Process Analysis	How do I do it? How is it done?
Comparison and Contrast	How are these similar and dissimilar?
Cause and Effect	What is the reason for this? What is the outcome?
Definition	What does this term mean?

In most informative writing, these various methods of organizing and developing thought are used in combination, with one method dominating according to the writer's purpose for explaining. The other forms of discourse can be used in combination with these. You have already learned that narration and description are frequently used for expository purposes. In Chapter 14 you will see how persuasive and expository writing are often blended, becoming interdependent.

Writing Essays of Exemplification

Exemplification means using examples to explain, convince, or amuse. Lending interest and information to writing, exemplification is one of the most common and effective ways of developing ideas. Examples may be developed in a sentence or more, or they may be only phrases or even single words, as in the following sentence: "Children like packaged breakfast foods, such as *Wheaties, Cheerios,* and *Rice Krispies."*

Characteristics of Good Examples

As supporting information, the best examples are specific, vivid, and representative. These three qualities are closely linked; collectively, they must support the topic sentence of a paragraph and the thesis of an essay.

You use examples to inform or convince your reader. Of course, an example by itself does not necessarily prove anything. We know that examples can be found on either side of an argument, even at the extreme edges. Therefore, in addition to providing specific examples so that your reader can follow you precisely and vivid ones so that your reader will be interested, you should choose examples that are representative. Representative examples are examples that your reader can consider, accept as appropriate, and even match with examples of his or her own. If you are writing about cheating and you give one specific, vivid, and representative example, your reader should be able to say, "That's exactly what happens. I can imagine just how the incident occurred, and I could give some examples that are similar."

Techniques for Finding Examples: Listing and Clustering

Writing a good essay of exemplification begins, as always, with prewriting. The techniques you use will depend on what you are writing about. If you were writing about cheating at school, you might work effectively with a list, perhaps including a few insights into your topic if you have not already formulated your controlling statement. The following is one such list compiled by student Lara Olivas. This is her controlling statement: Cheating students often put themselves under more stress than honest students. She has circled items she thinks she can use.

Student Cheating

When I copied homework

Looking at a friend's test answers

A student with hand signals

Jake and his electronic system

Time for planned cheating

Those who got caught

(A person who bought a research paper)

Jess, who copied from me

The Internet "Cheaters" source

The two students who exchanged identities

(More work than it's worth)

(More stress than it's worth)

The teacher's assistant and his friends

(The girl from the biology class)

If you are pretty well settled on your subject and you expect to use several different kinds of examples, clustering may work very well for you. Student Garabed Yegavian first used clustering to explore and then transferred much of his information to an outline. Yegavian's cluster is shown on page 168.

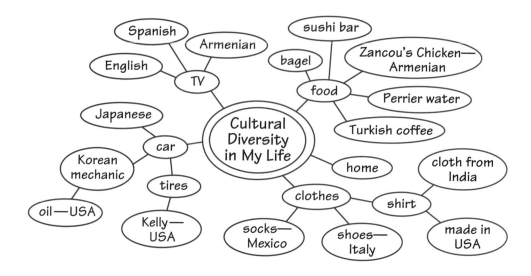

Number and Order of Examples

After you have explored your topic and collected information, you must decide whether to use only one example with a detailed explanation, a few examples with a bit less information, or a cluster of examples. A well-stated topic sentence or thesis will guide you in making this decision. When you are writing about a personal topic, you will probably have far more examples than you can use.

If your example is an incident or a series of incidents, you will probably use time order, reinforcing that arrangement with terms such as *next, then, soon, later, last,* and *finally.* If your examples exist in space (maybe in different parts of a room), then you would use space references (*up, down, left, right, east, west, north,* and *south*). Arranging examples by emphasis means going from the most important example to the least important or from the least to the most important.

Connecting Sources and Writing

Student Essay

April McClure became a full-time college student after she was paroled from the California Institution for Women near Chino, California. As she examined a list of prompts for her college writing assignment, one caught her eye:

> Write about an article of clothing, an accessory, or an expression of body art that you have seen change in acceptance or popularity from one time to another or from one place to another. Use specific examples.

Prison Tattoos

April McClure

Imagine my surprise when I was paroled and discovered that, in the free world, tattoos were cool! Of course, I had watched television and seen a few movies. I knew NBA players wore tattoos. I knew rock stars flaunted them. But I did not know the extent to which even the goody-two-shoes were getting inked up. My God, I was in style. And I had come from a place where tattoos were just like articles of clothing, except we could not take them off so easily.

> The upshot of it all is that now when people find out I have done time, they look at my butterfly and bird illustrations and ask how tattooing fits in with prison life.

Example

For one thing, tattooing is a trade on the yard. A person with a bit of talent in basic art finds clients waiting. All that person needs is a tattoo gun, some ink, and a pattern book. An electric tattoo gun can be made out of a motor from an electric shaver, a barrel from a ball point pen, a spoon, a guitar cord, and some tape. My friend Frisco is the best in the business. She made a gun, got some ditto masters for designs, and burned black dominos and styrofoam for ink. In two years she became the main tattooist on the yard.

Example

The kinds of tattoos convicts get are as varied as are the convicts, which is quite varied. Some want humor. I knew this woman named Dawson who had fleas tattooed along her hairline. They looked real. She also had "sweet" and "sour" over her breasts, and a little man with a lawnmower headed down her stomach. Then an inmate called Sunshine had a list of men's names tattooed on her arm, seven at last count. All but the last one was crossed out. She said he was about ready to go; then she would cross his name off and find another guy.

Example

Many tattoos are about love—family, boyfriend, or girlfriend. They're likely to come with hearts or flowers. One inmate I knew named Paula paid Frisco to tattoo a heart with "I love you, Maria" inside it. Then a guard saw the tattoo when it was half finished, and he wrote her up. She was told that if the tattoo was finished, she would get extra time. For two years she carried around the image of a heart with "I lo" inside. Her prison nickname became *Ilo,* and it still was when I left.

Example

Some prison women get religion. Then they want to get rid of devil, monster, and dragon tattoos. A woman named Shirley got born again and had a blood-dripping dagger on her arm covered up with Our Lady of Guadalupe. The funny thing was that there was a tiger under Our Lady's feet. Shirley liked to play the piano, and when she did, her muscles rippled and Our Lady seemed to be dancing on the tiger's back.

For every woman who sincerely gets religion, several make connections with the prison crime scene. <u>Their tattoos are likely to be about dope, gangs, and rebellion.</u> Of course, it is stupid for a person who is going to break the law to get any tattoo, because tattoos are identifiable marks and, therefore, useful to all law enforcement.

Example

Once a convict named Ruby Red talked her way out of the San Bernardino County Jail and escaped. Soon she was caught after someone recognized her by the pistol tattooed on her ankle.

<u>I am glad some people in the free world like tattoos.</u> That makes it easier for folks like me to walk the streets. But still in the general public, tattoos are a liability. Tattooed people may get some favorable glances, but mainly, from what I can see, they still get glares and stares, and they lose out on a lot of good jobs. Pinto, my last

Example

roommate, is back there in prison with tattoos all over her arms. When she returned last time, she told me her mother had made her wear long-sleeved shirts around the house. What her mother does not know is that her daughter now has tattoos on her hands. I guess Pinto will have to wear gloves.

Exercise 1   DISCUSSION AND CRITICAL THINKING

1. Circle the thesis.

2. Underline topic sentences.

3. Identify each specific example by writing the word *example* in the margin beside each one.

Practicing Patterns of Exemplification

The simple patterns in Exercise 2, based on "Prison Tattoos," will help you see the relationship between purpose and example(s).

Exercise 2   COMPLETING PATTERNS OF EXEMPLIFICATION

Clustering is a helpful strategy for developing ideas by exemplification. Fill in the empty bubbles.

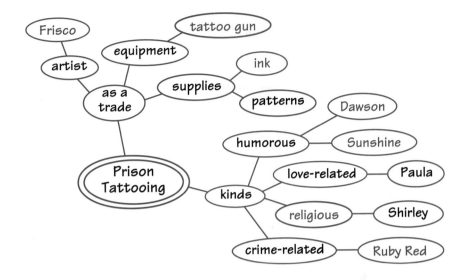

Clustering in Stage One of your writing will help you recall examples and decide on headings for your outline. You will probably cluster more examples than you will need in your final essay. Fill in the blanks in this outline. If necessary, refer back to "Prison Tattoos."

Thesis: When people discover that I have done time, they ask me about tattooing and prison life.

I. Tattooing as a trade in prison

    A. Necessary equipment and supplies

        1. Tattoo gun

        2. Ink

        3. Pattern book

    B. Frisco, an example of a prison tattoist

II. Kinds of prison tattoos

    A. Humorous

        1. Dawson's tattoos

        2. Sunshine's tattoos

    B. Love tattoos, with example

    C. Religious tattoos, with example

    D. Crime-related tattoos, with example

Student Documented Essay

Jason Alford considered a list of subjects for his essay with information from one or more sources. The idea of apathy appealed to him, and then his instructor suggested that he read a well-known essay titled "Why Don't We Complain?" by William F. Buckley, Jr.

After photocopying the essay, he underlined and annotated it; then he reflected on Buckley's ideas. He was surprised to discover that one of the reasons people do not complain more was not discussed by Buckley. He had his topic: He would summarize Buckley's essay and add to its insights, with examples from his own experience.

Biting My Tongue—Sometimes

Jason Alford

Complainers, as I use the word, are not whiners, wailers, or whimperers—people who harp about weather, sore feet, rock music, and other people's tattoos. They are people who do not like what is happening; they are concerned with things they think should be changed, usually of a personal nature. Unlike whining, complaining can be a good thing. But, as William Buckley, Jr., points out in his essay "Why Don't We Complain?", we all too frequently don't complain. He has some good explanations for our hesitancy, but I think he misses one of the main reasons.

From his experience, Buckley offers several examples of situations worthy of complaint. Once he was on a train that was 85 degrees in the passenger car; no one complained about the heat. He was in the movie theater and the picture was out of focus; no one complained. He was served his milk late after having asked for it repeatedly in the restaurant; he did not complain. He was on the airplane and an attendant was not responsive to his needs; he did not complain (62–64). They did not complain because they thought someone else would, because they were apathetic, because they were shy, because they did not want to make a scene. But Buckley overlooks one reason for not complaining: possible retaliation.

Retaliation can take two forms in school: open and silent. We all know the danger of complaining about a bully. My brother was bullied on campus in junior high school. When my parents learned about it, they went to the principal. The bullying stopped on campus, but it was taken off campus and became worse, even after my parents talked to the bullies' parents. Although one has to complain in that situation, retaliation may be the only result if one is dealing with irrational people, or the complaint is not handled in just the right way.

Example

Example

<u>The silent retaliation is worse.</u> In elementary school all my teachers but one were good. She was overbearing and impatient, and she brought religion into every subject with values. My parents complained to her, then to the principal. Although I had done well in other classes, I did not get picked for awards in her class, I was not tested for the advanced program, although others with similar qualifications were. (I was tested the next year and was accepted.) Years later a law was passed that parents could review the cumulative files kept by teachers. Out of curiosity, my parents reviewed mine and found that the teacher had inserted a number of negative comments about both me and my interfering parents. Those were comments that were available to all my teachers for the next nine years. Some parents, having decided that one teacher would not spoil their child's education, would not have complained.

Example

<u>Complainers do not get written up in restaurants, but they may get zapped in other ways, ways that are also silent.</u> While I was still in high school, I worked as a busboy in a restaurant. I remember that it was not uncommon for a table server to punish a complainer by substituting regular coffee for decaffeinated, which would make a grouchy customer even grouchier, but only after he or she left the building. Everyone has heard about servers or cooks spitting in the

Example

food. I saw it happen only once. It is more likely that a server will be "slow" in delivering food, the check, or change to a complainer. Now, most of these complainers were well justified in their grievances, but some were complaining to the wrong people, in the wrong way, or at the wrong time. Mostly, if retaliation occurred, it was in response to the way they complained. But a lot of the complainers got punished. Not all of them knew just how.

Example

<u>The same thing can happen to people living in apartment buildings.</u> There are so many things to complain about: the heavy feet above, the loud music, the loud talking, the pets, the kids, the trash, the unruly pool parties, the parking, and a few more. If one needs to complain, complaints should be phrased with care. I recall one instance in an apartment building when a tenant complained about a barking dog (dogs were not permitted) to the owner. After that complaint was rebuffed, the complainer went to the landlord. The landlord had the dog removed. The dog owner retaliated by harassing the complainer with late-night phone calls and finally vandalism of his car. Nothing could be proved. The complainer relocated.

Buckley is right in saying we should complain when something is wrong. He even offers some good insights into why we often don't complain. But he overlooks the retaliation point. Caution should not make us into cowards, yet caution should lead us to making deliberate choices of occasion, language, and demeanor. After all, among the good people out there are the tired, the irrational, the vindictive, and, yes, in varying degrees, even the lunatics.

Work Cited

Buckley, William F. Jr. "Why Don't We Complain?" *Patterns of Exposition.* Ed. Robert A. Schwegler. Boston: Longman, 2000. 61–69.

Example 3   **DISCUSSION AND CRITICAL THINKING**

1. Circle the thesis.

2. Underline the topic sentences.

3. Annotate Alford's examples by writing the word *example* in the margin beside each one.

4. What does Alford apparently mean by his title "Biting My Tongue— Sometimes"?
   He probably means that in some instances a complaint may aggravate problems.

5. How do your experiences in places such as school, restaurants, work, and apartments compare with those of Alford?
   Answers will vary.

Lessons from a Control Freak

Rebecca Barry

In this defense of control freaks, Rebecca Barry offers lessons on how to accept and appreciate what people like her do for and to others. At once a confession and an appeal by a power mom, this essay first appeared in *Redbook*.

1   I'm a control freak. I know this because it's come up in therapy and my friend Lisa often reminds me. "Remember how you bossed everyone around at your last party?" Well, boss is a little strong. I simply found a nice man standing alone by the vegetable dip and suggested that he dance with my neighbor, Mrs. Howland. (Okay,

so I gave him a little push in her direction, but it was gentle, more like a friendly tap.) "And what about that time at Laura's dinner party when you took over the stereo?" Yeah. So? People danced, didn't they?

2   While conventional wisdom says that control freaks are brittle, authoritarian psychos, I think we're just trying to maintain a sense of order in our lives. We can't help that we're good at it. Sure, some of us go too far—refusing to work with people who don't keep their pencils as sharp as ours, or following our daughters around on their dates—when they're 30. In moderation, however, a few controlling tendencies can do a body good.

Ruling the Work Scene

3   A wicked (okay, obsessive) eye for detail has paid off for Paula Currie, 42, executive director of Catholic Charities in Cortland, New York. "In everything—managing my staff, writing proposals and grants—detail is very important. For example, when the instructions for a grant proposal say, 'Leave a one-inch margin on the right side,' that's the kind of thing I notice, and need to notice," she says. (And she's never had a proposal kicked back for messy margins.) A control freak like me may brood for days about a single sentence, and I may call my editor back three times to discuss it, but in the end I know the story will be better for it. (You're enjoying this one, aren't you?)

4   The business world smiles on this kind of dedication. It's unlikely that a control freak will ever skip a step, miss a deadline, or be late for lunch (we check traffic reports). A manager's delight, a control freak always looks professional and seems meeting-ready. She consistently generates coffee stain-free work and is sure not to say inappropriate things about the company in front of clients. "I do things so carefully that I know I won't be wrong," says Courtney Adams, 30, manager of human resources at a consulting firm in San Francisco. "If I send something out and someone questions me about it, I will have my research on hand to back myself up. I even spell-check my e-mails to friends." In the boss's chair, control freaks can make you want to please them and inspire you to develop skills you didn't even know you had.

Tackling Domestic Challenges

5   As for husbands and boyfriends . . . well, they're another story. A marriage is a partnership, and many control freaks, driven by the belief that their way is the best and only way, might secretly (or blatantly) prefer a dictatorship. (Is that so wrong?) "My husband

recently said that being married to me is like being in the driver's seat but never quite being able to reach the steering wheel," says Marya Montoya, 32, a software salesperson in Denver.

Raising Very Well-Behaved Guests and Children

6   There are, however, many benefits to having a control freak under your roof. We anticipate problems, and we get things done. We make sure the plumber shows up—and stays until he fixes the leak. We steer the finances clear of debt territory. ("I have never bounced a check," Currie says with pride.) The car won't fall apart because no one changed the oil, the housework and bills will never be an issue because the control freak takes care of them.

7   And let's be honest. Control freaks can be downright charming. Our parties, planned down to the last dance, are beautiful and fun. We won't shrink into the background. In love, we are very good at asking for what we want. It doesn't matter if I'm from Saturn and he's from France, my mate won't be wandering around in a hazy fog, trying to figure out why he wasn't greeted at the door with a full-blown kiss. "I'll make my husband a list if he wants to know what to change," says Montoya.

8   Rules and structure, two things at which a control freak is very good, are also essential to child rearing. In Montoya's experience, children respond remarkably well to order. "We've instituted an allowance policy where he has something to work for," she says of her 12-year-old stepson. "He gets a certain amount for each chore he does, and I think it makes him feel good to know that if he wants to buy something, he can because he's earned it." Most control freaks pass a strong work ethic along to their kids. "I taught my children that if they didn't do a chore right the first time they'd have to go back and do it again," says Currie. "When my son went to sleep-away camp, he wrote us a letter saying he hated the food, but that he was the only one who didn't have to clean the latrine twice."

9   Kids feel safe knowing that their mothers are in charge. "I don't want to be that mom who doesn't show up on parent/teacher visiting day," says Marjorie Cohn, a senior vice president at Nickelodeon in New York. To prevent her worst fears from coming to life, she tacks a two-week calendar on the fridge where she writes down every important event in her child's schedule.

10   And since control freaks are master planners, our kids are rarely bored. "I try not to sit him in front of the TV set," says Adams of her 3-year-old son. "I take him to museum exhibits, I read to him, I encourage him to color. I think it will make him a brighter, happier person." (Of course it will—as long as he learns to color within the lines.)

You Know You're Too Controlling When

your family salutes when you come into the room.

your children call you their "smother."

you stay late at the office Friday to proofread your husband's chore list for Saturday.

you close most of your staff meetings with, "Never mind, I'll do it myself."

you redo your children's homework so often that their teacher mistakes your handwriting for theirs.

the last time you were wrong was 1976, and even then it was due to a misprint in *Consumer Reports.*

the phrase "remote control" makes you nervous.

Here's how to deal with your anal-retentive loved ones:

- *Understand the nature of the beast.* Control is about comfort, says Monica Basco, Ph.D., author of *Never Good Enough: Freeing Yourself from the Chains of Perfectionism.* "People get angry and assume the controlling person is being mean, but she's really trying to reduce her own anxieties."

- *Choose your battles.* "If you can live with letting them have their way in a situation, do it," suggests Deborah Luepnitz, Ph.D., a psychotherapist in Philadelphia. Sit quietly when your boss notes that there are no Os in Bermuda after you turn in your vacation memo (as long as she still okays your days off).

- *Develop a thick skin.* "If you share close quarters with a control freak, you can't be on the defensive all the time," says Dan Neuharth, Ph.D., author of *If You Had Controlling Parents. . . .* It will help if you realize that she has a lot on her shoulders—making sure her checkbook is balanced down to the penny, and her kids have dirt-free sneakers. If she's mad, it's probably not at you, but at the dust on that shelf in the bathroom.

- *Celebrate his or her successes.* "A control freak spends lots of energy trying to avoid criticism from others, or always feeling like the ax is going to fall when there is no ax," says Dr. Basco. The result is that while a control freak may appear confident, she may never quite fully give herself the credit she deserves.

- *Urge the control freak to let go now and then.* Wresting your beloved's power away may seem daunting, but it's good practice for both of you. As Dr. Neuharth says, "A relationship is a dance. If one person is always leading, it gets really boring."

Exercise 4	DISCUSSION AND CRITICAL THINKING

1. What is Rebecca Barry's main point?

   That in moderation a few controlling tendencies can do a body good.

2. How does Barry define *control freak?*

   She says that control freaks are just trying to "maintain a sense of order in [their] lives."

3. According to Barry, how does conventional wisdom define *control freak?*

   "Brittle, authoritarian psychos."

4. Name the individuals who are used in examples to support the idea that control freaks have some good effects on others.

   Paula Currie (paragraph 3), Courtney Adams (paragraph 4), Marya Montoya (paragraph 5), and Marjorie Cohn (paragraph 9).

5. Are control freaks in moderation really control freaks? Why or why not?

   Answers will vary.

6. Do you see this essay as an explanation or a rationalization?

   Answers will vary.

7. If you take each example and push it beyond moderation, what do you have?

   Paula Currie: May obsess so much over achieving perfection that she cannot function as a writer.

   Courtney Adams: May impose her standards and behavioral patterns on others, stifling them.

   Marya Montoya: May become a dictator.

   Marjorie Cohn: May make puppets of children.

8. How might this essay by a confessed control freak be perceived as an attempt to control?

   Answers will vary. At the least, it is an attempt to persuade readers that not all effects of controlling persons are bad. To some readers, this might be just another opportunity for a control freak to tell others how to think.

I'm Outta Here!

David Levine

Every day, three thousand students give up on high school—for good. They push open the doors and walk out. Turn their backs on it. Drop out. Now what? Using colorful examples, freelance author David Levine provides some of the answers.

1   Think about it. In some ways it seems perfect. Quit school. Just say No—no more pressure, no more stupid rules, no more deadlines, no more uncaring teachers, no more snobby, clique-conscious peers. Nearly every high school student has imagined what it would be like.

2   Beth Kierny* did more than imagine. A few months into her senior year at Columbia High School, in East Greenbush, New York, she dropped out of school.

Example

3   Beth is a shy eighteen-year-old with dark, curly hair who hated getting up early for classes. She was spending most of her time "gypping," leaving the building (or never showing up) and hanging out with her friends instead. Her parents didn't know; she was having problems with them and had moved in with her boyfriend, Dave, who had dropped out a few years earlier. When Beth found out she had missed so many days that she couldn't take her exams, she figured: Why not just leave?

Example

4   She thought it would be great. She'd just get a job like Dave, sleep in later, work at some cool place instead of sitting in boring classes, and lead an easier, more interesting life.

Example

5   But without a diploma, Beth found it difficult to get a job. She had to finally settle for one at the Hessmart gas station a few miles down Route 20. Being the youngest and newest employee, she got stuck working the worst shifts. Often she had to get up even earlier than she had to for school—sometimes she had to be *at work* by 7:00 A.M. Or she'd have to work the midnight shift, which was scary because you never knew if the place might get held up. Or she'd have to work weekends, when her friends were all out partying.

6   The money was terrible—at minimum wage she cleared maybe $90 a week—and she couldn't afford a car, so she had to take cabs to and from work, which cost almost ten bucks a day. That didn't leave much for her share of the $425 a month in rent on their small apartment behind the Burger King.

7   And if Dave, a part-time carpenter, found himself out of work, things were really tight. They were weeks and weeks late with the rent and got letters from the landlord threatening eviction (they'd already been thrown out of another place only a few months earlier). The bills wouldn't stop coming. The electricity was turned off. The telephone was disconnected. She and Dave fought all the time, mostly about money, sometimes about stupid things.

8   Then spring came, and her friends still in school were talking about the prom and the parties, and she found herself left out. Then came graduation, with its class rings and college plans and

*Names with asterisks have been changed.

yearbooks, and Beth felt like a total outsider. She was more depressed than she'd ever been in her life.

9   Like many students, Beth thought that school was hard and the world outside of school would be easier. Instead, she found that the world outside of school was hard, too.

10   Everyone knows kids like Beth, who for one reason or another believe they can't handle school and decide to quit. What you might not realize is that all those kids add up to a dropout epidemic. Every day, up to three thousand kids leave school—that's between thirty and sixty busloads of students. Although the estimates vary, about half a million leave each year. The national graduation rate, which has been dropping for years, is now 71 percent, meaning nearly one in three students don't finish school. In some urban areas, the dropout rate can be over 50 percent. While the majority of high school dropouts—60 percent—are white and do not live in cities, minorities as a group are hardest hit: Hispanic students, for example, have a dropout rate more than twice the national average. One recent study found that one in four black guys will drop out, while one in five black girls will. One study found that 62 percent of Hispanic students dropped out, along with 53 percent of black students and 42 percent of Native American students. Overall, boys are only slightly more likely to drop out than girls.

11   Within this larger puzzle are the individual pieces—the reasons why kids quit school. According to the Department of Education, there are six things that put students at higher risk. They include having a dropout sibling, coming from a single-parent family, coming from a household with an income below $15,000, being home alone more than three hours a day, not speaking English well, and having parents who didn't finish high school. What makes any student actually quit is harder to assess. Caroline Abbott, sixteen, who lives in Charlotte, North Carolina, never stopped going to school entirely, she just missed a lot of days. "I'd sit home, go to a friend's house," she says. "A good friend of mine dropped out, and I wanted to, too. I just wanted to be with her."

Example

12   "Poor attendance is a symptom, not the disease," says Joseph Markham, director of pupil personnel services for the Albany City School District, in New York. And these days there are many diseases.

13   A student's initial trouble may come from parents' marital problems, domestic violence, drug or alcohol use, or physical abuse. For Darrell Maynard,* now a tenth grader in Columbia, South Carolina, it was moving when he was in the eighth grade. "I didn't know no one," he says. So he started to hang out, and soon after

Example

that he began to sell drugs. He says he didn't like doing it. "It was kind of scary, really," Darrell says. "Other students looked at us as gangsters, and the teachers were afraid to get involved." But he felt as if he had nothing else in his life. "My mom keeps foster kids," he says. "She wasn't paying attention to me. My dad was away all week working." Eventually, he was caught with a machete in school and got kicked out. "When my dad found out, he said I had to go to work every day with him. I didn't want that."

Example   14   Curt Niedrach, seventeen, is a junior at Jackson Alternative School, in Jackson Township, New Jersey. All of his closest friends have dropped out. "They didn't think about how it was really going to be outside of school," he says. "They want to be free, but they don't think about what they're losing. Mostly, they don't want to be organized or deal with other people's deadlines, like showing up for class. Also, no one wants to get hassled if they don't fol-

Example   low every little rule." Edwin Soto, a sophomore at Bayard Ruskin High School, in New York City, has a lot of friends who've dropped out, too. "A typical day in their lives is getting up about 10:00 A.M., then finding each other and all the other guys from around the way," he says. "They try to gather as much money as possible to buy weed and go to the park to hang out. Later on, they head to pick up their girlfriends at school. After that, they go back to the park to hang out some more."

15   Some students leave school because they feel as if nobody cares. "Classes were too big, with thirty-five or more students in

Example   them," says Heather Murphy, seventeen, from Miami, who dropped out when she was fourteen. "I wasn't getting anything from my school in return for going. Teachers didn't have time for me, so why should I go?" Given the size and impersonal nature of some public high schools, finding help can be hard. Forty percent of the girls who drop out every year leave because they're pregnant. Other students quit because they feel it's a way of sparing themselves the failure.

Example   16   Take Caroline. In eighth grade everything was great: honor roll, cheerleading. She loved school, had lots of friends. Everyone told her that high school would be great, too. But it wasn't. "I hated it," she says. "They weren't friendly people. I wasn't interested in the classes." Caroline's ex-boyfriend—who had left the state—came back to the town. She couldn't keep her mind on school.

17   Still, she was trying, really trying. But when she failed algebra, something in her snapped. "You think, I'm trying so hard, I must be doing well, then one thing turns it all around. So I thought, Well, forget it. Why try so hard and accomplish nothing? I thought I was just dumb. So I just stopped trying. I gave up."

18   "To think that all dropouts or potential dropouts leave school because they aren't smart enough to hack it is to miss the point," says John K. Dougherty, Ph.D., president of alternative education for the state of New Jersey. Many kids lack motivation, and they aren't getting enough support at home to overcome that. Absenteeism pushes them further behind, so they can't perform well when they do show up at school. The discouragement spirals.

19   Some of the blame for the high dropout rate must fall on the schools themselves. Unfortunately, much of traditional education is uninspiring, and some experts believe it's simply obsolete. Teachers aren't paid well, and budget and staff cuts have left them unsupported. Classes are regularly overcrowded, and, too often, quiet or uninvolved kids are overlooked.

20   Schools are trying to adapt and respond to the crisis. Cities In Schools, Inc. (CIS), a national organization designed to get dropout-prone students into personalized programs that address their problems, believes that schools have to do more than educate. CIS president Bill Milliken says that what's needed is a sense of community, a sense that adults really care. He says schools should abandon the system of churning out graduates on an assembly line and bring the resources to the kids. "You have to build the community," he says. "If they don't have positive relationships at home and have negative ones on the street, then we have to build positive ones for them at school."

21   There's no denying that a high school diploma opens doors; staying in school and graduating extends the range of options of what you can do with your life. It's also a fact that the consequences of dropping out are severe and the prospects for dropouts are bleak. According to the National Dropout Prevention Center, less than 50 percent of dropouts find jobs when they leave school. When they do, they earn 60 percent less than high school graduates (over a lifetime, that adds up to $250,000). They are not accepted into military service and are 50 percent more likely to be on welfare. Eighty-eight percent of female dropouts under age thirty who head households live in poverty.

Example

22   More than half of Curt Niedrach's friends are now enrolled in a GED (general equivalency diploma) program. Beth Kierny is also going for her GED, but she's afraid that even this might not be good enough. "A lot of jobs want a diploma, not a GED," she says. Things are better with her parents—they're talking again, at least—but the pressures of her life still don't let up. She and Dave are looking for their third place to live in eighteen months. "It's hard, because a lot of places don't want to rent to kids," she says.

23   Because she's taking classes again, Beth has had to quit her job at the Hessmart and support herself with baby-sitting jobs. She's making even less money than she was before. Dave has decided to join the army. Beth, because she doesn't yet have a GED, can't.

24   There just aren't many options. "You have to finish school to get a decent job and to afford a car. You can't make it on minimum wages, working at gas stations or restaurants on weekends," she says. "You just can't."

Exercise 5   **DISCUSSION AND CRITICAL THINKING**

1. Circle the sentence that most clearly indicates the student view that Levine will explore.

   Both, but more on effects.

2. Is this essay concerned mainly with cause or effects, or a combination?

   Effects.

3. Are most of the examples used to show causes or effects?

   Both, but mainly to persuade.

4. Is Levine's purpose to inform or to persuade, or both?

5. Annotate Levine's examples by writing the word *example* in the margin beside each one.

   Time. Note that the extended examples of Beth and Dave move through their struggles.

6. Is the order of presentation more that of time or space?

Making the Grade

Kurt Wiesenfeld

Grading for academic performance, a concept taken for granted for most, is disregarded by about 10 percent of Kurt Wiesenfeld's physics students at Georgia Tech. These students are more concerned with negotiating and bargaining. This essay was first published in *Newsweek*.

1   It was a rookie error. After 10 years I should have known better, but I went to my office the day after final grades were posted.

Example

Example

Example

Example

Example

There was a tentative knock on the door. "Professor Wiesenfeld? I took your Physics 2121 class? I flunked it? I wonder if there's anything I can do to improve my grade?" I thought: "Why are you asking me? Isn't it too late to worry about it? Do you dislike making declarative statements?"

2   After the student gave his tale of woe and left, the phone rang. "I got a D in your class. Is there any way you can change it to 'Incomplete'?" Then the e-mail assault began: "I'm shy about coming in to talk to you, but I'm not shy about asking for a better grade. Anyway, it's worth a try." The next day I had three phone messages from students asking *me* to call *them*. I didn't.

3   Time was, when you received a grade, that was it. You might groan and moan, but you accepted it as the outcome of your efforts or lack thereof (and, yes, sometimes a tough grader). In the last few years, however, some students have developed a disgruntled-consumer approach. If they don't like their grade, they go to the "return" counter to trade it in for something better.

4   What alarms me is their indifference toward grades as an indication of personal effort and performance. Many, when pressed about why they think they deserve a better grade, admit they don't deserve one but would like one anyway. Having been raised on gold stars for effort and smiley faces for self-esteem, they've learned that they can get by without hard work and real talent if they can talk the professor into giving them a break. This attitude is beyond cynicism. There's a weird innocence to the assumption that one expects (even deserves) a better grade simply by begging for it. With that outlook, I guess I shouldn't be as flabbergasted as I was that 12 students asked me to change their grades *after* final grades were posted.

5   That's 10 percent of my class who let three months of midterms, quizzes and lab reports slide until long past remedy. My graduate student calls it hyperrational thinking: if effort and intelligence don't matter, why should deadlines? What matters is getting a better grade through an unearned bonus, the academic equivalent of a freebie T shirt or toaster giveaway. Rewards are disconnected from the quality of one's work. An act and its consequences are unrelated, random events.

6   Their arguments for wheedling better grades often ignore academic performance. Perhaps they feel it's not relevant. "If my grade isn't raised to a D I'll lose my scholarship." "If you don't give me a C, I'll flunk out." One sincerely overwrought student pleaded, "If I don't pass, my life is over." This is tough stuff to deal with. Apparently, I'm responsible for someone's losing a scholarship, flunking out or deciding whether life has meaning. Perhaps

these students see me as a commodities broker with something they want—a grade. Though intrinsically worthless, grades, if properly manipulated, can be traded for what has value: a degree, which means a job, which means money. The one thing college actually offers—a chance to learn—is considered irrelevant, even less than worthless, because of the long hours and hard work required.

7   In a society saturated with surface values, love of knowledge for its own sake does sound eccentric. The benefits of fame and wealth are more obvious. So is it right to blame students for reflecting the superficial values saturating our society?

8   Yes, of course it's right. These guys had better take themselves seriously now, because our country will be forced to take them seriously later, when the stakes are much higher. They must recognize that their attitude is not only self-destructive, but socially destructive. The erosion of quality control—giving appropriate grades for actual accomplishments—is a major concern in my department. One colleague noted that a physics major could obtain a degree without ever answering a written exam question completely. How? By pulling in enough partial credit and extra credit. And by getting breaks on grades.

9   But what happens once she or he graduates and gets a job? That's when the misfortunes of eroding academic standards multiply. We lament that schoolchildren get "kicked upstairs" until they graduate from high school despite being illiterate and mathematically inept, but we seem unconcerned with college graduates whose less blatant deficiencies are far more harmful if their accreditation exceeds their qualifications.

10   Most of my students are science and engineering majors. If they're good at getting partial credit but not at getting the answer right, then the new bridge breaks or the new drug doesn't work. One finds examples here in Atlanta. Last year a light tower in the Olympic Stadium collapsed, killing a worker. It collapsed because an engineer miscalculated how much weight it could hold. A new 12-story dormitory could develop dangerous cracks due to a foundation that's uneven by more than six inches. The error resulted from incorrect data being fed into a computer. I drive past that dorm daily on my way to work, wondering if a foundation crushed under kilotons of weight is repairable or if this structure will have to be demolished. Two 10,000-pound steel beams at the new natatorium collapsed in March, crashing into the student athletic complex. (Should we give partial credit since no one was hurt?) Those are real-world consequences of errors and lack of expertise.

Example

Example

Example

11 But the lesson is lost on the grade-grousing 10 percent. Say that you won't (not can't, but won't) change the grade they deserve to what they want, and they're frequently bewildered or angry. They don't think it's fair that they're judged according to their performance, not their desires or "potential." They don't think it's fair that they should jeopardize their scholarships or be in danger of flunking out simply because they could not or did not do their work. But it's more than fair; it's necessary to help preserve a minimum standard of quality that our society needs to maintain safety and integrity. I don't know if the 13th-hour students will learn that lesson, but I've learned mine. From now on, after final grades are posted, I'll lie low until the next quarter starts.

| Exercise 6 | **VOCABULARY HIGHLIGHTS** |

Write a short definition of each word as it is used in the essay. (Paragraph numbers are given in parentheses.) Be prepared to use the words in your own sentences.

tentative (1)	eroding (9)
cynicism (4)	blatant (9)
intrinsically (6)	accreditation (9)
saturated (7)	jeopardize (11)
eccentric (7)	integrity (11)

| Exercise 7 | **DISCUSSION AND CRITICAL THINKING** |

1. Circle the thesis.

2. Is this essay concerned with mainly causes, effects, or both?
   Both.

3. Annotate Wiesenfeld's examples by writing the word *example* in the margins beside each one.

4. What does Wiesenfeld think grades should represent?
   Academic performance.

5. What does Wiesenfeld believe grades represent to the wheedling 10 percent of his students?
   A commodity to be bargained for material gain.

6. Which paragraph contains examples that suggest the possible consequences of lowered academic standards?
   Paragraph 10.

7. Does Wiesenfeld have a solution to the problem? Explain.

He recommends, "Say that you won't . . . change the grade they deserve to what they want" (paragraph 11). This recommendation may or may not change students' attitudes, but it will at least make them think!

8. Do you have a solution?

Answers will vary.

9. Can one make an argument for extra credit, special testing, and selective (your definition) generosity?

Answers will vary.

Underground Dads

Wil Haygood

As a child, Wil Haygood did not have an actual dad around the house. But he was fortunate. He had men around who gave him the love and guidance he needed. Three men in particular were his surrogate fathers, and he learned important lessons from each. This essay was first published in the *New York Times Magazine*.

1   For years, while growing up, I shamelessly told my playmates that I didn't have a father. In my neighborhood, where men went to work with lunch pails, my friends thought there was a gaping hole in my household. My father never came to the park with me to toss a softball, never came to see me in any of my school plays. I'd explain to friends, with the simplicity of explaining to someone that there are, in some woods, no deer, that I just had no father. My friends looked at me and squinted. My mother and father had divorced shortly after my birth. As the years rolled by, however, I did not have the chance to turn into the pitiful little black boy who had been abandoned by his father. There was a reason: other men showed up. They were warm, honest (at least as far as my eyes could see) and big-hearted. They were the good black men in the shadows, the men who taught me right from wrong, who taught me how to behave, who told me, by their very actions, that they expected me to do good things in life.

2   There are heartbreaking statistics tossed about regarding single-parent black households these days, about children growing up fatherless. Those statistics must be considered. But how do you count the other men, the ones who show up—with perfect timing, with a kind of soft-stepping loveliness—to give a hand, to take a boy to watch airplanes lift off, to show a young boy the

beauty of planting tomatoes in the ground and to tell a child that all of life is not misery?

3   In my life, there was Jerry, who hauled junk. He had a lean body and a sweet smile. He walked like a cowboy, all bowlegged, swinging his shoulders. It was almost a strut. The sound of his pickup truck rumbling down our alley in Columbus, Ohio, could raise me from sleep.

4   When he wasn't hauling junk, Jerry fixed things. More than once, he fixed my red bicycle. The gears were always slipping; the chain could turn into a tangled mess. Hearing pain in my voice, Jerry would instruct me to leave my bike on our front porch. In our neighborhood, in the 60's, no one would steal your bike from your porch. Jerry promised me he'd pick it up, and he always did. He never lied to me, and he cautioned me not to tell lies. He was, off and on, my mother's boyfriend. At raucous family gatherings, he'd pull me aside and explain to me the importance of honesty, of doing what one promised to do.

5   And there was Jimmy, my grandfather, who all his life paid his bills the day they arrived: that was a mighty lesson in itself—it taught me a work ethic. He held two jobs, and there were times when he allowed me to accompany him on his night job, when he cleaned a Greek restaurant on the north side of Columbus. Often he'd mop the place twice, as if trying to win some award. He frightened me too. It was not because he was mean. It was because he had exacting standards, and there were times when I didn't measure up to those standards. He didn't like shortcutters. His instructions, on anything, were to be carried out to the letter. He believed in independence, doing as much for yourself as you possibly could. It should not have surprised me when, one morning while having stomach pains, he chose not to wait for a taxi and instead walked the mile to the local hospital, where he died a week later of stomach cancer.

6   My uncles provided plenty of good background music when I was coming of age. Uncle Henry took me fishing. He'd phone the night before. "Be ready. Seven o'clock." I'd trail him through woods—as a son does a father—until we found our fishing hole. We'd sit for hours. He taught me a patience and an appreciation of the outdoors, of nature. He talked, incessantly, of family—his family, my family, the family of friends. The man had a reverence for family. I knew to listen.

7   I think these underground fathers simply appear, decade to decade, flowing through the generations. Hardly everywhere, and hardly, to be sure, in enough places, but there. As mystical, sometimes, as fate when fate is sweet.

8   Sometimes I think that all these men who have swept in and out of my life still couldn't replace a good, warm father. But inasmuch as I've never known a good, warm father, the men who entered my life, who taught me right from wrong, who did things they were not asked to do, have become unforgettable. I know of the cold statistics out there. And yet, the mountain of father-son literature does not haunt me. I've known good black men.

Exercise 8   **DISCUSSION AND CRITICAL THINKING**

1. Copy here the sentence that focuses on the main idea of the essay.
   "There was a reason: other men showed up."

2. Paraphrase the thesis.
   Surrogate parents can shape the lives of children in positive ways just as real parents do.

3. Name the three examples used to support Haygood's main idea.
   Jerry (paragraph 3), Jimmy (paragraph 5), and Henry (paragraph 6).

4. What did Haygood learn from each man?
   Jerry: honesty; Jimmy: work ethic; Henry: patience and an appreciation of the outdoors.

5. How does Haygood relate his experiences shown in the examples to statistics?
   Statistics showing the negative side of single-parent black households are well known, but Haygood knows from experience that children can have surrogate parents who shape their young lives in positive ways.

✎ Topics for Writing Exemplification

Writing Process Worksheet

You will find a Writing Process Worksheet in Appendix A, page 531. It can be photocopied and enlarged, filled in, and submitted with each assignment if your instructor directs you to do so.

Source-Based Topics

Each essay developed from these suggested source-based topics should include at least one reference to the reading selection by the author's name and the title. Quotations should be enclosed in quotation marks. Follow your instructor's directions in documenting the ideas you borrow. Whether you use informal or formal documentation, the form is not complicated, and you will soon learn to use it for these essays without checking each time. See pages 78 and 79 for a discussion of MLA style and informal documentation.

Underlining and annotating reading selections will help you in finding support material. In prewriting brief essays, consider marking your outline to indicate where you will use quotations or other borrowed ideas. If the quotations or reworded statements are short and few, you could even insert them inside parentheses or circles in your outline; if you do, also include the author's last name and the page number. A sound system, consistently used, will save you time and ensure technically strong papers.

"Prison Tattoos"

1. Write an essay about people you know who have tattoos. Use specific examples. Unify the essay around a specific idea, such as one of the following: Tattoos are more easily acquired than removed. Tattoos help people define themselves for others. We need stricter laws to protect juveniles from tattooists.

"Biting My Tongue—Sometimes"

2. Write about the effectiveness of complaining, if the process is handled thoughtfully. Provide three or more examples.

3. Using this essay as a model, discuss the problems that can sometimes occur as the result of complaining, especially if the complaining is not handled well. Use your own examples. Refer directly to Alford's essay, and consider referring to Buckley's ideas as noted by Alford.

"Lessons from a Control Freak"

4. Rebecca Barry says that controlling in moderation is beneficial. Write an essay in which you argue that controlling is inherently bad. Use quotations from Barry's essay and examples from your own experience. Consider these questions: Have you ever been controlled? Have you observed someone who has been controlled for a long period of time? Have you ever tried to control others?

5. Write an essay in which you agree with Barry's thesis. Quote her and use your own examples.

"I'm Outta Here!"

6. Write an essay in which you make the same argument as Levine. Give Levine credit for the ideas you borrow and provide your own examples.

"Making the Grade"

7. Write an essay in which you side with Wiesenfeld. Provide your own examples.

8. Write an essay in which you question whether most grading is truly based on academic achievement. To what extent are Wiesenfeld's standards typical? Refer to courses you have taken, experiences you

have had, and stories you have heard. Discuss important knowledge or skills you have acquired that were never tested properly. Refer to extra-credit projects, if any.

"Underground Dads"

9. Write about mother or father figures who influenced you in special ways as you grew up. Who were they? Exactly how did they help? Might a mother or father have provided what they did?

Career-Related Topics

10. Use specific examples to support one of the following statements as applied to business or work.

It's not what you know, it's who you know.

Don't burn your bridges.

Like Legos, business is a matter of connections.

Tact is the lubricant that oils the wheels of industry.

The customer is always right.

If you take care of the pennies, the dollars will take care of themselves.

A kind word turns away wrath.

11. Use another common saying or invent one of your own and illustrate it with an example or examples.

12. Discuss how a specific service or product can benefit its users. Use an example or examples.

General Topics

13. Choose one of the following statements as a thesis for an essay. Support the statement with specific examples.

Television commercials are often amusing [misleading, irritating, sexist, racist, useless, fascinating].

Rap music often carries important messages [makes me sick, brings out the best in people, brings out the worst in people, degrades women, promotes violence, presents reality, appeals to our better instincts, tells funny stories].

Rock groups don't have to be sensational in presentation and appearance to be popular.

A person can be an environmentalist in everyday life.

Many people who consider themselves law-abiding citizens break laws on a selective basis.

Television news is full of stories of violence, but we can also find acts of kindness in everyday life.

Car salespeople behave differently depending on the kind of car they are selling and the kind of customer they have.

The kinds of toys people buy for their children tell us much about their social values.

People who do not have a satisfying family life will find a family substitute.

One painful experience reminded me of the importance of human rights [student rights, worker rights, gender rights].

Drug abuse, including alcohol abuse, may be a problem even with people who seem to be functioning well.

Country music appeals to some of our most basic concerns.

Writer's Guidelines: Exemplification

1. Use examples to explain, convince, or amuse.

2. Use examples that are vivid, specific, and representative.
   - Vivid examples attract attention.
   - Specific examples are identifiable.
   - Representative examples are typical and therefore the basis for generalization.

3. Tie your examples clearly to your thesis.

4. Draw your examples from what you have read, heard, and experienced.

5. Brainstorm a list or cluster of possible examples before you write.

6. The order and number of your examples will depend on the purpose stated in your thesis.

8

Analysis by Division: Examining the Parts

THE QUIGMANS   by Buddy Hickerson

I'm afraid you have a compound, compound, compound, fracture, fracture, fracture, fracture.

Writing Analysis by Division

*I*f you need to explain how something works or exists as a unit, you will write an analysis by division. You will break down a unit (your subject) into its parts and explain how each part functions in relation to the operation or existence of the whole. The most important word here is *unit*. You begin with something that can stand alone or can be regarded separately: a poem, a heart, a painting, a car, a bike, a person, a school, a committee. The following procedure will guide you in writing an analysis by division. Move from subject to principle, to division, to relationship.

Step 1: Select something that is a unit.

Step 2: State one principle by which the unit can function.

Step 3: Divide the unit into parts according to that principle (the perceived purpose or role).

Step 4: Discuss each of the parts in relation to the unit.

Here's how a writer might apply this general procedure to a real object (unit).

Step 1: For the unit, I choose a pencil.

Step 2: For my principle, I see the pencil as a writing instrument.

Step 3: For dividing the unit into parts based on the principle of a pencil as a writing instrument, I divide the pencil into an eraser, an eraser holder, a wooden barrel, and a thin graphite core with a sharpened point.

Step 4: For my discussion of the parts in relation to the unit, I might say: "At the top of the wooden barrel is a strip of metal encircling an eraser and clamping it to the barrel. In the center of the barrel is a core of graphite that can be sharpened to a point at the end and used for writing. The eraser is used to remove marks made by the graphite point. Thus I have a complete writing tool, one that marks and erases marks."

Like many things, a pencil can be regarded in different ways. For example, an artist might *not* consider a pencil mainly as a writing tool. Instead, an artist might look at a pencil and see it as an object of simple functional beauty that could be used as a subject in a still-life painting. Here is how an artist might follow the procedure.

Step 1: For the unit, I choose a pencil.

Step 2: For the principle or way of regarding the unit, I see the pencil as an object of simple functional beauty.

Step 3: For the division into parts based on my principle, I divide the pencil into texture, shape, and color.

Step 4: For the discussion of parts in relation to the unit, I will explain how the textures of the metal, graphite, and wood, along with their shapes and colors, produce a beautiful object.

Either treatment of the same unit, the pencil, is valid, but mixing the treatments by applying more than one principle at a time causes problems. For example, if we were to say that a pencil has an eraser, an eraser holder, a wooden barrel, a graphite core, and a beautiful coat of yellow paint, we would have an illogical analysis by division, because all parts but the "beautiful coat of yellow paint" relate to the pencil as a writing instrument.

Organization

In an essay of analysis by division, the main parts are likely to be the main points of your outline or main extensions of your cluster. If they are anything else, reconsider your organization. For the pencil, your outline might look like this:

I. Eraser

II. Eraser holder

III. Wooden barrel

IV. Graphite core with point at one end

Sequence of Parts

The order in which you discuss the parts will vary according to the nature of the unit and the way in which you view it. Here are some possible sequences for organizing the parts of a unit.

Time: The sequence of the parts in your composition can be mainly chronological, or time-based (if you are writing about something that functions on its own, such as a heart, with the parts presented in relation to stages of the function).

Space: If your unit is a visual object and if, like the pencil, it does nothing by itself, you may discuss the parts in relation to space. In the example about the pencil, the parts of the pencil begin at the top with the eraser and end at the bottom with the graphite point.

Emphasis: Because the most emphatic part of any piece of writing is the end (the second most emphatic part is the beginning), consider placing the most significant idea of the unit at the end. In the example, both space and emphasis govern the placement of the pencil point at the end of the order.

Connecting Sources and Writing

Student Essay

When asked to write an essay about a unit that could be divided into three or more parts for discussion, Hsiao Chin Yu turned to her culture. One special occasion stood out: Chinese New Year. The main feature of the celebration was a family feast. The food was delicious; it was served in courses, and each item was assigned symbolic value.

A Chinese New Year's Feast

Hsiao Chin Yu

Throughout my childhood, the traditional Chinese New Year's Feast was prepared by my grandmother at her house every year. My two aunts and three uncles and their families joined my family for the celebration. By then my grandmother was a widow, who had raised six children by herself since 1943. She was responsible for holding our family close together, and it was the Feast each year that helped connect us to our Chinese culture, because each dish had a symbolic meaning. The grownups already knew the traditions, but we children were learning. The food was served in three courses.

The first course was *chuen hop,* a tray for togetherness that contained eight kinds of sweet meats, each carrying a special meaning. For instance, candied lotus meant that our family would have sons. Candied melon promoted growth and health. Candied coconuts represented togetherness. Watermelon seeds symbolized having plenty. Peanuts promoted giving birth more than once. Thus the generations would keep growing, and our family would be as one.

The second course consisted of a fried fish, a whole boiled chicken (including the head and feet), and roasted pork with its skin attached. A whole pig could be purchased in a local butcher's shop, but most years my grandmother bought only the amount of pork we could eat that day. As we ate it, we were told that pork stood for luck. The fish symbolized the special nature of desire. The chicken symbolized newness. With these foods, we wished each other much extra good luck for a New Year.

These three items would be offered to our ancestors first in a ceremony during which we burned incense and prayed for them. After the ceremony, these dishes were cut and served with other foods at our dining table. The other foods included steamed dumplings (*yuan pao*), which were shaped like coins. In fact, to the delight of us children, my grandmother always hid some coins in the dumplings she gave us.

The third course featured egg rolls, prepared to observe the banishing of the old kitchen god and the welcoming of the new. A sweet rice cake (*nyuen kao*) and sweet fruits (usually tangerines) accompanied the egg rolls. A square red paper, which proclaimed "happiness and luck," decorated the top of the rice cake, which indicated that the New Year would be even better than the last. Then came the noodles, representing a long life.

My grandmother is now with my ancestors, but the knowledge of Chinese culture and our family are still with us. She gave me ideas and inspiration that I will try to pass on to my children.

Exercise 1	**DISCUSSION AND CRITICAL THINKING**

1. Underline the thesis.

2. What terms would you use for the three courses?
   Answers will vary. Perhaps, appetizers, main course, and dessert.

3. What terms would you use to generalize the symbols represented in each course?
   The first pertains to health, family, and prosperity. The second represents extra good luck for the new year. The third is good luck and happiness, conditions that should be even better in the new year, on the way to a long life.

4. In what way is this meal an educational experience for the children?
   The children learn Chinese cultural values.

Student Documented Essay

Emmett Davis faced an assignment in analysis by division in which he would discuss the qualities that made a person successful. He was expected to refer to at least two sources. Davis turned to the early days of rock and roll, his special interest. Almost every source he skimmed, both on the Internet and in his college library's database, contained discussion of Elvis Presley, who became his subject.

Elvis Presley: Twentieth-Century Legend

Emmett Davis

After having moved a few years into the twenty-first century, we still look back and revise lists of top people of the previous one hundred years. One much-discussed category is the Greatest Performers in Popular Music. Although I have trouble choosing the top person in some areas, in this case I have no problem. Of course, it's

Elvis Presley. Four factors stand out and make my choice easy: he was good looking, he could sing, he had style, and he influenced the main world of popular music, which we call "rock 'n' roll."

Looks

As for his looks, he was darkly handsome, some would say even beautiful, with thick, unruly hair and a sneering smile that appealed to the rebellious side of young people. Dick Clark, producer and host of *American Bandstand* for four decades, said that youth "copied his style. People imitated his gestures, dressed like him, wanted to be him (or his woman)" (148). Much has been made of the young Elvis and the old Elvis. The young was the person of slender body in a leather jacket. From that image he soon morphed into his spangled outfit phase, a reflection of his ties with country music entertainers but also becoming the model for the glitter look of numerous rock stars. Unfortunately, toward the end of his life, he put on too much weight and favored white bejeweled jump suits.

Voice

As for singing, he had a powerful, deep voice with a wide range similar to the big voices in rhythm and blues and black gospel music he had listened to and loved as he grew up in Mississippi and Tennessee. Early in his career he was sometimes criticized for not sounding more like traditional crooners. Although it was true that he did howl, wail, and shout in certain arrangements, he could sing religious songs and simple love ballads such as "Teddy Bear" and "Love Me Tender" with great clarity and warmth.

Style

When he was on stage, his style was personal, as he shook his hips and belted out songs like "Heartbreak Hotel" and "You Ain't Nothin' But a Hound Dog." While making the guitar respectable, he popularized the driving rhythm of rock. He made music more personal and more aggressive. His body language may look tame today, but in the 1950s, it was revolutionary.

Influence

Because he was so different and so good, he influenced and inspired others who would become famous artists of rock 'n' roll. Groups like the Beatles and the Rolling Stones gave him credit for his innovations. His influence even extends to academia. In 1995 the University of Mississippi convened an international conference entitled "In Search of Elvis." Professor Vernon Chadwick, who helped organize the conference, said that Elvis "is better known and in many cases more influential than William Faulkner" (Geier 14). Though Chadwick's statement may have upset some of his colleagues, it is well in line with what many of his fans believe.

Some fanatical fans believe Elvis is off hiding in the witness protection program and shopping at the K-Marts and Wal*Marts of the world, but, to me, he's alive in a more important way: he's a legend—he's the Greatest Performer in Popular Music for the Twentieth Century.

Works Cited

Clark, Dick. "Remembering 'Presleymania.'" *Newsweek* 8 June 98: 148.
Geier, Thom. "Eggheads for Elvis." *U.S. News & World Report* 7 August 1995: 14.

Exercise 2	**DISCUSSION AND CRITICAL THINKING**

1. Circle the thesis.

2. What is the unit being considered?
   Elvis Presley.

3. What is the principle for dividing the unit?
   Greatest entertainer of the twentieth century.

4. Underline the topic sentences that indicate the parts of the unit and, in the margin to the left, use single words to annotate those parts.

Practicing Patterns of Analysis by Division

In analysis by division, Roman numeral headings almost always indicate parts of the unit you are discussing as your subject. Learning to divide the unit into parts will help you move through your assignment quickly and efficiently.

Exercise 3	**COMPLETING PATTERNS OF ANALYSIS BY DIVISION**

Fill in the blanks to complete an Outline of Emmett Davis's "Elvis Presley: Twentieth-Century Legend" on page 197.

   I. Appearance
     A. Rugged good looks
     B. Dress
     C. Grooming
  II. Singing ability
     A. Range
     B. Quality

III. Style

    A. <u>Personal   </u>

    B. Animal magnetism

IV. <u>Influence   </u>

    A. Innovative

    B. Inspiring

A Brush with Reality
Surprises in the Tube

David Bodanis

For many years, David Bodanis taught a survey of intellectual history at Oxford University. He is the author of several books, including *The Secret Family* and the bestseller *The Secret House*, from which this excerpt is taken. A native of Chicago, he lives in London, England.

1   Into the bathroom goes our male resident, and after the most pressing need is satisfied it's time to brush the teeth. The tube of toothpaste is squeezed, its pinched metal seams are splayed, pressure waves are generated inside, and the paste begins to flow. But what's in this toothpaste, so carefully being extruded out?

2   Water mostly, 30 to 45 percent in most brands: ordinary, everyday simple tap water. It's there because people like to have a big gob of toothpaste to spread on the brush, and water is the cheapest stuff there is when it comes to making big gobs. Dripping a bit from the tap onto your brush would cost virtually nothing; whipped in with the rest of the toothpaste the manufacturers can sell it at a neat and accountant-pleasing $2 per pound equivalent. Toothpaste manufacture is a very lucrative occupation.

3   Second to water in quantity is chalk: exactly the same material that schoolteachers use to write on blackboards. It is collected from the crushed remains of long-dead ocean creatures. In the Cretaceous seas chalk particles served as part of the wickedly sharp outer skeleton that these creatures had to wrap around themselves to keep from getting chomped by all the slightly larger other ocean creatures they met. Their massed graves are our present chalk deposits.

4   The individual chalk particles—the size of the smallest mud particles in your garden—have kept their toughness over the aeons, and now on the toothbrush they'll need it. The enamel outer coating of the tooth they'll have to face is the hardest substance in the body—tougher than skull, or bone, or nail. Only the chalk particles in toothpaste can successfully grind into the teeth during brushing, ripping off the surface layers like an abrading wheel grinding down a boulder in a quarry.

5   The craters, slashes, and channels that the chalk tears into the teeth will also remove a certain amount of build-up yellow in the carnage, and it is for that polishing function that it's there. A certain amount of unduly enlarged extra-abrasive chalk fragments tear such cavernous pits into the teeth that future decay bacteria will be able to bunker down there and thrive; the quality control people find it almost impossible to screen out these errant super-chalk pieces, and government regulations allow them to stay in.

6   In case even the gouging doesn't get all the yellow off, another substance is worked into the toothpaste cream. This is titanium dioxide. It comes in tiny spheres, and it's the stuff bobbing around in white wall paint to make it come out white. Splashed around onto your teeth during the brushing it coats much of the yellow that remains. Being water soluble it leaks off in the next few hours and is swallowed, but at least for the quick glance up in the mirror after finishing it will make the user think his teeth are truly white. Some manufacturers add optical whitening dyes—the stuff more commonly found in washing machine bleach—to make extra sure that that glance in the mirror shows reassuring white.

7   These ingredients alone would not make a very attractive concoction. They would stick in the tube like a sloppy white plastic lump, hard to squeeze out as well as revolting to the touch. Few consumers would savor rubbing in a mixture of water, ground-up blackboard chalk, and the whitener from latex paint first thing in the morning. To get around that finicky distaste the manufacturers have mixed in a host of other goodies.

8   To keep the glop from drying out, a mixture including glycerine glycol—related to the most common car antifreeze ingredient—is whipped in with the chalk and water, and to give *that* concoction a bit of substance (all we really have so far is wet colored chalk) a large helping is added of gummy molecules from the seaweed *Chondrus Crispus*. This seaweed ooze spreads in among the chalk, paint, and antifreeze, then stretches itself in all directions to hold the whole mass together. A bit of paraffin oil (the fuel that flickers in camping lamps) is pumped in with it to help the moss ooze keep the whole substance smooth.

9   With the glycol, ooze, and paraffin we're almost there. Only two major chemicals are left to make the refreshing, cleansing substance we know as toothpaste. The ingredients so far are fine for cleaning, but they wouldn't make much of the satisfying foam we have come to expect in the morning brushing.

10   To remedy that, every toothpaste on the market has a big dollop of (detergent) added too. You've seen the suds detergent will make in a washing machine. The same substance added here will duplicate that inside the mouth. It's not particularly necessary, but it sells.

11   The only problem is that by itself this ingredient tastes, well, too like detergent. It's horribly bitter and harsh. The chalk put in toothpaste is pretty foul-tasting too for that matter. It's to get around that gustatory discomfort that the manufacturers put in the ingredient they tout perhaps the most of all. This is the flavoring, and it has to be strong. (Double rectified peppermint) oil is used—a flavorer so powerful that chemists know better than to sniff it in the raw state in the laboratory. (Menthol crystals) and (saccharin) or other sugar simulators are added to complete the camouflage operation.

12   Is that it? Chalk, water, paint, seaweed, antifreeze, paraffin oil, detergent, and peppermint? Not quite. A mix like that would be irresistible to the hundreds of thousands of individual bacteria lying on the surface of even an immaculately cleaned bathroom sink. They would get in, float in the water bubbles, ingest the ooze and paraffin, maybe even spray out enzymes to break down the chalk. The result would be an uninviting mess. The way manufacturers avoid that final obstacle is by putting something in to kill the bacteria. Something good and strong is needed, something that will zap any accidentally intrudant bacteria into oblivion. And that something is (formaldehyde)—the disinfectant used in anatomy labs.

13   So it's chalk, water, paint, seaweed, antifreeze, paraffin oil, detergent, peppermint, formaldehyde, and (fluoride) (which can go some way towards preserving children's teeth)—that's the usual mixture raised to the mouth on the toothbrush for a fresh morning's clean. If it sounds too unfortunate, take heart. Studies show that thorough brushing with just plain water will often do as good a job.

| Exercise 4 | **VOCABULARY HIGHLIGHTS** |

Write a short definition of each word as it is used in the essay. (Paragraph numbers are given in parentheses.) Be prepared to use the words in your own sentences.

splayed (1)   carnage (5)

extruded (1)   errant (5)

lucrative (3)   dollop (10)

aeons (4)   gustatory (11)

abrading (4)   intrudant (12)

| Exercise 5 | **DISCUSSION AND CRITICAL THINKING** |

1. What is the unit?
   Toothpaste.

2. What is the principle of Bodanis's division?
   He is concerned with the actual ingredients in the toothpaste.

3. Circle the words indicating the parts of the division as they first appear.

4. Bodanis is discussing a chemical formula. Does he address a general reading audience or a reading audience with a specific knowledge of industrial chemistry?
   General reading audience.

5. Explain how Bodanis's use of definitions of the ingredients suggests the audience for whom this essay is intended.
   Instead of giving technical formulas, he makes a lot of comparisons. He says that the chalky substance is the same material that is used in chalk in classrooms. The whitening is like bleach. The paraffin oil is used in campfire lamps. The glycerine glycol is related to car antifreeze. The detergent is like that used in clothes washing machines.

6. How would you characterize the *tone* (how the author regards his subject material and his audience) of the article?
   Humorous, breezy, and highly informal.

7. Give some examples of word choice that contribute to that tone.
   "Gob" (paragraph 2), "chomped" (paragraph 3), "bunker down" (paragraph 5), "goodies" (paragraph 7), "glop" (paragraph 8), "ooze" (paragraph 8), "dollop" (paragraph 10), "antifreeze" (paragraph 12), and "zap" (paragraph 12).

8. Why did Bodanis select the humorous tone?
   If he had used an objective and more scientific approach, he would have sacrificed reader interest. It's fun to read this lively descriptive analysis of an everyday product.

Designer Babies

Michael D. Lemonich

Designer drugs, designer foods, designer music—what's next? Michael D. Lemonich, staff writer for *Time*, says it may be babies. Ordinarily, we analyze a person for his or her qualities according to the person's development. Now science has provided us with a way to pick the qualities before birth. The technological decisions may be much easier to make than the ethical ones. This essay was first published in a special January 1999 issue, "The Future of Medicine."

1   Until just a few years ago, making a baby boy or a baby girl was pretty much a hit-or-miss affair. Not anymore. Parents who have access to the latest genetic testing techniques can now predetermine their baby's sex with great accuracy—as Monique and Scott Collins learned to their delight two years ago, when their long-wished-for daughter Jessica was born after genetic prescreening at a fertility clinic in Fairfax, Va.

2   And baby Jessica is just the beginning. Within a decade or two, it may be possible to screen kids almost before conception for an enormous range of attributes, such as how tall they're likely to be, what body type they will have, their hair and eye color, what sorts of illnesses they will be naturally resistant to, and even, conceivably, their IQ and personality type.

3   In fact if gene therapy lives up to its promise, parents may someday be able to go beyond weeding out undesirable traits and start actually inserting the genes they want—perhaps even genes that have been crafted in a lab. Before the new millennium is many years old, parents may be going to fertility clinics and picking from a list of options the way car buyers order air conditioning and chrome-alloy wheels. "It's the ultimate shopping experience: designing your baby," says biotechnology critic Jeremy Rifkin, who is appalled by the prospect. "In a society used to cosmetic surgery and psychopharmacology, this is not a big step."

4   The prospect of designer babies, like many of the ethical conundrums posed by the genetic revolution, is confronting the world so rapidly that doctors, ethicists, religious leaders and politicians are just starting to grapple with the implications—and trying to decide how they feel about it all.

5   They still have a bit of time. Aside from gender, the only traits that can now be identified at the earliest stages of development are about a dozen of the most serious genetic diseases. Gene ther-

apy in embryos is at least a few years away. And the gene or combination of genes responsible for most of our physical and mental attributes hasn't even been identified yet, making moot the idea of engineering genes in or out of a fetus. Besides, say clinicians, even if the techniques for making designer babies are perfected within the next decade, they should be applied in the service of disease prevention, not improving on nature.

6   But what doctors intend is not necessarily what's going to happen. Indeed, the technology that permitted the Collins family to pick the sex of their child was first used to select for health, not gender per se. Adapting a technique used on livestock, researchers at the Genetics & IVF Institute in Fairfax took advantage of a simple rule of biology: girls have two X chromosomes, while boys have one X and one Y. The mother has only Xs to offer, so the balance of power lies with the father—specifically with his sperm, which brings either an X or a Y to the fertilization party.

7   As it happens, Y chromosomes have slightly less DNA than Xs. So by staining the sperm's DNA with a nontoxic light-sensitive dye, the Virginia scientists were able to sort sperm by gender—with a high rate of success—before using them in artificial insemination. The first couple to use the technique was looking to escape a deadly disease known as X-linked hydrocephalus, or water on the brain, which almost always affects boys.

8   But while the technique is ideal for weeding out this and other X-linked disorders, including hemophilia, Duchenne muscular dystrophy and Fragile X syndrome, most patients treated at Genetics & IVF want to even out their families—a life-style rather than a medical decision. The Fairfax clinic has been willing to help, but such a trend doesn't sit well with some other practitioners. "Our view at the moment," says Dr. Zev Rosenwaks, director of the Center for Reproductive Medicine and Infertility at Cornell Medical Center in New York City, "is that these techniques should be used for medical indications, not family balancing."

9   But now that parents know that the technology is available, and that at least some clinics will let them choose a child's gender for nonmedical reasons, it may be too late to go back. In a relatively short time, suggests Princeton University biologist Lee Silver, whose book *Remaking Eden* addresses precisely these sorts of issues, sex selection may cease to be much of an issue. His model is in vitro fertilization, the technique used to make "test-tube" babies. "When the world first learned about IVF two decades ago," he says, "it was horrifying to most people, and most said that they wouldn't use it even if they were infertile. But growing demand

makes it socially acceptable, and now anybody who's infertile demands IVF."

10   That's not to say in vitro fertilization hasn't created its own set of ethical problems, including custody battles over fertilized embryos that were frozen but never used, questions about what to do with the embryos left over after a successful pregnancy, and the increased health risks posed by multiple births. Yet no one is suggesting the practice be stopped. Infertile couples would never stand for it.

11   Sex selection will undoubtedly raise knotty issues as well. Societies that value boys more highly than girls, including China and India, are already out of balance; this could tip the scales even further. Such an outcome is unlikely in the U.S., where surveys show that equal numbers of parents want girls as boys. But the same polls report that Americans believe an ideal family has a boy as the oldest child. Boys often end up being more assertive and more dominant than girls, as do firstborn children; skewing the population toward doubly dominant firstborns could make it even harder to rid society of gender-role stereotypes.

12   The ethical issues raised by techniques emerging from the genetic labs are likely to be even more complex. What if parents can use preimplantation genetic diagnosis to avoid having kids with attention-deficit disorder, say, or those predestined to be short or dullwitted or predisposed to homosexuality? Will they feel pressure from friends and relations to do so? And will kids who are allowed to be born with these characteristics be made to feel even more like second-class citizens than they do now?

13   Even thornier is the question of what kinds of genetic tinkering parents might be willing to elect to enhance already healthy children. What about using gene therapy to add genes for HIV resistance or longevity or a high IQ? What about enhancements that simply stave off psychological pain—giving a child an attractive face or a pleasing personality? No one is certain when these techniques will be available—and many professionals protest that they're not interested in perfecting them. "Yes, theoretically you could do such things," says Baylor University human-reproduction specialist Larry Lipshultz. "It's doable, but I don't know of anyone doing it."

14   Sooner or later, however, someone will do it. In countries with national health services, such as Canada and Britain, it tends to be easier to dictate what sorts of genetic enhancement will be permitted and what will be forbidden. But in the U.S., despite the

growth of managed care, there will always be people with enough money—or a high enough limit on their credit cards—to pay for what they want. "Typically," says Princeton's Silver, "medical researchers are moved by a desire to cure disease more effectively. Reprogenetics [a term Silver coined] is going to be driven by parents, or prospective parents, who want something for their children. It's the sort of demand that could explode."

15   Silver even contemplates a scenario in which society splits into two camps, the "gen-rich" and the "gen-poor," those with and those without a designer genome. The prospect is disturbing, but trying to stop it might entail even more disturbing choices. "There may be problems," admits James Watson, whose co-discovery of the structure of DNA in 1953 made all this possible. "But I don't believe we can let the government start dictating the decisions people make about what sorts of families they'll have."

| **Exercise 6** | **DISCUSSION AND CRITICAL THINKING** |

1. Apply the following aspects of an analysis by division to paragraph 2. What is the unit?
   Kids.

   What is the principle of dividing the unit into parts?
   Someday it will be possible to design children according to attributes.

   What are the main parts of the division?
   Attributes: tallness, body type, hair and eye color, disease limitations, and IQ and personality type.

2. Of the attributes that may be selected for children, which ones do clinicians say should be the only concern for development (paragraph 5)?
   Disease prevention.

3. What does Lemonich say is likely to be in the future of baby designing, regardless of what appears to be the prevailing ethical view?
   He believes that it is inevitable that researchers will go beyond disease limitation and experiment with other attributes such as those listed in paragraph 2.

4. Of the attributes mentioned in paragraphs 2, 12, and 13, which ones should be allowed in designing babies?
   Answers will vary.

5. What controls on baby designing can and should be imposed?
   Answers will vary.

Optimism, Tenacity Lead Way Back to Life

William Helmreich

William Helmreich is Professor of Sociology and Jewish Studies at City University Graduate Center and City College of New York and co-director of the City College Conflict Resolution Center. Author of ten books, Helmreich has written for metropolitan newspapers and numerous scholarly journals. In this article for the *Los Angeles Times,* he writes about the traits that enabled Holocaust survivors to function well again in society.

1   Accounts of tragedy and catastrophe have been much in the news: hurricanes in Florida and Hawaii, famine in Somalia and Sudan. The media focus tends to be on death and destruction and the terrible aftereffects on human beings. This is not surprising, but there are other, more hopeful, lessons to be learned from calamity.

2   I have spent the last six years traveling the United States, from New York to California, from Wisconsin to Mississippi, hearing from hundreds of people who lived through the greatest horror of the 20th Century, the Holocaust.* I was curious as to how the lives of these Jews had turned out and whether they were able to recover from their terrible experiences.

3   The results, when compared with the stereotypical anecdotal accounts of survivors who succumb to depression, anxiety and hopelessness, were highly surprising. While many survivors did have these serious emotional problems, the great majority did not. They led relatively normal lives, holding down jobs, having and raising children and contributing to the communities in which they settled. Some, such as Rep. Tom Lantos (D-Burlingame); Abraham Resnick, former vice mayor of Miami; Maj. Gen. Sidney Shachnow and the director of the Anti-Defamation League, Abraham Foxman, achieved considerable fame in their chosen fields. Others, not so well-known, became musicians, tailors, businessmen, teachers and farmers.

4   Naturally, all of the survivors are still affected, even haunted, by what happened to them. But they also constitute, on the

*The Holocaust was an era of persecution of Jews and other minorities that was part of German leader Adolf Hitler's plan to exterminate all Jewish people. Hitler led the Nazi Party.

whole, a community whose members display a zest for life and who have faith in the future.

5   How did they do it, I wondered? How, after experiencing betrayal and unspeakable cruelty in the Nazi death camps and elsewhere in Europe, were the survivors able to learn to live again, trust again, love again, and bring children into a world that had inflicted such pain on them? The answers contain lessons for everyone who goes through crisis and adversity, be it loss of a loved one, crippling illness, natural disaster or even a job reversal.

6   Most of the survivors who succeeded in rebuilding their lives possessed several traits:

7   First was flexibility, a willingness to adapt to new situations, much like what faces the survivors of Hurricanes Andrew and Iniki. In addition, there was a need to be assertive—a recognition that help given by others would be temporary and that ultimately they were on their own. Related to this was tenacity, an approach to life that refused to accept initial setbacks as the status quo.

8   One of the most crucial survivor characteristics was optimism. More than not thinking about the past, it reflected a certain mindset. Alex Gross, a real estate developer who survived Auschwitz and Buchenwald,* later lost his only son, at 14, in a farming accident. When he saw the mangled body, he resolved never to reveal the details of the death to his wife. Alas, that was not the end of Gross's woes. Nine years later his wife was murdered. Despite this double tragedy, Alex Gross has remarried and is active in his community. He is a survivor.

9   Survivors who did well were intelligent. This trait, which includes "street smarts," amounts to an ability to think quickly, analyze a situation and act. Another key feature was distancing ability, the capacity to view the Holocaust as a unique event requiring certain behavior that was appropriate then but not now. This was accompanied by group consciousness, the forging of a common bond with others who shared their tragedy.

10   Related to this was a more subtle trait, assimilation of the knowledge that they survived. This amounted to using the fact that one has prevailed over hardship as a source of strength. Of equal significance was finding meaning in one's life. For some it was their work, for others religion, and for many it was the bonds of love within the family structure.

11   Finally, there was courage. Simply continuing with life was an act of bravery. Specifically, however, it took many forms—fighting

---

*Auschwitz and Buchenwald were the names of two concentration camps.

back from debilitating illness, taking risks in business or standing up to bigotry.

12   Those who have lived through the riots in Los Angeles or the siege in Sarajevo, those who have lived through earthquakes, hurricanes and floods, can draw strength and sustenance from Hitler's survivors. The reason is that the success story of the survivors is not one of remarkable people. Rather, it is one of just how remarkable people can be.

Exercise 7   VOCABULARY HIGHLIGHTS

Write a short definition of each word as it is used in the essay. (Paragraph numbers are given in parentheses.) Be prepared to use the words in your own sentences.

stereotypical (3)	adversity (5)
anecdotal (3)	assertive (7)
succumb (3)	assimilation (10)
constitute (4)	debilitating (11)
inflicted (5)	sustenance (12)

Exercise 8   DISCUSSION AND CRITICAL THINKING

1. What is the unit?
   Holocaust victims.

2. What is the principle by which that unit functions; that is, what does the unit do or represent from this perspective? Write the answer here, and circle the passage that states or suggests the principle.
   How they survived to rebuild their lives (especially paragraph 6).

3. What are the ten parts (traits) that make up the unit according to this principle? Underline them in the text, and write them here.
   Flexibility, assertiveness, tenacity, optimism, intelligence, distancing ability, group consciousness, pride in survival, finding meaning in life, and courage.

4. Go back to your answer to question 3 and number the traits to indicate your view of the relative importance of each one.
   Answers will vary.

5. What is the order of the parts (time, space, emphasis, or a combination) in Helmreich's essay?
   Emphasis.

Three Generations of Native American Women's Birth Experience

Joy Harjo

Joy Harjo, a Native American of Creek, Cherokee, and white ancestry, has written screenplays, three books of poetry, and numerous essays, all about her culture. She is a consultant for the National Indian Youth Council and the Native American Broadcasting Consortium, and a professor of creative writing at the University of New Mexico. Here she gives accounts of childbirth experienced by her mother, herself, and her daughter.

1   It was still dark when I awakened in the stuffed back room of my mother-in-law's small rented house with what felt like hard cramps. At 17 years of age I had read everything I could from the Tahlequah Public Library about pregnancy and giving birth. But nothing prepared me for what was coming. I awakened my child's father and then ironed him a shirt before we walked the four blocks to the Indian hospital because we had no car and no money for a taxi. He had been working with another Cherokee artist silk-screening signs for specials at the supermarket and making $5 a day, and had to leave me alone at the hospital because he had to go to work. We didn't awaken his mother. She had to get up soon enough to fix breakfast for her daughter and granddaughter before leaving for her job at the nursing home. I knew my life was balanced at the edge of great, precarious change, and I felt alone and cheated. Where was the circle of women to acknowledge and honor this birth?

2   It was still dark as we walked through the cold morning, under oaks that symbolized the stubbornness and endurance of the Cherokee people who had made Tahlequah their capital in the new lands. I looked for handholds in the misty gray sky, for a voice announcing this impending miracle. I wanted to change everything; I wanted to go back to a place before childhood, before our tribe's removal to Oklahoma. What kind of life was I bringing this child into? I was a poor, mixed-blood woman heavy with a child who would suffer the struggle of poverty, the legacy of loss. For the second time in my life I felt the sharp tug of my own birth cord, still connected to my mother. I believe it never pulls away, until death, and even then it becomes a streak in the sky symbol-

izing that most important warrior road. In my teens I had fought my mother's weaknesses with all my might, and here I was at 17, becoming as my mother, who was in Tulsa, cooking breakfasts and preparing for the lunch shift at a factory cafeteria as I walked to the hospital to give birth. I should be with her; instead, I was far from her house, in the house of a mother-in-law who later would try to use witchcraft to destroy me.

3   After my son's father left me, I was prepped for birth. This meant my pubic area was shaved completely, and then I endured the humiliation of an enema, all at the hands of strangers. I was left alone in a room painted government green. An overwhelming antiseptic smell emphasized the sterility of the hospital, a hospital built because of the U.S. government's treaty and responsibility to provide health care to Indian people.

4   I intellectually understood the stages of labor, the place of transition, of birth—but it was difficult to bear the actuality of it, and to bear it alone. Yet in some ways I wasn't alone, for history surrounded me. It is with the birth of children that history is given form and voice. Birth is one of the most sacred acts we take part in and witness in our lives. But sacredness seemed to be far from my lonely labor room in the Indian hospital. I heard a woman screaming in the next room with her pain, and I wanted to comfort her. The nurse used her as a bad example to the rest of us who were struggling to keep our suffering silent.

5   The doctor was a military man who had signed on this watch not for the love of healing or out of awe at the miracle of birth, but to fulfill a contract for medical school payments. I was another statistic to him; he touched me as if he were moving equipment from one place to another. During my last visit I was given the option of being sterilized. He explained to me that the moment of birth was the best time to do it. I was handed the form but chose not to sign it, and am amazed now that I didn't think too much of it at the time. Later I would learn that many Indian women who weren't fluent in English signed, thinking it was a form giving consent for the doctor to deliver their babies. Others were sterilized without even the formality of signing. My light skin had probably saved me from such a fate. It wouldn't be the first time in my life.

6   When my son was finally born I had been deadened with a needle in my spine. He was shown to me—the incredible miracle nothing prepared me for—then taken from me in the name of medical progress. I fell asleep with the weight of chemicals and awoke yearning for the child I had suffered for, had anticipated in the months proceeding from this unexpected genesis when I was

still 16 and a student at Indian school. I was not allowed to sit up or walk because of the possibility of paralysis (one of the drug's side effects), and when I finally got to hold him, the nurse stood guard as if I would hurt him. I felt enmeshed in a system in which the wisdom that had carried my people from generation to generation was ignored. In that place I felt ashamed I was an Indian woman. But I was also proud of what my body had accomplished despite the rape by the bureaucracy's machinery, and I got us out of there as soon as possible. My son would flourish on beans and fry bread, and on the dreams and stories we fed him.

7   My daughter was born four years later, while I was an art student at the University of New Mexico. Since my son's birth I had waitressed, cleaned hospital rooms, filled cars with gas (while wearing a miniskirt), worked as a nursing assistant, and led dance classes at a health spa. I knew I didn't want to cook and waitress all my life, as my mother had done. I had watched the varicose veins grow branches on her legs, and as they grew, her zest for dancing and sports dissolved into utter tiredness. She had been born with a caul* over her face, the sign of a gifted visionary.

8   My earliest memories are of my mother writing songs on an ancient Underwood typewriter after she had washed and waxed the kitchen floor on her hands and knees. She too had wanted something different for her life. She had left an impoverished existence at age 17, bound for the big city of Tulsa. She was shamed in a time in which to be even part Indian was to be an outcast in the great U.S. system. Half her relatives were Cherokee full-bloods from near Jay, Oklahoma, who for the most part had nothing to do with white people. The other half were musically inclined "white trash" addicted to country-western music and Holy Roller† fervor. She thought she could disappear in the city; no one would know her family, where she came from. She had dreams of singing and had once been offered a job singing on the radio but turned it down because she was shy. Later one of her songs would be stolen before she could copyright it and would make someone else rich. She would quit writing songs. She and my father would divorce and she would be forced to work for money to feed and clothe four children, all born within two years of each other.

9   As a child growing up in Oklahoma, I liked to be told the story of my birth. I would beg for it while my mother cleaned and ironed. "You almost killed me," she would say. "We almost died."

---

*A caul is part of the membrane enclosing the fetus.
†Holy Rollers are fundamentalist Christian enthusiasts, who sometimes go into trances and roll on the floor.

That I could kill my mother filled me with remorse and shame. And I imagined the push-pull of my life, which is a legacy I deal with even now when I am twice as old as my mother was at my birth. I loved to hear the story of my warrior fight for my breath. The way it was told, it had been my decision to live. When I got older, I realized we were both nearly casualties of the system, the same system flourishing in the Indian hospital where later my son Phil would be born.

10   My parents felt lucky to have insurance, to be able to have their children in the hospital. My father came from a fairly prominent Muscogee Creek family. *His* mother was a full-blood who in the early 1920s got her degree in art. She was a painter. She gave birth to him in a private hospital in Oklahoma City; at least that's what I think he told me before he died at age 53. It was something of which they were proud.

11   This experience was much different from my mother's own birth. She and five of her six brothers were born at home, with no medical assistance. The only time a doctor was called was when someone was dying. When she was born her mother named her Wynema, a Cherokee name my mother says means beautiful woman, and Jewell, for a can of shortening stored in the room where she was born.

12   I wanted something different for my life, for my son, and for my daughter, who later was born in a university hospital in Albuquerque. It was a bright summer morning when she was ready to begin her journey. I still had no car, but I had enough money saved for a taxi for a ride to the hospital. She was born "naturally," without drugs. I could look out of the hospital window while I was in labor at the bluest sky in the world. Her father was present in the delivery room—though after her birth he disappeared on a drinking binge. I understood his despair, but did not agree with the painful means to describe it. A few days later Rainy Dawn was presented to the sun at her father's pueblo and given a name so that she will always be recognized as a part of the people, as a child of the sun.

13   That's not to say that my experience in the hospital reached perfection. The clang of metal against metal in the delivery room had the effect of a tuning fork reverberating fear in my pelvis. After giving birth, I held my daughter, but they took her from me for "processing." I refused to lie down to be wheeled to my room after giving birth; I wanted to walk out of there to find my daughter. We reached a compromise, and I rode in a wheelchair. When we reached the room, I stood up and walked to the nursery and

demanded my daughter. I knew she needed me. That began my war with the nursery staff, who deemed me unknowledgeable because I was Indian and poor. Once again I felt the brushfire of shame, but I'd learned to put it out much more quickly, and I demanded early release so I could take care of my baby without the judgment of strangers.

14   I wanted something different for Rainy, and as she grew up I worked hard to prove that I could make "something" of my life. I obtained two degrees as a single mother. I wrote poetry, screenplays, became a professor, and tried to live a life that would be a positive influence for both of my children. My work in this life has to do with reclaiming the memory stolen from our peoples when we were dispossessed from our lands east of the Mississippi; it has to do with restoring us. I am proud of our history, a history so powerful that it both destroyed my father and guarded him. It's a history that claims my mother as she lives not far from the place her mother was born, names her as she cooks in the cafeteria of a small college in Oklahoma.

15   When my daughter told me she was pregnant, I wasn't surprised. I had known it before she did, or at least before she would admit it to me. I felt despair, as if nothing had changed or ever would. She had run away from Indian school with her boyfriend and they had been living in the streets of Gallup, a border town notorious for the suicides and deaths of Indian peoples. I brought her and her boyfriend with me because it was the only way I could bring her home. At age 16, she was fighting me just as I had so fiercely fought my mother. She was making the same mistakes. I felt as if everything I had accomplished had been in vain. Yet I felt strangely empowered, too, at this repetition of history, this continuance, by a new possibility of life and love, and I steadfastly stood by my daughter.

16   I had a university job, so I had insurance that covered my daughter. She saw an obstetrician in town who was reputed to be one of the best. She had the choice of a birthing room. She had the finest care. Despite this, I once again battled with a system in which physicians are taught the art of healing by dissecting cadavers. My daughter went into labor a month early. We both knew intuitively the baby was ready, but how to explain that to a system in which numbers and statistics provide the base of understanding? My daughter would have her labor interrupted: her blood pressure would rise because of the drug given to her to stop the labor. She would be given an unneeded amniocentesis and would have her labor induced—after having it artificially

17 My daughter's induced labor was unnatural and difficult, monitored by machines, not by touch. I was shocked. I felt as if I'd come full circle, as if I were watching my mother's labor and the struggle of my own birth. But I was there in the hospital room with her, as neither my mother had been for me, nor her mother for her. My daughter and I went through the labor and birth together.

18 And when Krista Rae was born, she was born to her family. Her father was there for her, as were both her grandmothers and my friend who had flown in to be with us. Her paternal great-grandparents and aunts and uncles had also arrived from the Navajo Reservation to honor her. Something *had* changed.

19 Four days later, I took my granddaughter to the Saguaro forest before dawn and gave her the name I had dreamed for her just before her birth. Her name looks like clouds of mist settling around a sacred mountain as it begins to speak. A female ancestor approaches on a horse. We are all together.

Exercise 9   **DISCUSSION AND CRITICAL THINKING**

1. How are the generations of Harjo's family different? On what basis other than time can they be divided?

   The birth experiences are remarkably similar, with women being attended by those who do not know or do not care. They can be divided at least in the sense of awareness and determination to change things. Her mother accepted what was available without question; so did the author on the birth of her son; but when her daughter came, she was more independent and more critical; finally, when her daughter gave birth, she witnessed many of the same attitudes, but she is determined to make things different.

2. In what way is this essay optimistic?

   Harjo has made sure that "when Krista Rae was born, she was born to her family." The father, grandparents, and others were there. "Something *had* changed."

3. What strains of pessimism do you find in this essay?

   Very little has changed in the attitudes of others toward Native Americans and in the basic circumstances of birth.

4. What does Harjo see as the key to improvement for Native American culture?

   Family, tradition, heritage, and sticking up for one's rights.

5. Argue for or against calling the three generations described here the old, the transitional, and the new.

   Answers will vary.

✎ Topics for Writing Analysis by Division

Writing Process Worksheet

You will find a Writing Process Worksheet in Appendix A, page 531. It can be photocopied and enlarged, filled in, and submitted with each assignment if your instructor directs you to do so.

Source-Based Topics

Each essay developed from these suggested source-based topics should include at least one reference to the reading selection by the author's name and the title. Quotations should be enclosed in quotation marks. Follow your instructor's directions in documenting the ideas you borrow. Whether you use informal or formal documentation, the form is not complicated, and you will soon learn to use it for these essays without checking each time. See pages 77 and 78 for a discussion of MLA style and informal documentation.

Underlining and annotating reading selections will help you in finding support material. In prewriting brief essays, consider marking your outline to indicate where you will use quotations or other borrowed ideas. If the quotations or reworded statements are short and few, you could even insert them inside parentheses or circles in your outline; if you do, also include the author's last name and the page number. A sound system, consistently used, will save you time and ensure technically strong papers.

"A Chinese New Year's Feast"

1. Write about a holiday feast or other cultural event that can be discussed as a unit with parts.

"Elvis Presley: Twentieth-Century Legend"

2. If you are familiar with Elvis, write your own analysis by division, providing your own support.

3. If you disagree with the view of Emmett Davis, summarize his essay and explain why you think he is wrong. Preserve the basic form of unit, principle, parts, and relationship of parts.

4. Write about someone else who you believe has achieved legendary status. Use Davis's essay as a model for organization as you discuss your candidate's qualities for excellence in a particular field such as politics, entertainment, athletics, or art.

"A Brush with Reality: Surprises in the Tube"

5. Using this essay as a model, write about another product with ingredients. Consider makeup, breakfast cereal, bread, soft drinks, beer, perfume, insect repellant, mouthwash, and chewing gum. If you have difficulty in defining some of the terms, consider checking with

your campus experts in departments such as chemistry, biology, and health sciences. Also consult the Internet; try "chewing gum [or any other term] and ingredients." Try to discover how the common ingredients are used in other concoctions.

"Designer Babies"

6. Borrowing the list of attributes in paragraph 2, discuss which ones would and would not be acceptable according to your value system. Explain what kinds of people might favor certain attributes for their babies.

"Optimism, Tenacity Lead Way Back to Life"

7. Using this essay as a model, discuss the traits that were necessary in any significant struggle that you have witnessed or heard about. The significant struggle might be of a large magnitude involving a great number of people or it might pertain to only one individual, perhaps yourself. At the individual level it might involve death, illness, divorce, betrayal, unemployment, or relocation to another country or to a different cultural group.

"Three Generations of Native American Women's Birth Experience"

8. Using this essay as a model, write about three generations of birth experience in a family you are familiar with. Consider discussing your project with family members.

9. Summarize Harjo's essay by using this pattern for organization: unit, principle, parts, relationships of parts. Include comments on the differences in the three generations and point out both progress and lack of progress. Use a combined summary and reaction or a two-part response (summary separated from the reaction, as discussed in Chapter 4).

10. Using this essay as a model, write about three generations of people within a family you are familiar with, focusing on marriage (circumstances, ceremonies, customs, tone), education (opportunities, achievements), independence (circumstances of leaving home as a young person), or work.

Career-Related Topics

11. Explain how the parts of a product function together as a unit.

12. Explain how each of several qualities of a specific person—such as his or her intelligence, sincerity, knowledgeability, ability to communicate, manner, attitude, and appearance—makes that individual an effective salesperson, manager, or employee.

13. Explain how the demands or requirements for a particular job represent a comprehensive picture of that job.

14. Explain how the aspects of a particular service (such as friendly, competent, punctual, confidential) work together in a satisfactory manner.

General Topics

Some of the following topics are too broad for a short writing assignment and should be narrowed. For example, the general "a wedding ceremony" could be narrowed to the particular: "José and María's wedding ceremony." Select a topic from the following list. Narrow the topic, divide it into parts, and analyze it in a short essay.

15. A machine such as an automobile, a computer, a camera

16. A city administration, a governmental agency, a school board, a student council

17. An offensive team in football (any team in any game)

18. A family, a relationship, a gang, a club, a sorority, a fraternity

19. An album, a performance, a song, a singer, an actor, a musical group, a musical instrument

20. A movie, a television program, a video game

21. Any well-known person—athlete, politician, criminal, writer

Writer's Guidelines: Analysis by Division

Almost anything can be analyzed by division—for example, how the parts of the ear work in hearing, how the parts of the eye work in seeing, or how the parts of the heart work in pumping blood throughout the body. Subjects such as these are all approached with the same systematic procedure.

1. This is the procedure.
   - Step 1. Begin with something that is a unit.
   - Step 2. State the principle by which that unit functions.
   - Step 3. Divide the unit into parts according to the principle.
   - Step 4. Discuss each of the parts in relation to the unit.

2. This is the way you might apply that procedure to a good boss.
   - *Unit.* Manager
   - *Principle of function.* Effective as a leader
   - *Parts based on the principle.* Fair, intelligent, stable, competent in field
   - *Discussion:* Consider each part in relation to the person's effectiveness as a manager.

3. This is how a basic outline of analysis by division might look.

Thesis: To be effective as a leader, a manager needs specific qualities.

  I. Fair
  II. Intelligent
  III. Stable
  IV. Competent in field

9

Classification: Establishing Groups

THE QUIGMANS   by Buddy Hickerson

© Tribune Media Services, Inc. All Rights Reserved. Reprinted with permission.

Writing Classification

To explain by classification, you put persons, places, things, or ideas into groups or classes based on their characteristics. Whereas analysis by division deals with the characteristics of just one unit, classification deals with more than one unit, so the subject is plural.

To classify efficiently, try following this procedure:

1. Select a plural subject.

2. Decide on a principle for grouping the units of your subject.

3. Establish the groups, or classes.

4. Write about the classes

Selecting a Subject

When you say you have different kinds of neighbors, friends, teachers, bosses, or interests, you are classifying; that is, you are forming groups.

In naming the different kinds of people in your neighborhood, you might think of different groupings of your neighbors, the units. For example, some neighbors are friendly, some are meddlesome, and some are private. Some neighbors have yards like Japanese gardens, some have yards like neat-but-cozy parks, and some have yards like abandoned lots. Some neighbors are affluent, some are comfortable, and some are struggling. Each of these sets is a classification system and could be the focus of one paragraph in your essay.

Using a Principle to Avoid Overlapping

All the sets in the preceding section are sound because each group is based on a single concern: neighborly involvement, appearance of the yard, or wealth. This one concern, or controlling idea, is called the *principle*. For example, the principle of neighborly involvement controls the grouping of neighbors into three classes: friendly, meddlesome, and private.

All the classes in any one group must adhere to the controlling principle for that group. You would not say, for example, that your neighbors can be classified as friendly, meddlesome, private, and affluent, because the first three classes relate to neighborly involvement, but the fourth, relating to wealth, refers to another principle. Any of the first three—the friendly, meddlesome, and private—might also be affluent. The classes should not overlap in this way. Also, every member should fit into one of the available classes.

Establishing Classes

As you name your classes, rule out easy, unimaginative phrasing such as *fast/medium/slow, good/average/bad,* and *beautiful/ordinary/ugly.* Look for creative, original phrases and unusual perspectives.

Subject: neighbors

Principle: neighborhood involvement

Classes: friendly, meddlesome, private

Subject: neighbors

Principle: yard upkeep

Classes: immaculate, neat, messy

Subject: neighbors

Principle: wealth

Classes: affluent, comfortable, struggling

Using Simple and Complex Forms

Classification can take two forms: simple and complex. The simple form does not go beyond main divisions in its groupings.

Subject: Neighbors

Principle: Involvement

Classes: I. Friendly

II. Meddlesome

III. Private

Complex classifications are based on one principle and then subgrouped by another related principle. The following example classifies neighbors by their neighborly involvement. It then subgroups the classes on the basis of motive.

I. Friendly
   A. Civic-minded
   B. Want to be accepted
   C. Gregarious

II. Meddlesome
   A. Controlling
   B. Emotionally needy
   C. Suspicious of others

III. Private

    A. Shy

    B. Snobbish

    C. Secretive

Here are two examples by professional writers on other topics, one organized as a simple form and the other organized as a complex form.

Simple:

Subject
Development of classes
I. Some do not listen.
II. Some only half-
listen.
III. Some listen with
passive acceptance.
IV. Some listen with
discrimination.

Glenn R. Capp, *Listen Up!*

Listeners can be classified into four groups: (1) Some do not listen; they "tune the speaker out" and think of matters foreign to the speaker's subject. They get little from a speech. (2) Some only half-listen; their spasmodic listening fluctuates all the way from careful attention to no attention. They understand fragments of the speech, but they do not see the idea as a whole. (3) Some listen with passive acceptance; they accept all the speaker says without question. Because of their lack of discrimination, they add little to what the speaker says from their own experiences. (4) Some listen with discrimination; this critical type of listener gets the most from a speech.

Complex:

Subject
Main class I

There are two principal types of <u>glaciers;</u> the <u>continental</u> and the <u>valley.</u> The <u>continental glaciers</u> are great sheets of ice, called ice caps, that cover parts of continents. The earth has two continental glaciers at present: one spreads over most of Greenland and one over all of Antarctica save for a small window of rock and the peaks of several ranges. The Greenland ice sheet is over 10,000 ft. thick in the central part and covers an area of about 650,000 sq. miles. The Antarctic sheet has been sounded, in one place at least, to a depth of 14,000 ft., and it spreads over an area of 5,500,000 sq. miles. This is larger than conterminous United States in the proportion of 5½:3. It is calculated to store 7 million cu. miles of ice, which if melted would raise the ocean level 250 ft.

Main class II

Subclass A
(conventional)

Subclass B

Subclass C

<u>Valley glaciers</u> are ice streams that originate in the high snow fields of mountain ranges and flow down valleys to warmer climates, where they melt. <u>Some break up</u> into icebergs and eventually melt in the ocean. In certain places the valley glaciers flow down the mountain valleys to adjacent plains and there spread out as lobate feet. These are called <u>expanded-foot glaciers.</u> Generally the sprawling feet of several valley glaciers coalesce to form one major sheet, and this is called a <u>piedmont glacier.</u>

Notice that the valley glacier is subdivided:

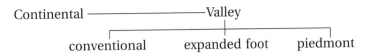

As you can see, glaciers are of two types based on their location (with implications for size): (1) the continental glacier, such as the huge one in the Antarctic, and (2) the valley glacier. The valley glacier can be subdivided into the conventional valley glacier, flowing straight; the expanded-foot glacier, which spreads out; and the piedmont glacier, which is made up of several expanded-foot glaciers. This information could be organized in an outline as follows:

I. Continental glacier
II. Valley glacier
    A. Conventional
    B. Expanded-foot
    C. Piedmont

This outline on glaciers could be cut down to just the "valley glacier" part and developed into an essay. Moving in the other direction, we can say that almost all classifications can be part of a higher level of classification. For example, glaciers are one type of earth-altering process. (Others include earthquakes, volcanoes, and wind erosion.)

Most essays of classification will be simple (based on one principle) in concept, informative in purpose, and organized class by class.

Exercise 1   AVOIDING OVERLAPPING CLASSES

Mark each set of classes as OK or OL (overlapping); circle the classes that overlap.

	Subject	Principle	Classes
	Example:		
OL	speech	uses	formal informal (garbled)
OL	1. shoppers	intentions	one item bargains looking (aggressive)
OL	2. gym members	needs	body building (young) good health social

___OL___	3. fast foods	ownership	franchise
			company
			individual
			(popular)

___OL___	4. local politicians	motives	connections
			step to higher office
			(controversial)
			community service

___OK___	5. graffiti	purposes	artistic
			political
			gang

Connecting Sources and Writing

Student Essay

In prison, Jolene Carter had become a student of human behavior. Then, given the opportunity to write about such matters, she knew she was surrounded by a wealth of highly original raw material. One of the suggested general topics in her textbook was the classification of people according to how they deal with unwanted and uninvited intruders, such as pesky insects, sneaky rodents, unruly neighborhood pets, rambunctious visiting children, aggressive store salespersons, annoying telemarketers, snoopy neighbors, and zealous religious proselytizers. She did not have to go beyond the first item on the list.

Types of Fly Fighters

Jolene Carter

One of the major annoyances here at the women's prison is flies. Situated as it is in the middle of an agricultural zone where breeding sites for flies abound, the prison attracts them by the millions. Inmates, even those who have seldom dealt with fly infestation, must learn to cope with the problem, especially at eating time, when the flies want to share our meals. In observing what goes on at different tables in the dining hall, I have discovered that there are three kinds of (fly fighters): the shooers, the hiders, and the baiters.

Thesis

Class 1

The shooers are the most unimaginative. They wave their hands at the flies, shooing them after they have landed, or by constant waving trying to keep them from landing. This technique requires an almost constant movement, one which is contrary to the movements associated with eating and is almost as difficult as patting one's head while rubbing one's stomach. At any time one can look around the dining room and see the women waving their hands and the flies waving their wings as if they are all communicating. If so, the flies have the last word.

Class 2

The hiders, the second class, practice stealth, figuring that any human being should be intelligent enough to hide food from a small-brained creature like a fly. After using several napkins to enshroud food, the hiders, head bent forward to close space, scoop food from under the covering and "chow down." Unfortunately, the food often saturates the napkin, or flies manage to crawl under the covering. But overall, this technique is fairly successful and is probably the most popular.

Class 3

The baiters, the third class, while being the most clever, are probably the most cynical. They have concluded that flies will succeed in some fashion. The baiters offer a self-serving compromise to the flies. Upon taking a seat at the table, they will immediately deposit a spoonful of food near the edge of the tray or even on the table itself. The next step is to use the hiders' technique of covering the major portion of food. While flies swarm to the exposed portion—the bait—the baiters, often with a smug look of superiority, eat and then carry the bait away to the dump zone.

Although the baiting method is probably the most successful, it is used the least. Most women shoo flies or hide food as an expression of their good manners and dignity. If you believe that last statement, I have a very entertaining fly farm kit I am selling for only $29.95

Exercise 2   **DISCUSSION AND CRITICAL THINKING**

1. Circle the subject (what is being classified) the first time it appears in the essay. Write it here.
   Fly fighters.

2. What is the principle of the classification (on what basis is the classifying being done)?
   Behavior.

3. Underline the topic sentences that contain the classes.

4. State the thesis (the author's exact words or your own phrasing).
   "There are three kinds of fly fighters: the shooers, the hiders, and the baiters."

5. Is the main purpose to inform or to persuade?
   To inform.

6. What is the basis of the humor in this piece?
   Wording, especially at the end. The topic itself is amusing: The author is discussing how people devise strategies to outsmart or compromise with flies.

Practicing Patterns of Classification

Because the basic pattern of classification consists of classes, the initial outline is predictable: It uses Roman numeral headings for the classes, although some classes may be longer and more complex than others.

Exercise 3   **COMPLETING PATTERNS OF CLASSIFICATION**

Fill in the blanks in this outline based on "Types of Fly Fighters."

Thesis: I have discovered that there are three types of fly fighters.

I. Shooers

    A. Wave their hands

    B. Always in motion

II. Hiders

    A. Use napkins to cover food

    B. Scoop food from under napkins

III. Baiters

    A. Hide some food

    B. Drop some food on table for bait

    C. Let flies eat bait

    D. Scoop food and eat it

Student Documented Essay

For an essay assignment in freshman composition, Joel Follette was asked to read the essay "College Pressures" and to apply its basic ideas to his experience at the community college he attended. Initially, he thought he was writing about two opposing worlds, Yale and Mt. San Antonio College, but then he found some similarities.

Community College Pressures
Joel Follette

All college students have pressures. In his essay "College Pressures," William Zinsser describes the "modern undergraduate primarily as a driven creature," who is "fearful of risk" and "goal-obsessed." He says various harmful pressures exist "throughout American education" (78). Although he has some good insights, his focus is on Yale University, not a community college, such as the one I attend. The pressures he writes about—economic, parental, peer, and self-induced—do exist at Mt. San Antonio College in Southern California to some extent, but they take very different forms.

Zinsser says the Yale students feel economic pressure because they are looking for a "passport to security," and only good grades will get that for them (74). They are competing for slots in famous programs in law and medicine, such as the ones at Yale and Harvard. Other economic pressures come from the cost of education. He says some Yale students work part time during the school year and full time during the summer and still get loans. Students I know in the evening program at my school also have economic problems. I have a full-time job the year round in a company that makes cardboard boxes. I work overtime whenever I can get it without missing classes. I have a wife, who works part time, and two children in elementary school. I, too, have loans, but they're for a little house we bought last year and for a car that I first leased and then bought in a foolish transaction. Unlike Yale, my school only costs a few hundred dollars a year for the three classes I take in evening school each semester, but I passed on a job offer with a good salary because the new hours would have interfered with my class schedule.

Zinsser links economic pressure with parental pressure (75). The parents of most Yale students are paying for their education, and those parents expect results. They expect their offspring to do well in class and to major in a field that will pay well. He says the students want "to fulfill their parents' expectations." They often feel guilty if they do not do well and neglect their own preferences in what to study. Although that may exist to a lesser degree at my community college, usually the parents themselves do not have a college degree and now they are not paying all the college costs for their children, although a large percentage of students in day school still live at home. Most evening students work full time, and the family pressure comes from a spouse and maybe children. When I get home on class nights at ten-thirty and see my kids sleeping and my tired wife, I know why I'm going to college, and I feel guilty if I don't do well. And, to some extent like the students at Yale, I'm thinking about security, not so much about being a doctor but about having a better job.

The other two pressures discussed by Zinsser, the peer and self-induced (76), are also linked. Again, there are big differences between the students at Yale and Mt. San Antonio College. Zinsser says that Yale students are very competitive, and they often "do more than they are expected to do" in order to excel (77). He uses the term "grade fever" (77). I have a *B* average and I know I have to make some *A*s to offset some *C*s, but I don't feel I am competing with my peers. We talk about grades, and usually ask each other about grades when we get tests or papers back. But I haven't seen a lot of competition. Of course, we have our pride, and we're embarrassed if we don't do well. Then we feel as if we've let ourselves and others down. According to my friend at UCLA, the students there are so grade conscious they hardly talk about their grades. Last semester one of his peers jumped to his death from a high-rise dorm room after finals. We don't jump here. I did see a guy kick a trash can one day after getting low marks on a research paper.

At all schools, pressures do exist. They may come from different sources and arrive in different degrees, but they're out there. Sometimes we do it to ourselves, and sometimes people do it to us. Pressures are the forces that may get in the way of our getting a good education, because we become too practical. But pressures are also what keep us going when we're dog-tired, sleepy, and cranky. I think Zinsser would say that if we didn't have so many of these pressures that we might just sit down and read a good book—and that just might be the best education of it all.

Work Cited

Zinsser, William. "College Pressures." *Blair & Ketchum's Country Journal* 4 (April 1979): 72–78.

Exercise 4   **DISCUSSION AND CRITICAL THINKING**

1. Circle the thesis and underline all topic sentences.

2. What is the main pressure?
   Answers will vary. Probably economic.

3. Which pressure differs to the greatest extent between Yale students and evening division community college students?
One can make a case for either economic or parental.

4. Is Follette a typical community college student? Discuss.
Answers will vary. He is fairly typical in that he is a part-time student, with three classes each semester; he has a young family; and he is working outside school.

Coworkers from Hell and How to Cope

Erica Monfred

Not all types of coworkers are classified here by Erica Monfred. Just the ones from hell. Along with her classification, she provides suggestions about how to send those obnoxious people back to their fiery place of origin. This essay was first published in *Cosmopolitan* in 1997.

1   In every workplace, there are congenial, supportive colleagues. . . . and then there are the other kind—the ones you fantasize about while pummeling the punching bag at the gym. Is there an officemate sabotaging your success? Here is a primer on how to handle the most common culprits.

1. Petty Bureaucrats

2   The petty bureaucrat is either the gatekeeper to someone important or in charge of something everyone desperately needs, like health insurance or paper clips. She doesn't actually have the authority to get things done, but she does have the power to prevent things from getting done.

3   Let's say your department needs another copier. You've noticed that accounting has three machines, one of which is almost never used. The head of that department says it's okay to take her extra copier, but the petty bureaucrat in charge of office equipment demands a long memo explaining in excruciating detail why you need it—with cc's to at least five other people who also have to give their approval, including the CEO, who happens to be in Belgrade for the month and can't be reached due to political upheaval.

4   How to cope? If you wait patiently, you'll be ready for retirement before the order comes through. Getting angry will just make

the petty bureaucrat gloat with satisfaction, because frustrating others' wishes is her game.

5   There's only one way to deal with this type: You must befriend her. Remember: She's insecure, a lonely misfit, desperate for a kind word or smile, shunned because she's so self-important and hateful. If you want that copier, start sucking up. Ask her to lunch. Show an excessive interest in her prize geraniums and philandering husband over your tuna melt and you'll be whizzing through that pile by the end of the day.

2. Credit Grabbers

6   In most cases, the thief is your boss, which puts you in a bind. Psychologist William Knaus, author of *Change Your Life Now,* says this is the problem Lee Iacocca* ran into with Henry Ford. "Iacocca talks about how threatened Ford was when he [Iacocca] started to get a lot of good publicity," Knaus explains. "Iacocca tried to make it work at Ford, but it was a losing proposition, because his credit-grabber boss was the most powerful person in the organization."

7   Eventually, Ford fired Iacocca, which was the best thing that ever happened to him—he went on to great success at Chrysler. "There are some people you simply shouldn't work for," Knaus asserts. "Life is too short to spend month after month, year after year, reporting to a parasitic boss who's going to damage your self-esteem."

8   If the culprit is a peer or subordinate, however, you have more options. The key is to document, document, document. After any meeting with a credit grabber, instantly send a memo to her and a copy to your boss, summarizing whatever ideas you contributed. If you team up on a project, create a computerized system outlining each of your responsibilities under the guise of getting organized. And keep quiet about any terrific ideas until they're documented as belonging to you.

3. Backstabber

9   Many backstabbers are what Michael Zey, M.D., author of *Winning With People,* calls friendly enemies. They're helpful and encouraging when you're down, he says, "but when you finally get that raise or promotion, they subtly start undermining your confidence and questioning your abilities." Even more insidious are those who remain friendly to your face and do their nasty work behind the scenes.

*Lee Iacocca is a former CEO at Chrysler.

10   Rumormongering is their most common and malignant tactic. Rumors can be impossible to counter once they've been spread, but you can insulate yourself against them by developing a network of supportive colleagues who'll report all office gossip to you. If you know who the fiend is, enlist their help to defeat her by confronting her directly, spreading a counter-rumor, or reporting her to management.

4. Nonstop Talkers

11   She plops down in your office, regardless of what you're doing at the moment, and launches into a litany of complaints about how the boss doesn't appreciate her; how she was overcharged when she took her incontinent dog, Spot, to the vet; how unfair it is that international terrorism is forcing her to wait in long lines at the airport. The usual signals, like saying, "I'm on deadline and can't talk now," don't deter her in the least.

12   Courtesy stops most of us from employing the kind of drastic tactics that actually work with this bulldozer. Recognize that divesting yourself of a motormouth may call for behavior your mother wouldn't approve of. First, try the kind of preemptive strike employed by media mogul Ted Turner. Turner tells people at the outset of a conversation how much time he can give them. When the allotted period has elapsed, he'll say something like "Your five minutes are up, and I've gotta go."

13   If that doesn't work, most experts agree that it's okay to employ even more abrupt measures. If she corners you at the water cooler, mumble an apology and take off in the opposite direction. If she has you trapped behind your desk, tell her you have to make a call, then pick up the phone and start talking very loudly. Even the most relentless blatherers will get the message eventually and start approaching colleagues who are nicer than you. You can bet your rude behavior will be at the top of their nonstop complaint list.

5. Alarmists

14   This corporate Chicken Little constantly races into your office with doomsday reports: You're getting a new boss who's so tyrannical he makes Attila the Hun* look like Leo Buscaglia†; such radical downsizing is on the way that the cleaning person will be doing your job. You have a panic attack every time you see this squawker coming down the hall.

*Attila the Hun was a violent barbarian of ancient Asia and Europe.
†Leo Buscaglia is a contemporary public relations expert.

15   Unfortunately, these days the sky really is falling on so many hardworking women that the office alarmist may be spreading an all too-accurate message. Be smart and use her latest warning as a wake-up call. Think about what you'd do if you did lose your job. Who would hire you? Do you have a network of contacts who'll help you? Talk to a few headhunters* and find out what's out there. Then, when the alarmist comes around, you can greet her latest disaster scenario by saying, "Who cares?"

6. Control Freaks

16   Control freaks are probably the most infuriating and hardest to handle of all difficult coworkers because they're so completely relentless. These obsessive-compulsives don't stop at a hands-on approach; they need to have a stranglehold on everything they touch. Your work is continually met with such comments as "Let's just check those figures one more time" and "I don't think that'll work; why don't we do it my way?" According to psychiatrist John M. Oldham, coauthor of *The New Personality Self Portrait: Why You Think, Work, Love, and Act the Way You Do,* control freaks "are tense, strained, anxious, and overwhelmed by the amount of work they have to do." Yet they're willing to devote so much time and energy to their jobs that they tend to move up in their professions, so chances are, you'll someday run into an overbearing higher-up.

17   According to psychologist Barry Lubetkin, of the Institute for Behavior Therapy in New York, passive resistance is the most effective way of dealing with these types. "Confrontation will only trigger even more controlling behavior," he says, "so avoid arguments and power struggles at all costs." When this coworker obsesses about some insignificant detail, make a neutral comment like "I understand what you're saying," then go about your business. He'll think you agreed with him and feel reassured.

7. Snoops

18   You can't leave a single piece of paper on your desk, because she always manages to read everything, personal and work-related. She grills you about your private life during business discussions, and you've even seen her lurking behind doorways while you chat with your boss.

19   Unlike backstabbers, who accumulate information to use against you, snoops have no ulterior motive; they just love to gossip. They're the kind of people for whom the saying "Get a life" was invented. The solution: Give them something to feed on with-

*Headhunters are people who find employees for companies.

out revealing personal secrets—so make stuff up! Leave hot fictional love notes from imaginary boyfriends on your desk. When she inquires about your personal life, tell her a lurid tale of multiple marriages and affairs with celebrities. When other colleagues come back to you asking if these stories are true, laugh and say, "I made all that up to get Mary Jane off my back."

8. Put-down Artist

20 "It took you a whole month to do this report."

21 "I can't believe they hired you with only a year's experience."

22 Verbal zingers act like sandpaper, rubbing slowly across your sense of self, eventually wearing it away. If you work for a put-down artist or with the kind of coworkers who constantly throw barbs your way, you'll soon dread coming into the office.

23 The first step in self-defense is acknowledging you've been hurt. Then set up a defense. Jennifer James, author of *Defending Yourself Against Criticism,* offers these strategies for countering an attack:

24 • Agree with everything the sniper says. This works with people who are so dense that nothing else gets to them or who have a sense of humor. For example:

25 *Put-down:* "Are you sure you spoke with the sales department before using these figures? They don't look right to me."

26 *Defense:* "Sales department? Why would I speak to them?"

27 • Register the hit. Say something like "Ooh, that really hurt," and go on with the conversation. This is a signal that you're not easy prey, and the tactic should stop everyone but the worst offenders.

28 • Send it back. For example:

29 *Put-down:* "Are you sure you should be eating that doughnut?"

30 *Defense:* "What I eat is a personal matter."

9. Bullies

31 Most of us adhere to an unspoken social contract that includes a modicum of considerate behavior. Bullies are unaware that such an agreement exists. Their no-holds-barred tactics include public humiliation, making scenes, threatening to get you fired, and generally treating you like an unruly two-year-old instead of an adult.

32 Why do these outrageous tactics work? In his book *Coping With Difficult People,* psychologist Robert Bramson explains that bullies possess tremendous power because of the typical responses

their behavior arouses in their victims: "confusion, mental or physical flight, a sense of helpless frustration that leads to tears or a tantrumlike rage." In other words, they get away with it because we let them.

33   The traditional wisdom about a schoolyard bully applies as well to the corporate type: You have to stand up to her. Bullies will often back down if you show you're willing to fight. Your strategy:

34   • Use positive body language. Don't let your shoulders droop and eyes drop when intimidated. Look her in the eye, and don't retreat.

35   • Give her time to cool down. "Remain in place and wait," recommends Bramson. "When the attack begins to lose momentum, jump in."

36   • Don't become paralyzed by fear. Even if you're so distraught you can't come up with the right retort, say something—anything to counter the onslaught.

37   • Stay rational. Ignore the intimidation, and slowly and reasonably make your case.

Exercise 5	**VOCABULARY HIGHLIGHTS**

Write a short definition of each word as it is used in the essay. (Paragraph numbers are given in parentheses.) Be prepared to use the words in your own sentences.

pummeling (1)   litany (11)

excruciating (3)   divesting (12)

parasitic (7)   mogul (12)

insidious (9)   ulterior (19)

insulate (10)   modicum (31)

Exercise 6	**DISCUSSION AND CRITICAL THINKING**

1. What is the main subject for the classification?
   Coworkers from hell.

2. What is the principle, or basis, of the classification?
   The destructive ways that coworkers behave.

3. How many classes are there?
   Nine.

4. How would you rank the classes, starting with the most troublesome?
   Answers will vary.

5. Why don't you tell them just to go back where they came from?
   You have to work with them. Some may be your bosses.

6. Which of the classes of coworkers can be identified most easily?
   Answers will vary. Probably the nonstop talkers, the control freaks, the put-down artists, and the bullies.

7. Which groups also exist in settings other than work-related on campus?
   Answers will vary. Perhaps in the classroom, on athletic teams, in clubs, and in hangout groups.

8. This passage has no conclusion. Should there be one? Explain why this form works or does not work for you.
   Answers will vary. The passage is more of a list. Moving from one point to another, the last class is enough finality.

Dangerous Curves
from Men's Health Magazine

Eve Golden

Freelance author Eve Golden has written mainly about women for a general reading audience, most notably the biographies *Platinum Girl: The Life and Legends of Jean Harlow* and *Vamp: The Rise and Fall of Theda Bara*. Here she addresses men, giving them advice on the kinds of women they should avoid in what she refers to as the "Dating Game from Hell."

1   My girlfriends and I spend an inordinate amount of time grousing about the terrible guys we fall for. So far the winner is Marie, who dated a guy who (1) lived in a trailer park because he liked it; (2) slept with a gun under the pillow; and (3) kept holy water in the freezer to *keep it holy longer.*

2   But—as the guys in my life are constantly making clear to me—men make the exact same mistakes, and fall for just as many of the wrong women. So in an effort to "C'mon, be fair about this, okay?" I've gone in search of *Five Women You Should Never Fall For.* . . . I spoke with Atlanta psychiatrist Frank Pittman, M.D., author of *Man Enough: Fathers, Sons and the Search for Masculinity.* After I described some of the terrible romances the men I know have wound up in, Dr. Pittman, who spends much time counseling couples with dysfunctional relationships, didn't let me

down. "The women you mention are all Incomplete Women," he told me, making me feel nicely superior. "They seem safe to incomplete men," he added, thus explaining my current lack of social life: A complete, dangerous woman, that's me.

3   In fact, all of the women you're going to learn to avoid have some very attractive qualities, qualities that many men instinctively fall for. That's what makes it so critical for you to avoid them. So without further ado, let's meet our contestants in the Dating Game from Hell.

The Damsel in Distress

4   She's the woman you see on those made-for-TV movies starring Barry Bostwick or Stephen Collins, about a good-natured guy who winds up entangled with some woman from the *Twilight Zone* (usually played by Meredith Baxter). She's helpless and heartbroken and just waiting for a big, strong man like you to come and sweep her off her feet. Does that sound a little anti-feminist, coming from a card-carrying NOW member? Remember, these women do exist. And they should all come equipped with big signs reading "Dangerous Curves Ahead."

5   "She is a disaster for everybody," Dr. Pittman states flat out. "Damsels in distress are never capable of knowing who is St. George and who is the dragon. If she is being abused by everyone in her life and you try to rescue her, I promise you it will only be a matter of time before you're seen as the next abuser."

6   My friend Rick agrees, having been the Stephen Collins character in one of those relationships. He tells me a sob story about his personal Damsel. "Ultimately, I stayed with her because she needed rescuing. I stuck around for a year and a half and never did rescue her. I learned from her, though: If there's a problem, get out early before it starts to affect your psyche."

7   How can you recognize the Damsel type? Dr. Pittman referees a lot of these relationships. "Any woman who falls in love with you too quickly, too desperately, too completely, must be nuts." Gee, there goes the plot of every movie made between 1929 and 1950. If you're married, you'll be able to spot her easily—she's the one making eyes at you from across the room. "These women are the sort of people who fall into affairs with married men," Dr. Pittman says. "Normal women don't do that." What makes a guy dumb enough to fall back? "A victim—a woman with more problems than you've got—will distract you from your problems. Briefly. Men are all too eager to believe that they're heroes, and that someone has finally noticed it." The lesson: Don't think too highly

of yourself, and don't think too highly of anyone who thinks too highly of you.

The (S)motherer

8   You know how sometimes a man and a woman will have the exact same cold, yet the woman's up making hot tea and the man's in bed moaning, "Call a priest"? Some men just invite mothering, and some women (not me, not on your life) love playing Mama. Maybe 100 years ago, when women didn't have actual lives, that was a good way to vent emotional and physical energy. But nowadays, any woman who puts 100 percent of her hopes, dreams, fears and desires on her man's life rather than her own is not someone you need.

9   Dr. Pittman, of course, agrees. "A motherer doesn't require that you give anything back. She's so constantly giving that you end up feeling like a child." Surprisingly, this kind of woman still exists in the 1990s. I have to admit, I couldn't find any Big Mamas or their admirers around my New York digs, so I called my friend Norman, whose Deep-South sister is June Cleaver II. "Oh, she bought a vacuum cleaner for one boyfriend," says Norman. "She made payments on his truck, she did his laundry. He just ate it up."

10   You can see how this kind of relationship can be wonderful for a guy, at least for a while. But it can't be permanent. Eventually, you'll want to give something back, and she won't want what you have to offer. All she wants, Dr. Pittman says, is to live vicariously through you, and living two people's lives is a little bit more of a burden than most anyone would want to tackle. What ever happened to Norman's sister's boyfriend? "He got some other girl pregnant and married her," Norman says. "The guys who are attracted to my sister tend to be young and immature." Which reinforces my belief: that guys who fall for motherly types are entirely too much in touch with their inner child. Do us all a favor, will you, and get in touch with your inner adult?

The Chameleon

11   You know the type: Suddenly she has a Boston accent, and suddenly she loves touch football, just because she's dating a Kennedy. "She's never an equal partner," Dr. Pittman says of this clinging vine, "because she gets her identity from adapting to the guy."

12   Oh, and I do know one or two chameleons. Very nice gals, but not with the best of self-images. Blanche was understandably defensive when I approached her on the topic, though she happily

admitted that she indeed fit the bill. "I dress like my boyfriend. I think it's good," she says philosophically. "We can share clothes." Blanche went on to try and explain herself. "Guys' opinions and ways of doing things just rub off from being around them. It's an ego thing for them." But doesn't it show kind of a lack of ego on Blanche's part? So far, Blanche and her boyfriend seem happy, though she is starting to look more and more like him every day and everyone's pretty much hoping he doesn't start sporting a mustache.

13   Yet this type of one-sided relationship will eventually drag a man under. "The guy finds it flattering for a while, but neither the man nor the woman has the possibility of give-and-take, of being able to adapt to the other," Dr. Pittman says. "They naturally begin to feel something's missing." I talked to one of Blanche's ex-boyfriends, Max. Why did they break up? "We were just bored," he said. "We fell into a rut. Doing the same thing"—his thing, I might add—"night after night." Didn't the fact that Blanche brought nothing to the ball game have something to do with this? Max claimed not to know what I was talking about. "Well, yeah, we had a lot of the same interests, that's why we had such a great time together, isn't it?" I've known Blanche for years, I told him, and she was never the slightest bit interested in basketball, Van Damme films or Japanese food before they met. "Yeah?" His eyes light up; he's obviously delighted. "Well, I guess she got a few things out of the relationship, then, right?"

The Uptown Girl

14   You know her, or at least you've seen her: She's Sharon Stone, Geena Davis, whoever's on the cover of *Sports Illustrated* this year. Happily, most men don't go around shooting U.S. presidents to impress her. But it's hard not to fall for a woman who's just—let's face it—out of your league.

15   The most insidious thing about this unattainable glamour girl is that she thinks she's Just Folks. I tried to reach Sharon Stone, Drew Barrymore and Kelly Lynch for their opinions on the topic, but they proved to be, well, unattainable. I did, however, get my friend Lauren, a successful film producer, to comment. Lauren has natural red hair, looks like a more glamorous Jodie Foster, as sweet as you'd wish. But she started back in horror when I described her as Unattainable. "But I'm not!" she squealed, as a male friend rolled his eyes helplessly behind her. "I mean, I'm not gorgeous or anything like that!" She does admit that men seem afraid to approach her, but puts that down to shyness. She's

utterly wrong. My not-too-terribly-shy friend Rick admits even he's intimidated by women like Lauren. "I just gaze at them with sheep eyes."

16   "There are women who just don't notice the guys who are pursuing them: that's what makes them unattainable," Dr. Pittman says. The men who pursue these glamorous ghosts "don't really want a woman. They're like dogs chasing cars. It's great exercise, as long as you know you'll never catch one. This is the perfect set-up for the guy who wants to be in love without all the problems of having a relationship. It's safe. Plus, he gets an identity from feeling the love he holds for her."

17   On the other hand, if you have normal, mutual relationships with other women, there's nothing wrong with having a crush on someone now and then. Dr. Pittman sheepishly admits that "I have that relationship with Susan Sarandon—whom I've never met, of course."

The Cruise Director

18   Okay, I have a confession. When my editor described this kind of Woman to Avoid, I thought he was being sarcastic and describing me: opinionated, always in control, bossy, having to make all the plans and double-check them afterward. This type of woman may be nerve-racking, but I hasten to add she always gets her stories in on deadline.

19   "She sounds real nice," agrees Dr. Pittman. "I have entirely too many pleasures in life to waste time running my life. I prefer having someone else do it for me. A Cruise Director can be someone who frees you up to be successful, to be creative."

20   That's fine as long as you're happy to leave your social life up to someone else's whims, and as long as she's willing to play cruise director for an extended tour. But it doesn't always work out that way. My friend Walter refused to talk about his ex-wife, but his new wife, Carol, was delighted to help. "Oh, she was such a pushy type," Carol enthused. "She ran everything, which was fun for both of them, at least for a while. But then the challenge was over, and she and Walter split up." Dr. Pittman says there can indeed be downsides to dating a Cruise Director. "If you're scared of women and you've got one who runs your life, you're going to feel controlled, that your autonomy is impinged upon, like an adolescent. She's for a guy who's got something to do that's more important than proving that women can't tell him what to do. But for the guy who's scared of female control, she'd be a disaster."

21   So maybe you're smart enough to avoid the above bachelorettes. Or maybe you're the type who clings to one after the other like Tarzan swinging through the vines. What's Dr. Pittman's advice for guys who keep falling for the wrong woman? "Get into a permanent, full-time committed relationship with someone with whom you don't get along terribly well and are basically incompatible." Yikes! He continues: "That puts you in the position of having to constantly examine yourself, develop new skills, learn to see the world from another perspective—it's a great maturing process." So is running away to join the circus, but I wouldn't recommend it for everyone.

22   "Seriously," Dr. Pittman explains, "you need incompatibility in a relationship. Of course, you need compatibility, too—to make you feel comfortable, safe, understood. But compatibility is never complete, and never permanent. It takes a certain amount of conflict to give a relationship life."

23   If that's the hard way, here's the easy one: Guys, if you want to have a relationship in the worst way, take it from me, you will. There's this odd notion today that if you're not involved in a romantic/sexual relationship, you're somehow half a person and cannot possibly be happy.

24   Bull. How many hours have you spent on the phone with friends, moaning to your barkeep or to your therapist about how unhappy you are in one relationship or another? Take my advice and think long and hard next time you fall. As my wise old Aunt Ida once told me, "It's better to be alone than to wish you were."

("Dangerous Curves" by Eve Golden from *Men's Health Magazine.* Reprinted by permission of *Men's Health Magazine.* Copyright 1994 Rodale, Inc. All rights reserved. For subscription information, call 1-800-666-2303.)

| **Exercise 7** | **DISCUSSION AND CRITICAL THINKING** |

1. What is being classified?
   Women with whom men should avoid having a relationship.

2. What are Golden's main sources of support?
   Her experience; her friends; and Dr. Frank Pittman, a psychiatrist.

3. From what field does Golden draw her examples and why?
   Show business. She probably thinks readers will be familiar with her examples and the kinds of movies in which they have been featured.

4. What do all her types have in common?
   They are all "incomplete women."

5. After men remove these types from their prospective dating pool, about how many are left (in a percentage figure)?
   Answers will vary.

6. Golden refers to these women as types. Discuss the possibility that some of these women are only posing as these types as a technique for attracting men and then reverting to what they really are. If that occurs, is it all bad?

   Answers will vary. Some women probably do pose as these types. It is not all bad if the women revert to something more genuine and solid.

7. Do some men project the need for some of the types of women discussed here? Explain.

   Answers will vary.

8. What are the qualities a stable, normal man should look for in a woman?

   A stable, normal woman. Pittman says a man should find someone who is different from himself.

Confessions of a Former Smoker

Franklin E. Zimring

Distinguished author and professor of law Franklin E. Zimring has written about a variety of social ills. Here he reflects on his own personal experience to explain and classify the different kinds of ex-smokers. His books include *Capital Punishment and the American Agenda* (1986) and *American Youth Violence* (1998). This essay first appeared in *Newsweek*.

1   Americans can be divided into three groups—smokers, non-smokers, and that expanding pack of us who have quit. Those who have never smoked don't know what they're missing, but former smokers, ex-smokers, reformed smokers can never forget. We are veterans of a personal war, linked by that watershed experience of ceasing to smoke and by the temptation to have just one more cigarette. For almost all of us ex-smokers, smoking continues to play an important part in our lives. And now that it is being restricted in restaurants around the country . . . , it is vital that everyone understand the different emotional states cessation of smoking can cause. I have observed four of them; and in the interest of science I have classified them as those of the zealot, the evangelist, the elect, and the serene. Each day, each category gains new recruits.

2   Not all antitobacco zealots are former smokers, but a substantial number of fire-and-brimstone opponents do come from the

ranks of the reformed. Zealots believe that those who continue to smoke are degenerates who deserve scorn, not pity, and the penalties that will deter offensive behavior in public as well. Relations between these people and those who continue to smoke are strained.

3   One explanation for the zealot's fervor in seeking to outlaw tobacco consumption is his own tenuous hold on abstaining from smoking. But I think part of the emotional force arises from sheer envy as he watches and identifies with each lung-filling puff. By making smoking in public a crime, the zealot seeks reassurance that he will not revert to bad habits; give him strong social penalties and he won't become a recidivist.

4   No systematic survey has been done yet, but anecdotal evidence suggests that a disproportionate number of doctors who have quit smoking can be found among the fanatics. Just as the most enthusiastic revolutionary tends to make the most enthusiastic counterrevolutionary, many of today's vitriolic zealots include those who had been deeply committed to tobacco habits.

5   By contrast, the antismoking evangelist does not condemn smokers. Unlike the zealot, he regards smoking as an easily curable condition, as a social disease, and not a sin. The evangelist spends an enormous amount of time seeking and preaching to the unconverted. He argues that kicking the habit is not *that* difficult. After all, *he* did it; moreover, as he describes it, the benefits of quitting are beyond measure and the disadvantages are nil.

6   The hallmark of the evangelist is his insistence that he never misses tobacco. Though he is less hostile to smokers than the zealot, he is resented more. Friends and loved ones who have been the targets of his preachments frequently greet the resumption of smoking by the evangelist as an occasion for unmitigated glee.

7   Among former smokers, the distinctions between the evangelist and the elect are much the same as the differences between proselytizing and nonproselytizing religious sects. While the evangelists preach the ease and desirability of abstinence, the elect do not attempt to convert their friends. They think that virtue is its own reward and subscribe to the Puritan* theory of predestination. Since they have proved themselves capable of abstaining from tobacco, they are therefore different from friends and relatives who continue to smoke. They feel superior, secure that their salvation was foreordained. These ex-smokers rarely give per-

*The Puritans were an early American religious group.

sonal testimony on their conversion. They rarely speak about their tobacco habits, while evangelists talk about little else. Of course, active smokers find such bluenosed behavior far less offensive than that of the evangelist or the zealot, yet they resent the elect simply because they are smug. Their air of self-satisfaction rarely escapes the notice of those lighting up. For active smokers, life with a member of the ex-smoking elect is less stormy than with a zealot or evangelist, but it is subtly oppressive nonetheless.

8   I have labeled my final category of former smokers the serene. This classification is meant to encourage those who find the other psychic styles of ex-smokers disagreeable. Serenity is quieter than zealotry and evangelism, and those who qualify are not as self-righteous as the elect. The serene ex-smoker accepts himself and also accepts those around him who continue to smoke. This kind of serenity does not come easily, nor does it seem to be an immediate option for those who have stopped. Rather it is a goal, an end stage in a process of development during which some former smokers progress through one or more of the less-than-positive psychological points en route. For former smokers, serenity is thus a positive possibility that exists at the end of the rainbow. But all former smokers cannot reach that promised land.

9   What is it that permits some former smokers to become serene? I think the key is self-acceptance and gratitude. The fully mature former smoker knows he has the soul of an addict and is grateful for the knowledge. . . . He doesn't regret that he quit smoking, nor any of his previous adventures with tobacco. As a former smoker, he is grateful for the experience and memory of craving a cigarette.

10   Serenity comes from accepting the lessons of one's life. And ex-smokers who have reached this point in their worldview have much to be grateful for. They have learned about the potential and limits of change. In becoming the right kind of former smoker, they developed a healthy sense of self. This former smoker, for one, believes that it is better to crave (one hopes only occasionally) and not to smoke than never to have craved at all. And by accepting that fact, the reformed smoker does not need to excoriate, envy, or disassociate himself from those who continue to smoke.

Exercise 8	**VOCABULARY HIGHLIGHTS**

Write a short definition of each word as it is used in the essay. (Paragraph numbers are given in parentheses.) Be prepared to use the words in your own sentences.

zealot (1)   unmitigated (6)

tenuous (3)   proselytizing (7)

recidivist (3)   predestination (7)

anecdotal (4)   foreordained (7)

vitriolic (4)   excoriate (10)

Exercise 9	**DISCUSSION AND CRITICAL THINKING**

1. What are the division and subdivision of classification that Zimring uses in the first paragraph?

   The main groups are the smokers, the nonsmokers, and those who have quit. Those who have quit are divided into the zealot, the evangelist, the elect, and the serene.

2. On what basis does Zimring divide the ex-smokers in his classification?

   On the basis of how each person who stops smoking goes into an emotional state.

3. With which classes do you associate the following words?
   arrogance: elect
   acceptance: serene
   preachy: evangelist
   hostility: zealot

4. What are some other categories of ex-smokers?

   Answers will vary. Perhaps the recently reformed, who chew gum, wear patches, suck toothpicks, and openly lust for tobacco.

5. How would you compare ex-smokers with ex-drinkers, ex-meat eaters, and ex-couch potatoes?

   Answers will vary.

Shaking Hands

Glen Waggoner

Shaking hands is a necessary part of many of our greetings. In this brief essay, former *Esquire* senior writer Glen Waggoner explains that different people have different styles and that most of the styles are wrong. This essay was first published in *Esquire*.

1   A handshake tells you a lot about a man. For one thing, it tells you that he's probably an American. Europeans hug when they greet each other, the English nod, the Japanese bow, but Americans shake hands. And that's the way it is.

2   Extending an empty hand to show that you have no weapon, grasping another's hand to signify your human bond—you have to admit the handshake has impeccable symbolic credentials. Too bad that it has become so commonplace as to have lost much of its original meaning. Anyway, it's our way of saying hello, so we might as well get straight once and for all the main kinds of handshake; especially the only one that is correct.

The Politician's Pump

3   A familiar face with a toothy grin that materializes out of a crowd as its owner grabs your right hand in a firm grip, while simultaneously seizing your right forearm in his left hand. Two short, strong shakes and you find yourself being moved sideways as Teeth swivels to mug the next voter. (Also known as the Receiving-Line Two-Hand when practiced by college presidents.)

The Preemptive Squeeze

4   All fingers and thumb. Your extended hand is caught just short of its target by a set of pincers that encloses your four fingers at the second knuckle and leaves your thumb pointing west. No palm contact whatsoever. One quick squeeze, a side-to-side waggle, and your hand is unceremoniously dropped, leaving it utterly frustrated.

The Limp Fish

5   The most hated of all. Someone puts his fingers in your hand and leaves them there. Excusable in foreigners, who are still grappling with a language where *gh* and *f* sound alike (as in "tough fish"). For others, unacceptable.

The Macho Man

6   The old bone-crusher, the familiar signature of the emotionally insecure but physically strong. If you're alert, you can see this one coming in time to take countermeasures. The best defense is a good offense: grab his hand toward the base of the palm, cutting down on his fingers' leverage, and start your grip before he starts his. Of course, if he's strong enough and macho enough, it won't work, and he'll bond your individual digits into a single flipper for trying to thwart him.

The Preacher's Clasp

7 As your right hands join, his left folds over the top and immobilizes them both (okay, all three, but who's counting?). Always accompanied by steady eye contact (no way you won't be the first to blink), and usually by a monologue delivered two inches closer to your face than is really necessary. Once the exclusive province of Presbyterian ministers, the Clasp is now practiced by a broad spectrum of the relentlessly sincere, including motivational speakers and honors graduates of weekend-therapy marathons. The worst thing about it is that it makes your hand sweat.

The Right Way

8 A firm, full-handed grip, a steady squeeze, and a definite but understated downward snap (but no up-and-down pumping, unless you're contemplating a disabling karate move), followed at once by a decisive release accompanied by eye contact and performed only if both parties are standing (the ritual implies mutual respect and equality, after all). Sounds easy enough, but how frequently do you encounter a really good one?

Footnote: Shaking Hands with Women

9 No difference in grip (the Right Way is always right), but convention has it that you should wait for her to extend her hand first. These days, chances are good she will.

Exercise 10   **DISCUSSION AND CRITICAL THINKING**

1. Underline the thesis.

2. On what principle is the classification based?
   How the handshake is performed.

3. On what other principles might a classification of handshaking be based?
   Purpose. Culture. Age.

4. This article was written for *Esquire,* so the audience was mainly men. Is the footnote pertaining to shaking hands with women enough?
   Answers will vary.

✎ Topics for Writing Classification

Writing Process Worksheet

You will find a Writing Process Worksheet in Appendix A, page 531. It can be photocopied and enlarged, filled in, and submitted with each assignment if your instructor directs you to do so.

Source-Based Topics

Each essay developed from these suggested source-based topics should include at least one reference to the reading selection by the author's name and the title. Quotations should be enclosed in quotation marks. Follow your instructor's directions in documenting the ideas you borrow. Whether you use informal or formal documentation, the form is not complicated, and you will soon learn to use it for these essays without checking each time. See pages 77 and 78 for a discussion of MLA style and informal documentation.

Underlining and annotating reading selections will help you in finding support material. In prewriting brief essays, consider marking your outline to indicate where you will use quotations or other borrowed ideas. If the quotations or reworded statements are short and few, you could even insert them inside parentheses or circles in your outline; if you do, also include the author's last name and the page number. A sound system, consistently used, will save you time and ensure technically strong papers.

"Types of Fly Fighters"

1. Use this essay as a model for the same prompt that Carter used: Write a classification of people according to how they deal with unwanted and uninvited intruders, such as pesky insects, sneaky rodents, unruly neighborhood pets, rambunctious visiting children, aggressive store salespersons, annoying telemarketers, snoopy neighbors, and zealous religious proselytizers.

"Community College Pressures"

2. Using Follette's basic framework, write about your own college pressures.

"Coworkers from Hell and How to Cope"

3. Select one of the classes and subdivide it for your own essay of classification.

4. Using the relevant classes from Monfred's essay, discuss the coworkers from hell whom you encountered at a particular job. Use specific examples.

"Dangerous Curves"

5. Write an essay of classification in which you warn women about how to identify certain types of men, thereby avoiding dysfunctional

relationships. Following Golden's lead, use examples of well-known people from popular culture (movie stars, other entertainers, politicians) to illustrate your classes.

"Confessions of a Former Smoker"

6. Using Zimring's categories as a model, discuss the behavior of people who were formerly heavy drinkers, meat eaters, nonexercisers, or frequent television viewers, and are now teetotalers, vegetarians, exercise buffs, or television abstainers.

"Shaking Hands"

7. Using Waggoner's classification as a model, write about different ways of hugging, waving, kissing, or saying goodbye.

Career-Related Topics

8. Discuss different types of managers you have encountered (democratic, authoritative, autocratic, buddy, aloof).

9. Discuss different types of customers with whom you have dealt (perhaps according to their purpose for seeking your services or products).

10. Discuss different types of employees you have observed.

11. Discuss different qualities of products or services available in a particular field.

12. Discuss different kinds of chat rooms on the Internet.

General Topics   Write an essay using one of the topics listed here. Divide your topic into groups according to a single principle.

13. Intelligence	23. Dopers	32. Mothers or fathers
14. Waitresses	24. Sports fans	33. Rock music
15. Dates	25. Churchgoers	34. Talkers on the telephone
16. Smokers	26. Laughs	35. Pick-up lines (as in a bar)
17. Smiles	27. Bus drivers	36. Chicken eaters
18. Liars	28. Riders on buses or airplanes	37. Surfers (Internet or ocean)
19. Gossips	29. Junk food	38. Beards
20. TV watchers	30. Graffiti	39. Pet owners
21. Styles in clothing	31. Home computers	
22. Sports		

Writer's Guidelines: Classification

1. Follow this procedure for writing essays of classification:
   - Select a plural subject.
   - Decide on a principle for grouping the units of your subject.
   - Establish the groups, or classes.
   - Write about the classes.

2. Avoid uninteresting phrases for your classes, such as *good/average/bad*, *fast/medium/slow*, and *beautiful/ordinary/ugly.*

3. Avoid overlapping classes.

4. The Roman numeral parts of your outline will probably indicate your classes.

   I. Class one

   II. Class two

   III. Class three

5. If you use subclasses, clearly indicate the different levels.

6. Following your outline alternative, give somewhat equal (however much is appropriate) space to each class.

10

Process Analysis: Writing about Doing

THE QUIGMANS   by Buddy Hickerson

"Hey, hey, hey! How am I supposed to kiss
you if you keep holdin' your nose?"

Writing Process Analysis

*I*f you have any doubt about how frequently we use process analysis, just think about how many times you have heard people say, "How do you do it?" or "How is [was] it done?" Even when you are not hearing those questions, you are posing them yourself when you need to make something, cook a meal, assemble an item, take some medicine, repair something, or figure out what happened. In your college classes, you may have to discover how osmosis occurs, how a rock changes form, how a mountain was formed, how a battle was won, or how a bill goes through the legislature.

If you need to explain how to do something or how something was (is) done, you will engage in *process analysis*. You will break down your topic into stages, explaining each so that your reader can duplicate or understand the process.

Two Types of Process Analysis: Directive and Informative

The questions How do I do it? and How is (was) it done? will lead you into two different types of process analysis—directive and informative.

Directive process analysis explains how to do something. As the name suggests, it gives directions for the reader to follow. It says, for example, "Read me, and you can bake a pie [tune up your car, read a book critically, write an essay, take some medicine]." Because it is presented directly to the reader, it usually addresses the reader as "you," or it implies the "you" by saying something such as "First [you] purchase a large pumpkin, and then [you]. . . ." In the same way, this textbook addresses you or implies "you" because it is a long how-to-do-it (directive process analysis) statement.

Informative process analysis explains how something was (is) done by giving data (information). Whereas the directive process analysis tells you what to do in the future, the informative process analysis tells you what has occurred or what is occurring. If it is something in nature, such as the formation of a mountain, you can read and understand the process by which it emerged. In this type of process analysis, you do not tell the reader what to do; therefore, you will seldom use the words *you* or *your.*

Working with Stages

Preparation or Background

In the first stage of the directive type of process analysis, list the materials or equipment needed for the process and discuss the necessary setup arrangements. For some topics, this stage will also provide technical terms and definitions. The degree to which this stage is detailed will depend on both the subject itself and the expected knowledge and experience of the projected audience.

The informative type of process analysis may begin with background or context rather than with preparation. For example, a statement explaining how mountains form might begin with a description of a flat portion of the earth made up of plates that are arranged like a jigsaw puzzle.

Steps or Sequence

The actual process will be presented here. Each step or sequence must be explained clearly and directly, and phrased to accommodate the audience. The language, especially in directive process analysis, is likely to be simple and concise; however, avoid dropping words such as *and, a, an, the*, and *of*, and thereby lapsing into "recipe language." The steps may be accompanied by explanations about why certain procedures are necessary and how not following directions carefully can lead to trouble.

Order

The order will usually be chronological (time based) in some sense. Certain transitional words are commonly used to promote coherence: *first, second, third, then, soon, now, next, finally, at last, therefore, consequently,* and—especially for informative process analysis—words used to show the passage of time such as hours, days of the week, and so on.

Basic Forms

Consider using this form for the directive process (with topics such as how to cook something or how to fix something).

How to Prepare Spring Rolls

    I. Preparation

        A. Suitable cooking area

        B. Utensils, equipment

        C. Spring roll wrappers

        D. Vegetables, sauce

    II. Steps

        A. Season vegetables

        B. Wrap vegetables

        C. Fold wrappers

        D. Deep fry rolls

        E. Serve rolls with sauce

Consider using this form for the informative process (with topics such as how a volcano functions or how a battle was won).

How Coal Is Formed

I. Background or context
    A. Accumulation of land plants
    B. Bacterial action
    C. Muck formation
II. Sequence
    A. Lignite from pressure
    B. Bituminous from deep burial and heat
    C. Anthracite from metamorphic conditions

Combined Forms

Combination process analysis occurs when directive process analysis and informative process analysis are blended, usually when the writer personalizes the account. For example, if I tell you from a detached view how to write a research paper, my writing is directive process analysis, but if I tell you how I once wrote a research paper and give you the details in an informative account, then you may very well learn enough so that you can duplicate what I did. Thus, you would be both informed and instructed. Often the personalized account is more interesting to the general reader, but if you need to assemble a toy the night before your child's birthday, for example, you just want directions.

Many assignments are done as a personalized account. A paper about planting radish seeds may be informative, but it would probably be uninspiring. However, a paper about the time you helped your grandpa plant his spring garden (giving all the details) may be informative, directive, and entertaining. It is often the cultural framework provided by personal experience that transforms an ordinary directive account into something memorable. That's why some instructors ask their students to explain how to do something within the context of experience.

Useful Prewriting Procedure

All the strategies of freewriting, brainstorming, and clustering can be useful in writing a process analysis. However, if you already know your subject well, you can simply make two lists, one headed *Preparation* or *Background* and the other *Steps* or *Sequence*. Then jot down ideas for each. After you have finished with your listing, you can delete parts, combine parts, and rearrange parts for better order. That editing of your lists will lead directly to a formal outline you can use in Stage Two of the writing process. Following is an example of listing for the topic of how to prepare spring rolls.

Preparation (Background)	Steps
stainless steel bowl	slice and mix vegetables
deep-fry pan	add sauce to vegetables
spoon	beat eggs
damp cloth	place wrappers on damp cloth
spring roll wrappers	add 2 to 3 tablespoons of vegetables
eggs	per wrapper
sauce	fold and seal wrapper with egg
cabbage	freeze for later or deep fry immediately
celery	serve with sweet and sour sauce
carrots	
bean sprouts	

Connecting Sources and Writing

Student Essay

Watching football games, most of us have observed cornerbacks harassing wide receivers. One person wants to catch the ball thrown by the quarterback; however, an opponent is there to interfere. In this essay, Brian Landry, a former high school football player, explains that the successful cornerback is doing much more than being annoying; he is actually playing a game within a game.

Guarding a Wide Receiver

Brian Landry

Unlike golf, one of the ultimate individual sports, football is a team sport, and many people think of it as one machine facing off against another. What those people miss is that each player has a specific role, and often an individual player is engaged in a game within a game against another player who is executing his own battle plan. Few match-ups offer more challenges to individuals than the one between the cornerback and the wide receiver. As a corner-back, I finally discovered an effective process, one that begins with preparation before the game and ends with strategic action on the field during a pass play.

Thesis

The most important part of winning is in the preparation. First, you need to be mentally and physically fit. Mental fitness involves studying your opposing team and its strategies, as well as knowing your own defensive schemes and having a winning attitude. Physical fitness is self-explanatory. You must have stamina, strength, and speed. Next is equipment. You must wear the appropriate gear and,

Preparation

especially, the shoes that suit the playing surface. With that preparation completed, you are ready for the wide receiver poised just across the line from you, his mind focused on making you look foolish on the next pass play.

Step 1

Initially you must control the distance between yourself and the receiver. Before the ball is snapped, keep yourself five to ten yards from the receiver, depending on his speed. If the receiver is fast, you can either give him a couple of yards distance so it will neutralize his speed, or you can bump him at the line so he doesn't get to use his speed. When the ball is about to be hiked, if you know the receiver is slow, get close to him, about one yard away. Always keep your feet shoulder-wide apart. Crouch down slightly, bringing your weight over your toes. This should be a very balanced position. Look the receiver in the eyes and try to intimidate him.

Step 2

Body contact should be just right, not too much or too little. When the ball is snapped, thrust your arms forward, striking the receiver just below his shoulder pads, making sure you are maintaining balance. If this is accomplished, then try to keep him there. Avoid grasping, because this will cause a penalty. More often than not, the receiver will move to avoid this procedure. Do not let him get inside of you. Push him towards the sidelines. Now you need to turn with him, keeping him within touching distance. You want to be between him and the quarterback. Try to remain always in contact with him. Use your outside arm for this procedure. Don't push him too much after five yards because this is another penalty.

Step 3

Your eyes now become your main tools. Look into the receiver's eyes, watching his reactions. Don't get in front of him because he can then stop and turn back. Watch his moves and be his shadow. Remember to keep your balance so you can turn quickly when he does. As you are watching his eyes, you are looking for two things. If his eyes become extremely big, as if a present is coming his way, or they become fixed on an object, then you must react quickly. This means the ball is usually en route there. Turn your head away from the receiver and back toward the quarterback. Pick up the ball as quickly as possible, still keeping in touch with the receiver, with your outside arm.

Step 4

At some point you may play the ball as well as the receiver. Once you see the ball, if it is off target with the receiver, run to where it is headed and catch it. If it is coming in your direction, don't let the receiver get between you and the ball. Judge the distance, and when the ball is close enough for you to jump and catch it, do so. Always catch the ball at its highest point. This technique keeps a receiver from stealing it at the last second. Remember that the receiver is trying for the ball too. You must want it more than he does. If the receiver has positioned himself in front of you, then you must react. When the ball is about to touch his hands, you must hit the ball, his hands, or both. Keep the arm that is away from the ball wrapped around his body. This way if he does catch it, you can make the tackle.

After the play is done, the key to all good cornerbacks is having a short memory. If the play went against you, forget it. There is always the next one. Remember that mental and physical preparation and the right equipment are prerequisites to the process on the field. Then you have a chance to become an effective cornerback.

| Exercise 1 | DISCUSSION AND CRITICAL THINKING |

1. Is this essay directive or informative process analysis?
   Directive.

2. Although this essay explains how to do something, an interested audience might have a broader base than just football players. Who might also be interested readers?
   Football fans, those who just watch.

3. Landry mentions that good cornerbacks should be both mentally and physically fit. Is one more important than the other? Discuss how the two work together.
   Landry says physical fitness is self-evident and necessary. But it is the mental powers that make the physical accomplishments possible, and he concentrates on that part of preparation.

4. On the basis of what Landry says, would you rather have a cornerback of average physical fitness and high mental ability or one with high physical fitness and average mental ability?
   Answers will vary.

5. Underline the thesis for the essay and double underline the topic sentences for the support paragraphs.

Practicing Patterns of Process Analysis

A definite pattern underlies a process analysis. In some presentations, such as directions with merchandise to be assembled, the content reads as mechanically as an outline, and no reader objects. The same can be said of most recipes. In other presentations, such as your typical college assignments, the pattern is submerged in flowing discussion. The directions or information must be included, but the writing should be well-developed and interesting. Regardless of the form you use or the audience you anticipate, keep in mind that in process analysis the pattern will provide a foundation for the content.

Exercise 2	COMPLETING PATTERNS OF PROCESS ANALYSIS

Fill in the missing parts of the outline.

Thesis: As a cornerback, I finally discovered an effective process, one that begins with preparation before the game and ends with strategic action on the field during a pass play.

    I. Preparation

        A. Fitness

            1. Mental _____

            2. Physical _____

        B. Equipment _____

    II. Steps

        A. Control of the distance between yourself and the receiver _____

        B. Use appropriate body contact _____

        C. Watch the receiver _____

        D. Play the receiver and the ball _____

Student Documented Essay

Balancing her roles as mother and wife, full-time realtor, and part-time student, Kay Eckert is a busy, energetic woman. Her assignment in a freshman composition class was to write a process analysis paper about one phase of work she is doing or has done. She was expected to give credit to any sources she used for information. Reflecting on her job as a realtor, all activities pointed to the paired objectives of customer service and sales. She decided to write about the prerequisite to company sales: obtaining a listing of property to sell.

How to Obtain a Real Estate Listing

Kay Eckert

Selling real estate is a highly competitive business. But closing a deal is often well down the line from the first essential step: getting a listing. <u>Usually other agents are also making their pitches, and a successful person must know how to prepare for that crucial first meeting with the potential clients and then how to get the contract.</u>

Preparation

1

2

3

4

5

The first task in the preparation, that of evaluating a home and arriving at a potential sales price, pertains to gathering facts about the home itself and the most recent sales in the neighborhood. For my research, I use the Title Company, a business service that provides up-to-date details about recent sales. A property profile provides all important information about the subject property and the surrounding neighborhood. Whatever information the owners (assuming for this presentation that there are two) have provided me is factored in. Another tool I use is the Multiple Listing Service of the Board of Realtors. Then I make my comparison, focusing on square footage, lot size, and amenities, and do my calculations.

6

7

8

With that information organized, I am ready to prepare a package of information for the sellers. This package must be easy to read and understand. It should include an area map to make it easy for the homeowners to locate homes that have recently sold in the neighborhood, and a clear set of recorded sales. Now it is time to pack the briefcase. It is important to take all I am likely to need: information sheets, maps, listing forms, a calculator, magazines, newspaper ads, and letters of recommendation. It is also important not to carry in too much and intimidate the property owners. Above all, I must appear to be organized and prepared; if I am apparently not, I certainly will not get the listing. This encounter will be my one and only opportunity.

Steps

1

Now is the time to meet the homeowners. Both should be present. After I greet the owners with a smile, I always try to "break the ice" by making a comment about a positive feature of the property—the landscaping, structure, or interior decoration. Many times the owners are nervous and self-conscious. I know that I am the intruder, often regarded as a necessary component in this stressful operation. Therefore, I do what I can to make them feel comfortable and relaxed.

2

3

4

5

As soon as we are acquainted, I ask the owners to show me through the house. I make a few notes, but mainly I make mental notes that I will transcribe back in my car. I remind myself of a little six-word quotation from my favorite real estate textbook, by

6

Danielle Kennedy: "Always move and act with confidence" (197–198). Strategically, I will make sure that our tour ends in the kitchen, because most important decisions in families are made at the kitchen table. It also gives owners the feeling that they are beginning the negotiations in their territory.

7

8

9

10

11
12
13

After I am invited to sit down, I take out the information package and explain in detail the material to both homeowners. I ask them to interrupt me and ask questions at any time. I point out recent home sales in their neighborhood and explain how these compare with their home. If they say they have used the Internet to obtain information about comparative sales and mention a service such as Yahoo! Real Estate (Yahoo), I explain that the Internet is useful, but the Title Company that I use concentrates on regional and local property and gives me the most reliable figures. Together we review my marketing plan, the listing forms, and the financial aspects of the transaction. After all questions are answered, I ask the owners: "Are you ready to list your home with me now?" If they intend to bring in other agents, then my chances of getting the listing are greatly reduced. If the owners have no further questions, I can start to fill out the contract. All that is left is for my new clients to sign on the dotted lines. We will then talk for a few more minutes and then I will leave with the smile I came with, my hope having turned to fulfillment.

During the next days, weeks, or months I will almost certainly be returning to this location with buyers. The relationship I have established with my clients, the preparation I made, and the listing procedures all make up a foundation for a good sale and perhaps for recommendations for years to come.

Works Cited

Kennedy, Danielle. *How to List and Sell Real Estate.* New York: Prentice Hall, 1983.

Exercise 3   **DISCUSSION AND CRITICAL THINKING**

1. Underline the thesis.

2. Use annotation and a vertical line in the margin to mark the preparation stage; then number the parts of the preparation.

3. Use annotation and a double vertical line in the margin to mark the steps; then number the steps in the process.

How to Paint a Fresco

Adam Goodheart

Enriching his comments with numerous references stretching back five hundred years, Adam Goodheart explains a much-admired but now seldom-used method of painting—the fresco. We learn how it was done in ancient times and, at the same time, we learn how we could do it now. This article was first published in *Civilization* in 1995.

Equipment

Lime	The bristles of a white hog
Sand	The hair of bears, sables and martens
Water	The quills of vultures, geese, hens
A trowel	and doves
Paper	Ocher, burnt grapevines, lapis lazuli
A needle	Egg yolks
A small bag of charcoal dust	Goat's milk

1   1. *Preparing the wall.* Cennino Cennini, a Tuscan master, advised pupils in 1437 to "begin by decking yourselves with this attire: Enthusiasm, Reverence, Obedience, and Constancy." You'd do better to deck yourself with some old clothes, though, since the first stage of the process is quite messy. Soak the wall thoroughly and coat it with coarse plaster, two parts sand to one part lime, leaving the surface uneven. (Andrea Pozzo, a 17th-century expert, recommended hiring a professional mason to do this, since "the lime makes a foul odor, which is injurious to the head.")

2   2. *Tracing your design.* You should already have extensive drawings for your fresco—these will be much sought by scholars and collectors in centuries to come. Make a full-size sketch, on sturdy paper, of a section of the fresco that you can paint in a day. Then go over the drawing with a needle, pricking holes along

every line. Lay a coat of fine plaster on a section of the wall corresponding to the location, size, and shape of the sketch, and press the sketch against the plaster. Fill a loosely woven bag with charcoal dust and strike it lightly all over the surface of the paper. Now peel the sketch off. Your design will be outlined in black dots on the wet plaster, giving you a guide for the day's work.

3   3. *Painting.* Time is of the essence: You must paint the plaster while it is wet, so that the pigments bind chemically with the lime. That gives you about six hours, although some painters had tricks to prolong drying. (Piero della Francesca packed the plaster with wet rags; problem was, this left indentations that are still visible after 500 years.) Use top-quality brushes. One 17th-century Flemish master recommended those made of "fish hair" (he probably meant seal fur), but most painters made brushes from bear, marten, or sable hairs inserted in hollow quills. Cennini suggested the bristles of a white hog for the coarser work. As for paints, every artist had his own favorite recipes, but all agreed that mineral pigments such as ocher or ground stone mixed with water were best. Avoid white lead. . . . A few pigments, such as dark blue azurite (often used for the Virgin Mary's mantle), must be mixed with egg yolk or goat's milk and added after the fresco is dry. Such colors will prove less durable.

4   Money is a consideration in choosing materials. When Michelangelo frescoed the Sistine ceiling, expenses came out of his fee, so he used cheap blue smalt for the sky. Twenty years later, when he did the *Last Judgment,* Michelangelo used semiprecious lapis lazuli for blue, since the pope was paying for the paint. (He made up for it by using burnt grapevines for black.)

5   4. *Casualties of style.* Realism, while a worthy goal, has its perils. Spinello Aretino, a 14th-century Tuscan, is said to have painted a fresco that depicted Lucifer with such hideous accuracy that the Evil One himself came to the artist in a dream and demanded an explanation. Spinello went half-mad with fear and died shortly thereafter. On the other hand, a Florentine woodcut from 1500 depicts a painter who has portrayed the Virgin so skillfully that when he falls off the scaffold, she reaches out of the fresco and saves him.

Warning

6   Frescoing ceilings can be rough on your back. While working on the Sistine Chapel, Michelangelo wrote a poem complaining: "I've already grown a goiter at this drudgery . . . With my beard toward

heaven . . . I am bent like a bow." Don't be discouraged, though. Bad posture is a small price to pay for immortality.

| Exercise 4 | DISCUSSION AND CRITICAL THINKING |

1. Is this a directive or informative process analysis?
   Directive.

2. What part of the essay represents the preparation stage?
   Equipment.

3. How many steps are included in the process and what are their numbers?
   Three. Numbers 1, 2, and 3.

4. How does Goodheart humanize his set of directions and give perspective to his subject material?
   He uses examples, anecdotes, and other information from hundreds of years ago when frescoing was a common method of painting.

5. As the author explains steps, he refers to individuals who made contributions to the art of fresco painting. Are these references examples of formal or informal documentation?
   Informal.

6. What is the purpose of paragraphs 5 and 6?
   The author provides information for entertainment and enlightenment.

7. What kind of audience does the author anticipate? How do you know?
   He is writing for an educated audience, one with some knowledge of art, world history, and geography. He assumes that his readers will be familiar with art, other historical times, and place names, such as "Tuscan" (paragraph 1), "Flemish" (paragraph 3), "Umbrian" (paragraph 3), and "Florentine" (paragraph 5).

Six Clicks from Death

Cynthia Joyce

Like so many of us, Cynthia Joyce had a health problem and turned to the Internet for answers. Unfortunately, her adventure in cyberspace was worse than her disease. Looking back with humor on her frantic search, she highlights where she went right and wrong. This article was first published in the April 1997 edition of *Salon* at http://www.salonmagazine.com.

1   I woke up one morning last fall and the entire right side of my face felt like it had been injected with Novocaine. I ran to the mirror to see what was going on and attempted a series of Jim Carrey* impersonations to work the numbness out of my face. The left side went along willingly, but the right side stared back at me, unblinking and totally expressionless.

2   By the time I made it to work, it had gotten worse. The right side of my face now looked like a fallen soufflé, and the right half of my tongue felt like rubber. I tried to downplay how scared I was, offering lame little jokes like, "Is this what they mean by 'self-effacing'?" My jokes didn't have the desired effect of putting my co-workers at ease because by now my speech was so slurred I sounded drunk. By midafternoon, the right side of my face was completely paralyzed—yet, oddly, my hearing on that side was amplified. I felt like a cross between a stroke victim and the Bionic Woman.†

3   My doctor took one look at me and, ruling out the possibility of a stroke (rare for healthy twenty-seven-year-olds), diagnosed me with Bell's palsy—a typically temporary condition resulting from damage to the seventh cranial nerve. He said no one knows what causes this damage, but most people fully recover in four to six weeks. He didn't tell me what happens to the *other* people, and I didn't ask. Although I understood that I was probably going to look like Bill the Cat‡ for at least a month, I was relieved that my doctor didn't seem overly concerned. As I went to fill his prescription for steroids, I vowed to keep busy, stay away from mirrors for a while, and learn everything I could about my syndrome.

4   As it turned out, staring at my distorted reflection would prove to be far less threatening a pastime than staring into the kaleidoscope of information on the Web.

5   The first thing I did when I returned to work the next morning was search the Web for information on Bell's palsy—beginning a series of self-misdiagnoses that did more lasting damage than the palsy itself. Because I didn't know where to find reliable health information, I started a general search on AltaVista. The first article that turned up was a *Healthgate* document from the National Library of Medicine's *Medline* database titled "Management of Bell's palsy." I read the abstract: "The natural history of Bell's palsy is favorable. Eighty-four percent show satisfactory recovery without any treatment; however, 16 percent suffer moderate to severe sequelae."

*Jim Carrey is a comedian and actor.
†The Bionic Woman was a character on a TV show who had superhuman abilities.
‡Bill the Cat is a comic-strip character.

6   *Sequelae?* Good God, what could that be? I'd never heard of it before. I quickly did a new search on sequelae. My heart was beating in my ears as I waited for the search results. I tried to picture what sequelae might look like. I imagined myself in scarf and gloves, trying to conceal the sequelae that covered my neck and hands. I pictured friends and co-workers recoiling in horror as sequelae spewed from my right ear. I wondered if sequelae was contagious—would I have to be quarantined?

7   The sequelae search results finally appeared, barely staving off my hysteria. I clicked on an article from the *Journal of Clinical Oncology* titled "Late Psycho-Social Sequelae in Hodgkin's Disease Survivors: A French Population-Based Case-Control Study." Of course, I'd never suffered from Hodgkin's disease, but it didn't matter. My line of reasoning went something like this: the incidence of sequelae in French populations must be pretty high to merit a control study being based on it. My mother's side of the family is French. As far as I was concerned, this constituted conclusive data. But I was forced to admit I was probably off-track when I calmed down enough to notice that the dreaded *s* word wasn't even mentioned in the conclusion.

8   I went back to the original search and followed the second entry, titled simply "Sequelae." It read: "Sequelae . . . may include persistent hypesthesia and dysesthesia, persistent motor weakness, infection, amputation, and death. These are the direct result of nerve and muscle injury." The various *-thesias* didn't mean anything to me, but seeing the words "nerve damage" and "amputation and death" so close together within the same paragraph threw me into a panic.

9   And it didn't end there. By the time I finally bothered to look up *sequelae* in Webster's and found that it means only "something that follows," I had diagnosed myself with a brain tumor, encephalitis, Lyme disease, and two different strains of the herpes virus. Whatever Web page I started from, I never seemed to be more than six clicks from a death sentence.

10   As my doctor predicted, I recovered fully within four weeks. He didn't tell me about the 16 percent who never recover or suffer the dreaded "sequelae" of recurring paralysis because he correctly assumed I'd automatically count myself among them. And since Bell's palsy may be linked to stress, he wisely decided not to give me cause for more. Nonetheless, during those four weeks, I think I found every single one of those 16 percent online.

11   Although I didn't know it at the time, it's safe to assume that because Bell's palsy usually goes away after several weeks, the people posting in online support groups like the Neurology Web

Forum represented a disproportionate segment of those Bell's palsy sufferers whose symptoms never faded. I certainly had no reason to distrust their accounts—but lots of reasons why I didn't need to hear them just then. Still, I opened every one of those links, and needless to say, with subject heads like "SCARED," "10 years later . . ." and "BELL'S STRIKES AGAIN," the stories only added to my hysteria.

12   Clearly, of course, people with serious illnesses—particularly those who have been properly diagnosed—can greatly benefit from online support groups. Dr. Allison Szapary, a resident at the University of California at San Francisco, believes that although younger residents like herself typically use medical databases like *Medline* "every day, all day," online support groups are far more useful for patients than such data-heavy sites. "I think the Web is better for offering emotional support than for actually giving good factual information," she says. "For people going through serious illnesses, it's important for them to feel connected to others going through the same thing."

13   One reason it's so useful, especially for people with chronic or degenerative illnesses, is that people can describe even their most embarrassing health problems without having to look someone in the eye—and in such situations, unlike in other kinds of Web conferences, the anonymity actually encourages more honesty.

14   As a cancer survivor, health writer, and producer for the popular *Ask Dr. Weil* alternative medicine site, Steven Petrow knows firsthand both the advantages and dangers of online medical resources.

15   "When I researched medical libraries like the University of Pennsylvania site, I wound up with more information than I knew how to interpret. When I went to my doctor I was a mess—I thought I was going to die," he says. "I've been a health writer for more than ten years, and when I read a study, I have to read all the footnotes very carefully, and sometimes I still don't understand. So you can only assume your average consumer would be confused some of the time."

16   Several sites, such as Reuters Health, offer information under two separate categories for consumers and professionals to help alleviate this problem. Patients still have access to medical research but can get it in layman's terms. Without that option, Petrow points out, having all the latest info "doesn't cure your problems—it could actually create new ones."

17   The editors of the *Journal of the American Medical Association* attempted to address some of these issues in an April 16 editorial in which they warned that "health care professionals and patients

alike should view with equal parts delight and concern the exponential growth of . . . the Web as a medical information delivery tool. Delight because the Internet hosts a large number of high-quality medical resources and poses seemingly endless opportunities to inform, teach, and connect professionals and patients alike. Concern because the fulfillment of that promise remains discouragingly distant."

18 Part of the problem with the Web, they argue, is that "science and snake oil may not always look all that different on the Net." Petrow agrees that the unregulated proliferation of health information sites on the Web makes it easier for consumers to be duped, especially by sites promoting alternative medicine.

19 "I think it's easier to scam people online," he says. "Some of us are hoping there will be some kind of oversight in terms of fraud on the Web because right now there isn't. With print magazines, at least you have to have 'advertisement' written on the page if it's an ad. It's hard for someone to tell what's legitimate or not, and part of the problem is when fraud is actually being committed, you don't have an actual physical location where someone could be prosecuted. The consumer law needs to evolve to a national level that incorporates the Web."

20 The authors of the *JAMA* editorial take a different view. They argue that because the Web is a global and decentralized medium, government regulation isn't the answer. Instead, they favor a standard set of guidelines for authorship, attribution, disclosure, and currency that online resources wishing to establish their reliability would adopt. "Web publishers of all stripes—ourselves included—should be free to post whatever they like and live with the consequences. Let a thousand flowers bloom. We just want those cruising the information superhighway to be able to tell them from the weeds."

21 But as my doctor, Jesse Dohemann, points out, even by-the-book science can start to smell like snake oil* if the doctor-patient relationship is eroded. "I had a guy in here recently who had horrible hives, so I sent him to all the top allergists, and no one could figure out what it was," Dohemann recalls. "He got in touch with a doctor from New York online who prescribed him medication normally used to treat people with Parkinson's disease. The hives did get better, but the guy was now taking a combination of drugs that would have crippled him within ten years. This doctor may have been a real M.D., but he was also a ding-dong."

*Snake oil is a fraudulent medicine.

22   As the rise of the HMO* has put greater emphasis on primary and preventive health care, alternative medical information like that provided by *Ask Dr. Weil* has become a growth industry. And the kind of general advice to people such sites provide—watch less news, eat more broccoli—would probably keep them out of legal trouble, even without the prominently displayed liability disclaimer, a standard feature of most sites offering free health advice.

23   But the "free" part of that equation may soon come to an end for the online services of more traditional medical institutions. Because many health-related sites offer interactive elements— like the Internist's Casebook, which lets you play medical detective—their mix of straight advice and "infotainment" allows them to rely on advertising revenue. But sites that cater more to health-care professionals, like Medscape, Medline and the Mayo Clinic, may soon be forced to charge subscription fees. "I think the love affair with free information is going to be coming to an end," Petrow predicts. "And the question seems to be, you pay for this type of information now; why wouldn't you have to pay for it on the Web?"

24   Looking back on my experience with Bell's palsy, it wasn't all a nightmare—in retrospect, it even seems pretty funny. And I did, in the end, discover an entire range of health resources, as well as develop a great new pastime—albeit a rather obsessive one.

25   For a while there, I was researching my every sneeze online. I no longer needed a *Physician's Desk Reference* to tell me which drugs I couldn't take with alcohol—I could look it up at PharmInfoNet. I could find out everything I never wanted to know about the freckles on my shoulders, my receding hairline, and why I get leg cramps. I even found an interactive ovulation site—one of my personal favorites—featuring the What-If Ovulation Calendar. Believe me, figuring out the last day of your menstrual cycle has never been so much fun.

26   But as my experience showed, too much information can sometimes be a real health hazard. So do the Web a favor: if you've ever suffered a debilitating, embarrassing, or long-lasting illness and been lucky enough to live to tell about it, then please do. You may not cure anyone of whatever ails them, but you just might keep them from going crazy.

*HMO: health maintenance organization.

Exercise 5   **VOCABULARY HIGHLIGHTS**

Write a short definition of each word as it is used in the essay. (Paragraph numbers are given in parentheses.) Be prepared to use the words in your own sentences.

kaleidoscope (4)	anonymity (13)
sequelae (5)	proliferation (18)
constituted (7)	disclaimer (22)
chronic (13)	retrospect (24)
degenerative (13)	obsessive (24)

Exercise 6   **DISCUSSION AND CRITICAL THINKING**

1. In what ways can this information process analysis be thought of as having directive use?

   If you were to conduct a similar search, you could consider Joyce's mistakes and have fewer problems than she. You could also better understand the limitations of obtaining medical information from the Web.

2. Which paragraphs provide the background of this analysis?

   Paragraphs 1 through 3.

3. What is Joyce's first step in her search?

   Her general search on AltaVista.

4. Which paragraphs include the steps of the process?

   Paragraphs 5 through 9.

5. In her quest for information about Bell's palsy, Joyce often needed to double back to reexamine what she had found and to redefine terms. Was that movement because of her ineptitude or the nature of researching information on the Web? Explain.

   It is because of the nature of researching information on the Web. Researching information on the Web will seldom move forward site by site. One will naturally make some wrong site selections and sometimes need to do collateral research to understand what one has found.

6. In what ways is pursuing a question on the Web similar to the writing process?

   Writing is recursive, meaning that as one writes one often needs to return to earlier strategies (to clusters, lists, controlling statements, outlines, preliminary drafts) to clarify and modify. In writing, one may have to change the focus, reword the thesis, add information, subtract information, and supply definitions.

7. How do paragraphs 10 through 26 relate to paragraphs 1 through 9 (the process analysis part)?

   Paragraphs 10 through 26 comment on the value of a search such as the one Joyce made. It also highlights the benefits of medical research, all of which she discovered as a result of her quest.

8. What did you learn from this essay that you can apply when you need to research some medical issue?
<small>Answers will vary.</small>

Attitude

Garrison Keillor

Author, humorist, and storyteller, Garrison Keillor is best known as host of *A Prairie Home Companion* straight from Lake Wobegon, long featured on National Public Radio. In this essay, first published in *The New Yorker*, he tells us how to play with "attitude."

1   Long ago I passed the point in life when major-league ball-players begin to be younger than yourself. Now all of them are, except for a few aging trigenarians and a couple of quadros who don't get around on the fastball as well as they used to and who sit out the second games of doubleheaders. However, despite my age (thirty-nine), I am still active and have a lot of interests. One of them is slow-pitch softball, a game that lets me go through the motions of baseball without getting beaned or having to run too hard. I play on a pretty casual team, one that drinks beer on the bench and substitutes freely. If a player's wife or girlfriend wants to play, we give her a glove and send her out to right field, no questions asked, and if she lets a pop fly drop six feet in front of her, nobody agonizes over it.

2   Except me. This year. For the first time in my life, just as I am entering the dark twilight of my slow-pitch career, I find myself taking the game seriously. It isn't the bonehead play that bothers me especially—the pop fly that drops untouched, the slow roller juggled and the ball then heaved ten feet over the first baseman's head and into the next diamond, the routine singles that go through outfielders' legs for doubles and triples with gloves flung after them. No, it isn't our stone-glove fielding or pussyfoot base-running or limp-wristed hitting that gives me fits, though these have put us on the short end of some mighty ridiculous scores this summer. It's our attitude.

3   Bottom of the ninth, down 18–3, two outs, a man on first and a woman on third, and our third baseman strikes out. *Strikes out!* In slow-pitch, not even your grandmother strikes out, but this guy does, and after his third strike—a wild swing at a ball that bounces

on the plate—he topples over in the dirt and lies flat on his back, laughing. *Laughing!*

4 Same game, earlier. They have the bases loaded. A weak grounder is hit toward our second baseperson. The runners are running. She picks up the ball, and she looks at them. She looks at first, at second, at home. We yell, "Throw it! Throw it!" and she throws it, underhand, at the pitcher, who has turned and run to back up the catcher. The ball rolls across the third-base line and under the bench. Three runs score. The batter, a fatso, chugs into second. The other team hoots and hollers, and what does she do? She shrugs and smiles ("Oh, silly me"); after all, it's only a game. Like the aforementioned strikeout artist, she treats her error as a joke. They have forgiven themselves instantly, which is unforgivable. It is *we* who should forgive them, who can say, "It's all right, it's only a game." They are supposed to throw up their hands and kick the dirt and hang their heads, as if this boner, even if it is their sixteenth of the afternoon—*this* is the one that really and truly breaks their hearts.

5 That attitude sweetens the game for everyone. The sinner feels sweet remorse. The fatso feels some sense of accomplishment; this is no bunch of rumdums he forced into an error but a team with some class. We, the sinner's teammates, feel momentary anger at her—dumb! dumb play!—but then, seeing her grief, we sympathize with her in our hearts (any one of us might have made that mistake or one worse), and we yell encouragement, including the shortstop, who, moments before, dropped an easy throw for a force at second. "That's all right! Come on! We got 'em!" we yell. "Shake it off! These turkeys can't hit!" This makes us all feel good, even though the turkeys now lead us by ten runs. We're getting clobbered, but we have a winning attitude.

6 Let me say this about attitude: Each player is responsible for his or her own attitude, and to a considerable degree you can *create* a good attitude by doing certain little things on the field. These are certain little things that ballplayers do in the Bigs, and we ought to be doing them in the Slows.

7 1. When going up to bat, don't step right into the batter's box as if it were an elevator. The box is your turf, your stage. Take possession of it slowly and deliberately, starting with a lot of back-bending, knee-stretching, and torso-revolving in the on-deck circle. Then, approaching the box, stop outside it and tap the dirt off your spikes with your bat. You don't have spikes, you have sneakers, of course, but the sig-

nificance of the tapping is the same. Then, upon entering the box, spit on the ground. It's a way of saying, "This here is mine. This is where I get my hits."

2. Spit frequently. Spit at all crucial moments. Spit correctly. Spit should be *blown,* not ptuied weakly with the lips, which often results in dribble. Spitting should convey forcefulness of purpose, concentration, pride. Spit down, not in the direction of others. Spit in the glove and on the fingers, especially after making a real knucklehead play; it's a way of saying, "I dropped the ball because my glove was dry."

3. At bat and in the field, pick up dirt. Rub dirt in the fingers (especially after spitting on them). Toss dirt, as if testing the wind for velocity and direction. Smooth the dirt. Be involved with dirt. If no dirt is available (e.g., in the outfield), pluck tufts of grass. Fielders should be grooming their areas constantly between plays, flicking away tiny sticks and bits of gravel.

4. Take your time. Tie your laces. Confer with your teammates about possible situations that may arise and conceivable options in dealing with them. Extend the game. Three errors on three consecutive plays can be humiliating if the plays occur within the space of a couple of minutes, but if each error is separated from the next by extensive conferences on the mound, lace-tying, glove adjustments, and arguing close calls (if any), the effect on morale is minimized.

5. Talk. Not just an occasional "Let's get a hit now" but continuous rhythmic chatter, a flow of syllables: "Hey babe hey babe c'mon babe good stick now hey babe long tater take him downtown babe . . . hey good eye good eye."

Infield chatter is harder to maintain. Since the slow-pitch pitch is required to be a soft underhand lob, infielders hesitate to say, "Smoke him babe hey low heat hey throw it on the black babe chuck it in there back him up babe no hit no hit." Say it anyway.

6. One final rule, perhaps the most important of all: When your team is up and has made the third out, the batter and the players who were left on base do not come back to the bench for their gloves. *They remain on the field, and their teammates bring their gloves out to them.* This requires some organization and discipline, but it pays off big in morale. It says, "Although we're getting our pants knocked off, still we must conserve our energy."

14   Imagine that you have bobbled two fly balls in this rout and now you have just tried to stretch a single into a double and have been easily thrown out sliding into second base, where the base runner ahead of you had stopped. It was the third out and a dumb play, and your opponents smirk at you as they run off the field. You are the goat, a lonely and tragic figure sitting in the dirt. You curse yourself, jerking your head sharply forward. You stand up and kick the base. How miserable! How degrading! Your utter shame, though brief, bears silent testimony to the worthiness of your teammates, whom you have let down, and they appreciate it. They call out to you now as they take the field, and as the second baseman runs to his position he says, "Let's get 'em now," and tosses you your glove. Lowering your head, you trot slowly out to right. There you do some deep knee bends. You pick grass. You find a pebble and fling it into foul territory. As the first batter comes to the plate, you check the sun. You get set in your stance, poised to fly. Feet spread, hands on hips, you bend slightly at the waist and spit the expert spit of a veteran ballplayer—a player who has known the agony of defeat but who always bounces back, a player who has lost a stride on the base paths but can still make the big play.

15   This is *ball,* ladies and gentlemen. This is what it's all about.

| **Exercise 7** | **DISCUSSION AND CRITICAL THINKING** |

1. Is the process analysis part of this essay informative or directive?
Directive.

2. What is the source of "attitude," as Keillor would like to see it demonstrated on his slow-pitch team?
Major league baseball.

3. Why does he skip over the preparation stage?
He has already given the background. The team is his. The game is slow-pitch. The players are equipped and they know how to play (to some extent). But they do not play with a winning attitude. All of that is understood.

4. Keillor provides us with six steps. Are the steps to be performed in a particular order?
No particular order.

5. In what other sports is attitude important? Give some examples of attitude-building rituals in other sports.
Answers will vary.

6. What attitude-building behavior is used by people outside sports: at school, at work, at worship, on the road.
Answers will vary.

7. What is the tone of this essay and what does Keillor expect readers to do?

The tone is humorous and Keillor expects his readers to laugh.

Stars

Usha Lee McFarling

In simple, direct terms, Usha Lee McFarling, a science writer for the *Boston Globe*, explains a process of enormous magnitude and complexity.

1   A star starts out life from what seems like nothing at all. Stars are born in huge clouds of gas that are actually far less dense than the space immediately surrounding Earth.

2   "These clouds are so spread out, they make the 'vacuum' of the space around the Earth that the space shuttle flies through seem as thick as chicken soup," says Jeff Hester, an astronomer at Arizona State University in Tempe. But because the clouds are so big, they contain a lot of molecules—enough, eventually, to build massive stars.

Background

3   How big are these clouds that serve as star nurseries? They can be a light-year across—so enormous it would take light one year to cross one. In contrast, it takes light only one-seventh of a second to travel the nearly 25,000-mile distance that equals the circumference of tiny Earth.

Steps

1

4   The key to star formation is gravity, says Hester. Gravity causes the multitude of spread-out molecules to move toward each other and pulls them toward the center of the cloud. "The cloud starts to collapse under the force of its own gravity," says Hester, who studies the process of star formation. This collapsing process happens relatively quickly (by cosmic standards)—only about 30 million years, or less.

2

5   Over time the cloud gets smaller and smaller. As the cloud contracts, it also begins to spin faster. (This is due to a little something called conservation of angular momentum—the same phenomenon that allows a figure skater like Nancy Kerrigan to speed up her spin when she pulls her arms in toward her body. As the mass of gas moves toward the center, the cloud spins faster.)

6   Next, the cloud starts to flatten. "It's just like when you make an honest pizza," says Hester. "The dough flattens as it spins."

3

Finally, because gravity becomes so strong in the center of the cloud, the center starts to collapse in on itself as it continues to rotate. At this point, you have a disk that's a few times the size of our solar system. (The disk would be about a couple of light-days across, if you're keeping track of the size of things.) As the disk continues to rotate, matter in the center of the disk starts to migrate further inward and a big clump forms in the middle of the disk. This clump, says Hester, is a protostar.

7
What happens to the matter that's left over further out in the disk? In our solar system, it went on to become the planets. (In essence, Earth is made up of leftovers.)

8
Protostars are very hot because so much of the gravitational energy that was once contained in the loose cloud of interstellar gas has been converted into heat. Protostars are spectacular, glowing with dull red light and infrared light. As a protostar emits this light, it continues to shrink and gets hotter and hotter. Finally, it's hot enough for real star business to begin—nuclear fusion.

4

9
At high enough temperatures, atoms slam together at incredibly fast speeds. When this happens, lighter atoms like hydrogen can fuse together to make heavier atoms like helium. One reaction releases massive amounts of energy; add all the reactions together, and "that's the energy that makes the stars shine," Hester says. Once nuclear fusion begins, that's truly when a star is born.

5

10
After a star "turns on," he says, its power can wreak havoc on the surrounding environment. A young star expands, ripping apart the cloud that formed it. In a case of stellar sibling rivalry, new stars often disrupt neighboring stars before they can form. It's hard to overstate what a powerful process star formation is. Even as they are forming, protostars eject huge amounts of material in jets and streams and create violent solar winds.

11
Astronomers have identified stellar nurseries within our galaxy—places where new stars are forming, and the Hubble telescope has taken some startling photos of the process of star formation in the Eagle nebula. Without a telescope, says Hester, you can see a stellar nursery by looking at the Milky Way in summer and looking to the south near the constellation Sagittarius. In the middle of the Milky Way, says Hester, you'll see dark splotches. These aren't areas that are free of stars, he says, "rather, they are the shadows of dense interstellar clouds that block the light from stars behind them." These clouds are the nurseries of future stars.

| Exercise 8 | **VOCABULARY HIGHLIGHTS** |

Write a short definition of each word as it is used in the essay. (Paragraph numbers are given in parentheses.) Be prepared to use the words in your own sentences.

molecules (2)   infrared (8)

angular (5)   fusion (8)

momentum (5)   stellar (10)

phenomenon (5)   sibling (10)

protostar (6)   nebula (11)

| Exercise 9 | **DISCUSSION AND CRITICAL THINKING** |

1. Is this essay directive or informative process analysis?
   Informative.

2. Annotate the essay by drawing a vertical line beside the paragraphs that present the background to this process.

3. Annotate the essay by writing numbers alongside paragraphs to show the steps by which stars are formed.

4. What is the function of paragraph 10?
   Paragraph 10 explains what happens after the star is born.

5. Paragraph 11 is the conclusion. How does it relate to paragraphs 1 and 2, the introduction?
   McFarling brings us back to the original setting—unimaginably large clouds of gas—and continues with the speaker (Jeff Hester) from the introduction, finally saying that we can see "the nurseries of future stars."

✎ Topics for Writing Process Analysis

Writing Process Worksheet

You will find a Writing Process Worksheet in Appendix A, page 531. It can be photocopied and enlarged, filled in, and submitted with each assignment if your instructor directs you to do so.

Source-Based Topics

Each essay developed from these suggested source-based topics should include at least one reference to the reading selection by the author's name and the title. Quotations should be enclosed in quotation marks. Follow your instructor's directions in documenting the ideas you borrow. Whether you use informal or formal documentation, the form is not complicated, and you will soon learn to use it for these essays without

checking each time. See pages 77 and 78 for a discussion of MLA style and informal documentation.

Underlining and annotating reading selections will help you in finding support material. In prewriting brief essays, consider marking your outline to indicate where you will use quotations or other borrowed ideas. If the quotations or reworded statements are short and few, you could even insert them inside parentheses or circles in your outline; if you do, also include the author's last name and the page number. A sound system, consistently used, will save you time and ensure technically strong papers.

"Guarding a Wide Receiver"

1. Write about how to play another position on a football team. Use this essay as an example.

2. Write about a person playing the position of wide receiver, and refer directly to this essay in explaining techniques for outsmarting and outplaying the cornerback.

3. Write an essay about how to play any sport. Limit your topic so that you can cover it in some detail. You might write about how to shoot a free throw in basketball or how to serve in tennis. If you are writing about a team sport, concentrate on one player or on one strategy or maneuver, such as a "suicide squeeze" in baseball.

"How to Obtain a Real Estate Listing"

4. Using this essay as a model and one or more basic sources as documented aids, explain how to do something related to a job you know well through observation or practice. Consider finding information about the job in printed company guidelines, on the Web, or in library sources.

"How to Paint a Fresco"

5. Using this essay as a model, explain how to paint with oils, acrylics, or watercolors. You could strengthen your writing by including some information about artists who have excelled in the form you choose. Use your library and the Internet in your search for sources.

6. Explain how to perform in another visual art, such as sculpting or photography. Include some background information to enlighten your readers and to heighten interest.

"Six Clicks from Death"

7. Explain in detail how you have searched for information on a similar topic. Indicate what you learned in the process and discuss how your search was similar to and different from Joyce's.

8. Explain in detail how you searched for any information on the Internet: genealogy, career, consumer goods, the truth about _____.

9. Conduct a search on the Internet, keep notes of your experience, and write an informative process analysis detailing what went right and wrong. Here are some health topics: Angelman's syndrome, hepatitis C, prostatitis, carcinoma, tonsil removal, herbs as food supplements.

"Attitude"

10. Using Keillor's essay as a model of form and tone, write a process analysis about how one could master a winning attitude in other fields: a particular vocation, education (either in the role of educator or student), another sport (basketball, football, tennis, golf, skating, soccer, track and field).

11. Write about professional wrestling as a "sport" that owes much of its popularity to the bizarre exhibitions of "winning attitude." Explain exactly what steps those professional wrestlers take. Name wrestlers and describe antics.

"Stars"

12. Write an informative process analysis essay about another topic from the physical sciences: earthquake, tsunami, hurricane, tornado, volcano eruption, famous flood, mountain building, tectonic plates.

Career-Related Topics

13. Explain how to display, package, sell, or demonstrate a product.

14. Explain how to perform a service or to repair or install a product.

15. Explain the procedure for operating a machine, computer, piece of equipment, or other device.

16. Explain how to manufacture, construct, or cook something.

General Topics   Most of the following topics are directive as they are phrased. However, each can be transformed into a how-it-was-done informative topic by personalizing it and explaining stage by stage how you, someone else, or a group did something. For example, you could write either a directive process analysis about how to deal with an obnoxious person or an informative process analysis about how you or someone else dealt with an obnoxious person. Keep in mind that the two types of process analysis are often blended, especially in the personal approach. Many of these topics will be more interesting to you and your readers if they are personalized.

Select one of the following topics and write a process analysis essay. Most of the topics require some narrowing to be treated in a brief essay. For example, writing about playing baseball is too broad; writing about how to throw a curve ball may be manageable.

17. How to end a relationship without hurting someone's feelings.

18. How to pass a test for a driver's license

19. How to get a job at _____

20. How to eat _____

21. How to perform a magic trick

22. How to repair _____

23. How to assemble _____

24. How to learn about another culture

25. How to approach someone you would like to know better

Writer's Guidelines: Process Analysis

1. Decide whether your process analysis is mainly directive or informative, and be appropriately consistent in using pronouns and other designations.

   • For the directive analysis, use the second person, addressing the reader as *you*. The *you* may be understood, even if it is not written.

   • For the informative analysis, use the first person, speaking as *I* or *we*, or the third person, speaking about the subject as *he, she, it,* or *they*, or by name.

2. Consider using these basic forms.

Directive	*Informative*
I. Preparation	I. Background
A.	A.
B.	B.
II. Steps	II. Sequence
A.	A.
B.	B.
C.	C.

3. Listing is a useful prewriting activity for this form. Begin with the Roman numeral headings indicated in guideline number 2.

4. The order of a process analysis will usually be chronological (time based) in some sense. Certain transitional words are commonly used to promote coherence: *first, second, third, then, soon, now, next, finally, at last, therefore,* and *consequently.*

Comparison and Contrast: Showing Similarities and Differences

THE QUIGMANS   by Buddy Hickerson

Comparison and Contrast Defined

Comparison and contrast is a method of showing similarities and differences between subjects. *Comparison* is concerned with organizing and developing points of similarity; *contrast* serves the same function for differences. In some instances, a writing assignment may require that you cover only similarities or only differences. Occasionally, an instructor may ask you to separate one from the other. Usually, you will combine them within the larger design of your paragraph or essay. For convenience, the term *comparison* is often used for both comparison and contrast, because both use the same techniques and are regularly combined into one operation.

This chapter will help you deal with topics and choose strategies for developing comparison and contrast.

Generating Topics and Working with the 4 *P*'s

Comparison and contrast are basic to your thinking. In your daily activities, you consider similarities and differences between persons, things, concepts, political leaders, doctors, friends, instructors, schools, nations, classes, movies, and so on. You naturally turn to comparison and contrast to solve problems and make decisions in your life and in your writing. Because you have had so much experience with comparing, finding a topic to write about is likely to be easy and interesting. Freewriting, brainstorming, and listing will help you generate topics that are especially workable and appropriate for particular assignments.

Many college writing assignments will specify a topic or direct you to choose one from a list. Regardless of the source of your topic, the procedure for developing your ideas by comparison and contrast is the same. That procedure can appropriately be called the 4 *P*'s; purpose, points, patterns, and presentation.

Purpose

In most of your writing, the main purpose will be either to inform or to persuade.

Informative Writing

If you want to explain something about a topic by showing each subject in relationship with others, then your purpose is informative. For example, you might be comparing two composers, Beethoven and Mozart. Both were musical geniuses, so you might decide that it would be senseless to argue that one is superior to the other. Instead, you choose to reveal interesting information about both by showing them in relation to each other. The emphasis of your writing would be on insights into their characteristics, the insights heightened because the characteristics are placed alongside each other.

Persuasive Writing

If you want to show that one actor, one movie, one writer, one president, one product, or one idea is better than another, your purpose will be persuasive. Your argument will take shape as you write, beginning with emphasis in the topic sentence or thesis and reinforcement by repetition throughout your paper, in each case indicating that one side is superior.

Let's say, as an extended illustration, that you are taking a course in twentieth-century European history and you are asked to write about two leaders. You choose to write about Mussolini and Hitler as dictators. In freewriting, you discover that you know quite a bit about the two leaders. By brainstorming, you come up with some specific information.

Who?	Mussolini and Hitler
What?	fascist leaders, racists—with Hitler being more extreme
Where?	in Italy and Germany, respectively
When?	the decade before and during World War II
Why?	greed, morals, possible psychological problems, with Hitler being more extreme
How?	setting up totalitarian states

You tentatively decide that your purpose will be to persuade readers that, although both men were fascists, Hitler was more extreme in all important respects. If you need more information, you will have to consult your textbooks, your lecture notes, or sources in the library or on the Internet.

Points

The points are the ideas that will be applied somewhat equally to both sides of your comparison and contrast. They begin to emerge in freewriting, take on more precision in brainstorming, acquire a main position in listing, and assume the major part of the framework in the outline.

When writing on an assigned topic based on lectures and reading, you will probably be able to decide these points quickly. The subject material itself may dictate the points. For example, if you were comparing the governments of the United States and Great Britain, you would probably use these three points: executive, legislative, and judicial.

Using listing as a technique for finding points is simple. Follow this procedure:

1. Select one side of your two-part subject (the side you know better) and compose a list in relation to a basic treatment you expect to extend to your comparative study.

<u>Hitler</u> <u>was a fascist dictator with racist views.</u>
    subject   **treatment**

2. Make a list of points (about Hitler as a fascist dictator).

    commitment

    racial views

    beliefs

    fascism

    flexibility

    militaristic designs

3. Decide which points can also be applied in a useful way to the other subject, in this case, Mussolini. (You can also reverse the approach.) In this instance, all of the points can be applied in a useful way.

4. Select the points for your thesis.

    racial views

    commitment

    militaristic designs

5. Incorporate these points into a thesis. (Your final thesis need not specify the points.)

<u>Although Mussolini and Hitler were both fascist dictators,</u>
                subject

<u>they</u> <u>were significantly different in their racial views,</u>
         treatment (with points)

<u>commitment, and militaristic designs.</u>

You now have a purpose and points. An outline or outline alternative will help you select and develop a pattern for your comparison.

Patterns

Now you will choose between two basic patterns of organization: (1) subject by subject (opposing) or (2) point by point (alternating). In long papers you may mix the two patterns, but in most college assignments, you will probably select just one and make it your basic organizational plan.

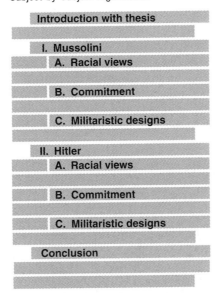

Figure 11.1
Subject-by-Subject Organization

Introduction with thesis

I. Mussolini
  A. Racial views

  B. Commitment

  C. Militaristic designs

II. Hitler
  A. Racial views

  B. Commitment

  C. Militaristic designs

Conclusion

Figure 11.2
Point-by-Point Organization

Introduction with thesis

I. Racial views
  A. Mussolini

  B. Hitler

II. Commitment
  A. Mussolini

  B. Hitler

III. Militaristic designs
  A. Mussolini

  B. Hitler

Conclusion

In comparison and contrast, the outline works especially well in indicting relationships and sequence. As with most other writing forms, the sequence of a comparison-and-contrast essay can be based on time, space, or emphasis. Emphasis is the most likely order.

Figures 11.1 and 11.2 show you the two patterns as they are applied to the essay.

In the subject-by-subject approach, organize your material around the subjects—the sides of the comparative study, as shown in Figure 11.1. In the point-by-point approach, organize your paper mainly around the points that you apply to the two subjects, as shown in Figure 11.2.

Presentation

The two patterns of organization—subject by subject and point by point—are equally valid, and each has its strengths for presentation of ideas.

As shown in Figure 11.1, the subject-by-subject pattern presents material in large blocks, which means the reader can see a body of material that is complete. However, if the material is also complex, the reader has the burden of remembering ideas while going from one part to the next. Parallel development of ideas and cross-references in the second portion of the essay can often offset that problem. Transitional words and phrases also help to establish coherence.

The point-by-point pattern shown in Figure 11.2 provides an imme-diate and direct relationship of points to subject. Therefore, it is especially useful in arguing that one side is superior to the other, in dealing with complex topics, and in working with longer compositions. But because of its systematic nature, if development is not sufficient, it can appear mechanical and monotonous. You can avoid that appearance by developing each idea thoroughly.

Some writers believe that the subject-by-subject form works best for short (paragraph-length) assignments, and the point-by-point form works best for longer pieces (essays).

In the following example, the topic of Mussolini and Hitler is presented in the final draft stage of the essay form, using a point-by-point arrangement.

Introduction with thesis

Hitler and Mussolini have often been thought of as twin dictators, but there were considerable differences between the two men and their regimes, and Hitler was more extreme. These differences become apparent when one considers their racial views, their commitment, and their militaristic designs.

Topic sentence

(Middle paragraph)

Racism is justly associated with all fascism at that time; therefore, Mussolini, along with Hitler, is implicated. It should be pointed out, however, that the Italians' blatant racism occurred after Mussolini's deep association with Hitler. Prior to that, for many years there had been no racial doctrine in Italian fascist ideology. But Hitler held racist views from the beginning of his political movement, and it was a main motive in the Nazi movement. To resolve the "Jewish problem," he eventually slaughtered at least six million people.

Topic sentence

(Middle paragraph)

Their degree of commitment to act also varied. From a distance toward the end of the war, they may have seemed quite similar, but over the span of their reigns, they were different. Mussolini merely talked and strutted for the most part. He had few fixed doctrines and increasingly accommodated himself to circumstances. But Hitler meant every bit of his bellicosity and was willing to wage the most frightful war of all time.

Topic sentence

(Middle paragraph)

A study of their involvement in that war, however, reveals striking differences. Italian fascism was comparatively restrained and conservative until the Nazi example spurred it to new activity. Mussolini talked of a militaristic policy, but he followed a more temperate course in practice and kept the peace for thirteen years, knowing that Italy could not gain from a major war. In contrast, Hitler's radical and dynamic pace hardly flagged from January 1933 to April 1945. In the process, anti-Semitism, concentration camps, and total war produced a sadistic nightmare without any parallel in the Italian experience.

Conclusion

Thus, though both were fascist, history shows the two men to be different in both ideas and actions. Only at the end of their relationship, when Mussolini succumbed to Hitler's domination, do the two leaders appear as twin dictators, but beneath appearances it is Hitler who was the true believer, the fascist dictator.

Connecting Sources and Writing

Student Essay

Daphne Lee's assignment in her freshman composition class was to write a comparison and contrast essay of 600 to 900 words. Among her topics was one on fast food establishments, in which she would be expected to use personal experience and preferences to show that one business was superior to the other in certain respects. A bit of freewriting confirmed that this was the right topic for her.

A Fast Food Face-Off

Daphne Lee

"Burger joints are all alike. Their food is all the same—salty and greasy—so who cares which one you select!" Those were the lines I rehearsed silently while pulling my car into a Wendy's parking lot somewhere in the city of Orange, California. We were on our way to the semi-annual medical checkup for my daughter Angelina when she dramatically stated that she was so hungry she could die any second now. Pathetically, I am one of those hopelessly-in-love-with-my-child kinds of mothers, so I drove around in an unfamiliar city trying to find her a McDonald's, the only fast food restaurant she would tolerate since she was two years old. Oddly, there were no McDonald's restaurants within a five-mile radius, so I hesitantly pulled up to the nearest fast food place, which turned out to be a Wendy's. Obviously, Angelina was really hungry, for she entered with me without a protest. This was our first time at a Wendy's, and I truly expected it to probably be my last. But it was during my visit to Wendy's that I changed my opinion about fast food chains.

Although McDonald's and Wendy's serve about the same clientele, the restaurants are more different than similar.

When I entered Wendy's, I immediately noticed the distinct difference between Wendy's and McDonald's in their ambiance. The interior design of Wendy's is simple and plain: a few booths, tables, and chairs. Mainly earthy tones such as natural wood and leafy green surrounded me. The design offered homely comfort. No bold decorations on walls, tables, or seats demanded my attention. Another difference was the smell. When I walked into Wendy's, no familiar scent of fried foods and hamburgers greeted me. As I looked around while standing in line, I noticed how quiet the place was. There were only subdued chatterings from diners, plus some noises from the kitchen and the cashier area, but for a fast food restaurant environment Wendy's was almost silent.

On the other hand, the McDonald's interior design, including but not limited to the booth seats, tables, chairs, décor on the walls, is all done with their color scheme of bright red and yellow. It seems to grab and captivate customers' visual sensation in an instant. In the olfactory department, McDonald's is filled with the scent of French fries and burgers and is accompanied by a hint of sweetness. These odors attack customers' olfactory receptors like a typhoon and jostle their digestive systems into overdrive. Yet the most prominent difference from Wendy's is probably the noise level. At McDonald's there are always children running up and down the aisles, jumping and going wild in the Jungle Gyms, tugging and giggling under the tables—all of this punctuated by disciplinary warnings loudly "whispered" by the parents. No doubt, McDonald's is an optimal place for sensory overload.

Studying Wendy's menu, I found that, although many of the items are similar to those of McDonald's, Wendy's provides a wider selection, including some foods that wouldn't be considered fast. Among the 99-cent mainstays are baked potatoes with sour cream and chives, chili, and stuffed pitas. There is even a well-stocked salad bar. On the minus side, for dessert Wendy's has only a few selections of milk shakes and chocolate chip cookies. Predictably, McDonald's is long on the sandwich list and short on nontraditional foods. Instead of everyday specialties, their promotional items are usually restricted to certain days. But Mac wins in the dessert lineup, with two kinds of cookies, milk shakes, apple turnovers, and soft-serve ice cream decorated by an assortment of sprinkles.

Angelina and I pondered the menu for a while before placing our order. I never hesitate in McDonald's. I get a large diet Coke, we share an extra large order of French fries, and she gets a Chicken McNuggets Happy Meal. Faced with more choices at Wendy's, we decided on a Spicy Chicken Sandwich Combo that came with a large order of French fries and a large diet Coke, an orange drink, an order of Chicken Nuggets, and a baked potato loaded with sour cream and chives. Angelina did not want a Wendy's Kid's Meal because the toy was not as "cool" as the one offered at McDonald's.

After picking up the food, we took a seat near a large window for our taste test. Examining and carefully blowing on a piece of hot chicken, Angelina dipped it into the sweet and sour sauce and then took a small bite. To my surprise, she continued to eat and even started on the French fries without complaint. I was skeptical as well; I took a breath and bit into the Spicy Chicken Sandwich. I was delighted. It has a soft bun, a crispy piece of lettuce and tomato, a hint of spices, and crunchy chicken meat, not excesively greasy tasting. In contrast, the McDonald's Spicy Chicken Sandwich, which I once considered the only palatable sandwich, usually has soggier chicken meat and greasier taste, although their buns are probably better tasting than those at Wendy's. McDonald's also supplies more lettuce than Wendy's. Next, I tried the Wendy's Chicken Nuggets, and I knew why Angelina liked them. They are meatier with thinner breading than McDonald's, so they are juicier and lighter tasting than Chicken McNuggets. When it comes to the taste of the French fries, we both agreed that McDonald's is the champion, but Wendy's is the first runner-up.

This visit to Wendy's has changed my preconception about fast food restaurants. The fast food restaurants are not all the same for me, anymore. In fact, we have been exploring other fast food establishments since that visit to Wendy's. At this point, our choice or, rather, my daughter's choice has been Wendy's more frequently than McDonald's. While we think that Wendy's surpasses McDonald's in many areas, it is difficult for us not to visit McDonald's occasionally. For Angelina, there is always a "cool" toy that McDonald's is advertising, which she must have. As for me, McDonald's brings back the memories of my little baby girl's face gleaming with smiles as she excitedly played at the Jungle Gym, or the way her eyes lit up when she tasted the French fries with ketchup for the first time. The foods served in fast food places generally are considered to be unhealthful, but for busy families fast foods are likely the next best things to home-cooked meals. Now my range of choices has widened.

Exercise 1	**DISCUSSION AND CRITICAL THINKING**

1. Circle the thesis.

2. Is the pattern point by point or subject by subject?
   Point by point.

3. Is Lee's purpose to inform or to persuade?
   To persuade.

4. Based on your experiences, are Lee's assessments of Wendy's and McDonald's sound?

Answers will vary.

5. How do the first two sentences of the essay reconcile with the next-to-the-last sentence?

Fast foods are, for the most part, salty and greasy, and, comparatively, they could be called unhealthful.

Practicing Patterns of Comparison and Contrast

Understanding the two basic patterns of comparison and contrast—subject by subject and point by point—and knowing which one to use for a particular assignment will serve you well in writing for all occasions.

Exercise 2   **COMPLETING PATTERNS OF COMPARISON AND CONTRAST**

Fill in the blanks to complete the comparisons and contrasts in the following skeletal outlines based on "A Fast Food Face-Off."

Point by Point

  I. Ambiance

    A. Wendy's

    B. McDonald's

 II. Menu

    A. Wendy's

    B. McDonald's

III. Taste test

    A. Wendy's

    B. McDonald's

Subject by Subject

  I. Wendy's

    A. Ambiance

    B. Menu

    C. Taste test

II. McDonald's _____

    A. Ambiance _____

    B. Menu

    C. Taste test _____

Student Documented Essay

For her comparison and contrast assignment, Lydia Hsiao was asked to read an essay of personal experience from her textbook and to relate it point by point to her life. In her textbook, *Rereading America,* she found an excerpt from *The Woman Warrior* by Maxine Hong Kingston. The result was essentially a comparative study, one that helped Hsiao understand her own struggle and triumph. Hsiao's instructor asked her to document her essay formally. (However, essays written from single textbook sources are often presented with only informal references to indicate quoted and otherwise borrowed material.)

Struggling Against Silence

Lydia Hsiao

In "Silence," a selection from Maxine Hong Kingston's autobiographical *The Woman Warrior,* the author portrays herself as an individual with timid characteristics. I have much in common with this author. Since both of us are Chinese and learned English as a second language, our experiences in school are very similar.

As I read of her struggle to communicate, her thoughts blend with my thoughts and her words become my words.

We both come from a strict Chinese background and were taught that "a ready tongue is an evil" (Kingston 252). We were also taught to keep to ourselves. We were never taught to communicate with those outside our culture. This background may have caused my self-consciousness and my paralyzing fear of being embarrassed. During my first year in the United States, I attended middle school in Riverside, California. I was constantly teased about my Chinese accent, even though initially I felt certain I did not have one, for I had attended an American school in Taiwan. Perhaps my fellow students reacted as they did because I was the only Chinese girl in school. Nevertheless, as a result of this treatment, I became silent whenever possible, and if I mispronounced a word during class, I could not help but be disgusted by my own mistake, causing me even greater embarrassment. Kingston says, "[They] scared the voice away" (254). The result was that, like Kingston, my potential was for years undiscovered.

In the same way Kingston allowed silence to "[paint] layers of black over [her life]" (254), silence continued to create a thicker darkness in *my* life. It first embarrassed me; then it soon robbed me of my self-esteem. As Kingston says, "[Talking] takes up that day's courage" (252). It was almost as if silence was more than a curtain. It seemed to grow its own body and walk beside me. That silence became my sinister friend, taking advantage of my willingness to accept this cruel school life, tricking me into believing that home was the only place I could find my voice. The monster silence kept me quiet.

As my keeper, that silence also sent a message to others. It was often a signal for people not to intrude, and, of course, it was used to prevent rejection. Like Kingston, "I enjoyed the silence" (253). It concealed words that would lead to my embarrassment, sounds that might make my already cracked confidence shatter into millions of pieces like safety glass in a car crash. Thus, in Kingston's words, soon "it did not occur to me [that] I was supposed to talk" (253). But Kingston also said that "if [she couldn't] talk, [she] couldn't have a personality" (254). Thus, silence, my wicked companion that protected me from getting hurt, now led me into retreat from life.

But both Kingston and I would achieve a breakthrough against silence. Kingston defeated her silence when she became a writer and published her writings, making her voice known. I made my voice known through my high school experience. When I moved to an area where more Asians lived, I made a supreme attempt to connect and associate with people who were willing to accept my differences in speaking. I was determined not to give in to silence. Through those interactions with new friends, silence slowly lost its hold on me. However, I still often ask people whether or not I have an accent. Interestingly enough, my Chinese friends say I do, and my Caucasian friends say I do not. I can never understand why that would be the case. Maybe a Chinese accent can be detected only by someone who knows the accent, or maybe a Chinese accent is something to be expected and, therefore, some people imagine they hear it. No matter what, I am still curious and, sometimes, feeling a bit insecure. I listen to myself. Again I am not far from Kingston, who said that even when she recited her Chinese lessons, she was two persons, "one chanting, one listening."

Now, when I begin to lose confidence and the dark curtain begins to fall or the monster begins to stir (Is it one, or both?), I remind myself that the best way to fight, as Kingston says, "is not to pause or stop to end the embarrassment, [but to keep] going until . . . the last word" (255). Like Kingston, I intend "to let people know [I] have a personality and a brain" (253).

Work Cited

Kingston, Maxine Hong. "Silence." *The Woman Warrior. Rereading America*. Ed. Gary Colombo, Robert Cullen, and Bonnie Lisle. New York: Bedford/St. Martin's, 1998. 252–255.

Exercise 3	DISCUSSION AND CRITICAL THINKING

1. Is Hsiao's purpose to inform or to persuade?
   To inform.

2. Circle the thesis.

3. Is Hsiao's pattern of organization point by point or subject by subject?
   Point by point.

4. Which image, the curtain or the monster, best fits her experience with silence?
   Answers will vary.

5. Can silence be caused by factors other than cultural? If so, what are they?
   Yes. Bad parenting, oppressive situations, new or unusual circumstances, lack of confidence, low self-esteem, fear.

The Baby Boomers and the Generation Xers

Philip Kotler and Gary Armstrong

Among the many influences on generational behavior is the economic. Here, Philip Kotler and Gary Armstrong, two professors of business, discuss what two groups will represent in both the work place and the marketplace of the future. This excerpt was published in *Principles of Marketing* (2000).

1   Demographics involve people, and people make up markets. Thus, marketers track demographic trends and groups carefully. Two of today's most important demographic groups are the so-called *baby boomers* and the *generation Xers*.

The Baby Boomers

2   The postwar baby boom, which began in 1946 and ran through 1964, produced 75 million babies. Since then, the baby boomers have become one of the biggest forces shaping the marketing environment. The boomers have presented a moving target, creating new markets as they grew through infancy to preadolescent, teenage, young-adult, and now middle-age years.

3   The baby boomers account for a third of the population but make up 40 percent of the work force and earn over half of all personal income. Today, the aging boomers are moving to the suburbs, settling into home ownership, and raising families. They are also reaching their peak earning and spending years. Thus, they constitute a lucrative market for housing, furniture and appliances, children's products, low-calorie foods and beverages, physical fitness products, high-priced cars, convenience products, and financial services.

4   The older boomers are now in their fifties; the younger are in their thirties. Thus, the boomers are evolving from the "youthquake generation" to the "backache generation." They're slowing up, having children, and settling down. They're experiencing the pangs of midlife and rethinking the purpose and value of their work, responsibilities, and relationships. The maturing boomers are approaching life with a new stability and reasonableness in the way they live, think, eat, and spend. The boomers have shifted their focus from the outside world to the inside world. Community and family values have become more important, and staying home with the family has become their favorite way to spend an evening. The upscale boomers still exert their affluence, but they indulge themselves in more subtle and sensible ways.

The Generation Xers

5   Some marketers think that focusing on the boomers has caused companies to overlook other important segments, especially younger consumers. Focus has shifted in recent years to a new group, those born between 1965 and 1976. Author Douglas Coupland calls them "Generation X," because they lie in the shadow of

the boomers and lack obvious distinguishing characteristics. Others call them baby busters, or twentysomethings, or Yiffies—young, individualistic, freedom-minded, few.

6   Unlike the boomers, the Xers do not share dramatic and wrenching experiences, such as the Vietnam War and Watergate, that might have unified their subculture and lifestyle. However, they do share a different set of influences. Increasing divorce rates and higher employment for mothers have made them the first generation of latchkey kids. Whereas the boomers created a sexual revolution, the Xers have lived in the age of AIDS. Having grown up during times of recession and corporate downsizing, they have developed a pessimistic economic outlook. This outlook is aggravated by problems in finding good jobs—the management ranks already are well stocked with boomers who won't retire for another 20 years or more.

7   As a result, the Xers are a more skeptical bunch, cynical of frivolous marketing pitches that promise easy success. They know better. The Xers buy lots of products, such as sweaters, boots, cosmetics, electronics, cars, fast food, beer, computers, and mountain bikes. However, their cynicism makes them more savvy shoppers. Because they often did much of the family shopping when growing up, they are experienced shoppers. Their financial pressures make them value conscious, and they like lower prices and a more functional look. The Generation Xers respond to honesty in advertising, as exemplified by Nike ads that focus on fitness and a healthy lifestyle instead of hyping shoes. They like irreverence and sass and ads that mock the traditional advertising approach.

8   Generation Xers share new cultural concerns. They care about the environment, and respond favorably to companies such as The Body Shop and Ben & Jerry's, which have proven records of environmentally and socially responsible actions. Although they seek success, the Xers are less materialistic. They want better quality of life and are more interested in job satisfaction than in sacrificing personal happiness and growth for promotion. They prize experience, not acquisition.

9   The Generation Xers will have a big impact on the work place and marketplace of the future. There are now 40 million of them poised to displace the lifestyles, culture, and materialistic values of the baby boomers. By the year 2010, they will have overtaken the baby boomers as a primary market for almost every product category.

Exercise 4   VOCABULARY HIGHLIGHTS

Write a short definition of each word as it is used in the essay. (Paragraph numbers are given in parentheses.) Be prepared to use the words in your own sentences.

demographics (1)   segments (5)

constitute (3)   wrenching (6)

lucrative (3)   aggravated (6)

evolving (4)   skeptical (7)

affluence (4)   cynicism (7)

Exercise 5   DISCUSSION AND CRITICAL THINKING

1. Are Kotler and Armstrong trying to inform or to persuade?
   To inform.

2. What is their main focus?
   The work place and the marketplace.

3. Is the pattern point by point or subject by subject?
   Subject by subject.

4. Underline the sentences in the Generation Xers section that link it to the Baby Boomers section to show contrast.

5. The authors discuss Baby Boomers and Generation Xers in considerable detail. Which characteristics do you agree with and which do you not agree with? Do you know a lot of individuals within these groups that do not fit the descriptions provided in this essay?
   Answers will vary.

6. Should we expect exceptions to the descriptions given for groups such as these?
   Of course. The authors refer to these characteristics as group characteristics. We would expect exceptions. We would also expect a range of commitment even for the individuals who do match the descriptions given for these groups. Not all Xers are environmentalists, for example.

7. Have you noticed any trends that have started to develop in the time since this material was written (in 2000)? If so, describe them.
   Answers will vary.

That Lean and Hungry Look

Suzanne Britt

Fat people, unite! And let this essay be your bible. Put its phrases on your bumper stickers. In a weight-conscious world, Suzanne Britt has written a revolutionary tract. Either be fat or wish you were, for the fat guys and gals are the good ones. This essay was originally published in *Newsweek*, and was later published in an anthology titled *Show and Tell*.

1   Caesar was right. Thin people need watching. I've been watching them for most of my adult life, and I don't like what I see. When these narrow fellows spring at me, I quiver to my toes. Thin people come in all personalities, most of them menacing. You've got your "together" thin person, your mechanical thin person, your condescending thin person, your tsk-tsk thin person, your efficiency-expert thin person. All of them are dangerous.

2   In the first place, thin people aren't fun. They don't know how to goof off, at least in the best, fat sense of the word. They've always got to be adoing. Give them a coffee break, and they'll jog around the block. Supply them with a quiet evening at home, and they'll fix the screen door and lick S & H green stamps.* They say things like "there aren't enough hours in the day." Fat people never say that. Fat people think the day is too damn long already.

3   Thin people make me tired. They've got speedy little metabolisms that cause them to bustle briskly. They're forever rubbing their bony hands together and eyeing new problems to "tackle." I like to surround myself with sluggish, inert, easygoing fat people, the kind who believe that if you clean it up today, it'll just get dirty again tomorrow.

4   Some people say the business about the jolly fat person is a myth, that all of us chubbies are neurotic, sick, sad people. I disagree. Fat people may not be chortling all day long, but they're a hell of a lot *nicer* than the wizened and shriveled. Thin people turn surly, mean and hard at a young age because they never learn the value of a hot-fudge sundae for easing tension. Thin people don't like gooey soft things because they themselves are neither gooey nor soft. They are crunchy and dull, like carrots. They go straight to the heart of the matter while fat people let things stay all blurry and hazy and vague, the way things actually

---

*S & H green stamps were rebate stamps that could be redeemed for merchandise.

are. Thin people want to face the truth. Fat people know there is no truth. One of my thin friends is always staring at complex, unsolvable problems and saying, "The key thing is . . ." Fat people never say that. They know there isn't any such thing as the key thing about anything.

5   Thin people believe in logic. Fat people see all sides. The sides fat people see are rounded blobs, usually gray, always nebulous and truly not worth worrying about. But the thin person persists. "If you consume more calories than you burn," says one of my thin friends, "you will gain weight. It's that simple." Fat people always grin when they hear statements like that. They know better.

6   Fat people realize that life is illogical and unfair. They know very well that God is not in his heaven and all is not right with the world. If God was up there, fat people could have two doughnuts and a big orange drink anytime they wanted it.

7   Thin people have a long list of logical things they are always spouting off to me. They hold up one finger at a time as they reel off these things, so I won't lose track. They speak slowly as if to a young child. The list is long and full of holes. It contains tidbits like "get a grip on yourself," "cigarettes kill," "cholesterol clogs," "fit as a fiddle," "ducks in a row," "organize" and "sound fiscal management." Phrases like that.

8   They think these 2,000-point plans lead to happiness. Fat people know happiness is elusive at best and even if they could get the kind thin people talk about, they wouldn't want it. Wisely, fat people see that such programs are too dull, too hard, too off the mark. They are never better than a whole cheesecake.

9   Fat people know all about the mystery of life. They are the ones acquainted with the night, with luck, with fate, with playing it by ear. One thin person I know once suggested that we arrange all the parts of a jigsaw puzzle into groups according to size, shape and color. He figured this would cut the time needed to complete the puzzle at least by 50 percent. I said I wouldn't do it. One, I like to muddle through. Two, what good would it do to finish early? Three, the jigsaw puzzle isn't the important thing. The important thing is the fun of four people (one thin person included) sitting around a card table, working a jigsaw puzzle. My thin friend had no use for my list. Instead of joining us, he went outside and mulched the boxwoods. The three remaining fat people finished the puzzle and made chocolate, double-fudged brownies to celebrate.

10   The main problem with thin people is they oppress. Their good intentions, bony torsos, tight ships, neat corners, cerebral

machinations and pat solutions loom like dark clouds over the loose, comfortable, spread-out, soft world of the fat. Long after fat people have removed their coats and shoes and put their feet up on the coffee table, thin people are still sitting on the edge of the sofa, looking neat as a pin, discussing rutabagas. Fat people are heavily into fits of laughter, slapping their thighs and whooping it up, while thin people are still politely waiting for the punch line.

11   Thin people are downers. They like math and morality and reasoned evaluation of the limitations of human beings. They have their skinny little acts together. They expound, prognose, probe and prick.

12   Fat people are convivial. They will like you even if you're irregular and have acne. They will come up with a good reason why you never wrote the great American novel. They will cry in your beer with you. They will put your name in the pot. They will let you off the hook. Fat people will gab, giggle, guffaw, gallumph, gyrate and gossip. They are generous, giving and gallant. They are gluttonous and goodly and great. What you want when you're down is soft and jiggly, not muscled and stable. Fat people know this. Fat people have plenty of room. Fat people will take you in.

Exercise 6   **DISCUSSION AND CRITICAL THINKING**

1. Is Britt trying mainly to inform or to persuade?
   To persuade.

2. Does she use the point-by-point or subject-by-subject pattern?
   Point by point.

3. Is Britt really serious about her characterizations of fat and thin people?
   Answers will vary.

4. If you were to put the issue of weight aside, what two opposing philosophies of life would still be advanced by Britt?
   Some people are reasonable and systematic about almost everything; they are critical, stingy, serious, task-oriented, and rigid. Others live lives of feeling; they are sympathetic, forgiving, outgoing, flexible, fun-loving, and generous. Britt likes the "others."

5. Do your experiences confirm what Britt says?
   Answers will vary.

Two Ways of Viewing the River

Mark Twain

Early in his career as a journalist, Samuel Langhorne Clemens adopted the pen name Mark Twain, which means "two fathoms deep," a phrase used in making soundings on the Mississippi River. He would go on to become one of the most respected persons in American letters in a long and celebrated career. Twain's most famous book is *The Adventures of Huckleberry Finn*. This passage is taken from his autobiographical *Life on the Mississippi*. Published in 1883, it is written from the perspective of Twain as a riverboat pilot.

1   Now when I had mastered the language of this water and had come to know every trifling feature that bordered the great river as familiarly as I knew the letters of the alphabet, I had made a valuable acquisition. But I had lost something, too. I had lost something which could never be restored to me while I lived. All the grace, the beauty, the poetry, had gone out of the majestic river! I still kept in mind a certain wonderful sunset which I witnessed when steamboating was new to me. A broad expanse of the river was turned to blood; in the middle distance the red hue brightened into gold, through which a solitary log came floating, black and conspicuous; in one place a long, slanting mark lay sparkling upon the water; in another the surface was broken by boiling, tumbling rings, that were as many-tinted as an opal; where the ruddy flush was faintest, was a smooth spot that was covered with graceful circles and radiating lines, ever so delicately traced; the shore on our left was densely wooded and the somber shadow that fell from this forest was broken in one place by a long, ruffled trail that shone like silver; and high above the forest wall a clean-stemmed dead tree waved a single leafy bough that glowed like a flame in the unobstructed splendor that was flowing from the sun. There were graceful curves, reflected images, woody heights, soft distances, and over the whole scene, far and near, the dissolving lights drifted steadily, enriching it every passing moment with new marvels of coloring.

2   I stood like one bewitched. I drank it in, in a speechless rapture. The world was new to me and I had never seen anything like this at home. But as I have said, a day came when I began to cease from noting the glories and the charms which the moon and the

sun and the twilight wrought upon the river's face; another day came when I ceased altogether to note them. Then, if that sunset scene had been repeated, I should have looked upon it without rapture, and should have commented upon it inwardly after this fashion: "This sun means that we are going to have wind tomorrow; that floating log means that the river is rising, small thanks to it; that slanting mark on the water refers to a bluff reef which is going to kill somebody's steamboat one of these nights, if it keeps on stretching out like that; those tumbling 'boils' show a dissolving bar and a changing channel there; the lines and circles in the slick water over yonder are a warning that that troublesome place is shoaling up dangerously; that silver streak in the shadow of the forest is the 'break' from a new snag and he has located himself in the very best place he could have found to fish for steamboats; that tall dead tree, with a single living branch, is not going to last long, and then how is a body ever going to get through this blind place at night without the friendly old landmark?"

3   No, the romance and beauty were all gone from the river. All the value any feature of it had for me now was the amount of usefulness it could furnish toward compassing the safe piloting of a steamboat. Since those days, I have pitied doctors from my heart. What does the lovely flush in a beauty's cheek mean to a doctor but a "break" that ripples above some deadly disease? Are not all her visible charms sown thick with what are to him the signs and symbols of hidden decay? Does he ever see her beauty at all, or doesn't he simply view her professionally and comment upon her unwholesome condition all to himself? And doesn't he sometimes wonder whether he has gained most or lost most by learning his trade?

Exercise 7   **VOCABULARY HIGHLIGHTS**

Write a short definition of each word as it is used in the essay. (Paragraph numbers are given in parentheses.) Be prepared to use the words in your own sentences.

trifling (1)	radiating (1)
acquisition (1)	somber (1)
conspicuous (1)	splendor (1)
opal (1)	wrought (2)
ruddy (1)	compassing (3)

Exercise 8   DISCUSSION AND CRITICAL THINKING

1. What is Twain's subject?
   The river, before and after knowledge.

2. Is he trying to inform or to persuade?
   To inform.

3. Does he use the point-by-point or the subject-by-subject pattern?
   Subject by subject.

4. What technique (conjunctive adverbs, such as *however*, or *conse-quently;* repeated words in the same order; italics, numbered entries) does he use in paragraph 2 to show the clear, parallel contrasts with items in paragraph 1? Give some examples.
   He repeats phrases, but this time with a new perspective. Examples are "sun," "floating log," "tumbling 'boils,'" and "slanting mark."

5. Paragraph 1 deals with aesthetics, that which is beautiful, and the language is appropriate for that concern. Paragraph 2 comes with the voice of reason and knowledge and deals with more objective description. Give some examples of the evocative (emotional) language in the first paragraph and the more objective language in the second paragraph.

   Emotional word choices: "river was turned to blood," "red hue brightened into gold," "many-tinted as an opal," and several others.

   Objective word choices: "we are going to have wind," "the river is rising," "dissolving bar and a changing channel," and several others.

6. How does the tone (the way the author regards his subject material and his audience) change from paragraph 1 to paragraph 2?
   In paragraph 1, Twain is poetic and emotional, wanting to move his reader's feelings. In paragraph 2, he is rational and objectively descriptive, wanting to inform.

Everyday Use

Alice Walker

This story is concerned with differences, differences of many kinds. It begins and ends with a mother's consideration of two very different daughters, one lacking in self-esteem and the other in humility. Finally, the mother had to take sides. So will you, as a reader. In 1983, the author, Alice Walker, won the Pulitzer Prize for *The Color Purple*. Because this short story is a narrative account, you can use the basic framework presented in Chapter 5—situation, conflict, struggle, outcome, meaning—for your analysis.

1   I will wait for her in the yard that Maggie and I made so clean and wavy yesterday afternoon. A yard like this is more comfortable than most people know. It is not just a yard. It is like an extended living room. When the hard clay is swept clean as a floor and the fine sand around the edges lined with tiny, irregular grooves, anyone can come and sit and look up into the elm tree and wait for the breezes that never come inside the house.

2   Maggie will be nervous until after her sister goes: she will stand hopelessly in corners, homely and ashamed of the burn scars down her arms and legs, eyeing her sister with a mixture of envy and awe. She thinks her sister has held life always in the palm of one hand, that "no" is a word the world never learned to say to her.

3   You've no doubt seen those TV shows where the child who has "made it" is confronted, as a surprise, by her own mother and father, tottering in weakly from backstage. (A pleasant surprise, of course: What would they do if parent and child came on the show only to curse out and insult each other?) On TV mother and child embrace and smile into each other's faces. Sometimes the mother and father weep, the child wraps them in her arms and leans across the table to tell how she would not have made it without their help. I have seen these programs.

4   Sometimes I dream a dream in which Dee and I are suddenly brought together on a TV program of this sort. Out of a dark and soft-seated limousine I am ushered into a bright room filled with many people. There I meet a smiling, gray, sporty man like Johnny Carson* who shakes my hand and tells me what a fine girl I have. Then we are on the stage and Dee is embracing me with tears in her eyes. She pins on my dress a large orchid, even though she has told me once that she thinks orchids are tacky flowers.

5   In real life I am a large, big-boned woman with rough, man-working hands. In the winter I wear flannel nightgowns to bed and overalls during the day. I can kill and clean a hog as mercilessly as a man. My fat keeps me hot in zero weather. I can work outside all day, breaking ice to get water for washing; I can eat pork liver cooked over the open fire minutes after it comes steaming from the hog. One winter I knocked a bull calf straight in the brain between the eyes with a sledge hammer and had the meat hung up to chill before nightfall. But of course all this does not show on television. I am the way my daughter would want me to be: a hundred pounds lighter, my skin like an uncooked barley

---

*Johnny Carson was a late-night television personality.

pancake. My hair glistens in the hot bright lights. Johnny Carson has much to do to keep up with my quick and witty tongue.

6   But this is a mistake. I know even before I wake up. Who ever knew a Johnson with a quick tongue? Who can even imagine me looking a strange white man in the eye? It seems to me I have talked to them always with one foot raised in flight, with my head turned in whichever way is farthest from them. Dee, though. She would always look anyone in the eye. Hesitation was no part of her nature.

7   "How do I look, Mama?" Maggie says, showing just enough of her thin body enveloped in pink skirt and red blouse for me to know she's there, almost hidden by the door.

8   "Come out into the yard," I say.

9   Have you ever seen a lame animal, perhaps a dog run over by some careless person rich enough to own a car, sidle up to someone who is ignorant enough to be kind to him? That is the way my Maggie walks. She has been like this, chin on chest, eyes on ground, feet in shuffle, ever since the fire that burned the other house to the ground.

10   Dee is lighter than Maggie, with nicer hair and a fuller figure. She's a woman now, though sometimes I forget. How long ago was it that the other house burned? Ten, twelve years? Sometimes I can still hear the flames and feel Maggie's arms sticking to me, her hair smoking and her dress falling off her in little black papery flakes. Her eyes seemed stretched open, blazed open by the flames reflected in them. And Dee. I see her standing off under the sweet gum tree she used to dig gum out of; a look of concentration on her face as she watched the last dingy gray board of the house fall in toward the red-hot brick chimney. Why don't you do a dance around the ashes? I'd wanted to ask her. She had hated the house that much.

11   I used to think she hated Maggie, too. But that was before we raised the money, the church and me, to send her to Augusta to school. She used to read to us without pity; forcing words, lies, other folks' habits, whole lives upon us two, sitting trapped and ignorant underneath her voice. She washed us in a river of make-believe, burned us with a lot of knowledge we didn't necessarily need to know. Pressed us to her with the serious way she read, to shove us away at just the moment, like dimwits, we seemed about to understand.

12   Dee wanted nice things. A yellow organdy dress to wear to her graduation from high school; black pumps to match a green suit she'd made from an old suit somebody gave me. She was deter-

mined to stare down any disaster in her efforts. Her eyelids would not flicker for minutes at a time. Often I fought off the temptation to shake her. At sixteen she had a style of her own: and knew what style was.

13   I never had an education myself. After second grade the school was closed down. Don't ask me why: in 1927 colored asked fewer questions than they do now. Sometimes Maggie reads to me. She stumbles along good-naturedly but can't see well. She knows she is not bright. Like good looks and money, quickness passed her by. She will marry John Thomas (who has mossy teeth in an earnest face) and then I'll be free to sit here and I guess just sing church songs to myself. Although I never was a good singer. Never could carry a tune. I was always better at a man's job. I used to love to milk till I was hooked in the side in '49. Cows are soothing and slow and don't bother you, unless you try to milk them the wrong way.

14   I have deliberately turned my back on the house. It is three rooms, just like the one that burned, except the roof is tin; they don't make shingle roofs any more. There are no real windows, just some holes cut in the sides, like the portholes in a ship, but not round and not square, with rawhide holding the shutters up on the outside. This house is in a pasture, too, like the other one. No doubt when Dee sees it she will want to tear it down. She wrote me once that no matter where we "choose" to live, she will manage to come see us. But she will never bring her friends. Maggie and I thought about this and Maggie asked me, "Mama, when did Dee ever *have* any friends?"

15   She had a few. Furtive boys in pink shirts hanging about on washday after school. Nervous girls who never laughed. Impressed with her they worshiped the well-turned phrase, the cute shape, the scalding humor that erupted like bubbles in lye. She read to them.

16   When she was courting Jimmy T she didn't have much time to pay to us, but turned all her faultfinding power on him. He *flew* to marry a cheap city girl from a family of ignorant flashy people. She hardly had time to recompose herself.

17   When she comes I will meet—but there they are!

18   Maggie attempts to make a dash for the house, in her shuffling way, but I stay her with my hand. "Come back here," I say. And she stops and tries to dig a well in the sand with her toe.

19   It is hard to see them clearly through the strong sun. But even the first glimpse of leg out of the car tells me it is Dee. Her feet

were always neat-looking, as if God himself had shaped them with a certain style. From the other side of the car comes a short, stocky man. Hair is all over his head a foot long and hanging from his chin like a kinky mule tail. I hear Maggie suck in her breath, "Uhnnnh," is what it sounds like. Like when you see the wriggling end of a snake just in front of your foot on the road. "Uhnnnh."

20   Dee next. A dress down to the ground, in this hot weather. A dress so loud it hurts my eyes. There are yellows and oranges enough to throw back the light of the sun. I feel my whole face warming from the heat waves it throws out. Earrings gold, too, and hanging down to her shoulders. Bracelets dangling and making noises when she moves her arm up to shake the folds of the dress out of her armpits. The dress is loose and flows, and as she walks closer, I like it. I hear Maggie go "Uhnnnh" again. It is her sister's hair. It stands straight up like the wool on a sheep. It is black as night and around the edges are two long pigtails that rope about like small lizards disappearing behind her ears.

21   "Wa-su-zo-Tean-o!" she says, coming on in that gliding way the dress makes her move. The short stocky fellow with the hair to his navel is all grinning and he follows up with "Asalamalakim, my mother and sister!" He moves to hug Maggie but she falls back, right up against the back of my chair. I feel her trembling there and when I look up I see the perspiration falling off her chin.

22   "Don't get up," says Dee. Since I am stout it takes something of a push. You can see me trying to move a second or two before I make it. She turns, showing white heels through her sandals, and goes back to the car. Out she peeks next with a Polaroid. She stoops down quickly and lines up picture after picture of me sitting there in front of the house with Maggie cowering behind me. She never takes a shot without making sure the house is included. When a cow comes nibbling around the edge of the yard she snaps it and me and Maggie *and* the house. Then she puts the Polaroid in the back seat of the car, and comes up and kisses me on the forehead.

23   Meanwhile Asalamalakim is going through motions with Maggie's hand. Maggie's hand is as limp as a fish, and probably as cold, despite the sweat, and she keeps trying to pull it back. It looks like Asalamalakim wants to shake hands but wants to do it fancy. Or maybe he don't know how people shake hands. Anyhow, he soon gives up on Maggie.

24   "Well," I say. "Dee."

25   "No, Mama," she says. "Not 'Dee,' Wangero Leewanika Kemanjo!"

26   "What happened to 'Dee'?" I wanted to know.

27 "She's dead," Wangero said. "I couldn't bear it any longer, being named after the people who oppress me."

28 "You know as well as me you was named after your aunt Dicie," I said. Dicie is my sister. She named Dee. We called her "Big Dee" after Dee was born.

29 "But who was *she* named after?" asked Wangero.

30 "I guess after Grandma Dee," I said.

31 "And who was she named after?" asked Wangero.

32 "Her mother," I said, and saw Wangero was getting tired. "That's about as far back as I can trace it," I said. Though, in fact, I probably could have carried it back beyond the Civil War through the branches.

33 "Well," said Asalamalakim, "there you are."

34 "Uhnnnh," I heard Maggie say.

35 "There I was not," I said, "before 'Dicie' cropped up in our family, so why should I try to trace it that far back?"

36 He just stood there grinning, looking down on me like somebody inspecting a Model A car. Every once in a while he and Wangero sent eye signals over my head.

37 "How do you pronounce this name?" I asked.

38 "You don't have to call me by it if you don't want to," said Wangero.

39 "Why shouldn't I?" I asked. "If that's what you want us to call you, we'll call you."

40 "I know it might sound awkward at first," said Wangero.

41 "I'll get used to it," I said. "Ream it out again."

42 Well, soon we got the name out of the way. Asalamalakim had a name twice as long and three times as hard. After I tripped over it two or three times he told me to just call him Hakim-a-barber. I wanted to ask him was he a barber, but I didn't really think he was, so I didn't ask.

43 "You must belong to those beef-cattle peoples down the road," I said. They said "Asalamalakim" when they met you, too, but they didn't shake hands. Always too busy: feeding the cattle, fixing the fences, putting up salt-lick shelters, throwing down hay. When the white folks poisoned some of the herd the men stayed up all night with rifles in their hands. I walked a mile and a half just to see the sight.

44 Hakim-a-barber said, "I accept some of their doctrines, but farming and raising cattle is not my style." (They didn't tell me, and I didn't ask, whether Wangero (Dee) had really gone and married him.)

45 We sat down to eat and right away he said he didn't eat collards and pork was unclean. Wangero, though, went on through

the chitlins and corn bread, the greens and everything else. She talked a blue streak over the sweet potatoes. Everything delighted her. Even the fact that we still used the benches her daddy made for the table when we couldn't afford to buy chairs.

46   "Oh, Mama!" she cried. Then turned to Hakim-a-barber. "I never knew how lovely these benches are. You can feel the rump prints," she said, running her hands underneath her and along the bench. Then she gave a sigh and her hand closed over Grandma Dee's butter dish. "That's it!" she said, "I knew there was something I wanted to ask you if I could have." She jumped up from the table and went over in the corner where the churn stood, the milk in it clabber by now. She looked at the churn and looked at it.

47   "This churn top is what I need," she said. "Didn't Uncle Buddy whittle it out of a tree you all used to have?"

48   "Yes," I said.

49   "Uh huh," she said happily. "And I want the dasher, too."

50   "Uncle Buddy whittle that, too?" asked the barber.

51   Dee (Wangero) looked up at me.

52   "Aunt Dee's first husband whittled the dash," said Maggie so low you almost couldn't hear her. "His name was Henry, but they called him Stash."

53   Maggie's brain is like an elephant's," Wangero said, laughing. "I can use the churn top as a centerpiece for the alcove table," she said, sliding a plate over the churn, "and I'll think of something artistic to do with the dasher."

54   When she finished wrapping the dasher the handle stuck out. I took it for a moment in my hands. You didn't even have to look close to see where hands pushing the dasher up and down to make butter had left a kind of sink in the wood. In fact, there were a lot of small sinks; you could see where thumbs and fingers had sunk into the wood. It was beautiful light yellow wood, from a tree that grew in the yard where Big Dee and Stash had lived.

55   After dinner Dee (Wangero) went to the trunk at the foot of my bed and started rifling through it. Maggie hung back in the kitchen over the dishpan. Out came Wangero with two quilts. They had been pieced by Grandma Dee and then Big Dee and me had hung them on the quilt frames on the front porch and quilted them. One was in the Lone Star pattern. The other was Walk Around the Mountain. In both of them were scraps of dresses Grandma Dee had worn fifty and more years ago. Bits and pieces of Grandpa Jarrell's Paisley shirts. And one teeny faded blue piece, about the size of a penny matchbox, that was from Great Grandpa Ezra's uniform that he wore in the Civil War.

56   "Mama," Wangero said sweet as a bird. "Can I have these old quilts?"

57   I heard something fall in the kitchen, and a minute later the kitchen door slammed.

58   "Why don't you take one or two of the others?" I asked. "These old things was just done by me and Big Dee from some tops your grandma pieced before she died."

59   "No," said Wangero. "I don't want those. They are stitched around the borders by machine."

60   "That'll make them last better," I said.

61   "That's not the point," said Wangero. "These are all pieces of dresses Grandma used to wear. She did all this stitching by hand. Imagine!" She held the quilts securely in her arms, stroking them.

62   "Some of the pieces, like those lavender ones, come from old clothes her mother handed down to her," I said, moving up to touch the quilts. Dee (Wangero) moved back just enough so that I couldn't reach the quilts. They already belonged to her.

63   "Imagine!" she breathed again, clutching them closely to her bosom.

64   "The truth is," I said, "I promised to give them quilts to Maggie, for when she marries John Thomas."

65   She gasped like a bee had stung her.

66   "Maggie can't appreciate these quilts!" she said. "She'd probably be backward enough to put them to everyday use."

67   "I reckon she would," I said. "God knows I been saving 'em for long enough with nobody using 'em. I hope she will!" I didn't want to bring up how I had offered Dee (Wangero) a quilt when she went away to college. Then she had told me they were old-fashioned, out of style.

68   "But they're *priceless!*" she was saying now, furiously; for she has a temper. "Maggie would put them on the bed and in five years they'd be in rags. Less than that!"

69   "She can always make some more," I said. "Maggie knows how to quilt."

70   Dee (Wangero) looked at me with hatred. "You just will not understand. The point is these quilts, *these* quilts!"

71   "Well," I said, stumped. "What would *you* do with them?"

72   "Hang them," she said. As if that was the only thing you *could* do with quilts.

73   Maggie by now was standing in the door. I could almost hear the sound her feet made as they scraped over each other.

74   "She can have them, Mama," she said, like somebody used to never winning anything, or having anything reserved for her. "I can 'member Grandma Dee without the quilts."

75 I looked at her hard. She had filled her bottom lip with checker-berry snuff and it gave her face a kind of dopey, hangdog look. It was Grandma Dee and Big Dee who taught her how to quilt her-self. She stood there with her scarred hands hidden in the folds of her skirt. She looked at her sister with something like fear but she wasn't mad at her. This was Maggie's portion. This was the way she knew God to work.

76 When I looked at her like that something hit me in the top of my head and ran down to the soles of my feet. Just like when I'm in church and the spirit of God touches me and I get happy and shout. I did something I never had done before: hugged Maggie to me, then dragged her on into the room, snatched the quilts out of Miss Wangero's hands and dumped them into Maggie's lap. Mag-gie just sat there on my bed with her mouth open.

77 "Take one or two of the others," I said to Dee.

78 But she turned without a word and went out to Hakim-a-barber.

79 "You just don't understand," she said, as Maggie and I came out to the car.

80 "What don't I understand?" I wanted to know.

81 "Your heritage," she said. And then she turned to Maggie, kissed her, and said, "You ought to try to make something of your-self, too, Maggie. It's really a new day for us. But from the way you and Mama still live you'd never know it."

82 She put on some sunglasses that hid everything above the tip of her nose and her chin.

83 Maggie smiled; maybe at the sunglasses. But a real smile, not scared. After we watched the car dust settle I asked Maggie to bring me a dip of snuff. And then the two of us sat there just enjoying, until it was time to go in the house and go to bed.

Exercise 9   **DISCUSSION AND CRITICAL THINKING**

1. How is the narrator's life different from the television fantasy she relates?

   She is a plain, ordinary person who does "man's work" on the farm. She says she is not quick-witted, clever, and confident as is her counterpart on the television show.

2. How is the narrator different from each of her two children?

   She is not worldly, educated, and ambitious as Dee is, but she has a sense of place and oneness with her life and heritage. She is different from Maggie in that she has more confidence and more understanding of the importance of family relationships, and probably is brighter.

3. What is the significance of the characters' names and name changes?

   Dee is a name taken from another member of the family, and is thus a direct tie to her heritage. When she changes her name, she makes an important symbolic break. She now returns to look at her heritage from a detached perspective—she now objectifies as Wangero. She wanted to become someone else and she succeeded.

4. **What does the incident of the house burning reveal about Dee?**

   Dee hated the house and wanted it obliterated. Although the author presents no evidence, some may be tempted to suspect that Dee set the fire.

5. **When Dee returns, in what way does she seem to regain a spontaneous connection with her family experiences?**

   The only time she seems to regain her affinity with the family is during the meal. Whereas her companion feels ill at ease, she eats hungrily, naturally, as she enjoys the food of her younger life.

6. **What do the quilts represent?**

   The quilt is a product of Dee's immediate heritage, one she has "outgrown." Maggie and the mother, to the contrary, would use the quilt, as they embrace the culture.

7. **How does the idea of the quilts relate to the idea of the burning home?**

   Both represent detachment. Dee wanted to separate herself from her younger life, of which the house represented a significantly onerous part. The quilt is something from her past that interests her, but she has separated herself from it, too. The house was to burn; the quilt is to hang on a wall, if she has her way.

8. **What is the significance of Dee's taking pictures of the house and her mother and sister?**

   It showed where she came from, who she was. The pictures will feed her ego. They represent the separation of her "true" self from her humble, impoverished childhood.

9. **Do you blame Dee for wanting to leave the simple, impoverished country life? Why or why not?**

   Answers will vary. It seems that Dee has less goodness, or basic humanity, than those who remained behind. But that "behind" is a restricted, impoverished world for some.

10. **What is lacking in Dee's character?**

    See answers 8 and 9. She has tried to find another life. Evidently she has succeeded in leaving the old life behind along with the people who are sincere, compassionate, sensitive, and easygoing. She has also abandoned what little she had of those qualities. Her new life, complete with new wardrobe and name, has not been assimilated well. She postures and pretends.

11. **In the end, does the narrator simply favor one daughter over the other or does she discover something deeper?**

    She accepts her life, her lot, and the simple, natural goodness of Maggie. As they sit out in the yard, dipping snuff, and "just enjoying," they are at one with their heritage.

✎ Topics for Writing Comparison and Contrast

Writing Process Worksheet

You will find a Writing Process Worksheet in Appendix A, page 531. It can be photocopied and enlarged, filled in, and submitted with each assignment if your instructor directs you to do so.

Source-Based Topics

Each essay developed from these suggested source-based topics should include at least one reference to the reading selection by the author's name and the title. Quotations should be enclosed in quotation marks. Follow your instructor's directions in documenting the ideas you borrow. Whether you use informal or formal documentation, the form is not complicated, and you will soon learn to use it for these essays without

checking each time. See pages 77 and 78 for a discussion of MLA style and informal documentation.

Underlining and annotating reading selections will help you in finding support material. In prewriting brief essays, consider marking your outline to indicate where you will use quotations or other borrowed ideas. If the quotations or reworded statements are short and few, you could even insert them inside parentheses or circles in your outline; if you do, also include the author's last name and the page number. A sound system, consistently used, will save you time and ensure technically strong papers.

"A Fast Food Face-Off"

1. Using this essay as a model, write a comparison and contrast essay about two other fast food establishments, two supermarkets, two department stores, or two products. Consider personalizing it as Lee did. You may want to find some supporting information in the library or on the Internet.

2. Write a comparative study of two fast food places, with a focus on healthfulness of their products. Most establishments have charts on fat and calorie content of their main dishes. The Internet has numerous sites devoted to health and eating out.

"Struggling Against Silence"

3. Find an essay of personal experience in this textbook (consult the table of contents) and write a comparison and contrast between your experience and views and those of the author. Use formal or informal documentation, as directed by your instructor. Use ample quotations and references.

"The Baby Boomers and the Generation Xers"

4. Using the characteristics (points) from this essay, write a well-structured statement in which you provide examples of people you know who represent the two generations. You may want to focus on one person for each generation.

5. If you disagree with the generalizations offered by the authors, use examples and reasoning to write a comparison and contrast essay of your views and those in this essay.

"That Lean and Hungry Look"

6. Using Britt's views (points) and some examples from your own experience, write an essay of comparison and contrast to argue that she is correct.

7. Using Britt's views (points) and some examples from your own experience, write an essay of comparison and contrast to argue that she is incorrect.

8. Using Britt's views in a comparison and contrast essay, argue that she is wrong about the weight aspect but right about her philosophy of life.

"Two Ways of Viewing the River"

9. Using Twain's essay as a model, write about something that you have experienced from both an emotional and a rational view or that you have encountered before and after you became knowledgeable. Examples include a piece of music before you studied music and after you studied music; a triple-cheeseburger before you studied nutrition and after you studied nutrition; birds singing before you studied ornithology and after you studied ornithology; an election before you became deeply involved in politics and after you became deeply involved in politics; a sporting event before you understood the business operations and after you understood the business operations.

"Everyday Use"

10. Write a comparison and contrast essay about the two daughters in this short story.

11. Write a comparison and contrast essay about a person you know and one character from the short story.

Career-Related Topics

12. Compare and contrast two pieces of office equipment or two services with the purpose of showing that one is better.

13. Compare and contrast two management styles or two working styles.

14. Compare and contrast two career fields to argue that one is better for you.

15. Compare and contrast a public school with a business.

16. Compare and contrast two computers or two software programs.

General Topics

Compare and contrast one or more of the following topics. After you limit your topic, personalize it or do some research so that you will have specific support.

17. Two generations of college students

18. Two automobiles, bicycles, motorcycles, snowmobiles

19. Two types of (or specific) police officers, doctors, teachers, preachers, students, athletes

20. Two famous persons—authors, generals, actors, athletes

21. Two philosophies, religions, ideologies

22. Downhill skiing and snowboarding

23. Living at college and living at home

24. A small college and a large college or a four-year college and a community college

25. Two gangs or two kinds of gangs

26. Two roommates, neighbors, friends, dates

27. Two movies, television shows, commercials, songs, singers

28. Dating and going steady, living together and being married, a specific person before and after marriage

29. Shopping malls and neighborhood stores

30. Two political candidates or office holders

Writer's Guidelines: Comparison and Contrast

1. *Purpose:* During the exploration of your topic, define your purpose clearly.

   • Decide whether you are writing a work that is primarily comparison, primarily contrast, or balanced.

   • Determine whether your main purpose is to inform or to persuade.

2. *Points*

   • Indicate your points of comparison or contrast, perhaps by listing.

   • Eliminate irrelevant points.

3. *Pattern*

   • Select the subject-by-subject or the point-by-point pattern after considering your topic and planned treatment. The point-by-point pattern is usually preferred in essays. Only in long papers is there likely to be a mixture of patterns.

   • Compose an outline reflecting the pattern you select.

   • Use this basic subject-by-subject pattern:

   I. Subject X
      A. Point 1
      B. Point 2

    II. Subject Y

       A. Point 1

       B. Point 2

- Use this basic point-by-point pattern:

    I. Point 1

       A. Subject X

       B. Subject Y

    II. Point 2

       A. Subject X

       B. Subject Y

4. *Presentation*

- Give each point more or less equal treatment. Attention to each part of the outline will usually ensure balanced development.
- Use transitional words and phrases to indicate comparison and contrast and to establish coherence.
- Use a carefully stated topic sentence for a paragraph and a clear thesis for an essay. Each developmental paragraph should have a topic sentence broad enough to embrace its content.

Cause and Effect: Determining Reasons and Outcomes

THE QUIGMANS   by Buddy Hickerson

© Tribune Media Services, Inc. All Rights Reserved. Reprinted with permission.

Writing Cause and Effect

C auses and effects deal with reasons and results; they are sometimes discussed together and sometimes separately. Like other forms of writing to explain, writing about causes and effects is based on natural thought processes. The shortest, and arguably the most provocative, poem in the English language—"I/Why?"—is posed by an anonymous author about cause. Children are preoccupied with delightful and often exasperating "why" questions. Daily we encounter all kinds of causes and effects. The same subject may raise questions of both kinds.

> The car won't start. Why? (*cause*)
> The car won't start. What now? (*effect*)

At school, from the biology lab to the political science classroom, and at work, from maintaining relationships to changing procedures, causes and effects are found everywhere.

Exploring and Organizing

One useful approach to developing a cause-or-effect analysis is listing. Write down the event, situation, or trend you are concerned about. Then on the left side, list the causes, and on the right side, list the effects. From them you will select the main causes or effects for your essay. Here is an example.

Causes	Event, Situation, or Trend	Effects
Low self-esteem	Joining a gang	Life of crime
Drugs		Drug addiction
Tradition		Surrogate family relationship
Fear		
Want surrogate family		Protection
Need protection		Ostracism
Want neighborhood status		Restricted vocational opportunities

As you use prewriting techniques to explore your ideas, you need to decide whether your topic should mainly inform or mainly persuade. If you intend to inform, your tone should be coolly objective. If you intend to persuade, your tone can be subjective. In either case, you should take into account the views of your audience as you phrase your ideas. You should also take into account how much your audience understands about your topic and develop your ideas accordingly.

Composing a Thesis

Now that you have listed your ideas under causes and effects, you are ready to focus on the causes, on the effects, or, occasionally, on both.

Your controlling idea, the thesis, might be one of the causes: "It is not just chance; people have reasons for joining gangs." Later, as you use the idea, you would rephrase it to make it less mechanical, allowing it to become part of the flow of your discussion. If you wanted to personalize the work—thereby probably making it more interesting—you could write about someone you know who joined a gang. You could use the same basic framework, the main causes, to indicate why this particular person joined a gang.

Writing an Outline

Your selection of a controlling idea takes you to the next writing phase: completing an outline or outline alternative. You need to

- consider kinds of causes and effects.
- evaluate the importance of sequence.
- introduce ideas and work with patterns.

In its most basic form, your outline, derived mainly from points in your listing, might look like one of the following:

Essay of causes

Thesis: It is not just chance; people have reasons for joining gangs.

  I. Low self-esteem (cause 1)
 II. Want surrogate family (cause 2)
III. Need protection (cause 3)

Essay of effects

Thesis: One is not a gang member without consequences.

  I. Restricted vocational opportunities (effect 1)
 II. Life of crime (effect 2)
III. Drug addiction (effect 3)
IV. Ostracism from mainstream society (effect 4)

Considering Kinds of Causes and Effects

Causes and effects can be primary or secondary, immediate or remote.

Primary or Secondary

Primary means "major," and *secondary* means "minor." A primary cause may be sufficient to bring about the situation (subject). For example, infidelity may be a primary (and possibly sufficient by itself) cause of divorce for some people but not for others, who regard it as secondary. Or if country X is attacked by country Y, the attack itself, as a primary cause, may be sufficient to bring on a declaration of war. But a diplomatic blunder regarding visas for workers may be of secondary importance, and, though significant, it is certainly not enough to start a war.

Immediate or Remote

Causes and effects often occur at a distance in time or place from the situation. The immediate effect of sulfur in the atmosphere may be atmospheric pollution, but the long-range, or remote, effect may be acid rain and the loss of species. The immediate cause of the greenhouse effect may be the depletion of the ozone layer, whereas the long-range, or remote, cause is the use of CFCs (commonly called Freons, which are found in such items as Styrofoam cups). Even more remote, the ultimate cause may be the people who use the products containing Freons. Your purpose will determine the causes and effects appropriate for your essay.

Evaluating the Importance of Sequence

The sequence in which events occur(red) may or may not be significant. When you are dealing with several sequential events, determine whether the sequence of events has causal connections; that is, does one event bring about another?

Consider this sequence of events: Joe's parents get divorced, and Joe joins a gang. We know that one reason for joining a gang is to gain family companionship. Therefore, we may conclude that Joe joined the gang to satisfy his needs for family companionship, which he lost when his parents were divorced. But if we do so, we may have reached a wrong conclusion, because Joe's joining the gang after the family breakup does not necessarily mean that the two events are related. Maybe Joe joined the gang because of drug dependency, low self-esteem, or a need for protection.

In each case, examine the connections. To assume that one event is *caused* by another just because it *follows* the other is a logical error called a *post hoc* ("after this") fallacy. An economic depression may occur after a president takes office, but that does not necessarily mean the depression was caused by the new administration. It might have occurred anyway, perhaps in an even more severe form.

Order

The order of the causes and effects you discuss in your paper may be based on time, space, emphasis, or a combination.

- *Time:* If one stage leads to another, as in a discussion of the causes and effects of upper atmospheric pollution, your paper would be organized best by time.

- *Space:* In some instances, causes and effects are best organized by their relation in space. For example, the causes of an economic recession could be discussed in terms of local factors, regional factors, national factors, and international factors.

• *Emphasis:* Some causes and effects may be more important than others. For instance, if some causes of divorce are primary (perhaps infidelity and physical abuse) and others are secondary (such as annoying habits and laziness), a paper about divorce could present the secondary causes first, and then move on to primary causes to emphasize the latter as more important.

In some situations, two or more factors (such as time and emphasis) may be linked; in that case, select the order that best fits what you are trying to say, or combine orders.

Introducing Ideas and Working with Patterns

In presenting your controlling idea—probably near the beginning for an introductory paragraph for an essay—you will almost certainly want to perform two functions:

1. *Discuss your subject.* For example, if you are writing about the causes or effects of divorce, begin with a statement about divorce as a subject.

2. *Indicate whether you will concentrate on causes or effects or combine them.* That indication should be made clear early in the paper. Concentrating on one—causes or effects—does not mean you will not mention the other; it only means you will emphasize one of them. You can bring attention to your main concern(s)—causes, effects, or a combination—by repeating key words such as *cause, reason, effect, result, consequence,* and *outcome.*

The most likely pattern for your work is shown in Figure 12.1.

Figure 12.1
Pattern for Essay

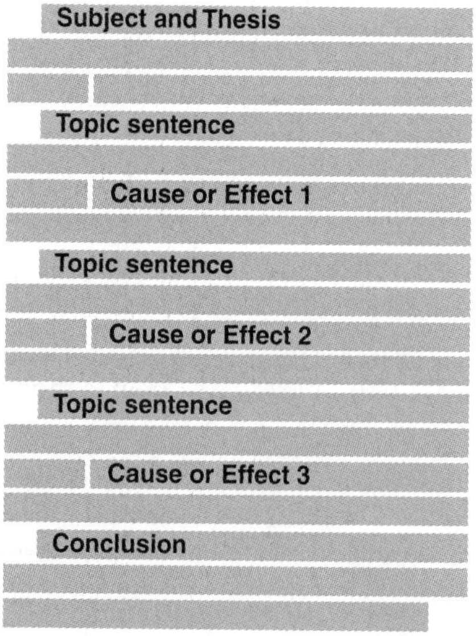

Subject and Thesis

Topic sentence
Cause or Effect 1

Topic sentence
Cause or Effect 2

Topic sentence
Cause or Effect 3

Conclusion

Exercise 1   **COMPLETING PATTERNS OF CAUSE AND EFFECT**

Complete the following cluster on teenage marriage. Then select three or more primary causes or three or more primary effects that could be used in writing an essay on this topic.

Answers will vary.

Causes   **Effects**

Primary causes   Primary effects

1. _____   1. _____

2. _____   2. _____

3. _____   3. _____

4. _____   4. _____

Connecting Sources and Writing

Student Essay

Victims of abuse do not always feel sorry for themselves. They also do not always protect others who are being abused. These are the shocking conclusions reached by Shandra Morgan, a thoughtful victim.

Kick Me! Kiss Me!

Shandra Morgan (pseudonym)

I can identify with people who were physically abused as children. I am one of them, and I've got all kinds of scars. In prison, I am surrounded by people with a background similar to mine. Like me, they are trying to leave a whole pattern of thinking and behavior behind. Here in prison, a woman I know filed a grievance against a guard who, she said, had struck her numerous times. When the Watch Commander read the statement, he said, "You didn't fill in this part that says, 'Action Requested?'" Her answer was immediate. "I want people to stop beating me unless I deserve it." A former victim of child abuse, she was taking an important step. The final one would occur when she stopped believing that she should be beaten for any reason. Some people might think that point is simple, but it isn't. First, one has to understand what happens to a person who gets beat on every day.

When I was a little kid, my father used to beat me—in ways I don't want to describe just yet. Abuse was a common part of my life. He especially liked to throw things such as ashtrays, books, the TV remote control, and beer cans (usually with beer in them). Then if he missed, he'd get even madder and chase me down and pound me with his fists. Naturally I figured out it would be better to be hit with a flying object than to be pounded, so I learned to move toward whatever he threw. He never seemed to catch on. I'd lunge toward something like an ashtray, and it'd hit me—fleshy parts like my seat were the best targets—and then I'd cry, and he'd stop. Sometimes he'd say how sorry he was and how I got him all upset. It always was my fault.

Of course, I believed it was my fault. Whenever he hit me, however he did it, I knew I deserved it, if not for the immediate mischief, for something else—I was wicked. I always felt more guilt than anger. My life was full of guilt-producing incidents. I received bad grades in school. I embarrassed him in front of his friends. I got in his way around the house. The food I cooked was never as good as that cooked by my mother, who'd disappeared two years after I was born—which was another source of guilt because she probably didn't like me. There were plenty of reasons for me to feel guilty, and I didn't neglect any of them.

But I wasn't the only one around the house who felt guilty. My little brother had his share of guilt feelings. For him, it was not my father he had to watch out for. My father thought Joey could do no wrong. I was the one who beat Joey. When my father was out, I slapped Joey around and threw things—ashtrays, books, hair brushes, whatever I had. Pretty soon I had me a little whiner to pick

Thesis

Effect

Effect

Effect

Effect

on, so I could feel better. I even had him apologizing, acting mousier than I ever did, and even cutting on himself.

Effect

Finally, when I went to school with bruises for the hundredth time, a teacher took me to the principal, and I told all. <u>The result was juvenile hall, followed by a half-dozen foster homes and a pattern of beating by adults in all kinds of situations—even by men I lived with.</u>

Effect

Being abused is bad. It made me feel guilty. <u>It made me want to be abused. And it made me want to be an abuser.</u> Now I'm working on undoing the pattern of thinking that I've had all these years. I want to take the "Kick me" sign off my back and replace it with one that reads "Kiss me." But right now I'm all so mixed up in changing that if someone did kiss me, I don't know whether I'd kick or kiss back.

Exercise 2   **DISCUSSION AND CRITICAL THINKING**

1. What is the subject (situation, circumstance, or trend) that is at the center of this discussion?
   Being abused.

2. Circle the sentence that most clearly indicates the author's intention of writing about cause, effect, or a combination.

3. Is this passage concerned more with causes, effects, or a combination?
   Effects.

4. Underline the sentences that indicate the specific causes or effects.

5. In what order (time, emphasis, or a combination) are the parts presented?
   Time.

6. Is the author's purpose mainly to inform or to persuade?
   To inform.

Practicing Patterns of Cause and Effect

A detailed outline and your subsequent writing may include a combination of causes and effects, but you almost always will emphasize one concern—either causes or effects—over the other. The emphasis will

provide the main structure, reflecting your purpose. Whether you are writing a basic outline for an assignment outside class without a significant time constraint or you are writing in class under the pressure of time, you will always have time to jot down prewriting lists and create cause and effect outlines.

| **Exercise 3** | **COMPLETING PATTERNS OF CAUSE AND EFFECT** |

Review the following cluster on the topic of being abused, then fill in the blanks to complete the effects outline. Note how the outline headings came from the clustering strategy.

Clustering (Demonstration)

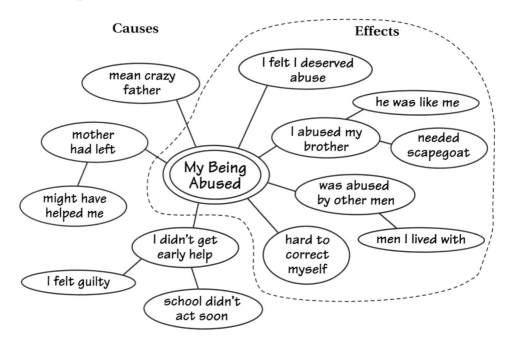

Effects outline

<u>A person who gets beat on every day</u> <u>may feel she deserves it, but she</u>
          subject   **treatment**
<u>may still beat on others.</u>

    I. Was injured   (Effect)

      A. Physical

      B. <u>Psychological</u>

    II. Felt guilty   (Effect)

III. Became <u>abuser</u>   (Effect)
   A. Abused <u>my brother</u>
   B. Felt <u>good about it</u>
IV. Found other <u>abusive relationships</u>   (Effect)

Student Documented Essay

Student Max Dunlop immediately thought of boxing when he received an assignment to write an essay of cause and effect that was in some way connected to entertainment. Recently, he had read a persuasive essay about boxing, "Blood on Their Hands," by Pete Hamill. It dealt mainly with the effects of boxing. Pursuing the topic, Dunlop went to the library. Using the *Reader's Guide to Periodical Literature* and the Electric Library, an electronic database, he found a few other sources. From them, he selected two he would use with the Hamill article.

It's Time to KO Boxing
Max Dunlop

We have heard the charges against boxing: The so-called sport exploits the poor, fosters crime, and destroys human bodies. The counterargument is that boxing should just be regulated more carefully. That would be fine for the first two charges. Strictly enforced rules could reduce exploitation and curtail crime, but the third charge is beyond remedy: boxing has as its objective the injury of human bodies. Unfortunately for participants, the results of body pounding take several untreatable forms.

The most untreatable of the forms is death. The *Washington Post* reported on July 4, 2001, that nationally "more than fifty professional fighters have died from boxing injuries since 1970" (D3). This figure pertains to the individuals whose deaths are clearly tied to what happened in the ring, usually with the sequence of a knockout, prolonged unconsciousness, and death. Other fatalities occur well after the brain is injured and often go unreported.

Among the long-term effects is one that can be called a slow or partial death: "dementia pugilistica." As Pete Hamill, noted sports journalist observes, this boxer is said to be punch-drunk. In the final stages, which occur between seven and sixteen years after "retirement," the boxer experiences "a decrease in general cognitive functions, memory deficits, impaired hearing, hyperreflexia, dysarthia, intention tremor, and incoordination" (93). Reporting from medical literature, Hamill continues, "This syndrome affects 9 to 25 percent of professional fighters" (94). These victims go on living but usually drift off into their separate worlds where they stumble around over invisible objects, hearing mysterious voices and dodging imaginary punches.

These shambling figures are often fortunate compared with other boxers whose injuries are thought to have been the triggers to the disabling conditions called Parkinson's disease, multiple sclerosis, and frontal-lobe tumors. All of those diseases are more common among pugilists than the general population (Hamill 94). We have all heard about links between traumas and the onset of Alzheimer's disease. We have witnessed the fate of Muhammad Ali, who suffers from Parkinson's.

Having no doubt about the effects of body pounding, the medical profession has been overwhelming in its recommendation of a ban of boxing. Amateur boxing is thought to be less dangerous, for the careers are shorter, the regulations are more strictly enforced, and the matches are shorter. But even with those factors considered, the American Academy of Pediatrics "opposes the sport of boxing for children, adolescents, and young adults. . . . Boxing [exposes] participants to potentially devastating neurologic and ocular injuries" ("Participation in Boxing" 134). The American Medical Association and the World Health Organization concur that boxing should not be legal. The medical profession has not prevailed for obvious reasons: Boxing fans look at their sport from a distance. They say things like, "That was a beautiful knockout." They never say, "That was a beautiful brain concussion."

Of course, a boxing critic should take on the popular argument of many boxing fans that no one is required to box. People volunteer to do it. A few become famous. A few are paid well. It is true that boxers do choose to participate for fame and fortune. But would we say that anyone who is willing to do anything for recognition and money should be given that choice? What if we were to place two combatants in an arena, each one armed with an AK-47, and then offer a big prize to the one who guns down the other? If the prize were large enough, some individuals would almost certainly volunteer for a shootout. If you agree that this activity should, nevertheless, not be allowed, then we both believe that in some instances people should not be permitted to do what they would willingly choose.

The final point is whether the sport of boxing should be legal. The medical community says no. Many of us join in following the evidence to its logical conclusion. This so-called sport with the primary objective of harming the opponent should be banned. It is not a split decision. Boxing should go the way of the gladiators.

Works Cited

"Boxing-Related Deaths." *Washington Post* 4 July 2001: D3.
Hamill, Pete. "Blood on Their Hands." *Esquire* June 1996: 92–100.
"Participation in Boxing by Children, Adolescents, and Young Adults."
Pediatrics 99 (Jan. 1997): 134–135.

Exercise 4   **DISCUSSION AND CRITICAL THINKING**

1. Is this essay concerned mainly with causes or effects?
   Effects.

2. Circle the thesis.

3. Underline each sentence that introduces a set of effects.

4. What are the main causes and the effect in the sixth paragraph?

   Causes: fame and fortune

   Effect: injury to individual

5. Does Dunlop attempt mainly to inform or to persuade?
   To persuade.

6. Do you agree with Dunlop's conclusion? Explain.
   Answers will vary.

7. What would Dunlop say to those who say that boxing is the way for
   some poor kids to get out of the ghetto or barrio?
   Answers will vary.

8. Does this apply equally to the growing sport of women's boxing?
   Yes, but answers will vary.

Multiple Sources on Love, Marriage, and Divorce

Unfortunately for individuals and society, the title of this selection of essays, "Love, Marriage, and Divorce," defines an all-too-common sequence of events. Many of us have grown up thinking about only the first two in that continuum. Surely, love is an almost magical chemistry that is followed by marriage as a natural commitment, with divorce lurking out there somewhere—for others, not ourselves.

The four authors of the following selections represent different perspectives, and each offers a special insight. Anne Roiphe is concerned with how and why people fall in love and marry, but she focuses on psychological reasons, pointing out that our subconscious often leads us to re-create what we experienced as children in a family. Therefore, a marriage may be a satisfying fulfillment or—unless the partners work at changing negative patterns—a failure. Ian Robertson places "romantic love, courtship, and marriage" in a sociological, historical context. Taking Cupid out of the picture, he explains why the practices of loving, courting, and marrying have developed and why they have been sustained. He points out that in a different culture we might never fall in love and would not expect to do so. Moreover, he says, "A courtship system is essentially a marriage market," and people who become partners almost certainly have characteristics in common, such as age, class, and religion. In "Female Mea Culpa," Lin Rolens takes a personal look at relationships. We're all familiar with the saying, "Just what does a woman (or man) want?" Rolens has a practical suggestion. Each person in a relationship should make up a list and present that list to the significant other. For starters, Rolens offers her own preliminary list. Daniel Goleman digs deeper for the roots to the problem of love and marriage strife. There he finds the different views of men and women responsible for the divisiveness in relationships.

Why Marriages Fail

Anne Roiphe

As novelist and journalist, Anne Roiphe has been especially concerned with the topic of contemporary relationships. In this essay, first published in *Family Weekly*, she concentrates on two phenomena all too frequently linked: marriage and divorce.

1   These days so many marriages end in divorce that our most sacred vows no longer ring with truth. "Happily ever after" and "Till death do us part" are expressions that seem on the way to becoming obsolete. Why has it become so hard for couples to stay together? What goes wrong? What has happened to us that close to one-half of all marriages are destined for the divorce courts? How could we have created a society in which 42 percent of our children will grow up in single-parent homes? If statistics could only measure loneliness, regret, pain, loss of self-confidence and fear of the future, the numbers would be beyond quantifying.

2   Even though each broken marriage is unique, we can still find the common perils, the common causes for marital despair. Each

marriage has crisis points and each marriage tests endurance, the capacity for both intimacy and change. Outside pressures such as job loss, illness, infertility, trouble with a child, care of aging parents and all the other plagues of life hit marriage the way hurricanes blast our shores. Some marriages survive these storms and others don't. Marriages fail, however, not simply because of the outside weather but because the inner climate becomes too hot or too cold, too turbulent or too stupefying.

3 When we look at how we choose our partners and what expectations exist at the tender beginnings of romance, some of the reasons for disaster become quite clear. We all select with unconscious accuracy a mate who will recreate with us the emotional patterns of our first homes. Dr. Carl A. Whitaker, a marital therapist and emeritus professor of psychiatry at the University of Wisconsin, explains, "From early childhood on each of us carried models for marriage, femininity, masculinity, motherhood, fatherhood, and all the other family roles." Each of us falls in love with a mate who has qualities of our parents, who will help us rediscover both the psychological happiness and miseries of our past lives. We may think we have found a man unlike Dad, but then he turns to drink or drugs, or loses his job over and over again or sits silently in front of the TV just the way Dad did. A man may choose a woman who doesn't like kids just like his mother or who gambles away the family savings just like his mother. Or he may choose a slender wife who seems unlike his obese mother but then turns out to have other addictions that destroy their mutual happiness.

4 A man and a woman bring to their marriage bed a blended concoction of conscious and unconscious memories of their parents' lives together. The human way is to compulsively repeat and recreate the patterns of the past. Sigmund Freud* so well described the unhappy design that many of us get trapped in: the unmet needs of childhood, the angry feelings left over from frustrations of long ago, the limits of trust and the recurrence of old fears. Once an individual senses this entrapment, there may follow a yearning to escape, and the result could be a broken, splintered marriage.

5 Of course people can overcome the habits and attitudes that developed in childhood. We all have hidden strengths and amazing capacities for growth and creative change. Change, however, requires work—observing your part in a rotten pattern, bringing difficulties out into the open—and work runs counter to the basic

---

*Sigmund Freud was an Austrian neuropsychologist who founded psychoanalysis.

myth of marriage: "When I wed this person all my problems will be over. I will have achieved success and I will become the center of life for this other person and this person will be my center, and we will mean everything to each other forever." This myth, which every marriage relies on, is soon exposed. The coming of children, the pulls and tugs of their demands on affection and time, place a considerable strain on that basic myth of meaning everything to each other, of merging together and solving all of life's problems.

6 Concern and tension about money take each partner away from the other. Obligations to demanding parents or still-dependent-upon parents create further strain. Couples today must also deal with all the cultural changes brought on in recent years by the women's movement and the sexual revolution. The altering of roles and the shifting of responsibilities have been extremely trying for many marriages.

7 These and other realities of life erode the visions of marital bliss the way sandstorms eat at rock and the ocean nibbles away at the dunes. Those euphoric, grand feelings that accompany romantic love are really self-delusions, self-hypnotic dreams that enable us to forge a relationship. Real life, failure at work, disappointments, exhaustion, bad smells, bad colds and hard times all puncture the dream and leave us stranded with our mate, with our childhood patterns pushing us this way and that, with our unfulfilled expectations.

8 The struggle to survive in marriage requires adaptability, flexibility, genuine love and kindness and an imagination strong enough to feel what the other is feeling. Many marriages fall apart because either partner cannot imagine what the other wants or cannot communicate what he or she needs or feels. Anger builds until it erupts into a volcanic burst that buries the marriage in ash

9 It is not hard to see, therefore, how essential communication is for a good marriage. A man and a woman must be able to tell each other how they feel and why they feel the way they do; otherwise they will impose on each other roles and actions that lead to further unhappiness. In some cases, the communication patterns of childhood—of not talking, of talking too much, of not listening, of distrust and anger, of withdrawal—spill into the marriage and prevent a healthy exchange of thoughts and feelings. The answer is to set up new patterns of communication and intimacy.

10 At the same time, however, we must see each other as individuals. "To achieve a balance between separateness and closeness is one of the major psychological tasks of all human beings at every

stage of life," says Dr. Stuart Bartle, a psychiatrist at the New York University Medical Center.

11   If we sense from our mate a need for too much intimacy, we tend to push him or her away, fearing that we may lose our identities in the merging of marriage. One partner may suffocate the other partner in a childlike dependency.

12   A good marriage means growing as a couple but also growing as individuals. This isn't easy. Richard gives up his interest in carpentry because his wife, Helen, is jealous of the time he spends away from her. Karen quits her choir group because her husband dislikes the friends she makes there. Each pair clings to each other and is angry with each other as life closes in on them. This kind of marital balance is easily thrown as one or the other pulls away and divorce follows.

13   Sometimes people pretend that a new partner will solve the old problems. Most often extramarital sex destroys a marriage because it allows an artificial split between the good and the bad—the good is projected on the new partner and the bad is dumped on the head of the old. Dishonesty, hiding and cheating create walls between men and women. Infidelity is just a symptom of trouble. It is a symbolic complaint, a weapon of revenge, as well as an unraveler of closeness. Infidelity is often that proverbial last straw that sinks the camel to the ground.

14   All right—marriage has always been difficult. Why then are we seeing so many divorces at this time? Yes, our modern social fabric is thin, and yes the permissiveness of society has created unrealistic expectations and thrown the family into chaos. But divorce is so common because people today are unwilling to exercise the self-discipline that marriage requires. They expect easy joy, like the entertainment on TV, the thrill of a good party.

15   Marriage takes some kind of sacrifice, not dreadful self-sacrifice of the soul, but some level of compromise. Some of one's fantasies, some of one's legitimate desires have to be given up for the value of the marriage itself. "While all marital partners feel shackled at times, it is they who really choose to make the marital ties into confining chains or supporting bonds," says Dr. Whitaker. Marriage requires sexual, financial and emotional discipline. A man and a woman cannot follow every impulse, cannot allow themselves to stop growing or changing.

16   Divorce is not an evil act. Sometimes it provides salvation for people who have grown hopelessly apart or were frozen in patterns of pain or mutual unhappiness. Divorce can be, despite its

initial devastation, like the first cut of the surgeon's knife, a step toward new health and a good life. On the other hand, if the partners can stay past the breaking up of the romantic myths into the development of real love and intimacy, they have achieved a work as amazing as the greatest cathedrals of the world. Marriages that do not fail but improve, that persist despite imperfections, are not only rare these days but offer a wondrous shelter in which the face of our mutual humanity can safely show itself.

Exercise 5   **VOCABULARY HIGHLIGHTS**

Write a short definition of each word as it is used in the essay. (Paragraph numbers are given in parentheses.) Be prepared to use the words in your own sentences.

obsolete (1)	projected (13)
perils (2)	symbolic (13)
turbulent (2)	chaos (14)
concoction (4)	myths (16)
erode (7)	persist (16)

Exercise 6   **DISCUSSION AND CRITICAL THINKING**

1. What is the subject (a situation, circumstance, or trend) at the center of this discussion?
   The failure of marriages.

2. Is this essay concerned more with causes, effects, or a combination?
   Both causes and effects but mainly causes.

3. Roiphe points out that marriages fail because of both internal and external factors.
   a. What outside pressures cause stress in marriages (paragraph 2)?
   Job loss, illness, infertility, trouble with a child, care of aging parents, and others.

   b. What pressures inside individuals cause stress in marriage (paragraphs 3, 4)?
   Unconscious attempts to re-create our childhood emotional patterns. For better or worse, we select mates similar to our parents. Thus, if our childhood was troubled, we will have problems to deal with in our marriages.

4. If it is true that we select marriage partners with qualities that will enable us to re-create our childhood experiences, both good and bad, then are those of us who had mostly bad childhood experiences trapped into reproducing those bad patterns?
   Roiphe says that "people can overcome the habits and attitudes that developed in childhood" (paragraph 5). We need to address our problems.

5. According to Roiphe, what specific realities puncture the dreams of romantic love (paragraph 7)?

"Real life, failure at work, disappointments, exhaustion, bad smells, bad colds and hard times."

6. What are the components (and thus the causes) of a good marriage?

"Adaptability, flexibility, genuine love and kindness and an imagination strong enough to feel what the other is feeling" (paragraph 8).

Romantic Love, Courtship, and Marriage

Ian Robertson

Romantic love, courtship, and marriage are more than matters of the heart. According to Ian Robertson, they are all perfectly understandable parts of our culture, and they do not exist in the same way outside our culture. In this excerpt from his college textbook, *Sociology*, Robertson explains the causes of our loving, courting, and marrying. He says that, often without thinking about what we are doing, we respond to the needs of both society and ourselves.

Romantic Love

1 The American family is supposed to be founded on the romantic love of the marital partners. Traces of a more pragmatic attitude persist in the American upper classes, where daughters are expected to marry "well"—that is, to a male who is eligible by reason of family background and earning potential. Most Americans, however, tend to look askance at anyone who marries for money or some other practical reason in which love plays no part.

2 Happily enough, romantic love defies a clinical definition. It is a different kind of love, though, from the love you have for your parents or your dog. It involves physical symptoms, such as pounding heart and sexual desire, and psychological symptoms, such as obsessive focus on one person and a disregard for any resulting social or economic risks. Our culture encourages us to look for this love—to find that "one and only," perhaps even through "love at first sight." The phenomenon of romantic love occurs when two people meet and find one another personally and physically attractive. They become mutually absorbed, start to behave in what may appear to be a flighty, even irrational manner, decide that they are right for one another, and may then enter

a marriage whose success is expected to be guaranteed by their enduring passion. Behavior of this kind is portrayed and warmly endorsed throughout American popular culture, by books, magazines, comics, records, popular songs, movies, and TV.

3   Romantic love is a noble idea, and it can certainly help provide a basis for the spouses to "live happily ever after." But since marriage can equally well be founded on much more practical considerations, why is romantic love of such importance in the modern world? The reason seems to be that it has the following basic functions in maintaining the institution of the nuclear family:

4   1. *Transfer of loyalties.* Romantic love helps the young partners to loosen their bonds with their family of orientation, a step that is essential if a new neolocal nuclear family is to be created. Their total absorption in one another facilitates a transfer of commitment from existing family and kin to a new family of procreation, something that would be unlikely to happen under the extended family system.

5   2. *Emotional support.* Romantic love provides the couple with emotional support in the difficulties that they face in establishing a new life of their own. This love would not be so necessary in an extended family, where the relatives are able to confront problems cooperatively. In an extended family, in fact, romantic love might even be dysfunctional, for it could distract the couple from their wider obligations to other kin.

6   3. *Incentive to marriage.* Romantic love serves as a bait to lure people into marriage. In the extended family system of traditional societies, it is automatically assumed that people will marry, but in the modern world, people have considerable choice over whether they will get married or not. A contract to form a lifelong commitment to another person is not necessarily a very tempting proposition, however: to some, the prospect may look more like a noose than like a bed of roses. Without feelings of romantic love, many people might have no incentive to marry.

7   To most of us, particularly to those who are in love, romantic love seems to be the most natural thing in the world, but sociological analysis shows that it is a purely cultural product, arising in certain societies for specific reasons. In a different time or in a different society, you might never fall in love, nor would you expect to.

Courtship and Marriage

8   A courtship system is essentially a marriage market. (The metaphor of the "market" may seem a little unromantic, but in fact, the participants do attempt to "sell" their assets—physical appear-

ance, personal charms, talents and interests, and career prospects.) In the matter of mate selection, different courtship systems vary according to how much choice they permit the individual. The United States probably allows more freedom of choice than any other society. A parent who attempts to interfere in the dating habits or marriage plans of a son or daughter is considered meddlesome and is more likely to alienate than persuade the young lover.

9   In this predominantly urban and anonymous society, young people—often with access to automobiles—have an exceptional degree of privacy in their courting. The practice of dating enables them to find out about one another, to improve their own interpersonal skills in the market, to experiment sexually if they so wish, and finally to select a marriage partner.

10   Who marries whom, then? Cupid's arrow, it turns out, does not strike at random. Despite the cultural emphasis on love as something mysterious and irrational, the selection of marital partners is more orderly and predictable than romantics might like to think. In general, the American mate-selection process produces *homogamy*, marriage between partners who share similar social characteristics. Among the characteristics that seem to attract people to one another are the following:

11   1. *Similar age.* Married partners tend to be of roughly the same age. Husbands are usually older than their wives, but this difference in age has been gradually declining throughout the century, from about 4 years in 1900 to 2.4 years today.

12   2. *Social class.* Most people marry within their own social class. The reasons are obvious: we tend to live in class-segregated neighborhoods, to meet mostly people of the same class, and to share class-specific tastes and interests. Interclass marriages are relatively more common, however, among college students. When there are class differences in a marriage, it is most often the wife who marries upward.

13   3. *Religion.* Most marriages are between people sharing the same religious faith, although Protestant interdenominational marriages are fairly common. Many people change their religion to that of their partner before marriage.

14   4. *Education.* Husbands and wives generally have a similar educational level. The college campus is, of course, a marriage market in its own right, and college-educated people are especially likely to marry people who have a similar education achievement.

15   5. *Racial and ethnic background.* Members of racial and ethnic groups are more likely to marry within their own group than outside it. In particular, interracial marriages are extremely rare.

Until the 1960s, several states had laws prohibiting interracial marriages, and such marriages still attract some social disapproval. Interracial marriages between blacks and whites are particularly unusual; in the majority of these cases, the husband is black and the wife white.

16   6. *Propinquity.* Spatial nearness is a common feature of those who marry one another, for the obvious reason that people are likely to have more social interaction and similarities with neighbors, coworkers, or fellow students than with others who are physically more distant.

Exercise 7   **DISCUSSION AND CRITICAL THINKING**

1. What is the subject (a situation, circumstance, or trend) at the center of this discussion?

   Romantic love, courtship, and marriage.

2. Is this piece concerned mainly with causes, effects, or a combination of both?

   Mainly causes.

3. What are the three cultural needs or causes (also called functions) that make romantic love useful in our society?

   (1) Transfer of loyalties; (2) emotional support; (3) incentive to marriage.

4. How would you rank the three functions of romantic love in order of importance?

   Answers will vary.

5. On the basis of what assets do individuals attempt to sell themselves on the "marriage market"?

   "Physical appearance, personal charms, talents and interests, and career prospects" (paragraph 8).

6. What six causes (or "characteristics") does Robertson list for why people fall in love?

   (1) Similar age, (2) social class, (3) religion, (4) education, (5) racial and ethnic background, (6) propinquity.

7. In your estimation, which of the six causes are the most important?

   Answers will vary.

8. Are the assets or the characteristics more important? Should they be?

   Answers will vary.

Female Mea Culpa

Lin Rolens

Freelance author Lin Rolens has a proposal to end all this animosity between the sexes. It is based on openness, and it starts and finishes with a list of needs and considerations, which are thinly veiled grievances. Ideally, this solution would be an exchange of lists. This essay was first printed in the *Santa Barbara News Press Magazine* in 1999.

1   For years now I've wanted a man who comes with a list: how he likes his coffee, what he won't eat, how he really feels about the remote control, how he likes his socks folded. I don't want the complete list, that would take volumes, but a starter list would be nice. And I don't want it presented with great ceremony; I want it slipped quietly into my pocket at just the right moment to make both our lives easier.

2   Of course, there should be a reciprocal list of all my little quirks, foibles, needs, pleasures and the like. Some of this is particular to me (I take my coffee with milk, will eat anything but okra, believe the remote should enjoy shared custody and will take my socks folded any way he cares to fold them), but certainly there are some general things about women that men would do well to know, some things that seem to escape them.

3   I offer a generalized starter list:

4   In our female hearts, we know, if there were any justice in the world, courtship would not be a phase in a relationship: It would be a way of life. Never mind dating, which is generally exhausting, but we really love, and even feel we deserve, all the little touches and enthusiasms, all those wonderful surprises and attentions that helped convince us you were the right one in the first place.

5   We love flowers: It isn't by accident that one of the features of our local farmers' market is masses of women leaving with great armfuls of flowers. We are, simply, suckers for flowers, and they often move us as words can't; men of sensibility know that women of sensibility never have too many flowers. The size of the bouquet decidedly is not the issue: We would rather receive a hand-selected nosegay than a floral display ordered through a secretary. And, this is important, flowers given for no apparent reason are flowers given for the best reason.

6   In the complicated logic of women, it is generally accepted that the only flowers not worth receiving are guilt flowers, those flowers proffered as moral groin cover or in lieu of a real apology. I

have shoved more than one rose bouquet in the trash compactor because the sender mistakenly believed I would have a total brain lapse about some recent transgression when I received them.

7   While we usually know what we want, we don't want to tell you what we want. Yes, we'll provide hints, murmured suggestions, but we don't want to have to lay it on the line. We want you to know; it's no mystery to us, and it's difficult to understand why it seems to be such a mystery to you. This goes for everything from where we want to vacation to what we would give if you just don't wear that particular pair of pants to the family reunion. Don't ask me to explain.

8   Talk is often balm, and truly being listened to is one of life's great luxuries. When the day or our lives overwhelm us, it is the wine of talk that proves settling. As we air whatever it is that disturbs us, the problem doesn't go away, but it deflates to a point where we see it in context.

9   Our rituals count; they are important and often meditative indulgences that help us center ourselves. Whether it's painting our toenails yet again in the color that horrifies you or taking long steamy baths or, as one of my friends recently did, spending an entire evening re-ironing all the cloth napkins in her linen closet, these endeavors prove healing. When we return to the fray, we will be better versions of ourselves.

10   When we buy new clothes, we want you to like them—a lot. We want to be adored, validated, or, if you can manage it, occasionally worshipped. (See "fat" for further clarification.)

11   Although it is all right, even inevitable, that we believe, whatever our current weight, that we are fat, it is never all right if you believe we are fat. We need and expect that you will find us just right, whatever our weight. While we are free to loathe extra dimples, bumps, lumps and curves, we trust that you will adore them with the same vigor that you adored our original youthful and girlish figures.

12   Food is not just food. When we cook for you, it is a way of loving you, and we'd appreciate it if you received it in the spirit in which it is given. This is particularly true when we make not only your favorite dinner or our own stellar specialty, but something, say, like your mother's secret spaghetti sauce recipe.

13   There is a widely held belief that we want to change you, that we see men as delicious raw material and that, by careful and patient encouragement or insistence, a good man can be molded into an excellent one. This is actually a problem of semantics: As we see it, we are simply providing you the opportunity to become your best self.

14   Finally, we like chick flicks, that's how they got the name. Action films are fine, but we bring hankies to the movies for a reason.

15   So that's it, a starter list. I'm sure every woman will have her own additions and variations, but it might be worth a try simply to slip this into his pocket.

Exercise 8	**VOCABULARY HIGHLIGHTS**

Write a short definition of each word as it is used in the essay. (Paragraph numbers are given in parentheses.) Be prepared to use the words in your own sentences.

reciprocal (2)   transgression (6)

quirks (2)   balm (8)

foibles (2)   meditative (9)

sensibility (5)   semantics (13)

in lieu of (6)

Exercise 9	**DISCUSSION AND CRITICAL THINKING**

1. Why does Rolens use flowers to explain "the complicated logic of women" (paragraph 6)?
   She believes that gifts should be tokens of love and feelings, not payoffs for injuries.

2. What does she mean when she compares "talk" to "balm" (paragraph 8)?
   She also refers to talk as "wine." It does not take trouble away, but it can soften troubled times and ease the pains.

3. What does Rolens mean when she says, "While we usually know what we want, we don't want to tell you what we want" (paragraph 7)?
   A loving person who wants to show consideration will be sensitive to the needs of others and doesn't need to be told.

4. Is Rolens really serious about making lists? After all, she did say, "We don't want to tell you what we want."
   She is not serious. This essay is her way of saying that men should be better than they are. Otherwise, the above statement would contradict her idea for making lists.

5. In making her list, is Rolens mainly concerned with herself or the man?
   She is concerned with both, but if men were more considerate, she would not have to make a list.

6. Explain what she means by referring to courtship as a "way of life" (paragraph 4).
   Courtship is the purest expression of what a loving relationship should be. We fall in love with and marry courtship. We live in the next phase.

7. Does Rolens believe that women are superior to men in showing respect and consideration? Is she right?

Answers will vary. If both men and women believed in their hearts that courtship should be a way of life, lists (or this essay) would not be necessary. She is writing about the female heart.

His Marriage and Hers: Childhood Roots

Daniel Goleman

A respected scholar, Daniel Goleman has written numerous books on psychology, including *Vital Lies, Simple Truths, The Meditative Mind,* and *Working with Emotional Intelligence.* Here he discusses how conflicts within relationships are caused especially by conditioning.

1   As I was entering a restaurant on a recent evening, a young man stalked out the door, his face set in an expression both stony and sullen. Close on his heels a young woman came running, her fists desperately pummeling his back while she yelled, "Goddamn you! Come back here and be nice to me!" That poignant, impossibly self-contradictory plea aimed at a retreating back epitomizes the pattern most commonly seen in couples whose relationship is distressed: She seeks to engage, he withdraws. Marital therapists have long noted that by the time a couple finds their way to the therapy office they are in this pattern of engage-withdraw, with his complaint about her "unreasonable" demands and outbursts, and her lamenting his indifference to what she is saying.

2   This marital endgame reflects the fact that there are, in effect, two emotional realities in a couple, his and hers. The roots of these emotional differences, while they may be partly biological, also can be traced back to childhood, and to the separate emotional worlds boys and girls inhabit while growing up. There is a vast amount of research on these separate worlds, their barriers reinforced not just by the different games boys and girls prefer, but by young children's fear of being teased for having a "girl-friend" or "boyfriend."[1] One study of children's friendships found that three-year-olds say about half their friends are of the opposite sex; for five-year-olds it's about 20 percent, and by age seven almost no boys or girls say they have a best friend of the opposite

sex.[2] These separate social universes intersect little until teenagers start dating.

3 Meanwhile, boys and girls are taught very different lessons about handling emotions. Parents, in general, discuss emotions—with the exception of anger—more with their daughters than their sons.[3] Girls are exposed to more information about emotions than are boys; when parents make up stories to tell their preschool children, they use more emotion words when talking to daughters than to sons; when mothers play with their infants, they display a wider range of emotions to daughters than to sons; when mothers talk to daughters about feelings, they discuss in more detail the emotional state itself than they do with their sons—though with the sons they go into more detail about the causes and consequences of emotions like anger (probably as a cautionary tale).

4 Leslie Brody and Judith Hall, who have summarized the research on differences in emotions between the sexes, propose that because girls develop facility with language more quickly than do boys, this leads them to be more experienced at articulating their feelings and more skilled than boys at using words to explore and substitute for emotional reactions such as physical fights; in contrast, they note, "boys, for whom the verbalization of affects is de-emphasized, may become largely unconscious of their emotional states, both in themselves and others."[4]

5 At age ten, roughly the same percent of girls as boys are overtly aggressive, given to open confrontation when angered. But by age thirteen, a telling difference between the sexes emerges: Girls become more adept than boys at artful aggressive tactics like ostracism, vicious gossip, and indirect vendettas. Boys, by and large, simply continue being confrontational when angered, oblivious to these more covert strategies.[5] This is just one of many ways that boys—and later, men—are less sophisticated than the opposite sex in the byways of emotional life.

6 When girls play together, they do so in small, intimate groups, with an emphasis on minimizing hostility and maximizing cooperation, while boys' games are in larger groups, with an emphasis on competition. One key difference can be seen in what happens when games boys or girls are playing get disrupted by someone getting hurt. If a boy who has gotten hurt gets upset, he is expected to get out of the way and stop crying so the game can go on. If the same happens among a group of girls who are playing, the *game stops* while everyone gathers around to help the girl who is crying. This difference between boys and girls at play epito-

mizes what Harvard's Carol Gilligan points to as a key disparity between the sexes: boys take pride in a lone, tough-minded independence and autonomy, while girls see themselves as part of a web of connectedness. Thus boys are threatened by anything that might challenge their independence, while girls are more threatened by a rupture in their relationships. And, as Deborah Tannen has pointed out in her book *You Just Don't Understand,* these differing perspectives mean that men and women want and expect very different things out of a conversation, with men content to talk about "things," while women seek emotional connection.

7   In short, these contrasts in schooling in the emotions foster very different skills, with girls becoming "adept at reading both verbal and nonverbal emotional signals, at expressing and communicating their feelings," and boys becoming adept at "minimizing emotions having to do with vulnerability, guilt, fear and hurt."[6] Evidence for these different stances is very strong in the scientific literature. Hundreds of studies have found, for example, that on average women are more empathic than men, at least as measured by the ability to read someone else's unstated feelings from facial expression, tone of voice, and other nonverbal cues. Likewise, it is generally easier to read feelings from a woman's face than a man's; while there is no difference in facial expressiveness among very young boys and girls, as they go through the elementary-school grades boys become less expressive, girls more so. This may partly reflect another key difference: women, on average, experience the entire range of emotions with greater intensity and more volatility than men—in this sense, women *are* more "emotional" than men.[7]

8   All of this means that, in general, women come into a marriage groomed for the role of emotional manager, while men arrive with much less appreciation of the importance of this task for helping a relationship survive. Indeed, the most important element for women—but not for men—in satisfaction with their relationship reported in a study of 264 couples was the sense that the couple has "good communication."[8] Ted Huston, a psychologist at the University of Texas who has studied couples in depth, observes, "For the wives, intimacy means talking things over, especially talking about the relationship itself. The men, by and large, don't understand what the wives want from them. They say, 'I want to do things with her, and all she wants to do is talk.'" During courtship, Huston found, men were much more willing to spend time talking in ways that suited the wish for intimacy of their wives-to-be. But once married, as time went on the men—

especially in more traditional couples—spent less and less time talking in this way with their wives, finding a sense of closeness simply in doing things like gardening together rather than talking things over.

9   This growing silence on the part of husbands may be partly due to the fact that, if anything, men are a bit Pollyannaish* about the state of their marriage, while their wives are attuned to the trouble spots: in one study of marriages, men had a rosier view than their wives of just about everything in their relationship — lovemaking, finances, ties with in-laws, how well they listened to each other, how much their flaws mattered.[9] Wives, in general, are more vocal about their complaints than are their husbands, particularly among unhappy couples. Combine men's rosy view of marriage with their aversion to emotional confrontations, and it is clear why wives so often complain that their husbands try to wiggle out of discussing the troubling things about their relationship. (Of course this gender difference is a generalization, and is not true in every case; a psychiatrist friend complained that in his marriage his wife is reluctant to discuss emotional matters between them, and he is the one who is left to bring them up.)

10   The slowness of men to bring up problems in a relationship is no doubt compounded by their relative lack of skill when it comes to reading facial expressions of emotions. Women, for example, are more sensitive to a sad expression on a man's face than are men in detecting sadness from a woman's expression.[10] Thus a woman has to be all the sadder for a man to notice her feelings in the first place, let alone for him to raise the question of what is making her so sad.

11   Consider the implications of this emotional gender gap for how couples handle the grievances and disagreements that any intimate relationship inevitably spawns. In fact, specific issues such as how often a couple has sex, how to discipline the children, or how much debt and savings a couple feels comfortable with are not what make or break a marriage. Rather, it is *how* a couple discusses such sore points that matters more for the fate of their marriage. Simply having reached an agreement about *how* to disagree is key to marital survival; men and women have to overcome the innate gender differences in approaching rocky emotions. Failing this, couples are vulnerable to emotional rifts that eventually can tear their relationship apart. . . . [T]hese rifts are far more likely to develop if one or both partners have certain deficits in emotional intelligence.

*Pollyanna was an extremely optimistic character in a book for children.

Notes

1. The separate worlds of boys and girls: Eleanor Maccoby and C. N. Jacklin, "Gender Segregation in Childhood," in H. Reese, ed., *Advances in Child Development and Behavior* (New York: Academic Press, 1987).
2. Same-sex playmates: John Gottman, "Same and Cross Sex Friendship in Young Children," in J. Gottman and J. Parker, eds., *Conversation of Friends* (New York: Cambridge University Press, 1986).
3. This and the following summary of sex differences in socialization of emotions are based on the excellent review in Leslie R. Brody and Judith A. Hall, "Gender and Emotion," in Michael Lewis and Jeannette Haviland, eds., *Handbook of Emotions* (New York: Guilford Press, 1993).
4. Brody and Hall, "Gender and Emotion," p. 456.
5. Girls and the arts of aggression: Robert B. Cairns and Beverley D. Cairns, *Lifelines and Risks* (New York: Cambridge University Press, 1994).
6. Brody and Hall, "Gender and Emotion," p. 454.
7. The findings about gender differences in emotion are reviewed in Brody and Hall, "Gender and Emotion."
8. The importance of good communication for women was reported in Mark H. Davis and H. Alan Oathout, "Maintenance of Satisfaction in Romantic Relationships: Empathy and Relational Competence," *Journal of Personality and Social Psychology* 53, 2 (1987), pp. 397–410.
9. The study of husbands' and wives' complaints: Robert J. Sternberg, "Triangulating Love," in Robert Sternberg and Michael Barnes, eds., *The Psychology of Love* (New Haven: Yale University Press, 1988).
10. Reading sad faces: The research is by Dr. Ruben C. Gur at the University of Pennsylvania School of Medicine.

Exercise 10   **VOCABULARY HIGHLIGHTS**

Write a short definition of each word as it is used in the essay. (Paragraph numbers are given in parentheses.) Be prepared to use the words in your own sentences.

pummeling (1)	ostracism (5)
poignant (1)	vendettas (5)
epitomizes (1)	disparity (6)
intersect (2)	empathic (7)
articulating (4)	innate (11)

Exercise 11   **DISCUSSION AND CRITICAL THINKING**

1. This essay uses two forms of discourse extensively: (1) contrast and (2) causes and effects. What does Goleman say is the effect of the contrasts he shows?
   Conflict between men and women.

2. According to Goleman, what are the roots of the different ways men and women express emotions?

"Boys and girls are taught very different lessons about handling emotions" (paragraph 3). Generally parents talk more about emotions and show more emotions to girls than boys.

3. According to Goleman, are the behavioral differences between males and females mainly a result of biology or training?

He admits that the differences may be partly biological in origin, but he knows that they can be traced back to childhood experiences.

4. What does Goleman say are the male and female views on communication in marriage?

Communication is much more significant to women than men. "In general, . . . women come into a marriage groomed for the role of emotional manager . . ." (paragraph 8). For men, communication and courtship go together, not marriage and communication. See paragraph 8.

5. Why don't men talk about marital problems more?

Compared with women, men are less aware of the problems, Goleman says. He points out also that men are slow in seeing that women are in distress. See paragraphs 9 and 10.

6. What is "emotional intelligence" (paragraph 11)?

Being able to understand, articulate, and deal with emotional states, especially troubled ones.

✎ Topics for Writing Cause and Effect

Writing Process Worksheet

You will find a Writing Process Worksheet in Appendix A, page 531. It can be photocopied and enlarged, filled in, and submitted with each assignment if your instructor directs you to do so.

Source-Based Topics

Each essay developed from these suggested source-based topics should include at least one reference to the reading selection by the author's name and the title. Quotations should be enclosed in quotation marks. Follow your instructor's directions in documenting the ideas you borrow. Whether you use informal or formal documentation, the form is not complicated, and you will soon learn to use it for these essays without checking each time. See pages 77 and 78 for a discussion of MLA style and informal documentation.

Underlining and annotating reading selections will help you in finding support material. In prewriting brief essays, consider marking your outline to indicate where you will use quotations or other borrowed ideas. If the quotations or reworded statements are short and few, you could even insert them inside parentheses or circles in your outline; if you do, also include the author's last name and the page number. A sound system, consistently used, will save you time and ensure technically strong papers.

"Kick Me! Kiss Me!"

1. Write about a similar case of physical abuse (child or spousal). Concentrate on either the causes or the effects.

2. Write about the effects of verbal abuse on an individual you know.

"It's Time to KO Boxing"

3. Take the other side of the argument, that boxing is worthwhile, has many good features, and can and should be preserved. Use your own sources, and, perhaps, refer to Dunlop's argument.

4. Write a critique of Dunlop's essay in which you take issue with his points one at a time. Use your own sources for your refutation of his ideas.

5. Write about another sport, such as hockey or football, that arguably should be regulated, especially at the youth level.

"Why Marriages Fail"

6. Explain the effects of a divorce on a person you know, either the child of divorced parents or a partner in a divorce. Consider both the immediate and the long-range effects. Don't forget that Roiphe maintains that divorce is not necessarily a bad idea.

7. Roiphe says that "we all select with unconscious accuracy a mate who will recreate with us the emotional patterns of our first homes" (paragraph 3). Either agree or disagree with that statement and support your views by discussing the causal factors in a marriage you are familiar with.

8. Discuss an ideal marriage (a particular one, if possible) and explain what made it that way (causes). Consider paragraphs 8 through 13 for ideas on what Roiphe believes makes a good marriage.

9. Roiphe says, "People can overcome the habits and attitudes that developed in childhood." Write an essay in which you show that she is right, or one in which you point out the difficulties in overcoming those habits and attitudes. Use specific examples and stress the causes or effects.

"Romantic Love, Courtship, and Marriage"

10. Write a piece in which you relate all or most of the six "characteristics that seem to attract people to one another" to a marriage or a relationship you are familiar with (paragraphs 11 through 16). Your example may support Robertson's views or it may show that a marriage can be very good, even though the partners do not share several of the six characteristics.

11. Write about a marriage that failed because the partners were too different, that is, they shared few or none of the six characteristics.

12. Write an essay in which you argue that the assets that prospective mates try to "sell" each other on (appearance, charm, common interests, career prospects) either are or are not more important than the six characteristics that attract people to each other. Use references to the article and your own examples.

13. Write an essay in which you rank the six "characteristics that seem to attract people to one another" and explain the reason for your ranking.

14. Apply the six "characteristics that seem to attract people to one another" to a particular culture other than middle-class American. Which ones fit? Which ones do not? To what degree do some fit?

15. Discuss to what extent the six characteristics apply to same-sex relationships.

"Female Mea Culpa"

16. Write an essay in which you discuss why you think it would or would not be easier (stressing effects) if men and women came with a list of their likes and dislikes, perhaps exchanging lists along with wedding vows. Should there be negotiations?

17. Write a male version of this essay, or write a modification of this female version.

18. Pick several statements by Rolens and write an essay with a paragraph about each one, stressing causes, effects, or both on relationships.

    Suggestions: "Women of sensibility never have too many flowers" (paragraph 5).

    "We don't want to tell you what we want" (paragraph 7).

    "Truly being listened to is one of life's great luxuries" (paragraph 8).

    "Food is not just food" (paragraph 12).

"His Marriage and Hers: Childhood Roots"

19. Using Goleman's ideas and your own experiences, discuss the differences that exist between men's and women's ways of expressing themselves.

20. Write about a marriage you are familiar with and discuss the relationship in terms of communication and "emotional intelligence" (paragraph 11).

Multiple Sources on Love, Marriage, and Divorce

21. Consider the relationship between a couple you know or know about and write of the causes of their problems in terms of insights found in two or more of the multiple sources.

22. Consider the relationship between a couple you know or know about and write of the effects of their problems in terms of insights found in two or more of the multiple sources.

23. Consider the relationship between a couple you know or know about and write of their successful relationship in terms of insights found in two or more of the multiple sources.

Career-Related Topics

24. Discuss the effects (benefits) of a particular product or service on a business community, family life, society generally, a specific group (age, income, interest), or an individual.

25. Discuss the needs (thus the cause of development) by individuals, families, or institutions for a particular product or type of product.

26. Discuss the effects of using a certain approach or philosophy in sales, human resources management, or customer service.

General Topics

Select one of the topics below as a subject (situation, circumstance, or trend) for your essay and then determine whether you will concentrate on causes, effects, or a combination.

27. Attending or completing college

28. Having or getting a job

29. Change in policy or administration

30. Change in coaches, teachers, officeholder(s)

31. Alcoholism

32. Gambling

33. Moving to another country, state, or home

34. Exercise

35. Passing or failing a test or course

36. Popularity of a certain TV program or song

37. Early marriage

You can probably write a more interesting, well-developed, and therefore successful essay on a topic you can personalize. For example, a discussion about a specific young person who contemplated, attempted, or committed suicide is probably a better topic idea than a general discussion of suicide. If you do not personalize the topic, you will probably have to do some basic research to supply details for development.

Writer's Guidelines: Cause and Effect

1. Determine whether your topic should mainly inform or mainly persuade, and use the right tone for your purpose and audience.

2. Use listing to brainstorm cause-and-effect ideas. This is a useful form:

Causes	Event, Situation, or Trend	Effects
1.		1.
2.		2.
3.		3.
4.		4.

3. Decide whether to concentrate on causes, effects, or a combination of causes and effects. Short essays generally discuss causes and effects but will use one as the framework for the piece. A typical basic outline might look like this:

   Thesis of the essay

      I. Cause or Effect 1

     II. Cause or Effect 2

    III. Cause or Effect 3

4. Do not conclude that something is an effect merely because it follows something else in time.

5. Emphasize your main concern(s)—causes, effects, or a combination—by repeating key words such as *cause, reason, effect, result, consequence,* and *outcome.*

6. Causes and effects can be primary or secondary, immediate or remote.

7. The order of causes and effects in your paper may be based on time, space, emphasis, or a combination.

Definition:
Clarifying Terms

THE QUIGMANS   by Buddy Hickerson

"I don't care if all my friends say you're primitive,
Sven. I love you from your sloping, suborbital-
ridge forehead to your hairy, prehensile toes."

© Tribune Media Services, Inc. All Rights Reserved. Reprinted with
permission.

Writing Definition

ost definitions are short; they consist of a *synonym* (a word or phrase that has about the same meaning as the term to be defined), a phrase, or a sentence. For example, we might say that a hypocrite is a person "professing beliefs or virtues he or she does not possess." Terms can also be defined by *etymology,* or word history. *Hypocrite* once meant "actor" (*hypocrites*) in Greek because an actor was pretending to be someone else. We may find this information interesting and revealing, but the history of a word may be of little or no use because the meaning has changed drastically over the years. Definitions can occupy an entire essay. The short definition is called a *simple definition;* the longer one is known as an *extended definition.*

Techniques for Writing Simple Definitions

If you want to define a term without being abrupt and mechanical, you have several alternatives. All of the following techniques allow you to blend the definition into your developing thought.

- *Basic dictionary meaning.* You can quote the dictionary's definition, but if you do, you are obliged to indicate your source, which you should do directly and explicitly. Always give the complete title of the dictionary, such as "*The American Heritage Dictionary* says," not simply "Webster says." Dozens of dictionaries use the "Webster" designation.

- *Synonyms.* Although no two words have exactly the same meaning, synonyms often follow as if in parentheses.

Example: He was guilty of the ancient sin of *hubris,* of excessive pride.

- *Direct explanation.* You can state the definition.

Example: This spontaneous and loyal support of our preconception—this process of finding "good" reasons to justify our routine beliefs—is known to modern psychologists as *rationalizing*—clearly a new name for a very ancient thing.

James Harvey Robinson, "On Various Kinds of Thinking"

- *Indirect explanation.* You can imply the definition.

Example: Trance is a similar abnormality in our society. Even a mild mystic is *aberrant* in Western civilization.

Ruth Benedict, *Patterns of Culture*

- *Analytical or formal definition.* In using this method, you define by placing the term (the subject) in a class (genus) and then identifying it with characteristics that show how it differs from other members of the same class, as the following examples show:

Subject	Class	Characteristics
A democracy	is a form of government	in which voters elect representatives to manage society.
A wolf	is a dog-like mammal	that is large and carnivorous, with coarse fur, erect, pointed ears, and a bushy tail.
Jazz	is a style of music	that features improvisation and performance.

Exercise 1   **WRITING SIMPLE DEFINITIONS**

Complete the following formal definitions.
Answers will vary.

Subject	Class	Characteristics
1. A workaholic	is a person	who lives to work instead of works to live.
2. Dreadlocks	is a natural hairstyle	in which hair is twisted into long matted or ropelike locks.
3. A hawk	is a bird of prey	that has a short, hooked bill and strong claws.
4. Hay fever	is an allergic condition	affecting the mucous membranes of the upper respiratory tract and the eyes, causing sneezing, runny nose, and itchy, watery eyes.
5. A muumuu	is a dress	made of loose material that hangs free from the shoulders.
6. Bongos	are two connected drums	that are fine-tuned and played by beating with hands.
7. A patriot	is an individual	who loves, supports, and defends his or her country.
8. A desert	is a large land area	that is dry, supports few plants, and has extreme temperatures.
9. Jealousy	is a state of mind	characterized by envy, suspicion, and fear.
10. Sociology	is the study of human behavior	with emphasis on the origins, organization, institutions, and development of human society.

Dictionary Entries—Which One to Use

Suppose that you do not know the meaning of the term in italics in the following sentence:

> That kind of cactus is *indigenous* to the Mojave Desert.

As you consider the term in context, you look at the dictionary definitions.

in•dig•e•nous (ĭn-dĭj´ə-nəs) *adj.* **1.** Originating and living or occurring naturally in an area or environment. See synonyms at native **2.** Intrinsic; innate. [From Latin *indigena,* a native. See INDIGEN.]

The first definition seems to fit the context of *indigenous.* It is followed by a reference: See synonyms at **native.** Then you look at the second set of definitions: "Intrinstic, innate." The words are synonyms. You can see that only *native* fits. To provide more information for the reader, the dictionary also presents *native* with a special treatment of synonyms as indicated by the reference.

Looking under the word *native,* you find this definition:

Synonyms   *native, indigenous, endemic, autochthonous, aboriginal*   These adjectives mean of, belonging to, or connected with a specific place or country by virtue of birth or origin. *Native* implies birth or origin in the specified place: *a native New Yorker; the native North American sugar maple. Indigenous* specifies that something or someone is native rather than coming or being brought in from elsewhere: *an indigenous crop; the Ainu, a people indigenous to the northernmost islands of Japan.* Something *endemic* is prevalent in or peculiar to a particular locality or people: *endemic disease. Autochthonous* applies to what is native and unchanged by outside sources: *autochthonous folk melodies. Aboriginal* describes what has existed from the beginning; it is often applied to the earliest known inhabitants of a place: *the aboriginal population; aboriginal nature.* See also synonyms at **crude.**

Usage Note   When used in reference to a member of an indigenous people, the noun *native,* like its synonym *aborigine,* can evoke unwelcome stereotypes of primitiveness or cultural backwardness that many people now seek to avoid. As is often the case with words that categorize people, the use of the noun is more problematic than the use of the corresponding adjective. Thus a phrase such as *the peoples native to northern Europe* or *the aboriginal inhabitants of the South Pacific* is generally much preferable to *the natives of northern Europe* or *the aborigines of the South Pacific.* • Despite its potentially negative connotations, *native* is enjoying increasing popularity in ethnonyms such as *native Australian* and *Alaska Native,* perhaps due to the wide acceptance of *Native American* as a term of ethnic pride and respect. These compounds have the further benefit of being equally acceptable when used alone as nouns (*a native Australian*) or in an adjectival construction (*a member of a native Australian people*). Of terms formed on this model, those referring to peoples indigenous to the United States generally capitalize *native*, as in *Alaska Native* (or the less common *Native Alaskan*) and *Native Hawaiian*, while others usually style it lowercase.

In the synonyms at the close of the entry, did you observe the various shades of meaning, especially the meaning of *indigenous* and *native?* A dictionary is an invaluable aid to definition, but it must be used with care if you want to express yourself clearly and precisely. No two words have exactly the same meaning, and a word may have many meanings, some that extend to very different concepts.

Avoiding Common Problems

- Do not use the expression *is where* or *is when* in beginning the main part of the definition. The verb *is* (a linking verb) should be followed by a noun, a pronoun, or an adjective.

Weak: A stadium is where they hold sports spectaculars.

Better A stadium is a structure in which sports spectaculars are held.

Weak: Socialism is when the ownership and operation of the means of production and distribution are vested in the community as a whole.

Better: Socialism is a theory or system of community organization that advocates that the ownership and control of the means of production, capital, land, and so forth, be vested in the community as a whole.

- Do not use the *circular definition*, a practice of defining a term with the term itself.

Circular: An aristocracy is a form of government based on rule by the aristocrats.

Direct: An aristocracy is a form of government in which the power resides in the hands of the best individuals or a small privileged class.

- Do not define the subject in more complicated language than the original.

Murky: *Surreptitious* means "clandestine."

Clear: *Surreptitious* means "secret."

- Do not substitute the example for the definition; the example may be excellent for clarification, but it does not completely define.

Weak: Political conservatives are people like William F. Buckley, Jr., and Pat Robertson.

Better: Political conservatives are people who are dedicated to preserving existing conditions. Examples of conservatives are William F. Buckley, Jr., and Pat Robertson.

Techniques for Writing Extended Definitions

Essays of definition can take many forms. Among the more common techniques for writing a short essay of definition are the patterns we have worked with in previous chapters. Consider each of those patterns when you need to write an extended definition. For a particular term, some forms will be more useful than others; use the pattern or patterns that best fulfill your purpose.

Each of the following questions takes a pattern of writing and directs it toward definition.

- *Narration:* Can I tell an anecdote or story to define this subject (such as *jerk, humanitarian,* or *citizen*)? This form may overlap with description and exemplification.

- *Description:* Can I describe this subject (such as *a whale* or *the moon*)?

- *Exemplification:* Can I give examples of this subject (such as naming individuals, to provide examples of *actors, diplomats,* or *satirists*)?

- *Analysis by Division:* Can I divide this subject into parts (for example, the parts of a *heart, cell,* or *carburetor*)?

- *Process Analysis:* Can I define this subject (such as *lasagna, tornado, hurricane, blood pressure,* or any number of scientific processes) by describing how to make it or how it occurs? (Common to the methodology of communicating in science, this approach is sometimes called the "operational definition.")

- *Cause and Effect:* Can I define this subject (such as *a flood, a drought, a riot,* or *a cancer*) by its causes and effects?

- *Classification:* Can I group this subject (such as kinds of *families, cultures, religions,* or *governments*) into classes?

Subject	*Class*	*Characteristics*
A republic	is a form of government	in which power resides in the people (the electorate).

- *Comparison and Contrast.* Can I define this subject (such as *extremist* or *patriot*) by explaining what it is similar to and different from?

If you are defining *orangutan* to a person who has never heard of one but is familiar with the gorilla, then you could make comparison-and-contrast statements. If you want to define *patriot,* then you might want to stress what it is not (the contrast) before you explain what it is: a patriot is not a one-dimensional flag waver, not someone who hates "foreigners" because America is always right and always best.

When you use prewriting strategies to develop ideas for a definition, you can effectively consider all the patterns you have learned by using a modified clustering form (Figure 13.1). Put a double bubble around the subject to be defined. Then put a single bubble around each pattern and add appropriate words, extending from that pattern. If a pattern is not

Figure 13.1
Bubble cluster showing how a term could be defined using different essay patterns.

relevant to what you are defining, leave it blank. If you want to expand your range of information, you could add a bubble for a simple dictionary definition and another for an etymological definition.

Order

The organization of your extended definition is likely to be one of emphasis, but it may be space or time, depending on the subject material. You may use just one pattern of development, such as narration or analysis by division, for the overall sequence. If so, you would use the principles of organization discussed in previous chapters.

Introduction and Development

Consider these ways of introducing a definition: with a question, with a statement of what it is not, with a statement of what it originally meant, or with a discussion of why a clear definition is important. You may use a combination of these ways or all of them before you continue with your definition.

Development is likely to represent one or more of the patterns of narration, description, exposition (with its own subdivisions), and argumentation.

Whether you personalize a definition depends on your purpose and your audience. Your instructor may ask you to write about a word from a subjective or objective viewpoint.

Connecting Sources and Writing

Student Documented Essay (Single Source)

The assignment was to read several essays related to health and write a documented essay of extended definition about one health condition as it related to the student's experience. The final product would include at least two quotations and several paraphrases from the source, each to be formally identified. The source would be listed at the end, according to MLA form for an article in an anthology. (Your instructor may not ask you to formally document an essay based on a single textbook source.)

My-graines

Vincent Sheahan

The aura set in like a suffocating stillness before a tropical storm. "This is going to be a bad one," I told myself as I shut off the lights, took my medication, lay down, and prepared for the inevitable—the relentless throbbing in my temple. About three hours of incapacitating agony later, I recovered, feeling strangely drained, and skimmed through my reading assignment for my college English class. What a coincidence! It included "In Bed," an essay about migraines by Joan Didion. Because I had only recently been diagnosed with migraines (although I had long suffered), I naturally had enormous curiosity about the subject, and now homework coincided with my private need for information. By closely comparing my family history, my triggers for attacks, and my personality with Joan Didion's, perhaps I could find some informed answers to my questions and be able to define *migraines* more precisely.

A year ago when I decided to seek medical help, the matter of family history was of immediate concern. At my first appointment, my neurologist informed me that, although no one knows why, migraines tend to run in families. I said the only person in my family who has migraines is my Uncle Joe, my father's brother. For Didion, the family connection is more apparent and pervasive: Both of her grandmothers, her father, and her mother all suffer from migraine headaches. But she does go on to explain, "One inherits, of course, only the predisposition" (59). Therefore, it is possible that everyone on my father's side has carried the gene for migraines, but only Uncle Joe has ever actually developed the headaches.

After the doctor asked his questions, I had one of my own: What actually causes migraine headaches? I was fearful that my job as an emergency medical technician (E.M.T.), with its debilitating stress and irregular hours, was the main reason. He explained that the exact causes are not completely understood and that my fatigue and irregular sleep patterns are not the causes of my migraines, because there are plenty of E.M.T.s who have the same sleep patterns as I do yet do not have migraines. Nevertheless, the fatigue and irregular sleep may trigger migraine headaches. For Didion, the triggers are varied. She says, "Almost anything can trigger a specific attack of migraine: stress, allergy, fatigue, an abrupt change in barometric pressure, a contretemps over a parking ticket. A flashing light. A fire drill" (60). Yet she explains that her headaches are not triggered at times when she needs to be alert and thinking clearly, such as an emergency situation, but instead, they are triggered when she is feeling overwhelmed or extremely stressed (60).

In addition to the exposure to these triggers, a migraine sufferer like me usually has what is called a "migraine personality." Didion offers a good definition of that term, saying that she is typical, a perfectionist who is "ambitious, inward, intolerant of error, rather rigidly organized" (60). But she points out that not all perfectionists have migraines and not all people with migraines are perfectionists. She says that she is a perfectionist about writing, not housekeeping (60). And, as for me, I try—probably harder than most—to be organized when it comes to my education, work, and personal life.

Like Joan Didion, I am intensely interested in migraines, and I am learning about them. We migraine sufferers have much in common, though each of us has his or her own family history of migraines, triggers, and migraine personality. Knowing that others go through what I do and having more information about my condition make it easier for me to deal with the pain of my migraines. I will continue to do the same thing Joan Didion does when she has an aura: I won't try to fight it. I will lie down and endure. When it's finally over, I will count my blessings.

Work Cited

Didion, Joan. "In Bed." *Health Views.* Ed. Marjorie Ford and Jon Ford. Boston: Houghton Mifflin, 1998. 58–61.

Exercise 2   **DISCUSSION AND CRITICAL THINKING**

1. Circle the thesis and underline the topic sentences in the support paragraphs.

2. Forms of writing other than definition are often used to define. Which form provides structure for this extended definition?
Comparison and contrast.

3. How is Sheahan's introduction connected to his conclusion?
Both are concerned with an aura and an attack, the first as it occurred and the last hypothetically.

4. How do you explain Sheahan's change of verb tenses?
He uses past tense in referring to his experiences and in making observations. He uses present tense in discussing Didion's ongoing condition and his ongoing condition.

Practicing Patterns of Definition

Doing the following exercise will help you remember the patterns of writing used in extended definitions.

| Exercise 3 | COMPLETING PATTERNS OF DEFINITION |

Fill in the double bubble with a term to be defined. You might want to define culturally diverse society, educated person, leader, role model, friend, infatuation, true love, success, or intelligence. Then complete a bubble on the right for each paragraph or essay pattern. If the pattern does not apply (that is, if it would not provide useful information for your definition), mark it NA ("not applicable). If you were actually writing an essay on the topic you selected, you would use ideas from your cluster to form points in an outline.

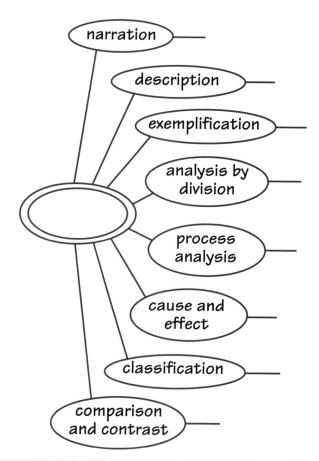

Student Documented Essay (Multiple Sources)

The assignment was to write an extended definition of an abstract term used in a college subject other than English. Proctor, a current student in Psychology 3, selected *motivation*. She was expected to use at least three sources from which she would quote and paraphrase. Her English instruc-

tor pointed out that she could include discussion of more than one definition, an approach that fit her term.

Perspectives on Motivation

Michelle Proctor

What is *motivation?* It is basically defined as any action or behavior that drives people to satisfy their biological or psychological needs.
There are three very good theories that give different perspectives
on motivation: Darwin's Instinct Theory, Hull's Drive Reduction Theory, and Maslow's Hierarchy of Needs Theory.

Charles Darwin's Instinct Theory explains that our basic
instincts are what motivate us. The salmon's basic instincts tell it
when to swim a thousand miles across an ocean to a river and up
into the gravel bed where it was spawned years before and where it
will spawn now. Instinct theorists regard motivation in several
ways. They believe our curiosity drives us to learn and acquire
more. Our jealousy of others and yet our fearfulness of being alone
motivates us to behave, while our needs of sociability lead us to do
many things in order to be accepted. This theory seems to be good
for defining much biological motivation, but it does not explain
much of behavior. Douglas A. Bernstein points out that theorists
have "named more than 10,000 instincts" and that instincts have
"become meaningless labels describing behavior without explaining
it" (259).

The Drive Reduction Theory was brought forth in 1943 by Clark
Hull. He believed motivation came from primary drives and secondary or acquired drives. Primary drives are the need for sleep,
food, water, and other basic needs. Secondary needs would be our
affiliation with others and our contact with them. If a person were
dying of thirst and came to a town where he could find water, then
the primary need would be to get water while his secondary need
would be to socialize with the townspeople. The fault in Drive
Reduction Theory is that after our primary needs have been filled,
our behavior does not stop. Our relationship with our environment
is a good example of this. In earlier years we were motivated by a
need to survive in our environment. Now that that need has been
met, we still want to master our environment to the point that we
may pollute it until no one will survive. Connecting with our
everyday experience, Rod Plotnik says that "drive-reduction theory
has difficulty explaining why, after we satisfy our hunger need with
a complete meal, and say we are full, we then eat a dessert" (330).

Margin annotations:

Example

Division
Cause and effect

Division

Example
Cause and effect

Example

Division

Cause and effect

Cause and effect

Comparison and contrast

The third theory on motivation came from Abraham Maslow in 1970. <u>Maslow's Hierarchy of Needs is explained in a pyramid of five steps, starting from the lowest need, the biological, to the highest need, self-actualization.</u> Each step may be reached only by the completion of the previous step. In Maslow's pyramid the first need that must be met is biological. This contains our basic needs of food, water, and sleep. After that has been fulfilled, then safety must be met. We must be physically and psychologically secure in our environment and our surroundings to reach the next stage of love and belongingness. Here we must be able to love someone or something to receive love in return. This is where step four, self-esteem, comes into play, and self-esteem must be very high for us to reach the final step, self-actualization. Of course, not all people do that. In *Theories and Systems of Psychology,* Robert Lundin says, "Maslow allows that only a small percentage (perhaps 10 percent) of people really become self-actualized, or 'fully human'" (373). Maslow himself says, "There are no perfect human beings" (Lundin 374). But to some extent, we can all accept our environment and work to help others learn and survive in their surroundings.

The first two theories define *motivation* primarily on the basis of our biological needs. Both contributed valuable insights into our understanding of why we behave as we do. Maslow was able to build on the ideas the other social scientists had developed. His Hierarchy of Needs is more comprehensive, offering a combination of biological and psychological needs. It represents the best definition we now have.

Works Cited

Bernstein, Douglas A., and Peggy W. Nash. *Essentials of Psychology.* 2nd ed. Boston: Houghton Mifflin, 2002.

Lundin, Robert W. *Theories and Systems of Psychology.* 5th ed. Lexington, Mass.: D.C. Heath, 1996.

Plotnik, Rod. *Introduction to Psychology.* 5th ed. Belmont, Calif.: Wadsworth, 1999.

Exercise 4   **DISCUSSION AND CRITICAL THINKING**

1. Is the purpose mainly to persuade or to inform?
    To inform.

2. Underline definitions in the second, third, and fourth paragraphs.

3. In the left margin, annotate the text by indicating the form(s) of discourse used for defining: example, analysis by division, comparison and contrast, cause and effect.

4. If Proctor uses one form more than others, list it here.
Cause and effect, the form used in the second, third, and fourth paragraphs.

5. Circle the sentence that best defines *motivation*.

Paired Sources on Bullying

Few people go through school without being bullied. The victims may also at times be the perpetrators. Bullies come in different guises and in different sexes. Their destructive work takes different forms. In "Disarming the Rage," the team of reporters says, "Children all over the country are feeling fear, hopelessness and rage, emotions that turn some of them into bullies and others into their victims." In the companion essay, "Bully, Bully," John Leo acknowledges a severe problem but sees part of the current concern over bullying to be an overreaction. He says that some of us have been "taking a lot of harmless and minor things ordinary children do and turning them into examples of bullying." The difference between the views of these two essays must begin with definitions. What is a bully? What is bullying?

Disarming the Rage

Richard Jerome, Ron Arias, Mary Boone, Lauren Comander, Joanne Fowler, Maureen Marrington, Ellen Mazo, Jamie Reno, Don Sider, Gail Cameron Wescott

This team of *People* magazine writers reports on efforts in the United States to curb bullying in schools in response to school shootings. In brief case studies, they explain how acts of violent reprisals are linked to bullying and define *bullying, bullies,* and *victims.*

1   Across the country, thousands of students stay home from school each day, terrified of humiliation or worse at the hands of bullies. In the wake of school shootings—most recently in

California and Pennsylvania—parents, teachers and lawmakers are demanding quick action.

Example

Description

Narration

Cause and effect

Example

2   In the rigid social system of Bethel Regional High School in Bethel, a remote town in the tundra of southwest Alaska, Evan Ramsey was an outcast, a status earned by his slight frame, shy manner, poor grades and broken family. "Everybody had given me a nickname: Screech, the nerdy character on *Saved by the Bell,*" he recalls. "I got stuff thrown at me, I got spit on, I got beat up. Sometimes I fought back, but I wasn't that good at fighting." Taunted throughout his years in school, he reported the incidents to his teachers, and at first his tormentors were punished. "After a while [the principal] told me to just start ignoring everybody. But then you can't take it anymore."

3   On the morning of Feb. 19, 1997, Ramsey, then 16, went to school with a 12-gauge shotgun, walked to a crowded common area and opened fire. As schoolmates fled screaming, he roamed the halls shooting randomly—mostly into the air. Ramsey would finally surrender to police, but not before killing basketball star Josh Palacios, 16, with a blast to the stomach, and principal Ron Edwards, 50, who was shot in the back. Tried as an adult for murder, Ramsey was sentenced to 210 years in prison after a jury rejected a defense contention that he had been attempting "suicide by cop," hoping to be gunned down but not intending to kill anyone. Still, Ramsey now admits in his cell at Spring Creek Correctional Center in Seward, Alaska, "I felt a sense of power with a gun. It was the only way to get rid of the anger."

4   Unfortunately Ramsey is not alone. Children all over the country are feeling fear, hopelessness and rage, emotions that turn some of them into bullies and others into their victims. Some say that is how it has always been and always will be—that bullying, like other adolescent ills, is something to be endured and to grow out of. But that view is changing. At a time when many parents are afraid to send their children to school, the wake-up call sounded by the 13 killings and 2 suicides at Columbine High School in Colorado two years ago still reverberates. It is now clear that Columbine shooters Dylan Klebold and Eric Harris felt bullied and alienated, and in their minds it was payback time.

5   In recent months there have been two other horrifying shooting incidents resulting, at least in part, from bullying. On March 5, 15-year-old Charles "Andy" Williams brought a .22-cal. pistol to Santana High School in Santee, Calif., and shot 15 students and adults, killing 2. He was recently certified to stand trial for murder as an adult. His apparent motive? Lethal revenge for the torment

he had known at the hands of local kids. "We abused him pretty much, I mean verbally," concedes one of them. "I called him a skinny faggot one time."

Example
Cause and effect

6   Two days after the Williams shooting, Elizabeth Bush, 14, an eighth grader from Williamsport, Pa., who said she was often called "idiot, stupid, fat, ugly," brought her father's .22-cal. pistol to school and shot 13-year-old Kimberly Marchese, wounding her in the shoulder. Kimberly, one of her few friends, had earned Elizabeth's ire by allegedly turning on her and joining in with the taunters. Bush admitted her guilt and offered apologies. A ward of the court until after she turns 21, she is now in a juvenile psychiatric facility. Kimberly, meanwhile, still has bullet fragments in her shoulder and is undergoing physical therapy.

Cause and effect

7   As school enrollment rises and youths cope with the mounting pressures of today's competitive and status-conscious culture, the numbers of bullied children have grown as rapidly as the consequences. According to the National Education Association, 160,000 children skip school each day because of intimidation by their peers. The U.S. Department of Education reports that 77 percent of middle and high school students in small midwestern towns have been bullied. And a National Institutes of Health study newly released in the *Journal of the American Medical Association* reveals that almost a third of 6th to 10th graders—5.7 million children nationwide—have experienced some kind of bullying. "We are talking about a significant problem," says Deborah Prothrow-Stith, professor of public health practice at Harvard, who cites emotional alienation at home as another factor in creating bullies. "A lot of kids have grief, loss, pain, and it's unresolved."

Cause and effect

8   Some experts see bullying as an inevitable consequence of a culture that rewards perceived strength and dominance. "The concept of power we admire is power over someone else," says Jackson Katz, 41, whose Long Beach, Calif., consulting firm counsels schools and the military on violence prevention. "In corporate culture, in sports culture, in the media, we honor those who win at all costs. The bully is a kind of hero in our society." Perhaps not surprisingly, most bullies are male. "Our culture defines masculinity as connected to power, control and dominance," notes Katz, whose work was inspired in part by the shame he felt in high school when he once stood idly by while a bully beat up a smaller student.

Cause and effect

9   As for the targets of bullying, alienation runs like a stitch through most of their lives. A study last fall by the U.S. Secret Service found that in two-thirds of the 37 school shootings since 1974, the attackers felt "persecuted, bullied, threatened, attacked or injured." In

more than three-quarters of the cases, the attacker told a peer of his violent intentions. William Pollack, a clinical psychologist and author of *Real Boys' Voices,* who contributed to the Secret Service study, said that several boys from Columbine described bullying as part of the school fabric. Two admitted to mocking Klebold and Harris. "Why don't people get it that it drives you over the edge?" they told Pollack. "It isn't just Columbine. It is everywhere."

Example

10   That sad fact is beginning to sink in, as the spate of disturbing incidents in recent years has set off desperate searches for answers. In response, parents have begun crusades to warn and educate other families, courts have seen drawn-out legal battles that try to determine who is ultimately responsible, and lawmakers in several states—including Texas, New York and Massachusetts—have struggled to shape anti-bullying legislation that would offer remedies ranging from early intervention and counseling to the automatic expulsion of offenders.

11   One of the most shocking cases of victimization by bullies took place near Atlanta on March 28, 1994. That day, 15-year-old Brian Head, a heavyset sophomore at suburban Etowah High School, walked into economics class, pulled out his father's 9-mm handgun and pressed it to his temple. "I can't take this anymore," he said. Then he squeezed the trigger. Brian had been teased for years about his weight. "A lot of times the more popular or athletic kids would make him a target," his mother, Rita, 43, says of her only child, a sensitive boy with a gift for poetry. "They would slap Brian in the back of the head or push him into a locker. It just broke him." Not a single student was disciplined in connection with his death. After his suicide, Rita, a magazine copy editor, and her husband, Bill, 47, counseled other parents and produced a video for elementary school students titled *But Names Will Never Hurt Me* about an overweight girl who suffers relentless teasing.

Example

12   Georgia residents were stunned by a second child's death on Nov. 2, 1998. After stepping off a school bus, 13-year-old Josh Belluardo was fatally punched by his neighbor Jonathan Miller, 15, who had been suspended in the past for bullying and other infractions. In that tragedy's wake Georgia Gov. Roy Barnes in 1999 signed an anti-bullying law that allows schools to expel any student three times disciplined for picking on others.

Example

Narration

13   On the other side of the continent, Washington Gov. Gary Locke is pressing for anti-bullying training in schools, following two high-profile cases there. Jenny Wieland of Seattle still cannot talk of her only child, Amy Ragan, shot dead at age 17 more than eight years ago, without tearing up. A soccer player and equestrian in her senior year at Marysville-Pilchuck High School, Amy was heading

Example

to the mall on the night of Nov. 20, 1992, when she stopped at a friend's apartment. There, three schoolmates had gathered by the time Trevor Oscar Turner showed up. Then 19, Turner was showing off a .38-cal. revolver, holding it to kids' heads, and when he got to Amy, the weapon went off. Turner pleaded guilty to first-degree manslaughter and served 27 months of a 41-month sentence.

14   "I can't help but wonder what Amy's life would be like if she was still alive," says Wieland today. "I wonder about her career and if she'd be in love or have a baby." Wieland turned her grief into action. In 1994 she helped start Mothers Against Violence in America (MAVIA), an activist group patterned after Mothers Against Drunk Driving. She left her insurance job to become the program's director and speaks annually at 50 schools. In 1998 she became the first director of SAVE (Students Against Violence Everywhere), which continues to grow, now boasting 126 student chapters nationwide that offer schools anti-harassment and conflict-resolution programs. "People ask how I can stand to tell her story over and over," she says. "If I can save just one child, it's well worth the pain."

Example
Narration

15   Not long after Amy Ragan's death, another bullying scenario unfolded 50 miles away in Stanwood, Wash. Confined to a wheelchair by cerebral palsy, Calcutta-born Taya Haugstad was a fifth grader in 1993, when a boy began calling her "bitch" and "retard." The daily verbal abuse led to terrible nightmares. By middle school, according to a lawsuit Taya later filed, her tormentor—a popular athlete—got physical, pushing her wheelchair into the wall and holding it while his friends kicked the wheels. Eventually Taya was diagnosed with posttraumatic stress disorder. "Imagine that you can't run away or scream," says her psychologist, Judith McCarthy. "Not only was she traumatized, she's handicapped. She felt terribly unsafe in the world." Her adoptive parents, Karrie and Ken Haugstad, 48 and 55, complained to school authorities and went to court to get a restraining order against the bully, but it was never issued. Taya sued the school district and the boy in 1999.

Cause and effect

The judge awarded her $300,000 last year, ruling that the school was negligent in its supervision, thus inflicting emotional distress. (The ruling is under appeal.) Taya, now 19 and a high school junior, hopes to study writing in college. She says she holds no grudge against her nemesis, who received undisclosed punishment from the school. "I don't think about him," she says.

Example

16   But Josh Sneed may never forgive the boys he refers to as the Skaters. It was in 1996, late in his freshman year at Powell High School in Powell, Tenn., when, he says, a group of skateboarders began to terrorize him. With chains clinking and baseball bats

Narration

pounding the pavement, he claims, they chased him and threatened to beat him to death. Why Josh? He was small and "a country boy," says his homemaker mother, Karen Grady, 41. "They made fun of him for that. They told him he was poor and made fun of him for that."

Narration

17   Then on Oct. 17, 1996, "I just snapped," her son says. As Jason Pratt, known as one of the Skaters, passed him in the cafeteria, Sneed whacked him on the head with a tray. "I figured if I got lucky and took him out, all the other nonsense would stop." But after a few punches, Josh slipped on a scrap of food, hit his head on the floor and lost consciousness as Pratt kneed him in the head several times. Finally a football player leapt over two tables and dragged Sneed away, likely saving his life. Four titanium plates were needed to secure his shattered skull, and he was so gravely injured that he had to relearn how to walk and talk. Home-schooled, Sneed eventually earned his GED, but he hasn't regained his short-term memory. Assault charges against both him and Pratt were dismissed, but Pratt (who declined to comment) was suspended from school for 133 days.

18   Grady sued the county, claiming that because the school knew Josh was being terrorized but never disciplined the tormentors, they effectively sanctioned the conditions that led to the fight. Her attorney, James A.H. Bell, hopes the suit will have national implications. "We tried to make a statement, holding the school system accountable for its failure to protect," he says. In February Sneed and Grady were awarded $49,807 by a judge who found the county partly at fault. A tractor buff who once aspired to own a John Deere shop, Josh now lives on his grandfather's farm, passing his days with cartoons, video games and light chores. "Everybody's hollering that they need to get rid of guns, but it's not that," he says. "You need to find out what's going on in school."

19   Around the country, officials are attempting to do precisely that, as many states now require a safe-school plan that specifically addresses bullying. Most experts agree that metal detectors and zero-tolerance expulsions ignore the root of the problem. Counseling and fostering teamwork seem most effective, as evidenced by successful programs in the Cherry Creek, Colo., school district and DeKalb County, Ga. "We create an atmosphere of caring—it's harder to be a bully when you care about someone," says John Monferdini, head counselor at the DeKalb Alternative School, which serves 400 county students, most of whom have been expelled for bullying and violent behavior. Apart from academics, the school offers conflict-resolution courses and team-oriented outdoor activ-

ities that demand cooperation, "Yeah, I'm a bully," says Chris Jones, 15. "If I'm with friends and we see someone coming along we can jump on, we do it. It's like, you know, an adrenaline rush." But a stint in DeKalb is having a transformative effect. "When I came here, it was because we beat up a kid so badly—sticking his head in the bleachers—and the only thing I wished was that we'd had a chance to hurt him worse before we got caught. That's not the way I am now."

Example

20   One wonders if intervention might have restrained the bullies who tormented Evan Ramsey. Ineligible for parole until 2066, when he'll be 86, Ramsey, now 20, spends most days working out, playing cards, reading Stephen King novels and studying for his high school diploma. He also has plenty of time to reflect on the horrible error in judgment he made. "The worst thing is to resort to violence," he says. "I'd like to get letters from kids who are getting problems like I went through. I could write back and help them." His advice: "If they're being messed with, they have to tell someone. If nothing's done, then they have to go [to] higher and higher [authority] until it stops. If they don't get help, that's when they'll lose it and maybe do something bad—really bad. And the pain of doing that never really stops."

Exercise 5   **DISCUSSION AND CRITICAL THINKING**

1. Which two of the many forms used in defining terms—example, cause and effect, description, narration, and so on—do these authors use most extensively?
   Example and cause and effect.

2. Annotate the essay for the use of cause and effect, example, description, and narration. Note that some of the forms overlap.

3. Bullying is shown to be the immediate cause of many of the acts of violence discussed by the team of writers. What factors are suggested as two of the causes of the bullying? (See paragraph 7.)
   The mounting pressures of today's competitive and status-conscious culture and emotional alienation at home. Prothrow-Stith says, "A lot of kids have grief, loss, pain, and it's unresolved" (paragraph 7).

4. What are some of the feelings of emotional distress that both the bullies and the victims often share? (See paragraphs 4, 7, and 9.)
   Fear, hopelessness, rage, and alienation.

5. A single definition of bullying is not included. Compose a definition based on the material included in this essay.
   Answers will vary. Possible definition: Bullying is the repeated act of teasing, taunting, intimidating, or physically abusing a weaker person.

6. To what extent can school intervention curb bullying?
   Answers will vary.

7. Do you agree with Jackson Katz's view on the cultural causes of bullying: "The concept of power we admire is power over someone else. . . . In corporate culture, in sports culture, in the media, we honor those who win at all costs. The bully is a kind of hero in our society"?
   Answers will vary.

Bully, Bully

John Leo

John Leo, staff writer for *U.S. News and World Report,* offers his observations on the currently hot-button issue of bullying in the United States. Focusing on definitions in a national study, he argues that rumors and dirty looks and putting up with horrible classmates are all part of growing up and should not be classified as bullying.

Do Gossip and Rumors Count as Punishable Behavior?

1   Now we have a big national study on bullying, and the problem with it is right there in the first paragraph: Bullying behavior may be "verbal (e.g., name-calling, threats), physical (e.g., hitting), or psychological (e.g., rumors, shunning/exclusion)." Uh-oh. The study may or may not have put bullying on the map as a major national issue. But it rather clearly used a dubious tactic: taking a lot of harmless and minor things ordinary children do and turning them into examples of bullying. Calling somebody a jerk and spreading rumors counted as bullying in the study. Repeated teasing counted too. You achieved bully status if you didn't let the class creep into your game of catch, or if you just stayed away from people you didn't like (shunning, exclusion).

2   With a definition like that, the total of children involved in either bullying or being bullied themselves ought to be around 100 percent. But no, the bullying study says only 29.9 percent of the students studied reported frequent or moderate involvement—and that total was arrived at by lumping bullies and their victims together in the statistics.

3   **Debatable Definitions**   The low numbers and highly debatable definitions undercut the study's conclusion that bullying is "a

serious problem for U.S. youth." Of the 29.9 figure, 13.0 percent were bullies, 10.6 percent were targets of bullying, and 6.3 percent were both perpetrators and victims. The study, done by the National Institute of Child Health and Human Development, is based on 15,686 questionnaires filled out by students in grades six through 10 in public and private schools around the country.

4 We have seen this statistical blending of serious and trivial incidents before. The American Association of University Women produced a 1993 report showing that 80 percent of American students have been sexually harassed, including a hard-to-believe 76 percent of all boys. The AAUW got the numbers up that high by including glances, gestures, gossip, and naughty jokes. The elastic definition encouraged schools and courts to view many previously uncontroversial kinds of expression as sexual harassment. Before long, schools were making solemn lists of harassing behaviors that included winking, and calling someone "honey."

5 Another set of broad definitions appeared when zero-tolerance policies descended on the schools. Antidrug rules were extended to cover aspirin. Antiweapons regulations covered a rubber knife used in a school play. Just two months ago, a third grader in Monroe, La., was suspended for drawing a picture of G.I. Joe. Now the antibullying movement is poised to provide a third source of dubious hyperregulation of the young. One antibullying specialist says "hard looks" and "stare downs"—everyday activities for millions of hormone-driven adolescents—should be punishable offenses under student codes.

6 This has all the makings of an antibullying crusade with many of the same wretched excesses of the zero-tolerance and antiharassment campaigns. Serious bullying can be ugly. Parents and schools should stop it and punish offenders. And schools should do whatever they can to create a culture of civility and tolerance. But rumors and dirty looks and putting up with horrible classmates are a part of growing up. So are the teenage tendencies to form cliques and snub people now and then. Adults shouldn't faint when they see this behavior, or try to turn it into quasi-criminal activity.

7 Another pitfall: In focusing on gossip, rumors, and verbal offenses, the crusade has the obvious potential to infringe on free speech at schools. Will comments like "I think Catholicism is wrong," or "I think homosexuality is a sin," be turned into antibullying offenses? The crusade could also demonize those who bully, instead of helping them change. Some of the antibully litera-

ture circulating in Europe is hateful stuff. One screed calls "the serial bully" glib, shallow, evasive, incapable of intimacy, and a practiced liar who "displays a seemingly limitless demonic energy." Yet a lot of the academic literature reports that bullies often aren't very psychologically different from their victims. And the national study says a fifth of bullying victims are bullies themselves.

8   The example of Europe's more advanced antibullying crusade should make Americans cautious. The European campaign has expanded from schools into the adult world and the workplace. Several nations are considering antibullying laws, including Britain. Definitions are expanding too. A proposed antibullying law in Portugal would make it illegal to harass workers by giving them tasks for which they are overqualified. Deliberately giving employees erroneous information would count as bullying too. Ireland's antibullying task force came up with a scarily vague definition of bullying: "repeated inappropriate behavior, direct or indirect," which could "reasonably be regarded as undermining the individual's right to dignity at work." Imagine what the American litigation industry could do with wording like that.

9   It's time to stop and ask: Where is our antibullying campaign going?

Exercise 6	**DISCUSSION AND CRITICAL THINKING**

1. Circle the thesis sentence.

2. The definition in question defines *bullying* as "verbal, physical, or psychological" behavior directed against the victim. Of those three characteristics, which two does Leo find troublesome?
   Verbal and psychological.

3. Why does Leo find those two characteristics troublesome?
   To him, they are taken too broadly. "Verbal" can include mild name-calling (calling someone a "jerk"). "Psychological" can include using rumors and gossip or not mixing with those you don't like.

4. Does he have a good point in criticizing the definition or is he unfairly ridiculing the definition?
   Answers will vary. Obviously, someone in authority would have to interpret the rule. The rumors and gossip he mentions can be trivial, but they can also be destructive and traumatic. Not letting "the class creep into your game of catch" should not be considered bullying; not letting a person be a part of any significant activities both inside the classroom and out is not right.

5. Does Leo believe there should be no antibullying campaign?
   No. (See paragraph 6.) He just believes that this one "has all the makings" of going too far.

6. What does Leo have to say about bullying?
   "Parents and schools should stop it and punish offenders."

7. What part of the questioned definition does he say is actually part of growing up? (See paragraph 6.)
   "Rumors and dirty looks and putting up with horrible classmates."

8. How does Leo use comparison and contrast to evaluate the definition of *bullying,* according to the national study?
   In paragraphs 4 and 5, he compares the definitions of sexual harassment, illegal drugs, and weapons. In paragraph 8, he compares the definition of bullying at school in the United States with the definitions of bullying at work in Europe.

9. Leo does not provide us with his definition of *bullying.* Write a definition for him or explain what kind of regulation he would use to confront bullying.
   Answers will vary.

Paired Sources on Bosses and Workers, Good and Bad

Chances are, if you eavesdrop in a management meeting room, you will hear comments about good and bad workers. Conversely, if you listen in to a group gathering of workers, perspectives on good and bad bosses will be somewhere on the agenda. The paired sources here recognize that special workplace interest. The essay "You and Your Boss" relates directly to the restaurant business, but it has much broader applications. The interview "Why Many Good Workers Turn into Bad Bosses" focuses on roles and relationships.

You and Your Boss

Paul B. Hertneky

Of all businesses the typical person encounters, the food industry is probably the most visible. We watch the workers—the servers, the buspersons, the clerks, and the hosts and hostesses. We may even glimpse the kitchen personnel—the cooks and helpers. We may see less of the individual who oversees the operation, but the service and product we receive will certainly be affected by whether that person, called the boss, is "good" or "bad." This article was originally published in *Restaurant Hospitality*.

1   In the last thirty years, computers have shrunken from humongous to handheld. We can grow vegetables without dirt. We can watch television while getting a root canal. We can have breakfast in London and lunch in New York. But life with a boss has changed more slowly. Dilbert,* instead of Dagwood,[†] could just as easily be working for Mr. Dithers.[‡] And Ebenezer Scrooge[§] continues to remind us of bosses we've all known. Despite a tide of management books, seminars, and videotapes, and an invasion of MBAs, bosses will still be bosses.

2   In the restaurant business, managers come and go as independent operators and companies restructure their organizations. Mammoth foodservice firms serve stockholders above all others. Nearly everyone in this business reports to at least one boss. In fact, we have enough bosses, laid shoulder-to-shoulder, to sink Long Island. Vivienne Wildes, who runs The Waiters Association, bristles at the word "boss." She says it carries "negative connotations," preferring "supervisors" or "employers." Okay, enlightened bosses avoid bossing their employees around. They seek consensus and focus more on listening, drawing ideas from employees and developing their skills.

3   But the vast number of restaurants don't glow with enlightened bosses. Owners nicknamed "Vulture" and "Bubblebutt" bark orders, publicly humiliate, and harass their employees. Turnover rates are blamed on everything from low pay to transient workers, but veterans point to nasty, inept bosses.

4   Maryanne, a bartender who chose to remain anonymous, works part-time in four restaurants. Her experience spans a couple of decades and covers every job in the front of the house. She describes one of her bosses as a hands-off owner who pays well for competency; another as a chef for whom cooking and serving is a religion; another is a virginal owner and all-around nice guy; and yet another serves lousy food while tooling around on an ego trip.

5   Foodservice bosses come in more varieties than fried appetizers in a fern bar.[¶] But according to their employees, they share one dominant characteristic: a thriving ego. Their restaurants reflect their philosophies and lifestyles. Maryanne says "the best bosses I've had were chef/owners . . . their mission is clear and single-

---

*Dilbert is a contemporary cartoon character.
[†]Dagwood is a hapless cartoon character of the 1940s and 1950s.
[‡]Mr. Dithers is the boss who harasses Dagwood.
[§]Ebenezer Scrooge is the stingy main character who repents in Charles Dickens's *A Christmas Carol.*
[¶]A fern bar is an upscale social bar.

minded." Acknowledging that most operators fall in-between, Maryanne says the worst bosses allow their egos to "lead them into a lifestyle that undermines the restaurant . . . to lead them to the wrong side of the bar." A training director for a fast-growing chain had worked for too many operators who exhibited "egotism to a fault—out of control—hating to give credit or praise, and, most of all, not listening."

6   Bull-headed operators are a hallmark of this business and they may also be the scourge. Every day, we all face the balance between when to talk and when to listen. Listening comes harder to those who hold themselves and their ideas in high regard. One franchise vice president considers a boss's worst trait "a disregard for other's ideas." Her sentiments match those of a veteran free-lance waiter, who blames closed-mindedness for a manager's inability to adapt to situations, new hires, and new systems.

7   An open mind consistently discovers new frontiers, listening offers true leaders perspective and respect—two vision-related qualities that govern how a boss views his or her world and is viewed by it. Scrooge's lifetime of self-centeredness blinded him to the surrounding reality—to Tiny Tim*—and we all cheer as the ghosts† open his eyes to the reality of his miserly past, his egocentric present, and his miserable future.

8   Respect is the word most frequently uttered when restaurant workers talk about their bosses. "Once respect goes, it all tumbles down," says Maryanne, who has seen her share of failed restaurants. John, a sous chef, said that "once I realized that I'd lost all respect for a boss I was gone." And a former manager, now a high-profile waiter, insists "if ever there was a cog that makes the machinery of a restaurant run, it's respect—that ability to look at a situation calmly and view staff, suppliers, and customers with respect."

9   But respect can be a slippery idea. We know this: sometimes it must be earned and sometimes it is immediately granted and expected to be maintained; it means seeing the value of others' skills, ideas, the way they do their jobs and live their lives. So, a boss or employee who doesn't listen or show imagination and diligence won't get much respect. Respect also tends to come to those who respect others. One waiter referred to a manager, ten years his junior, who offered no respect and got none. "He wanted to be liked, and he was. But nobody respected him. After a while,

*Tiny Tim is an impoverished crippled lad who benefits from Scrooge's change of heart.
†The ghosts are the spirits who visit Scrooge to tell him what he was, what he is, and what he will be if he doesn't change.

he calmed down and began to notice and rely on the strength of his staff—now I have a great deal of respect for him."

10   Lack of respect is sad; disrespect is deplorable. "This business is just full of sexual harassment," whispered one franchise executive over the phone. "You know, there's innuendo and all that crap and I know sometimes bosses don't know how inappropriate their actions and words are. I think we overlook it," she said, "because we figure we're just not as professional as other businesses, and that it goes with the territory." She also pointed out that, in an industry scraping for good managers, "you're willing to tolerate more than if you had someone standing at the door waiting for a job."

11   Indeed, stupid bosses exhibit intolerance that keeps career-minded people away. And these bosses haunt all levels of the industry. One female job applicant recalled an interview in which she was quizzed about her sexual fantasies. When she was offered the job, she declined.

12   Good bosses? Great bosses? They know who they are. If you wonder about the qualities most valued in bosses, they are opposite the faults listed above. Their egos fit through doorways. They listen and treat everyone the way they would like to be treated. They extend themselves in an effort to appreciate those who are new and different. They set a good example. They take interest in the lives of their employees. They possess what it took Scrooge a couple of horrifying nights to acquire—eyes that are wide open, and hearts and minds that follow.

Exercise 7   DISCUSSION AND CRITICAL THINKING

1. Circle the thesis.

2. Underline the first definition of *good bosses*.

3. In paragraph 5, what does Maryanne mean when she says, "The best bosses I've had were chef/owners . . . their mission is clear and single-minded"?
   She probably means that the chef/owners see their mission as running a restaurant with good food, efficiently and pleasantly served. Their ego is appropriately connected with that mission, instead of the mission being connected to their enormous ego.

4. Why is a large ego a problem for bosses?
   An egotistic person hates to give credit or praise and does not allow listening.

5. How does not listening handicap the boss?
   Closed-mindedness makes the manager unable to adapt to situations, new hires, and a new system.

6. What does listening provide for the manager?

   "Listening offers true leaders perspective and respect—two vision-related qualities that govern how a boss views his or her world and is viewed by it" (paragraph 7).

7. How is a self-centered boss like Scrooge?

   Scrooge had to face his miserly past, his egocentric present, and his miserable future.

8. In paragraph 8, to what three targets is the idea of respect directed?

   To staff, suppliers, and customers.

9. What is worse than lack of respect?

   Disrespect.

10. What is the effect of bosses' intolerance?

    The absence of career-minded people.

11. Complete this definition based on Hertneky's essay: A good boss is a human resources manager who is selfless___, open-minded___, respectful___, and tolerant_____ (opposite of *egocentric, closed minded, disrespectful and unappreciative,* and *intolerant).*

Why Many Good Workers Turn into Bad Bosses

U.S. News & World Report Staff

It is a common assumption that employees, having proved themselves as workers, would naturally transfer their excellence to a management position. Not necessarily so, says noted human resources specialist Charles Dwyer in this interview.

1   **Q** Mr. Dwyer, why are so many people ineffective as bosses?

A For a couple of reasons. One is that people are not consciously sensitive to what is important to other people. But there's a far more subtle reason: My behavior is designed by me, however unconsciously, to take care of my values first. I can say: "I'm the boss, and I can tell him what to do. That feels good." That's one reason quality-control circles have been ineffective in this country. They scare supervisors who want to maintain control over people.

2   **Q** Doesn't that forceful approach often work in managing employees?

A I'll show you S.O.B.s by the legion who get to the top of their organizations through aversive behavior control. It does work. The empirical evidence shows you can go on for a long time using fear, intimidation and threat to get an awful lot of the behavior that you want.

3   **Q** What are the dangers in taking that approach?

A It is not a pragmatic way to manage in terms of investment and return of energy. If I threaten you, you don't like it but you do what I want. But you're also looking for a way out. You're pushing back up, like a spring. I have to use more energy to keep you down.

4   **Q** What are some of the other results?

A Good people start to leave. Absenteeism goes up. Tardiness starts to increase. You end up with slowdowns, lost paper, sabotage.

If those coping mechanisms don't work, people get sick. It starts to wear on them. That makes them less sharp. There are more accidents, more safety violations, more sick time and more people quitting.

5   **Q** Why do managers bother using this approach?

A Because it feels good. You are in control of people even though the system you are using is an inefficient way to be productive and profitable.

6   **Q** What would an effective boss do?

A If you want people to behave in certain ways, you appeal to what is important to them. Most people want respect and autonomy. They want to feel they have some control. They want recognition and some status. They want emotional as well as financial security. Some employees will be yours forever if you pat them on the head twice a week—with sincerity, assuming you think they deserve it. Recognition is a very effective device for influencing human behavior.

7   **Q** What other motivators work?

A Besides these things, employees want to have fun at work.

8   **Q** Did you say "fun"?

A Yes. People like to have fun. You can build fun deliberately into an organization—lay out a whole series of things that say, "We can have fun here as long as we reach production goals." You can have joke boards, candid photographs and all kinds of things.

9   **Q** What does this do for employee performance and morale?

A I've seen people come from dull-as-dust assembly-line jobs who just had a wonderful day. I've seen people come in to work when they were sick and should have stayed home. They wouldn't miss a day of work, not because the work was enjoyable or intrinsically satisfying, but because it was fun to be there.

10   **Q** What else is important in managing subordinates?

A Feedback is very important. People want to know how well they're doing. You can't imagine how many people don't have the vaguest notion of how they are doing until somebody seriously fills out one of those rarely useful performance appraisals.

There are fundamental human values you can appeal to. You can sometimes work wonders with assembly-line workers by unbolting their chairs and bins so that they can put them wherever they want them.

11   **Q** You haven't stressed money as an effective motivator of people—

A It is, sometimes. If used in piecework pay and commissions, money works if you don't violate people's sense of fairness. But most people are paid wages and salaries, so money doesn't motivate them on a daily basis. They know they'll get paid almost no matter what.

Money is very different from status, recognition, security, fun, affiliation, feeling good, respect and autonomy. You want money as a way to have fun, be amused, be secure and feel good about yourself. Even if I gave you those things directly, you still need some money to live in a decent place and to be able to do certain kinds of things. But money is not the only motivator. It is an instrument to all those other things that I may be able to give you directly.

12   **Q** What personal traits does the effective boss have?

A There's flexibility and simplicity. If you look at people who are respected in corporations, you will see they have clarity and breadth of vision. They have their priorities clearly in mind. They use their time effectively. They know when to ignore and neglect things and when to stop hitting their heads against the wall. They have a strong, as opposed to a big, ego. They have a tough skin and confidence in themselves.

13   **Q** Can these traits be learned?

A Yes, but I know many who never learn them. That's part of the current criticism of the training of MBAs in this country: They don't understand the politics of organizations, human behavior or human motivation.

14   **Q** Do some managers lack these traits because they are promoted beyond their ability?

A People can move out of their technical specialties into higher management without learning to deal with planning and coordination and without understanding people. For all their technical knowledge, they find themselves in positions for which they've never been trained. Unfortunately for them, it's impossible to admit this, and equally impossible to take a promotion and then find out it's not for them and move back down.

15   **Q** Which skills are most often lacking?

A   In middle to upper management, one mostly notices executives who cannot deal well with people. As one moves up the ladder, what are most often lacking are intellectual or conceptual skills—the breadth of vision, the planning, the ability to see multiple pieces come together.

16   **Q** What kind of questions should one ask in assessing whether he or she will be an effective boss?

A Ask yourself: What is important to me? Is deference important? Is being on top important? Do I have driving ambition? Is visibility important? Is a job well done important?

Try ranking those values. You may begin to see whether or not the position that you're aspiring to is likely to be satisfying. Also, know what is expected of you and what you expect of yourself.

17   **Q** Do you think a boss can change his or her behavior?

A Yes—even an MBA! I've been doing it with people for a long time. While I don't have careful empirical studies, there's a fair mass of anecdotal evidence from people who have said, "Hey, I realize something I never realized before," and they changed their behavior to become more effective.

18 **Q** How does a boss avoid becoming ineffective?

A Our culture seems to place a high value on deference, authority, moving up and status. These things may not breed effective behavior toward others and may even bring on wars within ourselves. But we can make our own choices—what to say through the intercom, how to greet people, how to treat people, when to listen and when to talk.

People should define their own concepts of value and not allow society, a business school or anyone else to do it for them.

Understand yourself, your values, your behavior and its effect on other people—to realize, in other words, what it costs you, in terms of effectiveness, to do and say certain kinds of otherwise satisfying things.

| **Exercise 8** | **DISCUSSION AND CRITICAL THINKING** |

1. According to Charles Dwyer, why are so many people ineffective bosses?

   (1) Many people are not consciously sensitive to what is important to other people and (2) many bosses want to maintain control over others.

2. What are the main negative results of the forceful approach to managing?

   Like a spring, those being pressured will push back. Also, increased absenteeism, tardiness, slowdowns, lost paper, and sabotage.

3. What does an effective manager do to give people what they want?

   The effective boss shows respect, allows autonomy, shares control, gives recognition, confers status, and provides emotional and financial security.

4. Dwyer says that employees want to have fun at work. To what extent is that possible at places where you have worked?

   Answers will vary.

5. Why is money overrated as an effective motivator?

   Because money is something expected. The motivators related to status, recognition, security, fun, affiliation, feeling good, respect, and autonomy are put in place by a good boss and are, therefore, given.

6. What is the difference between a strong ego and a big ego?

   The strong ego denotes confidence and toughness. The big ego represents self-centeredness and insecurity.

7. In Q&A 14, what does the phrase "promoted beyond their ability" mean?

   People who excel in technical areas are often promoted to management jobs requiring skills in dealing with complex interpersonal relationships, for which they are unprepared or unqualified.

8. What difficulty does the person promoted beyond his or her ability face?

   It's difficult to admit failure, and it's impossible to return to his or her previous job.

9. Does Dwyer say it is possible for ineffective bosses to become effective? Does your experience confirm that view?

   Yes. Answers will vary.

✎ Topics for Writing Definition

Writing Process Worksheet

You will find a Writing Process Worksheet in Appendix A, page 531. It can be photocopied and enlarged, filled in, and submitted with each assignment if your instructor directs you to do so.

Source-Based Topics

Each essay developed from these suggested source-based topics should include at least one reference to the reading selection by the author's name and the title. Quotations should be enclosed in quotation marks. Follow your instructor's directions in documenting the ideas you borrow. Whether you use informal or formal documentation, the form is not complicated, and you will soon learn to use it for these essays without checking each time. See pages 77 and 78 for a discussion of MLA style and informal documentation.

Underlining and annotating reading selections will help you in finding support material. In prewriting brief essays, consider marking your outline to indicate where you will use quotations or other borrowed ideas. If the quotations or reworded statements are short and few, you could even insert them inside parentheses or circles in your outline; if you do, also include the author's last name and the page number. A sound system, consistently used, will save you time and ensure technically strong papers.

"My-Graines"

1. Using this essay as a model, write an essay about anyone you know who suffers from the same condition or any other chronic illness.

2. Use the Internet or another source to investigate a disease and then discuss that disease by referring to your source and by using examples from personal experience or observation.

"Perspectives on Motivation"

3. Select an abstract term (for example, *depression, stress, stroke, enabler, manipulation, controlling personality*) from any field you have studied or are studying and write an extended definition. You may have a

textbook that will give you a basic definition and discussion. Include some examples from your experience to enliven your essay.

"Disarming the Rage"

4. Take the most basic definition you can derive from this essay and a few insights and apply them to situations with which you are familiar. Your examples may come from your childhood experiences.

5. Using the idea about the characteristics shared by bullies and victims, discuss bullies you observed when growing up.

6. If you had enormous power as an educator, what would you do to curtail bullying? Discuss the main characteristics of bullying in relation to your plan. Give credit to this essay or any other sources.

"Bully, Bully"

7. Write an analysis of Leo's essay, and evaluate his ideas. To what extent do you agree with him? Examine the definitions along with him and explain what you think is and is not workable. Ask your instructor if you should separate your main summary from your critical reaction.

8. Discuss Leo's reservations about the definition of *bullying* from the national study as they apply to the examples of bullying and consequent bullying in "Disarming the Rage." Explain how the definition should be narrowed, if at all.

Paired Sources on Bullying

9. Write about the practice of bullying as you have witnessed or experienced it. "Disarming the Rage" accepts the definition developed by the national study, whereas "Bully, Bully" rejects it as being too broad. Give your views on both positions in your essay, as you construct your own definition of the word *bully.*

"You and Your Boss"

10. Use Hertneky's definition of a bad boss (or, by reversing it, the definition of a good boss) and discuss bosses you have had. Instead of observations by his informants—Maryanne, the waiter, and the franchise vice president—use insights from your own informants, along with whatever you have observed or experienced. You may have to modify Hertneky's definition to fit bosses in business other than food service.

11. Using this essay as a model, discuss a good worker. This topic will work best if you can define a good worker in a particular job.

12. Write an essay about someone else that is good, for example, good teachers, good soldiers (person in military service), good preachers, good neighbors, good police officers, or good siblings.

"Why Many Good Workers Turn into Bad Bosses"

13. Using this title as your theme, write about someone you know or know about who has been promoted to a management job and then seemed to change. This will usually be a person who was well liked and respected in a job in which he or she excelled and then became a person disliked or not respected in the management job. In your essay, define *efficient boss* and *efficient worker* and explain why the roles are often not similar.

14. Using Dwyer's definition of an efficient boss, discuss some bosses with whom you are familiar

15. Using the questions from this selection, or modifications of those questions, interview a person or persons in management. Write up the interview in the same form. You may want to include comments on the differences between Dwyer's comments and those of your informant.

Paired Sources on Bosses and Workers, Good and Bad

16. Write an essay about a good or bad boss you have observed. Explain why that boss was promoted to the position he or she holds. What qualities did that boss have as a worker? How have those qualities contributed to the person's strength or weakness as a boss. Refer to both essays in your analysis. Make sure that you include a clear definition of a good boss.

Career-Related Topics

17. Define one of the following terms by using other patterns of development (such as exemplification, cause and effect, narration, comparison and contrast): *total quality management, quality control, business ethics, customer satisfaction, cost effectiveness, Internet, temporary workers, union, outsource,* or *downsize.*

18. Define a term from computer technology, such as *Internet, World Wide Web, search engine,* or *chat room.*

General Topics

Select one of the following topics and write an extended definition of it; most of these topics will also serve well for writing simple definitions.

19. Conservative	30. Educated	41. Chicano
20. Asian American	31. Gang	42. Jock
21. Bonding	32. Freedom	43. Hispanic American
22. Sexist	33. Body language	44. African American
23. Cult	34. Hero	
24. Biker	35. Druggie	45. Macho
25. Liberal	36. Convict	46. Cool
26. Workaholic	37. Teen slang	47. Native American
27. Surfer	38. Psychopath	
28. Personal space	39. School spirit	48. Jerk
29. Clotheshorse	40. Feminist	

Writer's Guidelines: Definition

Simple Definition

1. No two words have exactly the same meaning.

2. Several forms of simple definitions can be blended into your discussion: basic dictionary definitions, synonyms, direct explanations, indirect explanations, and analytical definitions.

3. For a formal or analytical definition, specify the term, class, and characteristic(s).

    Example: Capitalism is an economic system charactierzed by
                   term   class

    investment of money, private ownership, and free
                        characteristics

    enterprise.

4. Avoid "is where" and "is when" definitions, circular definitions, and the use of words in the definition that are more difficult than the word being defined.

Extended Definition

1. Use clustering to consider other patterns of development that may be used to define your term.

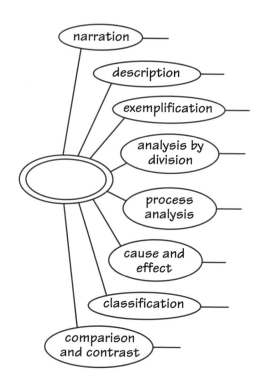

2. The organization of your extended definition is likely to be one of emphasis, but it may be space or time, depending on the subject material. You may use just one pattern of development for the overall organization.

3. Consider these ways of introducing a definition: with a question, with a statement of what it is not, with a statement of what it originally meant, or with a discussion of why a clear definition is important. You may use a combination of these ways before you continue with your definition.

4. Whether you personalize a definition depends on your purpose and your audience. Your instructor may ask you to write about a word within the context of your own experience or to write about it from a detached, clinical viewpoint.

14

Argument: Writing to Persuade

THE QUIGMANS   by Buddy Hickerson

"OH! So I'M paranoid, eh? Lemme ask you THIS, Mr. Peace-of-Mind: Does the fact that we're called BROILERS alarm you at all?"

Writing Essays of Argument

ersuasion is a broad term. When we persuade, we try to influence people to think in a certain way or to do something.

Argument is persuasion on a topic about which reasonable people disagree. Argument involves controversy. Whereas the idea of exercising appropriately is probably not controversial because reasonable people do not dispute its benefits, an issue such as gun control is controversial. In this chapter, we will be concerned mainly with the kind of persuasion that involves argument.

Techniques for Developing Argument

Statements of argument are informal or formal. An opinion column in a newspaper is likely to have little set structure, but an argument in college writing is likely to be tightly organized. Nevertheless, the opinion column and the college paper have much in common. Both provide an assertion (also commonly called a *proposition*), which is the main point of the argument, and both provide support, which is the evidence or the reasons that back up the assertion.

For a well-structured college essay, an organization plan is desirable. Consider these elements when you write an argument, and ask yourself the following questions as you develop your ideas:

Background: What is the historical or social context for this controversial issue?

Assertion (the thesis of the essay): What do I want my audience to believe or do?

Qualification of assertion: Can I limit my assertion so that those who disagree cannot easily challenge me with exceptions? If, for example, I am in favor of using animals for scientific experimentation, am I concerned only with medical experiments or with any use, including experiments for the cosmetic industry?

Refutation (taking the opposite view into account, mainly to point out its fundamental weakness): What is the view on the other side, and why is it flawed in reasoning or evidence?

Support: In addition to sound reasoning, can I use appropriate facts, examples, statistics, and opinions of authorities?

Note that the first letters in the terms make up the acronym BAQRS, pronounced "backers." This memory device will help you recall a useful procedure for quality control in your essays of persuasion and argument. This is the most commonly used pattern for an essay.

Figure 14.1
Common Essay Pattern

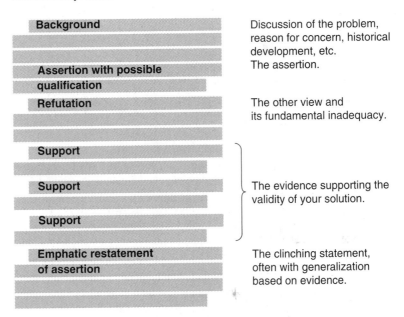

Background	Discussion of the problem, reason for concern, historical development, etc.
Assertion with possible qualification	The assertion.
Refutation	The other view and its fundamental inadequacy.
Support	
Support	The evidence supporting the validity of your solution.
Support	
Emphatic restatement of assertion	The clinching statement, often with generalization based on evidence.

There are, of course, other variants, and there are also several methods of developing the material within each pattern. You may organize the supporting facts by comparison, one side at a time or one issue at a time (present an issue favoring your position, then refute one of your opponent's claims). You may develop the argument (or persuasive writing, in a broader sense) by a method such as cause and effect, analysis by division, or a combination of methods.

Your Audience

Your audience may be uninformed, informed, biased, hostile, receptive, apathetic, sympathetic, empathetic—any one, a combination, or something else. The point is that you should be intensely concerned about who will read your composition. If your readers are likely to be uninformed about the social and historical background of the issue, then you need to set the issue in context. The discussion of the background should lead to the problem for which you have an assertion or solution. If your readers are likely to be biased or even hostile to your view, take special care to refute the opposing side in a thoughtful, incisive way that does not further antagonize them. If your readers are already receptive and perhaps even sympathetic, and you wish to move them to action, then you might appeal to their conscience and the need for their commitment.

Kinds of Evidence

In addition to sound reasoning generally, you can use these kinds of evidence: facts, examples, statistics, and authorities.

First, you can offer facts. Martin Luther King, Jr., was killed in Memphis, Tennessee, on April 4, 1968. Because an event that has happened is true and can be verified, this statement about King is a fact. But that James Earl Ray acted alone in killing King is to some questionable. That King was the greatest of all civil rights leaders is also opinion because it cannot be verified.

Some facts are readily accepted because they are general knowledge—you and your reader know them to be true, because they can be or have been verified. Other "facts" are based on personal observation and are reported in various publications but may be false or questionable. You should always be concerned about the reliability of the source for both the information you use and the information used by those with other viewpoints. Still other so-called facts are genuinely debatable because of their complexity or the incompleteness of the knowledge available.

Second, you can cite examples. Keep in mind that you must present a sufficient number of examples and that the examples must be relevant.

Third, you can present statistics. Statistics are numerical facts and data that are classified and tabulated to present significant information about a given subject.

Avoid presenting a long list of figures; select statistics carefully and relate them to things familiar to your reader. The millions of dollars spent on a war in a single week, for example, become more comprehensible when expressed in terms of what the money would purchase in education, highways, or urban renewal.

To test the validity of statistics, either yours or your opponent's, ask: Who gathered them? Under what conditions? For what purpose? How are they used?

Fourth, you can cite evidence from, and opinions of, authorities. Most readers accept facts from recognized, reliable sources—governmental publications, standard reference works, and books and periodicals published by established firms. In addition, they will accept evidence and opinions from individuals who, because of their knowledge and experience, are recognized as experts.

In using authoritative sources as proof, keep these points in mind:

- Select authorities who are generally recognized as experts in their field.

- Use authorities who qualify in the field pertinent to your argument.

- Select authorities whose views are not biased.

- Try to use several authorities.

- Identify the authority's credentials clearly in your essay.

Logical Fallacies

Certain thought patterns are inherently flawed. Commonly called *logical fallacies,* these thought patterns are of primary concern in argumentation. You should be able to identify them in the arguments of those on the other side of an issue, and you should be sure to avoid them in your own writing.

Eight kinds of logical fallacies are very common.

1. *Post hoc, ergo propter hoc* ("after this, therefore because of this"): When one event precedes another in time, the first is assumed to cause the other: "If *A* comes before *B,* then *A* must be causing *B.*"

    Examples: "I knew I'd have a day like this when I saw that black cat run across my driveway this morning."

    "What did I tell you? We elected him president, and now we are in a recession."

2. *False analogy:* False analogies ignore differences and stress similarities, often in an attempt to prove something.

    Examples: "Each driver has to get a driver's license because unqualified drivers could have bad effects on society. Therefore, couples should also have to get a license to bear children because unqualified parents can produce delinquent children."

    "The leader of that country is a mad dog dictator, and you know what you do with a mad dog. You get a club and kill it."

3. *Hasty generalization.* This is a conclusion based on too few reliable instances.

    Examples: "Everyone I met this morning is going to vote for Johnson, so I know Johnson is going to win."

    "How many people did you meet?"

    "Three."

4. *False dilemma:* This fallacy presents the reader with only two alternatives from which to choose. The solution may lie elsewhere.

    Examples: "Now, only two things can be done with the savings and loan places. You either shut them down or let them go bankrupt."

    "The way I see it, you either bomb them back into the Stone Age or let them keep on pushing us around."

5. *Argumentum ad hominem* (argument against the person): This is the practice of abusing and discrediting your opponent rather than keeping to the main issues of the argument.

   Examples: "Who cares what he has to say? After all, he's a wild-eyed liberal who has been divorced twice."

   "Let's put aside the legislative issue for a moment and talk about the person who proposed it. For one thing he's a Southerner. For another he's Catholic. Enough said."

6. *Begging the question:* This fallacy assumes something is true without proof. It occurs when a thinker assumes a position is right before offering proof.

   Examples: "Those savages can never be civilized."

   "I have one simple question. When is he going to stop ripping off his customers? Case closed."

7. *Circular reasoning:* This thought pattern asserts proof that is no more than a repetition of the initial assertion.

   Example: "You can judge good art by reading what good critics say about it."

   "But who are good critics?"

   "The people who spend their time judging good art."

8. *Non sequitur:* This fallacy draws a conclusion that does not follow.

   Examples: "He's my first cousin, so of course you can trust him."

   "You can count on Gizmo computers; they were designed in the Silicon Valley."

Exercise 1   **IDENTIFYING LOGICAL FALLACIES**

Identify the logical fallacies in the following sentences.

1. "This college should expand the English department because English is important."
   Circular reasoning.

2. "As they say, 'Variety is the spice of life.' Therefore, whether it be food or intimate relationships, I want to do a lot of sampling."
   False analogy.

3. "I've bought three Ford automobiles, and I can say for sure that Ford makes a good product."
   Hasty generalization.

4. "If you don't love this country, you should leave it."
   False dilemma.

5. "Of course, your Mercedes Benz is a great car. It's the product of German engineering."
   Non sequitur.

6. "I was scheduled to go to Dr. Mason for therapy, but then someone told me he had been divorced two times, and I canceled my appointment."
   Argumentum ad hominem.

7. "President Reagan was a great communicator because he talked so well."
   Circular reasoning.

8. "Soon after we increased the immigration quotas, crime went up. Now is the time to slam the gates shut."
   Post hoc.

9. "The inadequate federal welfare program should be abolished because far too many Americans are still poor."
   Begging the question.

10. "You can either fund digital high schools or let the next generation be computer illiterate."
    False dilemma.

Exercise 2   **WRITING EXAMPLES OF LOGICAL FALLACIES**

Provide examples of the following logical fallacies. Work in a group or individually as directed by your instructor.

Answers will vary.

1. *Post hoc:* _____

   _____

   _____

2. False analogy: _____

   _____

   _____

3. Hasty generalization: _____

   _____

   _____

4. False dilemma: _____

_____

_____

5. *Argumentum ad hominem:* _____

_____

_____

6. Begging the question: _____

_____

_____

7. Circular reasoning: _____

_____

_____

8. *Non sequitur:* _____

_____

_____

Connecting Sources and Writing

Student Essay

Even in this era of political correctness, a few social transgressions are allowed to go unchecked. Student Karen Peterson would like to persuade her audience to examine one of these free fire zones. If you meet her, you will see a woman who is hardworking, highly competent, and witty. She says she has experienced all of the negative things you are going to read about, but she accepts herself for what she is—a proud and beautiful woman with a lot of confidence, intelligence, sensitivity, and self-fulfillment, who just happens to be overweight.

Peterson's essay was in response to this prompt:

> Write an essay of persuasion in which you discuss the causes and effects of discrimination against a group of people with a common characteristic. Your essay should be between 500 and 800 words. Submit a completed Writing Process Worksheet, an early draft, and the final draft. Try to select a form of discrimination that you have witnessed from up close. Possible topics: the

causes and effects of discrimination in relation to name, race, region, body adornment, sexual preference, religion, weight, height, baldness, or physical handicap.

Walk in My Full-Figure Shoes
Karen Peterson

Let's play the *if* game. . . . If you have never experienced being called bubbles, two-ton Tessie, chunky, or plump; if you have never walked into a store and been told, "We don't carry your size"; if you have never experienced being left out of a trip to the beach by a group of your peers; if you have never been the last one chosen for a team and then sent to right field; if you have never been rejected by a friend who was becoming popular with the "in" crowd; if you have never been laughed at when you sat in a tiny chair; if you have never dreamed of being a cheerleader or a homecoming queen, then you have never been fat. But if you have, you know that society as a whole views being fat as unacceptable, and this stereotype has devastating psychological effects. Society seems to believe that fat people are unhealthy, unhappy, low in self-esteem, unmotivated, and lazy, to name just a few of the unwarranted labels.

Assertion

I am overweight, but I do not fit the stereotype. I am in great health. I am subject to the same emotions as those of a thin person. As far as having low self-esteem, I like myself and am secure in who I am. With regard to being unmotivated and lazy, I go to school full-time (17 semester units), and I take care of a household of four. I make the White Tornado look sluggish by comparison.

Support

The fashion industry, which is also dictated to by society, has long ignored the "full figure." When I was growing up, it was difficult to find fashionable, stylish clothing that fit me. Most clothing manufacturers designed clothes for the tall and thin figure, even though the world's population has few of those models. I often found myself going from store to store, discovering that the only place that carried my size was called something like Coleman Tents R Us. This may seem funny, but for a person like me, it can be traumatic.

Support

The media contribute to stereotyping by promoting the idea that in order to be beautiful, happy, healthy, and loved, a person must be thin. They promote this concept by showing thin people exclusively when they advertise cosmetics, clothing, cars, and alcohol. Only thin people are seen enjoying themselves on vacations. It's no wonder that fat people feel overwhelmed and defeated, when

Support

this is the image they continually see on virtually every television commercial, billboard, and magazine cover. These concepts and images create extreme pressure to conform. For instance, Oprah Winfrey was subjected to pressure and ridicule when one diet didn't work. She failed to fit the media's image. But she was still the same person. Surely a person is worth more than an image, heavy or light. Like her, I'm worth more than a perfect image.

Support   The worst offender of social stereotyping of fat people is the health-and-fitness industry. No other industry can do more psychological and physical damage while making a bundle of money by exploiting fat people. With all the fad diets, quick-weight-loss pills, "miracle" fat creams, and exercise weight-loss videos, it is no wonder that fat people don't know whom to believe, which weight-loss guru to follow, or simply how to lose weight successfully and safely. All of the marketed diets and solutions seem to place great emphasis on being fit and healthy. Yet in reality, many are detrimental. For most of my life, I have tried a variety of these so-called get-thin-quick regimens. The outcome at first was always great, but they fail to help me maintain the new, thin look. What resulted is commonly known as the yo-yo syndrome. I lost weight, but once I stopped dieting, the old habit and pounds returned, sometimes accompanied by even *more* pounds.

Restatement of main idea   But as pounds come and pounds go, people really need to look past the scales and accept others for what they are. I invite all to come walk in my full-figure shoes as we continue the *if* game. . . . If you have never cried yourself to sleep and wished for a fairy godmother to transform your body; if you have never been treated as if you were invisible and wished you really were; if you have never been made to feel unlovable by those who are unworthy of your love; if you have never forced yourself to laugh at a joke about weight and wanted the teller punished; if you have never known the pain of those things, then you have never been fat. Fat is only a word, not a human being. Fat cannot feel, need, or want as I have and as I still do.

| Exercise 3 | **DISCUSSION AND CRITICAL THINKING** |

1. Why is this essay one of persuasion but not argument?

   Argument implies that reasonable people could be divided on the issue.

2. Why is an essay of only persuasion, such as this one, less likely to have a refutation than an essay of argument?

   An essay of argument presupposes an opposition, one that has its own support. An essay of only persuasion attempts to convince but does not expect a reasonable opposition.

3. According to Peterson, does more discrimination occur during youth or adulthood?

   It is about equal, although it takes different forms.

4. How does Peterson make her support more specific?

   She gives personal examples.

5. What techniques does she use in writing her introduction and conclusion?

   She begins a what-if series in the introduction and then breaks away, develops her essay, then finally returns to it in the conclusion.

Practicing Patterns of Argument

The formal pattern of argument is not always followed in a set sequence, but the main components—the assertion and the support—are always included. You should also consider whether to qualify your assertion and whether to include a refutation.

| Exercise 4 | **COMPLETING PATTERNS OF ARGUMENT** |

This outline is the framework for "Walk in My Full-Figure Shoes." If necessary, refer to the essay as you fill in the blanks.

Assertion: Society as a whole views being fat as unacceptable.

I. Society stereotypes
   A. Unhealthy
   B. Unhappy
   C. Low in self-esteem
   D. Lazy
II. Fashion industry ignores the "full figure"
   A. Designs for the tall and thin
   B. Traumatic for the full-figure person

III. Media contribute
   A. Promote image of the thin instead of <u>the fat</u>
   B. Advertisements
   C. People with weight problem <u>ridiculed</u>
IV. Exploitation of the overweight by the health-and-fitness industry
   A. Fad <u>diets</u>
   B. Contradictory <u>advice</u>
   C. Ignore <u>typical results</u>

Student Documented Essay (Multiple Sources)

One option for the assignment in persuasive writing was to select a topic that could be discussed with the use of both personal experience and written sources. Tom Shields had worked in only one place and that in uncomplicated conditions, so he eliminated work as an area and considered family, school, and recreation. After a bit of freewriting, his mind went to youth sports. He had played Little League baseball, he had umpired some games, his father had coached, and his mother had been a Little League helper. Although he had liked the experience with Little League overall, he knew there were also major problems. He had found his subject.

Save Little League from Big Lugs

Tom Shields

With crime rates being high, with youth facilities not generally keeping up with population increases, and with more mothers and fathers working outside the home, organized youth sports programs can satisfy an extremely important recreational need. Little League is often regarded as the most successful of those programs. If one considers only the number of youngsters who have participated, it would be difficult to argue with the word *success*. But if one were to consider that more than 75 percent of the Little Leaguers quit before they were 13 (Siegenthaler 299), then the conclusion would be different. We would assume that for many of the quitters, the experience was not favorable. My proposal is to form an alternative to Little League, in which most adults would be banned as spectators.

This alternative, which I'll call KRB, for K-Rated Baseball, is a necessary measure in difficult times. The *K* stands for kids, and that's who would be allowed to attend games under my rules. Children can play. Children can spectate. Older children can coach,

Statistics

umpire, and run the snack bar. A few adults will be allowed to help organize, schedule, coach, and administer first aid, but they will be employed by the city recreation department, evaluated by the children, and moved often from team to team. Ushers will card all who wish to attend and deny passage to anyone over nineteen.

The formation of KRB is desirable because so many of that 75 percent who quit Little League had good motives for doing so. The following are some of the benefits of K-Rated Baseball:

KRB would be fun for youngsters. Of course, Little League has been fun for many youngsters, especially those who excelled. For many others it has been organized embarrassment and humiliation. In a study conducted by the University of Michigan, the main reason for youngsters dropping out was that "adults—particularly their own parents—have turned the playing of games into a joyless, negative experience" (Nack 88). Youngsters who like to play ball are dressed in complete uniforms, and their teams are often given names of famous teams. They are expected to play before hundreds of kibitzing fans, many with camcorders focused on the field. I remember that it was not unusual for certain parents to know the batting averages and RBI* totals of most team members. KRB would allow youngsters to play away from the pressure of parents and to have a good time.

Because the records would not be publicized, the coaches, who would be moved from team to team anyway, could spend more time helping youngsters perform well in a more relaxed atmosphere. The coaches would not be the zealots so often observed in Little League games. I was on one team on which we had a player who was a less skillful batter than others. The coach told him not to ever swing at the ball because it was unlikely he would ever get a hit, but the pitcher might walk him. This player—a nice kid, a good student— played an entire season and never swung the bat at a ball. Like the other less skillful players, he was required to play, but it was always right field. And sometimes the coach "forgot" to put him into the game. On another team, the coach required a player to bunt every time he came to bat. The coaches were both winners; the kids were both losers. I've heard coaches tell parents that their children will not be playing very much because the team is "very competitive." If the child drops out (part of the 75 percent), the coach doesn't have

Margin notes:

Authoritative statement

Example

Example

*RBI means runs batted in.

to play him. Most coaches will not victimize children, but far too many do. And the parents of other kids often want them to do so.

Of course, KRB would eliminate the violence, harassment, and intimidation that is so often a part of Little League games. Michael L. Sachs says, "Sports psychologists have long been concerned about what has been labeled 'Little League parent syndrome' (LLPS), named for those adults who get so wrapped up in their children's play that they yell and scream verbal abuse and, occasionally, get physically abusive" (63). Talk to any Little League umpire, and you will get stories about parents who are out of control. They yell at officials, they insult kid players, and they sometimes even berate their own children publicly. Every year we read about parents assaulting each other and officials. I can remember some scary times when I was a Little League umpire. Last week, I saw a television news spot about a woman who was attacked by parents at a game. Her son had just scored the winning run, when she was pummeled into unconsciousness and hit by a baby stroller. Violent behavior scares children and, at the same time, teaches them to be violent when they are displeased. I once heard a coach scream at the fans who were criticizing the players. He said, "After the game, I would like all the people who have been criticizing the players to come down here on the field, and we'll have a game in which adults can show youngsters how to play." The people shut up for a while. No one came to the field after the game.

Of course, there are other solutions. Parents could police themselves. Little League could require that parents attend sportsmanship classes. Kids could be treated as kids, not as alter egos for adults. As they say, one spoiled apple spoils the barrel, and that was yesterday; today there are too many spoiled apples. For the parents who are satisfied, let them continue. But for some of the parents of the 75 percent who drop out, how about some fresh air the Kid-Rated Baseball way. It may need some fine-tuning, but it could work.

Example

Example

Works Cited

Nack, William, and Lester Munson. "Violence in Sports." *Sports Illustrated* July 7, 2000: 86–95.

Sachs, Michael L. "Lighten Up, Parents!" *USA Today Magazine* Nov. 2000: 62–64.

Siegenthaler, K. L., and G. Leticia Gonzalez. "Youth Sports as Serious Leisure: A Critique." *Journal of Sport and Social Issues* 21 (Aug. 1997): 298–315.

Exercise 5   **DISCUSSION AND CRITICAL THINKING**

1. Indicate the following parts:
   Background:
   Growing, continuing problem with youngsters dropping out of Little League baseball.

   Assertion (thesis): (Circle it.)
   Qualification (of the assertion):
   Shields says that most parents are civil and supportive of youth sports in a positive way.

   Refutation (statement of the other side and response to it):
   Some would say that Little League is successful because of the huge enrollment, but Shields points out that most youngsters drop out of the program by the age of 13.

   Support: (Underline topic sentences, and use the words *statistics, authoritative statement,* and *example* as annotations in the left margin.)

2. Is Shields completely serious about this proposal?
   Answers will vary. The author probably realizes that KRB would be almost impossible to manage on a large scale, but it offers him an opportunity to talk about the real problems.

3. If you like some parts of his plan but not all, how would you modify it?
   Answers will vary.

Paired Sources on SUVs

Few drivers are in neutral about SUVs. In this pair of essays, the authors assume polar positions, gun their verbal motors, and gear up. Emotions derived from their experiences color their presentations. Ellen Goodman drives a Saab. Dave Shiflett commands a Toyota 4-Runner. Goodman is obviously sick and tired of SUV transgressions and is not going to take it anymore. Shiflett scoffs about the charges and flaunts macho pride. Surely you will take sides.

SUVs: Killer Cars

Ellen Goodman

Wasting no time, syndicated columnist Ellen Goodman identifies her enemy in the title of her essay. To her, sport utility vehicles are the pit bulls of the urban motoring world, and she would sterilize them all. She hates SUVs in more ways than Elizabeth Barrett Browning loved Robert, and longs for the days of fresh air, plentiful fuel, light traffic, and friendly drivers. This essay was first published in the *Boston Globe*.

1   For my second career, I want to write car ads. Or better yet, I want to live in a car ad.

2   In the real world, you and I creep and beep on some mis-nomered expressway, but in the commercial fantasy land, drivers cruise along deserted, tree-lined roads.

3   We stall and crawl on city streets, but the man in the Lexus races "in the fast lane"—on an elevated road that curves around skyscrapers. We circle the block, looking for a place to park, but the owner of a Toyota RAV4 pulls up onto the sandy beach. We get stuck in the tunnel, but the Escalade man navigates down empty streets because "there are no roadblocks."

4   The world of the car ads bears about as much resemblance to commuter life as the Marlboro ads bear to the cancer ward.

5   All of this is a prelude to a full-boil rant against the archenemy of commuters everywhere: sport utility vehicles. Yes, those gas-guzzling, parking space-hogging bullies of the highway.

6   These sport utility vehicles are bought primarily by people whose favorite sport is shopping and whose most rugged athletic event is hauling the kids to soccer practice.

7   The sales and the size of the larger SUVs have grown at a speed that reminds me of the defense budget. In the escalating highway arms race, SUVs are sold for self-defense. Against what? Other SUVs.

8   As someone who has spent many a traffic-jammed day in the shadow of a behemoth, I am not surprised that the high and weighty are responsible for some 2,000 additional deaths a year. If a 6,000-pound Suburban hits an 1,800-pound Metro, it's going to be bad for the Metro. For that matter, if the Metro hits the Suburban, it's still going to be bad for the Metro.

9   The problem with SUVs is that you can't see over them, you can't see around them and you have to watch out for them. I am by no means the only driver of a small car who has felt intimidated by the big wheels barreling past me. Their macho reputation prompted even the Automobile Club of Southern California to issue an SUV driver tip: "Avoid a 'road warrior' mentality. Some SUV drivers operate under the false illusion that they can ignore common rules of caution."

10   But the biggest and burliest of the pack aren't just safety hazards; they're environmental hazards. Until now, SUVs have been allowed to legally pollute two or three times as much as automobiles. All over suburbia there are people who conscientiously drive their empty bottles to the suburban recycling center in vehicles that get 15 miles to the gallon. There are parents putting big bucks down for a big car so the kids can be safe while the air they breathe is being polluted.

11   At long last some small controls are being promoted. The EPA has proposed for the first time that SUVs be treated like cars. If the agency, and the administration, has its way, a Suburban won't be allowed to emit more than a Taurus. That's an important beginning, but not the whole story.

12   Consider Ford, for example. The automaker produces relatively clean-burning engines. But this fall it will introduce the humongous Excursion. It's 7 feet tall, 80 inches wide, weighs four tons and gets 10 miles to the gallon in the city. No wonder the Sierra Club* calls it "the Ford Valdez†." This is a nice car for taking the kids to school—if you're afraid you'll run into a tank.

13   Do I sound hostile? Last week a would-be SUV owner complained to the *New York Times'* ethics critic that his friends were treating him as if he were "some kind of a criminal." The ethicist wrote back: "If you're planning to drive that SUV in New York, pack a suitcase into your roomy cargo area, because you're driving straight to hell."

14   I wouldn't go that far, though I have wished that hot trip on at least one SUV whose bumper came to eye level with my windshield. Still, the SUV backlash is growing so strong that today's status symbol may become the first socially unacceptable vehicle since cars lost their fins.

15   It's one thing to have an SUV in the outback and quite another to drive it around town. In the end, the right place for the big guy is in an ad. There, the skies are always clean, the drivers are always relaxed and there's never, ever another car in sight.

Exercise 6	**DISCUSSION AND CRITICAL THINKING**

Background, Assertion, Qualification, Refutation, and Support (BAQRS) are the main components in most arguments. Professional writers will usually be less procedural than student writers in presenting them. Locate and discuss the components that pertain to Goodman's essay.

1. *Background:* What setting does Goodman give to this essay? What does she provide to bring us to this account of her experiences and thinking pertaining to her topic?
    She leads with a scene from the commercial fantasy land, one that she probably expects readers to recall.

2. *Assertion:* If Goodman does not state her assertion in one sentence, write a one-sentence version here.
    SUVs should be banned from in-town driving.

---

*The Sierra Club is an environmental group.
†The Exxon Valdez was an oil tanker that ran aground and split open.

3. *Qualification:* To what extent does Goodman imply that there might be a place for SUVs?

   She points out that driving an SUV in the outback is more appropriate than driving it around town.

4. *Refutation:* What are some fundamental positions held by SUV supporters that Goodman finds without merit?

   Although Goodman provides little refutation, she does say that SUV owners are not buying something that has much to do with either sports or utility; mainly, she says, the vehicles are used for shopping trips and hauling kids.

5. What are Goodman's main points of support?

   SUVs are gas-guzzling, dangerous, parking space-hogging bullies.

6. What support does Goodman offer?

   Examples:
   She gives these examples: her testimony about her personal experience with SUVs (paragraph 8); Ford making even larger SUVs (paragraph 12); and the letter from the SUV owner to the *New York Times* (paragraph 13).

   Statistics and detailed information:
   SUVs and deaths (paragraph 8); size of new Ford SUV (paragraph 12).

   Statements by authorities:
   Automobile Club of Southern California (paragraph 9); EPA (paragraph 11); *New York Times* ethics critic (paragraph 13).

Guzzling, Gorgeous & Grand: SUVs and Those Who Love Them

Dave Shiflett

Freelance writer Dave Shiflett is not the David from the David and Goliath legend; in fact, he's closer to Goliath. Like the biblical giant, he thunders across the landscape in an SUV long on horsepower and short on charm. Not one to wallow in victimization, he's proud to be driving a socially unacceptable vehicle. This essay was originally published in the *National Review*.

1   Readers of Dickens* may occasionally imagine what it might have been like to peer from the guillotine and see Madame Defarge† knitting her Book of Sin. One would expect a look of ter-

---

*Charles Dickens was the English author of *A Tale of Two Cities,* a novel about the French Revolution, a triumph of the common people over the aristocrats.
†Madame Defarge is a character from Dickens' novel.

rifying certitude and ferocity, and while having one's head severed would constitute a profound setback on many fronts, one would at least be without her. As it happens, the old girl has many descendants in our own time, some of whom are glaring at me.

2   The indictment: Those of us who drive sport utility vehicles are guilty of crimes against fellow drivers, the environment, and world stability. We must be left horseless, if not headless.

3   This is a terrible turn of events. The fact is, we SUV drivers are peaceful, humble people of modest hopes and dreams, who happen to like driving around in large vehicles, often because they accommodate our heaving guts, which often reflect an infatuation with the handiwork of Harland Sanders* and August Busch.[†] Yet when we see ourselves denounced by our detractors, it is as if an alien race were being described.

4   We readily admit that our Big Rides use a bit more gas than the 48 horsepower vehicles (add 3hp when sails are raised) favored by those who would save the world from us. We are talking about the difference between the 27 miles per gallon average for regular automobiles and the 20 mpg rating of many SUVs. Because global warming is an article of faith among our critics, we're getting additional blame for melting icecaps, flooded coastlines, and the eventual appearance of palm trees in New York City.

5   We believe these charges are grossly exaggerated, and we also reject the assertion that our beloved tanks are killing machines. Official statistics tell us that around 4 percent of road fatalities are the result of SUV-auto crashes, which is of course terrible, but not all those accidents are our fault. Overall, SUVs are blamed for an additional 2,000 deaths per year, though as journalist Ken Smith has pointed out, that number is entirely speculative and must be taken very lightly.

6   Our critics are hardly inclined to do so. Sen. Dianne Feinstein, whose calmly sculptured coiffure cannot conceal what some call her Inner Inquisitor, calls us a subspecies of "energy gluttons" and backs legislation that would force us back into the slightly modified go-carts that pass for "mid-sized sedans." Ms. Geneva Overholser, whose placid first name cannot conceal a slightly hectoring personality, has denounced SUVs as "inexplicably popular extravagances" and "nonsensical, gas-guzzling behemoths." Geneva, who was once ombudsman for the *Washington Post,* even admitted that "I feel like a lunatic about SUVs and I hereby invite you to join me in raving."

---

*Harland Sanders is the founder of Kentucky Fried Chicken.
[†]August Busch is the founder of a brewery.

7   A line quickly formed. A. J. Nomai said the SUV "fad" is "all the rage among yuppies, suburban families and seemingly testosterone unbalanced males." Columnist Ellen Goodman called SUVs "gas-guzzling, parking space-hogging bullies of the highway." Bullying, as we have come to know, was the cause of the Columbine massacre, so this is a serious charge. Ms. Goodman also insists "the SUV backlash is growing so strong that today's status symbol may become the first socially unacceptable vehicle since cars lost their fins."

8   This all adds up to what crime specialists call a gang bang, and because we are suburban types who steer clear of that kind of activity, we're in shock. This is especially true when our kids join the fray. We understand, of course, that this kind of protest reflects our peaceful and prosperous times. The Cold War is over, and our youth, having had their molars sealed in infancy, have never even worried about tooth decay. As Bill Clinton (who goes around in very large vehicles) said after taking an egg in the ear, it's good for kids to be mad about something, and this is certainly a safe subject.

9   We can also chuckle over the fact that, for many of our critics, mass transit means taking an Airbus to Nice. We were especially gratified by recent news reports that DNC* chief Terry McAuliffe drives a Cadillac SUV that gets about 10 miles to the gallon, while Dick Gephardt,† currently on the warpath against "energy gluttons," drives a Ford SUV. These leaders, it was further reported, have garaged their Big Rides until the political assault on the president's energy policy is over.

10   Which, it seems, is what much of this criticism is about. We SUVers are mere pawns in a larger war. The people on the other side not only want us all to drive cars whose backseat passengers have to ride with their chins on their knees; they have a thing for windmills, solar panels, boarded-up nuclear-power plants, and kerosene lamps. They also tend to support mandatory-seatbelt laws, antismoking ordinances, and restrictions on home barbecuing. We understand that, in California, they went after weed whackers and leaf blowers—and won.

11   Now it is SUV drivers who are in the crosshairs of the new Defarges, and we're being demonized as irrational and "unbalanced" beings, making it all the easier to whack us. Yet we're not

---

*The DNC is the Democratic National Committee.
†Dick Gephardt is a congressional leader of the Democratic Party.

nearly the menaces we're cracked up to be, as perhaps my own story illustrates.

12   My first SUV was a 1989 Ford Bronco II. This was no bully machine, but instead a pathetic vehicle whose first engine went out at 52,000 miles (Ms. Goodman tells us she drives a Saab, which, of course, is just perfect.) The Bronco passed into the nether world after a roll-over accident, which critics will find pleasing. That the 16-year-old driver was doing 45 down a 15-mile-per-hour stretch of Hairpin Alley, swerved into a steep ditch, and overcorrected, may have had something to do with the crash, though one hates to point fingers. In any event, the mangled Bronco was replaced by a Toyota 4-Runner, purchased with 138,000 miles on the odometer. The SUV community, as it happens, admires diverse peoples, the Japanese among them, especially since they build machines that last. This one should go 300,000 miles, and because of my relatively light driving schedule that means 20 years of service, by which time we may well have been forced into vehicles that pass muster with environmental activists, such as rickshaws. This is not a complaint. I have sent my wife into training in anticipation of this development, and should it arrive we will go quietly, save for the occasional crack of the accelerator.

13   Meanwhile, our aged 4-Runner performs its commonplace duties, such as hauling sound equipment for a variety of humble bands that entertain humble citizens at humble watering holes. It also provides a place to sleep during music festivals and road trips. Ms. Goodman, who no doubt snoozes in her Saab between speaking engagements, should be able to empathize. Indeed, if she would only reach out to SUV owners as she does to members of other victim classes, she might find we are merely her fellow men.

14   Doubtful. It sometimes seems that another major beef against the Big Ride is curiously sexual in nature. Ms. Goodman makes the point: "I am old enough to remember when the shape of a car was female, Detroit's sex appeal was all curves and cars were pitched to men with blondes draped over their hood. Now we're sold bivouac cars with brawn. It's no accident, one reader reminded me, that the Nissan Pathfinder was nicknamed the 'hardbody.' If the minivan is the soccer mom, the SUV is the muscle man, even when it's driven by a woman."

15   Taken together with the observation about "testosterone unbalanced males," we start to sense that our critics are not merely out to park vehicles. They believe they're shutting down the four-wheeled version of the stag room. Many of us do not understand

how people got such an idea, though we are somewhat comforted in knowing that perhaps we're not the only loons in this dispute.

Exercise 7 VOCABULARY HIGHLIGHTS

Write a short definition of each word as it is used in the essay. (Paragraph numbers are given in parentheses.) Be prepared to use the words in your own sentences.

certitude (1)   behemoths (6)

ferocity (1)   ombudsman (6)

coiffure (6)   nether (12)

placid (6)   empathize (13)

hectoring (6)   bivouac (14)

Exercise 8 DISCUSSION AND CRITICAL THINKING

<u>B</u>ackground, <u>A</u>ssertion, <u>Q</u>ualification, <u>R</u>efutation, and <u>S</u>upport (BAQRS) are the main components in most arguments. Professional writers will usually be less procedural than student writers in presenting them. Locate and discuss the components that pertain to Shiflett's essay.

1. *Background:* What setting does Shiflett give to this essay? What does he provide to attract our attention and move us into his argument?
   He refers to a scene in Dickens's novel *A Tale of Two Cities,* in which scapegoat citizens are charged and summarily executed while people look on sadistically. He says that SUV drivers are also being unfairly persecuted.

2. *Assertion:* Since Shiflett does not state his assertion in one sentence, write a one-sentence version here.
   SUV drivers are being unfairly maligned. (Specifically, Shiflett is opposed to the indictment in paragraph 2.)

3. *Qualification:*
   He admits that SUVs use more gas than other family transportation vehicles and seems to acknowledge that the number of SUV-auto crashes and the SUV-related deaths are troubling. But he says the charges are grossly exaggerated.

4. *Refutation:*
   The entire essay is a refutation of the opposition's charge. See paragraph 2.

5. What are Shiflett's main points of support?
   He attacks others' views on SUV safety and gas consumption; he argues for SUV utility (hauling and transporting, as discussed in paragraph 13); he sees the attacks on SUVs as part of a political movement (see paragraphs 14 and 15).

6. What support does Shiflett offer?
   Examples:
   Personal experience of owning a 1989 Ford Bronco II and a Toyota 4-Runner (paragraph 12).

Statistics and detailed information:
Includes specific information about his SUVs (paragraph 12) and safety statistics (paragraph 5; although he calls them speculative).
Statements by authorities:
Statements by columnists, but they are discounted.

Background Information on the Abuse Defense

To provide you with additional information for your study of paired sources on the abuse defense following this section, Timothy W. Murphy, military attorney, presents an extended definition of the battered-spouse syndrome as it is commonly understood by psychologists. In the instance of homicide, the state of mind of the abused person who commits the crime is to be taken into account. It is in the spirit of this definition that legislation was passed to allow the battered-spouse syndrome as a defense. Murphy's complete essay was first published in the *Reporter,* 1992.

"Preparing, Prosecuting, and Understanding Battered Spouse Cases" by Timothy W. Murphy

"Battered Spouse Syndrome" describes the recurring pattern of physical abuse by a husband against his wife. Research indicates that, with few exceptions, the wife is the victim in incidents of domestic violence. It is estimated that only one-half of spouse abuse incidents are reported to law enforcement officials. Spouse abuse exists in all classes and levels of society. . . . While the reasons for a specific incident of violence may be unique, certain general characteristics are common to batterers, to battered women, and to their interaction in a violent marriage.

Dr. Lenore E. Walker, a leading expert in domestic violence, discovered that over 80 percent of batterers were exposed to domestic violence during their childhood. As a result, these men come to accept violence as a legitimate method of asserting control over their spouses. . . . Childhood experiences with violence contribute to a batterer's deeply rooted feelings of insecurity and inferiority, which he attempts to avoid by seeking to control his family. Control is exerted by attempting to isolate the wife from friends, family, outside employment, and interaction with others, and by demonstrating unreasonable jealousy of any of the wife's outside activities. Sexual jealousy and the use of sex as a means of rewarding and punishing his wife's behavior are common methods of control used by the batterer. Batterers tend to be extremely critical of their wives and defensive about their own shortcomings. They blame their wives for all of the problems existing in the relationship—including the acts of violence. The reasons battered women remain in abusive relationships has been the subject of much discussion, research, and debate among experts in the field. Two theories have emerged. The "minority" view contends that battered women suffer from some sort of psychological dependency, which attracts them to abusive relationships with men and renders them incapable of leaving the relationship. . . .

The "majority" view contends that the abused spouse learns to be helpless, and therefore accepts the abuse against her, as a result of violence exhibited during her childhood, the batterer's manipulation of her emotions through psychological and physical coercion, her isolation from others, and economic and emotional dependence on the abuser. Abused women have extremely low self-esteem and fear both their husbands and life itself.

The actual incidents of physical abuse occur in three predictable cycles. . . . The first phase, or "tension building" phase, is characterized by the husband's increased criticism of his wife, coupled with obsessive, jealous, and irritable behavior. The wife usually attempts to control the situation by compliant behavior. In some instances, the wife will provide an incident in order to have the tension decrease or end, and in order to exert some control of the situation.

The second phase is the battering phase, and is the shortest of the three. Battering may begin for no apparent reason. In some cases, the victim will also strike out at her husband during this phase, thereby releasing her frustration.

The third, and final, phase is termed the "loving contrition" phase. This phase is characterized by the abuser professing his deep sorrow for the incident and promising to stop violent behavior in the future. The batterer attempts to "win back" his wife's love by buying gifts, professing his love and devotion, and even agreeing to seek counselling. The abused spouse naively accepts her husband's assertions and part of the blame for the problem. . . . As a violent relationship continues to progress, the first phase becomes longer, the third shorter or nonexistent, and the battering more acute.

Paired Sources on the Abuse Defense

Prior to 1987, a person charged with attacking an abuser could not use the "battered-spouse syndrome" as a defense. The law passed in that year was welcomed by some as enlightened legislation and was opposed by others who saw it as a license for malicious assault. In this paired essay arrangement, Leslie Abramson supports the abuse defense and Alan W. Dershowitz opposes it.

The Abuse Excuse

Alan M. Dershowitz

In this excerpt from a book-long study by the same title, Alan M. Dershowitz gives his reasoned argument for why the battered-spouse syndrome is "junk science." A celebrated scholar and defense attorney, Dershowitz is also the author of *Letters to a Young Lawyer* and *The Genesis of Justice.*

1   The "abuse excuse"—the legal tactic by which criminal defendants claim a history of abuse as an excuse for violent retaliation—is quickly becoming a license to kill and maim. More and more defense lawyers are employing this tactic and more and more jurors are buying it. It is a dangerous trend, with serious and widespread implications for the safety and liberty of every American.

2   Among the recent excuses that have been accepted by at least some jurors have been "battered woman syndrome," "abused child syndrome," "rape trauma syndrome," and "urban survival syndrome." This has encouraged lawyers to try other abuse excuses, such as "black rage." For example, the defense lawyer for Colin Ferguson—the black man convicted in March 1995 of killing white commuters on the Long Island Railroad on December 7, 1993—has acknowledged that his black rage variation on the insanity defense "is similar to the utilization of the battered woman's syndrome, the post-traumatic stress syndrome and the child abuse syndrome in other cases to negate criminal accountability."

The Danger of Vigilantism

3   On the surface, the abuse excuse affects only the few handfuls of defendants who raise it, and those who are most immediately impacted by an acquittal or reduced charge. But at a deeper level,

the abuse excuse is a symptom of a general abdication of responsibility by individuals, families, groups, and even nations. Its widespread acceptance is dangerous to the very tenets of democracy, which presuppose personal accountability for choices and actions. It also endangers our collective safety by legitimating a sense of vigilantism that reflects our frustration over the apparent inability of law enforcement to reduce the rampant violence that engulfs us.

4   At a time of ever-hardening attitudes toward crime and punishment, it may seem anomalous that so many jurors—indeed, so many Americans—appear to be sympathetic to the abuse excuse. But it is not anomalous at all, since the abuse excuse is a modern-day form of vigilantism—a recognition that since official law enforcement does not seem able to prevent or punish abuse, the victim should be entitled to take the law into his or her own hands.

5   In philosophical terms, the claim is that society has broken its "social contract" with the abused victim by not according him or her adequate protection. Because it has broken that social contract, the victim has been returned to a "state of nature" in which "might makes right" and the victim is entitled to invoke the law of the jungle—"kill or be killed." Indeed, these very terms were used in a 1994 Texas case in which one black youth [Daimion Osby] killed two other blacks in a dangerous urban neighborhood. The result was a hung jury.

6   But vigilantism—whether it takes the old-fashioned form of the lynch mob or the new-fashioned form of the abuse victim's killing her sleeping husband—threatens the very fabric of our democracy and sows the seeds of anarchy and autocracy. The abuse excuse is dangerous, therefore, both in its narrow manifestation as a legal defense and in its broader manifestation as an abrogation of societal responsibility.

Affirmative Action in the Justice System

7   The other characteristics shared by these defenses is that they are often "politically correct," thus reflecting current trends toward employing different criteria of culpability when judging disadvantaged groups. In effect, these abuse-excuse defenses, by emphasizing historical discrimination suffered by particular groups, seek to introduce some degree of affirmative action into our criminal-justice system.

8   These abuse-excuse defenses are the daily fare of the proliferating menu of TV and radio talk shows. It is virtually impossible to

flip the TV channels during the daytime hours without seeing a bevy of sobbing women and men justifying their failed lives by reference to some past abuse, real or imagined. Personal responsibility does not sell soap as well as sob stories. Jurors who watch this stuff begin to believe it, despite its status as junk science. The very fact that Sally Jessy Raphael and Montel Williams* repeat it as if it were gospel tends to legitimate it in the minds of some jurors. They are thus receptive to it in the courtroom, especially when the defendant is portrayed as sympathetic, and his dead victim is unsympathetic. William Kunstler† is quick to point to public-opinion polls that show that "two-thirds of blacks and almost half the whites surveyed recognize the validity of our [black rage] theory of Mr. Ferguson's defense."

Most Victims Do Not Commit Violence

9   But neither public-opinion polls nor TV talk shows establish the empirical or normative validity of such abuse-excuse defenses. The basic fallacy underlying each of them is that the vast majority of people who have experienced abuses—whether it be sexual, racial, or anything else—do not commit violent crimes. Thus the abuse excuse neither explains nor justifies the violence. A history of abuse is not a psychological or a legal license to kill. It may, in some instances, be relevant at sentencing, but certainly not always.

10   Lest it be thought that the abuse excuse is credited only by radical defense lawyers, lay jurors, and talk-show-watching stay-at-homes, a quotation from the attorney general of the United States illustrates how pervasive this sort of thinking is becoming. In April 1993, Janet Reno‡ was quoted as commenting on urban riots as follows: "An angry young man who lashes out in violence because he never had a childhood might do the right thing," and when the "right thing" is in contradiction with the law, "you try to get the law changed." I wonder if the angry young man's innocent victim agrees that the violence directed against his shop was the "right thing" and that the law protecting his property should be "changed."

11   The worst consequences of these abuse excuses is that they stigmatize all abuse victims with the violence of the very few who have used their victimization as a justification to kill or maim. The

---

*Sally Jessy Raphael and Montel Williams are television talk-show hosts.
†William Kunstler was a liberal civil rights attorney.
‡Janet Reno was the attorney general in former President Clinton's Cabinet.

vast majority of abuse victims are neither prone to violence nor to making excuses.

Exercise 9   **VOCABULARY HIGHLIGHTS**

Write a short definition of each word as it is used in the essay. (Paragraph numbers are given in parentheses.) Be prepared to use the words in your own sentences.

syndrome (2)	autocracy (6)
negate (2)	abrogation (6)
vigilantism (3)	culpability (7)
rampant (3)	pervasive (10)
anarchy (6)	stigmatize 11)

Exercise 10   **DISCUSSION AND CRITICAL THINKING**

Background, Assertion, Qualification, Refutation, and Support (BAQRS) are the main components in most arguments. Professional writers will usually be less procedural than student writers in presenting them. Locate and discuss the components that pertain to Dershowitz's essay.

1. *Background:* What is the reason for concern over this issue?
   Dershowitz says that increasingly lawyers are using the abuse defense and that more and more jurors are sympathetic.

2. *Assertion:* What is Dershowitz's position?
   The last sentence in paragraph 1 contains his assertion: "It [the abuse defense] is a dangerous trend, with serious and widespread implications for the safety and liberty of every American."

3. *Qualification:* Is Dershowitz's assertion absolute or does he make exceptions?
   He makes no exception, although he does say the abusive circumstances may be relevant at sentencing in some cases.

4. *Refutation:* What are other views that can be disputed?
   • William Kunstler (paragraph 8)
   • Janet Reno (paragraph 10)
   • Dershowitz says (not in a single paragraph) that the facts of abuse are established in court trials and in television talk shows, but, as horrible as the cases are, most victims do not maim and kill their abusers.

5. What are Dershowitz's main points of support?
   • The abuse defense releases individuals from personal responsibility.
   • It promotes vigilantism; people take the law into their own hands.
   • It introduces affirmative action into the criminal-justice system.

6. What support does Dershowitz offer?
   Examples:
   • The Colin Ferguson case (paragraph 2)
   • The Daimion Osby case (paragraph 5)

Statistics and detailed information:
No statistics.

Statements by authorities:
For purposes of refutation: William Kunstler (paragraph 8) and Janet Reno (paragraph 10).

7. Do you agree or disagree with Dershowitz? Explain.
    Answers will vary.

Unequal Justice

Leslie Abramson

As a young defense attorney, Leslie Abramson frequently worked with abused clients and soon became convinced that justice pertained more to the letter of the law than to the spirit of the law. This essay was first published in *Newsweek*.

1   I never learned about "male justice" in school.

2   During my education in the New York City public schools, the City University of New York and the University of California, Los Angeles, School of Law, I was taught the noble fictions of our justice system. I was told that American justice is equal for all. I was instructed that the accused always is presumed innocent until proven guilty, and that the prosecution bears the burden of proving that guilt beyond a reasonable doubt.

3   By the end of my first year of practice I also had learned that much of what I'd been taught was naive. Most important, I discovered that the racism and sexism deforming so many of our institutions also infect the courts, producing a double standard of justice.

4   Much has been written about racism's insidious role in our criminal-justice system. But the recent cases of O.J. Simpson [acquitted of murder in October 1995], Lyle and Erik Menendez [charged with murdering their parents, their trial resulted in hung juries in January 1994], and Lorena Bobbitt [acquitted of maiming her husband in January 1994] have opened a public debate on how gender bias influences the way we perceive crime, criminal responsibility and justice.

Justice for "Wronged" Men and Abused Women

5   "Texas justice" was what we criminal lawyers used to call cases in which a man was acquitted after killing his wife and her lover

in *flagrante delicto*. It mattered not if the victims were unarmed or asleep when the "wronged" man blew them away in his fit of jealous rage. No one went to the talk shows to decry the "heat of passion" defense employed by men expressing their possessory rights over the women of their choice—including the right to kill. Of course, no such right to kill was expressly provided in the written law, but the unwritten law—what might be called the male bill of rights—was implicitly understood by sympathetic male jurors.

6   The law of macho, of course, does not extend to women and children who kill. They rarely kill, but when they do, they don't do it out of wounded pride or from affronts to their sexuality or in the anger of the rejected. The forces that drive them to act are fear and terror, the motivations of the weak, the oppressed, the tortured and the broken. And they are scorned and ridiculed and hated for it.

7   We guiltily admire the successful barroom brawler, the fastest gun, the aggressive forechecker, the crushing lineman. The law of self-defense as currently codified in most states recognizes this, and is a male version of survival—two physical and emotional equals duking it out or facing off *High Noon** style, pistols at the ready. Burning beds, parents united in abuse in their family den—these are not the images our male legislators had in mind when the criminal codes were written.

8   We've learned a lot since then about the psychology of abusive relationships, about the cruelty, oppression and inescapability of child abuse and molestation, about the terror that marks virtually every moment for the victims of chronic domestic violence. Despite this knowledge, the media, the self-anointed pundits and the self-promoting denizens of the law schools' ivory towers sanctimoniously declare their outrage when an abused person recounts a life of torment to explain why he or she succumbed at last to terror and struck out at the abuser. These critics label such explanations the "abuse excuse." They lament our loss of "personal responsibility."

9   This male model of justice pervades the public consciousness and explains why many people say they would sympathize with O.J. Simpson even if they believe he killed Nicole Brown Simpson and Ronald Goldman. It wouldn't matter, they say, even if they believed that these killings followed years in which this strong, physically fit professional athlete beat and emotionally abused his five-foot-eight 125-pound wife. O.J. Simpson may indeed be

---

*High Noon is a Western movie focusing on emotions surrounding a frontier-town duel.

innocent, as he is now legally presumed to be. What makes much of his support in the community troubling, however, is that it derives not from this presumption, but from the undercurrent of entitlement that the killing of an ex-wife engenders.

A Case of Psychological Abuse

10 The best and worst example of this double standard was graphically displayed to me in a case I handled a decade ago. My client, then a woman of fifty, had been raped on her way home from work years before and traumatized by the experience. Twenty years later she married a widower with a four-year-old daughter—and a shadowy past. Only after marrying this wealthy, domineering man did my client discover that he had produced his widowerhood by shooting his unarmed first wife to death as she spoke to a friend on the telephone while his infant daughter slept in the next room. He was convicted of manslaughter, served less than two years in prison and regained custody of the little girl upon his release.

11 During the course of their ten-year marriage the husband's highest form of amusement was to play the role of my client's former rapist by sneaking up on her from behind and grabbing her. He was the textbook battering husband, jealous, possessive, controlling his wife's every movement and human contact, belittling, explosively angry, sexually demanding. Finally, after a period of especially frequent outbursts, he threatened to do to my client what he had done to his first wife. She shot him, once, in the head while he was sleeping. She ran screaming down the hallway, called the police, confessed her crime. At her first trial she was convicted of second-degree murder and sentenced to five years to life in state prison. Her conviction was reversed on appeal due to prosecutorial and judicial misconduct.

12 That's when I entered the case. In her second trial, we presented evidence of the extreme psychological impairment this woman suffered. The jury hung; subsequently, she pleaded guilty to manslaughter and the judge granted her probation. At the sentencing hearing, the male deputy D.A. took my client's hand and said: "I want to apologize to you for that first conviction. You are not a murderer. I just didn't understand."

13 Score one for equal justice.

| Exercise 11 | **VOCABULARY HIGHLIGHTS** |

Write a short definition of each word as it is used in the essay. (Paragraph numbers are given in parentheses.) Be prepared to use the words in your own sentences.

insidious (4)   denizens (8)

flagrante delicto (5)   sanctimoniously (8)

implicitly (5)   engenders (9)

chronic (8)   impairment (12)

pundits (8)   subsequently (12)

| Exercise 12 | **DISCUSSION AND CRITICAL THINKING** |

Background, Assertion, Qualification, Refutation, and Support (BAQRS) are the main components in most arguments. Professional writers will usually be less procedural than student writers in presenting them. Locate and discuss the components that pertain to Abramson's essay.

1. *Background:* How does Abramson place this issue in historical perspective?

   She says that male and female justice have historically been different. She learned that through observation and through her experience as an attorney. She says that we can now look at crime, criminal responsibility, and justice. She cites the cases of Simpson, the Menendez brothers, and Bobbitt.

2. *Assertion:* What is Abramson's position?

   The last sentence in paragraph 3 is her assertion: "The racism and sexism deforming so many of our institutions also infect the courts, producing a double standard of justice." She is mainly concerned with gender bias here.

3. *Qualification:* Is Abramson's assertion absolute or does she make exceptions?

   She makes no exception.

4. *Refutation:* How does Abramson present the other side and show its flawed logic?

   In paragraph 2, she says that she "was taught the noble fictions of our justice system." She "was told that American justice is equal for all." She learned that from people who apparently believed what they said. However, she says, that is the justice for men and for certain groups, not for all.

5. What are Abramson's main points of support?

   • The law of macho takes into account a man's feelings at the time of certain acts of violence but not those of women.

   • The psychology of abusive relationships often explains violent behavior.

6. What support does Abramson offer?
   Examples:

   Her main example occupies paragraphs 10 through 12: the woman who kills her husband.

Statistics and detailed information:

She offers no statistics but does give some details in her extended example.

Statements by authorities:

None.

7. Do you agree or disagree with Abramson? Explain.

Answers will vary.

✎ Topics for Writing Argument

Writing Process Worksheet

You will find a Writing Process Worksheet in Appendix A, page 531. It can be photocopied and enlarged, filled in, and submitted with each assignment if your instructor directs you to do so.

Source-Based Topics

Each essay developed from these suggested source-based topics should include at least one reference to the reading selection by the author's name and the title. Quotations should be enclosed in quotation marks. Follow your instructor's directions in documenting the ideas you borrow. Whether you use informal or formal documentation, the form is not complicated, and you will soon learn to use it for these essays without checking each time. See pages 77 and 78 for a discussion of MLA style and informal documentation.

Underlining and annotating reading selections will help you in finding support material. In prewriting brief essays, consider marking your outline to indicate where you will use quotations or other borrowed ideas. If the quotations or reworded statements are short and few, you could even insert them inside parentheses or circles in your outline; if you do, also include the author's last name and the page number. A sound system, consistently used, will save you time and ensure technically strong papers.

"Walk in My Full-Figure Shoes"

1. Write an essay of persuasion in which you discuss the causes and effects of discrimination against a group of people with a common characteristic. Possible topics include the causes and effects of discrimination in relation to name, race, region, body adornment, sexual preference, religion, weight, height, baldness, or physical handicap.

"Save Little League from Big Lugs"

2. Write an essay on the same subject but with your own solution to the problem of overbearing adults in youth sports (or in a specific youth sport). You may agree or disagree with the view of Tom Shields. Use your own examples.

"SUVs: Killer Cars" and "Guzzling, Gorgeous & Grand: SUVs and Those Who Love Them"

3. Write an essay of argument reflecting your own reasoned opinion of SUVs. Refer directly to both essays and include documentation and references to other sources, as directed by your instructor. Include accounts of some of your own feelings and experiences.

"The Abuse Excuse" and "Unequal Justice"

4. Write an essay of argument in which you support or oppose the abuse defense. Refer to both essays and, perhaps, to the definitions by Murphy in the introduction of this pair of sources. Include documentation and references, as directed by your instructor.

5. Write a response to the following lyrics from a folk song about an actual case in California. Using your own reasoning and reasoning from the two essays, explain why you would or would not favor special consideration for this defendant. If you need more information, what information would you request? Explain why you would need that information.

I'd Still Pull the Trigger

the Board said "Are you sorry?"
when I came up for parole
and I knew I'd have to kneel and cry
or stay here in this hole

well, if they gave out second chances
and I could change my song
I'd still pull the trigger
but I wouldn't wait so long

"You always kill the one you love"
I've heard some people say
you may agree but as for me
it was the other way

he used to beat me and the kids
he punched and raped and lied
he was a short-time Dr. Jekyll
and a long-term Mr. Hyde

so if they gave out second chances
and I could change my song
I'd still pull the trigger
but I wouldn't wait so long.

Career-Related Topics

6. Write an essay of argument to convince people that workers at a particular company should or should not be laid off.

7. Write an essay of argument to convince people that workers in a particular service industry should or should not go on strike.

General Topics

Write an essay of argument on one of the following broad subject areas. You will have to limit your focus for an essay of argument. You may modify the topics to fit specific situations.

8. Sexual harassment

9. Juvenile justice

10. Endangered species legislation

11. Advertising tobacco

12. Homelessness

13. State-run lotteries

14. Jury reform

15. Legalizing prostitution

16. Censoring rap or rock music

17. Cost of illegal immigration

18. Installation of local traffic signs

19. Foot patrols by local police

20. Change in (your) college registration procedure

21. Local rapid transit

22. Surveillance by video (on campus, in neighborhoods, or in shopping areas)

23. Zone changes for stores selling liquor

24. Curfew for teenagers

25. Laws keeping known gang members out of parks

Writer's Guidelines: Argument

1. Ask yourself the following questions. Then consider which parts of the formal argument you should include in your essay.

   - *Background:* What is the historical or social context for this controversial issue?

   - *Assertion* (the thesis of the essay, also called the proposition): What do I want my audience to believe or do?

- *Qualification of assertion:* Can I limit my assertion so that those who disagree cannot easily challenge me with exceptions?

- *Refutation* (taking the opposing view into account, mainly to point out its fundamental weakness): What is the view on the other side, and why is it flawed in reasoning or evidence?

- *Support:* In addition to sound reasoning, can I use appropriate facts, examples, statistics, and opinions of authorities?

2. The basic pattern of an essay of argument is likely to be in this form:

Assertion (the thesis of the essay)

  I. Support 1

 II. Support 2

III. Support 3

15

The Research Paper

THE QUIGMANS   by Buddy Hickerson

The Research Paper Defined

*T*he *research paper* is a long documented essay based on a thorough examination of a topic and supported by explanations and by both references to and quotations from sources. The traditional research paper in the style of the Modern Language Association, typically called MLA style, includes a title page (sometimes omitted), a thesis and an outline, a documented essay (text), and a list of sources (called "Works Cited," referring to the works used specifically in the essay).

This chapter presents a logical, systematic plan for writing a research paper. Don't be apprehensive: If you can write an effective essay, you can write an effective research paper. Pick a feasible topic and stay on schedule. (The two main problems for students working on research papers are (1) they select topics that are too broad or too narrow and (2) they fall behind schedule.) The following ten illustrated steps will guide you smoothly and painlessly in selecting a workable topic, finding sources, incorporating the ideas of others into your work, correctly documenting your borrowed ideas, and writing a longer, more complicated assignment.

Ten Steps to Writing a Research Paper

1. Select a Topic

Select a topic, and make a scratch outline. Then, construct a thesis as you did for writing essays by choosing what you intend to write about (subject) and by deciding how you will limit or focus your subject (treatment). Your purpose will be either to inform (explain) or to persuade (argue).

- Your topic should interest you and be appropriate in subject and scope for your assignment.
- Your topic should be researchable through library and other relevant sources, such as the Internet. Avoid topics that are too subjective or are so new that good source material is not available.

To write a treatment for your subject, you may need to scan a general discussion of your topic area so you can consider it in perspective and begin to see the parts or aspects on which you will want to concentrate. Relevant sections of encyclopedias and comprehensive books, such as textbooks, are often useful in establishing the initial overview. At this point, the closer you can come to a well-defined topic with a functional scratch outline of its divisions, the more likely you are to make a smooth, rapid, effective journey through the process. Try to divide your thesis into its functional parts.

Student Example

Tentative thesis: Despite some valid criticism, <u>the zoo as an institution</u>
subject

<u>will probably survive because of its roles in entertainment, education,</u>
treatment

<u>and conservation.</u>

   I. Entertainment
      A. Money
      B. Problems

  II. Education
      A. General public
      B. Students

 III. Conservation
      A. Science
      B. Breeding

 IV. Criticism
      A. Pro
      B. Con

  V. Zoos of the future
      A. Education
      B. Conservation

2. Find Sources

Find sources for your investigation. With your topic and its divisions in mind, use the resources and the electronic databases available in your college library and the Internet to identify books, articles, and other materials pertaining to your topic. The list of these items, called the *bibliography,* should be prepared on cards in the form appropriate for your assignment (MLA style in this text). Seek different kinds of materials, different types of information (primary, meaning coming from direct study, participation, observation, involvement; and secondary, meaning coming from indirect means—usually reporting on what others have done, observed, or been involved in), and credible writers (authorities and relatively unbiased, reliable reporters on your topic).

The Traditional Library

The main parts of the library pertaining to most research papers are the book collection and the periodical collection. Books are arranged on shelves by subject according to the Library of Congress system or the

Dewey Decimal system. Periodicals, including newspapers, are stored in a variety of ways: in unbound form (very recent editions), in bound form, on microfilm, in databases, and in online computer systems.

Books

Today most academic and municipal libraries provide information about books on online computer terminals, with databases accessible by author, title, subject, or other key words. Usually a printout of sources is available. As with the Internet, selecting key words and their synonyms is crucial to effective use of these online terminals. A combination of words will help you focus your search. In the following sample printout on the topic *animal?* and *conservation,* the user has keyed in the topic and then clicked to the title to check for location and availability:

```
BOOK - Record 1 of 20 Entries Found                          Brief View
-----------------------------------------------------------------------
Title:          The atlas of endangered species
Published:      New York : Macmillan : Toronto : Maxwell Macmillan
                  Canada, 1991.
Subjects:       Endangered species.
                Endangered plants.
                Nature conservation.
                Rare animals.
                Rare plants.
                Wildlife conservation.
                Environmental protection.
-------------------------------------------------- + Page 1 of 2 -----------
Search Request: K-ANIMAL? AND CONSERVATION     MS<ENTER>-Book catalog
BOOK - Record 1 of 20 Entries Found                          Brief View
-----------------------------------------------------------------------
Title:          The atlas of endangered species
-----------------------------------------------------------------------
LOCATION:              CALL NUMBER:            STATUS:
REFERENCE SHELVES      333.9516 At65           Not checked out
(Non-Circulating)
```

Printed Material Other Than Books

For the typical college research paper, the main printed nonbook sources are periodicals, such as newspapers, magazines, and journals. Various indexes will provide you with information for finding the source material you need. Depending on the library and the publication, periodicals are listed in indexes printed on paper or in electronic form. The most common index in bound volumes is the *Readers' Guide to Periodical Literature* (now also computerized). It indexes more than 200 popular magazines such as *Time* and *Newsweek,* which means that it is useful for basic research but not for more scholarly studies. The *New York Times* and numerous other metropolitan newspapers are also covered by indexes. For more academic searches, check with a reference librarian for indexes in specific fields such as anthropology or art. Indexes are usually kept in one area of the reference section. The following figure shows three sample entries from the *Readers' Guide.*

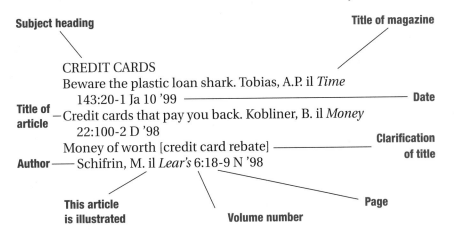

The Electronic Library

Computerized Indexes and Other Online Services

Computerized indexes, such as *InfoTrac, Periodical Abstracts,* and *Newspaper Abstracts Ondisc,* can be accessed in basically the same way as the online book catalogs, using key words and word combinations. They provide source information, perhaps with printouts. Some indexes include short abstracts (brief summaries) of the individual entries. Some indexes even provide the full text of material. One such index is *NEXIS,* an online service that can help you find sources and then provide the text of the original source material, all of which can be printed out.

An online essay originally published in, say, *Time* magazine, usually will be published without illustrations and in a different format. Therefore, it is important that you give full bibliographical information about your particular source (source citation instructions appear in Step 3).

Government publications, pamphlets, and other materials are cataloged in several ways. Procedures for searching all electronic indexes and sources routinely are posted alongside terminals, and librarians are available for further explanations and demonstrations. Many libraries also have pamphlets listing the periodicals they carry, their arrangements with other libraries for sharing or borrowing materials, access to the Internet, databases stored on CD-ROMS, and the availability of various online services. The availability of these indexes, catalogs, and databases varies greatly. Some libraries offer remote access to materials and the convenience of e-mailing the text of articles to home computers.

The Internet

A realistic view of what the World Wide Web offers will enable you to conduct a significant part of your research there.

Strengths:

- The Internet provides a mind-boggling number of easily accessible sources.

- The Internet can connect you instantly with people of shared interests.

- The Internet also allows you to do research around the globe from one computer in your home or at your library.

- Some governmental studies, scholarly journals, and other publications appear only on the Internet.

Weaknesses:

- The Internet slants toward current and recent events, offering little information on many topics set in the past.

- Although containing a wealth of material, most books and articles are still found only in the library.

- Always in a condition of change, most Internet sites add, change, and delete information constantly.

- Anyone—from expert to ignoramus—with the right equipment and the inclination can publish Internet material.

Thus, the Internet is a highly useful tool, but you would seldom rely on it entirely for a project. Here are some guidelines, strategies, and hints for conducting your research:

- Your search will probably begin with the location of search engines, of which there are hundreds available. No one search engine carries all material, and some examine the files of others.

- These are among the most popular search engines:

AltaVista	Excite
Lycos	Yahoo
HotBot	Google
Dogpile	

  You can enter those search engines through your Internet access button and save them on your "My Favorites" list.

- Because of the difficulty of retracing your research, when you come across material that may be useful, "Bookmark" or enter it on your "My Favorites" list. One useful strategy is to create a separate folder for your research paper topic.

- Make a copy of promising items, for they may have been altered or deleted when you return to the site. Having a copy will also allow you to underline and annotate material.

- Ask your librarian or your instructor for guidance on finding research addresses without going through search engines such as Google or Yahoo. Some of these are the Library of Congress, the U.S. Bureau of the Census, and the *New York Times.*

- To evaluate material, try to determine the expertise of the author(s), the sponsorship of the publication, and the reliability of supporting information.

3. List Sources

List tentative sources in a preliminary bibliography.

Bibliography and Works Cited, MLA Style

You will list source material in two phases of your research paper project: the preliminary bibliography and the works cited.

When you begin your research, make a list of works that may provide useful information on your topic. At this time, do not stop to make a careful examination and evaluation of each entry, although you should keep in mind that your material usually should come from a variety of sources and that they ideally should be objective, authoritative, and current. For various reasons, some sources may not find their way into your research paper at all. As you read, you may discover that some sources are superficial, poorly researched, overly technical, off the topic, or unavailable. The preliminary bibliography is nothing more than a list of sources to consider and select from.

The sources that you actually use in the paper—meaning those that you refer to by name or quote—become part of the Works Cited list at the end of the final draft.

The MLA research paper form is commonly used for both the preliminary bibliography and the list of works cited. This format is unlike the formats used in catalogs and indexes. The following examples show the difference between printout forms from library files and the MLA research paper forms.

Books

Printout Forms

```
Author:   DiSilvestro, Roger L.
Title:    The African elephant: twilight in Eden
Published: New York: Wiley, ©1991.
```

MLA Research Paper Form

Titles of longer works are either underlined or italicized. Be consistent.

DiSilvestro, Roger L. <u>The African Elephant: Twilight in Eden</u>. New York: Wiley, 1991.

Periodicals

Printout Form

Author: Ormrod, Stefan A.
Title: Boo for zoos.
Source: New Scientist v. 145 (Mar. 18 '95) p. 48.

MLA Research Paper Form

Ormrod, Stefan A. "Boo for Zoos." <u>New Scientist</u> 18 Mar. 1995: 48.

MLA Form for Printed Sources

Books

A Book by One Author

Twitchell, James B. <u>ADCULTusa: The Triumph of Advertising in American Culture</u>. New York: Columbia UP, 1996.

An Anthology

List the name of the editor, followed by a comma, a space, and "ed."

Grumet, Robert S., ed. <u>Northeastern Indian Lives</u>. Amherst: U of Massachusetts P, 1996.

Two or More Books by the Same Author

Walker, Alice. <u>The Color Purple: A Novel</u>. New York: Harcourt. 1982.

---, <u>Meridian</u>. New York: Harcourt, 1976.

A Book by Two or More Authors

Current, Richard Nelson, Marcia Ewing Current, and Louis Fuller. <u>Goddess of Light</u>. Boston: Northeastern UP, 1997.

Use *et al.* for four or more authors.

Comley, Nancy R., et al. <u>Fields of Writing</u>. New York: St. Martin's, 1997.

A Book with a Corporate Author

International City/County Management Association. <u>The Municipal Year Book: 1998</u>. Washington, DC: ICMA.

Articles

Article in a Journal
Butterick, George. "Charles Olson's 'The Kingfishers' and
the Poetics of Change." <u>American Poetry</u> 6.2 (1989):
28-59.

Article in a Weekly or Biweekly Magazine, Author Unknown
"How the Missiles Help California." <u>Time</u> 1 Apr. 1996: 45.

Article in a Monthly or Bimonthly Magazine
Fallows, James, "Why Americans Hate the Media." <u>Atlantic
Monthly</u> Feb. 1996: 45-64.

Newspaper Article
Gregory, Tina. "When All Else Fails." <u>Philadelphia
Inquirer</u> 2 Apr. 1990: C12.

Editorial
Lewis, Anthony, "Black and White." Editorial: <u>New York
Times</u> 18 June 1992, natl. ed.: A19.

A Work in an Anthology

Booth, Wayne C. "The Scholar in Society." <u>Introduction to
Scholarship in Modern Languages and Literatures</u>. Ed.
Joseph Gibaldi. New York: MLA, 1981. 116-143.

An Article in an Encyclopedia

Cheney, Ralph Holt, "Coffee." <u>Collier's Encyclopedia</u>.
1993 ed.

Government Publications

United States. Dept. of Transportation. National Highway
Traffic Safety Admin. <u>Driver Licensing Laws Annotated
1980</u>. Washington: GPO, 1980.

Citations from the *Congressional Record* require only a date and page
number.
<u>Cong. Rec.</u> 11 Sept. 1992: 12019-24.

Published Proceedings of a Conference

<u>Proceedings of the 34th Annual International Technical
Communication Conference</u>. Denver, 10-13 May 1987. San
Diego: Univelt, 1987.

Treat particular presentations in the proceedings as you would pieces in a collection.

```
Wise, Mary R. "The Main Event Is Desktop Publishing." Pro-
    ceedings of the 34th International Technical Communi-
    cation Conference. Denver, 10-13 May 1987. San Diego:
    Univelt, 1987.
```

A Lecture, Speech, or Address

```
Kern, David, "Recent Trends in Occupational Medicine."
    Memorial Hospital, Pawtucket, RI. 2 Oct. 1997.
```

A Personal Interview

```
Thomas, Carolyn. Personal Interview. 5 Jan. 2002.
```

A Film or Video Recording

```
Schindler's List. Dir. Steven Spielberg. Perf. Liam Neeson
    and Ben Kingsley. Universal, 1993.
```

MLA Form for Electronic Sources

Formats vary widely in electronic media because of rapidly changing systems and terms. The information you provide in your bibliography and works cited will inform your reader about such matters as the subject of each source, who has worked on it, where it came from originally, when it was first written and last changed, when you found it, where you found it, and how you found it. Be sure that you give enough information. If you cannot find directions for citing a source, you should identify a form used for similar content as a model, improvise if necessary, and be as consistent as possible.

Do not be intimidated by the length and seeming complexity of the citations. Every part is reasonable and every part is necessary. If you are not certain whether to include some information, you probably should. As you present your orderly sequence of parts in your entries, you must take great care in attending to detail, for a single keystroke can leave your source concealed in cyberspace with no electronic map for your reader.

The examples in this section follow MLA style. More details can be found at <www.mla.org>. Because the nature of electronic sources and references to them are constantly evolving, check each Web site for changes and updates.

This is the basic form for Internet and World Wide Web sources for your bibliography and works-cited entries:

- Author's (or editor's, compiler's, or translator's) last name, first name, middle initial

- "Title of article or other short work" or *Title of Book*

- Publication date or date of last revision for any printed version
- Subject of forum or discussion group
- Indication of online posting or Web page
- Title of electronic journal
- Editor's name (if available)
- Page numbers or the numbers of paragraphs or sections
- Name of institution or organization sponsoring or affiliated with Web site
- Date of access to the source
- <electronic address or URL>

Online Services—Library and Personal

Library Subscription Services (Database with Full Texts)
Online library subscription services provide databases mainly of articles in journals, magazines, and newspapers. They are accessed either at a library terminal or by the student's computer. They often include hundreds of publications and enable students to find and print out entire texts rapidly. Although most have complete printed versions, the illustrations are usually omitted, page numbers are changed or not given, and some material may be reformatted. For brief documented papers, instructors sometimes ask their students to include copies of the printouts with the final submission. Content ranges from works intended for the general reader to those written for scholarly purposes. Some are listed as "juried," which means that the selections have been evaluated for credible content by a group of experts in the field. Library online services include ProQuest Direct, Lexis-Nexis, and EBSCOhost.

The basic form is author, title, publication, information, service company, library, and date of access. Include the URL of the service in angle brackets if it is available.

```
Fox, Justin. "What in the World Happened to Economics?"
    Fortune 15 Mar. 1999: 90-102. ABI/INFORM Global. Pro-
    Quest Direct. Regional Community Coll. Lib., Little
    Rock. 2 Mar. 1999 <http://www.umi.com/proquest/>.
Rivenburg, Roy, "The Mean Season." Los Angeles Times 14
    July 1995: E-1. NewsBank InfoWeb. Mt. San Antonio
    Coll. Lib., Walnut, CA. 8 Sept. 1999.
```

Personal Subscription Services (Databases with Full Texts Supplied by Companies such as AOL)
Typically indicate author, title, publication information (if any), name of service, date of access, and the *Keyword* you used or the *Path* (sequence of topics) you followed in locating the source.

"Cloning." <u>BioTech's Life and Science Dictionary</u>. 30 June 1998. Indiana U. America Online. 4 July 1998. Path: Research and Learning; Science; Biology; Biotechnology Dictionary.

"Tecumseh." <u>Compton's Encyclopedia Online</u>. Vers. 3.0. 1998. American Online. 8 April 2000. Keyword: Compton's.

Professional Site

<u>MLA on the Web</u>. 25 November 1997. Modern Language Association of America. 25 Mar. 1998 <http://www.mla.org>.

Personal Site

Hawisher, Gail. Home page. University of Illinois Urbana-Champaign/The Women, Information Technology, and Scholarship Colloquium. 18 Mar. 1998 <http://www.art.uiuc.edu/wits/members/hawisher.html>.

Books

Conrad, Joseph. <u>Lord Jim</u>. London: Blackwoods, 1900. <u>Oxford Text Archive</u>. 12 July 1993. Oxford University Computing Services. 20 Feb. 1998 <ftp://ota.ox.ac.uk/pub/ota/public/english/conrad/lordjim.1924>.

Dickens, Charles. <u>A Christmas Carol</u>. London 1843. <u>The Electronic Text Center</u>. Ed. David Seaman. Dec. 1997. U of Virginia Library. 4 Feb. 1998 <http://etext.lib.virginia.edu/cgibin/browse=mixed?id=DicChri&tag=public&images=images/modeng&data=/lv1/Archive/eng=parsed>.

Poem

Hampl, Patricia. "Who We Will Love." <u>Woman Before an Aquarium</u>. Pittsburgh: U of Pittsburgh P, 1978: 27-28. A Poem a Week. Rice University. 13 Mar. 1998 <http://www.ruf.rice.edu/~alisa/Jun24html>.

Article in a Journal

Bieder, Robert A. "The Representation of Indian Bodies in Nineteenth-Century American Anthropology." <u>The American Indian Quarterly</u> 20.2 (1996). 28 Mar. 1998 <http://www.uoknor.edu/aiq/aiq202.html#beider>.

Killiam, Rosemary. "Cognitive Dissonance: Should Twentieth-Century Women Composers Be Grouped with Focault's Mad Criminals?" <u>Music Theory Online</u> 3.2 (1997): 30 pars. 10 May 1997 <http://smt.ucsb.edu/mto/mtohome.html>.

Article in a Magazine

Keillor, Garrison. "Why Did They Ever Ban a Book This Bad?" <u>Salon</u> 13 Oct. 1997. 14 Oct. 1997 <http://www.salon1999.com/feature/>.

Article in an Online Newspaper

"Tornadoes Touch Down in S. Illinois." <u>New York Times on the Web</u> 16 Apr. 1998. 20 May 1998 <http://www.nytimes.com/aponline/a/AP-Illinois-Storms.html>.

Newspaper Editorial

"The Proved and the Unproved." Editorial. <u>New York Times</u> 13 July 1997. 14 July 1997 <http://www.nytimes.com/yr/mo/day/editorial/13sun1.html>.

Review

Koeppel, Fredric. "A Look at John Keates." Rev. of <u>Keats</u>, by Andrew Motion. <u>Nando Times News</u> 16 Apr. 1998. 27 Aug. 1998 <http://www.nando.net/newsroom/ntn/enter/041698/enter30_20804.html>.

Posting to a Discussion List

Merrian, Joanne. "Spinoff: Monsterpiece Theatre." Online posting. 30 Apr. 1994. Shaksper: The Global Electronic Shakespeare Conf. 27 Aug. 1997 <http.//www.arts.ubc.ca/english/iemls/shak/MONSTERP_SPINOFF.txt>.

Inman, James. "Re: Technologist." Online posting. 24 Sept. 1997. Alliance for Computers in Writing. 27 Mar. 1998 <acw-1/unicorn.acs.ttu.edu>.

Gopher

Page, Melvin E. "Brief Citation Guide for Internet Sources in History and the Humanities." 20 Feb. 1996. 9

pp. 7 July 1996 <gopher://h-net.msu.edu/00/
lists/h-africa/internet-cit>.

Synchronous Communication (MOOs, MUDs)

Inept_Guest. Discussion of disciplinary politics in rhet/
comp. 12 Mar. 1998. LinguaMOO. 12 Mar. 1998
<telnet:lingua.utdallas.edu 8888>.

Scholarly Project

<u>Victorian Women Writers Project</u>. Ed. Perry Willett. Apr.
1997. Indiana U. 26 Apr. 1997 <http://www.
indiana.edu/~letrs/vwwp/>.

CD-ROM

West, Cornel. "The Dilemma of the Black Intellectual."
<u>Critical Quarterly</u> 29 (1987): 39-52. <u>MLA Interna-
tional Bibliography</u>. CD-ROM. Silver Platter.
Feb. 1995.

"About <u>Richard III</u>." <u>Cinemania 96</u>. CD-ROM. Redmond:
Microsoft, 1996.

Article in a Reference Database

"Fresco," <u>Britannica Online</u>. Vers. 97.1.1. Mar. 1997
Encyclopaedia Britannica. 29 Mar. 1997
<http://www.eb.com:180>.

Atwood, Margaret. "Memento Mori-but First. Carpe Diem."
Rev. of <u>Toward the End of Time,</u> by John Updike.
<u>New York Times Book Review</u> 12 Oct. 1997: 9-10. The
<u>New York Times</u> Books on the Web. 1997. The New
York Times Company. 13 Oct. 1997 <http://
search.nytimes.com/books/97/10/12/reviews/
971012.12atwood.html>.

Personal E-mail Message

Watkins, Jack. "Collaborative Projects." E-mail to
Gabriel Mendoza. 12 April 2002.

Exercise 1　　　**FORM FOR BIBLIOGRAPHY AND WORKS CITED**

Change the following items from printouts to MLA research paper form.

1. A Book by One Author
   Printout Form
   　　Author: Colin Tudge
   　　Title: Last Animals at the Zoo: How Mass Extinction Can Be Stopped
   　　Publisher: Hutchinson Radius
   　　Place of Publication: London
   　　Date of Publication (or Copyright): 1991

MLA Research Paper Form
   Tudge, Colin. <u>Last Animals at the Zoo: How Mass Extinction Can Be Stopped</u>. London: Hutchinson Radius, 1991.

2. A Work in an Anthology (May Be a Textbook)
   Printout Form
   　　Author of Work (Essay): Adam Goodheart
   　　Title of Essay: How to Paint a Fresco
   　　Title of Anthology: From Self to Sources: Essays and Documented Essays
   　　Editor of Anthology: Lee Brandon
   　　Publisher: Houghton Mifflin Company
   　　Place of Publication: Boston
   　　Date of Publication (or copyright): 2003
   　　Page Numbers of Work (Essay): 262–264

MLA Research Paper Form
   Goodheart, Adam. "How to Paint a Fresco." <u>From Self to Sources: Essays and Documented Essays</u>. Ed. Lee Brandon. Boston: Houghton Mifflin, 2003. 262–264.

3. Article in a Weekly or Biweekly Magazine
   Printout Form
   　　Author: Betsy Carpenter
   　　Title of Article: Upsetting the Ark
   　　Title of Magazine: U.S. News & World Report
   　　Date of Publication: August 24, 1992
   　　Page Numbers of Article: 57–61

MLA Research Paper Form
   Carpenter, Betsy. "Upsetting the Ark." <u>U.S. News & World Report</u> 24 Aug. 1992: 57–61.

4. Newspaper Article
   Printout Form
   　　Author of Article: Malcolm W. Browne
   　　Title of Article: They're Back! Komodos Avoid Extinction
   　　Title of Newspaper: New York Times

Date of Publication: March 1, 1994
Page Numbers of Article: C1 and C4

MLA Research Paper Form

Browne, Malcolm W. "They're Back! Komodos Avoid Extinction." <u>New York Times</u> 1 Mar. 1994:
C1, C4.

4. Take Notes

Takes notes in an organized fashion. Resist the temptation to write down everything that interests you. Instead, take notes that pertain to divisions of your topic as stated in your thesis or scratch outline. Locate, read, and take notes on the sources listed in your preliminary bibliography. Some of these sources need to be printed out from electronic databases or the Internet, some photocopied, and some checked out. Your notes will usually be on cards, with each card indicating key pieces of information:

A. Division of topic (usually the Roman number part of your scratch outline or the divisions of your thesis)

B. Identification of topic (by author's last name or title of piece)

C. Location of material (usually by page number)

D. Text of statement as originally worded (with quotation marks; editorial comments in brackets), summarized or paraphrased (in student's own words, without quotation marks), and statement of relevance of material, if possible

Student Example

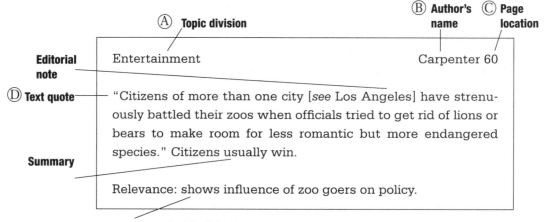

Exercise 2 **COMPLETING NOTE CARDS**

Transfer the following information to the blank note card below.

1. Quotation:
   "The lucky or well-born find homes at accredited zoos, but many are put to death or sold to game ranges, roadside menageries, amusement parks or circuses."

2. Author: Betsy Carpenter

3. Title: "Upsetting the Ark" (the only selection by Carpenter in this paper)

4. Location: p. 59

5. Division of Topic (how it relates to thesis): No easy solution to problem

---

No easy solution to problem   Carpenter 59

"The lucky or well-born find homes at accredited zoos, but many are put to death or sold to game ranges, roadside menageries, amusement parks or circuses."

Relevance: shows reality of situation.

---

5. Refine Your Thesis and Outline

Refine your thesis statement and outline to reflect more precisely what you intend to write.

Student Example

Thesis: Throughout the world, despite determined opposition, the modern zoo with a new image and compound purpose is taking shape.

I. Zoos as entertainment

  A. Attendance

  B. Income

  C. Customer preferences

II. Captive breeding success

  A. National

  B. International

III. Scientific success

    A. Embryo transfers

    B. Artificial insemination

    C. Test-tube fertilization

    D. Storage of eggs, sperm, and tissue

    E. Computer projects

        1. Lab studies

        2. Animal tracking

IV. Education

    A. Purpose--change attitude

    B. Basic idea--show animals in ecosystem

    C. School applications

V. Different models of zoos

    A. Zoo/park

    B. Safari park

    C. Regional zoo

6. Write Your First Draft

Referring to your thesis, outline, and note cards keyed to your outline, write the first draft of your research paper. Use the following guidelines to include proper MLA research paper form in documentation.

Plagiarism

Careful attention to the rules of documentation will help you avoid *plagiarism:* the unacknowledged use of someone else's words or ideas. It occurs when a writer omits quotation marks when citing the exact language of a source, fails to revise completely a paraphrased source, or gives no documentation for a quotation or paraphrase. The best way to avoid this problem is to be attentive in the following details.

When you copy a quotation directly into your notes, check to be sure that you have put quotation marks around it. If you forget to include them when you copy, you might omit them in the paper as well.

When you paraphrase, keep in mind that it is not sufficient to change just a few words or rearrange sentence structure. You must completely rewrite the passage. One of the best ways to accomplish this is to read the material you want to paraphrase; then cover the page so that you cannot see it and write down the information as you remember it. Compare your version with the original and make any necessary changes in the note. If you cannot successfully rewrite the passage, quote it instead.

The difference between legitimate and unacceptable paraphrases is shown in the following examples:

- *Source*

> "What is unmistakably convincing and makes Miller's theatre writing hold is its authenticity in respect to the minutiae of American life. He is a first-rate reporter; he makes the details of his observation palpable."

- *Unacceptable Paraphrase*

> What is truly convincing and makes Arthur Miller's theatrical writing effective is its authenticity. He is an excellent reporter and makes his observation palpable.

- *Legitimate Paraphrase*

> The strength of Arthur Miller's dramatic art lies in its faithfulness to the details of the American scene and in its power to bring to life the reality of ordinary experience.

The differences between these two versions of Clurman's statement are enormous. The first writer has made some token changes, substituting a few synonyms (*truly* for *unmistakably, excellent* for *first-rate*), deleting part of the first sentence, and combining the two parts of the second sentence into a single clause. Otherwise, this is a word-for-word copy of the original, and if the note were copied into the paper in this form, the writer would be guilty of plagiarism. The second writer has changed the vocabulary of the original passage and completely restructured the sentence so that the only similarity between the note and the source is the ideas.

Check to see that each of your research notes has the correct name and page number so that when you use information from that note in your paper, you will be able to credit it to the right source.

Documentation: Parenthetical References, MLA Style

Although you need not acknowledge a source for generally known information such as the dates of the Civil War or the names of the ships that carried Columbus and his followers to the New World, you must identify the exact source and location of each statement, fact, or original idea you borrow from another person or work.

In the text of the research paper, MLA style requires only a brief parenthetical source reference keyed to a complete bibliographical entry in the list of works cited at the end of the essay. For most parenthetical references, you will need to cite only the author's last name and the number of the page from which the statement or idea was taken, and, if you mention the author's name in the text, the page number alone is sufficient. This format also allows you to include within the parentheses additional information, such as title or volume number, if it is needed for clarity. Documentation for some of the most common types of sources is discussed in the following sections.

References to Articles and Single-Volume Books

Articles and single-volume books are the two types of works you will be referring to most often in your research paper. When citing them, either mention the author's name in the text and note the appropriate page number in parentheses immediately after the citation or acknowledge both name and page number in the parenthetical reference, leaving a space between the two. If punctuation is needed, insert the mark outside the final parenthesis.

- *Author's Name Cited in Text*

      Marya Mannes has defined euthanasia as "the
      chosen alternative to the prolongation of a
      steadily waning mind and spirit by machines
      that will withhold death or to an existence
      that mocks life" (61).

- *Author's Name Cited in Parentheses*

      Euthansia has been defined as "the chosen
      alternative to the prolongation of a steadily
      waning mind and spirit by machines that will
      withhold death or to an existence that mocks
      life" (Mannes 61).

- *Corresponding Bibliographic Entry*

      Mannes, Marya. <u>Last Rights</u>. New York: Morrow,
      1973.

References to Works in an Anthology

When referring to a work in an anthology, either cite in the text the author's name and indicate in parentheses the page number in the anthology where the source is located, or acknowledge both name and page reference parenthetically.

- *Author's Name Cited in Text*

      One of the most widely recognized facts
      about James Joyce, in Lionel Trilling's view,
      "is his ambivalence toward Ireland, of which
      the hatred was as relentless as the love was
      unfailing" (153).

- *Author's Name Cited in Parentheses*

      One of the most widely recognized facts
      about James Joyce "is his ambivalence toward
      Ireland, of which the hatred was as relentless
      as the love was unfailing" (Trilling 153).

- *Corresponding Bibliographic Entry*

> Trilling, Lionel, "James Joyce in His Letters." <u>Joyce: A Collection of Critical Essays</u>. Ed. William M. Chace. Englewood Cliffs: Prentice-Hall, 1974.

References to Works of Unknown Authorship

If you borrow information or ideas from an article or book for which you cannot determine the name of the author, cite the title instead, either in the text of the paper or in parentheses, and include the page reference as well.

- *Title Cited in Text*

> According to an article titled "Going Back to Booze," surveys have shown that most adult alcoholics began drinking heavily as teenagers (42).

- *Title Cited in Parentheses*

> Surveys have shown that most adult alcoholics began drinking heavily as teenagers ("Going Back to Booze" 42).

- *Corresponding Bibliographic Entry*

> "Going Back to Booze." <u>Time</u> 31 Nov. 1999: 41-46.

References to Internet Material

Treat Internet material as you would other material. If the author's name is not available, give the title. Include page and paragraph numbers if they are available; usually they are not.

References in Block Quotations

Quotations longer than four typewritten lines are indented ten spaces or one half inch without quotation marks, and their references are put outside end punctuation.

- *Reference Cited after End Punctuation*

> Implicit in the concept of Strange Loops is the concept of infinity, since what else is a loop but a way of representing an endless process in a finite way? And infinity plays a large role in many of Escher's drawings. Copies of one single theme often fit into each other, forming visual analogues to the canons of Bach. (Hofstadter 15)

• *Corresponding Bibliographic Entry*

Hofstadter, Douglas. <u>Gödel, Escher, Bach: An</u>
<u>Eternal Golden Braid</u>. New York: Vin-
tage, 1980.

| Exercise 3 | **GIVING CREDIT TO SOURCES** |

Complete the parenthetical references and punctuation according to MLA style.

1. Quotation, taken from page 60 of the source, is introduced with the author's name (with only one source by this author in this paper).

   Schmidt reports that the Cincinnati Zoo Center for Reproduction of Endangered Wildlife has frozen "eggs from a rare female Sumatran rhino that died, hoping one day to obtain some sperm and learn how to make test-tube rhino embryos" <u>   (60)   </u>.

2. Paraphrased information by James Rainey from an Internet source with no page numbers given (with only one source by this author in this paper).

   The Los Angeles Zoo faced similar opposition in 1994 when directors proposed a multimillion dollar expansion of the education program rather than spending that money on facilities for animals popular with zoo goers <u>   (Rainey).   </u>.

3. Quotation, from page 52 of the source, is introduced with the author's name. One other source by the same author is used in this paper. The title of this source is "Captive Audiences for Future Conservation."

   As Tudge points out, "Captive breeding is not an alternative to habitat protection. Increasingly, however, it is a vital backup" <u>("Captive Audiences for Future Conservation" 52).   </u>.

7. Revise Your First Draft

Evaluate your first draft, and amend it as needed (perhaps researching an area not well-covered for additional support material and adding or deleting sections of your outline to reflect the way your paper has grown).

Use the writing process guidelines as you would in writing any other essay:

• Write and then revise your paper as many times as necessary for <u>c</u>oherence, <u>l</u>anguage (usage, tone, and diction), <u>u</u>nity, <u>e</u>mphasis, <u>s</u>upport, and <u>s</u>entences (CLUESS).

- Correct problems in fundamentals such as <u>c</u>apitalization, <u>o</u>missions, <u>p</u>unctuation, and <u>s</u>pelling (COPS). Before writing the final draft, read your paper aloud to discover any errors or awkward sentence structure.

8. Prepare Your Works Cited Page

Using the same form as in the preliminary bibliography, prepare a Works Cited section (a list of works you have referred to or quoted and identified parenthetically in the text).

9. Write Your Final Draft

Write the final draft of your research paper with care for effective writing and accurate documentation. The final draft will probably include these parts:

1. Title page (sometimes omitted)

2. Thesis and outline (topical or sentence, as directed)

3. Documented essay (text)

4. List of sources used (Works Cited)

10. Submit Required Materials

Submit your research paper with any preliminary material required by your instructor. Consider using a checklist to make sure that you have fulfilled all requirements. A comprehensive checklist might look like this:

Research Paper Checklist

☐ Title page (sometimes omitted)

☐ Thesis and outline

☐ Documented essay (text)

_____ Approximate total number of words

_____ Approximate number of words quoted (usually more than 20 percent quoted words would be excessive)

☐ List of sources used (Works Cited)

_____ Number of sources used

☐ Preliminary materials, such as preliminary bibliography, note cards, and rough draft, as required

Student Example: Annotated Final Draft

Title page is optional; check with instructor.

Zoos—An Endangered Species?

Michael Chung

Professor Lee Brandon

English 1A

9 January 2002

Double-space throughout. Thesis and outline are optional; check with instructor.

<u>Thesis statement</u>: Throughout the world, despite determined opposition, the modern zoo with a new image and compound purpose is taking shape.

Align entries in columns.

I. Zoos as entertainment

    A. Attendance

    B. Income

    C. Customer preferences

        1. Favoring certain animals

        2. Favoring animals over education

II. Pandas for profit

    A. Criticism

    B. Benefits

        1. Money for zoo conservation projects

        2. Money back to natural habitat

III. Captive breeding success

    A. National

    B. International

IV. Scientific success

    A. Embryo transfers

    B. Artificial insemination

    C. Test-tube fertilization

    D. Storage of eggs, sperm, and tissue

        1. For use shortly

        2. Awaiting future development

    E. Computer projects

        1. Lab studies

        2. Animal tracking in field

Heading for all pages starting on the second page of the paper: last name, one space, page number (small Roman numerals for outline pages, Arabic for paper).

V. Education

    A. Purpose--change attitude

    B. Basic idea--show animals in ecosystem

    C. School applications

        1. Field trips

        2. Sleepovers

        3. Entire high school education in zoo

VI. Different models of zoos

    A. Zoo/Park

    B. Safari park

    C. Regional zoo

VII. Humane treatment of animals

    A. Problems without easy solution

        1. Unruly animals

        2. Animals with diseases

        3. Surplus animals

    B. Problems and solutions

        1. Providing better living areas

        2. Engaging animals in natural activities

VIII. Response to critics

    A. Acknowledging contributions

    B. Pointing out flaws

        1. Zoos and support for wildlife linked

        2. Much habitat destruction inevitable and irreversible

Chung 1

Michael Chung
Professor Lee Brandon
English 1A
9 January 2002

Zoos–An Endangered Species

½" from top

1" from top
Information here only
if you do not use a
title page.

Title—centered

Indent five spaces for
paragraph.
Uses historical
perspective for
introduction

Basic thesis idea as
question

1" side margin

Thesis

1" bottom margin

   Early zoos were usually little more than crude
holding pens where animals, often serving dually
with circuses, died off and were replaced by a seemingly inexhaustible supply from the wild. In the first
seven decades of the twentieth century, zoos evolved
into institutions that offered some education, a little
conservation of species, and, mostly, entertainment.
Meanwhile, numerous passionate critics emerged,
arguing for animal rights and questioning the effectiveness and appropriateness of zoo programs. They
brought into focus the question, Are zoos necessary?
   Since the 1970s, facing this criticism, zoos have
set out to justify their existence. The prevailing view
sides with the continuance of zoos. It generally
accepts the entertainment value but stresses education in different forms and conservation through
applied science. Worldwide, despite determined
opposition, the modern zoo is taking shape with a
new image and compound purpose.
   In any review of the questionable functions of a
zoo, the issue of entertainment at the expense of our

Chung 2

I. Zoos as entertainment

Quotation with statistics

fellow creatures must be considered. Indisputably, zoos are popular. According to Jeffrey Cohn, "An estimated 102 million people, more than attend professional football, baseball, and basketball games combined, visit the 162 accredited zoos and aquariums each year" ("Decisions at the Zoo" 659). Coming especially for entertainment, these visitors spend hundreds of millions of dollars, money that the zoos need for operation and projects, even for survival.

Quotation blended in

Example

Internet source

Naturally zoos tend to lure customers by giving them at least some of what they want to experience. Occasionally the zoos have met opposition when they tried to advance the issues of conservation and education over entertainment. In "Upsetting the Ark," Betsy Carpenter says that "citizens of more than one city have strenuously battled their zoos when officials tried to get rid of lions or bears to make room for less romantic but more endangered species" (60). The Los Angeles Zoo faced similar opposition in 1994 when directors proposed a multi-million dollar expansion of the educational program rather than spending that money on facilities for animals popular with zoo goers (Rainey). However, knowing what visitors want, zoos often take the lead in featuring eye-catching exhibits, and not all zoo officials are apologetic about doing so.

II. Pandas for profit

For the past several decades, giant pandas have been the most sought-after creatures for drawing

Chung 3

	crowds to zoos. With a limited number of these amusingly attractive creatures in the wild and only a few in captivity, demands for panda loans from the
Voice of expert	Chinese government have increased. Richard Block from the World Wildlife Fund says, "The zoos are using pandas to bring people through the gate without any real education or conservation programs attached (qtd. in Cohn, "Decisions at the Zoo," 656).
II, A. Criticism **Statistics** **Example**	Zoo officials and supporters argue otherwise. In 1987-88, the San Diego Zoo made about $7 million on a seven-month panda exhibit. Their directors argue that they were able to use more than fifteen percent of that sum to provide China with money, scientists,
II, B. Benefits	and equipment to help conserve pandas in their native habitat. Using a similar argument, the Columbus (Ohio) Zoo, amid continued controversy, signed a
Example	contract for a long-term loan. The contract was even more lucrative than previous contracts for the Chinese, with the exhibit including a talk, signs, and pamphlets. Critics still charged the zoo with token education and the Chinese government with cynically renting pandas for profit, pointing out that
Paraphrase	there is a financial incentive for keeping the panda population down to ensure a high rental fee for exhibits (Cohn, "Decisions at the Zoo," 657).
III. Captive breeding **success**	Quite aside from the entertainment aspect of zoos is the captive breeding program. In one spec-

Chung 4

tacular captive breeding success in 1992, the
National Zoo in Washington, D.C., may have saved
the endangered Komodo dragon from extinction by
successfully incubating thirty eggs. This ten-foot
dangerous, ugly creature that resembles a dinosaur
numbers only somewhere around 5,000-8,000 in the
wild but soon will be represented in numerous zoos
(Browne C1). Now that the incubation process is
established, the entire program offers opportunity to
restock the Komodo's habitat in Indonesia.

Not all captive breeding projects can end with a
reintroduction of the species to the wild. For those
species, the zoos have turned to science, which has
been used in a variety of ways. In "Preserving the
Genetic Legacies," Karen F. Schmidt says:

> Zoos are increasingly adapting the latest in human
> and agricultural reproductive technologies to aid
> beleaguered species by boosting their numbers,
> increasing gene variety in small populations and con-
> trolling inbreeding[. . .] . Although still in the early
> stages, embryo transfers, artificial insemination and
> even test-tube fertilization are seen by zoologists as
> having real or potential application in conserving
> endangered wildlife. (60)

These scientific endeavors began in the 1970s
and now some of them are commonplace. Female

III, A. Statistics

III, B. Paraphrased material

Citation

IV. Scientific success

Quotation introduced with title and author's name

Block-indented quotation, no quotation marks

Words omitted (ellipses)

Citation after period for long quotation

Chung 5

apes are on the pill and surrogate mother tigers are receiving embryos. Schmidt reports that the Cincinnati Zoo Center for Reproduction of Endangered Wildlife has frozen "eggs from a rare female Sumatran rhino that died, hoping one day to obtain some sperm and learn how to make test-tube rhino embryos" (60). In many zoos, eggs, sperm, and skin for DNA storage have been frozen in zoo labs, awaiting scientific development by future generations.

In current projects, computers have figured prominently. The California condor project at the Los Angeles Zoo used computer data to match males and females for effective breeding (Diamond 82). Karen Schmidt reports that in New York's Bronx Zoo, computer technology has involved a robot:

> One new tool to rescue the bird species is the "robo-egg," an egg-shaped electronic device that a mother bird treats as one of her own eggs. Sensors inside the robo-egg measure temperature and humidity in the nest and how often the mother bird turns the egg. The information is then relayed to researchers. (60)

Computers are also used in field studies of endangered animals. Some of these projects are coordinated by zoos. In the Malaysian Elephant Satellite Tracking Project, Malaysian, Smithsonian,

Reference introduced with author's name

Blended paraphrase and quotation

Citation after quotation marks for short quotation

IV, E. Computer projects

Block-indented quotation

Chung 6

Web site

and National Zoo officials have cooperatively used transmitters, satellites, and computers to track movements of elephants released in sanctuaries ("Project Technology").

Despite all these impressive contributions to wildlife conservation by zoos and other institutions, millions of species face extinction in the next half century, and little can be done to save most. Therefore, concerned people should do what is possible.

V, A. Education

Many conservationists believe that the zoo's top priority should be education. The director of the national Zoo, Michael Robinson, says that while zoos have an important role to play in captive breeding and science, a far more important one is in education.

Quotation from expert

He "contends that the only way to halt the destruction (of species) is to change people's attitudes and that zoos must evolve into institutions that teach people to treasure the natural world" (Carpenter 59).

After the Endangered Species Act became law in 1973, attitudes about the roles of zoos have generally changed within zoo management (Cohn, "The New Breeding Ground" 21). One of the most noticeable changes has been in the configuration of zoos, which now mostly reflect geographical areas or common ecosystems. Corresponding zoo signs and tours

V, B. Animals in ecosystem

have reinforced this idea of each species in relation

Chung 7

to its environment. Many zoos have established simulated ecosystems in an extraordinary fashion.

Good transition

V, C. School applications

  These new zoo facilities with special information and exhibits are correlated with formal educational programs. The National Zoo in Washington, D.C., has established a rain forest exhibit called "Amazonia," populating it with flora, fauna, and even recorded sounds. Staff pose as actual explorers of the jungle and work with young students on field trips. In Philadelphia, youngsters can see a magnified area through a plastic dome representing the eye of a bee. The Riverbanks Zoo in South Carolina provides sleepover opportunities for school kids and scouts. The Cincinnati Zoo takes the extended education concept one step forward by allowing junior and senior high students to attend high school full time at the zoo. The result is that seventy percent of the graduates go on to pursue animal-related studies (Tarpy 15-20). These are only a few examples of what top zoos are doing in education.

Examples

Statistics

VI. Different models of zoos

VI, A. Zoo/Park

  Several zoos have made education even more immediate and relevant by providing people with unusual perspectives, sometimes focusing on animals of the surrounding region. On the grandest design is the combination of museum, nature center, and zoo. In Kenya one park/zoo is seventy-three square miles (Tarpy 36). According to Ian and Oria

Examples
VI, B. Safari park

VI, C. Regional zoo

VII. Humane treatment of animals

VII, A. Problems without easy solution

Douglas-Hamilton, Kenyan citizens have learned that "live elephants are now worth far more than dead ones. In a good year they can earn Kenya $25 million or more in tourist revenue" (343). A safari park near London lets the animals run free and puts the people in cages, their cars ("Not Endangered" 56). The Arizona-Sonora Desert Museum near Tucson includes local animals and displays most of them unobtrusively. In New Orleans one can experience the reality of a Lousiana natural swamp in a zoo (Tarpy 21).

In keeping with these ecological concerns, the large contemporary zoo is likely to operate on the philosophy that animals should be provided with as much of their natural environment as possible, ensuring a higher degree of humane treatment than ever before. But, overall, obtaining humane treatment for zoo animals is quite complicated, and in practice it is somewhat uneven. Some zoos are better funded than others, and the problem of housing animals properly while also managing captive breeding and conducting educational programs at the same time is not always dealt with in perfect balance. Some animals, such as elephants, require much security (on the average, two elephant keepers are killed each year in North America), and others, such as the macaques, carry diseases (herpes B for the macaques) that can be transmitted to humans (Dia-

Chung 9

Paraphrase

Paraphrase

Quotation

VII, B. Problems and Solutions

Description

mond 80). The distribution of animals is also a problem. With more than eighty percent of the zoo population produced by the zoos (Carpenter 57), certain animals become too abundant. These surplus animals are expensive to maintain and sometimes difficult to trade. Carpenter says that "the lucky or well-born find homes at accredited zoos, but many are put to death or sold to game ranges, roadside menageries, amusement parks or circuses" (59). Those are just a few of the problems not easily addressed.

At the same time, the animals in accredited zoos are not being neglected. Responding to the criticism that animals often become neurotic in captivity, zoos have generally improved areas, replacing many cages with enclosed ranges. They have also often changed feeding practices. Instead of delivering the food, with fruit peeled and diced, meat cut, and vegetables chopped, some zoos have tried to involve the animals in a more natural way in obtaining their food. Thus, food is hidden, dangled, stuffed in holes drilled in logs—mainly made harder to get because in the wild many animals use most of their day hunting, not the ten minutes spent in the old-fashioned zoo. Some zoos provide whole live creatures such as fish and meal worms, though that practice is occasionally challenged by critics, because what seems

Chung 10

humane to one person may not seem humane to others (Diamond 80-84).

VIII. Response to critics

In all of the significant improvements in zoos, critics have played an important role and will continue to do so. Some still maintain that zoos are not humane in their treatment of animals, that the educational value of zoos is minimal, and that the zoo conservation effort is overstated. They say the more than $865 million spent each year on zoos could better be used for protecting habitat (Tarpy 47). The preponderance of evidence is on the other side. Education is highly significant and improving. Conservation, especially through science, is making well-documented advances, even preserving specimens for future developments. Colin Tudge, expert on wildlife management, cogently argues that "habitat destruction has already proceeded to the point where for

Quotation with words omitted

some animals [. . .] conservation by breeding in zoos is our only feasible alternative" (<u>Last Animals at the Zoo</u> 33). And as for the money spent on zoos, people are paying through taxes, fees, and the purchase of products. They respond to what they have learned about animals up close. It is unlikely that typical per-

VIII, B,1. Zoos and support for wildlife linked

sons would volunteer to support programs in remote areas to the same extent if there were no zoos to provide education, demonstrate conservation, and permit encounters with live animals.

Chung 11

The zoo of the future will almost surely be a projection of the contemporary model, one that teaches, conserves, explores, experiments, and, yes, even entertains. Captive breeding cannot save thousands of creatures facing extinction, but, as Tudge points out, "Captive breeding is not an alternative to habitat protection. Increasingly, however, it is a vital backup" ("Captive Audiences for Future Conservation" 51). Of course, the whole zoo operation must be monitored by those who know, appreciate, and understand animals. Nevertheless, zoos have demonstrated their value, and they have the potential to continue with their benefits.

Ends with emphasis on thesis

Chung 12

Works Cited

Browne, Malcolm W. "They're Back! Komodos Avoid Extinction." <u>New York Times</u> 1 Mar. 1994: C1, C4.

Carpenter, Betsy. "Upsetting the Ark." <u>U.S. News & World Report</u> 24 Aug. 1992: 57-61.

Cohn, Jeffrey. "Decisions at the Zoo." <u>Bioscience</u> Oct. 1992: 654-660.

--- "The New Breeding Ground." <u>National Parks</u> Jan./ Feb. 1997: 20-26.

Diamond, Jared. "Playing God at the Zoo." <u>Discover</u> Mar. 1995: 78-86.

Douglas-Hamilton, Ian and Oria. <u>Battle for the Elephants</u>. New York: Viking, 1992.

"Not Endangered." <u>The Economist</u> 13 Apr. 1991: 55-56.

"Project Technology." <u>The Malaysian Elephant Satellite Tracking Project</u> <http://www.si.edu/ elephant/eleintro.htm>. 3Jan.2002.

Rainey, James. "Dogfight at the Zoo." <u>Los Angeles Times</u>. 30 Jan. 1994: C1, C4 <http:// www.latimes.com/cgi-bin1994>. 3Jan.2002.

Schmidt, Karen F. "Preserving the Genetic Legacies." <u>U.S. News & World Report</u> 24 Aug. 1992: 60.

Tarpy, Cliff. "New Zoos." <u>National Geographic</u> July 1993: 6-37.

Tudge, Colin. "Captive Audiences for Future Conservation." <u>New Scientist</u> 28 Jan. 1995: 51.

---. <u>Last Animals at the Zoo: How Mass Extinction Can Be Stopped</u>. London: Hutchinson Radius, 1991.

Writer's Guidelines: The Research Paper

1. The research paper is a long documented essay based on a thorough examination of a topic and supported by explanations and by both references to and quotations from sources.

2. The research paper is no more difficult than other writing assignments if you select a good topic, use a systematic approach, and do not get behind with your work.

3. A systematic approach involves selecting a topic and making a scratch outline, developing a preliminary bibliography, taking notes keyed to divisions of your topic, creating a detailed outline based on your notes and insights, writing a rough draft with ideas supported by source material, revising the draft as many times as necessary, editing the paper, making a list of the works cited, and writing the final draft.

4. Your library almost certainly mixes traditional and electronic indexes and sources; you should become familiar with them.

5. Realistically viewed, the Internet can be a valuable source of material.

6. MLA style for works cited differs from that used in indexes such as the *Readers' Guide to Periodical Literature*.

7. You can avoid plagiarism by giving credit when you borrow someone else's words or ideas.

Handbook: Writing Effective Sentences

THE QUIGMANS   by Buddy Hickerson

© Tribune Media Services, Inc. All Rights Reserved. Reprinted with permission.

*T*his chapter presents rules and examples for grammar, usage, punctuation, and capitalization. In addition, it includes an exercise of twenty items for each unit. The answers to the first ten items within each exercise appear in the Answer Key near the end of this book. Another good way to practice basic writing skills is to write your own examples. In working with verb tense, for example, you could write sentences (perhaps similar to the model sentences) in which you apply the appropriate patterns. In working with punctuation, you could write sentences that demonstrate your ability to use different punctuation marks correctly.

Additional instruction in sentence writing can be found in Chapter 3, pages 58–60.

Identifying Parts of Speech

To classify a word as a part of speech, we observe two simple principles:

- The word must be in the context of communication, usually in a sentence.

- We must be able to identify the word with others that have similar characteristics—the eight parts of speech: nouns, pronouns, verbs, adjectives, adverbs, prepositions, conjunctions, or interjections.

The first principle is important because some words can be any of several parts of speech. The word *round,* for example, can function as five:

- I watched the potter *round* the block of clay. (verb)

- I saw her go *round* the corner. (preposition)

- She has a *round* head. (adjective)

- The Astronauts watched the world go *round.* (adverb)

- The champ knocked him out in one *round.* (noun)

1. Nouns

a. **Nouns are naming words.** Nouns may name persons, animals, plants, places, things, substances, qualities, or ideas—for example, *Bart, armadillo, Mayberry, tree, rock, cloud, love, ghost, music, virtue.*

b. **Nouns are often pointed out by noun indicators.** These noun indicators—*the, a, an*—signal that a noun is ahead, although there may be words between the indicator and the noun itself.

the slime	*a* werewolf	*an* aardvark
the green slime	*a* hungry werewolf	*an* angry aardvark

2. Pronouns

A **pronoun** is a word that is used in place of a noun.

a. Some pronouns may represent specific persons or things:

I	she	they	you
me	her	them	yourself
myself	herself	themselves	yourselves
it	he	we	who
itself	him	us	whom
that	himself	ourselves	

b. Indefinite pronouns refer to nouns (persons, places, things) in a general way:

each   everyone   nobody   somebody

c. Other pronouns point out particular things:

Singular	**Plural**
this, that	*these, those*
This is my treasure.	*These* are my jewels.
That is your junk.	*Those* are your trinkets.

d. Still other pronouns introduce questions:

Which is the best CD player?

What are the main ingredients of a Twinkie?

3. Verbs

Verbs show action or express being in relation to the subject of a sentence. They customarily occur in set positions in sentences.

a. **Action verbs** are usually easy to identify.

The aardvark *ate* the crisp, tasty ants. (action verb)

The aardvark *washed* them down with a snoutful of water. (action verb)

b. The **being verbs** are few in number and are also easy to identify. The most common *being* verbs are *is, was, were, are,* and *am.*

Gilligan *is* on an island in the South Pacific. (being verb)

I *am* his enthusiastic fan. (being verb)

c. The form of a verb expresses its tense, that is, the time of the action or being. The time may be in the present or the past.

> Roseanne *sings* "The Star-Spangled Banner." (present)
>
> Roseanne *sang* "The Star-Spangled Banner." (past)

d. One or more **helping verbs** may be used with the main verb to form other tenses. The combination is called a *verb phrase.*

> She *had sung* the song many times in the shower. (Helping verb and main verb indicate a time in the past.)
>
> She *will be singing* the song no more in San Diego. (Helping verbs and main verb indicate a time in the future.)

e. Some helping verbs can be used alone as main verbs: *has, have, had, is, was, were, are,* and *am.* Certain other helping verbs function only as helpers: *will, shall, should,* and *could.*

The most common position for the verb is directly after the subject or after the subject and its modifiers.

> At high noon only two men [subject] *were* on Main Street.
>
> The man with the faster draw [subject and modifiers] *walked* away alone.

4. Adjectives

Adjectives modify nouns and pronouns. Most adjectives answer the questions *What kind? Which one?* and *How many?*

a. Adjectives answering the **What kind?** question are descriptive. They tell the quality, kind, or condition of the nouns or pronouns they modify.

red convertible	*dirty* fork
noisy muffler	*wild* roses
The rain is *gentle.*	Bob was *tired.*

b. Adjectives answering the **Which one?** question narrow or restrict the meaning of a noun. Some of these are pronouns that become adjectives by function.

my money	*our* ideas	the *other* house
this reason	*these* apples	

c. Adjectives answering the **How many?** question are, of course, numbering words.

some people	*each* pet	*few* goals
three dollars	*one* glove	

d. The words *a, an,* and *the* are adjectives called *articles.* As noun indicators, they point out persons, places, and things.

5. Adverbs

a. **Adverbs** modify verbs, adjectives, and other adverbs. Adverbs answer the questions *How? Where? When?* and *To what degree?*

> **Modifying Verbs:**   They <u>did</u> their work <u>quickly.</u>
> $v$adv

> **Modifying Adjectives:**   They were <u>somewhat</u> <u>happy.</u>
> advadj

• Adverbs that answer the **How?** question are concerned with manner or way.

> She ate the snails *hungrily.*

> He snored *noisily.*

• Adverbs that answer the **Where?** question show location.

> They drove *downtown.*

> He stayed *behind.*

> She climbed *upstairs.*

• Adverbs that answer the **When?** question indicate time.

> The ship sailed *yesterday.*

> I expect an answer *soon.*

• Adverbs that answer the **To what degree?** question express extent.

> She is *entirely* correct.

> He was *somewhat* annoyed.

b. Most words ending in *-ly* are adverbs.

> He completed the task <u>skillfully.</u>
> adv

> She answered him <u>courteously.</u>
> adv

However, there are a few exceptions.

> The house provided a <u>lovely</u> view of the valley.
> adj

> Your goblin mask is <u>ugly.</u>
> adj

6. Prepositions

a. A **preposition** is a word or words that function as a connective. The preposition connects its object(s) to some other word(s) in the sentence. A preposition and its object(s)—usually a noun or pronoun—with modifiers make up a **prepositional phrase**.

Bart worked <u>against</u> great <u>odds.</u>

Everyone <u>in</u> his <u>household</u> cheered his effort.

The most common prepositions include the following:

about	before	but	into	past
above	behind	by	like	to
across	below	despite	near	toward
after	beneath	down	of	under
against	beside	for	off	until
among	between	from	on	upon
around	beyond	in	over	with

b. Some prepositions are composed of more than one word and are constructed using other parts of speech:

according to	as far as	because of	in spite of
ahead of	as well as	in back of	instead of
along with	aside from	in front of	together with

<u>According to</u> the weather <u>report</u>, a storm is forming.

c. **Caution:** Do not confuse adverbs with prepositions.

I went *across* slowly. (without an object—adverb)

I went *across* the field. (with an object—preposition)

We walked *behind* silently. (without an object—adverb)

We walked *behind* the mall. (with an object—preposition)

7. Conjunctions

a. A **conjunction** connects and shows a relationship between words, phrases, or clauses. A *phrase* is two or more words acting as a part of speech. A *clause* is a group of words with a subject and a verb. An independent clause can stand by itself: *She plays bass guitar.* A dependent clause cannot stand by itself: *when she plays bass guitar.*

b. There are two kinds of conjunctions: coordinating and subordinating.

- **Coordinating conjunctions** connect words, phrases, and clauses of equal rank: noun with noun, adjective with adjective, verb with verb, phrase with phrase, main clause with main clause, and subordinate clause with subordinate clause. The seven common coordinating conjunctions are *for, and, nor, but, or, yet,* and *so.* (They form the acronym FANBOYS.)

  Two Nouns: Bring a <u>pencil</u> <u>and</u> some <u>paper.</u>
  noun   conj   noun

  Two Phrases: Did she go <u>to the store</u> <u>or</u> <u>to the game?</u>
  prep phrase conj   prep phrase

  Paired conjunctions such as *either/or, neither/nor,* or *both/and* are usually classed as coordinating conjunctions.

  <u>Neither</u> the coach <u>nor</u> the manager was at fault.
  conj   conj

- **Subordinating conjunctions** connect dependent clauses with main clauses. The most common subordinating conjunctions include the following:

after	because	provided	whenever
although	before	since	where
as	but that	so that	whereas
as if	if	till	wherever
as long as	in order that	until	
as soon as	notwithstanding	when	

  Sometimes the dependent clause comes *before* the main clause, and is set off by a comma.

  <u>Although</u> <u>she</u> <u>was</u> in pain, she stayed in the game.

  conj   sub   v
  dependent clause

  Sometimes the dependent clause comes *after* the main clause, where it usually is *not* set off by a comma.

She stayed in the game <u>because</u> <u>she</u> <u>was needed.</u>

                                     conj   **sub**   **v**

                                           dependent clause

c. **Caution:** Certain words can function as either conjunctions or prepositions. It is necessary to look ahead to see if the word introduces a clause with a subject and verb—conjunction function—or takes an object—preposition function. Some of the words with two functions are these: *after, for, since,* and *until.*

> *After* the concert was over, we went home. (clause follows—conjunction)

> *After* the concert, we went home. (object follows—preposition)

8. Interjections

a. An **interjection** conveys strong emotion or surprise. When an interjection appears alone, it is usually punctuated with an exclamation mark.

> Wow!   Curses!   Cowabunga!   Yaba dabba doo!

b. When an interjection appears as part of a sentence, it is usually followed by a comma.

> Oh, I did not consider that problem.

c. The interjection may seem exciting, but it is seldom appropriate for college writing.

Exercise 1	**IDENTIFYING PARTS OF SPEECH**

Identify the part of speech of each italicized word or group of words by placing the appropriate abbreviations in the blanks. (See Answer Key for answers to 1 through 10.)

n	noun	pro	pronoun
v	verb	adj	adjective
adv	adverb	prep	preposition
conj	conjunction	interj	interjection

1. You *must attend* the three sessions *or* he will dock you a day's pay.

             <u>   v   </u>   <u> conj </u>

2. Roberto seemed *too tired* to answer any more questions.

             <u> adv </u>   <u> adj </u>

3. We *enjoyed* the movie *because* it was a good comedy.

___v___ ___conj___

4. *These* are very troubled times *that* require all our strength.

___pro___ ___pro___

5. The *work* was progressing *according to* schedule.

___n___ ___prep___

6. Will the girls practice *later than* they did last evening?

___adv___ ___conj___

7. *Among* the visitors was a *famous* novelist.

___prep___ ___adj___

8. *Red* is a very *common* autumn color.

___n___ ___adj___

9. *Politics* can be a *very* divisive topic of conversation.

___n___ ___adv___

10. For the winter formal, Shadu *bought himself* a new tuxedo.

___v___ ___pro___

11. *In spite of* the weather, we *found* the hidden cave.

___prep___ ___v___

12. Charley is a *far* wiser person *since* his defeat.

___adv___ ___prep___

13. *That* is an impossible *request,* which I know I cannot fulfill.

___pro___ ___n___

14. *Even though* Mitchico was *ill,* she went to her classes.

___conj___ ___adj___

15. The Pacific *fleet* was *nearly* destroyed in that attack.

___n___ ___adv___

16. It was a *thrilling* novel *of* the last war.

___adj___ ___prep___

17. What *kind* of individual can *he* be?

___n___ ___pro___

18. The player *who* caught the pass *is* Roy Patton.

___pro___ ___v___

19. Jonelle came to the meeting, *though* she could remain *only* a few minutes.

___conj___ ___adv___

20. We *should have seen* Gordon's car approaching
     earlier.   <u>   v   </u> <u> adv </u>

Identifying Subjects and Verbs

The **subject** is what the sentence is about, and the **verb** indicates what the subject is doing or is being.

Subjects

You can recognize the **simple subject** by asking Who? or What? causes the action or expresses the state of being found in the verb.

1. The **simple subject** and the **simple verb** can be single or compound.

     My *friend* and *I* have much in common.

     My friend *came* and *left* a present.

2. Although the subject usually appears before the verb, it may follow the verb.

     From tiny acorns grow mighty *oaks.*

3. The command, or **imperative,** sentence has a "you" as the implied subject, and no stated subject.

     (*You* understood) Read the notes.

4. Be careful not to confuse a subject with an **object of a preposition.**

     The *leader* [subject] of the *students* [object of the preposition] is dynamic.

Verbs

Verbs show action or express being in relation to the subject.

1. **Action verbs** suggest movement or accomplishment in idea or deed.

     He *dropped* the book. (movement)

     He *read* the book. (accomplishment)

2. **Being verbs** indicate existence.

     They *were* concerned.

3. Verbs may appear as single words or phrases.

     He *led* the charge. (single word)

     She *is leading* the charge. (phrase)

4. Verbs that are joined by a coordinating conjunction such as *and* and *or* are called **compound verbs.**

> She *worked* for twenty-five years and *retired.*

5. Do not confuse verbs with **verbals;** verbals are verblike words that function as other parts of speech.

> The bird *singing* [participle acting as an adjective] in the tree is defending its territory.
>
> *Singing* [gerund acting as a noun subject] is fun.
>
> I want *to eat* [infinitive acting as a noun object].

6. Do not confuse **adverbs** such as *never, not,* and *hardly* with verbs; they only modify verbs.

7. Do not overlook a part of the verb that is separated from another part in a question.

> "Where *had* the defendant *gone* on that fateful night?"

Exercise 2   **IDENTIFYING SUBJECTS AND VERBS**

Write the simple subject, without modifiers, in the first blank; write the verb in the second blank. Some sentences have compound subjects, compound verbs, or both. (See Answer Key for answers 1 through 10.)

1. My brother and his friend sold tickets for the field day.

   brother/friend   sold

2. Can somebody in command give us permission to moor our boat?

   somebody   can give

3. There were several excellent applicants for the position of dean of studies.

   applicants   were

4. Now comes the best part of the entertainment.

   part   comes

5. Please read the minutes of the previous meeting.

   (You)   read

6. During the first ten minutes of the game, our team, with two of the players out on fouls, scored two goals.

   team   scored

7. Never again will I be able to speak to Ruby about that.

   I   will be

8. There will be among your visitors today two agents from the Federal Bureau of Investigation.

agents	will be

9. Both the coach and the players were angered by a series of unjust penalties.

coach/ players	were angered

10. The cast was congratulated and given bonuses by a grateful producer.

cast	was congratu- lated/ given

11. Never again will Lewan help her with the work.

Lewan	will help

12. A tour of the churches and castles of Denmark is a worthwhile experience.

tour	is

13. Shut that window and take your seat.

(You)	shut/take

14. Rodrigo wanted to dig the foundation and to erect the framework of the new building.

Rodrigo	wanted

15. How many books are published each month on that particular subject?

books	are published

16. Two important items on the agenda were salaries and a pension plan.

items	were

17. Anna's unassuming attitude and careful concern for details impressed her employer.

attitude/ concern	impressed

18. The spectators stood, cheered, and waved their pennants.

spectators	stood/ cheered/ waved

19. Where have we placed those new suits?

we	have placed

20. Way up the steep mountain path stood Seth.

Seth	stood

Writing Different Kinds of Sentences

On the basis of number and kinds of clauses, sentences may be classified as simple, compound, complex, and compound-complex.

Clauses

1. A **clause** is a group of words with a subject and a verb that functions as a part or all of a complete sentence. There are two kinds of clauses: (1) independent (main) and (2) dependent (subordinate).

2. An **independent (main) clause** is a group of words with a subject and verb that can stand alone and make sense. An independent clause expresses a complete thought by itself and can be written as a separate sentence.

   I have the money.

3. A **dependent clause** is a group of words with a subject and verb that depends on a main clause to give it meaning. The dependent clause functions in the common sentence patterns as a noun, an adjective, or an adverb.

   When I have the money

Kinds of Sentences Defined

Kind	Definition	Example
1. Simple	One independent clause	She did the work well.
2. Compound	Two or more independent clauses	She did the work well, and she was paid well.
3. Complex	One independent clause and one or more dependent clauses	*Because she did the work well,* she was paid well.
4. Compound-Complex	Two or more independent clauses and one or more dependent clauses	*Because she did the work well,* she was paid well, and she was satisfied.

Punctuation

1. Use a comma before a coordinating conjunction (*for, and, nor, but, or, yet, so*) between two independent clauses.

   The movie was good, but the tickets were expensive.

2. Use a comma after a dependent clause (beginning with a subordinating conjunction such as *because, although, when, since,* or *before*) that occurs before the main clause.

   When the bus arrived, we quickly boarded.

3. Use a semicolon between two independent clauses in one sentence if there is no coordinating conjunction.

> The bus arrived; we quickly boarded.

4. Use a semicolon before and usually a comma after a conjunctive adverb (such as *however, otherwise, therefore, on the other hand,* and *in fact*), between two independent clauses (no comma after *then, also, now, thus,* and *soon*).

> The Dodgers have not played well this year; however, the Giants have won ten games in a row.

> Spring training went well; then the regular baseball season began.

Exercise 3   **WRITING DIFFERENT KINDS OF SENTENCES**

Indicate the kind of sentence by writing the appropriate abbreviations in the blanks. (See Answer Key for answers to 1 through 10.)

S	*simple*
CP	*compound*
CX	*complex*
CC	*compound-complex*

___S___ 1. William and Henry James contributed much to American philosophy and literature.

___CP___ 2. William was the philosopher, and Henry was the novelist and short-story writer.

___CX___ 3. Although William revolutionized philosophy, Henry is considered the better known.

___CC___ 4. Henry, who lived in England, wrote fiction; William stayed home and lectured.

___CX___ 5. He is taller than I am.

___CP___ 6. Some take up bicycling; others try swimming for their exercise.

___CC___ 7. Those who brought equipment went skiing; others stayed in the lodge.

___S___ 8. Colorful clothing styles have become popular, especially in California.

___S___ 9. To avoid foolish mistakes, always read the directions carefully.

___CX___ 10. Any money that I receive from the trust will be invested.

___CP___ 11. The wait seemed endless to the lovers, but at last the wedding day came.

___CC___ 12. I thought that I had given the right answer; however, I was proved wrong.

___S___ 13. His efforts to comfort the accident victim were endless.

___S___ 14. Dropped from the fifty-story window, the flowerpot shattered on the sidewalk.

___CX___ 15. Because I have debts, I will have to postpone my vacation.

___CC___ 16. I believed that he was honest; therefore, I gave him my wallet to hold.

___CP___ 17. Either you pay your rent this week, or you will be asked to move out.

___CX___ 18. Sandy, who can pitch, and Willie, who can catch, are valuable players.

___CC___ 19. Sandy, who could pitch, was retained, but Willie was released from his contract.

___CP___ 20. In the lion's carcass was honey; Samson took some.

Combining Sentences

Coordination

If you intend to communicate two equally important and closely related ideas, you certainly will want to place them close together, probably in a **compound sentence** (two or more independent clauses).

1. When you combine two sentence by using a **coordinating conjunction,** drop the period, change the capital letter to a small letter, and insert a comma before the coordinating conjunction.

> I like your home. I can visit for only three months.

> I like your home, but I can visit for only three months.

2. When you combine two sentences by using a **semicolon,** replace the period with a semicolon and change the capital letter to a small letter. If you wish to use a conjunctive adverb, insert it after the semicolon and usually put a comma after it.

> I like your home; I can visit for only three months.

> I like your home; however, I can visit for only three months.

Subordination

If you have two ideas that are closely related, but one is secondary or dependent on the other, you may want to use a **complex sentence.**

> My neighbors are considerate. They never play loud music.

> Because my neighbors are considerate, they never play loud music.

1. If the dependent clause comes before the main clause, set it off with a comma.

> Before you dive, be sure there is water in the pool.

2. If the dependent clause comes after the main clause, set it off with a comma only if you use the word *though* or *although,* or if the words are not necessary to convey the basic meaning in the sentence.

> Be sure there is water in the pool before you dive.

Coordination and Subordination

At times you may want to show the relationship of three or more ideas within one sentence. If that relationship involves two or more main ideas and one or more supporting ideas, the combination can be stated in a **compound-complex sentence** (two or more independent clauses and one or more dependent clauses).

> Before he learned how to operate a computer, he had trouble with his typewritten assignments, but now he produces clean, attractive material.

Use punctuation consistent with that of the compound and complex sentences.

Other Methods of Combining Ideas

1. Simple sentences can often be combined by using a prepositional phrase.

> Dolly Parton wrote a song about a coat. The coat had many colors.

> Dolly Parton wore a song about a coat *of many colors.*

2. To combine simple sentences, use an *appositive*, a noun phrase that immediately follows a noun or pronoun and renames it.

> Susan is the leading scorer on the team. Susan is a quick and strong player.

> Susan, *a quick and strong player,* is the leading scorer on the team.

3. Simple sentences can often be combined by dropping a repeated subject in the second sentence.

> Some items are too damaged for recycling. They must be disposed of.

> Some items are too damaged for recycling and must be disposed of.

4. Sentences can be combined by using a *participial phrase*, a group of words that includes a participle, which is a verblike word that usually ends in *-ing* or *-ed.*

> John rowed smoothly. He reached the shore.

> *Rowing smoothly,* John reached the shore.

| Exercise 4 | COMBINING SENTENCES |

Combine each group of sentences into a single sentence. Use coordination, subordination, or one of the other ways of combining ideas. (See Answer Key for answers to 1 through 10.)

1. The Joad family lived in Oklahoma.
   The time was the 1930s, during the Great Depression.
   During the Great Depression of the 1930s, the Joad family lived in Oklahoma.

2. The dust storms hit the area.
   The Joad family headed for California.

   When the dust storms hit the area, the Joad family headed for California.

3. In California the Joads were not welcome.
   Thousands of poor people had gone to California.
   In California, the Joads were not welcome because thousands of poor people had gone to California.

4. The poor people had heard of jobs in fruit picking.
They discovered that California had more job seekers than jobs.
The poor people had heard of jobs in fruit picking, but they discovered that California had more job seekers than jobs.

5. Some large farm owners took advantage of the workers.
The workers banded together.
After large farm owners took advantage of the workers, the workers banded together.

6. Jim Casey and Tom Joad became leaders.
The people learned to help themselves.
Jim Casey and Tom Joad became leaders, and the people learned to help themselves.

7. Edgar Allan Poe wrote a short story titled "The Cask of Amontillado."
In that story the narrator tells of his experience fifty years earlier.
Edgar Allan Poe wrote a short story titled "The Cask of Amontillado," in which the narrator tells of his experience fifty years earlier.

8. He wanted revenge against an enemy.
He walled that person up in a catacomb.
Because he wanted revenge against an enemy, he walled that person up in a catacomb.

9. At first his victim said it was surely a joke.
He begged to be freed.
At first his victim said it was surely a joke and begged to be freed.

10. The narrator refused.
The narrator cannot dismiss the experience from his mind after all these years.
The narrator refused; after all these years, he cannot dismiss the experience from his mind.

11. *Carrie* was Stephen King's first published novel.
In it King used some ideas from his experience as a high school teacher.
In *Carrie,* Stephen King's first published novel, King used some ideas from his experience as a high school teacher.

12. Carrie is not treated well.
She is insecure and unhappy.
Carrie, who is insecure and unhappy, is not treated well.

13. Some of Carrie's peers try to trick her for their amusement.
She is, at first, deceived.
When some of Carrie's peers try to trick her for their amusement, she is, at first, deceived.

14. She resorts to using a special power.
She gets revenge.
The town will not soon forget her.
Using a special power, she gets revenge, and the town will not soon forget her.

15. Tennessee Williams wrote *The Glass Menagerie.*
It is concerned with four people.
Each tries to escape reality.
The Glass Menagerie by Tennessee Williams is concerned with four people who try to escape reality.

16. The reality is harsh.
    Life is lonely and nightmarish.

    Because the reality is harsh, life is lonely and nightmarish.

17. Laura is one of the main characters.
    She has tried to escape into the world of her glass menagerie and her music.

    Laura, one of the main characters, has tried to escape into the world of her glass menagerie and her music.

18. Then she meets a young man she has long admired.
    He offers kindness to her.

    Then she meets a young man she has long admired, and he offers kindness to her.

19. The young man dances with Laura.
    For a brief time she has confidence.

    When the young man dances with Laura, for a brief time she has confidence.

20. But then she discovers she will never see him again.
    She returns to her glass menagerie and her music.

    But then she discovers she will never see him again, and she returns to her glass menagerie and her music.

Correcting Fragments, Comma Splices, and Run-Ons

Fragments

A correct sentence signals completeness; a **fragment** signals incompleteness—it doesn't make sense. You would expect the speaker or writer of a fragment to say or write more or to rephrase it.

1. A **dependent clause** cannot stand by itself because it begins with a subordinating word.

   > *Because* he left.

   > *When* she worked.

   > *Although* they slept.

2. A **verbal phrase,** a **prepositional phrase,** and an **appositive phrase** may carry ideas, but each is incomplete because it lacks a subject and verb.

   > verbal phrase: *have studied hard all evening*
   > sentence: Having studied hard all evening, John decided to retire.

   > prepositional phrase: *in the store*
   > sentence: She worked in the store.

appositive phrase: *a successful business*
sentence: Mars Brothers, a successful business, sells clothing.

3. Each complete sentence must have an **independent clause,** meaning a word or a group of words that contains a subject and a verb that can stand alone.

> *He enrolled* for the fall semester.

Comma Splices and Run-Ons

The **comma splice** consists of two independent clauses with only a comma between them.

> The weather was disappointing, we canceled the picnic.

A comma by itself cannot join two independent clauses.

The **run-on** differs from the comma splice in only one respect: it has no comma between the independent clauses. Therefore, the run-on is two independent clauses with *nothing* between them.

> The weather was disappointing we canceled the picnic.

Independent clauses must be properly connected.
Correct comma splices and run-ons:

1. Use a comma and a **coordinating conjunction** (*for, and, nor, but, or, yet, so*).

> We canceled the picnic, *for* the weather was disappointing.

2. Use a **subordinating conjunction** (such as *because, after, when, although, since, how, until, unless, before*) to make one clause dependent.

> *Because* the weather was disappointing, we canceled the picnic.

3. Use a **semicolon** (with or without a conjunctive adverb such as *however, otherwise, therefore, similarly, hence, on the other hand, then, consequently, also, thus*).

> The weather was disappointing; we canceled the picnic.

> The weather was disappointing; *therefore,* we canceled the picnic.

4. Make each clause a separate sentence. For a comma splice, replace the comma with a period and begin the second sentence (clause) with a capital letter. For a run-on, insert a period between the two independent clauses and begin the second sentence with a capital letter.

> The weather was disappointing. We canceled the picnic.

Exercise 5   **CORRECTING FRAGMENTS, COMMA SPLICES, AND RUN-ONS**

Write the appropriate identification in each blank and correct the errors. (See Answer Key for answers to 1 through 10.)

OK   correct
CS   comma splice
RO   run-on
FRAG   fragment

__CS__   1. Don Quixote was a good man who saw evil in the world, he decided to take action.

__CS__   2. He was old, nevertheless, he decided to become a knight.

__RO__   3. He was old nevertheless he decided to become a knight.

__OK__   4. He was old, but he decided to become a knight.

__OK__   5. He was old; nevertheless, he decided to become a knight.

__RO__   6. He made his armor from his materials the quality was not good.

__OK__   7. He used his own horse, an old nag with a sagging back.

__OK__   8. For a squire, he enlisted Sancho Panza, a peasant neighbor who would leave his family behind.

__FRAG__   9. The reason ~~being~~ **was** that he trusted and admired Don Quixote.

__FRAG__   10. Sancho Panza ~~riding~~ **rode** a mule.

__RO__   11. They went on many adventures together some were laughable.

__CS__   12. Don Quixote and Sancho Panza were deadly serious, they had a mission.

__RO__   13. Don Quixote would do what he could to rid the world of evil Sancho Panza would be rewarded with his own island kingdom.

__OK__   14. Because Don Quixote often misinterpreted reality, he mistook a servant for a noble woman and devoted himself to her.

RO_____ 15. He usually treated people of low social status and bad behavior very well they often responded by being better persons than they ordinarily were.

RO_____ 16. On one occasion he attacked a windmill he thought it was an evil giant.

OK_____ 17. The arms of the windmill knocked him off his horse, but he had an explanation for this misfortune.

RO_____ 18. Evil beings will sometimes change shapes Don Quixote would not be discouraged.
but

CS_____ 19. As he became famous, some people wanted to be near him so they could laugh however, they often went away with admiration for him.

CS_____ 20. He sometimes made mistakes nevertheless, he dedicated his life to virtue, beauty, and justice.

Working with Verb Forms

The twelve verb tenses are shown in this section. The irregular verb *drive* is used as the example. (See pages 485–486 for irregular verbs.)

Simple Tenses

Present
I, we, you, they *drive.*
He, she, it *drives.*

Present, may imply a continuation from past to future

Past
I, we, you, he she, it, they *drove.*

Past

Future
I, we, you, he, she, it they *will drive.*

Future

Pefect Tenses

Present Perfect
I, we, you, they *have driven.*
He, she, it *has driven.*

Completed recently in past, may continue in present.

Past Perfect
I, we, you, he, she, it, they *had driven.*   Prior to a specific time in the past

Future Perfect
I, we, you, he, she, it, they *will have driven.*   At a time prior to a specific time in the future

Progressive Tenses

Present Progressive
I *am driving.*
He, she, it *is driving.*   In progress now
We, you, they *are driving.*

Past Progressive
I, he, she, it *was driving.*   In progress in the past
We, you, they *were driving.*

Future Progressive
I, we, you, he she, it, they *will be driving.*   In progress in the future

Perfect Progressive Tenses

Present Perfect Progressive
I, we, you, they *have been driving.*   In progress before now or up to now
He, she, it *has been driving.*

Past Perfect Progressive
I, we, you, he, she, it, they *had been driving.*   In progress before another event in the past

Future Perfect Progressive
I, we, you, he, she, it, they *will have been driving.*   In progress before another event in the future

Past Participles

The past participle uses the helping verbs *has, have,* or *had* along with the past tense of the verb. For regular verbs, whose past tense ends in *-ed,* the past participle form of the verb is the same as the past tense.

Following is a list of some common regular verbs, showing the base form, the past tense, and the past participle. (The base form can also be used with such helping verbs as *can, could, do, does, did, may, might, must, shall, should, will,* and *would.*)

Regular Verbs

Base form (Present)	Past	Past Participle
ask	asked	asked
answer	answered	answered
cry	cried	cried
decide	decided	decided
dive	dived (dove)	dived
finish	finished	finished
happen	happened	happened
learn	learned	learned
like	liked	liked
love	loved	loved
need	needed	needed
open	opened	opened
start	started	started
suppose	supposed	supposed
walk	walked	walked
want	wanted	wanted

Whereas **regular verbs** are predictable—having an -*ed* ending for past and past-participle forms—**irregular verbs,** as the term suggests, follow no definite pattern.

Following is a list of some common irregular verbs, showing the base form (present), the past tense, and the past participle.

Irregular Verbs

Base Form (Present)	Past	Past Participle
arise	arose	arisen
awake	awoke (awaked)	awaked
be	was, were	been
become	became	become
begin	began	begun
bend	bent	bent
blow	blew	blown
break	broke	broken
bring	brought	brought
buy	bought	bought
catch	caught	caught
choose	chose	chosen
cling	clung	clung
come	came	come
creep	crept	crept
deal	dealt	dealt
do	did	done
drink	drank	drunk

Base Form (Present)	Past	Past Participle
drive	drove	driven
eat	ate	eaten
feel	felt	felt
fight	fought	fought
fling	flung	flung
fly	flew	flown
forget	forgot	forgotten
freeze	froze	frozen
get	got	got (gotten)
go	went	gone
grow	grew	grown
have	had	had
know	knew	known
lead	led	led
leave	left	left
lose	lost	lost
mean	meant	meant
read	read	read
ride	rode	ridden
ring	rang	rung
shine	shone	shone
shoot	shot	shot
sing	sang	sung
sink	sank	sunk
sleep	slept	slept
slink	slunk	slunk
speak	spoke	spoken
spend	spent	spent
steal	stole	stolen
stink	stank (stunk)	stunk
sweep	swept	swept
swim	swam	swum
swing	swung	swung
take	took	taken
teach	taught	taught
tear	tore	torn
think	thought	thought
throw	threw	thrown
wake	woke (waked)	woken (waked)
weep	wept	wept
write	wrote	written

"Problem" Verbs

The following pairs of verbs are especially troublesome and confusing: *lie* and *lay, sit* and *set,* and *rise* and *raise.* One way to tell them apart is to remember which word in each pair takes a direct object. A direct object answers the question *whom* or *what* in connection with a verb. The words *lay, raise,* and *set* take a direct object.

He *raised* the window. (He *raised* what?)

Lie, rise, and *sit,* however, cannot take a direct object. We cannot, for example, say "He rose the window." In the examples, the italicized words are objects.

Present Tense	Meaning	Past Tense	Past Participle	Example
lie	to rest	lay	lain	I lay down to rest.
lay	to place something	laid	laid	We laid the *books* on the table.
rise	to go up	rose	risen	The smoke rose quickly.
raise	to lift	raised	raised	She raised the *question*.
sit	to rest	sat	sat	He sat in the chair.
set	to place something	set	set	They set the *basket* on the floor.

Verb Tense

These rules about selecting a **tense** for certain kinds of writing are flexible, but you should be consistent, changing tense only for a good reason. Usually you should select the present tense to write about literature.

Moby Dick *is* a famous white whale.

Select the past tense to write about yourself (usually) or something historical (always).

I *was* eighteen when I *decided* I *was* ready for independence.

Exercise 6	**WORKING WITH VERB FORMS**

Write the correct verb in the blank. (See Answer Key for answers to 1 through 10.)

___lie___   1. If you (lie, lay) down, the exercise does you no good.

___drunk___   2. The doctor told him that his trouble was caused by the water he had (drank, drunk).

laid 3. The game began before the bets were (lain, laid) on the table.

supposed 4. The Halloween mask and costume made the children wonder who she was (suppose, supposed) to be.

sat 5. The audience ruined his act because it just (set, sat) there.

have 6. Nate wanted to do the right thing, but he didn't know what he should (had have) done.

set 7. The ball would not stop rolling even when she (set, sat) it between the two books.

used 8. In his thirties, Floyd (use, used) to rise at 8:00 and be at work by 9:00.

rise 9. The European audiences would (rise, raise) up in a body and applaud her for several minutes.

rang 10. The inspector accidentally (rang, rung) the bell that summoned the villagers to town meetings.

raised 11. She lived in the old house for thirty-two years, and the shades were never (risen, raised).

have 12. Given her confused testimony, she must (had, have) been guilty.

lie 13. Any good doctor would insist that a toddler (lie, lay) down every day to rest.

ate 14. Every day for three months, they (eat, ate) the same boring meals and complained as usual.

lying 15. Before his mother said a word, he told everyone he had been (lying, laying) down when the fire started.

burst 16. When Gloria said her balloon (busted, burst), the other employees sympathized.

sitting 17. Rubinstein refused to start until everyone was (setting, sitting) down.

rise 18. The last thing the board wanted was to have the president (rise, raise) from her chair and start the ticker tape.

<u>drunk</u>   19. The group at the church whispered that he had (drank, drunk) himself to death.

<u>lay</u>   20. Four kittens (lay, laid) in the basket like balls of white yarn.

Making Subjects and Verbs Agree

This section is concerned with number agreement between subjects and verbs. The basic principle of **subject-verb agreement** is that if the subject is singular, the verb should be singular, and if the subject is plural, the verb should be plural. There are ten major guidelines. In the examples under the following guidelines, the true subjects and verbs are italicized.

1. Do not let words that come between the subject and verb affect agreement.

   a. Modifying phrases and clauses frequently come between the subject and verb:

      The various *types* of drama *were* not *discussed.*

      Angela, who is hitting third, *is* the best player.

      The *price* of those shoes *is* too high.

   b. Certain prepositions can cause trouble. The following words are prepositions, not conjunctions: *along with, as well as, besides, in addition to, including,* and *together with.* The words that function as objects of prepositions cannot also be subjects of the sentence.

      The *coach,* along with the players, *protests* the decision.

   c. In compound subjects in which one subject is positive and one subject is negative, the verb agrees with the positive subject.

      Phillip, not the other boys, *was* the culprit.

2. Do not let inversions (verb before subject, not the normal order) affect the agreement of subject and verb.

   a. Verbs and other words may come before the subject. Do not let them affect the agreement. To understand subject-verb relationships, recast the sentence in normal word order.

      Are Juan and his *sister* at home? (question form)

      Juan and his *sister are* at home. (normal order)

   b. A sentence filler is a word that is grammatically independent of other words in the sentence. The most common fillers are *there* and *here.* Even though a sentence filler precedes the verb, it should not be treated as the subject.

There *are* many *reasons* for his poor work. (The verb *are* agrees with the subject *reasons*.)

3. A singular verb agrees with a singular indefinite pronoun.

   a. Most indefinite pronouns are singular.

      Each of the women *is* ready at this time.

      Neither of the women *is* ready at this time.

      One of the children *is* not paying attention.

   b. Certain indefinite pronouns do not clearly express either a singular or plural number. Agreement, therefore, depends on the meaning of the sentence. These pronouns are *all, any, none,* and *some.*

      All of the melon *was* good.

      All of the melons *were* good.

      None of the pie *is* acceptable.

      None of the pies *are* acceptable.

4. Two or more subjects joined by *and* usually take a plural verb.

      The *captain* and the *sailors were* happy to be ashore.

      The *trees* and *shrubs need* more care.

   a. If the parts of a compound subject mean one and the same person or thing, the verb is singular; if the parts mean more than one, the verb is plural.

      The *secretary* and *treasurer is* not present (one person)

      The *secretary* and the *treasurer are* not present. (more than one person)

   b. When *each* or *every* modifies singular subjects joined by *and,* the verb is singular.

      Each *boy* and each *girl brings* a donation.

      Each *woman* and *man has asked* the same questions.

5. Alternative subjects—that is, subjects joined by *or, nor, either/or, neither/nor, not only/but also*—should be handled in the following manner:

   a. If the subjects are both singular, the verb is singular.

      Rosa or *Alicia is* responsible.

   b. If the subjects are plural, the verb is plural.

      Neither the *students* nor the *teachers were* impressed by his comments.

c. If one of the subjects is singular and the other subject is plural, the verb agrees with the nearer subject.

> Either the Garcia *boys* or their *father goes* to the hospital each day.

> Either their *father* or the Garcia *boys go* to the hospital each day.

6. Collective nouns—*team, family, group, crew, gang, class, faculty,* and the like—take a singular verb if the noun is considered a unit, but a plural verb if the group is considered as a number of individuals.

> The *team is playing* well tonight.

> The *team are getting* dressed. (Here the individuals are acting not as a unit but separately. If you don't like the way this sounds, substitute "The members of the team are getting dressed.")

7. Titles of books, essays, short stories, and plays, a word spoken of as a word, and the names of businesses take a singular verb.

> *The Canterbury Tales was written* by Geoffrey Chaucer.

> *Markle Brothers has* a sale this week.

8. Sums of money, distances, and measurements are followed by a singular verb when a unit is meant. They are followed by a plural verb when the individual elements are considered separately.

> *Three dollars was* the price. (unit)

> *Three dollars were* lying there. (individual)

> *Five years is* a long time. (unit)

> The *first five years were* difficult ones. (individual)

9. Be careful of agreement with nouns ending in -*s*. Several nouns ending in -*s* take a singular verb—for example, *aeronautics, civics, economics, ethics, measles,* and *mumps.*

> *Mumps is* an extremely unpleasant disease.

> *Economics is* my major field of study.

10. Some nouns have only a plural form and so take only a plural verb—for example, *clothes, fireworks, scissors,* and *trousers.*

> His *trousers are* badly wrinkled.

> Mary's *clothes were* stylish and expensive.

Exercise 7   MAKING SUBJECTS AND VERBS AGREE

Write the correct verb in the blank. (See Answer Key for answers to 1 through 10.)

are   1. There (is, are) a number of wholesome foods on the menu.

were   2. After the explosion, (was were) there any people unaccounted for?

was   3. Not one of us (was, were) ready to promise not to fight.

has   4. Find out whether each of the skiers (have, has) lift tickets.

are   5. Most of the birds on the islands (are, is) related to the finch.

have   6. Only a few of the sheep (has, have) enough wool to shear.

appear 7. Every summer night a dark sky and the evening star (appears, appear) over the western horizon.

was   8. The owner and manager (was, were) pleased with the team's standing.

makes   9. Each camper and each boat (make, makes) trouble for commuters on the freeway.

has   10. Every glass and cup in the kitchen (has, have) lipstick on the rim.

have   11. Either the doctor or his lawyers (has, have) to testify.

was   12. Not only the oil tanks but also the office building (was, were) consumed.

spread 13. The whole town knew he was one of those people who (spread, spreads) gossip.

sail   14. The *Sea Gull* is one of the boats that (sail, sails) in the Honolulu race.

assembles 15. The troop, with its leaders, (assemble, assembles) in groups for contests.

become 16. Many helpers (become, becomes) necessary for milking the camels, tending the children, making rugs, and preparing meals.

<u>describes</u> 17. *Antarctic Caves* (describe, describes) a great hole that Admiral Byrd is said to have explored.

_____is_____ 18. The anthropologists believe semantics (is, are) within their discipline.

_____is_____ 19. All he needs for a new watch (is, are) five dollars more.

_____is_____ 20. The psychologist at our school believes a child's environment (is, are) more important than anything else.

Giving Verbs Voice

Which of these sentences sounds better to you?

> Ken Griffey, Jr., slammed a home run.

> A home run was slammed by Ken Griffey, Jr.

Both sentences carry the same message, but the first expresses it more effectively. The subject (*Ken Griffey, Jr.*) is the actor. The verb (*slammed*) is the action. The direct object (*home run*) is the receiver of the action. The second sentence lacks the vitality of the first because the receiver of the action is the subject; the doer is embedded in the prepositional phrase at the end of the sentence.

The first sentence demonstrates the active voice. It has an active verb (one that leads to a direct object), and the action moves from the beginning to the end of the sentence. The second exhibits the passive voice (with the action reflecting back on the subject). When given a choice, you should usually select the active voice. It promotes energy and directness.

The passive voice, though not usually the preferred form, does have its uses:

- When the doer of the action is unknown or unimportant.

> My car was stolen. (The doer, a thief, is unknown.)

- When the receiver of the action is more important than the doer

> My neighbor was permanently disabled by an irresponsible drunk driver. (The neighbor's suffering is the focus, not the drunk driver.)

As you can see, the passive construction places the doer at the end of a prepositional phrase (as in the second example) or does not include the doer in the statement at all (as in the first example). Instead, the passive voice places the receiver of the action in the subject position, and it presents the verb in its past-tense form preceded by a *to be* helper. The transformation is a simple one:

She read the book. (active)

The book was read by her. (passive)

Exercise 8   **GIVING VERBS VOICE**

Rewrite the following sentences, changing the passive-voice verbs to active voice.

1. The lecture <u>was given</u> by a famous scientist.
   A famous scientist gave the lecture.

2. The surgery <u>was performed</u> by Dr. Song.
   Dr. Song performed the surgery.

3. The opera <u>was produced</u> by the Vienna Boys' Choir.
   The Vienna Boys' Choir produced the opera.

4. The winning horse <u>was ridden</u> by Janice Baines.
   Janice Baines rode the winning horse.

5. The Wimbledon men's tennis tournament <u>was won</u> by Harold Stanton.
   Harold Stanton won the Wimbledon men's tennis tournament.

6. Lewis Carroll's *Alice's Adventures in Wonderland* <u>was read</u> by the class.
   The class read Lewis Carroll's *Alice's Adventures in Wonderland.*

7. The report for the mayor <u>was written</u> by Jan Brown.
   Jan Brown wrote the report for the mayor.

8. The rock star <u>was greeted</u> by thousands of fans.
   Thousands of fans greeted the rock star.

9. The album <u>was recorded</u> by Elvis on June 15, 1956.
   Elvis recorded the album on June 15, 1956.

10. The gun-control legislation <u>was passed</u> by both houses of the state assembly.
    Both houses of the state assembly passed the gun-control legislation.

Selecting Pronouns

A **pronoun** is a word that is used in place of a noun.

1. **Case** is the form a pronoun takes as it fills a position in a sentence.

   a. **Subjective pronouns** are *I, he,* and *she* (singular), and *we* and *they* (plural). *Who* can be either singular or plural.
      Subjective case pronouns can fill subject positions.

      > *We* dance in the park.

      > It was *she* who spoke. (referring back to and meaning the same as the subject)

   b. **Objective case pronouns** are *me, him,* and *her* (singular); and *us* and *them* (plural). *Whom* can be either singular or plural.
      Objective case pronouns fill object positions.

      > We saw *her* in the library. (object of verb)

      > They gave the results to *us*—Judy and *me.* (object of a preposition)

   c. Three techniques are useful for deciding what pronoun case to use.

      - If you have a compound element (such as a subject or object of a preposition), consider only the pronoun part.

        > They will visit Jim and (I, me). (Consider: They will visit me.)

      - If the next important word after *who* or *whom* in a statement is a noun or pronoun, the word choice will be *whom;* otherwise, it will be *who.* Disregard qualifier clauses such as *It seems* and *I feel.*

        > The person *who* works hardest will win.

        > The person *whom* judges like will win.

        > The person *who,* we think, worked hardest won. (ignoring the qualifier clause)

      - *Let's* is made up of the words *let* and *us* and means *"you let us";* therefore, when you select a pronoun to follow it, consider the two original words and select another object word—*me.*

        > Let's you and *me* go to town.

2. A pronoun agrees with its antecedent in person, number, and gender.

   a. Avoid needless shifting in **person,** which means shifting in point of view, such as from *I* to *you.*

      > *I* tried but *you* couldn't persuade her to return. (incorrect)

      > *I* tried but *I* couldn't persuade her to return. (correct)

b. Most problems with pronoun-antecedent agreement involve **number.** The principles are simple: If the antecedent (the word the pronoun refers back to) is singular, use a singular pronoun. If the antecedent is plural, use a plural pronoun.

> Jim forgot *his* notebook.

> Many students cast *their* votes today.

> Someone lost *his* or *her* [not *their*] book.

c. The pronoun should agree with its antecedent in **gender,** if the gender of the antecedent is specific. Masculine and feminine pronouns are gender-specific: *he, him, she,* and *her.* Others are neuter: *I, we, me, us, it, they, them, who, whom, that,* and *which.* The words *who* and *whom* refer to people. *That* can refer to ideas, things, and people, but usually not to people. *Which* refers to ideas and things, but never to people. In order to avoid a perceived sex bias, most writers and speakers prefer to use *he or she* or *his or her* instead of just *he* or *his;* however, many writers simply make antecedents plural.

> Everyone should work until *he* or *she* drops.

> People should work until *they* drop.

Exercise 9	**SELECTING PRONOUNS**

Write the correct pronoun in the blank. (See Answer Key for answers to 1 through 10.)

<u>Whom</u>   1. (Who, Whom) do you want me to call?

<u>me</u>   2. Give it to Matthew and (me, I).

<u>I</u>   3. Tony works faster than (I, me).

<u>me</u>   4. Let's you and (me, I) leave before midnight.

<u>him</u>   5. All but Maria and (he, him) left on the bus.

<u>Who</u>   6. (Who, Whom) do you think is the best person for the job?

<u>they</u>   7. Nevertheless, we were just as careful as (they, them).

<u>whomever</u>   8. I will accept (whoever, whomever) they select.

<u>ourselves</u>   9. We (ourself, ourselfs, ourselves) are ultimately responsible.

<u> him </u> 10. Do you expect the winner to be (he, him)?

<u> whoever </u> 11. I will try to help (whoever, whomever) asks.

<u> who </u> 12. Crystal was the person (who, whom) we thought would succeed.

<u> We </u> 13. (We, Us) citizens have a responsibility to be well informed.

<u> our </u> 14. They objected to (our, us) doing the work.

<u> he </u> 15. No one was more pleased than (he, him).

<u> us </u> 16. All of (we, us) residents signed the petition.

<u> whoever </u> 17. It will be read by (whoever, whomever) opens the mail.

<u> him </u> 18. I will ask Ruby and (he, him) to go.

<u> me </u> 19. Between you and (I, me), I am not interested in the idea.

<u> its </u> 20. The cat will not eat (its, it's) food.

Exercise 10   **MATCHING PRONOUNS AND ANTECEDENTS**

Write the correct pronoun in the blank. (See Answer Key for answers to 1 through 10.)

<u>he or she</u> 1. If anyone saw the accident, will (he or she, they) please tell me?

<u> her </u> 2. Ms. Johnson, the president and treasurer, left (their, her) home early for the meeting.

<u>his or her</u> 3. A person should always choose (his or her, their) friends with great care.

<u> itself </u> 4. Today a nation that does not educate its citizens may find (itself, themselves) unable to compete in international markets.

<u> it </u> 5. The audience was so delighted with the performance of the soprano that (it, they) rose and applauded her loudly.

<u> their </u> 6. The group of hikers carried a two-day supply of food in (its, their) knapsacks.

their   7. Neither Marcalena nor her friends have ever had (their, her) ears pierced.

his   8. Ahmad, the former owner and manager of the store, sold (his, their) stocks in the company.

his or her   9. Someone in this class forget (his or her, their) books yesterday.

its   10. The jury did (its, their) best to bring in a fair but quick verdict.

his or her   11. Every student at this school must join a club of (his or her, their) choice.

their   12. Either Curtis or his friends lost (his, their) way to the beach.

his   13. What kind of man would forget (his, their) promises to Danielle?

his or her   14. No one has any knowledge of what (his or her, their) assignments will be.

its   15. Brown & Company is having (its, their) spring clearance sale now.

who   16. All the workers (which, who) were fired met at his house Tuesday.

their   17. Karl was one of those students who were sure of (his or her, their) answers.

himself   18. Each boy bought a box of candy for (himself, theirselves, themselves).

he or she   19. A boxer must keep in top condition, if (you, he or she, they) expects to win consistently.

them   20. Leewan played tennis and basketball very well; she received letters in (it, them).

Using Adjectives and Adverbs

1. **Adjectives** modify (describe) nouns and pronouns and answer the questions *Which one? What kind?* and *How many?*

2. **Adverbs** modify verbs, adjectives, or other adverbs and answer the questions *Where? When? Why?* and *How?* Most words ending in *-ly* are adverbs.

3. If you settle for a common word such as *good* or a slang word such as *neat* to characterize something you like, you will be limiting your communication. The more precise the word, the better the communication. Keep in mind, however, that anything can be overdone; therefore, use adjectives and adverbs wisely and economically.

4. For making comparisons, most adjectives and adverbs have three different forms: the positive (one), the comparative (two), and the superlative (three or more).

   a. Adjectives
   - Add *-er* to short adjectives (one or two syllables) to rank units of two.

        Julian is *kinder* than Sam.

   - Ann *-est* to short adjectives (one or two syllables) to rank units of more than two.

        Of the fifty people I know, Julian is the *kindest.*

   - Add the word *more* before long adjectives to rank units of two.

        My hometown is *more beautiful* than yours.

   - Add the word *most* before long adjectives to rank units of three or more.

        My hometown is the *most beautiful* in all America.

   - Some adjectives are irregular in the way they change to show comparison: *good, better, best; bad, worse, worst.*

   b. Adverbs
   For most adverbs, use the word *more* to form the comparative modifier (two) and the word *most* to form the superlative modifier (three or more).

        Jim performed *skillfully.* (modifier)

        Joan performed *more skillfully* than Felix. (comparative modifier)

        But Susan performed *most skillfully* of all. (superlative modifier)

5. **Avoid double negatives.** Words such as *no, not, none, nothing, never hardly, barely,* and *scarcely* should not be combined.

> I *don't* have *no* time for recreation. (incorrect)

> I have no time for recreation. (correct)

6. Do not confuse adjectives with adverbs. Among the most commonly confused adjectives and adverbs are *good/well, bad/badly,* and *real/really.* The words *good, bad,* and *real* are almost always adjectives. *Well* is sometimes an adjective. The words *bad* and *really* are always adverbs. *Well* is usually an adverb.

7. Do not use an adverb such as *very, more,* or *most* before adjectives such as *perfect, round, unique, square,* and *straight.*

8. A modifier that gives information but doesn't refer to a word already in the sentence is called a **dangling modifier.**

> *Walking down the street,* a snake startled me. (dangling)

> Walking down the street, I was startled by a snake. (correct)

9. A modifier that is placed so that it modifies the wrong word or words is called a **misplaced modifier.**

> The sick man went to a doctor *with a high fever.* (misplaced)

> The sick man with a high fever went to a doctor. (correct)

Exercise 11	**USING ADJECTIVES AND ADVERBS**

The italicized word or words in each sentence should be omitted or corrected. Write the omission or correction in the blank. (See Answer Key for answers to 1 through 10.)

___older___   1. The father of the two boys admitted he liked the *oldest* one better.

___slowly___   2. After two weeks of prospecting, the old man was beginning to walk too *slow* to stay with the others.

___really___
___more___
___nearly___
___straight___   3. *The Tempest* has *real* elaborate stage directions.

4. Clem threw the ball *more straight* than he ever had before.

___bad___   5. The minister of finance felt *badly* when he discovered that the expedition had succeeded without his help.

rapidly 6. I'd rather work for someone who doesn't dictate so *rapid*.

more honest 7. The king's problem was always to decide which of his valets was *honester*.

surely 8. The early English writers *sure* borrowed a great deal from each other.

more easily 9. The wooden horse helped the Greeks win the war *easier*.

kinds 10. No one except the teacher liked those *kind* of plays.

hardest 11. Of the four years I spent in college, my sophomore year was the *harder*.

really 12. Gordon should have felt *real* good after recuperating in Patagonia.

really 13. Joan Ford and Nancy Montoya were *real* good friends.

whistled only 14. The little boy *only whistled* to show them he wasn't afraid.

any 15. I do not have *no* time to do the assignment.

really 16. It was agreed that the chapel was *real* good for the meeting.

low most 17. Washington's men got so cold that their spirits were *lowly*.

nearly perfect 18. Lauren had the *most perfect* voice for the role of Violetta of any who tried out.

well most 19. The doctor said, "He is doing really *good* now."

nearly round 20. The stadium was the *most* round structure on campus.

Exercise 12   ELIMINATING DANGLING AND MISPLACED MODIFIERS

In the blank, write "D" for dangling modifier, "M" for misplaced modifier, and "OK" for correct sentences. Revise the incorrect sentences. (See Answer Key for answers to 1 through 10.)

D   1. Through hard work, ~~writing can be learned~~. ^one can learn writing^

D   2. ~~Arriving~~ at the airport early, no one was waiting for them. ^When they arrived^

M   3. They installed the carpet │in the den│ with tough fiber.

_____D_____ 4. After waiting in line for three hours, ~~our patience was lost~~. ^{we lost our patience}

_____M_____ 5. They attempted to communicate secretly | when no one was looking.

_____OK_____ 6. Being alert and well trained, the dogs found the drugs.

_____M_____ 7. To build the house | with the inspector's signature, I had to secure permits.

_____M_____ 8. For a long time I had wanted | to dance with Pravina | in the worst way.

_____M_____ 9. They | only | worked for | three days in the mountain resort.

_____D_____ 10. Arriving late at the box office, ~~no tickets could be bought~~. ^{we could not buy tickets}

_____OK_____ 11. When people dance the twist, the music is a driving force.

_____D_____ 12. Driving late at night in the fog, ~~lights were very necessary~~. ^{we needed lights}

_____M_____ 13. We heard | that the Dodgers had won | on the radio.

_____M_____ 14. Soon after I arrived, I was told | on holidays | that the school is always closed.

_____M_____ 15. That kind of behavior is harmful | to my way of thinking.

_____M_____ 16. I tried | to | thoughtfully and carefully | consider the alternatives.

_____OK_____ 17. Being well prepared, Jarrett completed the assignment in an hour.

_____OK_____ 18. A person of established reputation, Kobe was immediately recognized.

_____M_____ 19. Irene rejected his proposal and drove away | from her suitor | with screeching wheels.

_____M_____ 20. Bill watched a large crow | with binoculars.

Balancing Sentence Parts

1. **Parallelism** means balancing one structure with another of the same kind—nouns with nouns, verbs with verbs, adjectives (words that can describe nouns) with adjectives, adverbs (words that can describe verbs) with adverbs, and so forth.

   > *Men, women,* and *children* [nouns] *enjoy* the show and *return* [verbs] each year.

   > She fell *in love* and *out of love* [phrases] in a few seconds.

   > *She fell in love with him,* and *he fell in love with her* [clauses].

2. Faulty parallel structure is awkward and draws unfavorable attention to what is being said.

   > *To talk* with his buddies and *eating* fast foods were his favorite pastimes. (The sentence should be *Talking . . . and eating* or *To talk . . . and to eat.*)

3. Some words signal parallel structure. All coordinating conjunctions (*for, and, nor, but, or, yet, so*) can give such signals.

   > The weather is hot *and* humid.

   > He purchased a Dodger Dog, *but* I chose Stadium Peanuts.

4. Combination words also signal the need for parallelism or balance. The most common are *either/or, neither/nor, not only/ but also, both/ and,* and *whether/or.*

   > We will *either* win this game *or* go out fighting. (verb following each of the combination words)

Exercise 13 **BALANCING SENTENCE PARTS**

In the blank, write "P" for parallel structure or "NP" for nonparallel structure. Correct nonparallel structures. (See Answer Key for answers to 1 through 10.)

___P___ 1. Both political parties were not only sure that their plat-

forms were needed but also happy that they were different.

                                                                      both

___NP___ 2. The drivers were suspected of changing the compression

of both the motor and the size of the wheels.

_____P_____   3. For thirty years, Senator Fogle has advocated federal work projects and urged regulative agencies to support them.

_____NP_____   4. The newspapers are filled with stories of how deserters are
working as spies and ˄*how* they create havoc in the provinces.

_____P_____   5. He believed that senior citizens make poor drivers and referred to his uncle as a good example.

_____NP_____   6. Boxing may be a dangerous sport, but ~~to box~~ *boxing* ˄ can also be a good discipline.

_____P_____   7. To increase sales, they hired a new advertising representative and held regular staff meetings.

_____NP_____   8. Unemployment seemed to be | the cause | not only | of the delinquency but also the reason for an increase in the number of divorces.

_____P_____   9. The new administration has taken over the control of food and drugs and the investigation of air and water pollution.

_____NP_____   10. Mr. James's resignation was as much a tragedy for the company as it was ~~victorious~~ *a victory* ˄ for him.

_____P_____   11. The leaders were trained in methods of organization, and the followers were coached in ways of cooperation.

_____NP_____   12. To get an English poet for the occasion and ~~paying~~ *to pay* ˄ the fee are two different matters.

_____P_____   13. Mars is about half the diameter of Earth and has only a tenth of its mass.

_____P_____ 14. Darwin thought of his century as a "golden age," but his

opponent disagreed.

_____NP_____ 15. One teacher simply ignored the cheating in his classes and

rationaliz~~ing~~^{ed} his position by saying the real students would

get an education anyway.

_____NP_____ 16. There are not only thousands of cars commuting daily to

the downtown hub but also vehicles of all kinds ~~that~~ never

leav~~e~~^{ing} the hub.

_____NP_____ 17. In Delhi, we enjoyed both the flowers that were always in

evidence and the climate ^{that} made them possible.

_____NP_____ 18. She would not put up with abstract and subjective interpre-

tations or ~~giving~~^{give} credit for unsupported generalizations.

_____P_____ 19. Madison Avenue takes people as they are and leaves them

there intellectually.

_____NP_____ 20. He was an undersized man with both an enormous head

and a conceited fool with delusions of grandeur.

Mastering Punctuation

1. The three marks of end punctuation are periods, question marks, and exclamation points.
   a. Periods
   Place a period after a statement.
   Place a period after common abbreviations.
   b. Question Marks
   Place a question mark at the end of a direct question.
   Use a single question mark in sentence construction that con-tain a double question—that is, a quoted question following a question.

Mr. Martin said, "Did he say, 'Are we going?'"

Do *not* use a question mark after an indirect (reported) question.

She asked me what caused the slide.

c. Exclamation Points
Place an exclamation point after a word or group of words that expresses strong feeling.
Do not overwork the exclamation point. Do not use double exclamation points.

2. The comma is used essentially to separate and to set off sentence elements.

a. Use a comma to separate main clauses joined by one of the coordinating conjunctions—*for, and, nor, but, or, yet, so.*

We went to the game, *but* it was canceled.

b. Use a comma after introductory dependent clauses and long phrases (generally, four or more words is considered long).

Before she and I arrived, the meeting was called to order.

c. Use a comma to separate words, phrases, and clauses in a series.

He ran *down the street, across the park,* and *into the arms of his father.*

d. Use a comma to separate coordinate adjectives not joined by *and* that modify the same noun.

I need a *sturdy, reliable* truck.

e. Use a comma to separate sentence elements that might be misread.

Inside, the dog scratched his fleas.

f. Use commas to set off nonessential (unnecessary for meaning of the sentence) words, phrases, and clauses.

Maria, who studied hard, will pass.

g. Use commas to set off nouns used as direct address.

Play it again, Sam.

h. Use commas to separate the numbers in a date.

June 4, 1965, is a day I will remember.

i. Use commas to separate the city from the state. No comma is used between the state and the ZIP code.

Walnut, CA 91789

j. Use a comma following the salutation and the complementary closing in a letter (but in a business letter, use a colon after the salutation).

> Dear John,

> Sincerely,

k. Use a comma in numbers to set off groups of three digits. However, omit the comma in dates and in long serial numbers, page numbers, and street numbers.

> The total assets were $2,000,000.

> I was born in 1980.

3. The semicolon indicates a stronger division than the comma. It is used principally to separate independent clauses within a sentence.

a. Use a semicolon to separate independent clauses not joined by a coordinating conjunction.

> You must buy that car today; tomorrow will be too late.

b. Use a semicolon between two independent clauses joined by a conjunctive adverb (such as *however, otherwise, therefore, similarly, hence, on the other hand, then, consequently, accordingly, thus*).

> It was very late; therefore, I remained at the hotel.

4. Quotation marks bring special attention to words.

a. Quotation marks are used principally to set off direct quotations. A direct quotation consists of material taken from the written work or the direct speech of others; it is set off by double quotation marks. Single quotation marks are used to set off a quotation within a quotation.

> He said, "I don't remember if she said, 'Wait for me.'"

b. Use double quotation marks to set off titles of shorter pieces of writing such as magazine articles, essays, short stories, short poems, one-act plays, chapters in books, songs, and separate pieces of writing published as part of a larger work.

> The book *Literature: Structure, Sound, and Sense* contains a deeply moving poem titled "On Wenlock Edge."

> Have you read "The Use of Force," a short story by William Carlos Williams?

> My favorite Elvis song is "Don't Be Cruel."

c. Punctuation with quotation marks follows definite rules.

- A period or comma is always placed *inside* the quotation marks.

> Our assignment for Monday was to read Poe's "The Raven."

> "I will read you the story," he said. "It is a good one."

- A semicolon or colon is always placed *outside* the quotation marks.

> He read Robert Frost's poem "Design"; then he gave the examination.

- A question mark, exclamation point, or dash is placed *outside* the quotation marks when it applies to the entire sentence and *inside* the quotation marks when it applies to the material in quotation marks.

> He asked, "Am I responsible for everything?" (quoted question within a statement)

> Did you hear him say, "I have the answer"? (statement within a question)

> Did she say, "Are we ready?" (question within a question)

> She shouted, "Impossible!" (exclamation)

> "I hope—that is, I—" he began. (dash)

5. Italic print (slanting type) is used to call special attention to certain words or groups of words. In handwriting or typing, such words are underlined.

   a. Italicize (underline) foreign words and phrases that are still listed in the dictionary as foreign.

      > *nouveau riche*   *Weltschmerz*

   b. Italicize (underline) titles of books (except the Bible), long poems, plays, magazines, motion pictures, musical compositions, newspapers, works of art, names of aircraft, ships, and letters, figures, and words referred to by their own name.

      > *War and Peace*   *Apollo 12*   leaving *o* out of *sophomore*

6. The dash is used when a stronger break than the comma is needed. It can also be used to indicate a break in the flow of thought and to emphasize words (less formal than the colon in this situation).

   > Here is the true reason—but maybe you don't care.

   > English, French, history—these are subjects I like.

7. The colon is a formal mark of punctuation used chiefly to introduce something that is to follow, such as a list, a quotation, or an explanation.

These cars are my favorites: Cadillac, Chevrolet, Buick, Oldsmobile, and Pontiac.

8. Parentheses are used to set off material that is of relatively little importance to the main thought of the sentence. Such material—numbers, parenthetical material, figures, supplementary material, and sometimes explanatory details—merely amplifies the main thought.

The years of the era (1961–1973) were full of action.

Her husband (she had been married only a year) died last week.

9. Brackets are used within a quotation to set off editorial additions or corrections made by the person who is quoting.

Churchill said: "It [the Yalta Agreement] contained many mistakes."

10. The apostrophe is used with nouns and indefinite pronouns to show possession, to show the omission of letters and figures in contractions, and to form the plurals of letters, figures, and words referred to as words.

man's coat   girls' clothes   *you're* (contraction of *you are*)   five *and*'s

11. The hyphen brings two or more words together into a single compound word. Correct hyphenation, therefore, is essentially a spelling problem rather than one of punctuation. Because the hyphen is not used with any degree of consistency, consult your dictionary for current usage. Study the following as a beginning guide.

    a. Use a hyphen to separate the parts of many compound words.

    about-face   go-between

    b. Use a hyphen between prefixes and proper names.

    all-American   mid-November

    c. Use a hyphen to join two or more words used as a single adjective modifier before a noun.

    first-class service   hard-fought game   sad-looking mother

    d. Use a hyphen with spelled-out compound numbers up to ninety-nine and with fractions.

    twenty-six   two-thirds

Note: Dates, street addresses, numbers requiring more than two words, chapter and page numbers, time followed directly by A.M. or P.M., and figures after a dollar sign or before measurement abbreviations are usually written as figures, not words.

Conquering Capitalization

In English, there are many conventions concerning the use of capital letters. Here are some of them.

1. Capitalize the first word of a sentence.

2. Capitalize proper nouns and adjectives derived from proper nouns.

   - Names of persons

        Edward Jones

   - Adjectives derived from proper nouns

        a Shakespearean sonnet   a Miltonic sonnet

   - Countries, nationalities, races, and languages

        Germany   English   Spanish   Chinese

   - States, regions, localities, and other geographical divisions

        California   the Far East   the South

   - Oceans, lakes, mountains, deserts, streets, and parks

        Lake Superior   Fifth Avenue   Sahara Desert

   - Educational institutions, schools, and courses

        Santa Ana College   Spanish 3   Joe Hill School
        Rowland High School

   - Organizations and their members

        Boston Red Sox   Boy Scouts   Audubon Society

   - Corporations, governmental agencies or departments, and trade names

        U.S. Steel Corporation   Treasury Department
        White Memorial Library

   - Calendar references such as holidays, days of the week, and month

        Easter   Tuesday   January

   - Historic eras, periods, documents, and laws

        Declaration of Independence   Geneva Convention
        First Crusade   Romantic Age

3. Capitalize words denoting family relationships when they are used before a name or substituted for a name.

        He walked with his nephew and Aunt Grace.
        but
        He walked with his nephew and his aunt.

Grandmother and Mother are away on vacation.
but
My grandmother and my mother are away on vacation.

4. Capitalize abbreviations after names.

Henry White, Jr.   William Green, M.D.

5. Capitalize titles of themes, books, plays, movies, poems, magazines, newspapers, musical compositions, songs, and works of art. Do not capitalize short conjunctions and prepositions unless they come at the beginning or the end of the title.

Desire Under the Elms   *Terminator*

Last of the Mohicans   *Of Mice and Men*

"Blueberry Hill"

6. Capitalize any title preceding a name or used as a substitute for a name. Do not capitalize a title following a name.

Judge Stone	Alfred Stone, a judge
General Clark	Raymond Clark, a general
Professor Fuentes	Harry Jones, the former president

Exercise 14   **INSERTING COMMAS**

Insert all necessary commas in the following sentences. (See Answer Key for answers to 1 through 10.)

1. John Steinbeck‸ a great American writer‸ was born in Salinas‸ California.

2. Using that area for a colorful setting‸ he wrote some of his best material.

3. In those highly descriptive works‸ he depicts common people.

4. Many of these common people are migrants and farm workers‸ and most are basically good.

5. His most famous novel‸ *The Grapes of Wrath‸* is set in the 1930s.

6. The main group of people is the Joad family in Oklahoma‸ a mostly rural state.

7. After the dust storms hit‸ the Joad family loses its farm to the bank executives‸ who are taking advantage of the poor.

8. Hearing of need for workers in California the Joads decide to leave.

9. On the trip to California these "Okies" are part of a migratory movement coming from other impoverished areas in or near Oklahoma.

10. Their trip which occupies the first part of the book is a story of suffering compassion and sacrifice.

11. They help themselves and they meet others in similar circumstances on the road.

12. Their will to survive is personified by Steinbeck's description of an ordinary determined turtle trying to cross a road.

13. Finally arriving at the California border the Joads discover that they are not welcome.

14. The large farm owners have advertised widely but they have no intention of employing all who come.

15. Instead they will cynically take advantage of the mass of poor desperate workers by paying starvation wages.

16. When the workers try to organize they are met with violence.

17. Despite the exploitation and suffering the farm workers behave with much courage and honor.

18. At the end of *The Grapes of Wrath* the workers have ennobled themselves in the struggle and have learned the importance of banding together for their human rights.

19. When the novel was published it was regarded largely as a political statement directed toward a current situation.

20. Now it has taken its place as a novel with universal appeal‸ one that

    celebrates the quest of every person for human dignity.

Exercise 15   **CHOOSING THE SEMICOLON OR THE COMMA**

Insert all necessary commas or semicolons in the following sentences. (See Answer Key for answers to 1 through 10.)

1. I had real friends among my relatives‸ and I had enemies among my

   former friends.

2. One mother sued the school for expelling her son‸ the expulsion was

   traumatic to her.

3. She thanked Khanh Doan, the editor; Raquel Perez, the critic; Richard

   Varay, her secretary‸ and Walter Ross, her agent.

4. The underdeveloped countries have about 69 percent of the world's

   adults‸ however, they have about 80 percent of the world's children.

5. It was impossible to move for the crowds were overwhelming.

6. The housetops were covered with people‸ cannons were lined up

   along the sidewalks, and the police officers were stationed at every

   corner.

7. Freud wanted to go to Rome, a city that fascinated him‸ but his pur-

   pose was never clear to me.

8. The lexicographer wanted to put all the names under three head-

   ings—philosophers, living or dead; artists, living or dead; and scien-

   tists‸ living or dead.

9. Albert Camus did not claim that the universe was rational‸ however,

   he agreed that humans are both rational and meaningful.

10. The teacher had us reading essays for speed in fact, we were even tested for reading time and comprehension.

11. It's true that Rome fell but most Roman buildings remained standing.

12. The human mind drives us to exploration, sometimes to destruction but not all people are explorers, nor, indeed, are all people capable of real exploration.

13. The novel was exciting and it was full of colorful descriptions.

14. We like talent yet we want it to pay off.

15. He didn't take himself seriously nevertheless, he was hurt when we ignored him.

16. We need moments of privacy for self-analysis, for looking inward; for making sense of others, for looking outward for catching up with life, for looking around; and for inspiration, for looking upward.

17. The mayor regarded herself as very fortunate in winning the election for she was only thirty years old.

18. He pitted Freud against Darwin and Freud won.

19. She treats the United States as a unit her purpose is to establish its unity in the reader's mind.

20. The great artists were also philosophers and scientists indeed, their contributions range through many areas and activities.

Exercise 16   **WORKING WITH ALL MARKS OF PUNCTUATION AND CAPITALIZATION**

One punctuation mark or capital letter is omitted in each of the following sentences. Insert them as needed. (Pairs of quotation marks are considered one unit.) (See Answer Key for answers to 1 through 10.)

1. We never felt that central Park was really centrally located in New York City.

2. Father claimed him as a son, but mother didn't.

3. "Oh I can't believe it's true!" cried Francisca.

4. Tiffany tried to justify her prejudice by getting out Huxleys *Collected Essays* and quoting from them.

5. You can't understand it without the punctuation; is it two boys hats or one?

6. It could be anyones, but its color makes me think it's mine.

7. History was easy compared to any of the french courses.

8. The whale's mouth, with its hundreds of curved slats, is full of hairy fibers commonly called hog's bristles.

9. Tucker said to them, "Remember that Papa said, The good die young!"

10. Wont the question of Clint's hour of birth hold up the astrologer's predictions?

11. The 1970s were good years for us; the clerks treated us with respect and we had more leisure.

12. It was something Truman said about the kitchen—was it about too many cooks?

13. Sooner or later every tourist has to answer one question Is the adventure worth the trouble?

14. We're all two selves—one egotistic and one gregarious—and we cant^ ' separate the two.

15. Lincoln—president by mandate—was thought of as the author of the emancipation Proclamation.

16. She had two reasons for going to correct her popularity poll and to demonstrate her courage.

17. Maugham can combine (as in his short story titled "On a Chinese Screen") warmth and horror in one paragraph.

18. He always said, "Make your choice and take the consequences."

19. The woman was a success, but certainly there was no mystery about it—being queen was well within the scope of Elizabeths talents.

20. Two brothers, Dale and Gilbert, called him uncle Sam.

Improving Spelling

Spelling Tips

The following tips will help you become a better speller.

1. Do not omit letters.

   Many errors occur because certain letters are omitted when the word is pronounced or spelled. Observe the omissions in the following words. Then concentrate on learning the correct spellings.

Incorrect	*Correct*	*Incorrect*	*Correct*
aquaintance	acquaintance	irigation	irrigation
ajourned	adjourned	libary	library
agravate	aggavate	paralell	parallel
aproved	approved	parlament	parliament
artic	arctic	paticulaly	particularly
comodity	commodity	readly	readily
efficent	efficient	sophmore	sophomore
envirnment	environment	stricly	strictly
familar	familiar	unconsious	unconscious

2. Do not add letters.

Incorrect	Correct	Incorrect	Correct
ath*e*lete	athlete	om*m*ission	omission
co*m*ming	coming	pas*t*time	pastime
drown*d*ed	drowned	privile*d*ge	privilege
folk*e*s	folks	simil*i*ar	similar
occa*s*sionally	occasionally	tra*d*gedy	tragedy

3. Do not substitute incorrect letters for correct letters.

Incorrect	Correct	Incorrect	Correct
benefi*s*ial	beneficial	offen*c*e	offense
bull*i*tins	bulletins	peculi*e*r	peculiar
*s*ensus	census	re*s*itation	recitation
d*i*scription	description	scre*a*ch	screech
d*e*sease	disease	substan*s*ial	substantial
dissen*t*ion	dissension	surpri*z*e	surprise
it*i*ms	items	techn*a*cal	technical

4. Do not transpose letters.

Incorrect	Correct	Incorrect	Correct
alu*nm*i	alumni	p*re*haps	perhaps
child*er*n	children	p*er*fer	prefer
dup*il*cate	duplicate	p*er*scription	prescription
irrev*el*ant	irrelevant	princip*el*s	principles
kind*el*	kindle	y*ei*ld	yield

Note: Whenever you notice other words that fall into any one of these categories, add them to the list.

5. Apply the spelling rules for spelling *ei* and *ie* words correctly.

Remember this poem?

> Use *i* before *e*
> Except after *c*
> Or when sounded like *a*
> As in *neighbor* and *weigh*.

i before e

achieve	chief	niece	relieve
belief	field	piece	shield
believe	grief	pierce	siege
brief	hygiene	relief	variety

Except after c

ceiling	conceive	deceive	receipt
conceit	deceit	perceive	receive

Exceptions: either, financier, height, leisure, neither, seize, species, weird

When sounded like a

deign	freight	neighbor	sleigh
eight	heinous	rein	veil
feign	heir	reign	vein
feint	neigh	skein	weigh

6. Apply the rules for dropping the final *e* or retaining the final *e* when a suffix is added.

   Words ending in a silent *e* usually drop the *e* before a suffix beginning with a vowel; for example, *accuse + ing = accusing.* Here are some common suffixes beginning with a vowel: *-able, -al, -age, -ary, -ation, -ence, -ing, -ion, -ous,* and *-ure.*

admire + *-able* = admirable	imagine + *-ary* = imaginary
arrive + *-al* = arrival	locate + *-ion* = location
come + *-ing* = coming	please + *-ure* = pleasure
explore + *-ation* = exploration	plume + *-age* = plumage
fame + *-ous* = famous	precede + *-ence* = precedence

   Exceptions: *dye* + *-ing* = *dyeing* (to distinguish it from *dying*), *acreage,* and *mileage.* Words ending in a silent *e* usually retain the *e* before a suffix beginning with a consonant; for example: *arrange + -ment = arrangement.* Here are some common suffixes beginning with a consonant: *-craft, -ful, -less, -ly, -mate, -ment, -ness,* and *-ty.*

Entire + *-ty* = entirety	manage + *-ment* = management
hate + *-ful* = hateful	safe + *-ly* = safely
hope + *-less* = hopeless	stale + *-mate* = stalemate
like + *-ness* = likeness	state + *-craft* = statecraft

   Exceptions: Some words taking the *-ful* or *-ly* suffixes drop the final *e:*

awe + *-ful* = awful	true + *-ly* = truly
due + *-ly* = duly	whole + *-ly* = wholly

   Some words taking the suffix *-ment* drop the final *e;* for example, *acknowledgment, argument,* and *judgment.*

   Words ending in silent *e* after *c* or *g* retain the *e* when the suffix begins with the vowel *a* or *o.* The final *e* is retained to keep the *c* or *g* soft before the suffixes.

advantag*e*ous	notic*e*able
courag*e*ous	peac*e*able

7. Apply the rules for doubling a final consonant before a suffix beginning with a vowel.

Words of one syllable

blot	blotted	get	getting	rob	robbed
brag	bragging	hop	hopped	run	running
cut	cutting	hot	hottest	sit	sitting
drag	dragged	man	mannish	stop	stopped
drop	dropped	plan	planned	swim	swimming

Words accented on the last syllable

acquit	acquitted	equip	equipped
admit	admittance	occur	occurrence
allot	allotted	omit	omitting
begin	beginning	prefer	preferred
commit	committee	refer	referred
concur	concurring	submit	submitted
confer	conferring	transfer	transferred
defer	deferring		

Words that are not accented on the last syllable and words that do
not end in a single consonant preceded by a vowel do not double the
final consonant (whether or not the suffix begins with a vowel).

Frequently Misspelled Words

a lot	business	divide	finally
absence	certain	dying	foreign
across	college	eighth	government
actually	coming	eligible	grammar
all right	committee	eliminate	grateful
among	competition	embarrassed	guarantee
analyze	complete	environment	guard
appearance	consider	especially	guidance
appreciate	criticism	etc.	height
argument	definitely	exaggerate	hoping
athlete	dependent	excellent	humorous
athletics	develop	exercise	immediately
awkward	development	existence	independent
becoming	difference	experience	intelligence
beginning	disastrous	explanation	interest
belief	discipline	extremely	interfere
benefit	discussed	familiar	involved
buried	disease	February	knowledge

laboratory	physically	rhythm	success
leisure	planned	ridiculous	suggest
length	pleasant	sacrifice	surprise
library	possible	safety	thoroughly
likely	practical	scene	though
lying	preferred	schedule	tragedy
marriage	prejudice	secretary	tried
mathematics	privilege	senior	tries
meant	probably	sense	truly
medicine	professor	separate	unfortunately
neither	prove	severely	unnecessary
ninety	psychology	shining	until
ninth	pursue	significant	unusual
nuclear	receipt	similar	using
occasionally	receive	sincerely	usually
opinion	recommend	sophomore	Wednesday
opportunity	reference	speech	writing
parallel	relieve	straight	written
particular	religious	studying	
persuade	repetition	succeed	

Understanding Confusing Words

The following are more words that are commonly misspelled or confused with one another. Some have similar sounds, some are often mispronounced, and some are only misunderstood.

a   An adjective (called an *article*) used before a word beginning with a consonant or a consonant sound, as in "I ate *a* donut."

an   An adjective (called an *article*) used before a word beginning with a vowel (*a, e, i, o, u*) or with a silent *h*, as in "I ate *an* artichoke."

and   A coordinating conjunction, as in "Sara *and* I like Johnny Cash."

accept   A verb meaning "to receive," as in "I *accept* your explanation."

except   A preposition meaning "to exclude," as in "I paid everyone *except* you."

advice   A noun meaning "guidance," as in "Thanks for the *advice.*"

advise   A verb meaning "to give guidance," as in "Will you please *advise* me of my rights?"

all right	An adjective meaning "correct" or "acceptable," as in "It's *all right* to cry."
alright	Not used in formal writing.
all ready	An adjective that can be used interchangeably with *ready,* as in "I am *all ready* to go to town."
already	An adverb meaning "before," which cannot be used in place of *ready,* as in "I have *already* finished."
a lot	An adverb meaning "much," as in "She liked him *a lot,*" or a noun meaning "several," as in "I had *a lot* of suggestions."
alot	Misspelling.
altogether	An adverb meaning "completely," as in "He is *altogether* happy."
all together	An adverb meaning "as one," which can be used interchangeably with *together,* as in "The group left *all together.*"
choose	A present tense verb meaning "to select," as in "Do whatever you *choose.*"
chose	The past tense form of the verb *choose,* as in "They *chose* to take action yesterday."
could of	A misspelled phrase caused by confusing *could've,* meaning *could have,* with *could of.*
could have	Correctly spelled phrase, as in "I *could have* left."
could've	Correctly spelled contraction of *could have,* as in "He *could've* succeeded."
affect	Usually a verb meaning "change," as in "Ideas *affect* me."
effect	Usually a noun meaning "result," as in "That *effect* was unexpected."
hear	A verb indicating the receiving of sound, as in "I *hear* thunder."
here	An adverb meaning "present location," as in "I live *here.*"
it's	A contraction of *it is,* as in "*It's* time to dance."
its	Possessive pronoun, as in "Each dog has *its* day."
know	A verb usually meaning "to comprehend" or "to recognize," as in "I *know* the answer."

no	An adjective meaning "negative," as in "I have *no* potatoes."
lead	A present tense verb, as in "I *lead* a stable life now," or a noun referring to a substance, such as "I sharpened the *lead* in my pencil."
led	The past tense form of the verb *lead,* as in "I *led* a wild life in my youth."
loose	An adjective meaning "without restraint," as in "He is a *loose* cannon."
lose	A present tense verb from the pattern *lose, lost, lost,* as in "I thought I would *lose* my senses."
paid	The past tense form of *pay,* as in "He *paid* his dues."
payed	Misspelling.
passed	The past tense form of the verb *pass,* meaning "went by," as in "He *passed* me on the curve."
past	An adjective meaning "former," as in "That's *past* history," or a noun, as in "He lived in the *past.*"
patience	A noun meaning "willingness to wait," as in "Job was a man of much *patience.*"
patients	A noun meaning "people under care," as in "The doctor had fifty *patients.*"
peace	A noun meaning "a quality of calmness" or "absence of strife," as in "The guru was at *peace* with the world."
piece	A noun meaning "part," as in "I gave him a *piece* of my mind."
quiet	An adjective meaning "silent," as in "She was a *quiet* child."
quit	A verb meaning "to cease" or "to withdraw," as in "I *quit* my job."
quite	An adverb meaning "very," as in "The clam is *quite* happy."
receive	A verb meaning "to accept," as in "I will *receive* visitors now."
recieve	Misspelling.
stationary	An adjective meaning "not moving," as in "Try to avoid running into *stationary* objects."
stationery	A noun meaning "paper material to write on," as in "I bought a box of *stationery* for Sue's birthday present."

than	A conjunction, as in "He is taller *than* I am."
then	An adverb, as in "She *then* left town."
their	An adjective (possessive pronoun), as in "They read *their* books."
there	An adverb, as in "He left it *there*," or a filler word, as in "*There* is no time left."
they're	A contraction of *they are,* as in "*They're* happy."
thorough	An adjective, as in "He did a *thorough* job."
through	A preposition, as in "She went *through* the yard."
to	A preposition, as in "I went *to* town."
too	An adverb meaning "exceeding or going beyond what is acceptable," as in "You are *too* late to qualify for the discount," or "also," as in "I have feelings, *too.*"
two	An adjective of number, as in "I have *two* jobs."
truely	Misspelling.
truly	An adverb meaning "sincerely" or "completely," as in "He was *truly* happy."
weather	A noun meaning "condition of the atmosphere," as in "The *weather* is pleasant today."
whether	A conjunction, as in "*Whether* he would go was of no consequence."
write	A present-tense verb, as in "Watch me as I *write* this letter."
writen	Misspelling.
written	A past-participle verb, as in "I have *written* the letter."
you're	A contraction of *you are,* as in "*You're* my friend."
your	A possessive pronoun, as in "I like *your* looks."

Your Spell Checker

Your computer spell checker is an important tool with many benefits and some limitations. With about 100,000 words in a typical database, the spell checker alerts you to problem words in your text that should be verified. If you agree that the spelling of a word should be checked, you can then select from a list of words with similar spellings. A likely substitute word will be highlighted. With a keystroke, you can correct a problem, add your own word to the database, or ignore the alert. With a few more keystrokes, you can type in your own correction, and you can add an unusual spelling or word to the database. You may even be able to program your spell checker to correct automatically your most frequent spelling or typing errors. You will be amazed at how many times your computer will catch misspellings that your eye did not see.

However, the spell checker has limitations. If you intended to type *he* and instead typed *me,* the spell checker will not alert you to a possible problem because the word you typed is spelled correctly. If you use the wrong word, such as *herd* instead of *heard,* the spell checker will not detect a problem. Thus, you should always proofread your writing after you have spell checked it. Do not be lulled into a false sense of spelling security simply because you have a machine on your side. As a writer, you are the final spell checker.

Correcting ESL Problems

If you came to the United States knowing little English, you probably acquired vocabulary first. Then you began using that vocabulary within the basic patterns of your own language. If your native language had no articles, you probably used no articles; if your language had no verb tenses, you probably used no verb tenses, and so on. Using the grammar of your own language with your new vocabulary may initially have enabled you to make longer and more complex statements in English, but eventually you learned that your native grammar and your adopted grammar were different. You may even have learned that no two grammars are the same, and that English has a bewildering set of rules and an even longer set of exceptions to those rules. This chapter presents grammar (the way we put words together) and rhetoric (the way we use language effectively) that can be applied to your writing. The following are some definitions, rules, and references that are of special help to writers who are learning English as a second language (ESL).

Using Articles in Relation to Nouns

Articles

Articles are either indefinite (*an, a*) or definite (*the*). Because they point out nouns, they are often called *noun determiners.*

Nouns

Nouns can be either singular (*book*) or plural (*books*) and are either count nouns (things that can be counted, such as "book") or noncount nouns (things that cannot be counted, such as "homework"). If you are not certain whether a noun is a count noun or a noncount noun, try placing the word *much* before the word. You can say, "much homework," so *homework* is a noncount noun.

Rules

- Use an indefinite article (*a* or *an*) before singular count nouns and not before noncount nouns. The indefinite article means "one," so you would not use it before plural count nouns.

Correct:	I saw a book. (count noun)
Correct:	I ate an apple. (count noun)
Incorrect:	I fell in a love. (noncount noun)
Correct:	I fell in love. (noncount noun)
Incorrect:	I was in a good health. (noncount noun)
Correct:	I was in good health. (noncount noun)

- Use the definite article (*the*) before both singular and plural count nouns that have specific reference.

Correct:	I read the book. (a specific one)
Correct:	I read the books (specific ones)
Correct:	I like to read a good book. (nonspecific, therefore the indefinite article)
Correct:	A student who works hard will pass. (any student, therefore nonspecific)
Correct:	The student on my left is falling asleep. (a specific student)

- Use the definite article with noncount nouns only when they are specifically identified.

Correct:	Honesty [as an idea] is a rare commodity.
Correct:	The honesty of my friend has inspired me. (specifically identified)
Incorrect:	I was in trouble and needed the assistance. (not specifically identified)
Correct:	The assistance offered by the paramedics was appreciated. (specifically identified)

- Place the definite article before proper nouns (names) of

  oceans, rivers, and deserts (for example, *the* Pacific Ocean and *the* Red River).

  countries, if the first part of the name indicates a division (*the* United States of America).

  regions (*the* South).

plural islands (*the* Hawaiian Islands).

museums and libraries (*the* Los Angeles County Museum).

colleges and universities when the word *college* or *university* comes before the name (*the* University of Oklahoma).

These are the main rules. For a more detailed account of rules for articles, see a comprehensive ESL book in your library.

Sentence Patterns

The Writing Different Kinds of Sentences section (p. 473) defines and illustrates the patterns of English sentences. Some languages include patterns not used in standard English. The following principles are well worth remembering.

- The conventional English sentence is based on one or more clauses, each of which must have a subject (sometimes the implied "you") and a verb.

  Incorrect: Saw the book. (subject needed even if it is obvious)

  Correct: I saw the book.

- English does not repeat a subject, even for emphasis.

  Incorrect: The book that I read it was interesting.

  Correct: The book that I read was interesting.

Verb Endings

- English indicates time through verbs. Learn the different forms of verb tenses and the combinations of main verbs and helping verbs.

  Incorrect: He watching the game. (A verblike word ending in *-ing* cannot be a verb all by itself.)

  Correct: He is watching the game. (Note that a helping verb such as *is, has, has been, will,* or *will be* always occurs before a main verb ending in *-ing.*)

- Take special care in maintaining consistency in tense.

  Incorrect: I went to the mall. I watch a movie there. (verb tenses inconsistent)

  Correct: I went to the mall. I watched a movie there.

All twelve verb tenses are covered with explanations, examples, and exercises in the Working with Verb Forms section of this chapter, pages 483–494.

Idioms

Some of your initial problems with writing English are likely to arise from trying to adjust to a different and difficult grammar. If the English language used an entirely systematic grammar, your learning would be easier, but English has patterns that are both complex and irregular. Among them are idioms, word groups that often defy grammatical rules and mean something other than what they appear to mean.

The expression "He kicked the bucket" does not mean that a person struck a cylindrical container with his foot; instead, it means that someone died. That example is one kind of idiom. Because the expression suggests a certain irreverence, it would not be the choice of most people who want to make a statement about death; but if it is used, it must be used with its own precise wording, not "He struck the long cylindrical container with his foot" or "He did some bucket-kicking." Like other languages, the English language has thousands of these idioms. Expressions such as "the more the merrier" and "on the outs" are ungrammatical. They are also very informal expressions and therefore seldom used in college writing, although they are an indispensable part of a flexible, effective, all-purpose vocabulary. Because of their twisted meanings and illogic, idioms are likely to be among the last parts of language that a new speaker learns well. A speaker must know the culture thoroughly to understand when, where, and how to use slang and other idiomatic expressions.

If you listen carefully and read extensively, you will learn English idioms. Your library will have dictionaries that explain them.

More Suggestions for ESL Writers

1. Read your material aloud and try to detect inconsistencies and awkward phrasing.

2. Have others read your material aloud for the same purposes.

3. If you have severe problems with grammatical awkwardness, try composing shorter, more direct sentences until you become more proficient in phrasing.

4. On your Self-Evaluation Chart, list the problems you have (such as articles, verb endings, clause patterns), review relevant parts of Chapter 16, and concentrate on your own problem areas as you draft, revise, and edit.

Exercise 17   **EXAMINING ESL PROBLEMS**

Make corrections in the use of articles, verbs, and phrasing (See Answer Key for answers.)

George Washington at Trenton

One of ^the^ most famous battles during the War of Independence ~~occur~~ *occurred* at Trenton, New Jersey, on Christmas Eve of ~~the~~ 1776. The colonists out- ^*were*^ matched in supplies and finances and ~~were~~ outnumbered in troop strength. Most observers in other countries ~~think~~ *thought the* rebellion would be put down soon. ^*The*^ British ^*were*^ overconfident and ~~believe~~ *believed* there would be no more battles until spring. But George Washington ~~decide~~ *decided* to fight one more time. That Christmas, while ^*a*^ large army of Britishers ^*were*^ having ^*a*^ party and thinking about the holiday season, ^*the*^ Americans set out for ^*a*^ surprise raid. They loaded onto boats used for carrying ore and rowed across ^*the*^ Delaware River. George Washington stood tall in ^*the*^ lead boat. According to legend, ^*the*^ drummer boy floated across ^*the*^ river on his drum, pulled by ^*a*^ rope tied to ^*a*^ boat. Because ^*the*^ British did not feel threatened by the ragtag colonist forces, they ^*were*^ unprepared to do battle. The colonists stormed ^*the*^ living quarters and the general assembly hall and achieved victory. It was good for the colonists' morale, something they needed, for they would endure ^*a*^ long, hard winter before fighting again.

Appendixes

THE QUIGMANS   by Buddy Hickerson

"The company has decided to automate, Quigman. Dr. Tensly here will be installing a Mac processor in your skull."

Appendix A: Writing Process Worksheet

The following page has been designed for you to photocopy and enlarge, if your instructor directs you to do so.

Writing Process Worksheet

TITLE _____

NAME _____ DUE DATE _____

ASSIGNMENT   In the space below, write whatever you need to know about your assignment, including information about the topic, audience, pattern of writing, length, whether to include a rough draft or revised drafts, and whether your paper must be typed.

PREWRITING STAGE ONE   **Explore**   Freewrite, brainstorm (list), cluster, or gather information as directed by your instructor. Use the back of this page or separate paper if you need more space.

PREWRITING STAGE TWO   **Organize**   Write a topic sentence or thesis; label the subject and the treatment parts.

Write an outline or an outline alternative.

WRITING STAGE THREE   **Write**   On separate paper, write and then revise your paper as many times as necessary for coherence, language (usage, tone, and diction), unity, emphasis, support, and sentences (CLUESS). Read your paper aloud to hear and correct any grammatical errors or awkward-sounding sentences.

Edit any problems in fundamentals, such as capitalization, omissions, punctuation, and spelling (COPS).

Appendix B: Student Demonstration of All Stages of the Writing Process

Here we see how Tanya worked through the entire writing process. In Stage One, she freewrote, brainstormed, and developed a cluster of ideas. In Stage Two, she composed a good thesis statement, developed further a part of her cluster from Stage One, and drew up an outline based on the cluster. Finally, in Stage Three, she wrote one of her first drafts, rewrote and edited that draft, and, finally, presented the finished version.

Note that Tanya has used a Writing Process Worksheet like the one provided in Appendix A for your major writing assignments. Her worksheet has been lengthened for you to be able to see all parts of her work.

· ·

Writing Process Worksheet

TITLE _Prison as a Community_

NAME _Tanya_   **DUE DATE** _Monday, June 5, 8 a.m._

ASSIGNMENT

In the space below, write whatever you need to know about your assignment, including information about the topic, audience, pattern of writing, length, whether to include a rough draft or revised drafts, and whether your paper must be typed.

The details included in this section would remind Tanya of her specific assignment. She would reread this section to make certain she was following directions.

Write an essay of 500 to 800 words on a specific group of people who function as a unit, such as a family, a work team, a sports team, a committee, an organization, or some kind of community. Consider social units you have studied or are studying in history, sociology, and psychology courses. Submit the Writing Process Worksheet and at least one preliminary draft with your final typed draft. List any sources you have used.

PREWRITING
STAGE ONE

Explore   Freewrite, brainstorm (list), cluster, or gather information as directed by your instructor. Use the back of this page or separate paper if you need more space.

This freewriting helped Tanya with the initial exploration of an idea and led to the generation of a topic.

Writing about a group of people gives me a lot of things to think about from where I am in my situation here in prison. I could write about gangs and there are plenty of them around and I could write about prison families and lots of different work stations all over the grounds and I could even write about the guards or correctional officers as they like to be called. And I could find a lot in my other classes that would give me information or at least some definitions and frameworks to work from. One thing I read about in my history book last week made me think even before this assignment. And that was <u>the walled cities</u> that sprung up in Europe more than a thousand years ago. They were little <u>communities. All inside walls.</u> Just <u>like the place where I live now.</u> When I came to prison I'd never been locked up before and I didn't know about prison and I guess I just thought of prison as a place where a bunch of people are locked up and sort of herded around. Then I came here and discovered that <u>prison is like</u> a <u>little town</u> in some ways and it has walls or fences just like the walled city I read about in my history book. Its just that <u>some one of them walled people out</u> and <u>one of them walls people in.</u> Reading the book made me think about my place here and how youve got most <u>everything here that you'll find in a regular city.</u> You've got <u>government, schools, churches,</u> a <u>post office,</u> a <u>hospital, rec space,</u> and <u>citizens</u> and a lot more. The place is called <u>the California Institution</u> for Women, but it has its own name, Frontera, and a separate zip code.

Unit
Walls and
fences

Town
walling in
parts

Clustering

Clustering helped Tanya further explore possible areas for development. The dotted lines mark the area of special interest.

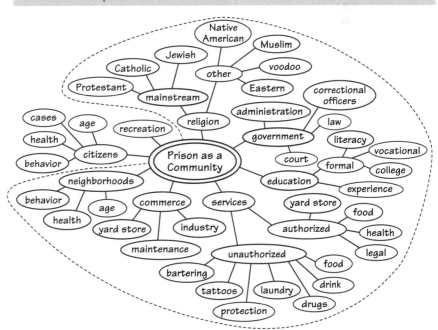

Brainstorming (Big-Six Questions)

Brainstorming helped her to focus.

Who? People at the California Institution for Women

What? A community with parts: government, education, religion, services, business, citizens, housing

Where? All the time

Why? Because the people make up a unit, a community

How? Each part of the prison relates to other parts

Listing

Listing helped Tanya find divisions for her outline.

(churches)	laundry
(schools)	(service providers)
(government)	(citizens)
cops	recreation
post office	housing
hospital	(industry)
cafeteria	stores
	maintenance

PREWRITING STAGE TWO

Organize   Write a topic sentence or thesis; label the subject and the treatment parts. This is Tanya's final thesis.

Thesis: Except for freedom, <u>this prison</u> <u>has all the components of a</u>
                                    subject   treatment
<u>typical community outside the fence.</u>

Write an outline or an outline alternative.

   I. Government as laws
     A. Administration
     B. Correctional officers
     C. Convicts

III. Housing
   A. Assignments
      1. Based on behavior
      2. Based on age
      3. Based on health
   B. Special units
III. Commerce and services
   A. Regular jobs
      1. Industry
         a. Free enterprise
         b. Prison products
      2. Prison operation
   B. Underground services
      1. Hustles
      2. Extent
IV. Religion
   A. Larger groups
      1. Protestant
      2. Catholic
      3. Jewish
   B. Others in smaller numbers
      1. Sweat lodge folks
      2. Muslims
      3. Inmate preacher
      4. Voodoo practitioner
V. Education
   A. Formal
      1. Literacy
      2. Vocational
      3. College
   B. Informal
      1. Survival
      2. Life improvement

> Tanya's outline shows the divisions of her topic. Each Roman numeral heading will become one or more paragraphs. Had this been a documented essay, Tanya would have either written in quotations and references on this sheet, or, more likely, she would have used note cards or a separate sheet of paper.

WRITING STAGE THREE

Write   On separate paper, write and then revise your paper as many times as necessary for coherence, langauge (usage, tone, and diction), unity, emphasis, support, and sentences (CLUESS). Read your paper aloud to hear and correct any grammatical errors or awkward-sounding sentences.

Edit any problems in fundamentals, such as capitalization, omissions, punctuation, and spelling (COPS).

The following is an early draft that shows Tanya's revision process. The draft also includes some editing (COPS).

Rough Draft: Writing, Revising, Editing

Prison as a Community

Few free world citizens ~~look at~~ regard the California Institution for Women
as a walled city but that's what it is. Before I was sent here, I ~~thought~~ imagined
~~of~~ prison as a bunch of scary people in a pen. Then I became a resident and discovered that, except for freedom, this place has all the
parts of a community outside the fence. ~~It was an import discovery.~~
It all begins with rules.
CIW has a goverment, one that is totalitarian not democratic.
The prison constitution is a set of laws passed by the state of California.
The warden and her ~~deputies~~ associates administer the laws ~~with wisdom~~. The
correctional officers enforce the laws ~~fairly~~. The convicts obey ~~with-~~
~~with grace.~~
~~out complaining. If you believe all of that, I have some friends around~~
~~here who just found some cash and would like to share it with you.~~
These laws also govern ~~housing~~ where we live in the prison. It is said that the
two most important things in prison are where one lives and where
one works. An inmate's address at prison can be determined by several factors ~~such as~~ behavior, reputation, age, and health; Therefore,
one can be assigned to a cell block with designations such as ordinary (general dorm, room, or cell), honors, geriatrics, convalescent, solitary,
protective custody, or psychiatric. At times special living units are
formed. Once there was a living unit at CIW called the AIDS ward, for
convicts who were HIV positive. ~~A strange procedure developed.~~ If
somebody approached these women as they were being escorted

across the yard a correctional officer would blow a whistle and shout, "Stay away! These inmates have AIDS! These inmates have AIDS!" The HIV positive women now live in housing for the general population, and staff is more enlightened.

The other part of the ~~mentioned~~ saying "where you work" is tied in with both ~~street~~ *free world* industry and the operation of the prison. For years CIW has produced clothing for the California Transportation Agency (CalTrans), made mostly of heavy orange fabric. *We have also manufactured jeans and underwear for California prisons for men.* Most jobs relate to food, laundry, maintenance, and clerical *services, such as* ~~services~~. All able-bodied women, even those in educational programs, must work. Some jobs provide ~~money~~ *compensation*, the so-called " pay slots ", but prison work is almost never connected with vocational training or with ~~street~~ *post-parole* jobs. The money is placed in a trust fund *, usually about fifteen to thirty dollars a month,* and can be used in the prison store for treats, smokes, *health aids,* hygiene items, or the like.

Another part of "work" at the prison ~~is tied~~ *relates* to the underground activities and economy. ~~No one keeps written records of those transactions.~~ The hustles include tattooing, gambling, drugs, food running, laundry service, body guarding *strong-arming*, and hootch *(a homemade alcohol product)* making. That list tells you more about prison than does the official line offered to the public.

In addition to the commonplace housing and the above and below ground work, CIW also offers religion a la carte. ~~Religion is really important.~~ Convicts have three full-time chaplains. Anyone one can attend a Jewish Sed*e*ar, a Catholic mass, or a Protestant spectacular. Last Sunday, I attended a foot-stomping, *woman-wailing* Gospel Bonanza put on by outside evangelists, the men in spandex and the women with big hair. The program

rivaled any free world revival in a three-post tent. Also available are

sweat lodge rituals for the Native Americans and services for Muslims.

Like the commercial and service areas, religion also has its

underground activities. ~~There are several examples.~~ Currently, an

who was an ordained minister on the streets,

inmate has been baptizing women in the shower (total immersion,

she argues) marrying lesbians, and performing exorcisms (including

Equally well known   recently

one on a schizoid yard cat named Blue Eyes). A voodooist has con-

structed personalized images for putting a hex on those she believes

have offended her, leading a number of terrified women to dispose of

ie

hair and other byproducts of personal hygeine only by the toilet

flushing technique.

Another component of the community

~~Then there~~ is school. It may be on an academically low level,

such as literacy, or somewhat advanced, such as the GED program.

Small college programs, such as the one I am now enrolled in, depend

on state funding, which in our case will be withdrawn next year.

At the practical level, in recent years, several vocational programs

have been offered and then discontinued: plumbing, graphic arts,

and hair styling.

Naturally, the other side of formal education at CIW is informal

education. No one leaves the same as she was upon entering. Each

either

inmate will learn from the prison and become better or worse. I wish

I could say that life improvement usually wins out over other forces.

For myself, against odds, I intend to make it so.

It does sometimes happen in this best of all criminal schools.

Yes, CIW is more than a holding pen for criminal types. It really is

a community/ but being a social unit does not make it a nice place to

live. The average person stays here for three to five years and moves

on, ~~which is~~ about the average for movement on the street. And not

all is bad. Some of us convicts do save ourselves. We occasionally get

For most, the help is not enough.
some help.

Final Draft

This is Tanya's final draft. As directed, she submitted all of the material in the unit.

Prison as a Community

Few free world citizens regard the California Institution for Women as a walled city, but that's what it is. Before I was sent here, I imagined prison as a bunch of scared and scary people in a fenced pen. Then I became a resident and discovered that, except for freedom, this place has all the parts of a community outside the fence.

It all begins with rules. CIW has a government, one that is totalitarian, not democratic. The constitution is a set of laws passed by the state of California. The warden and her associates administer the laws. The correctional officers enforce the laws. The convicts obey or else.

These laws also govern where we live in the prison. It is said that the two most important things in prison are where one lives and where one works. An inmate's address at prison can be determined by several factors: behavior, reputation, age, and health. Therefore, one can be assigned to a cell block with designations such as ordinary (general dorm, room, or cell), honors, geriatrics, solitary, convalescent, protective custody, or psychiatric. At times special living units are formed. Once there was a living unit at CIW called the AIDS ward, for convicts who were HIV positive. If somebody approached these women as they were being escorted across the yard, a correctional officer would blow a whistle and shout, "Stay away! These inmates have AIDS! These inmates have AIDS!" The HIV positive women now live in housing for the general population, and staff is more enlightened.

The other part of the saying "where you work" is tied in with both free world industry and the operation of the prison. For years CIW has produced clothing for the California Transportation Agency (CalTrans), made mostly of heavy orange fabric. We have also manufactured Levis and underwear for California prisons for men. Most jobs relate to services, such as food, laundry, maintenance, and clerical. All able-bodied women, even those in educational programs, must work. Some jobs provide compensation, the so-called "pay slots," but prison work is almost never connected with vocational training or with post-parole jobs. The money, usually about fifteen to thirty dollars a month, is placed in a trust fund and can be used in the prison store for treats, smokes, health aids, hygiene items, or the like.

Another part of "work" at the prison relates to the underground activities and economy. The hustles include tattooing, gambling, drugs, food running, laundry service, strong-arming, body guarding, and hootch (a homemade alcohol product) making. That list tells you more about prison than does the official line offered to the public.

In addition to the commonplace housing and the above and below ground work, CIW offers religion a la carte. Convicts have three full-time chaplains. Anyone can attend a Jewish Seder, a Catholic mass, or a Protestant spectacular. Last Sunday, I attended a foot-stomping, woman-wailing Gospel Bonanza put on by outside evangelists, the men in spandex and the women with big hair. The program rivaled any free world revival in a three-post tent. Also available are sweat lodge rituals for the Native Americans and services for Muslims.

Like the commercial and service areas, religion has its underground activities. Currently, an inmate, who was an ordained minister on the streets, has been baptizing women in the shower (total immersion, she argues), marrying lesbians, and performing exorcisms (including one on a schizoid yard cat* named Blue Eyes). Equally well known, a voodooist has recently constructed personalized images for putting a hex on those she believes have offended her, leading a number of terrified women to dispose of hair and other byproducts of personal hygiene only by the toilet flushing technique.

Another component of the community is school. It may be on an academically low level, such as literacy, or somewhat advanced,

*A yard cat is an unowned cat that runs free on the prison grounds.

such as the GED program. At the practical level, in recent years, several vocational programs have been offered and then discontinued; plumbing, graphic arts, and hair styling. Small college programs, such as the one I am now enrolled in, depend on state funding, which in our case will be withdrawn next year.

Naturally, the other side of formal education at CIW is informal education. No one leaves the same as she was upon entering. Each inmate will learn from the prison and become either better or worse. I wish I could say that life improvement usually wins out over other forces. It does sometimes happen in this best of all criminal schools. For myself, against odds, I intend to make it so.

Yes, CIW is more than a holding pen for criminal types. It really is a community. But being a social unit does not make it a nice place to live. The average person stays here for three to five years and moves on, about the average for movement on the street. And not all is bad. Some of us convicts do save ourselves. We occasionally get some help. For most, the help is not enough.

Appendix C: Taking Tests

Good test-taking begins with good study techniques. These techniques involve, among other things, how to read, think, and write effectively. Those skills have been covered in this book. Here we will discuss only a few principles that apply directly and immediately to the test situation.

At the beginning of the semester, you should discover how you will be tested in each course. Match your note-taking and underlining of texts to the kind or kinds of tests you will take. Objective tests will usually require somewhat more attention to details than will subjective or essay tests.

For both types of tests—and you will probably have a combination—you should carefully apportion your time, deciding how much to spend on each section or essay and allowing a few minutes for a quick review of answers. For both, you should also read the directions carefully, marking key words (if you are permitted to do so) as a reminder to you for concentration.

Objective Tests

Here are some tips on taking objective tests.

- Find out whether you will be graded on the basis of the number of correct answers or on the basis of number of right-minus-wrong answers. This is the difference: If you are graded on the basis of the number of correct answers, there is no penalty for guessing; therefore, if you want the highest possible score, you should leave no blanks. But if you are graded on the basis of right-minus-wrong (meaning one or a fraction of one is subtracted from your number of correct answers for every miss), then answer only if the odds of being right are in your favor. For example, if you know an answer is one of two possibilities, you have a 50 percent chance of getting it right; consequently, guess if the penalty is less than one because you could gain one by getting it right and lose less than one by getting it wrong. Ask your teacher to explain if there is a right-minus-wrong factor.

- If you are going to guess and you want to get some answers correct, you should pick one column and fill in the bubbles. By doing that, you will almost certainly get some correct.

- Studies show that in a typical four-part multiple-choice test section, more answers are B and C than A and D.

- Statements with absolutes such as *always* and *never* are likely to be false, whereas statements with qualifications such as *usually* and *probably* are likely to be true.

- If you don't know an answer, instead of fixating on it and getting frustrated, mark it with what seems right, put a dot alongside your answer, and go back later for a second look if time permits.

- When (and if) you go back to check your work, do not make changes unless you discover that you obviously marked one answer incorrectly. Studies have shown that first hunches are usually more accurate.

Subjective or Essay Tests

Here are some tips on taking subjective tests.

- Consider the text, the approach taken by the instructor in lectures, and the overall approach in the course outline and try to anticipate essay questions. Then, in your preparation, jot down and memorize simple outlines that will jog your memory during the test if you have anticipated correctly.

- Remember to keep track of time. A time-consuming A+ essay that does not allow you to finish the second half of the exam will result in a failing grade.

- Study the essay questions carefully. Underline key words. Each essay question will have two parts: the subject part and the treatment part. It may also have a limiting part. If you are required, for example, to compare and contrast President Jimmy Carter and President George H. W. Bush on their environmental programs, you should be able to analyze the topic immediately in this fashion:

  The *subject* is President Carter and President Bush.

  The *limitation* is their environmental programs.

  The *treatment* is comparison and contrast.

Hence, you might mark the question in this fashion:

<u>Compare and contrast</u> the <u>environmental programs</u> of
    treatment   **limitation**

<u>President Jimmy Carter</u> and <u>President George H. W. Bush</u>
                            subject

The treatment part (here "compare and contrast") may very well be one of the forms of discourse such as definition, classification, or analysis, or it may be something like "evaluate" or "discuss," in which a certain form or forms would be used. Regardless of what the treatment word is, the first step is to determine the natural points of division and to prepare a simple outline or outline alternative for organization.

- In writing the essay, be sure to include specific information as support for your generalizations.

Appendix D: Writing a Job Application Letter and a Résumé

Two forms of practical writing that you may need even before you finish your college work are the job application letter and the résumé. They will often go together as requirements by an employer. In some instances, the employer will suggest the form and content of the letter and résumé; in others, you will receive no directions and should adjust your letter and résumé to match the requirements and expectations as you perceive them. The models on pages 545 and 546 are typical of what job applicants commonly submit.

Job Application Letter

The following basic guidelines will serve you well:

- Use standard letter-size paper and type.

- Do not apologize, and do not brag.

- Do not go into tedious detail, but do relate your education, work experience, and career goals to the available job.

- Begin your letter with a statement indicating why you are writing the letter and how you heard about the job opening.

- End the letter by stating how you can be contacted for an interview.

Résumé

Employers are especially concerned about your most recent work experiences and education, so include them first, as indicated in the example of a traditional form on page 546. Then a listing of special relevant skills can add dimensions to your suitability. The heading "College Activities" can be replaced with "Interests and Activities." Your main concern is presenting relevant information in a highly readable manner. Always end with a list of references or information on how to contact references.

203 Village Center Avenue
Glendora, CA 91740
July 11, 2002

Mr. Roy Ritter
Computers Unlimited
1849 N. Granada Avenue
Walnut, CA 91789

Dear Mr. Ritter:

I am responding to your advertisement in the Los Angeles *Times* for the position of salesperson for used computers. Please consider me as a candidate.

In one more semester I will have completed my Associate in Arts degree at Mt. San Antonio College with a major in business management and a minor in computer technology.

My experience relates directly to the job you offer. As a result of my part-time work for two years as lab technician at my college, I have come to know the operations of several different computers. I have also learned to explain the operations to people who have very little knowledge of computers. In my business classes, I have studied the practical approaches to advertising and sales while also learning theory. Each semester for the past two years, I have worked in the college bookstore, where I helped customers who were buying various products, including computers. My fluency in Spanish has often been an asset there.

This job would coincide perfectly with my work at school, my work experience, and even my goal of being a salesperson with a large company.

Enclosed is my résumé with several references to people who know me well. Please contact them if you want information or if you would like a written evaluation.

I am available for an interview at your request.

Sincerely yours,

Benjamin Johanson

Benjamin Johanson

Benjamin Johanson
203 Village Center Avenue
Glendora, CA 91740
(626) 987-5555

POSITION DESIRED
Salesperson for used computers

WORK EXPERIENCE

Lab Technician in the Mt. San Antonio College Computer Lab	2000–02
Sales Clerk in the Mt. San Antonio College Bookstore	2000–02

EDUCATION

Full-time student at Mt. San Antonio College	2000–02
High school diploma from Glendora High School	2000

SPECIAL SKILLS
Fluent in Spanish
Proficient in word processing and computer research

COLLEGE ACTIVITIES
Hackers' Club (2000–02)
Chess Club (2000–02)
Forensics Club (2000–02)—twice a regional debate champion

REFERENCES
Stewart Hamlen
Chairperson, Business Department
Mt. San Antonio College
Walnut, CA 91789
(909) 594-5611, ext. 4410

Bart Grassmont
Human Resources Director, Bookstore
Mt. San Antonio College
Walnut, CA 91789
(909) 594-5611, ext. 4706

Answer Key: Chapter 16

Exercise 1: Identifying Parts of Speech

1. v, conj
2. adv, adj
3. v, conj
4. pro, pro
5. n, prep
6. adv, conj
7. prep, adj
8. n, adj
9. n, adv
10. v, pro

Exercise 2: Identifying Subjects and Verbs

1. brother/friend, sold
2. somebody, can give
3. applicants, were
4. part, comes
5. (You), read
6. team, scored
7. I, will be
8. agents, will be
9. coach/players, were angered
10. cast, was congratulated/given

Exercise 3: Writing Different Kinds of Sentences

1. S
2. CP
3. CX
4. CC
5. CX

6. CP

7. CC

8. S

9. S

10. CX

Exercise 4: Combining Sentences

Answers will vary.

1. During the Great Depression of the 1930s, the Joad family lived in Oklahoma.

2. When the dust storms hit the area, the Joad family headed for California.

3. In California, the Joads were not welcome because thousands of poor people had gone to California.

4. The poor people had heard of jobs in fruit picking, but they discovered that California had more job seekers than jobs.

5. After large farm owners took advantage of the workers, the workers banded together.

6. Jim Casey and Tom Joad became leaders, and the people learned to help themselves.

7. Edgar Allan Poe wrote a short story titled "The Cask of Amontillado," in which the narrator tells of his experience fifty years earlier.

8. Because he wanted revenge against an enemy, he walled that person up in a catacomb.

9. At first his victim said it was surely a joke and begged to be freed.

10. The narrator refused; after all these years, he cannot dismiss the experience from his mind.

Exercise 5: Correcting Fragments, Comma Splices, and Run-Ons

1. CS   world;

2. CS   old;

3. RO   old; nevertheless,

4. OK

5. OK

6. RO   materials;

7. OK

8. OK

9. FRAG   was

10. FRAG   rode

Exercise 6: Working with Verb Forms

1. lie
2. drunk
3. laid
4. supposed
5. sat
6. have
7. set
8. used
9. rise
10. rang

Exercise 7: Making Subjects and Verbs Agree

1. are
2. were
3. was
4. has
5. are
6. have
7. appear
8. was
9. makes
10. has

Exercise 8: Giving Verbs Voice

1. A famous scientist gave the lecture.

2. Dr. Song performed the surgery.

3. The Vienna Boys' Choir produced the opera.

4. Janice Baines rode the winning horse.

5. Harold Stanton won the Wimbledon men's tennis tournament.

6. The class read Lewis Carroll's *Alice's Adventures in Wonderland*.

7. Jan Brown wrote the report for the mayor.

8. Thousands of fans greeted the rock star.

9. Elvis recorded the album on June 15, 1956.

10. Both houses of the state assembly passed the gun-control legislation.

Exercise 9: Selecting Pronouns

1. Whom

2. me

3. I

4. me

5. him

6. Who

7. they

8. whomever

9. ourselves

10. him

Exercise 10: Matching Pronouns and Antecedents

1. he or she

2. her

3. his or her

4. itself

5. it

6. their

7. their

8. his

9. his or her

10. its

Exercise 11: Using Adjectives and Adverbs

1. *older* replaces *oldest*

2. *slowly* replaces *slow*

3. *really* replaces *real*

4. *more nearly straight* replaces *more straight*

5. *bad* replaces *badly*

6. *rapidly* replaces *rapid*

7. *more honest* replaces *honester*

8. *surely* replaces *sure*

9. *more easily* replaces *easier*

10. *kinds* replaces *kind*

Exercise 12: Eliminating Dangling and Misplaced Modifiers

1. D   one can learn writing

2. D   when they arrived

3. M   fiber in the den

4. D   we lost our patience

5. M   when no one was looking, they

6. OK

7. M   permits with the

8. M   wanted in the

9. M   worked for only

10. D   we could not buy tickets

Exercise 13: Balancing Sentence Parts

1. P
2. NP   both of
3. P
4. NP   and how
5. P
6. NP   boxing
7. P
8. NP   not only the cause
9. P
10. NP   a victory

Exercise 14: Inserting Commas

1. Steinbeck, a great American writer, . . . Salinas,
2. setting,
3. works,
4. workers,
5. novel, *The Grapes of Wrath,*
6. Oklahoma,
7. hit, . . . executives,
8. California,
9. California,
10. trip, . . . book, . . . suffering, compassion,

Exercise 15: Choosing the Semicolon or the Comma

1. relatives,
2. son;
3. secretary;
4. adults;
5. move,
6. people,
7. him;

8. scientists,

9. rational;

10. speed;

Exercise 16: Working with All Marks of Punctuation and Capitalization

1. Central

2. Mother

3. Oh,

4. Huxley's

5. boys'

6. anyone's

7. French

8. "hog's bristles."

9. 'The . . . young'

10. Won't

Exercise 17: Examining ESL Problems

George Washington at Trenton

One of most famous battles during the War of Independence occur [*the* inserted before "most"; *occurred* correcting "occur"]

at Trenton, New Jersey, on Christmas Eve of the 1776. The colonists out- [*the* struck out; *were* inserted]

matched in supplies and finances and were outnumbered in troop [*were* struck out]

strength. Most observers in other countries think rebellion would be put [*thought the* replacing "think"]

down soon. British overconfident and believe there would be no more [*The* inserted; *were* inserted; *believed* replacing "believe"]

battles until spring. But George Washington decide to fight one more [*decided* replacing "decide"]

time. That Christmas, while large army of Britishers having party and [*a* inserted before "large"; *were* inserted; *a* inserted before "party"]

thinking about the holiday season, Americans set out for surprise raid. [*the* inserted before "Americans"; *a* inserted before "surprise"]

They loaded onto boats used for carrying ore and rowed across Delaware [*the* inserted before "Delaware"]

River. George Washington stood tall in lead boat. According to legend, [*the* inserted before "lead boat"]

the   the   a

ᴧdrummer boy floated across ᴧriver on his drum, pulled by ᴧrope tied to

a   the

ᴧboat. Because ᴧBritish did not feel threatened by the ragtag colonist

             were   the

forces, they ᴧunprepared to do battle. The colonists stormed ᴧliving quar-

ters and the general assembly hall and achieved victory. It was good for

the colonists' morale, something they needed, for they would endure

a

ᴧlong, hard winter before fighting again.

Text Credits

Leslie Abramson, "Unequal Justice." From *Newsweek*, July 24, 1994, © 1991 Newsweek, Inc. All rights reserved. Reprinted by permission.

American Heritage Dictionary definitions. Copyright © 2000 by Houghton Mifflin Company. Adapted and reproduced by permission from *The American Heritage Dictionary of the English Language*, Fourth Edition.

Maya Angelou, "Soft Mornings and Harsh Afternoons," from *I Know Why the Caged Bird Sings* by Maya Angelou, copyright © 1969 and renewed 1997 by Maya Angelou. Used by permission of Random House, Inc.

Rebecca Barry, "Lessons from a Control Freak," originally published in *Redbook*, February 1999, Vol. 192, Issue 4, p. 67. © 1999 by Rebecca Dorfman by permission of The Wylie Agency.

David Bodanis, "A Brush with Reality: Surprises in the Tube," from *The Secret House*, Simon & Schuster, 1986. Reprinted by permission of the author.

Suzanne Britt, "That Lean and Hungry Look" first published in *Newsweek* is reprinted by permission of the author.

Alan M. Dershowitz, "The 'Abuse Excuse' Is Detrimental to the Justice System," from *The Abuse Excuse* by Alan Dershowitz. Copyright © 1994 by Alan M. Dershowitz. By permission of Little, Brown and Company, (Inc.).

Eve Golden, "Dangerous Curves" from *Men's Health Magazine*. Reprinted by permission of *Men's Health Magazine*. Copyright 1994 Rodale, Inc. All rights reserved. For subscription info, call 1-800-666-2303.

Daniel Goleman, "The Language of Love," from *Emotional Intelligence* by Daniel Goleman, copyright © 1995 by Daniel Goleman. Used by permission of Bantam Books, a division of Random House, Inc.

Adam Goodheart, "How to Paint a Fresco" by Adam Goodheart from *Civilization*, July/August 1995. Copyright © 1995 by Adam Goodheart. Reprinted by permission of The Wylie Agency, Inc.

Ellen Goodman, "SUVs: Killer Cars," Copyright 1999, The Boston Globe Newspaper Co./Washington Post Writers Group. Reprinted with permission.

Joy Harjo, "Three Generations of Native American Women's Birth Experience," from *MS. Magazine*, 1991. Reprinted by permission of the author.

Wil Haygood, "Underground Dads," *New York Times Magazine*, November 30, 1997. Copyright © 1997 by the New York Times Co. Reprinted by permission.

William Least Heat-Moon, "Tuesday Morning" from *Blue Highways* by William Least Heat-Moon. Copyright © 1982, 1999 by William Least Heat-Moon. By permission of Little, Brown and Company, (Inc.)

William Helmreich, "Optimism, Tenacity Lead Way Back to Life," *Los Angeles Times*, 11/25/92. Reprinted by permission of the author.

Paul B. Hertneky, "You and Your Boss," *Restaurant Hospitality*, vol. 80, 8/1/96, p. 78(2). Reprinted by permission.

Sue Hubbell, "On the Road: A City of the Mind," © 1985 by Sue Hubbell. Reprinted by permission of Darhansoff & Verrill.

Richard Jerome, Ronald F. Arias, and Joanne Fowler, "Disarming the Rage," *People*, June 4, 2001. People Weekly © 2001. Time Inc. All rights reserved.

Cynthia Joyce, "Six Clicks from Death," *Salon Magazine*, April '97. Reprinted by permission.

Garrison Keillor, "Attitude" originally from *The New Yorker*. Reprinted by permission of The Ellen Levine Literary Agency.

Philip Kotler and Gary Armstrong, "The Baby Boomers and the Generation Xers," *Principles of Marketing*, Prentice Hall, 2000. From *Principles of Marketing* 9/e by Kotler/Armstrong. © 2000.

Author and Title Index

Subject Index

Instructor's Guide

FROM SELF TO SOURCES

ESSAYS AND BEYOND

Lee Brandon
Mt. San Antonio College

HOUGHTON MIFFLIN COMPANY   BOSTON   NEW YORK

Editor in Chief: Patricia A. Coryell
Senior Sponsoring Editor: Mary Jo Southern
Associate Editor: Kellie Cardone
Senior Manufacturing Coordinator: Marie Barnes
Marketing Manager: Annamarie Rice

Printed in the U.S.A.

ISBN: 0-618-15065-X

123456789-VHG-06 05 04 03 02

Contents

Quizzes on Handbook Topics

To the Instructor

As the title suggests, *From Self to Sources* moves from spinning the personal narrative to working with the ideas of others. It focuses on reading-related, or text-based, writing. Learning to incorporate others' ideas will provide students with substance for their writing and prepare them to deal with content in the immediate English course, other English courses, courses across the curriculum, and careers. For freshman composition courses, this book will enable instructors to move students gradually and smoothly from single-source topics to simple multiple-source topics and then to the research paper without the usual scholarship-shock. The pattern and pace of those increments can be established easily by the instructor, depending on the students' needs and abilities. Students in developmental courses probably would not write a research paper.

Flexible

Accommodating instructors with somewhat different pedagogies and course lengths, *From Self to Sources* has been tested successfully in both freshman composition courses and developmental courses one level below freshman composition.

These are the two basic course patterns:

- A course concerned with writing both undocumented and documented essays (with the instructor phasing in documented writing at the appropriate time in the semester)
- A course concerned with the above and with a research paper

Comprehensive

From Self to Sources covers handbook material (with concern for ESL instruction), reading selections, explicit critical thinking activities, the research paper, and instruction for writing both undocumented and documented essays.

The following description of the book's organization shows its range and benefits.

Student Overview

This brief passage introduces students to the organization and principles of the book while demystifying and demythifying the process of writing. It encourages students to practice sound principles and introduces them to effective strategies for self-improvement, such as using the Writing Process Worksheet and the Self-Evaluation Chart.

Chapter 1

- Chapter 1 defines the simple essay (personal, without sources) and the documented essay.
- Working with examples and principles, this chapter involves students in examining and experimenting with the different parts of an essay: introduction, support paragraphs, and conclusion.

Chapter 2

- Using student work and providing exercises for practice, Chapter 2 explains the writing process, with emphasis on strategies for prewriting (collecting information, freewriting, brainstorming, listing, clustering, writing theses, and outlining).
- Examples from the classroom and exercises will help students master these strategies. In this chapter and the next, one student example shows all the prewriting and writing stages of the writing process.

Chapter 3

- Chapter 3 discusses systematic approaches to writing, revising, and editing.
- This chapter introduces an easily remembered acronym, CLUESS (Coherence, Language, Unity, Emphasis, Support, Sentences), to guide students in revision. Exercises allow students to practice this system.

Chapter 4

- Chapter 4 discusses techniques used for responding to reading-related assignments and briefly explains formal and informal documentation. This chapter also covers how to underline, annotate, outline, paraphrase, summarize, synthesize, and analyze. A two-part summary-reaction form helps students avoid merely repeating what they have read.

Patterns of Writing

Chapters 5–14

From Self to Sources features a different form of discourse for each of ten chapters. Chapters 5–14 are suitable for reading-related writing assignments based on single-sources. Chapters

12–14 also include some professional sources grouped by topics and, therefore, can be used for reading-related writing assignments based on multiple sources. The Thematic Table of Contents for Sources provides other opportunities for writing based on multiple sources. Each chapter includes one student undocumented essay, one student documented essay, and four professional sources.

The Research Paper

Chapter 15

Chapter 15 includes a ten-step approach to writing the research paper, a complete student research paper, as well as illustrated forms of MLA documentation and discussion of electronic and traditional libraries, online searching, plagiarism, and other research-related topics.

Handbook

Chapter 16

Chapter 16 provides handbook material with explanations, examples, and exercises. Half of the answers to exercises are given in the Student Key, allowing for both class work and independent work.

Appendixes

Appendixes

The Appendixes present several pieces of support material:

Appendix A is a blank Writing Process Worksheet that students can photocopy, fill in, and submit with written assignments.

Appendix B contains a student demonstration for all stages of the Writing Process Worksheet (explained more briefly in Chapters 2–3).

Appendix C is a guide for taking both objective and essay tests.

Appendix D includes instructions for writing a job application letter and a résumé.

Teaching Writing

From Self to Sources can be used either in upper-level developmental courses or freshman composition.

In **developmental courses** (where the research paper will probably not be assigned), reading-related writing with some simple informal and formal documentation will give students additional confidence and competency as they move along in the continuum of their writing programs toward freshman composition.

In **freshman composition**, we expect more sophisticated writing and require a research paper—tall orders for apprehensive students.

In my early years of teaching I struggled with the matter of how to challenge my students without overwhelming them. The research paper was in itself the main intimidator, and I witnessed far too many inexperienced writers going through the familiar pattern of fright (of the assignment), fight (against themselves, their loved ones, and me), and flight (from the course and, much worse, from college). The survivors were often just that, survivors.

Fortunately for all, I finally discovered that if I first took these troopers through miniature obstacle courses, they were less likely to notice when I marched them into the "big muddy," AKA, the research paper.

Reading-related writing in Chapters 5–14 can be the small obstacle courses. *From Self to Sources* allows the instructor to construct hurdles at speed-bump height and to space them on the semester time line. The variety of suggested topics for essay writing in each chapter provides much room for flexible design: Reading-Related Topics, Career-Related Topics, and General Topics.

Whenever you reach the time—immediately or later—for writing assignments clearly tied to reading selections, you have choices: You can simply tell your students that they are expected to refer to source(s), X number of times for particular assignments. Since the source material is in the textbook, you can say that the documentation can be informal, meaning clear references to the source with accurate use of quotation marks for words borrowed. Or you can ask them, even from the outset, to use MLA form for the Works Cited and the parenthetical footnotes. A few exercises (see Chapter 15) will help students use the form.

Initially, in most instances, students will be either writing about parallel experiences or developing their own ideas as they include one or more points from source materials. Student demonstrations of both undocumented and documented essays in *From Self to Sources* will be useful tools.

Cooperative Learning

Although *From Self to Sources* includes only occasional explicit directions for cooperative learning, numerous features enhance group work.

Most instructors use simple, well-tested procedures. First they have students count out numbers for three- or four-member groups (so as to mix abilities and personalities), instruct each group to appoint a recorder and director, and have groups work with some imposed structure that provides direction and standards. The review material discussion questions following reading selections, suggested writing topics, and points from the Writing Process Worksheet are all useful in group work.

Self-Evaluation Chart

If you have had the experience of marking a misspelled word, a sentence-structure problem, or a basic organizational problem repeatedly for a particular student while suspecting that the student has been making the same mistake for years, then you will understand the usefulness of the Self-Evaluation Chart. This chart gives students an opportunity (you can make it a requirement) to note repeated errors or problems (including those in content, form, and fundamentals) so that they will have a personal checklist to use when revising and editing papers. Students with many problems in writing should be directed to concentrate on those problems selectively, starting with the most important. Students who compile an enormous list of shortcomings near the beginning of the course may be discouraged. As students learn how to correct their writing, they can cross items off their chart. A filled-in example of the Self-Evaluation Chart appears in the Student Overview following the Preface. A blank chart is just inside the front cover of the textbook.

Grading: Saving Time and Sanity Without Compromising Your Standards

Make Students Responsible

Require students to use the Self-Evaluation Chart to help them avoid errors that they have made repeatedly.

Provide Standards for Students

Whether students are working independently or in peer groups, they need to know what to look for. This text provides easily remembered acronyms for revision and editing. The acronyms are CLUESS (coherence, language, unity, emphasis, support, and sentences) for revision and COPS (capitalization, omissions, punctuation, and spelling) for editing. The criteria represented by the acronyms are discussed in Chapter 3, reinforced in the Handbook, and demonstrated by a student in Appendix B. Students can remember these terms and apply the concepts. When they do, much of your work will be done before you read the final drafts. Of course, initially the students will need guidance, but finally, as students repeatedly apply the CLUESS and COPS points, you will move closer to the goal that we teachers all have—to make ourselves unnecessary to our student writers.

Have Students Use the Writing Process Worksheet

The Writing Process Worksheet furnishes the student with directions for both prewriting (exploring, writing a thesis, and outlining) and writing (writing, revising, and editing). It can be easily customized with adjustments for your approach.

A student can photocopy the form from Appendix A, complete the parts you require, and attach it to other parts of the assignment. A typical submission with the worksheet would include three parts: the completed form, the first draft with markings, and the final draft. At a glance, you can see exactly how a writer has complied with the parts of a sound writing process. Some instructors prefer to check the prewriting portion of the worksheet to make sure the thesis is well conceived and clearly stated and the organizational plan is adequate before allowing their students to proceed with writing, revising, and editing.

Lee Brandon
English Department
Mt. San Antonio College
1100 N. Grand Ave.
Walnut, CA 91789
(909) 594-5611 Ext. 4410
e-mail: BrandonBooks@AOL.com

Sample Syllabi

These syllabi represent two basic and direct approaches to using *From Self to Sources*. Each can be altered for the number and nature of assignments.

Sample 1 (for freshman composition)

Syllabus for a Course Requiring a Research Paper

5 essays (reading-related suggested, to correlate with the research paper project)
1 research paper
1 final examination (a documented essay, in-class or take-home assignment)

Week 1:   Introduction to course: diagnostic writing

Week 2:   Student Overview; read Chapters 1, 2, and 3 (selecting exercises to address current needs pertaining to the essay form and the writing process) ; work briefly in class with handbook exercises in response to problems revealed in diagnostic writing (This activity will be interspersed throughout the semester.)

Week 3:   Read Chapter 4 (introducing techniques for reading-related writing—summary, paraphrase, synthesis—with simple forms for crediting sources)

Week 4:   Read Chapter 5 (narration) or 6 (description) in preparation for Essay 1 including a single-source informal or formal reference (You may want to postpone this formally or informally documented paper until the next assignment.)

Week 5:   Read Chapter 16 (research paper); discuss the research paper as concept, referring to the documented essay as a miniature version; discuss topics and basic research; examine the ten steps to doing a research paper, and explain how they are also a form of the writing process; submit Essay 1

Week 6:   Read Chapter 7 (exemplification) or 8 (analysis by division) in preparation for Essay 2; discussion emphasizing the progression from topic to division, to outline, to support (including one or more references to a source), and to writing (with informal or formal documentation); submit research paper topics

Week 7:   Continue discussion of research paper topics: how to divide the topic for a basic outline, how to do basic research by keying notes to the divisions of a topic; submit Essay 2 (with formal or informal documentation of references to a source)

Week 8:   Read Chapter 9 (classification) or 10 (process analysis) in preparation for Essay 3; submit sampling of sources for the research paper according to MLA form and a simple outline for the research paper (Refer to Chapter 16 for examples.)

Week 9:   Submit Essay 3; submit a sampling of notes keyed to the beginning outline; discuss documented writing in the essay and the research paper

Week 10:   Read Chapter 11 (comparison and contrast) or 12 (cause and effect) in preparation for Essay 4 with one or two sources; submit an outline for the research paper

Week 11:   Submit Essay 4; discuss how to organize research papers and how to use supporting information

Week 12:   Read Chapter 13 (definition) in preparation for Essay 5 with two sources; submit a rough draft of the research paper

Week 13:   Submit Essay 5; discuss the research paper project

Week 14:   Read Chapter 14 (argument) for the final examination (and Essay 6) with two or more sources; submit the research paper with all stages

Week 15:   Discuss documented writing in essays and research papers

Week 16:   In-class final (perhaps allowing students to bring in an outline marked to show where source material will be inserted, note cards, works cited) or take-home final (two or more sources with MLA documentation)

Sample 2 (for an upper-level developmental English course or for freshman composition not requiring a research paper)

Syllabus for a Course Not Requiring a Research Paper

5 essays
1 final examination (a documented essay as an in-class or take-home assignment)

Week 1:   Introduction to course: diagnostic writing

Week 2:   Read Student Overview; read Chapters 1, 2, and 3 (selecting exercises to address current needs pertaining to the essay form and the writing process); work briefly in class with handbook exercises in response to problems revealed in diagnostic writing (This activity will be interspersed throughout the semester.)

Week 3:   Read Chapter 4 (introducing techniques for reading-related writing—summary, paraphrase, synthesis—with simple forms for crediting sources); practice with simple documentation

Week 4:   Read Chapter 5 (narration) or 6 (description) in preparation for Essay 1 including a single-source informal or formal reference (You may want to postpone this formally or informally documented paper until the next assignment.)

Week 5:   Submit Essay 1; read Chapter 7 (exemplification) or 8 (analysis by division) in preparation for Essay 2; discussion emphasizing the progression from topic to division, to outline, to support (including one or more references to a source), and to writing (with informal or formal documentation)

Week 6:   Discuss Essay 1; further preparation for Essay 2; review revision procedures (Chapter 3)

Week 7:   Submit Essay 2; read Chapter 9 (classification) or 10 (process) in preparation for Essay 3

Week 8:   Discuss Essay 2; further preparation for Essay 3

Week 9:   Read Chapter 11 (comparison and contrast) in preparation for Essay 4 with one or more references; submit Essay 3

Week 10:   Read Chapter 12 (cause and effect) in preparation for Essay 4 related to two sources; discuss Essay 3; review synthesis (Chapter 4)

Week 11:   Submit Essay 4; read Chapter 13 (definition) for Essay 5 with two sources

Week 12:   Discuss documented writing in essays and research papers (Read Chapter 4 as review and Chapter 12 as overview) for Essay 5; discuss Essay 4

Week 13:   Submit Essay 5; read Chapter 14 (argument) for Essay 6 with two sources

Week 14:   Submit Essay 5; prepare for Essay 6 based on multiple sources related to the thematic table of contents

Week 15:   Discuss Essay 5; further preparation for Essay 6; course review

Week 16:   In-class final (perhaps allowing students to bring in an outline marked to show where source material will be inserted, note cards, works cited) or take-home final (two or more sources and a specified minimum number of references presented with MLA documentation)

Quizzes on Selected Readings
(Chapters 5 through 14)

Chapter 5: "If Those Cobras Don't Get You, the Alligators Will"

Name: _____

True or False

_____ 1. The author, Richard Wolkomir, is known as "Mr. Urban Legend."

_____ 2. According to Jan Harold Brunvand, urban legends reflect our concerns.

_____ 3. "The Vanishing Hitchhiker" is purely American in origin.

_____ 4. These tall tales never have a hint of truth to them.

_____ 5. Urban legends are continually recycled.

_____ 6. Urban legends are studied at universities as folklore.

_____ 7. *FOAF* stands for "frightened of a fiend."

_____ 8. Professor Bill Ellis says that telling urban legends helps release anxiety.

_____ 9. One explanation for the success of the urban legend is that people like to be scared.

_____ 10. Newspaper reporters never report urban legends as facts.

Multiple Choice

_____ 11. *specters:* (a) guests (b) ghosts (c) eyeglasses (d) observers

_____ 12. *prototype:* (a) speed typing (b) illustration (c) original model (d) unlikely story

_____ 13. *rendezvous:* (a) meeting at an appointed place (b) bizarre death scene (c) circular (d) often repeated story

_____ 14. *proliferate:* (a) to elaborate (b) to diminish (c) to inspire fear (d) to grow or increase in number rapidly

_____ 15. *plummeted:* (a) rise rapidly (b) drop straight down (c) destroy reputations (d) study intently

Chapter 5: "On the Road: A City of the Mind"   Name: _____

True or False

_____ 1. "A City of the Mind" refers to early morning sleeplessness and drug abuse.

_____ 2. Transients are not treated as well as truck drivers.

_____ 3. Truckers are in and out of truck stops in half an hour.

_____ 4. In New Mexico, the waitress is embarrassed by the picture of a scantily clad woman.

_____ 5. In Oklahoma, the waitress figures out a good way to get $20 tips.

_____ 6. Flossie in Illinois has been waitressing for forty years.

_____ 7. Charlie and Coors want to pursue the conversation about chippies with Flossie.

_____ 8. The author always stays in the background, never involving herself.

_____ 9. Flossie isn't paid well, but she has a good work schedule.

_____ 10. Stripping away superficial aspects of setting, the truck stop cafes are remarkably similar.

Multiple Choice

_____ 11. *transients:* (a) those who are on the move   (b) residents   (c) students   (d) workers

_____ 12. *Formica:* (a) synthetic covering   (b) cement   (c) table   (d) chair

_____ 13. *obscure:* (a) lost   (b) unclear   (c) extreme   (d) apparent

_____ 14. *simulated:* (a) moved emotionally   (b) genuine   (c) at the same time   (d) not genuine

_____ 15. *jaded:* (a) world-weary   (b) energetic   (c) angry   (d) bright

Chapter 6: "The Discus Thrower"   Name: _____

True or False

_____   1. The author of this piece is a psychiatrist.

_____   2. The head nurse understands how the doctor feels.

_____   3. The patient is legless and blind.

_____   4. The patient has completely given up.

_____   5. The doctor admires the patient.

_____   6. The patient asks for shoes.

_____   7. The nurse feeds the patient scrambled eggs.

_____   8. The doctor sees himself as a spy.

_____   9. The patient likes to throw boiled eggs.

_____   10. The patient will live a long time because of his spirit.

Multiple Choice

_____   11. *furtive:* (a) at a great distance (b) secretive (c) angry (d) outward

_____   12. *vigor:* (a) strength (b) strict (c) diseased (d) lifeless

_____   13. *forceps:* (a) an instrument used for listening to the heart (b) towels
(c) a surgical instrument used for grasping (d) the muscles above the eyes

_____   14. *irony:* (a) using words to express opposite meanings (b) metallic (c) using
an example instead of a dictionary meaning (d) tragedy

_____   15. *accomplices:* (a) completes (b) friends (c) adjusts to (d) associates in
crime

Chapter 6: "Tuesday Morning"   Name: _____

True or False

_____   1.   The Navajo possess the largest reservation in the United States.

_____   2.   The Navajo are the largest tribe on a reservation in the United States.

_____   3.   The last true American cowboy is likely to be an Indian.

_____   4.   The Hopi have elaborate war dances.

_____   5.   The Hopi are related to the ancient Aztecs.

_____   6.   Adverse conditions give life to the bristlecone pines and the Hopi.

_____   7.   In Tuba City the children spoke only Hopi.

_____   8.   The Navajo language has many curse words.

_____   9.   The author has several conversations with the Navajo.

_____   10.   The whites now buy beads from the Indians.

Multiple Choice

_____   11.   *retribution:*   (a) forgetfulness   (b) retaliation   (c) celebration
                 (d) mourning

_____   12.   *comprise:*   (a) award   (b) include   (c) depart   (d) friend

_____   13.   *consorting:*   (a) twisting   (b) antagonistic to   (c) associating with
                 (d) detesting

_____   14.   *topographically:*   (a) musically   (b) stylistically   (c) quickly
                 (d) according to geographical features

_____   15.   *patina:*   (a) surface condition   (b) value   (c) charm   (d) covered porch

Chapter 7: "Lessons from a Control Freak"   Name: _____

True or False

_____   1. Author Rebecca Barry is an admitted control freak.

_____   2. Barry agrees with conventional wisdom that control freaks are brittle, authoritarian psychos.

_____   3. She believes in controlling in moderation.

_____   4. The business world has no use for control freaks.

_____   5. There are many benefits to having a control freak under the roof.

_____   6. Most control freaks pass a weak work ethic along to their kids.

_____   7. Children of control freaks are rarely bored.

_____   8. Dr. Basco says, "A control freak spends lots of energy trying to avoid criticism from others."

_____   9. Dr. Neuharth says that a loved spouse should be challenged now and then for the good of the relationship.

_____   10. Controlling others is a natural part of maintaining loving relationships.

Chapter 7: "I'm Outta Here!"   Name: _____

True or False

_____ 1. Overall, girls are only slightly more likely to drop out of school than boys.

_____ 2. A student's initial trouble may come from parents' marital problems, domestic violence, drug or alcohol use, or physical abuse.

_____ 3. Poor school attendance is a symptom, not a disease.

_____ 4. Some students leave school because they feel as if nobody cares.

_____ 5. Most dropouts leave school because they aren't smart enough.

_____ 6. Some believe much of traditional education is obsolete.

_____ 7. According to the National Dropout Prevention Center, more than 80 percent of dropouts find jobs when they leave school.

_____ 8. Over a lifetime, the typical high school graduate earns $250,000 more than the typical dropout.

_____ 9. Staying in school and graduating extends the range of options for students.

_____ 10. High school dropouts can always go into the military service.

Multiple Choice

_____ 11. *epidemic:* (a) affecting many persons at one time (b) a night-blooming plant (c) desperate (d) poor

_____ 12. *sibling:* (a) a competitor (b) a parent (c) a brother or sister (d) a caring teacher

_____ 13. *symptom:* (a) a plan (b) a large school (c) the result of a conflict (d) an indication

_____ 14. *potential:* (a) a possible development (b) a strong medicine (c) an answer to a problem (d) the cause of a problem

_____ 15. *obsolete:* (a) pure (b) out of date (c) before its time (d) inactive

Chapter 8: "A Brush with Reality"   Name: _____

True or False

_____   1. In most brands of toothpaste, more than 50 percent is water.

_____   2. The water in toothpaste is ordinary tap water.

_____   3. Chalk is the polishing agent of toothpaste.

_____   4. Chalk in toothpaste has no negative effects on teeth.

_____   5. Chalk also acts as a dye to make the teeth look white.

_____   6. Seaweed ooze and paraffin oil are used to keep toothpaste smooth.

_____   7. Detergent in toothpaste makes the suds.

_____   8. Peppermint oil is used to control the foaming action.

_____   9. Formaldehyde is used to kill bacteria.

_____   10. Despite the use of unsavory ingredients, studies show that only toothpaste will clean teeth effectively.

Multiple Choice

_____   11. *extruded:* (a) mixed (b) pushed out (c) sold (d) inserted

_____   12. *lucrative:* (a) profitable (b) ridiculous (c) clear (d) pleasant

_____   13. *abrading:* (a) way of styling hair (b) stirring (c) grinding (d) moving

_____   14. *dollop:* (a) run fast (b) small lump (c) pretty woman (d) a tube

_____   15. *gustatory:* (a) related to the sense of taste (b) a strong wind of short duration (c) related to the sense of smell (d) worthless

Chapter 8: "Designer Babies"   Name: _____

True or False

_____   1. Someday parents may be able to insert genes they want into their offspring.

_____   2. Biotechnology critic Jeremy Rifkin says that designing babies will be regarded by society as a huge step.

_____   3. Clinicians seem to agree that these new techniques for designing babies should be applied to the service of disease prevention.

_____   4. Whatever the doctors decide to do about designing babies is what will happen.

_____   5. Biologist Lee Silver suggests that sex selection may cease to be much of an issue.

_____   6. Boys often end up being more assertive and more dominant than girls.

_____   7. Firstborn children often end up being less assertive and less dominant than other children.

_____   8. Ethical issues will be easily dealt with by thoughtful legislation.

_____   9. Silver contemplates a society of the "gen-rich" and the "gen-poor."

_____   10. This essay clearly indicates the future of baby designing.

Chapter 9: "Coworkers from Hell and
How to Cope"

Name: _____

True or False

_____ 1. Petty bureaucrats have no power.

_____ 2. The best way to deal with petty bureaucrats is to get angry and show them who is boss.

_____ 3. In the presence of credit grabbers, you should document all your important contributions.

_____ 4. Rumors may be impossible to counter once they have spread.

_____ 5. Control freaks must be confronted immediately.

_____ 6. Fortunately for all, control freaks are almost never promoted to jobs with authority.

_____ 7. Snoops should be deprived of all information.

_____ 8. The first step in self-defense against a put-down artist is retaliation.

_____ 9. Bullies get away with their behavior because others let them.

_____ 10. Positive body language is one good defense against bullies.

Multiple Choice

_____ 11. *pummeling:* (a) beating (b) descending (c) failing (d) promoting

_____ 12. *insidious:* (a) large (b) treacherous (c) thoughtless (d) clever

_____ 13. *excruciating:* (a) highly competitive (b) expensive (c) painful (d) well-connected

_____ 14. *divesting:* (a) separating from a spouse (b) dressing (c) leaving (d) stripping away

_____ 15. *modicum:* (a) contemporary (b) small amount (c) large amount (d) good behavior

Chapter 9: "Confessions of a Former   Name: _____
            Smoker"

True or False

_____   1. Zimring divides Americans into two groups: the smokers and the nonsmokers.

_____   2. Antitobacco zealots are all former smokers.

_____   3. Zealots believe that those who continue to smoke deserve scorn.

_____   4. Few zealots have been deeply committed to tobacco habits.

_____   5. Evangelists regard smoking as an easily curable condition.

_____   6. Evangelists are well known for their testimonials about how much they miss tobacco.

_____   7. Evangelists spend much time seeking out and preaching to the unconverted.

_____   8. They elect to not attempt to convert their friends.

_____   9. Serene ex-smokers accept themselves and others who continue to smoke.

_____   10. Zimring has the least admiration for the serene ex-smokers.

Multiple Choice

_____   11. *zealot:* (a) a compulsive smoker   (b) a fanatic   (c) a legislator
               (d) a helper

_____   12. *tenuous:* (a) weak or slight   (b) complaining   (c) constructive
               (d) withdrawn or submissive

_____   13. *recidivist:* (a) inmate   (b) addict   (c) one who resists   (d) one who returns
               to a former state

_____   14. *vitriolic:* (a) caustic or biting   (b) loud   (c) unhappy   (d) aggressive

_____   15. *unmitigated:* (a) not softened   (b) not angry   (c) without dedication
               (d) weak

Chapter 10: "How to Paint a Fresco"   Name: _____

True or False

_____   1. The first step in painting a fresco is tracing the design.

_____   2. Preparing the wall will be a messy job only if you are inexperienced.

_____   3. You must transfer the design from a drawing to a coat of fine plaster on the wall.

_____   4. You must paint the plaster while it is still wet.

_____   5. Plaster takes about sixteen hours to dry.

_____   6. Using lead pain can cause problems.

_____   7. Michelangelo always used the most expensive paints.

_____   8. Spinello painted Lucifer with what was regarded as hideous accuracy.

_____   9. Frescoing ceilings can be rough on your eyes.

_____   10. Michelangelo used semiprecious lapis lazuli for blue paint in the *Last Judgment*.

Chapter 10: "Star"   Name: _____

True or False

_____   1. Stars are born in huge clouds of gas.

_____   2. These clouds are so large, it would take light one year to cross one.

_____   3. The key to star formation is gravity.

_____   4. As a star forms, the cloud gets larger.

_____   5. In our solar system after our sun (a star) was formed, the leftovers became the moon.

_____   6. In star formation, the protostar is formed just before the star itself.

_____   7. Once nuclear fusion begins, that's truly when a star is born.

_____   8. Once a star is born, it then protects the cloud that formed it.

_____   9. The Milky Way is the location of stellar nurseries.

_____   10. The dark splotches in the Milky Way are places without stars.

Multiple Choice

_____   11. *momentum:*   (a) brief unit of time   (b) heavy   (c) force of a moving body   (d) gravity

_____   12. *phenomenon:*   (a) observable fact or event   (b) outer space   (c) telescope   (d) cosmic cloud

_____   13. *fusion:*   (a) process of merging   (b) something difficult to understand   (c) explosion   (d) process of separating

_____   14. *stellar:*   (a) far away   (b) timeless   (c) slow process   (d) pertaining to stars

_____   15. *sibling:*   (a) mother or father   (b) brother or sister   (c) youngest family member   (d) cluster

Chapter 11: "The Baby Boomers and the Generation Xers"

Name: _____

True or False

_____ 1. The baby boomers account for one-third of the population in the United States.

_____ 2. The baby boomers are reaching their peak earning and spending years.

_____ 3. The boomers seldom think of the purpose of their work, responsibilities, and relationships.

_____ 4. The boomers created a sexual revolution.

_____ 5. Generation Xers have grown up during times of recession and corporate downsizing.

_____ 6. Generation Xers are inexperienced shoppers.

_____ 7. Xers are more materialistic than boomers.

_____ 8. Xers care about the environment.

_____ 9. Xers are more interested in job satisfaction than in sacrificing personal happiness and growth for promotion.

_____ 10. By the year 2010, the Xers will have overtaken the baby boomers as a primary market for almost every product category.

Multiple Choice

_____ 11. *constitute:* (a) make up (b) finance (c) destroy (d) increase spending

_____ 12. *affluence:* (a) poverty (b) wealth (c) informality (d) good disposition

_____ 13. *segments:* (a) parts (b) attempts (c) jobs (d) experiments

_____ 14. *skeptical:* (a) nervous (b) insecure (c) aggressive (d) doubting

_____ 15. *aggravated:* (a) make more severe (b) make better (c) make sad (d) make happy

Chapter 11: "That Lean and Hungry Look"

Name: _____

True or False

_____ 1. Suzanne Britt says that thin people don't know how to goof off.

_____ 2. She says that thin people are always busy trying to compensate for their low metabolism.

_____ 3. Thin people turn surly, mean, and hard at a young age.

_____ 4. Thin people want to avoid the truth.

_____ 5. Fat people know there is no truth.

_____ 6. Thin people believe in logic.

_____ 7. Fat people know what happiness is, they go after it, and they get it.

_____ 8. Thin people are the ones acquainted with the night, with luck, with fate, with playing it by ear.

_____ 9. Fat people are heavily into fits of laughter, slapping their thighs, and whooping it up.

_____ 10. Thin people like math and morality and reasoned evaluation of the limitations of human beings.

Chapter 12: "Why Marriages Fail"   Name: _____

True or False

_____   1. We all select a mate who will recreate with us the emotional patterns of our first homes.

_____   2. The human way is to compulsively reject the past.

_____   3. People can overcome the habits and attitudes that developed in childhood.

_____   4. Concern about money brings partners together.

_____   5. Communication is essential for a good marriage.

_____   6. A mate can never need too much intimacy.

_____   7. Mates must see each other as parts of a unit, not as individuals.

_____   8. Marriage has not always been difficult.

_____   9. Divorce is not an evil act.

_____   10. Marriage requires some level of compromise.

Multiple Choice

_____   11. *obsolete:* (a) harmful (b) stubborn (c) out of date (d) arrogant

_____   12. *perils:* (a) dangerous problems (b) shiny deposits found in oysters (c) opportunities (d) excuses

_____   13. *turbulent:* (a) settled (b) marked by unrest (c) hungry (d) seeking custody of children

_____   14. *concoction:* (a) failure (b) formal contract (c) something of mixed parts (d) living together without marriage

_____   15. *erode:* (a) defeat (b) wear away (c) improve (d) run over

Chapter 12: "Romantic Love, Courtship,   Name: _____
             and Marriage"

True or False   ·

_____   1. Romantic love is easily defined.

_____   2. Romantic love enables young partners to become independent.

_____   3. Romantic love is part of the ordinary behavior of human beings.

_____   4. A courtship system, according to the author, is essentially a marriage market.

_____   5. Parents should control the marriage plans and dating habits of a son or daughter in subtle, loving ways.

_____   6. Young people no longer have a high degree of privacy in their courting.

_____   7. Age differences between husband and wife declined during the twentieth century.

_____   8. Few people change their religion to that of their partner before marriage.

_____   9. Most people marry within their own social class.

_____   10. This piece is mostly objective.

Chapter 13: "Disarming the Rage"   Name: _____

True or False

_____   1. Some experts see bullying as an inevitable consequence of a culture that rewards perceived strength and dominance.

_____   2. About half of bullies are females.

_____   3. According to the U.S. Secret Service, in two-thirds of school shootings since 1974, victims felt they had been persecuted, bullied, threatened, attacked, or injured.

_____   4. Most experts agree that metal detectors and zero-tolerance expulsions ignore the root of the problem.

_____   5. Columbine shooters Dylan Klebold and Eric Harris did not feel bullied or alienated.

_____   6. The National Education Association reports that 160,000 children skip school each day because of intimidation by their peers.

_____   7. Most victims of bullying who intend to retaliate do not tell others of their plans.

_____   8. After Brian Head, the victim of bullying, committed suicide, numerous students were disciplined in connection with his death.

_____   9. Counseling and fostering teamwork seem most effective in dealing with bullying.

_____   10. The word *bullying* is defined mainly through examples.

Chapter 13: "Bully, Bully"   Name: _____

True or False

_____   1. According to a national study, bullying behavior may be verbal, physical, or psychological.

_____   2. John Leo believes the definition is too broad.

_____   3. Leo ridicules the idea that shunning and exclusion are forms of bullying.

_____   4. Leo agrees that "hard looks" and "stare downs" should be treated as bullying behaviors.

_____   5. He says that unrealistically broad definitions have led to a statistical blending of serious and trivial incidents.

_____   6. Leo believes that all so-called bullying is just ordinary juvenile behavior.

_____   7. He says teenage tendencies to form cliques and snub people now and then are all part of growing up.

_____   8. A national study says that about half of bullying victims are bullies themselves.

_____   9. Europe has been more restrained than America in crusading against bullying.

_____   10. Leo fears that our antibullying campaign is becoming increasingly too far-reaching.

Chapter 14: "SUVs: Killer Cars"   Name: _____

True or False

_____   1. Goodman describes car ads as depictions of unreality.

_____   2. Goodman says SUVs are the archenemy of commuters everywhere.

_____   3. She points out that most SUVs are owned by sportsmen.

_____   4. Goodman says SUVs are responsible for about 5,000 deaths a year.

_____   5. The Automobile Club of Southern California has issued an SUV driver tip to "avoid a 'road warrior' mentality."

_____   6. SUVs have been allowed to legally pollute two or three times as much as automobiles.

_____   7. Pollution controls for SUVs have never been promoted.

_____   8. Goodman sees a backlash forming against SUVs.

_____   9. Overall, Goodman writes an impersonal account.

_____   10. Goodman feels intimidated because she drives a small car.

Chapter 14: "Guzzling, Gorgeous, and Grand"

Name: _____

True or False

_____   1. Dave Shiflett says SUV owners are peaceful, humble people.

_____   2. Shiflett says SUVs travel an average of 20 miles per gallon of gas.

_____   3. He says regular automobiles get 27 MPG.

_____   4. Shiflett charges the Republican party leadership with hypocrisy.

_____   5. He sees the attack on SUV ownership as only part of a larger war.

_____   6. Shiflett associates criticism of SUVs with mandatory seatbelt laws and antismoking ordinances.

_____   7. He has owned two SUVs, both made in America.

_____   8. He points out that one major complaint about SUVs is sexual in nature.

_____   9. Shiflett says that Ellen Goodman sympathizes with SUV owners like him.

_____   10. Shiflett offers a concrete counterproposal.

Multiple Choice

_____   11. *placid:* (a) peaceful (b) unruly (c) affectionate (d) harmless

_____   12. *hectoring:* (a) measuring (b) confronting (c) controlling (d) withdrawing

_____   13. *ombudsman:* (a) secret agent (b) police officer (c) race car driver (d) complaint investigator

_____   14. *empathize:* (a) to stress (b) to ridicule (c) to identify with others (d) to give examples

_____   15. *bivouac:* (a) overnight (b) amphibious (c) temporary camp (d) flight

Quizzes on Handbook Topics

Quiz 1: Subjects and Verbs   Name: _____

Write the subject and verb of each of the following sentences in the space provided.

Subject   Verb

_____ _____   1. My brother and his friend sold tickets for the field day.

_____ _____   2. Can somebody in command give us permission to moor our boat?

_____ _____   3. There were several excellent applicants for the position of dean of students.

_____ _____   4. Now comes the best part of the entertainment.

_____ _____   5. Please read the minutes of the previous meeting.

_____ _____   6. During the first ten minutes of the game, our team, with two of the players out on fouls, scored two goals.

_____ _____   7. Never again will I be able to speak to her about that.

_____ _____   8. There will be among your visitors today two agents from the Federal Bureau of Investigation.

_____ _____   9. Both the coach and the players were angered by a series of unjust penalties.

_____ _____   10. The cast was congratulated and given bonuses by a grateful producer.

_____ _____   11. Never again will Helen help her with the work.

_____ _____   12. A tour of the churches and castles of Denmark is a worthwhile experience.

_____ _____   13. Shut that window and take your seat.

_____ _____   14. Bill will help us to dig the foundation of the new building.

_____ _____   15. How many books are published each month on that particular subject?

Quiz 2: Sentence Combining   Name: _____

Rewrite each set of sentences to make an effective compound, complex, or compound-complex sentence.

1. The Joad family lived in Oklahoma.
    The time was the 1930s, during the Great Depression.

    The dust storms hit the area.
    The Joad family headed for California.

2. In California the Joads were not welcome.
    Thousands of poor people had gone to California.

    The poor people had heard of jobs in fruit picking.
    They discovered that California had more job seekers than jobs.

3. Some large farm owners took advantage of the workers.
    The workers banded together.

    Jim Casey and Tom Joad became leaders.
    The people learned to help themselves.

4. Edgar Allan Poe wrote a short story entitled "The Cask of Amontillado."
    In that story the narrator tells of his experience fifty years earlier.

    He wanted revenge against an enemy.
    He walled up that person in a catacomb.

Quiz 3: Fragments   Name: _____

In the space provided, write **C** if the sentence is correct or **Frag** if the group of words is a fragment. Make the fragments into complete sentences.

_____   1. Let us begin at the beginning.

_____   2. After the party was over.

_____   3. The beer blast lasting all night.

_____   4. Hurriedly and ineffectively tried to smother the small fire.

_____   5. The discussion continued far into the night.

_____   6. The silhouetted figure standing in the doorway.

_____   7. The long-haired dog in the pen on the corner of the row.

_____   8. When the storm was over and the sun had broken through.

_____   9. My nephew is a smart child, of course.

_____   10. Locked file cabinets seem to arouse a busybody's curiosity.

_____   11. Since she was operated on a year ago.

_____   12. Slowly but confidently, opened the locked door.

_____   13. The space shuttle had been tested several times before.

_____   14. The rain swelling the waters behind the dam.

_____   15. The dam on the third-largest river in the state, a technological and engineering wonder.

Quiz 4: Comma Splices and Run-Ons   Name: _____

Mark correct sentences **C**, run-ons **RO**, and comma splices **CS** in the space provided.

___CS___   *Example:* In Hartford, Wisconsin, there is a small Chrysler plant, it makes
                   outboard motors.

_____   1.   In 1781 the Revolutionary War ended when General Cornwallis surrendered to
                   General Washington at Yorktown.

_____   2.   I did not understand that we were to go skiing this weekend, I have a book
                   report due on Monday.

_____   3.   Ray sold his house he moved to Santa Fe, where he was offered a job as a
                   systems analyst.

_____   4.   Derrick was not as bright as some of his classmates, however, because he
                   worked so diligently, he did better than those who had more ability.

_____   5.   James Webb, a graduate of the U.S. Naval Academy, is a former Secretary of
                   the Navy he has written several books about his experiences in the Marines
                   and as a midshipman.

_____   6.   Many Russian and French choreographers wrote ballets; some of these ballets
                   became popular in America.

_____   7.   In 1863 Abraham Lincoln delivered his often-quoted Gettysburg Address, he
                   was assassinated two years later in 1865.

_____   8.   Once Anita had decided to go back to school, she felt relieved that the
                   decision had been made however, she was a little apprehensive about
                   attending classes with students so much younger than she.

_____   9.   Geraldo hurried into the house; he took his coat off and hung it up, then he
                   yelled, "I'm home."

_____   10.   The desire to complete a job is frequently the key to completing it; someone told
                   me that truth a long time ago.

Quiz 5: Comma Splices and Run-Ons   Name: _____

Mark correct sentences **C**, run-ons **RO**, and comma splices **CS** in the space provided.

___CS___   *Example:* Linemen get very little credit for winning football games, however, they play important roles.

_____   1. Kinisha was the storyteller in her family she remembers making up stories for the younger children.

_____   2. There is a proliferation of "how-to" and "'self-help"' books on the market, they are frequently on the best-seller list.

_____   3. Curtis is the oldest of five children he is the only one to have graduated from college.

_____   4. Paper towels serve many useful purposes, and they are not very expensive.

_____   5. Juan's desk was cluttered with computer printouts the mess didn't seem to bother him.

_____   6. She broke the zipper on her evening dress her mother had to cut the dress off.

_____   7. The director of the research center has a top-level managerial position, the director reports directly to the vice president for research.

_____   8. Brothers and sisters can be best of friends, they can be worst of enemies.

_____   9. Swimming, running, and bicycling are three parts of a triathlon; it is now an Olympic event.

_____ 10. The environmentalists are urging the public to recycle trash however, few people are willing to separate their garbage.

Quiz 6: Subject-Verb Agreement   Name: _____

Circle the verb that agrees in number with the subject in each of the following sentences.

1. Juan and Marguerite (is, are) both lawyers.

2. Children's stories (contains, contain) many images of horror and create fear.

3. Neither Almeta nor her teachers (was, were) present at the assembly.

4. Economics, as well as mathematics, (is, are) difficult for many students.

5. Each of the members (is, are) ready for a new election.

6. The crew (is, are) servicing the plane at 6:00 A.M.

7. At the beginning of the semester, each student (is, are) given a basic skills test.

8. A good pair of running shoes (costs, cost) quite a bit more than old-fashioned sneakers.

9. Ricardo and his brothers (is, are) going to the family reunion.

10. One of Shakespeare's most popular plays (is, are) *Romeo and Juliet*.

11. At the back of the book (is, are) an envelope that contains pictures.

12. *The Cosby Show,* a long-running TV program, (has, have) gone off the air.

13. There (is, are) a lot left to be done.

14. (Isn't, Aren't) Mario going to the prom?

15. Where (is, are) the members of the Senior Committee?

Quiz 7: Pronoun Case   Name: _____

Circle the correct form of the pronoun *who*.

1. (Who, Whom) does the choir director think is the more talented of the two composers?

2. If this chartreuse umbrella does not belong to you, to (who, whom) does it belong?

3. You will have to ask (whoever, whomever) is on duty at the gate house how to get to the picnic area.

4. (Whoever, Whomever) is running that vacuum cleaner has succeeded in destroying my powers of concentration.

5. Everybody in camp (who, whom) had been hoping for a letter arrived at mail call.

6. (Whose, Who's) going to call Norman about our plans for the weekend?

7. The afternoon I met Ann and her bulldog, I couldn't decide who was walking (who, whom).

8. Neither of us knows (who, whom) the woman in that gorgeous sari is.

9. (Who, Whom) should we ask for when we get to the clinic?

10. The names of those to (who, whom) we have sent season tickets are posted in the box office.

11. (Who's, Whose) glasses are those lying on the beach towel?

12. Tell the Garcias to ask (whoever, whomever) is at the reception desk where the auditorium is.

13. You can be sure that Kim knows (who, whom) is responsible for the graffiti on the sidewalk.

14. A computer programmer (who, whom) used to work here now works in the Candler Building.

15. The programmer (who, whom) Ms. Newsome hired to take his place graduated a year behind us at State.

Quiz 8: Pronoun Agreement   Name: _____

Circle the pronoun that agrees in number with its antecedent in each sentence.

1. Each of the girls makes (her, their) own clothes.

2. The jury finally made (its, their) decision.

3. It often seems that television programmers are not concerned with (its, their) viewers.

4. Both Bill and Tony write (his, their) mothers twice a week from their army base.

5. Neither Damon nor his parents offered (his, their) advice.

6. Either of the two boys will offer (his, their) help.

7. Neither the Library of Congress nor the New York Public Library has (its, their) own film rooms.

8. Either the president or the senators will give (his or her, their) speeches today.

9. American citizens must protect (its, their, his) rights.

10. Every person should have (his or her, their) own savings account.

11. Neither the baseball players nor the managers want to lose (his, their) side of the argument.

12. Each student should turn in (his or her, their) paper now.

13. Does everyone have (his or her, their) textbook?

14. Everyone has the right to (his or her, their) own opinion.

15. Each of the first-year women called (her, their) home on the first day of the fall term.

Quiz 9: Adjectives and Adverbs   Name: _____

Underline any adjective or adverb that is incorrectly used. Then write the correct form at the left. Write **C** if the sentence is correct.

_____surely_____   *Example:* You <u>sure</u> do make a good lemon meringue pie.

_____   1. Jack and Fran painted steady all morning, finishing the deck just before lunch.

_____   2. My rolls didn't rise, and, to make matters worse, my cheesecake turned out bad.

_____   3. The train stopped so sudden that her coat and books spilled into the aisle.

_____   4. Of Joan's two watercolors in the show, this one is surely the best.

_____   5. His idea of a well morning is to sleep until he wakes up and then have his coffee and read the morning paper on the patio.

_____   6. The child stared uncertain at the clown, who was smiling broadly at the nursery school audience.

_____   7. The factory whistle sounded very clearly on that gray Monday afternoon.

_____   8. My father spoke plain to us children when he disapproved of our behavior.

_____   9. We always knew when Professor Coldham had arrived in the dining hall; his was a real good voice.

_____ 10. Thank you very muchly for bringing me the jacket I left in the golf cart.

_____ 11. Jessica's heart beat rapid when she heard the key turn in the lock.

_____ 12. Once the cloud cover had been burned away, the day grew somewhat warmerly.

_____ 13. Uncle Herman feels quite well now that he has given up his steady diet of tamales.

_____ 14. I'm glad to hear that he feels better; he's felt badly for days.

_____ 15. The harvest moon is real bright tonight.

Quiz 10: Commas   Name: _____

In the space provided, write **C** if the sentence is correctly punctuated. Write **P** if there is a comma error, and correct the error.

_____   1. My mother the lady in the pink suit is the president of this club.

_____   2. The Restoration poets who were most popular during the eighteenth century are famous for their wit and command of the English language.

_____   3. You must understand young fellow that a child's place is to be seen and not heard.

_____   4. "You're the thief" said the detective with astonishment.

_____   5. She decided to shift the responsibility onto Harry an ambitious young man.

_____   6. Phoenix a growing metropolis is developing pollution problems.

_____   7. The city that has the largest population of senior citizens is Miami.

_____   8. The tallest building in the world is now I believe the Sears Tower in Chicago.

_____   9. The Empire State Building which held first honors in height for over 40 years is now in third place.

_____   10. Mr. President the reporters are waiting.

_____   11. "Let them wait" he replied.

_____   12. Recitation although it is a required part of the course is a bore.

_____   13. The pine tree overbearing and wild cast a gloom over the whole house.

_____   14. The depressed teenager whispered "Life should be better."

_____   15. Mr. Wildermuth a tall and distinguished-looking man served as one of the ushers.

Quiz 11: Commas and Semicolons   Name: _____

Mark correctly punctuated sentences with **C**, and correct other sentences with a comma or a semicolon. Each sentence has no more than one error.

_____   1.   The road was slick in fact, my car lost traction numerous times.

_____   2.   I tried to obtain a loan however, all my friends said they had no money.

_____   3.   They said they had no money because they had problems with cash flow.

_____   4.   I said that I had no cash to flow under any circumstances I needed a friend with funds.

_____   5.   Paul was a pilot but most of us were afraid to fly with him.

_____   6.   His aircraft was an old Cessna that sounded like a large lawn mower.

_____   7.   Once I traveled with him to Palm Springs, California; Phoenix, Arizona and Taos, New Mexico.

_____   8.   After we landed in a farmer's field I returned home by bus.

_____   9.   The party started late and it ended just before sunrise.

_____   10.   If I had really understood the situation I would not have joined that club.

_____   11.   Steve Allen, who was a well-known actor, musician, and comedian, was active in show business but his main activity was writing books.

_____   12.   One of his popular books is *The Talk Show Murders* a novel in which Allen fictionalized some experiences of real-life talk-show hosts.

_____   13.   People of different backgrounds are killed on talk shows in front of live audiences, and the murderer is sought therefore, the book is classified as a detective novel.

_____   14.   The business implications of these wicked and shocking acts are tremendous however, no one can solve the crimes.

_____   15.   The talk-show industry is on the verge of collapse because future guests start canceling their appearances.

Quiz 12: Other Types of Punctuation   Name: _____

If the sentence is correctly punctuated, write **C** in the space provided. If there is a punctuation error, write **P** in the blank and then correct the error.

_____ 1. But do not let us quarrel any more is a famous line from one of Robert Browning's poems.

_____ 2. No, my Lucrezia; bear with me is the continuation of Browning's poem.

_____ 3. Have you ever thought about the word really?

_____ 4. What does the word mean?

_____ 5. "In the spring of that year 1643, there came a terrible flood."

_____ 6. There are a few things that are more important than money, such as health, happiness, love, and friendship.

_____ 7. Some educated people seem to be predisposed to ill health.

_____ 8. Stop prancing around! he yelled.

_____ 9. "She was you must believe me not involved," declared the distraught teenager.

_____ 10. Gold (long considered a precious metal) can function as a medium of exchange, not just as ornamentation.

_____ 11. "During the reign of Amhos, in the Year of the Great Sun 207 B.C., she assumed the mantle of state."

_____ 12. She said, "By the time we arrived at Phoenix, we decided the vacation was a mistake.

_____ 13. The newlyweds had a long shopping list a crock pot, a blender, a food processor, and a juice extractor.

_____ 14. "Her Majesty has declared Saturday next to be a 'Day of Awareness' for all who might benefit."

_____ 15. However, she intends to spend that day watching her favorite television show *Gilligan's Island.*

Answers to Selected Readings

Chapter 5: "If Those Cobras Don't Get You, the Alligators Will"

True or False

1. F
2. T
3. F
4. F
5. T
6. T
7. F
8. T
9. T
10. F

Multiple Choice

11. b
12. c
13. a
14. d
15. b

Chapter 5: "On the Road: A City of the Mind"

True or False

1. F
2. T
3. F
4. F
5. F
6. T
7. F
8. F
9. F
10. T

Multiple Choice

11. a
12. a
13. b
14. c
15. a

Chapter 6: "The Discus Thrower"

True or False

1. F
2. F
3. T
4. F
5. T
6. T
7. F
8. T
9. F
10. F

Multiple Choice

11. b
12. a
13. c
14. a
15. d

Chapter 6: "Tuesday Morning"

True or False

1. T
2. T
3. T
4. F
5. T
6. T
7. F
8. F
9. F
10. T

Multiple Choice

11. b
12. b
13. c
14. d
15. a

Chapter 7: "Lessons from a Control Freak"

True or False

1. T
2. F
3. T
4. F
5. T
6. F
7. T
8. T
9. T
10. F

Chapter 7: "I'm Outta Here!"

True or False

1. F
2. T
3. T
4. T
5. F
6. T
7. F
8. T
9. T
10. F

Multiple Choice

11. a
12. c
13. d
14. a
15. b

Chapter 8: "A Brush with Reality"

True or False

1. F
2. T
3. T
4. F
5. F
6. T
7. T
8. F
9. T
10. F

Multiple Choice

11. b
12. a
13. c
14. b
15. a

Chapter 8: "Designer Babies"

True or False

1. T
2. F
3. T
4. F
5. T
6. T
7. F
8. F
9. T
10. F

Chapter 9: "Coworkers from Hell and How to Cope"

True or False

1. F
2. F
3. T
4. T
5. F
6. F
7. F
8. F
9. T
10. F

Multiple Choice

11. a
12. b
13. c
14. d
15. b

Chapter 9: "Confessions of a Former Smoker"

True or False		*Multiple Choice*
1. F		11. b
2. F		12. a
3. T		13. d
4. F		14. a
5. T		15. a
6. F		
7. T		
8. T		
9. T		
10. F		

Chapter 10: "How to Paint a Fresco"

True or False

1. F
2. F
3. T
4. T
5. F
6. T
7. F
8. T
9. F
10. T

Chapter 10: "Star"

True or False		*Multiple Choice*
1. T		11. c
2. T		12. a
3. T		13. a
4. F		14. d
5. F		15. b
6. T		
7. T		
8. F		
9. T		
10. F		

Chapter 11: "The Baby Boomers and the Generation Xers"

True or False   *Multiple Choice*

1. T   11. a
2. T   12. b
3. F   13. a
4. T   14. d
5. T   15. a
6. F
7. F
8. T
9. T
10. T

Chapter 11: "That Lean and Hungry Look"

True or False

1. T
2. F
3. T
4. F
5. T
6. T
7. F
8. F
9. T
10. T

Chapter 12: "Why Marriages Fail"

True or False   *Multiple Choice*

1. T   11. c
2. F   12. a
3. T   13. b
4. F   14. c
5. T   15. b
6. F
7. F
8. F
9. T
10. T

Chapter 12: "Romantic Love, Courtship, and Marriage"

True or False

1. F
2. T
3. F
4. T
5. F
6. F
7. T
8. F
9. T
10. T

Chapter 13: "Disarming the Rage"

True or False

1. T
2. F
3. T
4. T
5. F
6. T
7. T
8. F
9. T
10. T

Chapter 13: "Bully, Bully"

True or False

1. T
2. T
3. T
4. F
5. T
6. F
7. T
8. F
9. F
10. T

Chapter 14: "SUVs: Killer Cars"

True or False

1. T
2. T
3. F
4. F
5. T
6. T
7. F
8. T
9. F
10. T

Chapter 14: "Guzzling, Gorgeous, and Grand"

True or False

1. T
2. F
3. T
4. F
5. T
6. T
7. F
8. T
9. F
10. F

Multiple Choice

11. a
12. c
13. d
14. c
15. c

Answers to Handbook Topics

Quiz 1: Subjects and Verbs

1. brother/friend, sold
2. somebody, can give
3. applicants, were
4. part, comes
5. (You), read
6. team, scored
7. I, will be
8. agents, will be
9. coach/players, were angered
10. cast, was congratulated/given
11. Helen, will help
12. tour, is
13. (You), shut/take
14. Bill, will help
15. books, are published

Quiz 2: Sentence Combining

Answers will vary.

1. During the Great Depression of the 1930s, the Joad family lived in Oklahoma.

   When the dust storms hit the area, the Joad family headed for California.

2. In California, the Joads were not welcome because thousands of poor people had gone to California.

   The poor people had heard of jobs in fruit picking, but they discovered that California had more job seekers than jobs.

3. After large farm owners took advantage of the workers, the workers banded together.

   Jim Casey and Tom Joad became leaders, and the people learned to help themselves.

4. Edgar Allan Poe wrote a short story titled "The Cask of Amontillado," in which the narrator tells of his experience fifty years earlier.

   Because he wanted revenge against an enemy, he walled up that person in a catacomb.

Quiz 3: Fragments

C	1.	
Frag	2.	The party was over.
Frag	3.	The beer blast lasted all night.
Frag	4.	They hurriedly and ineffectively tried to smother the small fire.
C	5.	
Frag	6.	The silhouetted figure stood in the doorway.
Frag	7.	The long-haired dog lived in the pen on the corner of the row.
Frag	8.	When the storm was over, the sun broke through.
C	9.	
C	10.	
Frag	11.	She was operated on a year ago.
Frag	12.	Slowly but confidently, he opened the locked door.

C	13.
Frag	14. The rain swelled the waters behind the dam.
Frag	15. The dam on the third-largest river in the state is a technological and engineering wonder.

Quiz 4: Comma Splices and Run-Ons

1. C
2. CS
3. RO
4. CS

5. RO
6. C
7. CS
8. RO

9. CS
10. C

Quiz 5: Comma Splices and Run-Ons

1. RO
2. CS
3. RO
4. C

5. RO
6. RO
7. CS
8. CS

9. C
10. RO

Quiz 6: Subject-Verb Agreement

1. are
2. contain
3. were
4. is
5. is

6. is
7. is
8. costs
9. are
10. is

11. is
12. has
13. is
14. Isn't
15. are

Quiz 7: Pronoun Case

1. Who
2. whom
3. whoever
4. Whoever
5. who

6. Who's
7. whom
8. who
9. Whom
10. whom

11. Whose
12. whoever
13. who
14. who
15. whom

Quiz 8: Pronoun Agreement

1. her
2. its
3. their
4. their
5. their

6. his
7. its
8. their
9. their
10. his or her

11. their
12. his or her
13. his or her
14. his or her
15. her

Quiz 9: Adjectives and Adverbs

1. steadily
2. badly
3. suddenly
4. better
5. good
6. uncertainly
7. clear
8. plainly
9. really
10. much
11. rapidly
12. warm
13. C
14. bad
15. really

Quiz 10: Commas

1. P   mother, the lady in the pink suit,
2. P   poets, . . . century,
3. P   understand, young fellow,
4. P   thief,"
5. P   Harry,
6. P   Phoenix, a growing metropolis,
7. C
8. P   now, I believe,
9. P   Building, . . . years,
10. P   President,
11. P   wait,"
12. P   Recitation, . . . course,
13. P   tree, overbearing and wild,
14. P   whispered,
15. P   Wildermuth, . . . man,

Quiz 11: Commas and Semicolons

1. slick;
2. loan;
3. C
4. circumstances;
5. pilot,
6. C
7. Phoenix, Arizona;
8. field,
9. late,
10. situation,
11. business;
12. *Murders,*
13. sought;
14. tremendous;
15. C

Quiz 12: Other Types of Punctuation

1. P   "But . . . more"
2. P   "No . . . me"
3. P   *really?*
4. C
5. P   [1643]
6. C
7. C
8. P   "Stop . . . around!"
9. P   was—you must believe me!—not
10. C
11. P   [207 B.C.]
12. P   mistake."
13. P   list:
14. C
15. P   show: